THE
EMERGENCE
OF POTTERY

Smithsonian Series in Archaeological Inquiry

Robert McC. Adams and Bruce D. Smith, Series Editors

The Smithsonian Series in Archaeological Inquiry presents original case studies that address important general research problems and demonstrate the values of particular theoretical and/or methodological approaches. Titles include well-focused edited collections as well as works by individual authors. The series is open to all subject areas, geographical regions, and theoretical modes.

Advisory Board

THE
EMERGENCE
OF POTTERY

TECHNOLOGY AND INNOVATION IN ANCIENT SOCIETIES

EDITED BY

**WILLIAM K. BARNETT
AND JOHN W. HOOPES**

SMITHSONIAN INSTITUTION PRESS   WASHINGTON AND LONDON

Copy Editor: Jane Kepp
Supervisory Editor: Duke Johns
Designer: Kathleen Sims

Library of Congress Cataloging-in-Publication Data
The emergence of pottery : technology and innovation in ancient
    societies / edited by William Barnett and John Hoopes.
        p.   cm.
    Includes bibliographical references and index.
    ISBN 1-56098-516-X.—ISBN 1-56098-517-8 (pbk.)
    1. Pottery, Prehistoric—Themes, motives.   2. Pottery,
Prehistoric—Classification.   3. Industries, Prehistoric.
I. Barnett, William (William K.)   II. Hoopes, John.
GN799.P6E44   1995
930.1′028′5—dc20   94-44464

British Library Cataloguing-in-Publication Data is available

Manufactured in the United States of America
02 01 00 99 98   5 4 3 2

♾ The paper used in this publication meets the minimum
requirements of the American National Standard for Information
Sciences—Permanence of Paper for Printed Library Materials
Z39.48-1984.

Contents

Illustrations

Tables

Contributors

C. Melvin Aikens is professor and head of the Department of Anthropology, University of Oregon, where he has taught for more than 25 years. He maintains research interests in the prehistory of western North America, with a recent focus on human ecology and settlement systems in the Great Basin, and in northeast Asia, with a focus on traditional continuity and the growth of sociocultural complexity in Japan. He wrote *Prehistory of Japan* with T. Higuchi and co-edited *Prehistoric Hunter-Gatherers in Japan* with T. Akazawa and *Pacific Northeast Asia in Prehistory* with S. N. Rhee.

Ian Armit is an inspector of ancient monuments for Historic Scotland. He has published widely on Scottish archaeology and on the Mesolithic/Neolithic transition in northern and western Europe. Armit is the editor of *Beyond the Brochs: Changing Perspectives on the Atlantic Scottish Iron Age* and the author of *The Later Prehistory of the Western Isles of Scotland*, *The Archaeology of Skye and the Western Isles*, and the forthcoming *Iron Age Scotland*.

Barbara Arroyo is a National Science Foundation Minority Postdoctoral Fellow at the University of Missouri Research Reactor Facility in Columbia, Missouri. Her research interests include the evolution of complex societies, origins of sedentary communities, and origins of pottery in southeastern Mesoamerica. She has recently surveyed for ancient clay sources and settlements on the southwest Pacific coast of Guatemala.

William K. Barnett is director of the Interdepartmental Laboratories and a research fellow in anthropology at the American Museum of Natural History. He is also a research fellow in archaeology at Boston University. His interests include the agricultural transition in the western Mediterranean, ceramic production and distribution, and the development of analytical methodologies for archaeological research.

Peter Bogucki is assistant dean for undergraduate affairs of the School of Engineering and Applied Sciences at Princeton University, having previously served as director of studies for Forbes College, also at Princeton. He has taught at Harvard, Princeton, the University of Pennsylvania, and the University of Massachusetts at Boston. Bogucki is the author of *Early Neolithic Subsistence and Settlement in the Polish Lowlands* and *Forest Farmers and Stockherders: Early Agriculture and Its Consequences in North-Central Europe*.

Renée M. Bonzani is a visiting scholar in the Department of Archaeology at the University of Calgary, Canada. Her research interests include paleoethnobotany, paleoecology, and ethnobotany of the neotropics. She is a doctoral candidate in the Department of Anthropology at the University of Pittsburgh.

John E. Clark is an assistant professor in the Department of Anthropology and director of the New World Archaeological Foundation at Brigham Young University. His research interests include technology, actualistic studies, political economy, cultural evolution, and theory. He has recently investigated the origins of Early Formative rank societies in Chiapas, Mexico.

Angela E. Close is an assistant professor of anthropology at the University of Washington; she previously taught at Ohio State University and Southern Methodist University. Her principal research interests are in the later phases of the Stone Age of North Africa and, most particularly, in the kinds of information that can be extracted from stone artifacts. She has published numerous books and articles on North African prehistory and is editor of the *Journal of World Prehistory*.

Richard Cooke is staff scientist (archaeology) at the Glen Tupper Center for Tropical Paleoecology at the Smithsonian Tropical Research Institute in Panama. He has lived and worked in Panama since 1969. Research topics that interest him specially are the history of tropical forest peoples, human adaptations to estuaries, and the archaeology of lower Central America. He recently supervised excavations at the Cerro Juan Días site in central Panama.

Patricia L. Crown is an associate professor in the Department of Anthropology at the University of New Mexico. She is particularly interested in the organization of ceramic production in the greater American Southwest. She has recently investigated pan-Southwestern changes in ceramic production during the fourteenth century.

Jonathan E. Damp is associate anthropologist at the Bishop Museum, Honolulu, Hawaii. His recent research includes Polynesian settlement systems and household organization and socioeconomic transformations in the archaeological record of coastal Ecuador.

Bill Finlayson is the manager of the Centre for Field Archaeology at the University of Edinburgh, coordinating the university's work in applied archaeological research with consultancy services. His main research interests are in hunter-gatherer archaeology and the analysis of wear traces on stone tools. His recent research has focused on the Mesolithic in Scotland as well as the transition to farming in western Europe.

Anne Birgitte Gebauer is an associated fellow in the Department of Anthropology at the University of Wisconsin, Madison. She has had a postdoctoral scholarship and taught at Århus University in Denmark. Gebauer is co-editor, with T. Douglas Price, of *Transitions to Agriculture in Prehistory* and *Last Hunters—First Farmers: New Perspectives on the Prehistoric Transition to Agriculture*.

Dennis Gosser is working toward his Ph.D. in the Department of Anthropology at Arizona State University. His research interests include cultural evolution and the development of chiefdoms in southern Mexico and eastern Polynesia. He has recently investigated the role of intoxicants in the creation of prestige economies.

Brian Hayden is a professor in the Department of Archaeology at Simon Fraser University, Burnaby, British Columbia. He is the author of *Archaeology: The Science of Once and Future Things,* as well as *The Structure of Material Systems: Ethnoarchaeology in the Maya Highlands* and *Paleolithic Reflections: Lithic Technology among Australian Aborigines.*

John W. Hoopes is an associate professor in the Department of Anthropology and associate curator at the Museum of Anthropology at the University of Kansas. His research interests include human ecology and cultural evolution in southern Central America. He has recently conducted investigations on prehistoric settlements in the Golfo Dulce region of southern Costa Rica.

William A. Longacre is a professor of anthropology and head of the Department of Anthropology at the University of Arizona in Tucson. He has taught at Yale University, the University of Hawaii, the University of the Philippines, and Silliman University. For more than 20 years he has conducted ethnoarchaeological research, focusing upon pottery, in the Philippines and, most recently, in southwestern China. He is the editor of *Ceramic Ethnoarchaeology* and, with James M. Skibo, of *Kalinga Ethnoarchaeology: Expanding Archaeological Method and Theory.*

Joni L. Manson has conducted research in the American Southwest and Midwest as well as in the former Yugoslav republics. She has published and presented papers on ceramic technology, trade and communication networks, and applications of archaeomagnetic analyses to archaeology. Manson has served as a technical assistant for the Ohio Historic Preservation Office and has carried out historical research on abandoned mine lands for the Ohio Department of Natural Resources.

Andrew M. T. Moore is associate dean for the social sciences in the Graduate School of Arts and Sciences at Yale University. His principal research interests are the beginning of farming and settled life in western Asia and the development of urban societies there. He has written extensively on these subjects and on his excavation of the early village of Abu Hureyra on the Euphrates in Syria.

Augusto Oyuela-Caycedo is a University Postdoctoral Fellow in the Department of Archaeology at the University of Calgary, Canada. He is also associated with the Center for Latin American Studies, University Center for International Studies at the University of Pittsburgh. His research interests are in the history of archaeology, the origins of sedentism and food production, and the rise of complex societies in the neotropics. He recently published an edited volume on the history of Latin American archaeology and directed a field research project in the savannas of northern Colombia.

Camilo Rodríguez is an environmental consultant for the Empresa Colombiana de Petróleos. He has conducted archaeological fieldwork in northern Colombia. His principal research focuses on preceramic cultures and the origins of agriculture in South America.

Anna C. Roosevelt is curator of archaeology at the Field Museum of Natural History and professor of anthropology at the University of Illinois at Chicago. Her research interests include human ecology and cultural evolution in the humid tropics. Her recent field investigations have been based in the Brazilian Amazon.

Kenneth E. Sassaman earned his Ph.D. in anthropology in 1991 from the University of Massachusetts, Amherst. He is employed as an archaeologist with the South Carolina Institute of Archaeology and Anthropology, University of South Carolina. With a long-standing interest in the anthropology of hunter-gatherers, Sassaman strives to bring alternative social perspectives to prehistories otherwise written from an ecological point of view.

Patricia Vargas is an Ecuadorian archaeologist trained at the Escuela Superior Politécnica del Litoral in Guayaquil. She has research interests in socioeconomic transformations in the archaeological record of coastal Ecuador.

Karen D. Vitelli is a professor of anthropology and director of the Graduate Program in Classical Archaeology at Indiana University, Bloomington. Her publications on prehistoric ceramics include *Franchthi Neolithic Pottery, vol. 1: Classification and Ceramic Phases 1 and 2.*

W. H. Wills is an associate professor in the Department of Anthropology at the University of New Mexico. His research interests include the origins of agriculture and the origins of village life. He has recently investigated early village social organization in the greater American Southwest.

Preface

The chapters in this book originated as contributions to two symposia at meetings of the Society for American Archaeology (SAA). These symposia brought together researchers who were developing theories about early pottery that went far beyond traditional culture history or functionalist interpretations to seek economic, political, and even individual factors behind the initial emergence of this singularly important technology.

The discussions that took place around the organization and execution of these symposia led to several realizations about the nature of early pottery. The invention of pottery was an oft-repeated process, and the initial utilization of ceramic technology, through either invention or adoption, varied widely among cultures and geographic regions. Nonetheless, there were similarities to be found among the diverse ways in which pottery emerged. Exploring themes of similarity and diversity with a comparative approach that drew upon information from around the globe invested our intellectual process with a great deal of dynamism and excitement. The chapters in this book are testimony to the enthusiasm of the archaeologists who undertake research on early pottery.

At the 1990 meeting of the SAA, one of us (Hoopes) organized a symposium entitled "New Perspectives on Early Ceramics and Formative Culture in the New World." It had two principal goals: to present the latest research on the earliest known ceramic complexes in the Americas, and to bring together archaeologists from different regions who were working on similar problems, many of whom had never met one another before. The papers covered geographical areas ranging from Ecuador to southern Mexico. The symposium fostered increased contact among the participants. Their willingness to share unpublished data and ideas had a significant effect on current research and interpretations. Three of the participants (all contributors to this book) have since completed dissertations that offer new models for the emergence of pottery in various parts of the New World. Seven of the ten papers in the symposium evolved into chapters for this book. Another became part of a separate monograph on early pottery in the Oaxaca Valley.

Independently, the other co-editor of this book (Barnett) had an intriguing discussion with Terry Hunt at the 1991 meeting of the SAA about similarities between the decoration, distribution, and rapid appearance of early western Mediterranean pottery and Lapita pottery, the earliest ware in Polynesia. This and subsequent discussions with other scholars focusing on early pottery led to the general realization that a great deal of new research by independent scholars revolved around the problem of the origins of pottery.

Barnett organized a second symposium, titled "The Emergence of Pottery," for the 1993 meeting of the SAA. It brought New World scholars together with Old World archaeologists, all of whom were working on ideas surrounding the origins of pottery. The principal objectives of the symposium were to appraise the status of early pottery research worldwide and to encourage further communication between archaeologists working in widely separated regions of the world. The symposium was well attended and both the quality and the quantity of postpresentation comments attested to its success. Papers presented at the 1993 symposium formed the basis for the majority of chapters in this book. They are supplemented by updated contributions from participants in the 1990 symposium and by invited chapters (by Aikens, Armit and Finlayson, Hayden, and Manson) that expand the book's geographical and theoretical scope.

The issues that emerged in these two symposia revealed that research on early pottery, a topic that had become moribund in the wake of processual critiques of traditional culture history during the 1970s and 1980s, was in fact alive and well. New directions in ceramic theory and interpretation ranged far from typological descriptions and diffusionistic explanations to offer models for the process of innovation and its acceptance. This recent research is characterized by more extensive use of archaeometric data, the integration of social, economic, and technological models, the consideration of gender-related factors, and a critical approach toward modeling relationships between the emergence of pottery and the evolution of food production, sedentism, and social complexity.

Assembling this volume posed an array of challenges. Ensuring consistency in ^{14}C date notation was our single greatest concern in bringing together chapters from scholars of diverse academic and geographical orientations. This diversity was compounded by the contributors' variable use of ^{14}C calibration. In our opinion, the conventions used by the British journal *Antiquity* provided each author with maximum freedom in date reporting within a consistent format. We therefore decided to adopt the following *Antiquity*-style notation: b.c. and b.p. denote uncalibrated radiocarbon dates; B.C., B.P., and A.D. denote calendar years or radiocarbon dates calibrated to calendar years. We worked closely with the contributors to ensure that this convention was adhered to throughout the volume. We hope it guarantees a consistency of date reporting without requiring that authors calibrate or present dates on a particular time scale.

Several people were instrumental in the successful completion of this book. Daniel Goodwin of the Smithsonian Institution Press encouraged the publication of our symposium contributions and supported us throughout the project. Cheryl Anderson and Duke Johns, also at the Smithsonian Institution Press, provided a great deal of assistance and guidance. Jane Kepp was an insightful manuscript editor. William Longacre and Prudence Rice offered perceptive comments and guidance as discussants at the "Emergence of Pottery" symposium. James Brown was especially helpful in the discussions surrounding the second symposium.

Considering the importance of pottery for the nutrition of infants and their mothers (see the chapter by Crown and Wills), it is probably significant that each of the co-editors experienced the birth of children during the preparation of this work. We would like to thank our wives for their patience and support, and we dedicate this book to our families.

1

The Shape of Early Pottery Studies

JOHN W. HOOPES AND
WILLIAM K. BARNETT

The invention and adoption of pottery are among archaeology's most compelling issues. For thousands of years, in a wide variety of settings, ceramics have persisted as an innovative technology with complex linkages to extremely different social, economic, environmental, and ideological systems. Until recently, prevailing models that concerned themselves with periods of ceramic innovation, although sophisticated in their interpretation of subsistence, ecological, and performance phenomena, failed to address social factors that interacted with these phenomena and affected the emergence of pottery use. These models have traditionally employed mentalist, adaptationist, "enabling" (usually through agriculture), or economic approaches (Brown 1989). Current models for the emergence of pottery, presented throughout this volume, represent a set of novel perspectives and a wider range of approaches to understanding the dynamics of prehistoric economic and social interaction. To better evaluate these models, it is necessary to deconstruct commonly held assumptions about prehistoric ceramics, some of which have been present in the literature for generations.

The origins of ceramic technology are as widely varied and idiosyncratic as the origins of stone tools, agriculture, village life, political organization, writing systems, and religions. Pottery was invented by a number of different societies, each of which developed and sustained the technology in the context of specific and distinct ecological, economic, and social conditions. Equally important were the dynamics that led people to incorporate and modify extant ceramic technologies —or not to do so—and the nature of the technologies' introduction. Archaeological investigations of the emergence of pottery have as their focus durable residues of past human activities. Their goals have been the pursuit and formulation of both specific and generalized models for phenomena as varied as culture change, the adoption of innovation, the application and development of new technologies, human communication by means of material culture, and the ways in which gender, economics, politics, and ethnicity affect people's choices for investing their ceramic manufacturing efforts.

As a class of archaeological remains, ceramics tend to be far better preserved than most other residues of prehistoric life. Ceramic assemblages are durable (though brittle) and abundant, and ceramic artifacts can display an infinite range of variation in technology, form, and decoration, providing rich sources of data for interpretation. Pottery is thoroughly "cultural," in

1

that its variation is almost completely dependent upon the ideas of the potter. The plasticity of the medium and the additive aspects of its manufacture, together with the fact that pots can be made by people of all ages and genders, invest pottery with a high information content relative to other archaeological remains.

Once pottery enters the archaeological record, it can become a source of information about a culture's technological adaptations, chronology, subsistence, household activities, trade and exchange, symbolic systems, and a wealth of other topics. Ecological, economic, and social models for the emergence of pottery have become increasingly testable as a result of improving information sets and archaeometric approaches for analyzing production, distribution, design, residues, use-wear, and taphonomy (see Rice 1987). The results of these analyses not only permit independent examination of existing hypotheses but also provide glimpses of facets of prehistoric dynamics, such as patterns of nonsubsistence economic and social interaction, that previously were difficult to detect.

The archaeological record makes it clear that pottery was most commonly produced by sedentary, agricultural societies; most mobile, foraging societies did not have pottery (Arnold 1985). It is a mistake, however, to infer the existence of either sedentism or agriculture from the presence of pottery alone. Like many other "Neolithic" innovations, such as ground stone axes, metallurgy, long-distance exchange, sedentary village life, monumental architecture, and complex social organization, pottery technology was utilized by complex hunter-gatherers. The chapters in this volume go a long way toward decoupling the emergence of pottery from any deterministic associations with either sedentism or agriculture. They furnish a caveat to those who would read more into the presence of early pottery than can be justified and force us all to reconsider the nature of pottery's emergence.

It is abundantly clear that the origins of ceramic technology varied widely in space, time, and cultural context. Rather than focusing on the ceramic objects themselves, many current studies of the emergence of pottery are concerned with reconstructing the ecological and social conditions that fostered innovation and promoted the retention and improvement of this new technology. In doing so, they effectively distinguish ceramic studies from typologically based culture histories. Models for the emergence of pottery are therefore of great relevance to the broader concerns of archaeology in explaining the complex interrelationships between human societies and material culture over time.

Technological innovation and the successes or failures of new technological systems are processes that have always had a profound effect on the human experience.

This book brings together recent research on the emergence of pottery and provides new perspectives on the nature of the invention and adoption of ceramic technology around the world. The contributors, utilizing principles from production and distribution models, ceramic ecology, and information theory, present a wealth of new information. It is hoped that the range of models, perspectives, and interpretations presented here will help to emphasize the importance of variation in human societies and the particular historical, environmental, and cultural contexts of early pottery. Why and when pottery appears are questions that spark inquiries into the nature of the societies that employed the then-new technology. Although we can arrive at some generalizations about the processes that may have led to the emergence and adoption of pottery, the particulars of individual cases are equally important.

The chapters in this book focus on the earliest pottery from the Middle East, North Africa, Europe, the Pacific, and the Americas, exploring ceramic innovation in the contexts of the origins and spread of agriculture, the development of sedentism and exchange systems, and the role of pottery in social and economic structures. The wide variety of models offered to explain ceramic innovation make its complexity abundantly clear and raise many fruitful questions for further investigations. These chapters are therefore relevant not only to those interested in ceramics but also to scholars investigating any period of change or innovation.

Origins of Pottery as a Technology

V. Gordon Childe (1951:76) noted that "pot-making is perhaps the earliest conscious utilization by man [*sic*] of a chemical change." Although the manufacture of useful objects of stone, bone, and other natural materials had reached a high level of sophistication by the end of the Paleolithic period, and although the earliest invention of ceramics—the first thoroughly artificial objects—can be credited to Gravettian figurine makers at Dolni Vestonice around 30,000 B.P., the use of pottery vessels is so far not known to have occurred until after the global changes that accompanied the advent of the Holocene.

There are myriad suggestions as to how ceramic vessels were "discovered." Childe (1951:76) suggested the accidental burning of clay-lined baskets, based on an association of crude sherds with Paleolithic materials from Kenya. He also suggested that the earliest pots were imitations of vessels made from natural forms such as gourds, bladders, skins, baskets, and even human skulls, and that the earliest decorations helped to reinforce connections between ceramic vessels and earlier materials (Childe 1951:79). The principle of fired clay is not difficult to understand, and it was probably observed at work in fire pits hundreds of thousands of years before it was ever utilized. The significant aspect of the discovery of pottery is the application of the firing principle to the solution of a problem.

Pottery vessels are tools (Braun 1983:107), and ceramic technology was invented or adopted in order to accomplish specific ends within a particular social milieu, including relations with other groups. These ends were as widely varied as the societies themselves. Uses of early pottery vessels ranged from short-term storage and transport of water and solids to cooking, brewing, serving, long-term storage, display, and exchange. Ceramic vessels played specific roles in status display and competition, the communication of ideas, and aesthetic expression.

The uses of pots conditioned (and were in turn conditioned by) the nature of the societies that used them as well as the vessels' physical qualities and the steps undertaken in their manufacture. Karen Vitelli (chapter 5), for example, notes that the technology of the earliest Neolithic pottery in the Aegean consists of infrequent potting by individuals who nonetheless invested a great deal of energy in each vessel. Vitelli concludes that this investment was due to the social value placed on each pot. Joni Manson (chapter 6) and Kenneth Sassaman (chapter 18) explore the roles of ceramic performance characteristics in the development of European Starčevo and North American Archaic pottery, respectively, and William Longacre's comments (chapter 22) stress the importance of measures of performance characteristics in ceramic research.

Theories on the Origins of Pottery

A predominant hypothesis is that pottery was invented in order to detoxify foods and make them more palatable. Processing was especially important in the case of plants that could not be consumed in any other way (see Arnold 1985:Table 6.1) and for potential staple grains such as wheat, maize, and rice (Arnold 1985:

135). Cooking and boiling in ceramic vessels that could be left on the fire was less energy intensive than stone boiling, a technique that can be used with perishable containers. The sterilization of foods through boiling, facilitated by ceramic vessels, improved and extended those foods' edibility and shelf life. Food preparation techniques such as soaking and cooking increased the nutritive value of plants such as maize and beans. Pottery could also be used to introduce new methods of food processing, such as baking, toasting, and brewing.

Another set of theories proposes that a principal function of early pottery was as a prestige good used in ritual displays, particularly in the context of competitive feasts. For Brian Hayden (1990; chapter 20), the invention of pottery accompanied the emergence of agriculture as a source of products that played key roles in a prestige economy based on competitive feasting. In comparison, Ian Armit and Bill Finlayson (chapter 21) and William Barnett (1990), through their evaluation of data from northwestern and southwestern Europe, respectively, discuss roles that early pottery may have played as symbols of ethnicity and social group identity. That numerous examples of early pottery are highly decorated or display a particular manufacturing technology, combined in some cases with evidence of transport or exchange, provides empirical support for the application of prestige or symbolic models to the appearance of ceramics.

John Clark and Dennis Gosser (chapter 17) interpret Barra ceramics—among the earliest in Mesoamerica—as representing a new type of valued prestige item that also happened to be a container. Pots enhanced the consumption and display of agricultural products, and therefore played a role that was as important in the construction of social networks and hierarchies as it was in nutrition. In Mesoamerica (Arroyo, chapter 16; Clark and Gosser, chapter 17), Central America (Cooke, chapter 14; Hoopes, chapter 15), and South America (Oyuela-Caycedo, chapter 11; Rodriguez, chapter 12; Roosevelt, chapter 10) the earliest pottery complexes included decorated vessels that may have been used to communicate status or other forms of social identity. In Europe, early decorated ceramics that may have fulfilled symbolic or prestige roles are known from North Africa (Close, chapter 3), the Aegean (Vitelli, chapter 5), the western Mediterranean (Barnett, chapter 7), eastern Europe (Manson, chapter 6), central Europe (Bogucki, chapter 8), and northern Europe (Armit and Finlayson, chapter 21). Farther to the east, the Incipient Jomon in Japan (Aikens, chapter 2) and

Lapita in Polynesia (Kirch and Hunt 1988) represent well-known examples of earliest decorated wares.

John Hoopes (chapter 15) points out that social uses of ceramic vessels may complement, rather than follow from, processes of domestication and cultivation. Whereas agricultural products eventually became the focus of ceramic use, pottery vessels also enhanced the value of wild food products in the context of social interaction based on plants' seasonal abundance and on periodic reciprocity between groups. There is evidence that in both the Old and New Worlds, early pottery played a key role in the preparation, serving, and consumption of special foods and beverages at feasts and other social gatherings (Barnett, chapter 7; Clark and Gosser, chapter 17). The nutritional advantages of food products made possible by the use of ceramic vessels may well have been secondary to the value of social contexts these foods helped to create. In cases where the introduction of pottery coincided roughly with the beginnings of agriculture, activities such as feasts may have made agricultural products available that only later were consolidated as the principal mode of subsistence (Zvelebil 1986). In other cases, social constraints may have acted to interfere with the adoption of pottery (Sassaman, chapter 18).

The Relationship of Pottery to Sedentism

Dean Arnold (1985:109–26) has been able to demonstrate a clear tendency for pottery-producing societies to be sedentary rather than mobile. But while the continued use and manufacture of pottery was undoubtedly connected with increased sedentism, the origins of pottery were not necessarily tied to permanence of site occupation. Pottery can be successfully employed by seasonally mobile foragers or by agropastoralists such as the Rarámuri (Graham 1993). Several chapters in this volume make it clear that pottery was frequently used by seasonally mobile populations. It is important to note, however, that pottery use itself occurs in the context of sedentary activity, even by groups that are mobile for part of the year.

The energy demands of pottery production are high. As Patricia Crown and Wirt Wills (chapter 19) note for the Southwestern United States, pottery manufacture did not represent an efficient use of time and energy for Late Archaic populations until patterns of sedentary occupation were established through the adoption of cultigens and improved techniques for processing gathered plant foods. Once sedentism became the

norm, the investment of energy in making pots paid off in terms of improved nutrition for the community as a whole and for women and children in particular.

There is no doubt that sedentism, even when seasonal, played a significant, positive role in the emergence of ceramic technology. Changes in the use of raw materials and the organization of labor that accompanied permanence of occupation had a direct effect on vessel quality, enhancing the vessels' practical and/or prestige value. The particular characteristics of foods gathered and produced in the context of sedentism—whether temporary or permanent—also influenced vessel form, function, and quality. At one end of the continuum, we find simple vessels with either general or special functions produced expeditiously from readily available materials during a short-term stay in one location. At the other end, permanent workshops and facilities produced high-quality vessels with expensive clays, tempers, and pigments for a variety of specialized uses.

The Relationship of Pottery to Agriculture

Theoretical linkages between pottery and the origins of agriculture can be traced to authors including E. B. Tylor (1871) and Lewis Henry Morgan (1877) and thus have a long tradition in the history of anthropological and archaeological research. Tylor suggested that the domestication of plants and animals divided the stage of Savagery from that of Barbarism in his scheme for the evolution of civilization. Morgan subdivided Tylor's Barbarism into Lower, Middle, and Upper stages. Agriculture marked the beginning of Lower Barbarism, whereas the subsequent invention of pottery characterized Middle Barbarism. Hence, pottery came after agriculture in these initial formulations, a presumption reinforced by the recognition of the complexity of preceramic Natufian villages and the existence of a "Pre-Pottery Neolithic" in the Levant (Moore, chapter 4).

Childe (1951:76) saw pottery as a virtually universal characteristic of Neolithic communities, and for decades ceramics were the prime marker for Neolithic period sites. More recently, Prudence Rice (1987:9) has characterized pottery as

part of the so-called Neolithic technocomplex. This is an assemblage of tools and containers for food preparation and storage, together with the associated technology of their manufacture and use, that correlates in a very general way with worldwide changes in human lifeways at the end of the

Paleolithic period or soon thereafter. These changes are dramatic, involving the adoption of food production rather than collecting, and settlement in villages rather than temporary encampments.

To consider pottery a "Neolithic" industry overlooks the context of its origins, especially given current interpretations of agriculture as the hallmark of the Neolithic period. Our chronological terminology mistakenly implies that pottery production, village life, food production, and complexity were intimately linked to one another, in spite of abundant data indicating that pottery often preceded those patterns labeled "Neolithic" in the Old World and "Formative" in the New World. Recent examinations of complex hunter-gatherers (e.g., Arnold 1993) contribute to the decoupling of agriculture from sedentism and complexity and thus from the capacity of foragers for ceramic production. The earliest pottery in Japan (Aikens, chapter 2) was produced by early Holocene fishermen. Pottery was being utilized by Ertebølle Mesolithic cultures of northern Europe centuries before the earliest appearance of domesticates (Gebauer, chapter 9). Angela Close (chapter 3) notes that pottery is also documented for the Khartoum Mesolithic. Despite the association of domesticates and pottery in the western Mediterranean, it is unclear that there was any great economic shift to agriculture associated with the appearance of early wares (Barnett, chapter 7).

In the New World, some earliest pottery from South America (Oyuela-Caycedo, chapter 11; Roosevelt, chapter 10) and North America (Sassaman, chapter 18) is associated with seasonally mobile, preagricultural societies. Despite the common usage of terms such as "Early Formative," "Early Preclassic," "Initial Period," and "Early Woodland" to refer to initial pottery cultures in the New World, and despite the fact that "Archaic" is still widely used as a synonym for "Preceramic," it is important to recognize that Gordon Willey and Philip Phillips (1958:110) pointed out that many "Archaic" cultures had a sophisticated pottery technology and that the earliest North American ceramics were made by Late Archaic hunters and gatherers. In many areas, early pottery may bear no more implications for sedentism or agriculture than do ground stone tools.

This is not to say that no important relationship exists between ceramics and agriculture in many parts of the world, but only that the two do not always go hand in hand, and there is no predictable cause-and-effect relationship between them. Increased reliance upon plant products, especially those that are seasonally abundant, appears to have resulted in situations favorable to the adoption of ceramics. The chapters by Close, Moore, Vitelli, Manson, Bogucki, Barnett, and Gebauer all trace the relationship and development of agriculture and ceramic technology, or the lack thereof, across the Old World. Plants, however, need not have been domesticated products. Indeed, consumption of wild fruits and seeds or small, abundant animal foods such as mollusks may lead to the emergence of pottery. Changes in the efficiency of food preparation that resulted from pottery use may have predisposed certain populations to the adoption of labor-intensive domesticates. As Hayden (1990) has suggested, however, the evolution of food production may have been driven by social competition rather than by nutritional advantages.

Just as pottery preceded agriculture in several instances, so the reverse was also true. In Mexico and the Levant, domestication preceded ceramic production by millennia. In both areas, containers such as gourds, skins, baskets, and ground stone vessels served many of the functions for which ceramic vessels were later utilized. In the Southwestern United States, pottery began to be used shortly after the initial use of cultivated plants as an energy-efficient means of increasing the nutritional value of land- and labor-intensive crops.

Who Made and Used Early Pottery?

The issue of who made and used the first pottery is a theme that runs throughout this volume. Was early pottery made by recognizable subsets of individuals in the societies that used it? Was there recognizable variation in the ways early vessels were used by members of a given society? How might ceramic artifacts help define social roles and condition modes of human interaction?

It is as difficult to recognize gender in ceramic production as it is in most other parts of the archaeological record. Yet ceramic use had the potential to affect the lives of women and children in ways different from those in which it affected the lives of adult men. Pottery facilitated the production of weaning foods, the extraction of fats and oils, the edibility of marginal plant and animal products, and both detoxification and preservation of a variety of second-choice foods. As a result, the nutrition of individuals who had the least access to the highest quality foods was dramatically improved. Pregnant and nursing women, whose foraging ranges were reduced by restricted mobility, are likely to have fared better with the kinds of foods that could be prepared using pottery. Women, as gatherers and as the individuals most closely associated with households, might also have been closer to the technologies and materials for making pottery (Vitelli, chapter 5) and better able to organize the diverse tasks (Wright 1991) necessary for manufacturing ceramics.

Crown and Wills (chapter 19) suggest that the adoption of pottery vessels was directly related to changing gender roles. Although it is difficult to determine whether distinct gender roles were well established within societies that were beginning to manufacture pottery, vessels that made it possible to increase the nutritional value and/or quantity of available foods are likely to have had a direct impact upon the health of the most vulnerable segment of human societies—babies and small children. These changes in turn affected nursing mothers and, by extension, women in general. The fact that early pottery vessels, when used for subsistence purposes, are likely to have had a more significant impact on women and children than on men provides some clues as to who may have been manufacturing them and why. Women's role in the invention and production of pottery within specific societies, however, must be demonstrated through multiple lines of evidence. Unfortunately, few other sorts of evidence are preserved as well as the ceramics themselves.

Pottery changed the nature of food preparation in a fundamental way. As Crown and Wills point out, although pottery required an extra investment of labor in its manufacture, it ultimately made it possible for individuals who did not range far for hunting (mostly women and children) to restructure many of their home-base activities. Often this restructuring meant greater responsibility for the preparation of valued food products than was typical of similar individuals in a preceramic culture. Individuals who invested the greatest energy in food preparation on a regular basis were also the most likely to be called upon when special preparation was required. In the case of feasting, although far-ranging individuals (mostly men) were required to gather or procure special or additional quantities of raw foods, close-ranging individuals were probably recruited for the preparation of special products or foods and beverages needed in quantity for a special occasion. In this way, pottery served to create new social roles and increase the potential for mobility and improvement of individual status. A person who had been one of several gatherers and grinders could, with pottery, become a cook.

The nature of the earliest ceramics also reveals information about who the users were within a given social structure. The elaborateness of ceramic vessels, such as the fancy Barra *tecomates* (Clark and Gosser, chapter 17), was intimately linked with the status of their users. Such pottery was used by individuals in public or private displays in which the vessels themselves—both as a new technology and as a medium with great symbolic potential—served to structure social interactions and condition the human behavior surrounding them.

The Significance of Early Pottery

Childe was among the first to suggest that the manufacture of pottery was also likely to have had an effect on human cognition. With pottery, humans created the first artificial medium. "To early man [*sic*] this change in the quality of the material must have seemed a sort of magic transubstantiation—the conversion of mud or dust into stone. It may have prompted some philosophical questions as to the meaning of substance and sameness" (Childe 1951:77). "The constructive character of the potter's craft reacted on human thought. Building up a pot was a supreme instance of creation by man. . . . In thinking of 'creation', the free activity of the potter in 'making form where there was no form' constantly recurs to man's mind" (Childe 1951:79).

None of the chapters in this book directly addresses the internalization of pottery manufacture. It is probably significant that the world's earliest ceramics were not containers but figurines, and that ceramic figurines were prominent in many early pottery complexes (Clark and Gosser, chapter 17; Moore, chapter 4). In situations where pottery emerged and persisted for its role in social interactions—as objects for prestige display, ritual gifts, serving of special foods and beverages, trade and exchange, or symbolizing inclusion or exclusion (Weissner 1984)—it affected actors of all ages and genders. Pottery became symbolic of the situations in which it was used as well as a medium on which symbols could be communicated. It joined objects of stone, wood, bone, and other substances as part of a society's material expression. The special significance with which it was imbued is challenging to interpret, even in the presence of abundant information from other sources.

Conclusions

The chapters in this volume highlight the variable and intricate relationships among the emergence of pottery, sedentism, agriculture, and complex systems. They provide a series of case studies of the ways in which material culture and other aspects of the human experience are interwoven through space and time. Collectively, they tend to acknowledge that the processes that resulted in village life, domestication, and ceramic production were closely related. But although it is true that pottery was frequently employed to facilitate the production of foods and beverages that were qualitatively and/or quantitatively different from those available to people without pottery, it is also important to recognize that pottery itself—even in the absence of special subsistence benefits—had qualities that enhanced its value in social contexts and varied independently of those benefits. Whereas previous models emphasized changing subsistence strategies as principal factors in the development of new technologies during the transition from mobile hunting and gathering to complex village lifeways, it is now clear that the emergence of technologies such as pottery was characterized by a complicated mix of ecological, historical, economic, and social factors that differed greatly among past human societies. It is important not to underestimate the potential for human societies to transform themselves through the invention or adoption of the ceramic craft.

References Cited

Arnold, Dean
  1985   *Ceramic Theory and Cultural Process.* Cambridge University Press, New York.
Arnold, Jeanne E.
  1993   Labor and the Rise of Complex Hunter-Gatherers. *Journal of Anthropological Archaeology* 12:75–119.
Barnett, William
  1990   Small-Scale Transport of Early Neolithic Pottery in the West Mediterranean. *Antiquity* 64:859–65.
Braun, David
  1983   Pots as Tools. In *Archaeological Hammers and Theories,* edited by J. A. Moore and A. S. Keene, pp. 107–34. Academic Press, New York.

Brown, James A.
  1989   The Beginnings of Pottery as an Economic Process. In *What's New? A Closer Look at the Process of Innovation,* edited by S. E. van der Leeuw and R. Torrence, pp. 203–24. Unwin Hyman, London.
Childe, V. Gordon
  1951   *Man Makes Himself.* New American Library of World Literature, London.
Graham, Martha
  1993   Settlement Organization and Residential Variability among the Rarámuri. In *Abandonment of Settlements and Regions,* edited by Catherine M. Cameron and Steve A. Tomka, pp. 25–42. Cambridge University Press, Cambridge.
Hayden, Brian
  1990   Nimrods, Pickers, Pluckers, and Planters: The Origins of Food Production. *Journal of Anthropological Archaeology* 9:31–69.
Kirch, Patrick V., and Terry L. Hunt, eds.
  1988   Archaeology of the Lapita Cultural Complex: A Critical Review. Thomas Burke Memorial Washington State Museum, Research Report no. 5, Burke Museum, Seattle.
Morgan, Lewis H.
  1877   *Ancient Society.* Holt, New York.
Rice, Prudence
  1987   *Pottery Analysis: A Sourcebook.* University of Chicago Press, Chicago.
Tylor, E. B.
  1871   *Primitive Culture.* Murray, London.
Wiessner, Polly
  1984   Reconsidering the Behavioral Basis for Style: A Case Study among the Kalahari San. *Journal of Anthropological Archaeology* 3:190–234.
Willey, Gordon R., and Phillip Phillips
  1958   *Method and Theory in American Archaeology.* University of Chicago Press, Chicago.
Wright, Rita P.
  1991   Women's Labor and Pottery Production in Prehistory. In *Engendering Archaeology: Women and Prehistory,* edited by Joan Gero and Margaret Conkey, pp. 194–223. Basil Blackwell, Oxford.
Zvelebil, Marek
  1986   Mesolithic Prelude and Neolithic Revolution. In *Hunters in Transition,* edited by Marek Zvelebil, pp. 5–15. Cambridge University Press, Cambridge.

The Old World

2

First in the World

The Jomon Pottery of Early Japan

C. MELVIN AIKENS

The Jomon pottery of Japan has been archaeologically prominent since it was described and illustrated in some detail by Edward S. Morse in his now-classic monograph *The Shell Mound of Omori*, published in 1879. Morse's research is widely recognized both in Japan and abroad as a milestone in the development of Japanese archaeology. In present-day Japan, archaeology is an industry of huge proportions, and the Jomon culture has by now been described and celebrated in thousands of published reports. These are, of course, virtually all in Japanese, but there is a growing literature in English as well, for which Kaner (1990) provides a valuable bibliographic review. Overviews of Japanese prehistory are offered by Aikens and Higuchi (1982) and Pearson et al. (1986), and illuminating treatments of the Jomon pottery tradition are provided by Kidder and Esaka (1968) and Bleed (1978). The most comprehensive recent survey of Jomon pottery is found in 55 papers published in Japanese in three volumes of a ten-volume series on Jomon research edited by Kato, Kobayashi, and Fujimoto (1981–84). In these volumes, specialists from all over Japan discuss Jomon pottery region by region and period by period. The present chapter combines a brief introduction to Jomon pottery and culture with an argument relating its beginnings to environmental change and cultural adaptation at the beginning of the Holocene.

The Jomon Sequence

Pottery is radiocarbon dated to about 12,700 b.p. in a good cultural and stratigraphic context at Fukui Cave, not far from Nagasaki City on Japan's southern island of Kyushu. So far, it remains the earliest well-dated pottery in the world. It marks the dawn of the Jomon tradition, which is divided into Incipient, Initial, Early, Middle, Late, and Final periods, each with internal subdivisions. In Hokkaido there is yet one more period, termed Continuing Jomon, that lasted on into the time of imported rice agriculture farther south.

From its first appearance in the south to its ultimate disappearance in the north, the Jomon tradition spans well over 10,000 years. Across this great stretch of space and time, Jomon pottery exhibits marked continuity even while expressing noteworthy temporal and regional variation (Table 2.1). So numerous are Jomon pottery types that an adequate excursion into their large and complex taxonomy would necessitate a major essay in itself; here, the discussion proceeds in terms of a few prominent categories of shape and de-

Table 2.1. Decorative Modes of Jomon Pottery from the Tokyo Region

Decorative Mode (All Pottery Types)	Jomon Period				
	Initial	Early	Middle	Late	Final
Incising			x	x	x
Grooving	x	x	x	x	x
Diagonal cord marking	x	x	x	x	
Zoned cord marking		x	x	x	
Bamboo stick marking	x	x	x		
Knotted cord marking		x			
Knotless cord marking		x			
Net marking		x			
Wheat pattern cord marking		x			
Oblique cord marking		x			
Shell scraping	x	x			
Shell impressing	x	x			
Shell imprinting	x	x			
Punctation	x	x			
Zigzag rouletting	x				
Lattice rouletting	x				
Elliptical rouletting	x				
Nail marking	x				
Linear relief	x				

Source: Kidder and Esaka 1968:282–83.

sign that are the general currency of such conversations among Japanese archaeologists. Regional style zones that have been proposed for the country as a whole will be briefly addressed following the chronological presentation.

INCIPIENT JOMON

Japan's earliest pottery is usually found at inland sites such as Fukui Cave and Sempukuji Rockshelter in Kyushu, Kamikuroiwa Rockshelter in Shikoku, and Ishigoya, Muroya, and Kosegasawa caves in central and northern Honshu, to name only a few well-known find spots. When such pottery was first being recognized some 30 years ago, it seemed to concentrate heavily in caves or rockshelters, but a more recent tabulation of Incipient Jomon sites shows only 20 out of 93 to be in such locations (Suzuki 1981:44). Still, this is a high percentage of sheltered sites in comparison with sites of all other Jomon periods. Also notable is that Suzuki's tabulation names only two shell mound sites, showing that littoral occupations—later overwhelm-

ingly numerous—were extremely rare at that early time.

In the Kyushu sites, the first pottery appears with microblade technologies like those of terminal Paleolithic, aceramic sites that are found widely in Japan. Farther north, where the first pottery appears somewhat later, it is associated with bifacial projectile points and scrapers of types that directly follow the microblade technologies there. Radiocarbon dates for these earliest pottery-bearing sites lie between about 12,700 and 10,000 b.p. (Fig. 2.1). Unmistakably, Japan is one place where pottery first came into use among hunter-gatherers, far removed from any conceivable influence of Neolithic food production.

The "Incipient Jomon" label used to characterize this period reflects both its position at the beginning of the Japanese pottery sequence and the fact that the pottery cannot properly be labeled simply "Jomon." That word refers to cord marking, a mode of decoration present on most early Japanese pottery but not on the very earliest. Archaeologists have debated whether this earliest pottery, because it is not cord marked, ought really to be considered part of the Jomon tradition at all, but it has come to be generally accepted as the obvious beginning of the sequence and therefore as part of the tradition.

The earliest sherds from Fukui Cave were small fragments of a well-fired, fairly thin ware decorated by parallel "linear relief" bands of clay pinched up from the vessel wall before firing. This type is widespread and is closely followed stratigraphically at Fukui Cave and elsewhere by a fingernail-incised ware. Subsequently there appear, still within the Incipient Jomon horizon, fiber-impressed and stick-rouletted motifs. Where complete vessels are known, it appears that the decorative elements are generally found near the rims, leaving most of the pot undecorated. Plain, undecorated sherds have, of course, generally been found along with the decorated specimens, but—unsurprisingly—a few sites of the period have also come to light that seem to yield only plain wares.

All of the earliest vessels appear to be small cooking pots. The site of Kamikuroiwa yielded sherds suggesting a deep, round-bottomed pot. Whole or nearly whole vessels from Muroya, Ishigoya, and other sites are deep pots with the greatest diameter at the rim and nearly straight sides tapering slightly toward rounded or slightly flattened bottoms.

INITIAL JOMON

The Igusa type marks the beginning of the Initial Jomon period, which dates between about 10,000 and 6000 b.p. Igusa pottery, found in the greater Tokyo region, establishes the pattern of cord-marked, pointed-bottom vessels that is characteristic of Initial Jomon throughout Japan. At Natsushima, on Tokyo Bay, Igusa ware is found in a loam stratum that immediately underlies a deep shell midden; other sites at water's edge also show its presence, though typically it occurs beneath the shell layers that attest the following stages of Initial Jomon. At Nishinojo shell mound, across the bay, Igusa pottery has been found in association with a semisubterranean house, and such sites are known in the interior as well, where they are associated with grinding tools, among other things (Sugihara and Serizawa 1957; Bleed 1978). These sites presage the broad-spectrum, hunting-fishing-gathering, pithouse-dwelling lifeway that characterizes the Jomon cultural tradition as a whole.

The Natsushima shell midden occupies a prominent place in Jomon research because a small fireplace found immediately beneath the earliest shell layer— among the first archaeological features to be radiocarbon dated in Japan—returned the startlingly early age

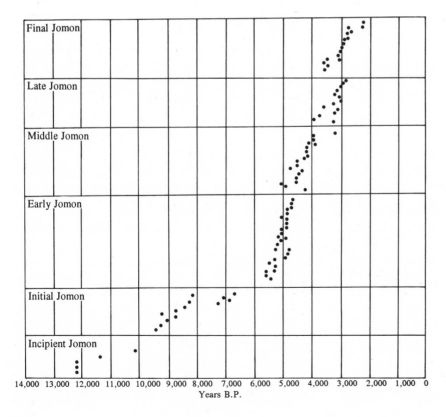

Fig. 2.1. Radiocarbon dates associated with Jomon pottery (based on Serizawa 1974:Fig. 285).

of 9240 b.p. A corresponding date on shell was 9450 b.p. (Crane and Griffin 1960:45). In 1960, when the Natsushima dates were published, this was about twice the age generally estimated for the Initial Jomon period; now, the high antiquity of the Jomon tradition is substantiated by a great many ^{14}C dates. Natsushima, yielding 34 species of shellfish, 17 species of marine fish, 11 species of mammals, and 7 species of birds, demonstrated a flourishing littoral economy. A great deal of pottery was found in the midden, along with flaked stone arrowpoints, bone fishhooks and gorges, flaked pebble adzes, and grinding stones.

The pottery of the shell layers was designated the Natsushima type. Not greatly different from the few small pieces of Igusa ware that preceded it, the Natsushima type was represented by more than 10,000 sherds. It demonstrated an overwhelming prevalence of cord marking, which covered vessel surfaces entirely. All of the restorable vessels were conical, with pointed or slightly rounded bottoms. So were all but a fraction of about 90 others for which basal fragments could be identified. The pointed bases, it has been suggested, would have facilitated pressing the pots into the coals of a cooking fire. In addition to the Natsushima type, many other types have been recognized in local sequences throughout Japan. Although the nuances are many, in general character all the Initial Jomon pottery is closely reminiscent of that from Natsushima.

EARLY JOMON

The period between about 6000 and 4500 b.p. saw the Jomon lifeway established in a substantially mature form. The basic house types and economic patterns that appeared earlier continued, though a notable innovation in northern Honshu was the appearance of large communal structures that occurred along with smaller dwellings of older types. The Jomon cultural tradition thereafter gave rise to increasingly dense populations and some notable local elaborations, but its fundamental adaptation to the Japanese environment did not change (Koyama 1978). Although a separate Jomon identity was finally lost in the great transformation of the Yayoi age, when an agricultural economy came to Japan, traditions of hunting, fishing, and gathering that were mature by the Early Jomon period have persisted strongly in the historical culture (Akimichi 1981; Koyama 1981, 1992; Matsuyama 1981; Aikens and Akazawa 1992).

Early Jomon pottery is dominated by deep vessels that are fundamentally of "flowerpot" shape, with broad open mouths and straight walls that taper slightly inward toward a flattened base. Pointed-bottom and round-bottom vessels reminiscent of Initial Jomon forms continue to be seen, and there are some pots with very narrow but flattened bottoms. Rims that flare outward near the top and vessels with bulging sides become more common later in the period. Fiber temper is general, though not universal, in Early Jomon pottery but largely disappears by the end of the period. Cord marking continues as a dominant decorative technique, with many variations, and shell marking or incising is often seen as well.

Many vessels and fragments show evidence of use as cooking pots, but it becomes increasingly clear during this period that storage was also a major function of much Jomon pottery. This is particularly evident in sites of northern Honshu such as Sugisawadai, Hatookazaki, and Taira, where huge amounts of pottery, including caches of many vessels, are found in association with large communal dwellings (Aomori-ken Kyoiku Iinkai 1980; Akita-ken Kyoiku Iinkai 1981; Iwate-ken Kyoiku Iinkai 1982). These have been dubbed "Snow Country Houses" and are seen as sites where whole communities concentrated themselves and their stores to last out the long, snowy winters of the region (Watanabe 1975).

Torihama, on the Japan Sea side of the country not far from Kyoto, is a waterlogged site that has preserved a detailed record of other technological items used along with the pottery of Early Jomon times (Torihama Shell Mound Research Group 1979–84). Wooden specimens recovered there include dugout canoes and carved paddles, hunting bows, and carefully shaped adze handles; more refined items that had been painted with red or black lacquer included a number of bowls and a wooden comb. Some fragments of lacquered pottery were recovered as well. Plant-fiber cordage, long attested for Jomon culture by the prevalent cord marking on pottery, was well represented at Torihama in a variety of gauges ranging from slender thread to substantial rope.

MIDDLE JOMON

Middle Jomon times, dated between about 4500 and 4000 b.p., produced the flamboyantly shaped and sculptured pottery that is surely the most widely known aspect of Jomon culture, inside or outside of Japan. The production of plain domestic vessels for cooking and storage certainly continued unabated, but the artistry and relative abundance of Middle Jomon ritual and display pottery forcefully draws attention to growing complexity in the sociopolitical realm. Middle Jomon culture flourished most richly in the Tokyo region and the adjacent mountainous region of central Honshu, where many large, long-occupied village sites are known (Fujimori 1965). Middle Jomon is recognizable throughout Japan, but the florescence that makes the period so notable was concentrated in a smaller region.

The concept of a "Jomon agriculture" that might have underpinned this growing social complexity has been discussed for a long time, but the crucial evidence that might conclusively demonstrate a productive agriculture this early remains lacking (Crawford and Takamiya 1990). What has become clear from continuing investigation, however, is the high productivity of the Japanese landscape under the Jomon hunter-fisher-gatherer regime and the degree to which native subsistence economics might have fostered patterns of settlement and harvesting behavior that mimicked or—in another view—presaged agricultural patterns (Nishida 1983).

Turning again to pottery, it seems likely that its manufacture continued to be a household industry, but it equally appears that the many spectacular and finely crafted pieces characteristic of this time were the work of specialists who produced for important people and important social rituals. Middle Jomon times surely saw the rise of significant sociopolitical elites, as I have argued elsewhere (Aikens 1981; see also Kobayashi 1992). The basic flowerpot shape continued in Middle Jomon times, but a variety of new, specialized forms also appeared. Where vessels of the basic flowerpot shape were elaborated, the work often consisted of sculpturing and modeling the rims, sometimes to a fantastic extent. The "flaming pottery" of the central mountains is one example (Kobayashi 1982); the rim designs can be easily imagined as licking flames. Serpents winding around the tops of vessels, their heads protruding above the level of the rim, are another common design, and protuberant anthropomorphic heads and other elements are often seen as well. Sometimes these elaborations made the vessels so top-heavy that extreme care must have been required to keep them from upsetting. Less overdone vessels often had simpler peaked or crenelated rims. Decoration by incising and applique overshadowed cord marking, although that technique persisted too.

In addition to the basic flowerpot shapes, there were large, deep vessels with straight, smooth rims, perforated all around, that may have accommodated skin drumheads laced across their tops; simple oval bowls;

and bowls with elaborated rims featuring handles or finger loops. Especially striking are small incense burners or lamps, often soot blackened, that feature overarching loop handles by which they might have been hung; these specimens in particular are often elaborately sculptured and richly decorated. Other distinctive shapes include footed bowls or goblets, narrow-necked jugs or pouring vessels, footed serving dishes, and even items that mimic seashells and other natural forms. Middle Jomon is also the period when there flourished elaborate, large, sculptured figurines, the most impressive of them having hollow bodies and large goggle eyes and wearing tunics and baggy trousers. The great majority of such figures are human females, as indicated by breasts, but male humans and a variety of zoomorphic items—often of solid rather than hollow construction—are also known. Excellent photographic essays illustrating the artistic richness of Middle Jomon pottery (and Jomon pottery generally) are available in Kidder and Esaka (1968) and Kobayashi (1977).

LATE JOMON

The Late Jomon dates between about 4000 and 3000 b.p. The pottery continues clearly in the tradition of Middle Jomon, but the fabric tends generally to be thinner and smoother, and the sculptural decoration is markedly less flamboyant. The top-heavy creations of Middle Jomon are rarely seen. Deep pots with straight or peaked rims continued as major forms, and ritual and display vessels continued as well, some new shapes being added to the inventory. The center of cultural elaboration at this period seems to have shifted from the central mountains to the Tokyo region, where large, long-occupied shell midden sites containing numerous pithouses and many burials are the best-known form of settlement.

The dominant decorative technique of Late Jomon was zoned cord marking, in which patterns outlined by deep incising or grooving were filled with cord marks. Outside the inscribed patterns—more often free-form or curvilinear than geometric—the surface was smoothed or polished. Ritual and prestige vessels continued the trend established in Middle Jomon. Incense burners, footed bowls, goblets, and zoomorphic forms persisted and took on new shapes, some of the footed serving dishes and goblets coming to stand on high pedestaled bases. Most striking is a proliferation of pouring vessels, which range from simple deep pots equipped with a small pouring spout near the rim to beautifully globular and elaborately decorated teapots of strikingly modern form that have pouring spouts, fitted lids, and overarching curved handles, or loops for the attachment of rope handles. Globular jars with tall, narrow necks, and jugs or pitchers with constricted openings and sometimes even thumb loops at the top, also represent pouring vessels. Obviously the ceremonious serving of beverages, heated or cooled, is well attested. The making of elaborate clay figurines also continued from Middle Jomon times.

FINAL JOMON

Radiocarbon dates for Final Jomon overlap conspicuously with those for the preceding Late Jomon (see Fig. 2.1). Age determinations associated with Final Jomon pottery place the period between about 3500 and 2000 b.p., a range that overlaps the end of Late Jomon by some 500 years. At the top of the Final Jomon time scale, the dates overlap by about the same amount with those for the Yayoi period, when the Jomon tradition lost its individual identity. In the former case, the overlapping dates seem to reflect no more than typological difficulties in drawing the line between Late and Final Jomon pottery types, which differ only in nuances. In the latter case, the new Yayoi pottery is distinctly different from the Jomon and is a marker intimately associated with the florescence of imported wet-rice agriculture. The overlap here reflects, most basically, the time involved in the spread of Yayoi agriculture and pottery from its southern point of ingress into the northern marches of Japan.

The center of elaboration of Final Jomon pottery was in far northern Honshu, where the Kamegaoka style flourished. The prestige forms—serving vessels, censers, teapots, zoomorphs—that characterized Late Jomon continued, and zoned cord marking persisted as a major decorative technique. Deep incising also remained important in tracing out a variety of curvilinear motifs. Perhaps most striking in this period is the high degree of finish that became commonplace, manifested in the polishing, burnishing, and even lacquering of pottery vessels. Also notable was the importance of small forms, some of which have been found as far south as the Kyoto region, where they were obviously trade items.

Other pottery products of what was obviously a prestige industry included anthropomorphic figurines (usually female), engraved pottery plaques, disks, earrings, and spherical beads, and even the elongate, curved beads called *magatama,* which—then made of semi-precious stone—became abundant in the subsequent Yayoi and Kofun periods of Japan and are recognized historically as important symbols of both Korean and Japanese imperial lineages. The highly refined Kamegaoka style represents the culmination, though not quite the end, of the Jomon pottery tradition.

CONTINUING JOMON

Under this heading may be briefly mentioned two ways in which the influence of the Jomon pottery tradition persisted beyond the period conventionally assigned to Jomon times. From about the Tokyo region northward, the Yayoi farmers who pioneered wet-rice cultivation in the region made a distinctive pottery that for the most part used the forms common in the Yayoi tradition but often used cord-marked decoration as well. Classified by archaeologists as Yayoi pottery, these wares manifestly continued a Jomon practice within a population that surely included both persistent Jomon hunter-fisher-gatherers and immigrant farmers from farther south (Aikens and Akazawa 1992).

In Hokkaido, cord-marked pottery more fully in the Jomon tradition and labeled by archaeologists as "Continuing Jomon" was similarly made for some centuries after the end of the Final Jomon period. This ware was used in the context of a fishing-hunting-gathering lifeway that was fundamentally Jomon in character and clearly persistent from earlier times. The so-called Continuing Jomon culture was ultimately supplanted, during what is known farther south as Kofun and Haji times, by a Satsumon culture. Satsumon included both surface-roughened pottery vaguely in the Jomon spirit and plain vessels that were clearly derivative of the new continental tradition introduced in Yayoi times. Satsumon culture also included, to some degree at least, the cultivation of wheat, millet, and other domesticates introduced from the continent (Crawford and Takamiya 1990).

Regional Variation in Jomon Pottery

Regional variation developed early in Jomon pottery and remained marked throughout the life of the tradition. A mapping by Kamaki (1965) is old but still widely cited, sometimes with slightly different subdivisions. Kamaki's map shows six broad regions in existence by Early Jomon times, spread across a northeast-southwest distance of about 2,000 kilometers (Fig. 2.2). Area I includes most of Hokkaido, from about

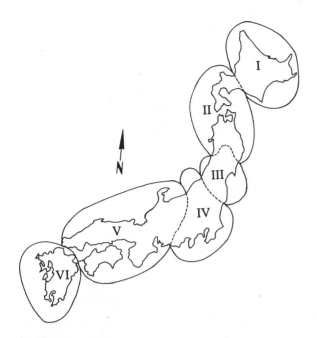

Fig. 2.2. Regional pottery distribution spheres of Early Jomon times (after Kamaki 1965:Fig. 4).

forest of the greater Tokyo region of central Honshu; an *Umataka-Chojigahara* area in the warm-temperate deciduous forest on the Japan Sea side of central Honshu, where winter snows lie deep; a *Katsusaka* area in the warm-temperate evergreen broadleaf and deciduous forest on the Pacific slope of central Honshu; a *Funamoto* area in the evergreen broadleaf forest of southwestern Honshu and Shikoku; and a *Sobata-Ataka* area in the evergreen broadleaf forest of Kyushu (Fig. 2.3). The names reflect the regional pottery typology, and the differing environmental settings imply that human adaptations to regional biotas defined interaction spheres within which certain habits of pottery manufacture were also shared. Another view of regionalism in Jomon culture, approached from data on subsistence technologies other than pottery, identifies groupings that are generally congruent with those named by Watanabe but less finely subdivided (Akazawa 1986).

Origin of the Jomon Pottery Tradition

The earliest pottery appeared in southwestern Japan just as the Pleistocene-Holocene transition was well under way. It then spread northeastward through the archipelago from Kyushu to Hokkaido over a period of several thousand years. At Fukui Cave, in southwestern Kyushu, the earliest ^{14}C date for pottery is 12,700 b.p.; at Kamikuroiwa in Shikoku, it is 12,200 b.p.; at Natsushima on Tokyo Bay, central Honshu, it is 9450 b.p.; and in Aomori Prefecture at the northern tip of Honshu, it is 8600 b.p. In Hokkaido the dates are less clear, but the inception of pottery is thought to lie between about 8500 and 7000 b.p. (Serizawa 1974; Esaka 1986). The ^{14}C dates provide minimum ages for the appearance of pottery because they are associated with specimens believed on stratigraphic and typological grounds not to be the very earliest in their respective regions.

The Pleistocene-Holocene transition was a period when higher postglacial sea levels created thousands of miles of productive new shoreline with innumerable small islands, bays, and inlets and corresponding opportunities for littoral and marine harvesting. It was also a time of major biotic shifts throughout the Japanese archipelago, equally linked to climatic change across the Pleistocene-Holocene boundary. Tsukada (1986:Fig. 8) charts data from 33 pollen sites distributed across Japan from 31 to 44 degrees north latitude. He shows that oaks, which glacial cold had kept in a

Sapporo onward to the northeast; Area II includes peninsular southern Hokkaido and northernmost Honshu; Area III comprises north-central Honshu; Area IV encompasses central Honshu; Area V covers the remainder of southwestern Honshu and the island of Shikoku; and Area VI comprises the island of Kyushu. This pattern persists, with some changes in the shape of the areas, through Middle and Late Jomon times. In Final Jomon times the pattern changes markedly, with two very large style zones dominating northeastern and southwestern Japan, respectively, and two much smaller zones centered on central Honshu's Tokyo region and on Hokkaido. By the end of the period, southwestern Japan was dominated by pottery of Yayoi type, and northeastern Japan by the last of the Jomon wares.

Watanabe (1974) has pointed out, in discussing various patterns of human adaptation to the natural environment, that the pottery style zones which persisted through much of the Jomon age correspond quite closely to biotic subregions. Dividing the pottery areas in northeast Honshu more finely than did Kamaki, and focusing on Early and Middle Jomon times, Watanabe identifies a *Hokuto* area in the needle-leaf forest of northeast Hokkaido; an *Ento* area in the cool-temperate deciduous forest of peninsular Hokkaido and northern Honshu; a *Daigi* area in the warm-temperate deciduous forest of south-central Honshu; an *Ukishima-Otama* area in the evergreen broadleaf

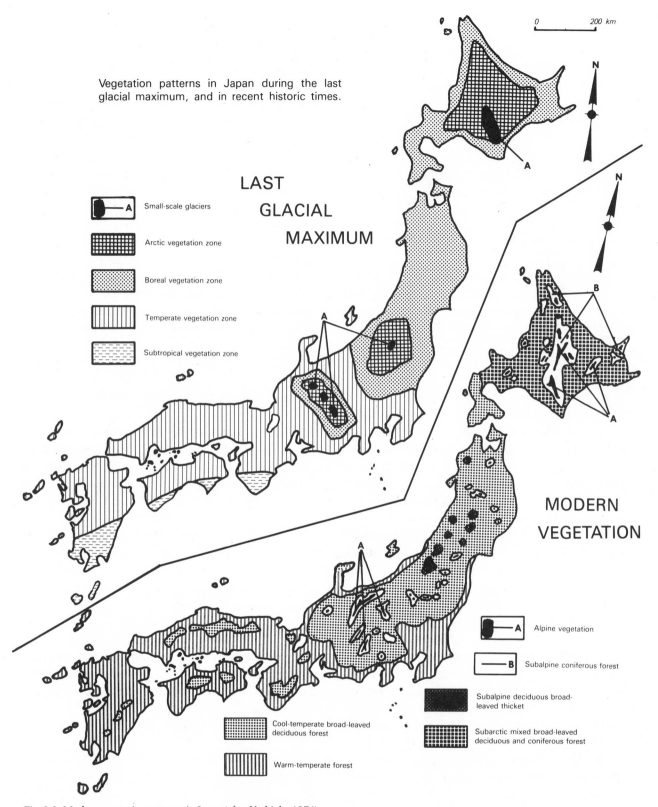

Vegetation patterns in Japan during the last glacial maximum, and in recent historic times.

LAST GLACIAL MAXIMUM

Small-scale glaciers

Arctic vegetation zone

Boreal vegetation zone

Temperate vegetation zone

Subtropical vegetation zone

MODERN VEGETATION

Alpine vegetation

Subalpine coniferous forest

Subalpine deciduous broad-leaved thicket

Subarctic mixed broad-leaved deciduous and coniferous forest

Cool-temperate broad-leaved deciduous forest

Warm-temperate forest

Fig. 2.3. Modern vegetation patterns in Japan (after Yoshioka 1974).

southern Kyushu refugium, spread rapidly northward after 12,000 b.p. They soon reached central Honshu and were in central Hokkaido by about 8000 b.p. Notably, the dates for the northward spread of pottery track closely the dates for northward expansion of broadleaf temperate forest.

An intimate linkage between the subsistence economy of the Jomon age and the diverse biota of Holocene littoral and forest settings has been overwhelmingly demonstrated. Monograph after monograph provides long lists of the shellfish, fish, bird, and mammal species found in archaeological sites. Direct plant macrofossil evidence is much less abundant, but remains of hard-shelled nuts such as acorns, walnuts, chestnuts, and buckeyes are common, and more than 40 edible plant species have been recovered from Jomon sites where conditions were favorable to preservation (Fujimori 1965; Watanabe 1975). Fishhooks, fish spears, net weights, projectile points, pit traps, milling slabs, nut stones, mortars, pestles, hoe/digging stick tips, and other tools, found everywhere, show how this bounty was taken and processed.

Unquestionably there was a direct practical connection between the making and use of pottery and the evolution of the broad-spectrum, hunting-fishing-gathering, woodland/waterside economy that Jomon people created in adapting to the new biotic conditions of Holocene times. The close juxtaposition of diverse resource zones in the topographically rugged and biotically rich Japanese environment early fostered stable settlements and growing populations. In the subsistence regime of these early Japanese, the cooking and storing of diverse animal and vegetal foods was fundamental to existence, and Jomon pottery served both purposes cheaply and effectively.

In trying to imagine the beginnings of Jomon pottery, it is immediately clear that the social and environmental context was all important. It was not some accidental concatenation of earth and fire that brought forth the earliest Japanese pottery. People everywhere surely had long known about the plasticity of wet earth, the hardening effects of fire, and the utility of containers. What was new at the beginning of the Holocene in Japan was a social and environmental context in which people needed cooking and storage containers in large quantity. In this context there were obvious advantages to fired earth vessels that could be made for a fraction of the labor required by skin bags, bark buckets, plant-fiber baskets, or hollowed-out containers of wood or stone.

Conclusions

Jomon pottery appeared during the transition from Pleistocene to Holocene environmental conditions. The tradition lasted long, and archaeologists have segmented it into many temporal and regional subdivisions. At first wholly utilitarian, the pottery came by Middle Jomon times to play also an important role in social ritual and social status display. The appearance of Jomon pottery in Japan was clearly fostered by new conditions of life at the beginning of the Holocene. Though its broader context is not addressed in the foregoing, the Jomon pottery of Japan was but the most precocious (so far as we now know) among traditions that developed over about the same period on the adjacent Asian mainland, evidently under quite similar conditions (Aikens 1992).

References Cited

Aikens, C. Melvin
  1981   The Last 10,000 Years in Japan and Eastern North America: Parallels in Environment, Economic Adaptation, Growth of Societal Complexity, and the Adoption of Agriculture. In *Affluent Foragers: Pacific Coasts East and West,* edited by S. Koyama and D. H. Thomas. Senri Ethnological Studies 9:261–73. National Museum of Ethnology, Osaka.
  1992   Hunting, Fishing, and Gathering in Pacific Northeast Asia: Pleistocene Continuities and Holocene Developments. In *Pacific Northeast Asia in Prehistory,* edited by C. M. Aikens and S. N. Rhee, pp. 99–104. Washington State University Press, Pullman.
Aikens, C. Melvin, and Takeru Akazawa
  1992   Fishing and Farming in Early Japan: Jomon Littoral Tradition Carried into Yayoi Times at the Miura Caves on Tokyo Bay. In *Pacific Northeast Asia in Prehistory,* edited by C. M. Aikens and S. N. Rhee, pp. 75–82. Washington State University Press, Pullman.
Aikens, C. Melvin, and Takayasu Higuchi
  1982   *Prehistory of Japan.* Academic Press, New York.
Akazawa, Takeru
  1986   Regional Variation in Procurement Systems of Jomon Hunter-Gatherers. In *Prehistoric Hunter-Gatherers in Japan: New Research Methods,* edited by T. Akazawa and C. M. Aikens, pp. 73–89. University of Tokyo Press, Tokyo.

Akimichi, Tomoya
1981   Riverine Fisheries in Nineteenth Century Hida. In *Affluent Foragers: Pacific Coasts East and West,* edited by S. Koyama and D. H. Thomas. Senri Ethnological Studies 9:141–56. National Museum of Ethnology, Osaka.

Akita-ken Kyoiku Iinkai
1981   Excavation Report on the Sugisawadai and Takesei Sites. *Akita-ken Bunkazai Chosa Hokokusho* 83. (In Japanese)

Aomori-ken Kyoiku Iinkai
1980   Excavation Report on the Taira Site. *Aomori-ken Maizo Bunkazai Chosa Hokokusho* 52. (In Japanese)

Bleed, Peter
1978   Origins of the Jomon Technical Tradition. *Asian Perspectives* 19(1):105–15.

Crane, H. R., and J. B. Griffin
1960   University of Michigan Radiocarbon Dates V. *Radiocarbon Supplement* 2:31–48.

Crawford, Gary, and Hiroto Takamiya
1990   The Origins and Implications of Late Prehistoric Plant Husbandry in Northern Japan. *Antiquity* 64(245):889–911.

Esaka, Teruya
1986   The Origins and Characteristics of Jomon Ceramic Culture: A Brief Introduction. In *Windows on the Japanese Past: Studies in Archaeology and Prehistory,* edited by R. J. Pearson, G. L. Barnes, and K. L. Hutterer, pp. 223–28. Center for Japanese Studies, University of Michigan, Ann Arbor.

Fujimori, Eiichi
1965   *Idojiri: A Middle Jomon Culture from the Southern Foothills of Yatsugatake.* Chuo Koron Bijutsu Shuppan, Tokyo. (In Japanese)

Iwate-ken Kyoiku Iinkai
1982   Tohoku Trunk Highway Buried Cultural Resources Excavation Report XV-2. *Iwate-ken Bunkazai Chosa Hokokusho* 70. (In Japanese)

Kamaki, Yoshimasa
1965   An Outline of Jomon Culture. In *Nihon no Kokogaku, II: Jomon Jidai,* edited by Yoshimasa Kamaki, pp. 2–28. Kawade Shobo Shinsha, Tokyo. (In Japanese)

Kaner, Simon
1990   The Western Language Jomon: A Review. In *Bibliographical Reviews of Far Eastern Archaeology 1990: Hoabinhian, Jomon, Yayoi, Early Korean States,* edited by G. L. Barnes. Oxbow Books, Cambridge.

Kato, Shinpei, Tatsuo Kobayashi, and Kyo Fujimoto
1981–84   *Jomon Culture Research,* vols. 3, 4, 5. Yuzankaku, Tokyo. (In Japanese)

Kidder, J. Edward, and Teruya Esaka
1968   *Prehistoric Japanese Arts: Jomon Pottery.* Kodansha, Tokyo.

Kobayashi, Tatsuo
1982   Echigo: Country of the Flaming Pottery. *The East,* March 1982:54–61.
1992   Patterns and Levels of Social Complexity in Jomon Japan. In *Pacific Northeast Asia in Prehistory,* edited by C. M. Aikens and S. N. Rhee, pp. 91–96. Washington State University Press, Pullman.

Kobayashi, Tatsuo (ed.)
1977   *Archaeological Treasures of Japan: Jomon Pottery.* Kodansha, Tokyo. (In Japanese, with English notes)

Koyama, Shuzo
1978   *Jomon Subsistence and Population.* Senri Ethnological Studies 2. National Museum of Ethnology, Osaka.
1981   A Quantitative Study of Wild Food Resources: An Example From Hida. In *Affluent Foragers: Pacific Coasts East and West,* edited by S. Koyama and D. H. Thomas. Senri Ethnological Studies 9:91–115. National Museum of Ethnology, Osaka.

Koyama, Shuzo (ed.)
1992   *Hunting and Fishing: Exploring the Sources of Japanese Culture.* Yuzankaku, Tokyo. (In Japanese)

Matsuyama, Toshio
1981   Nut Gathering and Processing Methods in Traditional Japanese Villages. In *Affluent Foragers: Pacific Coasts East and West,* edited by S. Koyama and D. H. Thomas. Senri Ethnological Studies 9:117–39. National Museum of Ethnology, Osaka.

Morse, Edward S.
1879   The Shell Mound of Omori. *Memoirs of the Science Department, University of Tokyo* 1(1).

Nishida, Masaki
1983   The Emergence of Food Production in Neolithic Japan. *Journal of Anthropological Archaeology* 2:305–22.

Pearson, Richard J., Gina Lee Barnes, and Karl L. Hutterer (eds.)
1986   *Windows on the Japanese Past: Studies in Archaeology and Prehistory.* Center for Japanese Studies, University of Michigan, Ann Arbor.

Serizawa, Chosuke (ed.)
1974   *Excavating Ancient History 1: The First Hunters.* Kodansha, Tokyo. (In Japanese)

Sugihara, Sosuke, and Chosuke Serizawa
1957   Shell Mounds of the Earliest Jomon Culture at Natsushima, Kanagawa Prefecture, Japan.

Meiji Daigaku Bungakubu Kenkyu Hokoku 5. (In
Japanese)

Suzuki, Yasuhiko
  1981   Incipient Jomon Pottery Types. In *Jomon
           Bunka no Kenkyu* 3:44–65. Yuzankaku, Tokyo.
           (In Japanese)

Torihama Shell Mound Research Group
  1979–84 *Torihama Shell Mound.* 4 vols. Fukui-ken
           Kyoiku Iinkai, Fukui Kenritsu Wakasa Rekishi
           Minzoku Shiryokan. (In Japanese)

Tsukada, Matsuo
  1986   Vegetation in Prehistoric Japan: The Last
           20,000 Years. In *Windows on the Japanese Past:
           Studies in Archaeology and Prehistory,* edited by
           R. J. Pearson, G. L. Barnes, and K. L.

Hutterer, pp. 11–56. Center for Japanese
Studies, University of Michigan, Ann Arbor.

Watanabe, Makoto
  1974   Various Patterns of Man's Adaptation to the
           Natural Environments in the Jomon Age. *The
           Quaternary Research* (Dai-Yonki Kenkyu)
           13(3):160–67. (In Japanese)
  1975   *Vegetable Foods of the Jomon Period.* Yuzankaku,
           Tokyo. (In Japanese)

Yoshioka, Kunji
  1974   Vegetation Map of Japan. In *The Flora and
           Vegetation of Japan,* edited by M. Numata,
           p. 295. Kodansha, Tokyo; Elsevier,
           Amsterdam.

3

Few and Far Between

Early Ceramics in North Africa

ANGELA E. CLOSE

The African invention of pottery occurred some time in the tenth millennium b.p. It took place within the zone that is now the southern Sahara and the Sahel, but probably neither west of the Hoggar Mountains nor east of the Nile Valley. The invention was made—perhaps more than once—among groups who ranged from (at most) semisedentary to highly mobile and whose subsistence was based almost entirely upon wild species. (The possession of domestic animals did not markedly affect the ways of life of the groups who had them.) In North Africa, as elsewhere in the western Old World, it is traditional to call "Neolithic" those groups with pottery, ground stone, domesticates, and permanent settlements and to take the presence of any one of these as sufficient proof of the existence of the others. It is now apparent that each of the four traits is independent of the others and that the first African pottery appeared in a variety of archaeological contexts in which it probably served socially and economically different purposes.

Initial Distributions in Time and Space

Pottery first appeared in North Africa in the mid-tenth to the early ninth millennium b.p. In the southern central Sahara, the earliest indication is from Temet, in the Ténéré of northern Niger (Fig. 3.1), where a fibrolite potter's comb was found in a cultural layer dated on charcoal to almost 9600 b.p. (Table 3.1). It was sealed under a thick layer of diatomite that yielded dates of about 9500 b.p. and 8500 b.p. (Roset 1987:220–25). No ceramics were found at Temet itself, but the nearby site of Adrar Bous 10 yielded numerous potsherds in a cultural layer that was, again, sealed under diatomite. Charcoal from the cultural layer has given three dates tightly clustered around 9100 b.p. (Roset 1987:222). Farther south, in the Aïr, sherds were also common in the archaeological deposit at Tagalagal—a deposit 70 cm thick preserved under a small rockshelter (Fig. 3.2). Associated charcoal yielded two dates of about 9300 b.p. There is a similar date associated with the ceramics of Tamaya Mellet to the west (Delibrias et al. 1974: 44) and a somewhat later—mid-ninth millennium—date for the pottery-bearing rockshelter of Gabrong in northern Chad (Gabriel 1972; Jäkel and Geyh 1982: 157).

In the Hoggar Mountains of Algeria in the central Sahara, the lower cultural layer of the Launey site is dated to about 9200 b.p. (Maître 1974:101). Farther to the east, in the Tadrart Acacus of western Libya, ce-

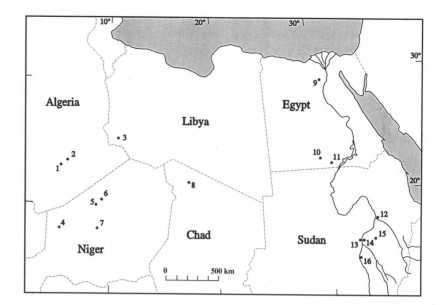

Fig. 3.1. North African ceramic-bearing sites discussed in chapter 3. Key: 1, Amekni; 2, Launey; 3, Wadi Ti-n-Torha; 4, Tamaya Mellet; 5, Temet; 6, Adrar Bous 10; 7, Tagalagal; 8, Gabrong; 9, Fayum; 10, Kiseiba; 11, Nabta; 12; Abu Darbein; 13; Sarurab; 14, Saggai, Geili; 15, Shaqadud; 16, Shabona.

Table 3.1. Radiocarbon-Dated Sites in North Africa with Early (≥8500 b.p.) Pottery

Site	Country	Age b.p.	Ref./Lab No.	Sample
Temet	Niger	9550 ± 100	Roset 1987	Charcoal
Adrar Bous 10	Niger	9130 ± 65	Roset 1987	Charcoal
Adrar Bous 10	Niger	9100 ± 150	Roset 1987	Charcoal
Adrar bous 10	Niger	9030 ± 190	Roset 1987	Charcoal
Tagalagal	Niger	9370 ± 130	Roset 1987	Charcoal
Tagalagal	Niger	9330 ± 130	Roset 1987	Charcoal
Tamaya Mellet	Niger	9350 ± 170	Gif-1728	Bone
Gabrong	Chad	8560 ± 120	Hv-3715	?
Launey	Algeria	9210 ± 115	UW-97	Charcoal
Ti-n-Torha East	Libya	8670 ± 60	R-1163α	Charcoal
Ti-n-Torha East	Libya	8640 ± 70	R-1035α	Charcoal
E-77-7 (Nabta)	Egypt	8960 ± 110	SMU-440	Charcoal
E-77-7 (Nabta)	Egypt	8870 ± 80	SMU-2591	Charcoal
E-79-8 (Kiseiba)	Egypt	9820 ± 380	SMU-858	Charcoal
E-79-8 (Kiseiba)	Egypt	9610 ± 150	SMU-928	Charcoal
E-79-8 (Kiseiba)	Egypt	9440 ± 230	SMU-758	Charcoal
E-79-8 (Kiseiba)	Egypt	9350 ± 120	SMU-927	Charcoal
E-79-8 (Kiseiba)	Egypt	9180 ± 140	SMU-914	Charcoal
E-79-8 (Kiseiba)	Egypt	9060 ± 80	SMU-861	Charcoal
E-79-8 (Kiseiba)	Egypt	8920 ± 130	SMU-757	Charcoal
E-80-4 (Kiseiba)	Egypt	9220 ± 120	SMU-925	Charcoal
Sarurab	Sudan	9370 ± 110	HAR-3475	Charcoal
Sarurab	Sudan	9340 ± 110	HAR-3476	Charcoal
Saggai	Sudan	10060 ± 150	Caneva 1983	Shell
Abu Darbein	Sudan	8640 ± 120	T-8624	Shell
Abu Darbein	Sudan	8560 ± 35	Q-3230	Shell
Abu Darbein	Sudan	8500 ± 100	T-6381	Shell

Fig. 3.2. Late tenth-millennium b.p. potsherds from Tagalagal, Niger (reproduced by permission from Roset 1987:Fig. 11.4).

ramics appear in the long cave sequences of the Wadi Ti-n-Torha by about 8700 b.p. (Barich 1987a:105).

In the eastern Sahara, ceramics are known from three early sites in southern Egypt, two (E-79-8 [Connor 1984:239–43] and E-80-4 [Close 1984b:346]) near Kiseiba and one (E-77-7 [H. Haas, personal communication 1992; Haas and Haynes 1980:Table A7.1]) near Nabta, which is only 100 kilometers from the Nile Valley. The ten dates for these sites (Table 3.1) range throughout almost the whole of the tenth millennium b.p. There is no close association, however, between the earlier dates and the potsherds, which might therefore be better placed within the later centuries of the tenth millennium.

In the central Nile Valley, there are two dates for ceramics of about 9300 b.p. from Sarurab, near Khartoum (Khabir 1987a). This age has not been universally accepted (Marks and Mohammed-Ali 1991:239), because the same site had previously been dated to about 6000 b.p. The younger dates, however, were run on samples of bone and shell (Mohammed-Ali 1984:118), whereas the tenth-millennium dates are on charcoal and may therefore be more reliable. They are not, in any case, discordant with the suite of early dates for pottery in North Africa as a whole (Table 3.1). Absolutely the earliest date for a ceramic horizon in North Africa is that of more than 10,000 years from Saggai, also near Khartoum. It may be too old, however: it is almost a thousand years earlier than the next oldest firmly associated dates, the sample was of Nile oyster shell rather than charcoal, and four other dates for the site fall in the second half of the eighth millennium b.p. (Caneva 1983:149–52). On the Atbara

River, pottery is firmly dated to the mid-ninth millennium b.p. at Abu Darbein (Haaland 1987b:49, and personal communication, 1993).

The distribution of the earliest ceramic-bearing sites in North Africa is essentially confined to what is or was the southern part of the Sahara (Fig. 3.1). More northerly parts of the desert, the Maghreb, the Mediterranean coast, and the lower Nile Valley were the provinces of groups whom archaeologists would see as more traditionally "Epipaleolithic," manufacturing fine bladelet tools but not pottery. This northern, aceramic Epipaleolithic persisted through the tenth and ninth millennia b.p. (summarized in Close 1987: 77–80), and, in some areas, even later. Pottery was known in the Saharan Atlas Mountains by the mid-eighth millennium (Aumassip 1986; Grébénart 1970) but did not appear in Cyrenaïca until about 7000 b.p. (McBurney 1967:271) and is completely lacking from the lower Nile Valley until 6300 b.p. (Ginter et al. 1985:27). Many of the early pottery-using groups in the desert flaked stone tools very similar to those of their Epipaleolithic contemporaries to the north, but the presence/absence dichotomy in ceramics remains striking.

Within the broad east-west zone of the southern Sahara, it is impossible to identify precisely one area where pottery-making technology was discovered. There is no geographical trend discernible among the radiocarbon dates (Table 3.1). This problem is compounded by the fact that all of the earliest ceramics occur in regions that had been previously unoccupied (or apparently so) for at least several millennia, so that there are no local precursors among whom we might hope to trace the development of ceramic technology. Despite persistent suggestions of a Saharan wet phase as late as 20,000 b.p. (for example, Petit-Maire 1988:20), most evidence now indicates that the region had become hyperarid and therefore uninhabitable by 50,000 b.p. (summarized by Schild et al. 1992) and that it remained so until the northward shift of the monsoon belt at the very end of the Pleistocene. The ceramic sites noted earlier represent some (but not all) of the first colonists of the desert after that northward shift.

The Nile, however, continued to flow, although sometimes sluggishly, throughout this period, and there is evidence for unbroken occupation of the valley as far south as the Second Cataract. In contrast, from the Second Cataract to Khartoum—a stretch that includes most of the early ceramic occurrences in the valley—there are no known late Pleistocene aceramic sites (Marks et al. 1987:137–38); the reason for this remains obscure. Our first sight of North African pottery makers is therefore always one of recent immigrants; this is certainly so in the desert and apparently so in the central Nile Valley. Their geographical distribution and their association with a northward shift of the monsoon belt suggest that they came from the south and that pottery might have even greater antiquity in what is now the Sahelian zone; this is, of course, pure speculation.

The Early Ceramics

Insofar as can be determined from what are often only a very few, very small sherds, the earliest pottery in North Africa encompassed a variety of simple vessel forms and a number of different decorative motifs, and it tended to be well and carefully formed and fired. This is so much the case that its excavators have often felt obliged to remark that it must have been preceded by a lengthy (though as yet undiscovered) period of development. Once the basic facts of shaping and firing clay had been mastered, however, a wide range of options would automatically have become possible: what Roset calls "the immediately available technological minimum" (1987:230). We should not expect early pottery to be simple or crude; indeed, in some sequences, cruder or coarser ceramics appear later, presumably indicating that pottery had by then become commonplace (see Vitelli, chapter 5).

The early pottery tends to be extensively decorated. In fact, the absence of undecorated sherds from some collections, such as those from Egypt and Niger, suggests that vessels may have been decorated all over (Nieves Zedeño, personal communication, 1992). In contrast, decoration on the earliest vessels from the Wadi Ti-n-Torha is concentrated on their upper parts (Barich 1987a:105). Plain sherds are always a minority, and usually a small minority, until the late Neolithic.

Most decorative motifs were created by comb impressions, often with a rocking technique, with lower frequencies of incisions, cord impressions, and impressions of single- or double-pronged wands. This decoration gives a feeling of homogeneity and consistency across the region until the appearance (also widespread) of burnished pottery about 6000 b.p. Many of the decorations can be seen as part of Arkell's (1949) vaguely defined Wavy Line and, especially, Dotted Wavy Line groups (consisting, respectively, of sets of parallel incised and parallel dot-impressed lines in which waviness seems to be entirely optional [Caneva 1987; Mohammed-Ali 1991:69–70]).

There also exist similarities in some other aspects of material culture (most notably barbed bone points, or "harpoons") between the central Sahara and the central Nile Valley. For these reasons, there have been attempts to place most or all of the southern ceramic sites into a single archaeological entity, such as the "Neolithic of Sudanese Tradition" (Camps 1969: 197), the "Saharo-Sudanese Neolithic" (Camps 1974: 221–61), or the "African Aqualithic" (Sutton 1974, 1977). Such lumping has always met some resistance (Haaland 1987a:19–20; Hays 1975:194–96), occasionally vigorous (Maître 1974:102–10). The increase in our knowledge over the last two decades now indicates that these entities were founded primarily upon our ignorance of the prehistoric complexity of the region. Unfortunately, although we can now see that complexity exists, we still cannot see enough to discern its outlines, and any attempt to define meaningful cultural groups within this vast area remains premature.

Physical and chemical analyses of early North African ceramics have not been common, and they have been concerned with clay and temper characterization rather than with pottery function (Adamson et al. 1987; Ali Hakem and Khabir 1989; Banks 1980; Chlodnicki 1989; de Paepe 1986a, 1986b, 1991; Echallier and Roset 1986; Francaviglia and Palmieri 1983, 1988; Hays and Hassan 1974a, 1974b; Khabir 1987b, 1991; Nordström 1972; Palmieri 1987; Zedeño and Wendorf 1993).

Although sherds themselves have been analyzed, there have rarely been complementary analyses (as opposed to broad geological characterizations) of the potential sources of raw materials (exceptions are Ali Hakem and Khabir [1989], Francaviglia and Palmieri [1988], and Zedeño and Wendorf [1993]), so that the value of even the existing studies is somewhat limited. Nonetheless, with few exceptions—and those exceptions are late in time (Francaviglia and Palmieri 1988: 357)—the sherds analyzed tend to cluster by site, even when the sites are within a few kilometers of each other. This suggests that pottery was made locally rather than in some central place of manufacture and distribution. In those cases where clay and temper sources have been analyzed, the overall results indicate that some or most ceramics were made locally (often *very* locally, from clays within tens or hundreds of meters of the site) but that others came from farther away, although not usually very far. In Egypt, most of the early ceramics from the Nabta and Kiseiba areas were made from clays found within the same basins as the sites themselves, but there was also occasional east-west movement of vessels between the two areas, a distance of about 100 kilometers (Zedeño and Wendorf 1993). At Adrar Bous 10, most of the raw materials occur within 15–20 kilometers of the site, although a few are from farther afield, whereas at Tagalalag, none of the raw materials occurs very close to the site, but almost all are within 25 kilometers (Echallier and Roset 1986).

Contexts of the Early Ceramics

Early North African pottery appears in an area that extends some 3,000 kilometers from east to west and over 1,000 kilometers from north to south. Within so large an area, a great deal of variability is to be expected in all aspects of human culture, but only parts of that pattern can yet be seen. Relatively few sites have been investigated, not all of those are fully published, and most sites simply do not yield material that will tell us much about the ways of life of their occupants: some sites have no bone preserved, and very few have floral remains other than scraps of charcoal. Rather than make bold generalizations across an archaeological map that is largely blank, I shall concentrate upon the three groups of sites for which the fullest information is presently available: the sites at Nabta and Kiseiba in the arid heart of the eastern Sahara; the sites of Wadi Ti-n-Torha in the massif of the Tadrart Acacus; and the Khartoum Mesolithic sites of the central Nile Valley.

THE EASTERN SAHARA

Today, the eastern Sahara is the driest part of the desert, and this seems also to have been true during the early Holocene. The greater aridity meant that some cultural responses seen in better-watered regions to the west and south—particularly semisedentism—were not possible. On the other hand, the greater challenge of mere survival in the eastern Sahara was met by the adoption of cattle pastoralism, for which there is no evidence farther west until perhaps 2,000 years later.

After the long period of late Pleistocene aridity, the rains returned to the eastern Sahara somewhat before 11,000 b.p. They did not return in quantity, however: estimates of annual rainfall during the early Holocene vary from less than 100 millimeters to 200 millimeters,

and being monsoonal, the rainfall would have been confined to a single, brief (summer) season (summarized by Close 1992:158). The wild herbivore faunas (other than micromammals) of the early Holocene are almost entirely limited to hares and small gazelles; oryx occurs but rarely. These are all desert-adapted creatures that need to drink only occasionally, if at all (Gautier 1984; Van Neer and Uerpmann 1989).

People began to return to the eastern Sahara in detectable numbers after about 9500 b.p. Because the rains came from the south, it would seem reasonable that the people should have come from the same direction. There is no evidence for this at all from Sudan, however, and the closest parallels in stone artifacts are with sites in the Nubian Nile Valley. All of the tenth-millenium and most of the ninth-millennium sites seem to be typical traces of the short-term camps of small groups of hunter-gatherers, characterized by flaked (and some ground) stone artifacts, mammal bones, ostrich eggshell, and charcoal (Wendorf and Schild 1980:103–28; Wendorf et al. 1984). However, all the faunal collections of any size (more than 41 identifiable bones) include a few bones of presumably domestic cattle (Close and Wendorf 1992), and several sites, including the earliest ones, have yielded potsherds (Fig. 3.3).

For the earliest sites, the only direct evidence for subsistence is the animal bones. Meat was obtained

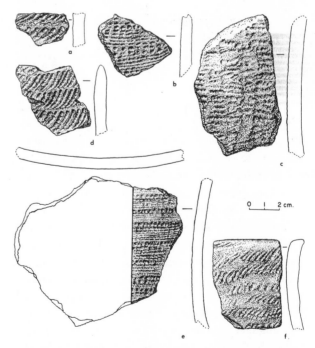

Fig. 3.3. Early potsherds from Site E-79-8 near Bir Kiseiba (eastern Sahara). Sherds *a*, *d*, and *f* are late tenth millennium b.p. in age; *b*, *c*, and *e* date to about 8000 b.p. (after Connor 1984:Fig. 11.15).

primarily by hunting hares and gazelles. Cattle bones are so rare that cattle were probably kept as living sources of protein—milk and blood—rather than for meat. They could also have served as water purification systems wherever the water was too brackish for human consumption (see Potts 1993:177). Some modern Sahelian pastoralists subsist for several months each year on milk, milk products, and very little else (Smith 1980). The eastern Sahara of the early Holocene was no more forgiving than the modern Sahel, and the possession of domestic animals may have been the factor that permitted people to colonize and survive there, providing insurance in a very precarious environment.

The consistent occurrence of grinding stones strongly indicates the use of plant foods throughout the early Holocene. The earliest identified remains are from E-75-6 at Nabta, dating to about 8000 b.p., where the commonest varieties are *Zizyphus* fruits and the grains of sorghum, which was morphologically wild although its lipid chemistry suggests the possibility of cultivation (Wendorf et al. 1992). These were accompanied by a range of other wild grasses (principally *Panicum, Setaria,* and *Echinochloa*), seeds of legumes, seeds probably of the mustard and caper families, unidentified tubers, and other, less frequent types. Wild grass grains have been harvested intensively by recent Saharan and Subsaharan groups. They seem to be more nutritious, important, and reliable foods than domestic cereals, especially in marginal areas (Harlan 1989).

Dwelling structures were apparently quite insubstantial until well after 8000 b.p., and all the evidence suggests a strictly nomadic way of life. The largest and richest sites (in terms of artifacts), and thus presumably those used for the longest periods, are in the lower parts of playa basins where wells were dug to obtain water in the dry season. Because these sites were seasonally flooded, they were also seasonally abandoned; other sites appear to have been even more ephemeral. Sedentism was unknown.

Thus, the archaeological record suggests that pottery was being made and used by small, highly mobile groups of hunter-gatherers who also herded domestic cattle but did not let this herding greatly affect their way of life. This scenario is strongly supported by linguistic evidence. Reconstruction of the Proto-Northern Sudanic language includes words for "temporary shelter" but not for permanent structures; for "cow," "to milk," and "to drive (domestic animals)"; for "grain," "ear of grain," and "grindstone" (according with the impor-

tance of wild grass seeds); and for "to make pottery" (Ehret 1993:110). Ehret dates the Proto-Northern Sudanic language to about 8000 B.C. (1993:Fig. 6.1), which would probably coincide rather closely with the radiocarbon dates if they could be calibrated.

What the pots were being used for in this context remains mysterious. Pots have traditionally been viewed as cooking vessels (Vitelli 1989:24–25). At E-75-6, four "house-floors" revealed hundreds of small (15–25 cm in diameter), hemispherical earth ovens in which plant foods were baked in hot ashes, but there were altogether only 12 potsherds. If containers were used, assuredly they were not ceramic vessels—but it is possible that there were no containers. Modern Zaghawa bake hard cakes by putting a mixture of *Zizyphus* and millet flours into a hole in the ground and burning fuel on the top (Tubiana and Tubiana 1977:20). Cakes of sorghum and *Zizyphus* thus baked might, after removal, leave archaeological traces similar to those found at E-75-6.

Indeed, one of the most remarkable aspects of the eastern Saharan pottery is its rarity: before about 7600 b.p., no site has more than a few sherds and many sites have none. (The richest site, E-79-2 near Kiseiba, dating to about 7600 b.p., has fewer than 10 sherds per cubic meter [Banks 1984].) This rarity contrasts markedly with the abundance of ostrich eggshells, which were used as water bottles: their fragments are almost ubiquitous and sometimes overwhelming in frequency. The contrast between the water bottles, which would have been common equipment and vital to survival in this arid environment, and the ceramics suggests that the principal role of the latter was not an economic one. As in the early Neolithic of Franchthi (Vitelli 1989; chapter 5), there simply are not enough potsherds for pots to have had regular importance in cooking, storage, holding water, or, indeed, any other everyday affair.

Their significance is more likely to lie within the social and symbolic spheres, but it is not possible to determine their precise roles. Most pots are found very close to the sources of raw material from which they were made (Zedeño and Wendorf 1993), and so probably did not travel far, if at all, during their use life. There was occasional movement of vessels, however, between the Nabta and Kiseiba areas. We know from the distributions of lithic raw materials that early Holocene groups brought flint, a prized material, from the Nabta area to Kiseiba (Close 1984a); the occasional exchange of pots—rare things in society at that time—may have cemented relations between the two areas. In a land where water and food resources were unpredictable from one year to another, great advantage would have been gained in having good relations with one's neighbours.

THE TADRART ACACUS

Rainfall over the Tadrart Acacus in the early Holocene may not have been significantly greater than it was over the eastern Sahara. The Acacus, however, has a high water table that fed permanent springs (Marcolongo 1987) and permitted a comparatively luxuriant vegetation (Barich 1992; Schulz 1987). This environment, in turn, supported a variety of medium-size and large animals unknown in the eastern Sahara and meant that neither humans nor other animals were dependent upon the rains for their survival from year to year. The Acacus was thus a much richer and more secure environment than the plains of the eastern Sahara, which may be why its first colonists came without the insurance of their own domestic protein-on-the-hoof. (This is also true of their counterparts in the Ténéré [Roset et al. 1990].)

Human occupation of the Tadrart Acacus is first documented late in the tenth millennium b.p. in the Wadi Ti-n-Torha (Barich 1974; Barich, ed. 1987). The earliest dates are from Two Caves (ca. 9300 b.p.), but the best information concerning ceramics lies in the sequence of the nearby shelter of Torha East, which begins about 9000 b.p. and thereafter parallels that of Two Caves. The first people were classically Epipaleolithic, using fine bladelet tools and some ground stone but almost no pottery. They specialized above all in the hunting of Barbary sheep, a mountain animal, along with much smaller numbers of gazelles, wild asses, and buffalo or hartebeests. Small mammals (hare, dassie, and hedgehog) are present but surprisingly uncommon (6 percent of the fauna in the lower levels of Torha East). Fish occur, indicating permanent water, but they are few and stunted; aquatic resources were never important at Ti-n-Torha (Gautier 1987; Gautier and Van Neer 1977–82), in contrast to Adrar Bous 10 in the Ténéré, where there was a large, permanent lake at this time (Roset et al. 1990).

Macroremains of plants have been recovered from Two Caves, dating to about 8600 b.p. (Barich 1992; Wasylikowa 1992). They consist exclusively of wild grasses, principally *Setaria, Brachiaria*, and *Urochloa*, with smaller quantities of *Panicum, Echinochloa*, and *Cenchrus*. This material gives even higher antiquity to the collecting of Saharan grasses than does the material from Nabta, but it differs curiously from the latter in being much less varied and in lacking completely Nabta's two most common plants, sorghum and *Zizyphus*. There is a kind of symmetry between the restricted animals and varied plants in the eastern Saharan diet and the varied animals and restricted plants in that of the Acacus, reflecting, perhaps, the more difficult conditions in the east.

For the late tenth millennium b.p. and the first half of the ninth, there is no evidence that the caves and shelters of Wadi Ti-n-Torha were used as more than temporary campsites. On the basis of the fauna, Gautier (Gautier and Van Neer 1977–82:101) has suggested that occupation probably took place during the dry season.

In the Torha East sequence, pottery first appears in something other than vanishingly small quantities at about 8700 b.p. (Barich 1987a:105; Fig. 3.4). Even the base of the sequence, however, at about 9000 b.p., may not have been strictly aceramic (Barbara Barich, per-

Fig. 3.4. Mid-ninth-millennium b.p. potsherds from Torha East (Tadrart Acacus) (reproduced by permission from Barich 1987b:Fig. 10.5).

sonal communication, 1993). The owners (and presumably the makers) of the pottery were nonsedentary hunters of mountain sheep and collectors of wild grasses. As in the eastern Sahara, we do not know the uses to which the pottery was put, but, again as in the eastern Sahara, the rarity of pottery in the early levels of Torha East (Barich 1974: Table V) suggests that it was not economically important.

Soon after the first pottery appeared in the Acacus, the earlier parallelism with the eastern Sahara changed markedly. During the main period of occupation of Torha East, about 8500–8000 b.p., a row of four or five huts was built along the back of the shelter, with substantial stone wall foundations. These are seen to indicate greater sedentism, perhaps in response to a more arid climatic phase documented elsewhere in the central Sahara (Barich 1987a: 102). Within the Torha East sequence itself, there is a significant decline at this time in larger herbivores (Barbary sheep, the wild ass, and gazelles) from 94 percent to 83 percent of the faunal remains, and a corresponding increase in smaller mammals (hare, dassie, and hedgehog) from 6 percent to 17 percent. This shift might reflect either the increased aridity or the hunting out of local large mammals by the more sedentary human groups (Gautier and Van Neer 1977–82: 102–104)—or, of course, both.

Coinciding with the construction of the huts, there was a sudden and sustained increase in the absolute quantity of pottery (Barich 1974: Table V). In light of the other evidence, it is tempting to conclude that although pottery had been known earlier, it was increasing sedentism that permitted it to assume a larger role in the lives of its makers. Pottery still was probably not of great economic importance, however, since even after a sevenfold increase in frequency, there were only 140–150 sherds per layer.

Although the use of pottery might relate to sedentism in the Acacus, it had nothing to do with food production. Subsistence throughout the occupation of Torha East was based entirely on wild species. The first domesticates, cattle, did not appear for at least another millennium (Barich 1987a: 116). This is, in fact, generally true of the early "Saharo-Sudanese Neolithic": ceramics and some degree of sedentism pre-date food production. At Amekni (Camps 1969), for example, on the western side of the Hoggar, pottery was known before 8000 b.p., but there is not a single domestic plant or animal in the entire sequence, which lasted up to about 5500 b.p.

THE CENTRAL NILE VALLEY

Economically and environmentally, the most important aspect of the central Nile Valley is its large and perennially flowing river, which not only provided water but also was a major source of food by virtue of the plants and animals living in it and along its margins. In addition, rainfall in the area during the early Holocene is estimated to have been about 500 millimeters per annum, sufficient to maintain a wooded savannah in the hinterlands away from the river (Wickens 1975). The central Nile Valley was, therefore, much more productive than the Acacus and incomparably more so than the eastern Sahara.

Pottery-making and pottery-using groups, called "Khartoum Mesolithic" in this part of North Africa, appear late in the tenth millennium b.p., full-blown and without local antecedents. Not surprisingly, they made significant use of the resources of the river—fish, molluscs, and reptiles (Peters 1991b)—hence Sutton's (1977) naming them part of his Aqualithic. The importance of riverine resources may, however, have been somewhat overstated. Haaland, for example, refers to the "intensification of aquatic resource utilization" (1992:48) beginning with the Khartoum Mesolithic; but 10,000 years earlier, at the largest of the sites in Wadi Kubbaniya (near Aswan), 98 percent of all identifiable bones were of fish (Close 1989:459). It is difficult to imagine how one could become much more specialized. In fact, the faunas of Khartoum Mesolithic sites in the Nile Valley include a wide array of land mammals, principally of medium and large antelopes and other large bovids but extending all the way up to elephants (Gautier 1989: Table 1). The Khartoum Mesolithic at Shaqadud, which is not in the valley, has no fish at all, although freshwater molluscs do occur (Peters 1991a: Table 10-1). Much of the fishing practiced by Khartoum Mesolithic groups involved the same techniques of floodplain "fish-harvesting" as are inferred for the late Paleolithic of the lower Nile Valley (Gautier and Van Neer 1989: 145–47; Peters 1991b: 38–39). The former groups differed from the latter not so much in "intensification" as in also having the technology to take deep-water fish, including ceramic and stone net sinkers and barbed bone points (fish gorges were known at Kubbaniya) and, by implication, boats or rafts, and in having available a much wider range of wild mammals to hunt.

On first principles, we assume that plants were important in the diet, and this assumption seems to be supported by the numerous grinding stones. Direct evidence, however, is remarkably rare; only Haaland reports *Setaria*, *Celtis*, and *Zizyphus* from sites on the Atbara (1987b:49, 1992:48), the last two occurring in clusters at Abu Darbein.

Much has been made of the apparent sedentism of Khartoum Mesolithic groups (Caneva 1988; Haaland 1992), a supposition that seems to be based upon the large size of some sites (but which is always less than a hectare and often considerably less) and their richness in cultural material. These factors do suggest a higher degree of sedentism than in the Wadi Ti-n-Torha, and certainly more than in the eastern Sahara, but permanent occupation has not been demonstrated for any site. What seems more probable is a pattern of seasonal movement like that suggested for Shabona (which could not have been permanently occupied because it was seasonally flooded [Clark 1989]), and reoccupation of the same sites. Reoccupation and short-distance movement are suggested by the use of special burial areas at some sites and by the existence of regional cultural differences within the Khartoum Mesolithic (Caneva 1988:368; this is also shown by the inability of Marks and Mohammed-Ali [1991:243–44] to seriate pottery from more than one site).

The sites of these perhaps semisedentary hunter-fisher-gatherers yield thousands or even tens of thousands of potsherds. The quantities seem to indicate that, in this case, ceramics were being used for everyday activities and were an unremarkable part of the material culture. However, apart from the use of broken pots to make apparent net sinkers, precise uses remain unknown and untested—though not, of course, unguessed. Caneva (1988:368) has suggested that vessels were used for food storage, specifically for storage of fats, thus permitting people to be even more sedentary and therefore to have more use for pots. Clark (1989:408–409) sees their importance rather in processing molluscs or in preserving or extracting oil from fish.

Haaland (1992) envisions a much more elaborate and seductive scenario in which the invention of pottery permitted the use of more fish, which led to sedentism. This process coincided with the invention of grinding stones, which permitted the consumption of grass seeds, which could be boiled in the recently invented pottery vessels, providing mush on which infants could be weaned. The earlier weaning of infants, in combination with sedentism, led to shorter intervals between births, faster population growth, and, ulti-

mately, food production. A somewhat similar process has been suggested for parts of North America (see Crown and Wills, chapter 19).

It is not apparent, however, why deep-water fish could not have been used in the absence of ceramics; the seasonally harvested fish (although admittedly not deep-water) at Kubbaniya were successfully processed without benefit of pottery, as were the smaller quantities of deep-water fish in the middle Paleolithic of Nubia (Greenwood 1968). The question of whether there really was increased use of riverine resources in the Khartoum Mesolithic has been discussed earlier in this chapter, as has the lack of positive evidence for sedentism. Contra Haaland (1992:48), grinding stones were not invented during the Holocene but were known in the Sahara as far back as the Last Interglacial (Close 1993:337–40) and were used heavily at Kubbaniya for grinding plant foods over 18,000 years ago. From the same sites, there are also the charred feces of infants who were apparently being weaned on "some sort of fine mush" (Hillman et al. 1989:165). Plant foods were cooked at Kubbaniya without pottery. Plant foods, including grass seeds, were also cooked without pottery by Neolithic people in the eastern Sahara, although pottery was known to them. The use of ceramic cooking vessels may have permitted more efficient use of plant foods (as noted in several chapters in this volume), but, as in southwestern Asia (Moore, chapter 4), the origins of plant consumption and of plant processing technology lie much deeper in the North African past.

The sheer numbers of potsherds in Khartoum Mesolithic sites mean that pottery was used in some important and common practice(s). Where clay sources have been investigated, the pots seem to have been made of local clays at each site, so we can exclude their use as containers in the transport of other goods or, indeed, their movement as goods in their own right; such movement is not attested until the fifth millennium b.p. (de Paepe 1986a:134–35). As Caneva (1988), Clark (1989), and Haaland (1992) have suggested, pots were probably used for storage or cooking or both; there seems at present to be no basis on which to select among these functions.

The importance of pots in everyday life may well have been permitted by the more sedentary habits of their makers (compared with dwellers in the Sahara), but there is little evidence that pottery, in turn, revolutionized those habits. There is no patterned, diachronic change in the Khartoum Mesolithic economy from its inception before 9000 b.p. until the Khartoum Neolithic at about 6000 b.p. The latter is marked by the presence of domestic cattle and caprovids, which, it is generally agreed, were brought into the central Nile Valley from regions to the west or northwest, where their presence is attested earlier (Haaland 1992:55; Krzyzaniak 1992:247). Their appearance coincided with that of burnished pottery, a local development by which the Khartoum Neolithic is defined, but the two phenomena were independent of each other (Marks and Mohammed-Ali 1991:240–41, 255).

Evidence for domestic plants is completely lacking from the Khartoum and late Neolithic. It is widely supposed that sorghum should have been domesticated or at least cultivated, but the earliest evidence for sorghum is a few impressions of (wild) grains in potsherds from several sites of the sixth and fifth millennia b.p. (Stemler 1990). This is not conclusively negative evidence, because sorghum could long have been cultivated and yet remained morphologically wild, depending on the techniques of harvesting and sowing (Stemler 1984), and because domesticated sorghum, which must have come from Africa, was present in eastern Arabia by 5000 B.P and possibly earlier (Potts 1993: 180, 182). Nevertheless, it seems telling, in terms of the relationship between sorghum and African ceramics, that the only good evidence for intensive collection of sorghum, whether cultivated or not, is from a site (E-75-6 at Nabta) where pottery was markedly rare.

Conclusions

We know that pottery making was invented in Africa by the late tenth millennium b.p., but we do not know exactly when. It was probably invented along the southern side of the Sahara, but we do not know exactly where. Once invented, pottery was evidently seen as desirable and spread quickly across a 3,000-kilometer belt of the continent. Manufacture was local but usually not in great quantity. Ceramic analysis in North Africa has concentrated upon techniques of manufacture and decoration, so that we actually know very little about what pottery was used for, but its notable rarity in some regions suggests a role beyond than that of cooking porridge.

If we consider its assocation with the other "classic" traits of the Neolithic, we find that pottery is always associated with grinding stones. The grinding of plant foods, however, has a much higher antiquity in North Africa than does pottery, and neither necessarily leads

to the other; the coincidence could be fortuitous. There does seem to be a correlation between the quantity of pottery used and the inferred degree of sedentism. This is not surprising, given the difficulty of transporting large numbers of pots. Even in the central Nile Valley, however, it is not certain that there was permanent sedentism during the early millennia of ceramic use. Except in the eastern Sahara, pottery was known two or three thousand years before plants or animals were domesticated, and even in the eastern Sahara, there is no obvious causal relationship between the making of pots and the domestication of cattle. In the pristine African context, food production and ceramic technology proceeded quite independently of each other. When the Southwest Asian suite of domesticates began to appear in Egypt—in the Fayum in the mid-seventh millennium b.p.—we do find ceramic vessels seated in basin-hearths, packed around with fuel and containing fish and other bones (Wetterstrom 1993:205). However, the purposes of those potters who followed the older and more southerly African tradition remain enigmatic.

Acknowledgments

I wish to thank Barbara Barich and Fred Wendorf for reading and commenting upon an earlier version of this chapter. I thank Barbara Barich, Randi Haaland, Jean-Pierre Roset, and Nieves Zedeño for discussing their results with me and for guiding me to sources I had overlooked or which were not yet published. Figures 3.2 and 3.4 are reproduced by kind permission of Jean-Pierre Roset and Barbara Barich, respectively, and Southern Methodist University Press.

References Cited

Adamson, D. A., J. D. Clark, and M. A. J. Williams
  1987   Pottery Tempered with Sponge from the White Nile, Sudan. *African Archaeological Review* 5:115–27.
Ali Hakem, A. M., and A. M. Khabir
  1989   Sarourab 2: A New Contribution to the Early Khartoum Tradition from Bauda Site. In *Late Prehistory of the Nile Basin and the Sahara,* edited by L. Krzyzaniak and M. Kobusiewicz, pp. 381–85. Poznan Archaeological Museum, Poznan, Poland.
Arkell, A. J.
  1949   *Early Khartoum.* Oxford University Press, London.

Aumassip, G.

1986   *Le Bas-Sahara dans la préhistoire.* Centre National de la Recherche Scientifique, Paris.

Banks, K. M.

1980   Appendix 3: Ceramics of the Western Desert. In *Prehistory of the Eastern Sahara,* by F. Wendorf and R. Schild, pp. 299–315. Academic Press, New York.

1984   Report on Site E-79-2. In *Cattle-Keepers of the Eastern Sahara: The Neolithic of Bir Kiseiba,* assembled by F. Wendorf and R. Schild, edited by A. E. Close, pp. 95–121. Department of Anthropology, Southern Methodist University, Dallas, Texas.

Barich, B. E.

1974   La serie stratigrafica dell'Uadi Ti-n-Torha (Acacus, Libia). *Origini* 8:7–184.

1987a   The Wadi Ti-n-Torha Facies. In *Archaeology and Environment in the Libyan Sahara: The Excavations in the Tadrart Acacus, 1978–1983,* edited by B. E. Barich, pp. 97–112. British Archaeological Reports, International Series 368, Oxford.

1987b   Adaptation in Archaeology: An Example from the Libyan Sahara. In *Prehistory of Arid North Africa: Essays in Honor of Fred Wendorf,* edited by A. E. Close, pp. 189–210. Southern Methodist University Press, Dallas, Texas.

1992   The Botanical Collections from Ti-n-Torha/Two Caves and Uan Muhuggiag (Tadrart Acacus, Libya): An Archaeological Commentary. *Origini* 16:109–23.

Barich, B. E. (ed.)

1987   *Archaeology and Environment in the Libyan Sahara: The Excavations in the Tadrart Acacus, 1978–1983.* British Archaeological Reports, International Series 368, Oxford.

Camps, G.

1969   *Amekni: Néolithique ancien du Hoggar.* Mémoires du Centre de Recherches Anthropologiques, Préhistoriques et Ethnographiques 10. Arts et Métiers Graphiques, Paris.

1974   *Les civilisations préhistoriques de l'Afrique du Nord et du Sahara.* Doin, Paris.

Caneva, I.

1987   Pottery Decoration in Prehistoric Sahara and Upper Nile: A New Perspective. In *Archaeology and Environment in the Libyan Sahara: The Excavations in the Tadrart Acacus, 1978–1983,* edited by B. E. Barich, pp. 231–54. British Archaeological Reports, International Series 368, Oxford.

1988   The History of a Middle Nile Environment: A Suggested Cultural Model. In *El Geili: The History of a Middle Nile Environment 7000 B.C.–A.D. 1500,* edited by I. Caneva, pp. 359–77. British Archaeological Reports, International Series 424, Oxford.

Caneva, I. (ed.)

1983   Pottery-Using Gatherers and Hunters at Saggai (Sudan): Preconditions for Food Production. *Origini* 12:7–278.

Chlodnicki, M.

1989   The Petrographic Analysis of the Neolithic Pottery of Central Sudan. In *Late Prehistory of the Nile Basin and the Sahara,* edited by L. Krzyzaniak and M. Kobusiewicz, pp. 369–73. Poznan Archaeological Museum, Poznan, Poland.

Clark, J. D.

1989   Shabona: An Early Khartoum Settlement on the White Nile. In *Late Prehistory of the Nile Basin and the Sahara,* edited by L. Krzyzaniak and M. Kobusiewicz, pp. 387–410. Poznan Archaeological Museum, Poznan, Poland.

Close, A. E.

1984a   Early Holocene Raw Material Economies in the Western Desert of Egypt. In *Origin and Early Development of Food-Producing Cultures in North-Eastern Africa,* edited by L. Krzyzaniak and M. Kobusiewicz, pp. 163–70. Poznan Archaeological Museum, Poznan, Poland.

1984b   Report on Site E-80-4. In *Cattle-Keepers of the Eastern Sahara: The Neolithic of Bir Kiseiba,* assembled by F. Wendorf and R. Schild, edited by A. E. Close, pp. 325–49. Department of Anthropology, Southern Methodist University, Dallas, Texas.

1987   The Lithic Sequence from the Wadi Ti-n-Torha (Tadrart Acacus). In *Archaeology and Environment in the Libyan Sahara: The Excavations in the Tadrart Acacus, 1978–1983,* edited by B. E. Barich, pp. 63–85. British Archaeological Reports, International Series 368, Oxford.

1989   Report on Site E-78-3: A Deeply Stratified Sequence of Early Kubbaniyan Occupations. In *The Prehistory of Wadi Kubbaniya, vol. 3: Late Paleolithic Archaeology,* assembled by F. Wendorf and R. Schild, edited by A. E. Close, pp. 375–469. Southern Methodist University Press, Dallas, Texas.

1992   Holocene Occupation of the Eastern Sahara. In *New Light on the Northeast African Past,* edited by F. Klees and R. Kuper, pp. 154–83. Africa Praehistorica 5. Heinrich-Barth-Institut, Köln.

1993   BT-14 Main Excavation: The Archaeological Sequence of the East Lake (1986 and 1987

Seasons). In *Egypt during the Last Interglacial: The Middle Paleolithic of Bir Tarfawi and Bir Sahara East,* by F. Wendorf, R. Schild, A. E. Close, and associates, pp. 288–344. Plenum Press, New York.

Close, A. E., and F. Wendorf
1992   The Beginnings of Food-Production in the Eastern Sahara. In *Transitions to Agriculture in Prehistory,* edited by A. B. Gebauer and T. D. Price, pp. 63–72. Prehistory Press, Madison, Wisconsin.

Connor, D. R.
1984   Report on Site E-79-8. In *Cattle-Keepers of the Eastern Sahara: The Neolithic of Bir Kiseiba,* assembled by F. Wendorf and R. Schild, edited by A. E. Close, pp. 217–50. Department of Anthropology, Southern Methodist University, Dallas, Texas.

Delibrias, G., M. T. Guillier, and J. Labeyrie
1974   Gif Natural Radiocarbon Measurements VIII. *Radiocarbon* 16:15–94.

de Paepe, P.
1986a   Etude minéralogique et chimique de la céramique néolithique d'El Kadada et ses implications archéologiques. *Archéologie du Nil Moyen* 1:113–40.
1986b   La provenance de la céramique néolithique du Gebel Uweinat (Libye): Évidence minéralogique et chimique. *Archéologie du Nil Moyen* 1:149–59.
1991   Ceramics from Shaqadud Studied by Physical Methods. In *The Late Prehistory of the Eastern Sahel: The Mesolithic and Neolithic of Shaqadud, Sudan,* edited by A. E. Marks and A. Mohammed-Ali, pp. 261–66. Southern Methodist University Press, Dallas, Texas.

Echallier, J. C., and J-P. Roset
1986   La céramique des gisements de Tagalagal et de l'Adrar Bous 10 (Aïr, République du Niger): Résultats des analyses. *Cahiers de l'Office de la Recherche Scientifique et Technique Outre-Mer Série Sciences Humaines* 2:151–58.

Ehret, C.
1993   Nilo-Saharans and the Saharo-Sudanese Neolithic. In *The Archaeology of Africa: Food, Metals and Towns,* edited by T. Shaw, P. Sinclair, B. Andah, and A. Okpoko, pp. 104–25. Routledge, London.

Francaviglia, V., and A. Palmieri
1983   Petrochemical Analysis of the "Early Khartoum" Pottery: A Preliminary Report. *Origini* 12:191–205.
1988   Ceramic Fabrics and Source Locations in the Khartoum Province. In *El Geili: The History of a Middle Nile Environment 7000 B.C.–A.D. 1500,* edited by I. Caneva, pp. 345–58. British Ar-

chaeological Reports, International Series 424, Oxford.

Gabriel, B.
1972   Terrassenentwicklung und vorgeschichtliche Umweltbedingungen im Enneri Dirennao (Tibesti, östliche Zentralsahara). *Zeitschrift für Geomorphologie N.F. Suppl. Bd.* 15:113–28.

Gautier, A.
1984   Archaeozoology of the Bir Kiseiba Region, Eastern Sahara. In *Cattle-Keepers of the Eastern Sahara: The Neolithic of Bir Kiseiba,* assembled by F. Wendorf and R. Schild, edited by A. E. Close, pp. 49–72. Department of Anthropology, Southern Methodist University, Dallas, Texas.
1987   The Archaeozoological Sequence of the Acacus. In *Archaeology and Environment in the Libyan Sahara: The Excavations in the Tadrart Acacus, 1978–1983,* edited by B. E. Barich, pp. 283–308. British Archaeological Reports, International Series 368, Oxford.
1989   A General Review of the Known Prehistoric Faunas of the Central Sudanese Nile Valley. In *Late Prehistory of the Nile Basin and the Sahara,* edited by L. Krzyzaniak and M. Kobusiewicz, pp. 353–57. Poznan Archaeological Museum, Poznan, Poland.

Gautier, A., and W. Van Neer
1977–82   Prehistoric Fauna from Ti-n-Torha (Tadrart Acacus, Libya). *Origini* 11:87–127.
1989   Animal Remains from the Late Paleolithic Sequence at Wadi Kubbaniya. In *The Prehistory of Wadi Kubbaniya, vol. 2: Stratigraphy, Paleo-economy, and Environment,* assembled by F. Wendorf and R. Schild, edited by A. E. Close, pp. 119–61. Southern Methodist University Press, Dallas, Texas.

Ginter, B., J. K. Kozlowski, and M. Pawlikowski
1985   Field Report on the Survey Conducted in Upper Egypt in 1983. *Mitteilungen des Deutschen Archäologischen Institut, Abteilung Kairo* 41:15–41.

Grébénart, D.
1970   Problèmes du néolithique près d'Ouled Djellal et Djelfa: Botma Si Mammar et Safiet bou Rhenan. *Libyca* 19:47–66.

Greenwood, P. H.
1968   Fish Remains. In *The Prehistory of Nubia,* edited by F. Wendorf, pp. 100–109. Fort Burgwin Research Center and Southern Methodist University Press, Dallas, Texas.

Haaland, R.
1987a   *Socio-Economic Differentiation in the Neolithic Sudan.* British Archaeological Reports, International Series 350, Oxford.
1987b   Problems in the Mesolithic and Neolithic

Culture-History in the Central Nile Valley, Sudan. In *Nubian Culture: Past and Present,* edited by T. Hägg, pp. 47–74. Kungl. Vitterhets Historie och Antikvitets Akademien, Konferenser 17. Almqvist and Wiksell, Stockholm.

1992   Fish, Pots and Grain: Early and Mid-Holocene Adaptations in the Central Sudan. *African Archaeological Review* 10:43–64.

Haas, H., and C. V. Haynes

1980   Appendix 7: Discussion of Radiocarbon Dates from the Western Desert. In *Prehistory of the Eastern Sahara,* by F. Wendorf and R. Schild, pp. 373–78. Academic Press, New York.

Harlan, J. R.

1989   Wild-Grass Seed Harvesting in the Sahara and Sub-Sahara of Africa. In *Foraging and Farming: The Evolution of Plant Exploitation,* edited by D. R. Harris and G. C. Hillman, pp. 79–98. Unwin Hyman, London.

Hays, T. R.

1975   Neolithic Settlement of the Sahara as It Relates to the Nile Valley. In *Problems in Prehistory: North Africa and the Levant,* edited by F. Wendorf and A. E. Marks, pp. 193–204. Southern Methodist University Press, Dallas, Texas.

Hays, T. R., and F. A. Hassan

1974a   Mineralogical Analysis of "Sudanese Neolithic" Ceramics. *Libyca* 22:157–65.

1974b   Mineralogical Analysis of Sudanese Neolithic Ceramics. *Archaeometry* 16:71–79.

Hillman, G., E. Madeyska, and J. Hather

1989   Wild Plant Foods and Diet at Late Paleolithic Wadi Kubbaniya: The Evidence from Charred Remains. In *The Prehistory of Wadi Kubbaniya, vol. 2: Stratigraphy, Paleoeconomy, and Environment,* assembled by F. Wendorf and R. Schild, edited by A. E. Close, pp. 162–242. Southern Methodist University Press, Dallas, Texas.

Jäkel, D., and M. A. Geyh

1982 ^{14}C-Daten aus dem Gebiet der Sahara. *Berliner Geographische Abhandlungen* 32:143–65.

Khabir, A. M.

1987a   New Radiocarbon Dates for Sarurab 2 and the Age of the Early Khartoum Tradition. *Current Anthropology* 28:377–80.

1987b   Petrographic and X-ray Analysis of Neolithic Pottery from Sarurab. *Nyame Akuma* 28:45–46.

1991   A Qualitative Change in the Texture of Temper of Neolithic Ceramics from the Central Nile Valley. *Sahara* 4:145–48.

Krzyzaniak, L.

1992   The Late Prehistory of the Upper (Main) Nile: Comments on the Current State of Research.

In *New Light on the Northeast African Past,* edited by F. Klees and R. Kuper, pp. 239–48. Africa Praehistorica 5. Heinrich-Barth-Institut, Köln.

McBurney, C. B. M.

1967   *The Haua Fteah (Cyrenaica) and the Stone Age of the South-East Mediterranean.* Cambridge University Press, Cambridge.

Maître, J-P.

1974   Nouvelles perspectives sur la préhistoire récente de l'Ahaggar. *Libyca* 22:93–143.

Marcolongo, B.

1987   Natural Resources and Palaeoenvironment in the Tadrart Acacus: The Non-Climatic Factors Determining Human Occupation. In *Archaeology and Environment in the Libyan Sahara: The Excavations in the Tadrart Acacus, 1978–1983,* edited by B. E. Barich, pp. 269–82. British Archaeological Reports, International Series 368, Oxford.

Marks, A. E., and A. Mohammed-Ali

1991   The Place of Shaqadud in Late Prehistory of the Central Nile Valley. In *The Late Prehistory of the Eastern Sahel: The Mesolithic and Neolithic of Shaqadud, Sudan,* edited by A. E. Marks and A. Mohammed-Ali, pp. 237–59. Southern Methodist University Press, Dallas, Texas.

Marks, A. E., J. Peters, and W. Van Neer

1987   Late Pleistocene and Early Holocene Occupations in the Upper Atbara River Valley, Sudan. In *Prehistory of Arid North Africa: Essays in Honor of Fred Wendorf,* edited by A. E. Close, pp. 137–61. Southern Methodist University Press, Dallas, Texas.

Mohammed-Ali, A. S.

1984   Sorourab I: A Neolithic Site in Khartoum Province, Sudan. *Current Anthropology* 25:117–19.

1991   The Mesolithic and Neolithic Ceramics from Shaqadud Midden. In *The Late Prehistory of the Eastern Sahel: The Mesolithic and Neolithic of Shaqadud, Sudan,* edited by A. E. Marks and A. Mohammed-Ali, pp. 65–93. Southern Methodist University Press, Dallas, Texas.

Nordström, H.

1972   A Qualitative Analysis of the Early and Middle Nubian Pottery. In *Neolithic and A-Group Sites,* edited by H. Nordström, pp. 48–49. Scandinavian University Books, Stockholm.

Palmieri, A. M.

1987   Chemical Analysis of the Acacus Pottery: A Preliminary Essay. In *Archaeology and Environment in the Libyan Sahara: The Excavations in the Tadrart Acacus, 1978–1983,* edited by B. E. Barich, pp. 221–29. British

Archaeological Reports, International Series 368, Oxford.

Peters, J.
1991a   The Faunal Remains from Shaqadud. In *The Late Prehistory of the Eastern Sahel: The Mesolithic and Neolithic of Shaqadud, Sudan*, edited by A. E. Marks and A. Mohammed-Ali, pp. 197–235. Southern Methodist University Press, Dallas, Texas.

1991b   Mesolithic Fishing along the Central Sudanese Nile and the Lower Atbara. *Sahara* 4:33–40.

Petit-Maire, N.
1988   Climatic Change and Man in the Sahara. In *Prehistoric Cultures and Environments in the Late Quaternary of Africa*, edited by J. Bower and D. Lubell, pp. 19–42. British Archaeological Reports, International Series 405, Oxford.

Potts, D. T.
1993   The Late Prehistoric, Protohistoric, and Early Historic Periods in Eastern Arabia (ca. 5000–1200 B.C.). *Journal of World Prehistory* 7:163–212.

Roset, J-P.
1987   Paleoclimatic and Cultural Conditions of Neolithic Development in the Early Holocene of Northern Niger (Aïr and Ténéré). In *Prehistory of Arid North Africa: Essays in Honor of Fred Wendorf*, edited by A. E. Close, pp. 211–34. Southern Methodist University Press, Dallas, Texas.

Roset, J-P., F. de Broin, M. Faure, M. Gayet, C. Guérin, and F. Mouchet
1990   La faune de Tin Ouaffadene et d'Adrar Bous 10, deux gisements archéologiques de l'Holocène ancien au Niger nord-oriental. *Géodynamique* 5(1):67–89.

Schild, R., F. Wendorf, and A. E. Close
1992   Northern and Eastern African Climate Changes between 140 and 12 Thousand Years Ago. In *New Light on the Northeast African Past*, edited by F. Klees and R. Kuper, pp. 81–96. Africa Praehistorica 5. Heinrich-Barth-Institut, Köln.

Schulz, E.
1987   Holocene Vegetation in the Tadrart Acacus: The Pollen Record of Two Early Ceramic Sites. In *Archaeology and Environment in the Libyan Sahara: The Excavations in the Tadrart Acacus, 1978–1983*, edited by B. E. Barich, pp. 313–26. British Archaeological Reports, International Series 368, Oxford.

Smith, S. E.
1980   The Environmental Adaptation of Nomads in the West African Sahel: A Key to Under-standing Prehistoric Pastoralists. In *The Sahara and the Nile: Quaternary Environments and Prehistoric Occupation in Northern Africa*, edited by M. A. J. Williams and H. Faure, pp. 467–87. Balkema, Rotterdam.

Stemler, A.
1984   The Transition from Food Collecting to Food Production in Northern Africa. In *From Hunters to Farmers: The Causes and Consequences of Food Production in Africa*, edited by J. D. Clark and S. A. Brandt, pp. 127–31. University of California Press, Berkeley.

1990   A Scanning Electron Microscopic Analysis of Plant Impressions in Pottery from the Sites of Kadero, El Zakiab, Um Direiwa and El Kadada. *Archéologie du Nil Moyen* 4:87–105.

Sutton, J. E. G.
1974   The Aquatic Civilization of Middle Africa. *Journal of African History* 15:527–54.

1977   The African Aqualithic. *Antiquity* 51:25–33.

Tubiana, M-J., and J. Tubiana
1977   *The Zaghawa from an Ecological Perpective.* A. A. Balkema, Rotterdam.

Van Neer, W., and H-P. Uerpmann
1989   Palaeoecological Significance of the Holocene Faunal Remains from the B.O.S. Missions. In *Forschungen zur Umweltgeschichte der Ostsahara*, edited by R. Kuper, pp. 307–41. Africa Praehistorica 2. Heinrich-Barth-Institut, Köln.

Vitelli, K. D.
1989   Were Pots First Made for Foods? Doubts from Franchthi. *World Archaeology* 21:17–29.

Wasylikowa, K.
1992   Exploitation of Wild Plants by Prehistoric Peoples in the Sahara. *Würzburger Geographische Arbeiten* 84:247–62.

Wendorf, F., A. E. Close, R. Schild, K. Wasylikowa, R. A. Housley, J. R. Harlan, and H. Krolik
1992   Saharan Exploitation of Plants 8,000 Years bp. *Nature* 359:721–24.

Wendorf, F., and R. Schild
1980   *Prehistory of the Eastern Sahara.* Academic Press, New York.

Wendorf, F., R. Schild (assemblers), and A. E. Close (ed.)
1984   *Cattle-Keepers of the Eastern Sahara: The Neolithic of Bir Kiseiba.* Department of Anthropology, Southern Methodist University, Dallas, Texas.

Wetterstrom, W.
1993   Foraging and Farming in Egypt: The Transition from Hunting and Gathering to Horticulture in the Nile Valley. In *The Archaeology of Africa: Food, Metals and*

Towns, edited by T. Shaw, P. Sinclair, B. Andah, and A. Okpoko, pp. 165–226. Routledge, London.

Wickens, G. E.
1975   Changes in the Climate and Vegetation of the Sudan since 20,000 B.P. *Boissiera* 24:43–65.

Zedeño, M. N., and F. Wendorf
1993   Ceramics and Nomads: The Development of Ceramic Production in the Eastern Sahara of Egypt. Ms. on file, Department of Anthropology, Southern Methodist University, Dallas, Texas.

4

The Inception of Potting in Western Asia and Its Impact on Economy and Society

A. M. T. MOORE

From the beginning of systematic studies of prehistory it was thought that the invention of potting coincided with the inception of the Neolithic and the development of farming. That was certainly the view of Mortillet (Mortillet and Mortillet 1881:Plates 55, 61) in his scheme of European prehistoric cultural development, and the earliest interpreters of the prehistory of Western Asia took it as a basic assumption (see, for example, Peake and Fleure 1927:iii). Childe (1936:101) espoused the same idea in his early writings on the Neolithic Revolution. Potting was regarded as an important technological innovation that, together with the domestication of plants and animals, enabled the people of the region to construct cultures more advanced than those of their hunter-gatherer Paleolithic forebears. The link was considered so fundamental that knowledge of potting was used by Neuville (1934:255) as a defining characteristic of the first post-Mesolithic culture in Palestine in one of the earliest attempts to establish a prehistoric cultural sequence for that area.

The Neolithic sites that were excavated across Southwest Asia in the first half of the twentieth century virtually all dated from the later stages of the Neolithic, and they contained pottery in a variety of wares. This evidence supported the apparently strong link between potting and the Neolithic way of life (Seton Williams 1948:34–35). Kenyon's excavations at Jericho during the 1950s, however, demonstrated that the beginning of farming and village life there preceded the inception of potting by two millennia. In recognition of this then-startling discovery, she called the two earliest phases of Neolithic settlement at Jericho Pre-Pottery Neolithic A and B (Kenyon 1979:26–31). At Jarmo in the Zagros foothills, Braidwood also found indications of a phase of Neolithic occupation that preceded the introduction of pottery (Braidwood and Howe 1960:49), thus demonstrating that the same cultural sequence obtained in Iraq. Shortly before his death, Childe (1957:15) revised his views to take account of these discoveries. Subsequent research has confirmed that potting began well after the beginning of the Neolithic in the Mesopotamian borderlands, the Zagros Mountains, and Anatolia.

Discussion of the inception of potting across Southwest Asia today, therefore, takes place in the context of a different sequence of development than was once envisaged, because the old idea of a presumed link between pottery and the beginnings of farming and village life there does not hold. The development of potting in Western Asia took place long after the inception of the Neolithic farming way of life and was, perhaps, a consequence of it. It began in the middle of the Neolithic period across Western Asia, but we need to determine precisely when and where in order to answer the question of whether this innovation had a single or multiple origin. It is important to determine the cultural context in which potting began, for that will help us to understand how it came about. We need to know, too, what connections there may have been between the inception of potting and other innovations in technology during the Neolithic. The development of a new craft, especially one that would have affected every household, has social implications that must be explored if we are to discern the role of this craft in Neolithic societies. The technical aspects of pottery manufacture and distribution also deserve attention. Finally, we would like to know something of the effects of the introduction of pottery for the people of Western Asia themselves.

Despite the obvious importance of pottery to archaeologists as a tool of chronological analysis, and despite our long-standing need to know how and why it developed, relatively few studies have been carried out on the prehistoric pottery of Western Asia. Thus it is impossible to provide detailed answers to all the questions just posed. My intention in this essay is to summarize our present state of knowledge about the beginnings of potting there and to offer some preliminary observations in partial answer to these questions. It is my hope that this essay will contribute to a better understanding of the processes of technological innovation (Torrence and van der Leeuw 1989:3) in the late prehistoric societies of Western Asia and elsewhere.

The Inception of Potting

We should begin by establishing where and when pottery first came into use, because conflicting claims have been made in the past (compare, for example, Mellaart 1975:110 and Cauvin 1978:103). In Anatolia, one of the best known sites at which pottery was first made is the very large settlement (ca. 12.5 ha) of Çatal Hüyük on the Konya Plain (Fig. 4.1). Some sherds were found in the lowest deposits of the site in level XII, dating to about 8300 b.p. (Mellaart 1975: 98).[1] This is one of the oldest dated records of pottery use anywhere in Southwest Asia. The use of pottery increased in later centuries at Çatal Hüyük, especially toward the end of occupation from about 7600 to 7400 b.p. The pottery was of the simplest kind, consisting of deep bowls and hole-mouth jars, light in color and

with burnished surfaces. Later on, darker, harder-fired vessels were made, though the surfaces of nearly all of them were undecorated. Baked clay was used to make a wide variety of other objects at the site, especially in the later levels. Among these objects were stamp seals with incised designs, beads and pendants, and a variety of animal and human figurines. Some of the latter were richly modeled (Mellaart 1967:Plate IX).

The bulk of the deposits at Çayönü, another large village (ca. 4 ha) in the upper Tigris basin that has been under excavation for many years, date from the earlier Neolithic before pottery was made. Some sherds have been found in the upper levels ascribed to phase II that date to about 8000 b.p. (Çambel 1981). The pottery was very simple and quite rough, although some vessels had a dark burnished surface. The beginning of pottery manufacture at the site coincided with a shift in the economy from farming combined with hunting and gathering in phase I, the main period of earlier Neolithic occupation, to farming and the raising of sheep and goats in phase II (van Zeist 1972; Lawrence 1982:189). Modest quantities of human and animal figurines and a variety of other artifacts were made in lightly baked clay throughout the Çayönü sequence (Broman Morales 1990). Thus the inhabitants had long been familiar with the basic skills of manufacturing baked clay objects.

The transition from an early Neolithic pre-dating the use of pottery to a later Neolithic when the craft came into general use has also been traced at Gritille in the Euphrates Valley south of the Anti-Taurus. The materials recovered from Gritille bear a close resemblance to those from sites in northern Syria. A few sherds of gray burnished ware were recovered from contexts dating to late in the Neolithic sequence, or about 7800 b.p. (Voigt 1988:225). Once again, the inhabitants of the site made a variety of figurines and other objects in baked clay for centuries before they began to make pots.

It seems that the Neolithic people of Anatolia at first made pottery in relatively modest quantities and in a restricted range of shapes, with little more surface treatment than smoothing and burnishing. It was several centuries before they made vessels in a greater variety of shapes and with more elaborate surface decoration. Later, they indulged in an exuberant enriching of their pottery tradition, best exemplified in the material from the village of Hacilar in Pisidia (ca. 7800–6900 b.p.; Mellaart 1970). The vessels from the earlier levels at Hacilar were still monochrome with a light gray or buff surface and occasional painted red lines.

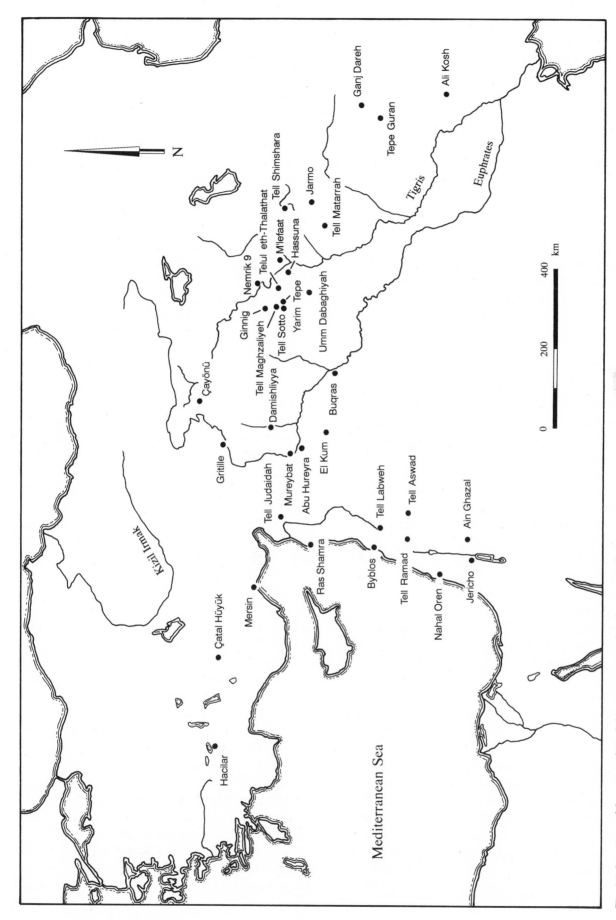

Fig. 4.1. Locations of the principal Neolithic sites mentioned in chapter 4.

By level VI, a wider range of jars and cups had come into use, some of them decorated with plain red slip and a few with designs of red on cream. Some cups were made in the shape of human heads, while others were zoomorphic. Among the most remarkable objects made of baked clay were numerous female figurines of striking appearance. In later levels the pots were decorated even more richly, with geometric patterns of extraordinary variety. These vessels seem to have been tableware, whereas the larger jars probably held liquids. Coarser vessels were used for cooking. Several potters' workshops found in level II indicate that pots were formed and finished within the village, although they were probably fired outside it.

In Cilicia, to the south of the Anatolian Plateau, the earliest known pottery comes from the Neolithic levels at the bottom of the Mersin mound (Garstang 1953: 11), dating from about 8000 b.p. The pottery was of two kinds, a fine burnished ware with brown or black surfaces and a more plentiful coarse ware. The pots were of much the same simple shapes in both wares, mainly hole-mouth vessels, bowls, and dishes. In later levels some of the pots were painted with abstract designs in red. The closest affinities of this painted pottery are with material from sites on the Konya Plain (Mellaart 1975:125; Moore 1978:318).

In the Levant, the inception of potting coincides with the transition from Neolithic 2 to Neolithic 3 and 4, or from the pre-pottery to the pottery Neolithic, dated to about 8000 b.p. The cultural transition can be traced at several sites, among them Ras Shamra and Abu Hureyra in the north, Tell Ramad in the central Levant, and Ain Ghazal farther south. Other sites ceased to be occupied just before the transition—for example, Mureybat, Tell Aswad (Damascus), and Nahal Oren—or, like Byblos and Tell Judaidah, were first settled as pottery was coming into use. At other settlements such as Jericho, a key site for the whole Neolithic sequence, the transition was marked by an interruption in occupation.

At Ras Shamra on the Syrian coast, pottery was first used soon after 7900 b.p. at the beginning of phase VB (Contenson 1992, 1:191–92). There was little change in its manufacture throughout phases VB and VA, which lasted until about 7000 b.p. The earliest pottery recovered was a lightly fired, crumbly ware. Slightly later, thick-walled, dark, plain wares with burnished surfaces began to be made, and this remained the most common kind of pottery throughout the rest of the Neolithic sequence at Ras Shamra (Contenson 1992, 1:147). The shapes were quite simple: hemispherical

bowls, hole-mouth jars, and necked jars. The surfaces of a few vessels were decorated with incisions and, occasionally, red paint. Some vessels were more finely made, with thinner walls, and were harder fired.

Perhaps the best-known early pottery from the northern Levant is the material from Tell Judaidah that has been ascribed to the A and B phases of the Amuq sequence. There, as elsewhere, hemispherical bowls and hole-mouth jars predominated, but the wares themselves varied. There were three main types: "dark-faced burnished ware," coarse simple ware, and washed impressed ware (Braidwood and Braidwood 1960). All varied considerably in color, hardness of firing, and coarseness of fabric. A few of the burnished vessels were decorated with incised patterns, while some red paint was used on other pots. A similar range of coarse and finer burnished wares, sometimes with simple incised or painted decoration, has been found on a variety of Neolithic 3 sites across the northern Levant.

Farther east, in the Euphrates Valley, the transition from Neolithic 2 to 3 and the advent of potting have been documented at Abu Hureyra. The economic shift that accompanied these cultural changes has been precisely dated to about 8300 b.p. (Moore 1992:856), but pottery seems to have come into use somewhat later. We found very few sherds in our excavation of the site, and most of them were of lightly fired, crumbly wares that did not survive well in the levels close to the surface that dated to the Neolithic 3 period. Thus it is not possible to state precisely when pottery began to be used at Abu Hureyra.

Large quantities of sherds were recovered from the second series of excavations at Buqras, farther down the Euphrates. This site was first occupied toward the end of Neolithic 2, about 8300 b.p., and pottery began to be used several centuries later, apparently around 8000 b.p. (Le Mière 1983; Contenson 1985a). Most of the vessels were lightly fired and beige in color, with a variety of surface treatments. Nearly all had been burnished, and a few were coated with red slip or painted with geometric designs in red. Some vessels resembled those produced on other northern Levantine sites, but Le Mière has noted that the closest parallels for the Buqras material are to be found on sites in northern Iraq such as Umm Dabaghiyah and Yarim Tepe I.

Recent excavations at Damishliyya on the Balikh River, a tributary of the Euphrates, have yielded evidence for the transition from Neolithic 2 to 3 (Akkermans 1991). The date for this change, and the accompanying inception of potting, was about 7900 b.p., virtually the same date as on sites farther west and north.

The transition from Neolithic 2 to 3 and the inception of potting seem to have taken place at about the same time or slightly later with the beginning of level III at Tell Ramad, southwest of Damascus (Contenson 1981:468, 1985b:24). Most of the vessels were relatively small bowls and jars, some of which had necks. They were usually brown or gray with burnished surfaces. A few had incised decoration, but use of paint was rare. These vessels were similar to the earliest pottery from Byblos on the Lebanese coast and also bore a general resemblance to the pottery from Ras Shamra VB. They had less in common with the pottery from the Euphrates sites.

Further regional variation can be seen in the earliest pottery found on sites in Palestine. The earliest pottery found at Jericho, for example, in the Pottery Neolithic A phase, was a rough, straw-tempered, lightly fired buff ware. A few vessels in a slightly finer ware had cream- or red-slipped geometric decoration (Kenyon and Holland 1982:ch. 2). The coarse wares of the next phase at Jericho, Pottery Neolithic B, were similar to those of Pottery Neolithic A, but a more delicate, finer ware was also made. This ware was thinner walled, though still lightly fired, and included a greater variety of shapes, among them carinated cups and bow-rim jars. Some of these vessels were decorated with red slip or red paint at the rim and occasional incised herringbone patterns. Somewhat similar pottery has been found over a wide area of the southern Levant, west and east of the Jordan River.

Evidence for the beginning of potting is more elusive at this end of the Fertile Crescent because there seems to have been greater disruption in patterns of settlement and material culture there than elsewhere in the Levant at the end of Neolithic 2. We know there was a break in the sequence at Jericho between Neolithic 2 and 3, but in the absence of radiocarbon dates for the pottery Neolithic from that site, we cannot be certain when occupation was resumed there and thus when potting began. The transition from Neolithic 2 to 3 has been documented at Ain Ghazal near Amman (Rollefson, Simmons, and Kafafi 1992). The earliest pottery from this site resembled that from Jericho Pottery Neolithic B. This material was found in the upper levels of the site and its date has not yet been clearly defined, but it appears to have postdated the end of the previous phase there, called Pre-Pottery Neolithic C, dated to about 7600 b.p. (Rollefson, Simmons, and Kafafi 1992:Table 1). On present evidence, therefore, it looks

as though potting began several centuries later in the southern Levant than farther north.

The third area we should consider consists of the lowlands of Mesopotamia and the valleys of the Zagros Mountains that mark their eastern border, because Neolithic sites have been found in both zones. Until recently, no evidence had been found for early Neolithic occupation of the Assyrian steppes of northern Mesopotamia. Excavations at a series of sites there in recent years, notably Tell Maghzaliyeh and Nemrik 9 (Bader 1989; Kozlowski 1990), have confirmed that this region was inhabited by early Neolithic farmers who lived in villages. Their counterparts in the Zagros were the inhabitants of villages such as Jarmo and Ganj Dareh, sites that have been known for some time and that date to the ninth millennium b.p. and earlier.

One site has been found in northern Mesopotamia that seems to span the transition from the earlier to later Neolithic when pottery was first made. This is the site of Ginnig, located on the open plains to the north of the Jebel Sinjar (Campbell and Baird 1990). The pottery from this site is thought to resemble that from Umm Dabaghiyah, probably the earliest ware to be made in northern Mesopotamia. The pottery at Umm Dabaghiyah itself (Kirkbride 1973:Plate 3) consisted of simple bowls and jars made of a coarse, lightly fired buff ware with vegetable temper. Some of the vessels were decorated with red paint, incised designs, and applied motifs. Similar material has been found at Tell Sotto and Telul eth-Thalathat (Fukai and Matsutani 1981:plates 35–37; Bader 1989), both to the west of Mosul.

This phase of initial pottery use in northern Mesopotamia was followed immediately by the best-known Neolithic culture in the region, named after the type-site of Hassuna. By now agriculture and stockbreeding were the mainstays of the economy, as the evidence from Hassuna itself and the related site of Yarim Tepe I indicates (Lloyd and Safar 1945; Merpert and Munchaev 1987:19). Hassuna pottery was a little more varied in shape than that of the preceding phase, but the most common vessels were still bowls and jars. Some of the latter had collars and everted rims. The wares were usually buff in color, and some vessels were decorated with designs in red or black paint or with incised designs on the rims and shoulders. A distinctive vessel was the so-called "husking tray," a heavy, flat-bottomed dish with incised grooves on the interior. Much of the pottery was coarse, though there were some finer wares also.

Very few radiocarbon dates have yet been obtained

for any of these sites, so caution is needed in deciding just when pottery came into use in northern Mesopotamia. A series of dates of uncertain accuracy was obtained many years ago for Tell Shimshara, an Hassunan site overlooking the valley of the Little Zab River in the foothills of the Zagros (Mortensen 1970: 136), that suggests this period probably began in the first half of the eighth millennium b.p. Support for this view comes from another date obtained long ago for Tell Matarrah (Braidwood and Howe 1960:161). If this estimate is correct, then the pottery from Ginnig and Umm Dabaghiyah would have been made about 8000 b.p., that is, at about the same time as the first pottery in the Levant and Anatolia.

What of the Zagros zone to the southeast? There the key site is Jarmo, one of the few that span the pre-pottery to the pottery Neolithic. The site was occupied for several centuries around 8000 b.p. (Braidwood 1983:538), and pottery seems to have been made for the first time shortly after that date. The vessels were chaff tempered and lightly fired (Adams 1983), with some smoothing and burnishing of the surfaces. The pots consisted of various kinds of bowls, some of which were carinated, jars, and dishes. A few of them were coated with a slip, and there was some use of red paint for decoration.

Several more Neolithic sites have been excavated in the high mountain valleys farther to the southeast along the Zagros chain. One of them, Tepe Guran, provides a good example of the context in which pottery was adopted. The mound lay at the side of the Hulailan Valley at an altitude of 950 meters, and the excavators estimated that the Neolithic settlement was inhabited from about 8500 to 7500 b.p. (Meldgaard, Mortensen, and Thrane 1963:104). The first inhabitants of the site were thought to have been transhumant goat herders who lived there in the winter. Then, at a date estimated to be about 8200 b.p., the settlement changed (Mortensen 1974:25): it became a permanent village of mud brick houses whose inhabitants were farmers, herders, and hunters who started to make pottery. The few sherds from the lowest levels of this village were of a simple gray-brown ware with smoothed surfaces that had been lightly fired. The bulk of the pottery from the later levels consisted of a plain buff, chaff-tempered ware used to make bowls, some of which were carinated. About 15 percent of the pottery consisted of a variety of vessels with painted decoration; the excavators have compared some of the designs to material from Jarmo. The inception of potting at Tepe Guran seems, then, to have taken place early and to have coincided with a shift from seasonal habitation to permanent settlement based on farming.

Neolithic villages have been found on the plains of Khuzistan on the eastern edge of southern Mesopotamia, but the oldest of these date only from the end of the early Neolithic. New dates obtained recently for one of them, Ali Kosh, indicate that it was occupied for a few centuries around 8000 b.p. (Hedges et al. 1990:231), much later than originally claimed by the excavators. The earliest pottery there seems to date from early in the eighth millennium b.p.

What does this review of the earliest evidence for pottery across Western Asia tell us about the origins of the craft? It seems that the beginning of pottery making was nearly synchronous across the region, the only exception being the southern Levant, where it may have started a little later. Thus the view expressed by Mellaart (1975:110) that potting began at Çatal Hüyük and spread southward to the Levant cannot be sustained. Indeed, the evidence does not support the idea of a single place of origin but suggests, rather, that pottery began to be made at about the same time over much of Western Asia. We should note in passing that the earliest pottery found at Knossos in Crete, at sites on the Greek mainland, and farther west around the shores of the Mediterranean all dates to about the same time or a little later. The new craft seems to have begun at approximately 8000 b.p. over a very wide area indeed.

The Context

The first potters were settled farmers who lived in villages. Their settlements were widely distributed across the Mediterranean woodland and moister steppe zones of the Fertile Crescent, in the rugged hill and mountain country that marked its outer rim, and on the Anatolian Plateau. Their ancestors had been farmers for up to 2,000 years. They were members of societies that were apparently egalitarian, and each community seems to have been largely self-sufficient in the necessities of daily life. Villages had intermittent contacts with their neighbors, in part through networks of exchange in raw materials, among them shells, obsidian, and other unusual stones. These long-standing relationships would have provided paths along which knowledge of innovations such as potting could have traveled swiftly.

The beginning of potting coincided with significant changes in economy, patterns of settlement, and culture across the region. The speed of these changes varied from place to place, but their effects seem to have been felt everywhere. The economy of most earlier Neolithic villages had been based on the cultivation of cereals and pulses, combined with some hunting and gathering of wild species. Herding of sheep and goats seems to have contributed little to the economy of most of these settlements. That changed across Southwest Asia beginning about 8000 b.p., as most people abandoned hunting and gathering and became full-time farmers and herders. At about the same time, the inhabitants of the steppe that formed the hinterland of the Levant started to leave their villages and move into the better-watered woodland zone along the inner edge of the Fertile Crescent. These changes seem to have occurred partly in response to a rise in temperature and a decrease in effective precipitation, and also because of the adverse impact the inhabitants of villages in the steppe had on their environs (Moore 1985:29, 52–54, 57).

Everywhere the beginning of potting marked the cultural transition from the earlier to the later Neolithic (Moore 1985:29, 37, 49). The change was a gradual one in Anatolia but more abrupt in Mesopotamia and the Levant. Crafts seem to have become more varied and productive in the later Neolithic, and there were other changes in artifact inventories. Villages in Mesopotamia and the Levant took on new configurations. Burial customs seem to have changed everywhere as people gave up the rituals of ancestor reverence implied by an earlier emphasis on skulls and subfloor interment and began to bury their dead away from their dwellings.

Technological Antecedents

The inhabitants of early villages across Western Asia used clay for a variety of purposes well before they commenced making pottery. Indeed, large-scale use of clay, especially for building, formed part of a set of innovations that marked the inception of the Neolithic. People started to make mud bricks to construct houses from the beginning of the Neolithic, about 10,000 b.p.—for example, at Jericho in the Pre-Pottery Neolithic A (Kenyon 1981:60, Plate 44a) and, on the eastern edge of Mesopotamia, at M'lefaat on the Khazir River, as revealed in recent excavations conducted there by Kozlowski and visited by the author in 1990. During the ninth millennium, mud bricks were manufactured on a very large scale to provide for the inhabitants of the numerous and sometimes very large villages of densely packed houses in which most people lived.

Plaster was used extensively to make floors for the houses in these early villages, notably in Anatolia and the Levant during the ninth millennium b.p. Floors would be renewed several times during the life of a house, so that prodigious quantities of plaster were required to maintain them. At sites like Abu Hureyra the plaster was usually made of gypsum, which is obtained by firing pieces of the raw material at low temperatures. Elsewhere, lime plaster was used, the lime for which was obtained by burning chalk or limestone at temperatures in excess of 800°C, probably in simple kilns (Gourdin and Kingery 1975).[2] The inhabitants of a single settlement might make many metric tons of lime during its existence (Garfinkel 1987:70), and so would consume a great deal of wood as fuel for firing —enough to remove most of the trees growing around a site.

Increasingly during the ninth millennium and into the eighth, the people of the Levant used gypsum and lime plaster to make a variety of containers (Contenson and Courtois 1979). These vessels of white ware, or vaisselle blanche, were frequently quite large; some of the ones we found at Abu Hureyra were built in the rooms where they were to be used and were clearly not intended to be moved. The wet plaster was apparently difficult to control, so vessels were often formed in molds made of baskets or other materials. The walls were built up in thin layers, each one being allowed to dry before the next one was applied. Many of the finished vessels probably held dry foodstuffs. The greatest quantities of white ware were made in the few centuries before and after 8000 b.p., just as pottery was coming into use. Several sites dating to this period, such as Tell Labweh (Kirkbride 1969:49) and El Kum (Dornemann 1986:11–22), have yielded large samples of this material. This abundance suggests that the need for large, durable containers to store foodstuffs indoors increased significantly during the ninth millennium, providing one reason, perhaps, for the invention of pottery. Once the craft of potting was firmly established, white ware ceased to be made as pottery took its place.

We should remember that plaster was used in ritual contexts in the earlier Neolithic of the Levant, notably to form human faces on skulls at Jericho (Kenyon 1981: 77, 310), Ain Ghazal (Rollefson 1983), Tell Ramad (Contenson 1971:281), and elsewhere. These three sites, all in the central and southern Levant, have also yielded models of human figures made of plaster and mud. Such artifacts apparently played a role in rituals connected with reverence for ancestors.

The people of Western Asia accumulated a great deal of experience concerning the uses of clay and plaster in the two millennia that separated the beginning of farming and the inception of potting. Most useful to them, perhaps, was the knowledge gained in firing materials at high temperatures and the working of clay and plaster into artifacts. This experience extended to the creation of a variety of small objects in clay, some of which were baked. The most distinctive were figurines of humans and animals, found at most early village sites across Western Asia. Among the larger collections of such objects are those from Jericho (Holland 1982), Tell Ramad (Contenson 1971:281), Çayönü (Broman Morales 1990), and Jarmo (Broman Morales 1983). To these may be added clay stamp seals, beads, and spindle whorls. Some of the most unusual clay artifacts were the models of houses found at Çayönü and possibly also at Jarmo (Broman Morales 1990:69, 1983: 390). The functions of many of these artifacts cannot be determined with certainty, but it does seem likely that most of them had symbolic significance for their makers. As Hodder has pointed out (1988:73), "the use of pottery is thus prefigured in a different and less practical context. . . . In some cases at least, later practical applications are made of an earlier ritual or symbolic use."

A few clay containers have survived from the earlier Neolithic, harbingers of vessels that were later to be made from more durable pottery. They are small cups, vases, and dishes fashioned from fine clay with often little or no tempering. Such vessels have been found at several sites across Western Asia, notably at Ganj Dareh in the Zagros (Smith and Crépeau 1983) and, on the Euphrates, at Mureybat (Cauvin 1978:fig. 19) and Abu Hureyra. Larger clay vessels were also found at Ganj Dareh that Smith believes were used to store foodstuffs. Of course, many more such artifacts may have been fashioned during this period, only to decay completely in the soil once they were buried.

The vessels from Ganj Dareh and Abu Hureyra were simply dried in the sun to impart a certain durability, but Cauvin thinks the cups from Mureybat were deliberately fired (1978:101). Certainly, many of the figurines that have been found at different sites seem to have been intentionally hardened, though some, of course, may have been burned accidentally. Nevertheless, it does look as though some people attempted to fire clay objects in modest quantities long before they made pottery. The clay vessels themselves, whatever their function, were too small to have held foodstuffs or anything else in quantity, so they cannot be regarded as functional precursors to pottery, unlike the containers made of white ware that were probably intended mainly for storage of dry goods.

Production and Use of the Earliest Pottery

From the beginning of potting in Western Asia the wares varied in fabric and decoration from region to region. Much the same range of shapes, however, was made from one area to another, at least in the earlier stages. This consistency probably indicates that the earliest pottery answered similar needs and served the same range of functions wherever it was made.

Most of the pottery recovered seems to have been made at the site where it was found, from local clays. The variations in the early pottery within each settlement suggest that potting was done by a number of people who probably resided in separate households. These potters possessed particular knowledge and skills and so may be regarded as specialist craftsmen, like other skilled artisans in the same communities (Moore 1981:452).

Vandiver (1987) has studied the manufacture of pottery at many of the villages where pottery was first made and has discovered that the same technique was used from the Mediterranean to the Indus. She has called it "sequential slab construction." Irregularly shaped slabs of clay were pieced together to form the pot, beginning at the bottom and working up the sides. Thicker pieces were used at the base and thinner ones at the rim. Sometimes the base was formed in a mold to keep it in shape. The surfaces were then smoothed over before the pot was fired. Within a few centuries it had become common practice to turn the pot on a mat to aid in thinning and smoothing the surface.

It had been suggested that many of the pots made in the earlier centuries of pottery manufacture were coil built—for example, at Çatal Hüyük (Mellaart 1967: 216) and Jericho (Moore 1973:52). It now seems likely that the lines visible in sherd cross-sections that have been interpreted as the separations of individual coils were the joins between slabs, as Vandiver's X-rays show (1987:Plate 3). Notwithstanding, further research may show that there were some variations in techniques of manufacture within and between sites. The sequential slab method of construction seems to have begun in the Neolithic and continued into much later times. It shared some elements with the manufacture of white ware and clay objects on earlier Neolithic sites—for example, the use of molds and construction of the walls of a pot in sections or layers—so it would be reasonable to conclude that the technique was derived in part from these prior experiences.

The fabric of the coarser pottery vessels was often tempered with straw, whereas grit was frequently used to temper the finer wares. The pots were finished by smoothing the wet surface with the hand or by wiping it with grass or straw. The surface was then often burnished to close the pores in order to make it more watertight, as well as for aesthetic reasons.

Firing techniques seem to have been irregular, judging by the variable surface coloring of the earliest pottery and the uneven hardness of many potsherds. Many of the vessels were probably fired in bonfires. Kilns for firing pottery have not been found on the sites that have yielded the earliest wares, although ovens, presumably for making bread, have been excavated in and near houses—for example, at Tepe Guran (Meldgaard, Mortensen, and Thrane 1963:fig. 7) and Abu Hureyra.

A recent study has demonstrated that a proportion of the pottery made on sites across the northern Levant and northern Mesopotamia was exchanged (Le Mière and Picon 1987). Traffic was restricted to the fine wares, and most of the vessels were exchanged between sites that were relatively close, although a few pots were brought in from regions as much as 400 kilometers away (Le Mière and Picon 1987:144). The trade in pots began as soon as the craft itself had developed, and it persisted throughout the eighth millennium into later times. The practice was probably common throughout Western Asia, as visual studies of pottery manufacture and distribution in other regions have suggested (Moore 1973:62; Mellaart 1975:120). It appears that earlier patterns of exchange in scarce raw materials such as obsidian and other exotic stones quickened in the later Neolithic with the systematic trading of pottery. Why was pottery, something that seems to have been made almost everywhere soon after the craft first developed, exchanged between settlements? It may have been because the finer wares that were traded were themselves considered sufficiently desirable to be acquired by others, or perhaps it was their perishable contents, such as special foods, as Le Mière and Picon have suggested (1987:145).

What was the earliest pottery used for? Most of the pots may be classified as coarse ware, but some finer vessels were made too, right from the beginning. The finer wares, consisting mostly of cups and small bowls, may have been used as "tableware," that is, dishes for serving food and drink. We have no evidence, incidentally, that tables or other kinds of furniture were used in the houses of later Neolithic settlements. Meals for a household were probably served in such dishes set on mats on the floor of one of the rooms in a house.

The coarse wares may have been used to store foodstuffs such as grains and pulses. We have seen that on sites in the Levant, the large storage containers that had been made out of "white ware" were gradually replaced by coarse pottery containers. Some pottery jars were strong enough and had a sufficiently dense fabric to have held water.

Many of the hole-mouth and other jars were apparently used for cooking. These pots have traces of soot on their sides. Baked clay pot stands were used at Çatal Hüyük to support such vessels in the fire (Turkish Ministry of Culture and Tourism 1983:52). Precisely what was cooked in them has not yet been determined, because organic residues in the potsherds themselves have not been analyzed. From what we know of the available foodstuffs, the most likely foods to have been cooked in such pots were meat, grains, and pulses.

The inhabitants of earlier Neolithic villages seem to have roasted their meat on open fires, judging from the signs of burning on the animal bones recovered from their settlements. Their descendants created a revolution in cuisine when they started to use pottery because it enabled them to cook casseroles and other more complex dishes in which the flavors of meat, vegetables, and herbs could be combined. Furthermore, cooking food in water provided a new way of rendering pulses and grains digestible.

Studies of the microwear on human teeth from Abu Hureyra support the interpretation that significant changes occurred in the preparation of food about this time (Molleson and Jones 1991; Molleson, Jones, and Jones 1993). In Abu Hureyra 2A (ca. 9400 to 8300 b.p.), teeth were severely abraded by eating grains prepared as dry, gritty muesli or as bread. Chewing of dried, dusty gazelle meat contributed to the effect. Beginning in 2B and continuing through 2C (8300 to 7000 b.p.), the mode of food preparation was modified in ways that reduced this wear. Grains, other plant foods, and meat were prepared in new ways, probably by cooking them in pots, which first came into use at the site late in period 2B (Molleson, Jones, and Jones 1993:465).

The development of potting coincided with a shift to large-scale herding of sheep, goats, and cattle, as we have already noted. This would have created a need for new containers in which to hold, process, and serve dairy products, especially milk, yogurt, and cheese. Some of these tasks could have been performed with animal skins and doubtless were—skin bags are still used by nomads in Arabia for making yogurt and buttermilk (Dickson 1949:402)—but pottery containers were more durable, among other advantages. Thus an important adjustment in the subsistence economy would have provided another incentive to make pottery. But this deduction, too, needs confirmation from organic residue analysis.

Reflections

The development of potting in Western Asia was apparently an indigenous phenomenon, judging from the regional varieties of wares and their styles of decoration. It seems to have owed nothing to advances in ceramic technology elsewhere, even though we now know that pottery was first made significantly earlier in one adjacent region, the southern fringes of the Sahara in Africa (Close, chapter 3). Its inception was rapid, and within a few centuries new shapes and styles of decoration had been created. The almost simultaneous adoption of pottery across Western Asia clearly indicates that the new craft answered a common set of needs over a wide area. The coincidence of its development with an episode of major economic and cultural change suggests that there were connections between these phenomena. Among these were the need to store and prepare the foods obtained from farming and herding in new, more effective containers and to prepare them in more varied and palatable ways that were less damaging to people's teeth and health.

The practical purposes for which pottery was used from the start suggest that functional potential was the most important reason for its development. The levels that have yielded the earliest pottery from several sites in Western Asia had few potsherds in them, but this phase was brief. By the mid-eighth millennium b.p., potsherds had become the most abundant durable artifact, chipped stone excepted, on Neolithic sites everywhere. Any symbolism that the pottery may have possessed seems to have been of secondary importance. There is a contrast here between the essentially practical role that early pottery served in Western Asia and the symbolic and social importance that Vitelli (chapter 5) has ascribed to the earliest pots at Franchthi Cave in Greece.

Potting was one more of a number of crafts that were either invented or refined throughout the Neolithic. We have already discussed the scale on which mud bricks and plaster were produced for building purposes in the earlier Neolithic. To those crafts may be added others: carpentry to work whole trees such as poplars and pines for building purposes and to make boxes, platters (Mellaart 1967:215), and a wide range of other organic objects that have since decayed; weaving of textiles, mats, and baskets; stone carving of bowls, beads, and other ornaments; flint tool manufacture; and the first attempts at working metals. Thus pottery takes its place alongside a number of other technological advances that marked the achievement of a mature Neolithic way of life.

The Next Stage: The Halaf and Ubaid Cultures

The transition to the Chalcolithic period at around 7000 b.p., a thousand years after the craft of potting began, saw major changes in modes of pottery production and distribution. We are learning, however, that these had their roots in the later Neolithic (Akkermans 1991:124). In Halaf times (ca. 7000–6500/6000 b.p.), pottery was produced on a larger scale and on a more systematic basis than during the Neolithic. Vessels were made in a greater variety of shapes, and the fine wares were given a much more elaborate finish. Indeed, the best of these are among the finest prehistoric pottery ever produced anywhere. The coarse wares, on the other hand, differed little from those made during the Neolithic and are often indistinguishable from them.

The technology of Halaf pottery manufacture has been surprisingly little studied, but there is some evidence to suggest that the methods used to construct pots were similar to those of the later Neolithic (Vandiver 1987:27). The fabric of the coarse wares continued to be tempered with chaff, and the vessels were irregularly fired using the simplest of techniques. Halaf potters, however, exerted considerable skill in making their fine wares. These were fashioned from selected clays that were tempered with fine sand to yield a smooth paste of even consistency. The walls of the vessels were thinned as much as possible, sometimes creating pots of considerable delicacy. A small proportion of vessels was made in shapes that exploited to the full the malleability of the paste. Among these were large open bowls and cups and other vessels with carinations and broad flared rims, the so-called "cream bowls." The fine wares were painted with small-scale designs, sometimes abstract, sometimes naturalistic, that could be extended to cover much of the surface of the pot. The colors used were tones of red, orange, and black. The finest of these vessels, in somewhat exaggerated shapes, were probably intended for display because they would not have withstood regular use, even as tableware.

The finer wares and those of intermediate quality were fired in kilns, some of which have been found on archaeological sites, notably at Yunus near Carchemish (Woolley 1934), Yarim Tepe II (Merpert and Munchaev 1973:112), and, best known of all, at Arpachiyah (Mallowan and Rose 1935) (Fig. 4.2). The establishment there seems to have been a veritable potter's workshop of more than local importance. This advance in firing technology was an important element in the improvement of the quality of the pottery and the expansion of the craft. The indications are that the pottery was made by skilled artisans who were part- or full-time specialists.

Many Halaf villages of medium and large size made their own pottery. Such appears to have been the case at Sabi Abyad on the Balikh in north Syria (Akkermans 1990:276–77). Some of the production of these local workshops was distributed to small settlements nearby. We have learned from neutron activation studies of potsherds and clays that a considerable trade in pottery developed in Halaf times in which the finer wares were exchanged over long distances (Davidson and McKerrell 1976:52–53; Davidson 1981:76). Certain sites, among them Arpachiyah, Chagar Bazar, Tell Brak, and Tell Halaf, served as major production centers. This trade was conducted on a much larger scale than anything seen in the Neolithic, though we can see now that it developed from those earlier antecedents.

The cultural context for these changes in pottery production was significantly different from that of the Neolithic. For the first time in Western Asia there is evidence from burials that society was becoming more differentiated (Hijara 1978). The settlements themselves ranged from small hamlets such as Tell Kreyn near Tabqa on the Euphrates to very large sites like Tell Halaf itself. Some of the larger sites, such as Yarim Tepe II, possessed structures that apparently served functions other than domestic (Merpert and Munchaev 1973:111).

These trends were carried farther during the succeeding Ubaid period (ca. 6500–5500 b.p.) when the first towns such as Eridu were built. The wares became much more standardized, with less variation in decoration, as production techniques improved. The fabric of the pottery and its shapes and designs were all remarkably uniform over very large distances: Ubaid pottery may readily be recognized on sites from the Middle Euphrates to the Persian Gulf.

Many Ubaid bowls and other vessels were made on turntables. Ubaid pots were fired at higher temperatures than Halaf ones, a testimony to increasing skills in the use of clays and kilns. Substantial pottery workshops with kilns have been found at Tell Abada that illuminate the scale and sophistication of the production process (Jasim 1985:208).

Pottery was still made at many settlements of modest size, but again, neutron activation analyses have shown that the vessels were regularly traded locally and also over considerable distances (Davidson and McKerrell 1980:164). The most remarkable example of this long-distance trade is the evidence that much of the pottery found at Ubaid sites along the shores of the Persian Gulf was carried there from southern Mesopotamia, particularly from the sites of Ur, Al Ubaid itself, and Eridu (Oates et al. 1977:232). On a visit to Al Ubaid and Eridu in 1990, T. J. Wilkinson and I found traces of extensive zones of pottery kilns marked by dense concentrations of ashes and Ubaid waster sherds, some of them vitrified, on the surfaces of both sites.[3] These were presumably the remains of the kilns in which some of the pottery found along the Gulf had been made.

We have seen that society became more complex during Chalcolithic times in Western Asia, with the development of social distinctions and the advent of the first towns. Advances in the production of pottery kept pace with these changes in the social sphere. The craft was organized to produce increasing quantities of pots to more standardized designs in more durable wares. Pottery had become an item of daily use during the later Neolithic, but in the Chalcolithic vast quantities of pots were produced that exceed in bulk any other category of artifact from the sites that have been excavated. In recent years we have learned that significant quantities of pottery were traded between sites from the inception of the craft, providing the clearest evidence yet for the degree of intercourse between contemporaneous Neolithic sites. The pace of that trade quickened considerably in Chalcolithic times when, for the only time in prehistory, regions of Western Asia far distant from each other seem to have been in regular communication. The political implications of those contacts remain to be determined.

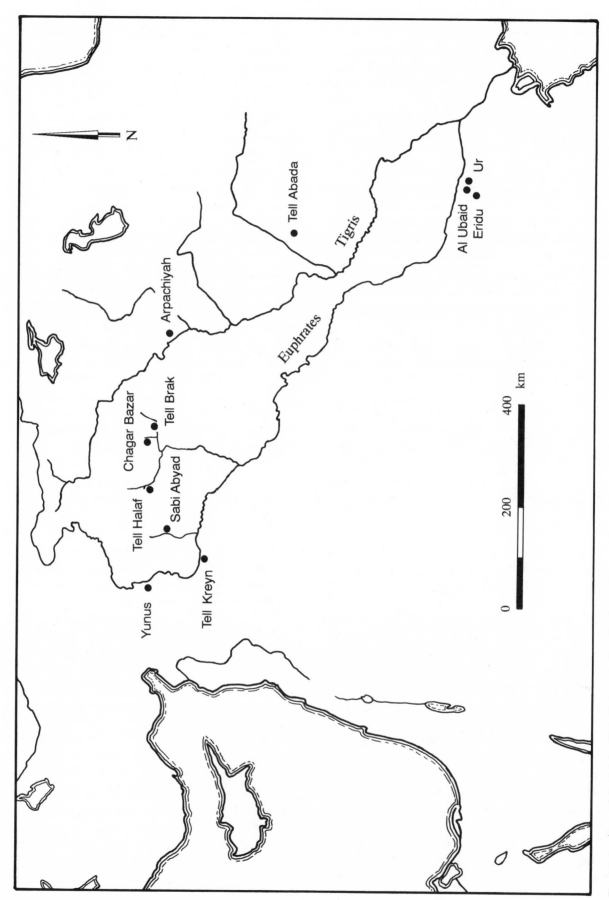

Fig. 4.2. Locations of the Halaf and Ubaid sites mentioned in chapter 4.

Notes

1. All the dates in this essay are given in radiocarbon years before present. They have not been calibrated.

2. Gypsum plaster was commonly used on sites in the interior of Syria and eastward across the Jezireh to the Tigris, in part because the raw material was readily available locally. Farther west and north, where limestone formed the local bedrock, lime plaster was made. For a recent study of the manufacture and use of plaster through the Neolithic into later times, see Rehhoff et al. 1990.

3. An account of this discovery is in preparation.

References Cited

Adams, R. McC.
1983   The Jarmo Stone and Pottery Vessel Industries. In *Prehistoric Archeology along the Zagros Flanks,* edited by L. S. Braidwood, R. J. Braidwood, B. Howe, C. A. Reed, and P. J. Watson, pp. 209–32. Oriental Institute Publications 105. The Oriental Institute, Chicago.

Akkermans, P. M. M. G.
1990   *Villages in the Steppe.* Universiteit van Amsterdam.
1991   New Radiocarbon Dates for the Later Neolithic of Northern Syria. *Paléorient* 17(1):121–25.

Bader, N. O.
1989   *Earliest Cultivators in Northern Mesopotamia.* Nauka, Moscow. (In Russian)

Braidwood, R. J.
1983   Jarmo Chronology. In *Prehistoric Archeology along the Zagros Flanks,* edited by L. S. Braidwood, R. J. Braidwood, B. Howe, C. A. Reed, and P. J. Watson, pp. 537–40. Oriental Institute Publications 105. The Oriental Institute, Chicago.

Braidwood, R. J., and L. S. Braidwood
1960   *Excavations in the Plain of Antioch,* vol. 1. Oriental Institute Publications 61. University of Chicago Press, Chicago.

Braidwood, R. J., and B. Howe
1960   *Prehistoric Investigations in Iraqi Kurdistan.* Studies in Ancient Oriental Civilization 31. University of Chicago Press, Chicago.

Broman Morales, V.
1983   Jarmo Figurines and Other Clay Objects. In *Prehistoric Archeology along the Zagros Flanks,* edited by L. S. Braidwood, R. J. Braidwood, B. Howe, C. A. Reed, and P. J. Watson, pp. 369–423. Oriental Institute Publications 105. The Oriental Institute, Chicago.
1990   *Figurines and Other Clay Objects from Sarab and Çayönü.* Oriental Institute Communications 25. University of Chicago Press, Chicago.

Çambel, H.
1981   Chronologie et organisation de l'espace à Çayönü. In *Préhistoire du Levant,* edited by J. Cauvin and P. Sanlaville, pp. 531–53. Actes du Colloque International 598. Centre National de la Recherche Scientifique, Paris.

Campbell, S., and D. Baird
1990   Excavations at Ginnig: The Aceramic to Early Ceramic Neolithic Sequence in North Iraq. *Paléorient* 16(2):65–78.

Cauvin, J.
1978   *Les premiers villages de Syrie-Palestine du IXème au VIIème millénaire avant J.C.* Maison de l'Orient, Lyon.

Childe, V. G.
1936   *Man Makes Himself.* Watts, London.
1957   *The Dawn of European Civilization.* 6th ed. Routledge and Kegan Paul, London.

Contenson, H. de
1971   Tell Ramad: A Village of Syria of the 7th and 6th Millennia B.C. *Archaeology* 24(3):278–85.
1981   Le néolithique de Damascène. In *Préhistoire du Levant,* edited by J. Cauvin and P. Sanlaville, pp. 467–70. Actes du Colloque International 598. Centre National de la Recherche Scientifique, Paris.
1985a   La campagne de 1965 à Bouqras. *Cahiers de l'Euphrate* 4:335–71.
1985b   La région de Damas au néolithique. *Les Annales Archéologiques Arabes Syriennes* 35:9–29.
1992   *Préhistoire de Ras Shamra.* 2 vols. Ras Shamra-Ougarit 8. Éditions Recherche sur les Civilisations, Paris.

Contenson, H. de, and L. C. Courtois
1979   A propos des vases en chaux: Recherches sur leur fabrication et leur origine. *Paléorient* 5:177–82.

Davidson, T. E.
1981   Pottery Manufacture and Trade at the Prehistoric Site of Tell Aqab, Syria. *Journal of Field Archaeology* 8:65–77.

Davidson, T. E., and H. McKerrell
1976   Pottery Analysis and Halaf Period Trade in the Khabur Headwaters Region. *Iraq* 38(1):45–56.
1980   The Neutron Activation Analysis of Halaf and 'Ubaid Pottery from Tell Arpachiyah and Tepe Gawra. *Iraq* 42(2):155–67.

Dickson, H. R. P.
1949   *The Arab of the Desert.* Allen and Unwin, London.

Dornemann, R. H.
1986   *A Neolithic Village at Tell El Kowm in the Syrian Desert.* Studies in Ancient Oriental Civilization 43. The Oriental Institute, Chicago.

Fukai, S., and T. Matsutani
1981   *Telul eth-Thalathat,* vol. 4. Institute of Oriental Culture, University of Tokyo.

Garfinkel, Y.
1987   Burnt Lime Products and Social Implications in the Pre-Pottery Neolithic B Villages of the Near East. *Paléorient* 13(1):69–76.

Garstang, J.
1953   *Prehistoric Mersin.* Clarendon Press, Oxford.

Gourdin, W. H., and W. D. Kingery
1975   The Beginnings of Pyrotechnology: Neolithic and Egyptian Lime Plaster. *Journal of Field Archaeology* 2:133–50.

Hedges, R. E. M., R. A. Housley, C. R. Bronk, and G. J. Van Klinken
1990   Radiocarbon Dates from the Oxford AMS System: *Archaeometry* Datelist 11. *Archaeometry* 32:211–37.

Hijara, I.
1978   Three New Graves at Arpachiyah. *World Archaeology* 10(2):125–28.

Hodder, I.
1988   Material Culture Texts and Social Change: A Theoretical Discussion and Some Archaeological Examples. *Proceedings of the Prehistoric Society* 54:67–75.

Holland, T. A.
1982   Figurines and Miscellaneous Objects. Appendix C in *Excavations at Jericho,* vol. 4, by K. M. Kenyon and T. A. Holland, pp. 551–63. British School of Archaeology in Jerusalem, London.

Jasim, S. A.
1985   *The Ubaid Period in Iraq.* 2 vols. British Archaeological Reports, International Series 267, Oxford.

Kenyon, K. M.
1979   *Archaeology in the Holy Land.* 4th ed. Benn, London.
1981   *Excavations at Jericho,* vol. 3. British School of Archaeology in Jerusalem, London.

Kenyon, K. M., and T. A. Holland
1982   *Excavations at Jericho,* vol. 4. British School of Archaeology in Jerusalem, London.

Kirkbride, D.
1969   Early Byblos and the Beqa'a. *Mélanges de l'Université Saint-Joseph* 45:43–60.
1973   Umm Dabaghiyah 1972: A Second Preliminary Report. *Iraq* 35:1–7.

Kozlowski, S. F.
1990   *Nemrik 9.* University of Warsaw.

Lawrence, B.
1982   Principal Food Animals at Çayönü. In *Prehistoric Village Archaeology in South-Eastern Turkey,* edited by L. S. Braidwood and R. J. Braidwood, pp. 175–99. British Archaeological Reports, International Series 138, Oxford.

Le Mière, M.
1983   Pottery and White Ware. In "Bouqras Revisited: Preliminary Report on a Project in Eastern Syria," by P. A. Akkermans, J. A. K. Boerma, A. T. Clason, S. G. Hill, E. Lohof, C. Meiklejohn, M. Le Mière, G. M. F. Molgat, J. J. Roodenberg, W. Waterbolk-van Rooyen, and W. Van Zeist, pp. 351–54. *Proceedings of the Prehistoric Society* 49:335–72.

Le Mière, M., and M. Picon
1987   Production locales et circulation des céramiques au VIe millénaire, au Proche-Orient. *Paléorient* 13(2):133–47.

Lloyd, S., and F. Safar
1945   Tell Hassuna. *Journal of Near Eastern Studies* 4:255–89.

Mallowan, M. E. L., and J. C. Rose
1935   Excavations at Tall Arpachiyah, 1933. *Iraq* 2:1–178.

Meldgaard, J., P. Mortensen, and H. Thrane
1963   Excavations at Tepe Guran, Luristan. *Acta Archaeologica* 34:97–133.

Mellaart, J.
1967   *Çatal Hüyük.* Thames and Hudson, London.
1970   *Excavations at Hacilar.* 2 vols. Occasional Publications of the British Institute of Archaeology at Ankara 9. British Institute of Archaeology at Ankara, Edinburgh.
1975   *The Neolithic of the Near East.* Thames and Hudson, London.

Merpert, N. Ya., and R. M. Munchaev
1973   Early Agricultural Settlements in the Sinjar Plain, Northern Iraq. *Iraq* 35:93–113.
1987   The Earliest Levels at Yarim Tepe I and Yarim Tepe II in Northern Iraq. *Iraq* 49:1–36.

Molleson, T., and K. Jones
1991   Dental Evidence for Dietary Change at Abu Hureyra. *Journal of Archaeological Science* 18:525–39.

Molleson, T., K. Jones, and S. Jones
1993   Dietary Change and the Effects of Food Preparation on Microwear Patterns in the Late Neolithic of Abu Hureyra, Northern Syria. *Journal of Human Evolution* 24:455–68.

Moore, A. M. T.
1973   The Late Neolithic in Palestine. *Levant* 5:36–68.

1978   *The Neolithic of the Levant.* D. Phil. thesis, University of Oxford. University Microfilms International, Ann Arbor, Michigan.

1981   North Syria in Neolithic 2. In *Préhistoire du Levant,* edited by J. Cauvin and P. Sanlaville, pp. 445–56. Actes du Colloque International 598. Centre National de la Recherche Scientifique, Paris.

1985   The Development of Neolithic Societies in the Near East. *Advances in World Archaeology* 4:1–69.

1992   The Impact of Accelerator Dating at the Early Village of Abu Hureyra on the Euphrates. *Radiocarbon* 34(3):850–58.

Mortensen, P.

1970   Tell Shimshara: The Hassuna Period. *Historisk-filosofiske Skrifter* 5(2):1–148. Munksgaard, Copenhagen.

1974   A Survey of Prehistoric Settlements in Northern Luristan. *Acta Archaeologica* 45:1–47.

Mortillet, G. de, and A. de Mortillet

1881   *Musée Préhistorique.* Reinwald, Paris.

Neuville, R.

1934   Le préhistorique de Palestine (1). *Revue Biblique* 43:237–59.

Oates, J., T. E. Davidson, D. Kamilli, and H. McKerrell

1977   Seafaring Merchants of Ur? *Antiquity* 51: 221–34.

Peake, H., and H. J. Fleure

1927   *Peasants and Potters.* Clarendon Press, Oxford.

Rehhoff, L., P. Akkermans, E. Leonardsen, and I. Thuesen

1990   Plasters: Gypsum or Calcite? A Preliminary Case Study of Syrian Plasters. *Paléorient* 16(2):79–87.

Rollefson, G. O.

1983   Ritual and Ceremony at Neolithic Ain Ghazal (Jordan). *Paléorient* 9(2):29–38.

Rollefson, G. O., A. H. Simmons, and Z. Kafafi

1992   Neolithic Cultures at 'Ain Ghazal, Jordan. *Journal of Field Archaeology* 19:443–70.

Seton Williams, M. V.

1948   Neolithic Burnished Wares in the Near East. *Iraq* 10:34–50.

Smith, P. E. L., and R. Crépeau

1983   Fabrication expérimentale de répliques d'un vase néolithique du site de Ganj Dareh, Iran: Recherche technologique. *Paléorient* 9(2): 55–62.

Torrence, R., and S. E. van der Leeuw

1989   Introduction: What's New about Innovation? In *What's New? A Closer Look at the Process of Innovation,* edited by S. E. van der Leeuw and R. Torrence, pp. 1–15. Unwin Hyman, London.

Turkish Ministry of Culture and Tourism

1983   *The Anatolian Civilisations I.* The Council of Europe XVIIIth European Art Exhibition.

Vandiver, P. B.

1987   Sequential Slab Construction: A Conservative Southwest Asiatic Ceramic Tradition, ca. 7000–3000 B.C. *Paléorient* 13(2):9–35.

van Zeist, W.

1972   Palaeobotanical Results of the 1970 Season at Çayönü, Turkey. *Helinium* 12:3–19.

Voigt, M. M.

1988   Excavations at Neolithic Gritille. *Anatolica* 15:215–32.

Woolley, C. L.

1934   The Prehistoric Pottery of Carchemish. *Iraq* 1:146–62.

5

Pots, Potters, and the Shaping of Greek Neolithic Society

Studies of prehistoric pottery begin with no a priori knowledge of why pots were made or what they were used for. We do know, however, that pots were *made* in a necessary series of stages by individuals whose choices and hence behavior at every stage of the process are recorded in their pots and sherds. That direct, secure relationship provides us with a rare glimpse of some of the behavior of prehistoric individuals. Those individual potters—even if making pots was but one of their contributions—should be among the important players in any archaeological discussion of the beginnings of ceramics.

The following account of the beginnings of pottery in the Aegean pays particular attention to what we can glean of some potters' behavior, primarily from sherds from Franchthi Cave in southern Greece (Fig. 5.1). Franchthi is the focus because I know it best and because it is one of the few Greek sites that permit the kind of analyses involved, but the larger record from the rest of the Aegean area conforms to much of what I present. Where it does not, the differences suggest that responses to the many innovations of the Neolithic were variable, even within the relatively small geographical area of Greece (see Perlès and Vitelli 1994).

This review begins late in the middle of the Neolithic sequence, sometime after about 5500 B.C., moves on to the Late and Final Neolithic (sometimes called Chalcolithic) in the next millennium, and then returns to the beginnings of pottery production in the Early Neolithic, about 6700 B.C.[1]

Middle Neolithic Potters

The late Middle Neolithic (MN) potters at Franchthi and throughout southern Greece worked in a ceramic tradition that had been developing without interruption since the Early Neolithic (EN), so they had about a thousand years of experience and experimentation upon which to draw. The high technical quality and the elegance of their pots speak eloquently of the time invested in each piece by skilled potters who took substantial risks.

Throughout the Peloponnese, potters used a common recipe for their clay body. The thickness of the vessel walls, rarely over 5 millimeters, is completely uniform around the circumference; vessels are well balanced and symmetrical, without overly thick or thin bottoms; and rims often fit perfectly on compass-drawn circles. The shapes they produced (Fig. 5.2) are sharply angular and often have tall and elegant bases

KAREN D. VITELLI

55

Fig. 5.1. Location of Franchthi Cave in Greece.

or pedestals. Many of the shapes are challenging to build, difficult to dry without stress cracks and breaks, and more difficult still to fire without mishap. The surfaces are superbly finished, with rare traces of tool depressions. Up to 25 percent of the vessels were given individualized painted decoration: no two pots have identical patterns—although the decorated pots are not always the most finely made. The rate of innovation is high, and the innovations appear throughout the region where the style is shared, although subtle local variations in their execution imply some local production at most sites.

Firing was an at least loosely controlled three-stage process that often successfully produced dark, reduced, iron-oxide-based paint on a light, oxidized background. Firings may have been done in a movable kiln (Vitelli 1994) and sometimes reached temperatures sufficient to begin vitrification of the paint and occasionally the body of the vessels. Indeed, in the latest MN, overfired sherds are common. Potters were willing to chance overfiring to achieve the occasional "perfectly" fired piece. Given the high level of technical expertise involved, the potters were surely specialists.

The Middle Neolithic potters developed, in a matter of a few centuries, most of the basic ceramic technology (minus the potter's wheel) relied on by later historical potters. The high rate of innovation, the experimentation, and the consequent risk run counter to our ethnographic models of the traditional conservative potter and suggest a pottery "industry" motivated by circumstances quite different from those of today's traditional potters. Indeed, today's potters all work in contexts that have long histories of ceramic production and use, and these contexts have developed within particular cultural settings. In the earlier Neolithic, *everything* concerning ceramics had to be discovered and worked out: from how to make, modify, and use a pot to the criteria for judging what constituted a good, excellent, or appropriate pot.

The risk taking that the MN potters engaged in suggests a kind of competition—some kind of power and importance, however fleeting—in the achievement of a new, difficult, extraordinary pot. The pots, then, must have been designed in some sense for social display. They are too obviously useful as containers never to have been put to that use, and foods, beverages, medicines, incense, poisons, and drugs are among the possible contents. But significance must also have been attached to the pot itself, and perhaps even to the process of its production. A pot was designed to perform, in its first use at least, at some special occasion.

Among the special designs the potters came up with are the first pots in the Franchthi sequence that retain evidence of actually having been used over a fire (Vitelli 1989, 1993:213–15). The examples are all from a single shape, essentially a stew pot (Fig. 5.2, top row). They occur in a special fabric that is similar to that of finer wares but was modified by the addition of larger nonplastics to improve its tolerance of repeated exposure to rapid temperature changes. Those larger nonplastics, together with a consistently lower firing temperature and the absence of burnishing or other embellishment aside from intentional blackening of all surfaces, qualify these cooking pots as "coarse" ware. The vessels are, however, very carefully built—as we should expect, since cooks are unlikely to entrust ingredients to a pot they fear might disintegrate.

The rim sherds of the cooking pots regularly fit exactly on compass-drawn circles; the surfaces are regular and even; and wall thicknesses rarely exceed 5 millimeters and are uniform on all parts of the vessel. The techniques and specifics of building and finishing the cooking pots are so similar to those of the fine ware that the same individuals probably made both. It makes sense that skilled, experienced, innovative potters would have the knowledge and creativity to design a vessel with specific properties suited to a specific task. In the general context of ceramic production aimed at social display, we should perhaps envision the first cooking pots as also intended for social occasions. Indeed, cooking pots account for only about 10 percent of the contemporaneous assemblage. With capacities of roughly 4 liters, they could have provided sufficient food for only a few special people or, conceivably, for more people but on infrequent special occasions.

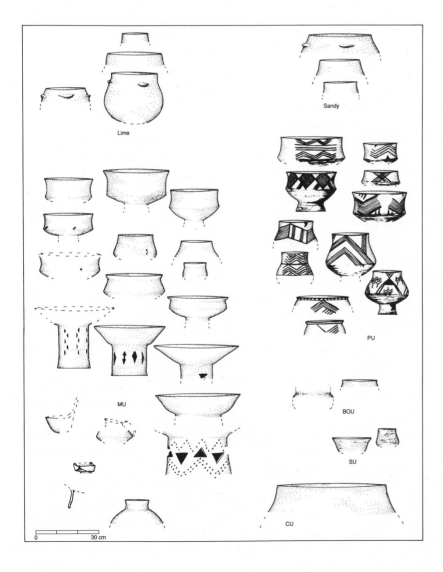

Fig. 5.2. Late Middle Neolithic coarse ware shapes from Franchthi Cave and Lerna.

Late Neolithic Potters

In the Late Neolithic (LN), potters abandoned the few but widespread styles of MN and created instead a wide array of new styles in fine wares, each apparently made in a limited geographical area (Perlès 1992:140). This change points to changes in the relationships among groups of potters, in their sharing of information, and perhaps in their movements and their affiliations and loyalties. Such changes in the organization of the production of pottery surely affected, and reflect, changes in the organization of the larger society.

The LN potters also directed a larger portion of their production to stew pots: approximately 20 percent in the earlier phase, and as much as 30–40 percent in the later. Whether the increase reflects changes in general food preparation practices or increases in special occasions or feasting is unclear.

Final Neolithic Potters

By Final Neolithic (FN) times, the production of coarse wares had become the potters' primary focus. Coarse wares account for 80–85 percent of assemblages, and nearly 100 percent at some sites.[2] A primary reason for the designation "coarse" is the quantity and size of nonplastics, which commonly are as large as 5–10 millimeters. Earlier coarse wares were made from standard ingredients. The FN nonplastics, which include occasional chunks of sherd and even fragments of retouched obsidian blades, seem to have been chosen randomly. It is hard to identify two pots made from the same clay body. That, along with the variable motor habits of the potters involved, points to large numbers of individuals involved in pottery production. It may be that for the first time in the Aegean we are seeing in the FN something close to household production for household consumption.

Up to this point, only one shape, a stew pot, was made in coarse wares. In the FN, potters created a variety of new shapes: large and small stew pots, shallow pans, sieves, "cheese" pots, and strange ovenlike objects (Fig. 5.3). The new shapes point to greater variety in the ways food was prepared and possibly to an increase in the variety of foods consumed (Demoule and Perlès 1993; Hansen 1991:145–64)—the first hints of development toward a cuisine (Goody 1982:105).

The surface finish of the FN coarse wares varies. Some vessels, especially the large, deep pots, are roughly comparable to earlier stew pots: they were scraped to a fairly uniform thickness and carefully smoothed. They appear to be pots a cook could trust. Others, however, still show building surfaces: smeared coil joints, pinching depressions, patches, and gouges, with no attempt to cover or remove them and no concern to scrape the walls to a regular thickness, which can be considerably over 1 centimeter. On the bottoms, the impressions of grasses and mats are still clear. All the coarse wares are low fired, with thick black cores. Some are so minimally fired that they melt if saturated with water.

These coarse sherds show us potters with the knowledge of what was necessary to make a pot that would serve a particular function, and what was unnecessary. They drew on the considerable body of experience that potters had accumulated over the previous millennia. Their pots also show us, for the first time, potters who were interested primarily in practical necessity and who spent little time on extra embellishments. This observation reinforces the impression of potters making pots for their own needs, as but one of many chores, and it stands in strong contrast with the practices and context of earlier pottery production.

Other consequences of the FN potters' redirection of effort should include effects on diet and nutrition (probably more dramatic ones than at any prior time); effects on the social aspects of food preparation and consumption; effects on the organization and allocation of work beyond pottery making; and effects on whatever aspects of life had formerly been affected by the elegant fine wares that were no longer made in any appreciable quantity.

Early Neolithic Potters

If it is not until the end of the Neolithic that we have a close association between pots and food preparation, then we need a new explanation for the original introduction of pottery in the Early Neolithic.[3] That explanation should take into account the role of the potters and the unbroken EN-MN ceramic tradition that includes specialist potters in the MN. An appreciation of beginning potters' behavior—gained from my nearly 20 years of teaching experimental pottery classes primarily to students with no prior experience of working clay—may contribute toward understanding the beginnings of pottery in Greece.

Early Neolithic (EN) pottery is generally described as coarse or even crude. In some cases the designations are apt, but not, I think, for the same reasons and with the same implications as for the later coarse wares.

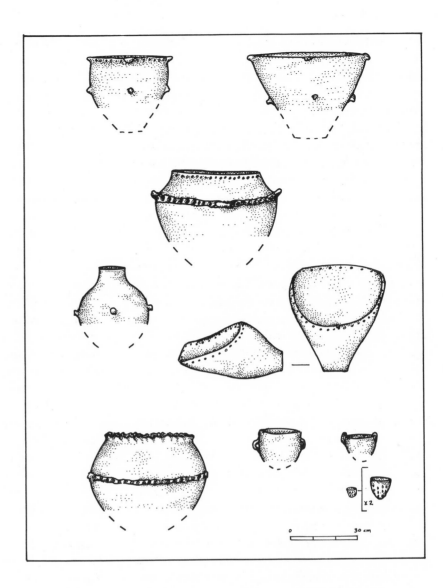

Fig. 5.3. Sample of Final Neolithic coarse ware shapes from Franchthi Cave and Lerna.

Some, but not all, EN wares in Greece have plentiful nonplastics, but the inclusions are neither as large as those in later coarse wares nor as random as those from the Final Neolithic. Quantity and size are variable, but the recipes called for standard ingredients. The nonplastics in the EN pottery, whether naturally occurring or intentionally added, do not represent an adjustment for particular ceramic properties related to intended uses, but rather represent the attempts of novice potters, with little prior knowledge to draw on, to produce a clay body that they could build with and dry and fire successfully.

Another determinant of coarseness is minimal surface finish, and in that respect few, if any, EN sherds deserve the label. All the EN sherds at Franchthi that preserve any original surface are burnished. Modern experiments confirm comments in the ethnographic record that burnishing is the most time-consuming

stage of producing a pot. Beginning experimental potters burnish their pots until their fingers cramp and their elbows ache, and with the right clay, achieve a high sheen—but their pieces still may look "crude" if they haven't discovered how to make the surface truly even and regular before they begin to burnish. Any crudeness in the EN vessel surfaces is of the same sort: it is not, as in FN examples, the result of too little effort but of too little knowledge and experience.

EN pots have also been called coarse because they tend to be lopsided and irregular, with walls that vary in thickness and often appear too thick for the size of the vessel. These traits are also typical of the work of inexperienced potters, even highly gifted ones. Once someone has discovered the tricks for producing a level rim or a high-gloss burnish, the tricks can be easily demonstrated to another potter. But to judge the thickness of a wall below the point one can feel directly with thumb and fingers is a problem that has no quick solution. It requires experience: regular practice, repeated failure, and a slowly acquired sense of how heavy a pot of a certain size "ought" to be. Symmetry, too, follows naturally from a well-paced working rhythm—from a set of sequential actions repeated so often they become second nature. It does not come from making three or four pots per year, the estimated production per potter in the EN at Franchthi (Vitelli 1993:210, 211n9).[4]

Low firing is another criterion for ceramic coarseness. The EN pots from Greece are soft fired and marked with firing clouds that betray the direct fuel firings used by the potters. Higher-temperature firings and the use of kilns can be documented as later additions to Neolithic technology. The EN potters were able to exert some control over the color of their pots. They had inherited long experience of making fires and adjusting heat and smoke with different fuels, but they had not yet learned to maintain and manipulate temperatures in the region needed to affect the hardness and other properties of ceramic materials. They did not choose to fire their pots in a particular way to affect properties other than color; they simply fired within the attainable limits.

The EN pots in Greece are pots made with the loving care and extended effort of most beginning potters, and they are crude and coarse in the same ways and for many of the same reasons. The EN pots are coarse not by the potters' choice, as were the coarse pots of later Neolithic potters, but because of the limitations imposed by their experience and knowledge of relevant technology. Viewed in the context of the available technology, they are excellent products. That they may also have been made by potters who were specialists, at least in the sense that few individuals made pots for use by others beyond the immediate family, becomes more likely when we look closely at the evidence from Franchthi.

At Franchthi, five distinctive wares occur throughout the Early Neolithic deposits. All were made in the same basic shapes and sizes (Fig. 5.4), but each ware was made using different nonplastics. The pots in each ware were scraped differently, were burnished with different tools and at different angles, had their rims finished with different motions and their lugs and bases added in subtly different ways, and were fired using different procedures and, probably, fuels. The largely unintentional differences in motor habits strongly suggest that, at any given time, a different potter was responsible for each ware. All the wares, with the possible exception of one, were made from local materials,

so the differences are not the result of exchange among different communities.

The five wares occur in all EN deposits, both inside the cave and out, in consistent relative frequencies, and in superimposed deposits that span the EN (^{14}C dates range from 6680 to 5640 B.C.). The consistent frequencies and occurrence over a number of generations indicate that the different wares are not the result of random selection of ingredients and procedures. Other southern Greek EN sites also have evidence for more than one ware in contemporaneous production, although reliable statistics on frequencies are not available.

At Franchthi, the only site where recovery techniques currently permit such calculations, total annual production in the EN can be estimated at some 12–13 pots per year (Vitelli 1993:210). Even if the estimate is off by a magnitude of two or three, production was still well within the capability of a single potter. The demand for pots did not require the services of five potters, yet something compelled at least five individuals to make an occasional pot using very specific ingredients and procedures.

The differences among the wares—their ingredients and procedures—should not have affected the properties of the resulting pots sufficiently to have limited the uses to which each could have been put. The differences are not random but intentional. Members of the small community at Franchthi must have known that different potters collected their materials from different places. They all likely knew which individual produced pots in which tradition or ware. Thus, who made a pot, and according to which traditional recipe, might have been an important part of each pot's function or meaning.

If we could suggest reasons why that might have been the case, we would be closer to understanding the reasons for the introduction of pottery. One way to proceed is to consider who might have had the knowledge and opportunity to discover or invent ceramic processes. The first potters everywhere must have had some prior knowledge of relevant materials and processes. We know what some of that knowledge must have been: how to recognize and where to find ingredients such as particular clays, rocks, shells, and ash and other vegetal materials. The knowledge should also have included ways of preparing those materials, such as crushing, grinding, and charring; proportions for mixing; techniques and timing for kneading or wedging; building techniques and stages; kinds of tools useful for various procedures; how to determine when a piece was ready to fire; when the wind and

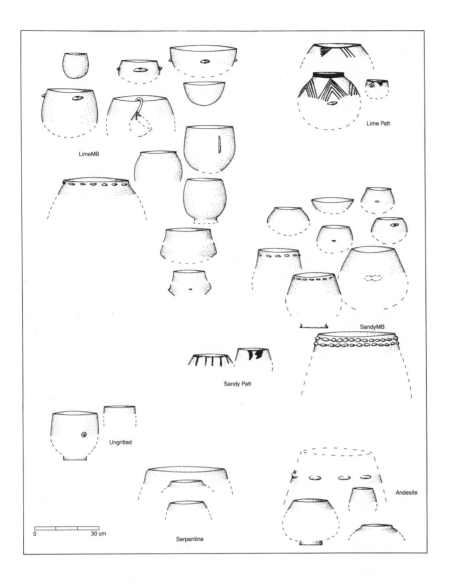

Fig. 5.4. The range of ceramic shapes in all five wares from the Early Neolithic at Franchthi Cave.

weather were right for firing; what fuels to use; how and when to place pot and fuel together; and a whole assortment of other small but potentially significant procedures that contribute to the success of a fired pot.

Most of this knowledge is also needed for finding, harvesting, and processing plants for food and other uses. To anyone who has done both, the parallels are obvious.[5] It seems logical that the parallels exist because individuals who were expert in one (and plant processing is the earlier) applied their knowledge and practices in developing the other. This is the primary reason I have suggested elsewhere that women, generally considered to have been the gatherers, were probably also the inventors and first practitioners of pottery making (e.g., Vitelli 1993:xx). In the EN, however, it does not appear that every woman made pottery, as may have been true in the FN. Why would only some

women have become potters? To answer this question we might return to the EN pots.

The EN wares at Franchthi are distinctive for their ingredients and, to a lesser extent, their coloring. Colors, including ceramic colors, have symbolic meaning in many cultures, such that color may limit the appropriate contexts for a vessel's use (e.g., Kaplan and Levine 1981:876–78; Rice 1987:331–32). Might the choice of ingredients for a pot also have had symbolic value, making one recipe more appropriate for a particular circumstance than another? Each ware had its own recipe, initially formulated, perhaps, by someone who also had expert knowledge of plants. That combination recalls the special ingredients for spells and cures utilized by the shamans, sorcerers, witches, diviners, and medicine men and women of the ethnographic record (e.g., McNaughton 1988:47 and passim; Prentice 1986:112–14; Ripinsky-Naxon 1992: 40; Spencer 1977). If only those individuals who had access to esoteric knowledge of "sacred" plants applied that knowledge to a new medium—clay—in the early years of the Neolithic, then only a few members of any community would have been potters, and their pots would have been symbols of their powers.

The potential relationship between a kind of magic and pottery making is perhaps made more plausible by the example of the blacksmiths of West Africa. Members of the blacksmith caste or clan transform ore-bearing rocks into a variety of tools and sculptures through their expert knowledge and control of fire (McNaughton 1988:156–60; Vaughan 1970:61–62).[6] They are also considered to have arcane knowledge and occult powers (McNaughton 1988:42–46 and passim). In an age without metal, that is, the Neolithic, potters would have been the ones with power to transform matter through the control of fire. Again, anyone who has made and fired a ceramic object has experienced the sense of the seemingly magical transformation that takes place during firing.

If it was individuals with shamanic powers who added the making of ceramic objects to their repertoire at the beginning of the Neolithic, that would explain the limitations imposed on who might make pottery. It would also explain the pre-pottery clay objects, the small numbers of pots made in the earliest Neolithic, the importance of the differences among early wares, the late introduction of pots for cooking, and the social/symbolic context of early pottery.[7] It would also provide an explanation for an "industry" that began as the domain of specialists, grew to a point of intense competition that spurred rapid technological and stylistic innovation focused on fine wares, and eventually moved to the realm of nonspecialists—by which time most related shamanic practices, usually associated with hunter-gatherers, must have lost their centrality in the Neolithic belief system.

Although the suggestion of early potters-as-shamans requires that we make several leaps of faith, it is grounded in and explains the actual detailed evidence of the pottery. The suggestion follows from focusing on the individuals who made pots and acknowledging that they had a role in shaping Neolithic society. It also hints that early Neolithic society, unlike societies in the modern Western world, might not have been organized around a hierarchical system of power and prestige based on the accumulation of goods and debts (cf. Hayden 1990).

Notes

1. See Jacobsen and Farrand (1987:plate 71) for a full listing of Franchthi ^{14}C dates.

2. Final Neolithic settlement patterns in southern Greece show an impressive increase in the use of caves and in new sites, often small in size, suggesting scattered farmsteads of a few families (Demoule and Perlès 1993). Many of the new sites are in previously marginal areas or areas that had been unoccupied (including the Cycladic islands), areas where the occupants would have been dependent on trade for many necessary items (Davis 1992:703–704).

3. For a disussion of the evidence for a "pre-pottery" phase in Greece, see Perlès and Vitelli (1994) and Vitelli (1993:37–40). Moore (chapter 4) also notes that at many eastern Mediterranean sites, figurines and other objects of baked clay were produced for centuries before pottery first appeared.

4. This is roughly my own production range as a potter. Even after 20 years at this level, the only time I achieved a semblance of symmetry comparable to some of the lower-quality MN vessels was late in an intensive 6-week pottery-making season in which I produced more than 20 pots. The observation is confirmed by another, more experienced experimental potter, Yves Garidel (personal communication, 1993).

5. In fact, it was the repeated, independent observations in the journals of students in my experimental pottery classes noting parallels between aspects of pottery making and traditional cooking practices that finally convinced me to pursue the relationship I suggest here.

6. McNaughton, among others, notes that "women in the blacksmith clans own the rights to make pottery" (1988:7). It would be interesting to discover the historical basis for this association.

7. Prentice's argument (1986) that shamans were responsible for the introduction of gourds (cucurbits) to North America, if applied to potters-as-shamans, provides many additional explanations, especially for the acceptance, spread, and exchange of pottery.

References Cited

Davis, Jack
  1992   Review of Aegean Prehistory I: The Islands of the Aegean. *American Journal of Archaeology* 96:699–756.
Demoule, Jean-Paul, and Catherine Perlès
  1993   The Greek Neolithic: A New Review. *Journal of World Prehistory* 7(3):355–416.
Goody, Jack
  1982   *Cooking, Cuisine and Class: A Study in Com-*

parative Sociology. Cambridge University Press, Cambridge.

Hansen, Julie M.
1991   *The Paleoethnobotany of Franchthi Cave.* Excavations at Franchthi Cave, Greece, fasc. 7. Indiana University Press, Bloomington.

Hayden, Brian
1990   Nimrods, Piscators, Pluckers, and Planters: The Emergence of Food Production. *Journal of Anthropological Archaeology* 9:31–69.

Jacobsen, Thomas W., and W. R. Farrand
1987   *Franchthi Cave and Paralia: Maps, Plans, and Sections.* Excavations at Franchthi Cave, Greece, fasc. 1. Indiana University Press, Bloomington.

Kaplan, Flora S., and David M. Levine
1981   Cognitive Mapping of a Folk Taxonomy of Mexican Pottery: A Multivariate Approach. *American Anthropologist* 83:868–84.

McNaughton, Patrick R.
1988   *The Mande Blacksmiths: Knowledge, Power and Art in West Africa.* Indiana University Press, Bloomington.

Perlès, Catherine
1992   Systems of Exchange and Organization of Production in Neolithic Greece. *Journal of Mediterranean Archaeology* 5:116–64.

Perlès, Catherine, and Karen D. Vitelli
1994   Technologie et fonction des premières productions céramiques de Grèce. In *Terre cuite et société. La céramique, document techniques, économique, culturel,* pp. 225–42. Actes des XIV Rencontres Internationales d'Archéologie et d'Histoire d'Antibes, 21–23 October 1993. CNRS, APDCA, Juan-les-Pins.

Prentice, Guy
1986   Origins of Plant Domestication in the Eastern United States: Promoting the Individual in Archaeological Theory. *Southeastern Archaeology* 5:103–19.

Rice, Prudence M.
1987   *Pottery Analysis: A Sourcebook.* University of Chicago Press, Chicago.

Ripinsky-Naxon, M.
1992   Shamanism: Religion or Rite? *Journal of Prehistoric Religion* 6:37–44.

Spencer, Robert F.
1977   Shamanism in Northwestern North America. In *The Anthropology of Power: Ethnographic Studies from Asia, Oceania, and the New World,* edited by Raymond D. Fogelson and Richard N. Adams, pp. 351–74. Academic Press, New York.

Vaughan, James H., Jr.
1970   Caste Systems in the Western Sudan. In *Social Stratification in Africa,* edited by Arthur Tuden and Leonard Plotnicov, pp. 59–92. The Free Press, New York; Collier-Macmillan Ltd., London.

Vitelli, Karen D.
1989   Were Pots First Made for Foods? Doubts from Franchthi. *World Archaeology* 21:17–29.
1994   Experimental Approaches to Thessalian Neolithic Ceramics: Gray Ware and Ceramic Color. In *La Thessalie. Quinze années de recherches archéologiques 1975–1990. Bilans et perspectives,* pp. 143–48. Actes du Colloque Internationale, Lyons, 17–22 April 1990, volume A. Greek Ministry of Culture, Athens.
1993   *Franchthi Neolithic Pottery, vol.1: Classification and Ceramic Phases 1 and 2.* Excavations at Franchthi Cave, Greece, fasc. 8. Indiana University Press, Bloomington.

6

Starčevo Pottery and Neolithic Development in the Central Balkans

JONI L. MANSON

The Starčevo culture and several closely related contemporaneous cultures are generally considered to represent the earliest Neolithic populations in the central Balkan region. In this part of the world, "Neolithic" is defined as relating to the beginning stages of an agricultural and stock-raising economy, along with the production of polished stone tools and ceramics (Benac et al. 1979). Unfortunately, the vast majority of sites in this region are undated and have been excavated without the systematic retrieval of botanical and animal remains that is necessary for detailed economic and ecological analyses. In practice, the interpretation of any particular site in this area as Neolithic commonly depends upon the presence or absence of one type of artifact—pottery.

Archaeology of the Starčevo Culture

The Starčevo culture derives its name from the archaeological site located just west of the small village of Starčevo, about 20 kilometers east-northeast of Belgrade, Yugoslavia (Serbia). The site lies on the northern (left) bank of the Danube and is also known as Starčevo-Grad (Fig. 6.1). The later Neolithic site of Vinča lies practically opposite Starčevo across the Danube River. Brief test excavations were performed at Starčevo-Grad in 1928 by M. Grbić, and larger-scale excavations were carried out in 1931 and 1932 by a joint Yugoslav-American team. The concept of an early Neolithic "Starčevo culture" was defined on the basis of these excavations (Fewkes et al. 1933; Ehrich 1977; Benac et al. 1979). Additional field work was conducted in 1969 and 1970, but by this time brick-making activities in the area had nearly obliterated the site.

Starčevo settlements are found in Croatia, Bosnia-Hercegovina, Macedonia, and particularly in Serbia, including the autonomous provinces of Vojvodina and Kosovo (Fig. 6.2). (All of the territories discussed in this chapter are delineated by the pre–civil war borders of the Yugoslav republics.) There is a great deal of similarity or overlap with neighboring cultures—particularly with the Anzabegovo-Vršnik culture (Macedonia), the Karanovo culture (southern Bulgaria), the Kremikovci culture (western Bulgaria), the Criş culture (Romania), and the Körös culture (Hungary) (Fig. 6.3). Starčevo sites stretch to the northwest as far as Bjelovar in Croatia. To the west and southwest, Starčevo sites are found in the Bosna and Drina valleys and on the Dinaric plains of Bosnia-Hercegovina (Brukner

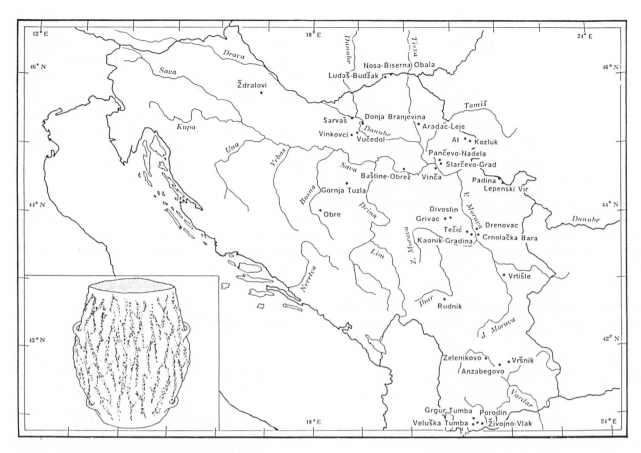

Fig. 6.1. Neolithic sites in the central Balkans.

et al. 1974; Dimitrijević 1979; Garašanin 1979). While the various culture names correspond roughly to modern political boundaries, they may also reflect slightly different adaptations to the many diverse microenvironments of the Balkan peninsula (Kaiser 1984:46).

Although Starčevo sites represent the earliest agricultural, cattle-breeding, ceramic-producing populations in the central Balkans, a comparison with sites to the south (especially in Greek Macedonia, Thessaly, and Thrace) shows that only the earliest Starčevo sites are properly attributed to an "early Neolithic" period (cf. Protosesklo and Presesklo). The majority are more comparable to "middle Neolithic" sites (e.g., Sesklo and early Dimini) in these southern regions (see Garašanin 1979:212).

The lack of stratified sites and paucity of radiocarbon dates for the Starčevo culture have resulted in a tendency to create typological ceramic sequences with little attention to absolute chronologies. The first attempt to devise a chronological sequence of pottery types from Starčevo sites was published by V. Milojčić (1950:108–18). Milojčić used pottery from various sites to establish a four-part ceramic sequence and rel-

ative chronology, Starčevo I through IV (Fig. 6.4). This was followed by the work of D. Arandjelović-Garašanin (1954), whose sequence closely paralleled that of Milojčić but recognized closer similarities between the middle periods. The stages were thus labeled Starčevo I, IIa, IIb, and III. Arandjelović-Garašanin based most of her analysis on some 50,000 sherds from the early excavations at Starčevo-Grad, particularly material from pit 5A, which she considered a closed, stratified feature. This ceramic sequence does appear to be supported at the few Starčevo sites that have vertical stratigraphy, especially Rudnik at Metohija (Garašanin 1979).

According to the Arandjelović-Garašanin (1954) system, painted ceramics are absent from Starčevo I. Fine, burnished monochrome ware is fairly common, although coarser wares, particularly barbotine ceramics, predominate. The term "barbotine" refers to a rough coating of clay on the exterior surface of a vessel. The coating may be irregularly spattered across the surface or applied and then streaked with fingers or sticks so that the coating appears to be organized into strips or ridges. Incised, finger-impressed, and appli-

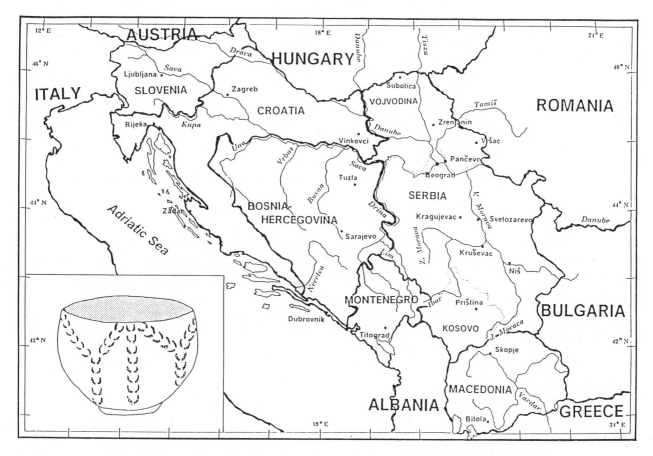

Fig. 6.2. Geopolitical map of the central Balkans. Boundaries shown are the pre–civil war borders of the Yugoslav republics.

quéd pottery of coarse and medium fabric is present but not common at this stage.

Starčevo II is considered the start of "classical" Starčevo. In Starčevo IIa, the percentage of fine ware increases slightly, though coarse ware still predominates. Barbotine remains the most common type of coarse ware. The proportion of appliquéd, incised, and impressed samples is slightly higher than in the preceding period. Painted pots appear—in white and dark colors and with linear and curvilinear motifs, including spirals. During Starčevo IIb, painted ceramics decrease in frequency, and white painted designs disappear entirely.

Starčevo III shows another increase in the percentage of fine ware. Barbotine still predominates among coarse wares, though impressed, appliquéd, and incised ceramics are present in greater numbers. The barbotine technique is more often found applied in an organized, regular manner during this period. The same types of dark painting continue, although spirals (especially in polychrome) are more common. There is an increase in the frequency of pots on high pedestals and biconical forms.

Critics of the Arandjelović-Garašanin typology have questioned the use of painted pottery as a major distinguishing characteristic, because painted specimens always constitute a very small portion (typically not more than 2 percent) of the total ceramic inventory. There has also been considerable debate about the reliability of the stratigraphy of pit 5A at Starčevo-Grad (see Korošec 1973; Ehrich 1977).

S. Dimitrijević (1974, 1979) offered an alternative ceramic sequence beginning with a "Preclassic" Starčevo period. The first part of Dimitrijević's Preclassic Starčevo is called the Monochrome phase; the second is the White Linear (Linear A) phase. His "Classic" Starčevo encompasses the Dark Linear (Linear B) phase and the Garlandoid phase. Classic Starčevo is characterized by the large numbers of barbotine ceramics found at these sites. The Dark Linear phase includes many dark painted linear designs—vertical bands, zigzags, triangles, and net motifs. As one would expect, the Garlandoid phase is characterized by painted pottery bearing a garland motif executed in white or dark paint. This Classic period mainly corresponds to Arandjelović-Garašanin's Starčevo II. Di-

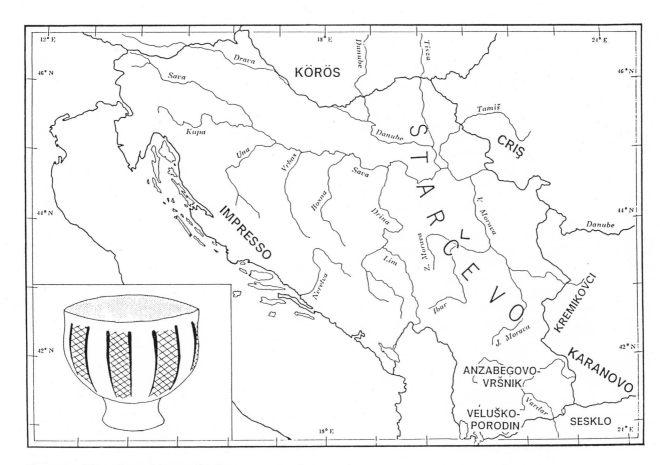

Fig. 6.3. Neolithic cultures of the central Balkans.

Milojčić 1950	Arandelović-Garašanin 1954	Garašanin 1979	Garašanin 1979	Gimbutas 1974	Srejović 1972	Dimitrijević 1974, 1979		Brukner 1979
						Final		
Starčevo IV	Starčevo III	Starčevo III	Veluška Tumba IV	Anzabegovo III	Classic Starčevo	LATE CLASSIC	Spiraloid B	Late Körös
							Spiraloid A	
Starčevo III	Starčevo IIb	Starčevo IIb				CLASSIC	Garlandoid	Early Körös
Starčevo II	Starčevo IIa	Starčevo IIa	Veluška Tumba III	Anzabegovo II			Dark Linear (Linear B)	
Starčevo I	Starčevo I	Starčevo I (Gura Baciului)	Veluška Tumba II	Anzabegovo I	Proto-Starčevo	PRECLASSIC	White Linear (Linear A)	
			Veluška Tumba I				Monochrome	

Fig. 6.4. Typological sequences of Starčevo ceramics.

mitrijević's "Late Classic" Starčevo period consists of the Spiraloid A and Spiraloid B phases and generally corresponds to the Starčevo III period of Arandjelović-Garašanin's scheme. Spirals appear during Spiraloid A and increase in frequency during Spiraloid B. Dimitrijević also proposed a "Final" Starčevo period, restricted to peripheral sites. A large proportion of the pottery consists of finger-streaked and spattered barbotine and appliquéd specimens. Dimitrijević (1979: 253) suggests that this Final Starčevo period was "a substratum for the roots of the linear banded pottery culture" of central Europe.

The Dimitrijević scheme has not been readily accepted by most archaeologists working in the region; indeed, his system seems to work best at the northern and western Starčevo sites. Thus, in spite of criticisms leveled against the Arandjelović-Garašanin sequence, her system is deeply entrenched in the literature of this region and continues to be used. In fact, because of the relative scarcity of radiocarbon dates for the Starčevo culture, this system often serves as the *only* source of chronological "control" for many sites (see, for example, Brukner 1979; M. Garašanin 1979; D. Garašanin 1984).

Chronology of the Starčevo Culture

The slow acceptance of the use of radiocarbon dating has hampered much archaeological research in the central Balkans. Only a small number of Starčevo sites have associated ¹⁴C dates. Throughout this chapter, radiocarbon dates are listed as years "b.c."; calibrated ("calendrical") dates are given as years "B.C." Calibration of radiocarbon dates was accomplished by means of the CALIB (rev. 2.0) program distributed by the Quaternary Isotope Laboratory of the University of Washington (see Stuiver and Reimer 1986).

The stratified site of Anzabegovo in Macedonia has eight radiocarbon dates from the earliest level (Anzabegovo I), spanning the period of about 5300 to 5150 b.c. (ca. 6100–6000 B.C.). The five dates from Anzabegovo II indicate a range of about 5100 to 4900 b.c. (ca. 5950–5700 B.C.). The five dates for Anzabegovo III appear to span a period from about 4900 to 4550 b.c. (ca. 5700–5450 B.C.) (Gimbutas 1974).

Two ¹⁴C dates have been published for the stratified site of Veluška Tumba in Macedonia. Veluška Tumba I dates to about 5000 b.c. (ca. 5800 B.C.). Veluška

Tumba II has a date of about 4750 b.c. (ca. 5600 B.C.) (Todorović et al. 1977).

In Serbia, the later excavations at Starčevo-Grad yielded five radiocarbon dates from bone samples, ranging from 4900 to 4700 b.c. (ca. 5700–5550 B.C.) (Ehrich 1977). The seven ¹⁴C dates from Divostin I range from about 5250 to 4950 b.c. (ca. 6050–5750 B.C.). The Starčevo occupation of Grivac is dated to around 5300 b.c. (ca. 6100 B.C.). Starčevo material from Banja dates to about 5100 b.c. (ca. 5950 B.C.) (McPherron 1988). In the Iron Gates region, radiocarbon dates from Padina indicate a Starčevo occupation from about 5150 to 4600 b.c. (ca. 6000–5450 B.C.) (Clason 1982).

A single radiocarbon date is available from the Starčevo settlement at Gornja Tuzla in Bosnia-Hercegovina. It indicates an occupation around 4700 b.c. (ca. 5550 B.C.) (Tasić and Tomić 1969).

Additional dates for Starčevo sites have been obtained by means of archaeomagnetic intensity analyses (Manson 1990; Manson and Schmidt 1991). When clay (which often contains magnetic minerals such as magnetite and hematite) is heated above the "blocking temperature" of these minerals, the magnetic particles may record the direction and strength of the earth's magnetic field at that location and time. In the case of stationary features such as hearths, both directional and intensity data are useful. For movable artifacts of baked clay such as figurines and pottery sherds, however, the directional data are of no value because it is impossible to determine the exact location and orientation of the sample during its firing and subsequent cooling. Fortunately, magnetic intensity values are independent of directional data and can be obtained from very small samples taken from any artifact of baked clay. These intensity values can then be compared with those of master regional curves that include associated radiocarbon dates (see Kovacheva 1977, 1980; Kovacheva and Veljovich 1985 for archaeomagnetic curves for the central Balkan region). In most cases, the archaeointensity values obtained for a Starčevo site allow it to be placed within a 100-year time span when correlated with the master regional curves. Manson (1990) also combined typological, radiocarbon, and archaeomagnetic data to propose the following absolute dates for the Arandjelović-Garašanin (1954) typological sequence of the Starčevo culture.

Starčevo I: at least 5300–5100 b.c. (ca. 6100–5950 B.C.)

Starčevo IIa: circa 5100–4850 b.c. (ca. 5950–5650 b.c.)

Starčevo IIb: circa 4850–4500 b.c. (ca. 5650–5400 b.c.)

Starčevo III: circa 4500–possibly 4200 b.c. (ca. 5400–5100 b.c.)

This more refined chronology has provided a better framework within which to search for patterns of behavior as reflected in the material remains of Starčevo populations.

Starčevo Settlement and Subsistence

Starčevo sites are generally located on river terraces, on gentle slopes close to springs and streams, or on low rises near swamps and marshes. They rarely occupy naturally defensible locations, although a few such sites are known (e.g., Vučedol). A few cave sites have been found, but most settlements are situated in open spaces. Vertical stratigraphy is rare—most sites have a single component with cultural deposits typically less than one meter in depth (Tringham 1971; Kaiser 1984). Starčevo sites often show evidence of disturbance from later occupations and/or natural causes.

House types include semisubterranean pithouses and quadrangular surface structures. House sizes suggest nuclear family residences, and household assemblages generally indicate a household mode of production. A variety of hearths and ovens, storage pits, and large (possibly communal) grinding stones have been found at Starčevo settlements.

Some inferences about seasonality and subsistence practices may also be made based on settlement observations. The wide range of available resources probably indicates that subsistence activities were also rather diverse (see Barker 1975). The small size and shallowness of many sites may indicate that these sites were occupied for no more than a single generation or that the inhabitants were only semisedentary. Some sites (e.g., Ludaš-Budžak) may have been occupied year-round, judging by the remains of certain animals and migratory birds (Whittle 1985). It is also possible that some Starčevo populations practiced transhumance and that some sites represent seasonal occupations (see Barker 1975, 1985; Benac 1979; Kosse 1979; Sherratt 1980; Chapman 1981).

Information on prehistoric economies depends on good conditions of preservation plus systematic recovery of floral and faunal materials. Unfortunately, pre-servation of organic materials is poor at many Starčevo sites, and careful recovery of plant and animal remains (including screening and flotation techniques) is rare. In addition, a priori assumptions about what a "Neolithic" economy *should* be have contributed to a somewhat haphazard approach to the study of Starčevo subsistence. Good economic data are available from only a handful of sites, including Nosa, Ludaš-Budžak, Lepenski Vir, Starčevo-Grad, Divostin I, Obre I, and Anzabegovo.

Domesticated plant species include broom-corn millet, emmer, einkorn, club wheat, field peas, lentils, and hulled six-row barley. Among wild plant species, beechnuts, acorns, apples, Cornelian cherries, wild grapes, and hazelnuts have been identified. The remains of domesticated dogs, cattle, sheep, goats, and pigs have been recovered. A considerable variety of wild animals is also represented at Starčevo sites, including red and roe deer, aurochs, wild pig, wild ass, brown bear, beaver, wolf, brown hare, fox, tortoise, catfish, pike, carp, and other unidentified fish, shellfish, and bird species. A general trend of decreasing reliance on domesticates can be observed as one moves northward through the Starčevo culture area.

It is unlikely that the shift to a fully agricultural, sedentary village life occurred before the later Vinča period in this area (see Kaiser and Voytek 1983; Kaiser 1984; Tringham and Krstić 1990). However, "if domestication is viewed as a 'process' rather than as a 'revolution,' then the questions concerning the origins of the 'first farmers' in southeastern Europe are of less interest than understanding how and why domesticates became such a significant part of the subsistence base and how changing economic practices may have affected subsequent technological and social development" (Manson 1990:146).

It is possible that some Neolithic groups should be viewed more as pastoralists than as farmers (see Menghin 1931; Narr 1956; Barker 1975; Sterud 1978; McPherron and Christopher 1988). Because stock breeding is generally well-attested to at Starčevo sites, the possibility of transhumant strategies should be examined more closely. More detailed faunal analyses, including age- and sex-specific mortality curves, are required to determine the importance of secondary animal products (e.g., milk and wool) in the subsistence economy (Greenfield 1988). Livestock can also serve as a means of food storage to reduce risks related to environmental fluctuations, and they may be a form of negotiable wealth—an exchange commodity with the added advantage of being able to move itself (Sherratt

1982). At this point, the available data are not sufficient for judging these possibilities.

Stone and Bone Artifacts

The lithic artifact assemblages include both flaked and ground stone tools. Most of the flaked stone artifacts are blades and worked flakes. Materials seem to have been mostly of local origin. Starčevo sites generally yield large numbers of polished stone tools, including axes, adzes, chisels, and various milling and hand stones.

Bone tools include needles, awls, polishers, fishhooks, and points. The most common bone tool recovered from Starčevo sites, however, is the spatula—a carefully made, well-polished bone object with a flattened surface at one end. These items are so common that Childe (1957) considered them a diagnostic artifact of the Starčevo culture. Striations on the edges of the spatulas point to their use in a scraping motion, possibly for scraping flour together on a grinding stone (Childe 1957; McPherron and Christopher 1988). Kutzián (1947) described them as spoons and suggested they may have been used to smooth and decorate ceramic vessels (see also Kalicz 1970).

Starčevo Pottery

The bulk of Starčevo assemblages consists of objects made of baked clay, including weights, spindle whorls, stamps, house models, "altars" (or lamps), anthropomorphic and zoomorphic figurines, and ceramic vessels. These items, particularly pots and potsherds, have received much attention from excavators and analysts. Indeed, potsherds make up some 95 percent of the total artifact assemblage at some Neolithic sites in the region (Dimitrijević 1979).

Starčevo pottery is generally described in terms of fabric, form, and decoration. Paste texture and surface decoration are the major criteria for determining ware types. Coarse ware predominates at all Starčevo sites. Although the clay itself may be relatively fine grained, the pottery also contains much chaff, mica, sand, and sometimes even small pebbles. The sand, mica, and pebbles may have occurred naturally as accessories in the raw clay material or they may have been intentionally added; the chaff (or some similar organic material) is assumed to have been added as tempering.

The organic tempering frequently burned out during firing, leaving a large number of elongated cavities and resulting in pottery vessels with high porosity (Manson 1990). Coarse ware vessels were frequently large and thick walled. The pottery appears to be low fired, with a thick, dark central core. Refiring of sherds from Starčevo-Grad indicates that the clay matrix was sufficiently dense to prevent oxidation at the core even at temperatures of 1,000°C (Horton 1938). In general, coarse wares have roughened (barbotine) surfaces.

Medium wares resemble coarse wares in texture and tempering material, though vessel walls are somewhat thinner. They, too, have thick, dark cores in cross-section. They may have incised, impressed, or appliquéd decoration, or they may have plain, burnished surfaces.

Fine wares contain little or no organic tempering, but fine sand or mica is commonly present. The walls are thin and typically even-colored in cross-section. They may have plain, highly burnished surfaces or painted decoration.

All Starčevo pottery was probably fired in an incompletely oxidizing atmosphere. Maniatis and Tite (1981) used scanning electron microscopy to determine that Starčevo sherds from Divostin I and Dobrovodica were fired at less than 750°C. The archaeomagnetic dating technique used by Manson (1990) provided another means of estimating firing temperatures. Since chemical remanent magnetization can occur when a sample is reheated to a temperature above its maximum firing temperature, evidence for high-temperature chemical change can be used to estimate the ancient firing temperature (see also Arbour and Schwartz 1982). Results of the archaeomagnetic analysis of Starčevo potsherds indicate the occurrence of high-temperature chemical changes between 500°C and 600°C, suggesting that this was the maximum firing temperature of much Starčevo pottery.

Starčevo pots are basically spherical or hemispherical in shape, regardless of fabric or overall size. There are also smaller numbers of shouldered pots with cylindrical necks and vessels with outflaring walls. Straight or slightly thickened bases and ring bases are common. Several (usually four) short legs or feet are occasionally found on globular vessels of medium ware. Higher, pedestal-type bases are associated with fine wares. Handles are sometimes present on larger vessels. They usually consist of protuberances, sometimes with horizontal or vertical holes to facilitate hanging or carrying. Tunnellike and bandlike handles are also known.

A Functional Analysis of Starčevo Pottery

Most analyses of Starčevo pottery are stylistic—they are primarily concerned with decoration and ceramic fabric. These studies are used to establish the typologies on which relative chronologies are based. While the establishment of temporal frameworks is an important step in archaeology, ceramic analyses focused on time and space relationships rarely consider the many other kinds of information that can be obtained from pottery. With few exceptions (e.g., Manson 1990, 1992), analyses of Starčevo ceramic assemblages do not include a functional analysis based on technological attributes and performance-related characteristics.

As a number of archaeologists have stressed in the past few years, however, pots are tools—they were made to be used (see Braun 1983:107). Furthermore, they are particularly useful for food storage and preparation. Ceramic vessels allow direct, sustainable, high-temperature heating of their contents, which is especially important when cooking small starchy seeds such as cereal grains. The nutritional value, palatability, and digestibility of many plant foods can be improved by boiling them. In addition, many cultigens (notably cereals and legumes) contain toxins that can be reduced or removed by cooking (see Leopold and Ardrey 1972; Liener and Kakade 1980; Braun 1983; Reid 1984, 1988; Arnold 1985; Katz and Voigt 1986; Myers 1989; Stahl 1989). Thus the use of pottery vessels can extend the range of potential food sources available to a population. Considering this information, it is reasonable to expect that as a population's reliance on these cultigens increases, pottery vessels will be modified to be better suited for their cooking.

The heating effectiveness of pottery depends to a large extent on attributes that influence thermal shock resistance, thermal conductivity, and thermal diffusivity. Thermal shock resistance allows a pot to withstand a sudden temperature change brought about by placing a pot over a heat source or by removing it from a heat source (Kingery 1955; Rye 1976). When a pot is placed over a heat source, the exterior portion of the vessel wall heats faster than the interior portion, causing tensile stresses that can lead to cracking or spalling. As a result, thick-walled pots are frequently less resistant to thermal shock than thinner-walled vessels. Thermal shock resistance also varies directly with porosity—as porosity increases, so does thermal shock resistance—because high porosity reduces thermal stresses and limits cracking (see Rye 1976, 1981; Shepard 1976; Plog 1980; Arnold 1985; Rice 1987).

Thermal shock resistance is closely related to the properties of thermal diffusivity and conductivity. Thermal conductivity is a measure of the ease with which heat is transferred from a vessel to its contents (Touloukian et al. 1970). Thermal diffusivity is a measure of the ease with which heat spreads through a vessel's walls (Touloukian et al. 1973; Steponaitis 1983). Thermal diffusivity testing, therefore, can be performed on sherds, whereas thermal conductivity experiments properly require whole vessels. Properties that increase thermal diffusion and conduction also increase thermal shock resistance because temperature gradients within the vessel walls are reduced. Based on these principles, vessels with good thermal diffusivity and conductivity should be the most effective for cooking (i.e., boiling or simmering) when the pot is placed on, in, or over a heat source. (Note that other principles would apply if cooking is carried out by adding hot rocks to the contents of a vessel; see, for example, Sassaman, chapter 18.)

It should be remembered that tests of performance characteristics of archaeological materials actually measure remnant, residual, or apparent properties that may differ from the original properties of the pot (Braun 1983; Rice 1987). Although the amount of degradation that occurred during the vessel's use-life and later burial cannot be determined, it is assumed that some general hypotheses about *relative* performance can be formulated from tests on archaeological materials.

An analysis of technological attributes related to the heating effectiveness of Starčevo pottery reveals several interesting patterns that can be used to draw inferences about behavioral changes among Starčevo populations. In a functional study of Starčevo sherds, high correlations ($p \leq .01$) were found between date and thermal coefficient, date and vessel wall thickness, and date and temper index (Manson 1990).

The thermal coefficient is a measure of thermal diffusivity that also controls for variation in sherd thickness, area, and mass. The thermal coefficient is created by comparing an "observed slope" of the rate of temperature increase over time for each sherd to a "predicted slope." The predicted slope is based on the application of a formula derived by subjecting experimental tiles (of known compositions but various dimensions) to thermal diffusivity testing (see Snyder 1989:154–65 for details on determining thermal coefficients). With size and shape differences controlled, variation in thermal coefficients most likely reflects differences in ceramic composition—for example, in the clay matrix, porosity, tempering material, and amount of tempering. Overall, the mean value of the thermal coefficient of Starčevo sherds decreases through time. In other words, the value of the observed slope approaches the value of the predicted slope, indicating an increasing emphasis by the potters on controlling compositional variables that affect thermal performance.

Wall thickness refers to a measure of the average thickness of a body sherd. In this study, only medium and coarse ware sherds were used in tests related to heating efficiency. Fine, painted pottery was not available from all sites, and ethnographic data tend to support the conclusion that such wares were generally used for storage, serving, or display rather than for cooking (see Lischka 1978; Plog 1980; Hally 1986; and others in this volume). There is a clear trend toward decreasing wall thickness over time. Wall thickness is related to vessel size and intended use. It affects thermal diffusivity and conductivity, mechanical strength, and thermal shock resistance. Generally, thicker walls have greater mechanical strength and offer greater stability to a vessel—important considerations for large storage vessels. Thinner walls are usually better heat conductors and have greater thermal shock resistance (Braun 1983; Smith 1985; Rice 1987; Skibo et al. 1989). Thus, the trend toward thinner walls may well be associated with greater concern for thermal performance.

The range of variation in sherd thickness and thermal coefficients *within* a site also appears to decrease and then level off through time. This trend suggests an increase in control and standardization in the pottery-making process. Variation in thickness and thermal coefficients seems to drop fairly steadily until about 5400 to 5300 B.C. and then levels off somewhat. The date of 5400 B.C. roughly corresponds to the transition from Starčevo IIb to Starčevo III.

The temper index is a method for determining the relative proportions of organic and mineral tempering in a sherd. In terms of vessel performance, there are advantages and disadvantages to either form of tempering. Organic-tempered pots tend to have high porosity and good thermal shock resistance and are relatively light weight. For good heating effectiveness, however, their interior surfaces often require additional treatment to reduce permeability. Mineral tempering gives a pot somewhat better mechanical stress resistance and heat transference without the need for additional postfiring treatment (Schiffer and Skibo 1987; Skibo et al. 1989).

None of the Starčevo sites in this study yielded all organically tempered pottery or all mineral-tempered pottery, but the proportions of organic and mineral tempering in the sherds did appear to vary from site to site. To test this observation, each sherd was assigned a number based on the relative amounts of organic and mineral tempering it contained (see Manson 1990). An average was calculated for each site; this number was considered the temper index number for that site. There appears to be a trend over time toward higher temper index numbers, indicating a gradual shift in emphasis from organic to mineral tempering in the Starčevo pottery.

Implications for Neolithic Development in the Balkans

Generally, societies that lack evidence of social stratification or craft specialization have a "domestic mode of production" (Kaiser 1983). In these societies (including Starčevo), the makers of the pots were also the users; potters were thus able to evaluate the effectiveness and convenience of particular materials, techniques, and attributes. Therefore, "where pottery making is a domestic craft, we can then assume a selective process" (Braun 1983:112). The attributes that contribute to a vessel's success can be expected to be selected for, and changes in performance-related attributes may indicate that other changes were occurring in the lifeways of the population.

Skibo, Schiffer, and Reid (1989) used ethnographic and experimental data to compare the choice of organic versus mineral tempering with a group's residential mobility. The ethnographic data showed a strong correlation between organic tempering and mobility. Experimental results suggested some reasons for this correlation. Vessels with organic tempering are noticeably lighter in weight, they can be made much more quickly, and they have a higher greenware strength than mineral-tempered vessels of the same size. The Starčevo tempering index showed a definite trend over time toward an increased use of mineral tempering in the pottery, suggesting increasing residential stability over time for Starčevo populations.

There was also an overall trend through time toward modifications that indicate increasing concern for heating effectiveness. Interestingly, the ceramics from the Late Archaic–Early Woodland transitional period and the Late Woodland period of the midwestern United States display some of the same changes in attributes that were found in the Starčevo ceramic assemblages. They, too, demonstrated a reduction in the average wall thickness of vessels (Braun 1983) and a shift from organic to mineral tempering (Schiffer and Skibo 1987). In the Midwest, these changes in ceramic attributes were associated with an economic shift from hunting and gathering (with a minor domesticated plant component) to a greater reliance on plant cultigens. It is likely that the same changes in pottery making among Starčevo peoples also reflect an increasing emphasis on the cooking of domesticated plant foods, particularly cereals.

Of course, a finished pottery vessel represents a decision-making process. It is a composite of the potter's decisions to balance costs, expectations, and needs, based on resource availability and the framework of knowledge within which the potter is operating (see Rice 1987). Much prehistoric pottery can be interpreted more meaningfully in terms of "acceptable" performance than in terms of optimal performance levels. Any changes in performance-related characteristics should be examined closely. Starčevo pottery may not have been "optimal" in many respects, but it apparently served the purposes for which it was intended. The fact that small modifications continued to be made to enhance the thermal performance of Starčevo pottery indicates an increasing concern for heating effectiveness and is a tribute to the technical knowledge and skills of these Neolithic potters.

The ceramic evidence for increasing residential stability and reliance on cultigens through time may support the hypothesis that Starčevo groups originally relied more heavily on pastoralism than on agriculture. Faunal remains demonstrate the importance of domesticated animals at many Starčevo sites, and it is possible that an economic strategy of transhumance was practiced. Hunting and gathering activities apparently continued throughout the entire Starčevo culture period. It is likely that domesticated plants played a significant role only in the economies of later Starčevo populations. Although the groundwork was laid during the Starčevo culture, a fully sedentary, agricultural village lifestyle probably did not appear in this region until the succeeding Vinča culture period.

In any case, the concept of an agricultural "revolution" in the central Balkans should be abandoned and attention focused on the transitional processes involved. The domestication of plants and animals, as well as their integration into an economic system, is a *process*, not merely a *feature* of the Neolithic period. An emphasis on identifying the first appearance of domesticates (or pottery) is misplaced—the critical questions concern how they became an essential part of an economic system. Ceramic cooking vessels with good heating effectiveness offer one explanation of how cultigens could have become increasingly important in the diets of Neolithic populations. Thus, functional analyses of pottery that can reveal evidence of technological changes related to performance are one way to look at processes of transition in the archaeological record. Analyses of cultural materials (including ceramics) must surely go beyond typological description and sequencing to better interpret the behavior of prehistoric peoples.

Acknowledgments

This article is based on research conducted for my dissertation. I gratefully acknowledge the financial assistance of the Institute for International Education (Fulbright Scholarship for Dissertation Research in Yugoslavia), Southern Illinois University at Carbondale (Doctoral Research Award), and the U.S. Department of Education (Jacob K. Javits Fellowship). All archaeomagnetic research was conducted at the Palaeomagnetism laboratory at the University of Pittsburgh. Members of my doctoral committee—Carroll Riley, Alan McPherron, Robert Rands, Lionel Bender, and Victor Schmidt—provided assistance at various stages of my research. I also thank David Snyder and Lisa Renken for their constructive comments on portions of earlier drafts of this material. A shorter version of this article was presented at the 57th annual meeting of the Society for American Archaeology in Pittsburgh, 1992.

References Cited

Arandjelović-Garašanin, Draga
    1954   *Starčevačka kultura*. Ljubljana.
Arbour, G., and E. J. Schwartz
    1982   Archeomagnetic Intensity Study of Indian Potsherds from Quebec, Canada. *Journal of Geomagnetism and Geoelectricity* 34:129–36.
Arnold, Dean E.
    1985   *Ceramic Theory and Cultural Process*. Cambridge University Press, Cambridge.
Barker, Graeme
    1975   Early Neolithic Land Use in Yugoslavia. *Proceedings of the Prehistoric Society* 41:85–104.

1985   *Prehistoric Farming in Europe.* Cambridge University Press, Cambridge.

Benac, Alojz
1979   Prelazna zona. In *Praistorija Jugoslavenskih zemalja II,* pp. 363–470. Akademija Nauka i Umjetnosti Bosne i Hercegovine, Sarajevo.

Benac, A., M. Garašanin, and D. Srejović
1979   Uvod. In *Praistorija Jugoslavenskih zemalja II,* pp. 11–31. Akademija Nauka i Umjetnosti Bosne i Hercegovine, Sarajevo.

Braun, David P.
1983   Pots as Tools. In *Archaeological Hammers and Theories,* edited by A. Keene and J. Moore, pp. 107–34. Academic Press, New York.

Brukner, Bogdan
1979   Körös-grupa. In *Praistorija Jugoslavenskih zemalja II,* pp. 213–26. Akademija Nauka i Umjetnosti Bosne i Hercegovine, Sarajevo.

Brukner, B., B. Jovanović, and N. Tasić
1974   *Praistorija Vojvodine.* Institut za Izučavanje Istorije Vojvodine i Savez Arheoloških Društava Jugoslavije, Novi Sad.

Chapman, John
1981   *The Vinča Culture of South-East Europe.* British Archaeological Reports, International Series 117, Oxford.

Childe, V. Gordon
1957   *The Dawn of European Civilization.* 6th ed. Routledge and Kegan Paul, London. (First published 1925)

Clason, A. T.
1982   Padina and Starčevo: Game, Fish and Cattle. *Palaeohistoria* 22:141–73.

Dimitrijević, Stojan
1974   Problem stupnjevanja Starčevačke kulture s posebnim obzirom na doprinos Južnopanonskih nalazišta rješavanju ovog problema. *Počeci ranih zemljoradničkih kultura u Vojvodini i Srpskom Podunavlju,* edited by N. Tasić. Srpsko Arheološko Društvo, Beograd i Gradski Muzej, Subotica, *Materijali* 10:59–93.
1979   Sjeverna zona. In *Praistorija Jugoslavenskih zemalja II,* pp. 229–360. Akademija Nauka i Umjetnosti Bosne i Hercegovine, Sarajevo.

Ehrich, Robert W.
1977   Starčevo Revisited. In *Ancient Europe and the Mediterranean,* edited by V. Markotic, pp. 59–67. Aris and Phillips, Warminster.

Fewkes, V., H. Goldman, and R. Ehrich
1933   Excavations at Starčevo, Yugoslavia, Seasons 1931 and 1932. *Bulletin of the American School of Prehistoric Research* 9:33–54.

Garašanin, Draga
1984   Naselje Starčevačke kulture. In *Vinča u Praistoriji i Srednjem Veku,* pp. 13–21. Galerija Srpske Akademije Nauka i Umjetnosti, Beograd.

Garašanin, Milutin
1979   Centralnobalkanska zona. In *Praistorija Jugoslavenskih zemalja II,* pp. 79–212. Akademija Nauka i Umjetnosti Bosne i Hercegovine, Sarajevo.

Gimbutas, Marija
1974   Anza, ca. 6500–5000 b.c.: A Cultural Yardstick for the Study of Neolithic Southeast Europe. *Journal of Field Archaeology* 1:26–66.

Greenfield, Haskel J.
1988   The Origins of Milk and Wool Production in the Old World. A Zoological Perspective from the Central Balkans. *Current Anthropology* 29:573–93.

Hally, David J.
1986   The Identification of Vessel Function: A Case from Northwest Georgia. *American Antiquity* 51:267–95.

Horton, Donald
1938   Note on a Microscopic Study of a Sample Group of Barbotine Sherds with Positive Appliqué from "Grad," Starčevo. *Proceedings of the American Philosophical Society* 78:397–402.

Kaiser, Timothy
1983   Specialization, Production, and Social Change in the Balkan Neolithic. Paper presented at the 48th annual meeting of the Society for American Archaeology, Pittsburgh, Pennsylvania.
1984   Vinča Ceramics: Economic and Technological Aspects of Late Neolithic Pottery Production in Southeast Europe. Ph.D. dissertation, University of California, Berkeley. University Microfilms, Ann Arbor, Michigan.

Kaiser, Timothy, and Barbara Voytek
1983   Sedentism and Economic Change in the Balkan Neolithic. *Journal of Anthropological Archaeology* 2:323–53.

Kalicz, Nándor
1970   *Clay Gods: The Neolithic Period and the Copper Age in Hungary.* Hereditas Series, no. 1. Corvina Kiadó, Budapest.

Katz, Solomon H., and Mary M. Voigt
1986   Bread and Beer: The Early Use of Cereals in the Human Diet. *Expedition* 28(2):23–34.

Kingery, W. D.
1955   Factors Affecting Thermal Stress Resistance of Ceramic Materials. *Journal of the American Ceramic Society* 38:3–15.

Korošec, Borut
1973   Application de methodes d'analyse statistique au problème de la chronologie du site de Starčevo. *Arheološki Vestnik—Acta Archaeologica* 24:271–302.

Kosse, Krisztina
1979   *Settlement Ecology of the Early and Middle Neolithic Körös and Linear Pottery Cultures in Hungary.* British Archaeological Reports, International Series 64, Oxford.

Kovacheva, Mary
1977   Archaeomagnetic Investigations in Bulgaria: Field-Intensity Determinations. *Physics of the Earth and Planetary Interiors* 13:355–59.
1980   Summarized Results of the Archaeomagnetic Investigation of the Geomagnetic Field Variation for the Last 8000 Years in South-Eastern Europe. *Geophysical Journal of the Royal Astronomical Society* 61:57–64.

Kovacheva, Mary, and Dushan Veljovich
1985   Arheomagnitno izsledvane na praistoricheski obekti ot NRB i SFRYU. *Arheologia* 4(2): 21–26.

Kutzián, I.
1947   *The Körös Culture.* Dissertationes Pannonicae, Budapest.

Leopold, A. Carl, and Robert Ardrey
1972   Toxic Substances in Plants and the Food Habits of Early Man. *Science* 176:512–14.

Liener, Irvin E., and Madhusudan L. Kakade
1980   Protease Inhibitors. In *Toxic Constituents of Plant Foodstuffs,* 2d ed., edited by I. E. Liener, pp. 7–71. Academic Press, New York.

Lischka, Joseph J.
1978   A Functional Analysis of Middle Classic Ceramics at Kaminaljuyu. In *The Ceramics of Kaminaljuyu, Guatemala,* edited by R. K. Wetherington, pp. 223–78. Monograph Series on Kaminaljuyu, Pennsylvania State University Press, University Park, Pennsylvania.

McPherron, Alan
1988   Radiocarbon Determinations. In *Divostin and the Neolithic of Central Serbia,* edited by A. McPherron and D. Srejović, pp. 379–83. Ethnology Monograph 10, University of Pittsburgh, Pittsburgh, Pennsylvania.

McPherron, Alan, and K. Chris Christopher
1988   The Balkan Neolithic and the Divostin Project in Perspective. In *Divostin and the Neolithic of Central Serbia,* edited by A. McPherron and D. Srejović, pp. 463–92. Ethnology Monograph 10, University of Pittsburgh, Pittsburgh, Pennsylvania.

Maniatis, Y., and M. Tite
1981   Technological Examination of Neolithic-Bronze Age Pottery from Central and Southeast Europe and from the Near East. *Journal of Archaeological Science* 8:59–76.

Manson, Joni L.
1990   A Reanalysis of Starčevo Culture Ceramics: Implications for Neolithic Development in the Balkans. Ph.D. dissertation, Southern Illinois University, Carbondale. University Microfilms, Ann Arbor, Michigan.
1992   Heating Effectiveness of Neolithic Pottery. Paper presented at the 57th annual meeting of the Society for American Archaeology, Pittsburgh, Pennsylvania.

Manson, Joni L., and Victor A. Schmidt
1991   Archaeomagnetic Dating of Neolithic Yugoslavian Potsherds. Paper presented at the 56th annual meeting of the Society for American Archaeology, New Orleans, Louisiana.

Menghin, O.
1931   *Weltgeschichte der Steinzeit.* Anton Scroll, Vienna.

Milojčić, Vladimir
1950   *Körös-Starčevo-Vinča.* Reinecke Festschrift, Mainz.

Myers, Thomas P.
1989   The Role of Pottery in the Rise of American Civilizations: The Ceramic Revolution. In *Ceramic Ecology, 1988: Current Research on Ceramic Materials,* edited by C. C. Kolb, pp. 1–28. British Archaeological Reports, International Series 513, Oxford.

Narr, K. J.
1956   Early Food-Producing Populations. In *Man's Role in Changing the Face of the Earth,* edited by W. L. Thomas, Jr., pp. 134–51. University of Chicago Press, Chicago.

Plog, Stephen
1980   *Stylistic Variation in Prehistoric Ceramics.* Cambridge University Press, Cambridge.

Reid, Kenneth C.
1984   Fire and Ice: New Evidence for the Production and Preservation of Late Archaic Fiber-Tempered Pottery in the Middle-Latitude Lowlands. *American Antiquity* 49:55–76.
1988   Simmering Down: A Second Look at Ralph Linton's "North American Cooking Pots." Paper presented at the 21st Great Basin Anthropological Conference, Park City, Utah.

Rice, Prudence M.
1987   *Pottery Analysis: A Sourcebook.* University of Chicago Press, Chicago.

Rye, Owen S.
1976   Keeping Your Temper under Control: Materials and the Manufacture of Papuan Pottery. *Archaeology and Physical Anthropology in Oceania* 11:106–37.

1981   *Pottery Technology: Principles and Reconstruc-
            tion.* Manuals on Archeology 4. Taraxacum,
            Washington, D.C.
Schiffer, Michael B., and James M. Skibo
1987   Theory and Experiment in the Study of
            Technological Change. *Current Anthropol-
            ogy* 28:595–622.
Shepard, Anna O.
1976   *Ceramics for the Archaeologist.* 9th printing.
            Carnegie Institution Publication 609,
            Washington, D.C.
Sherratt, Andrew
1980   Water, Soil and Seasonality in Early Cereal
            Cultivation. *World Archaeology* 11:313–30.
1982   Mobile Resources: Settlement and Exchange
            in Early Agricultural Europe. In *Ranking,
            Resource and Exchange,* edited by C. Renfrew
            and S. Shennan, pp. 13–26. Cambridge
            University Press, Cambridge.
Skibo, J. M., M. B. Schiffer, and K. C. Reid
1989   Organic-Tempered Pottery: An Experimental
            Study. *American Antiquity* 54:122–46.
Smith, Marion F., Jr.
1985   Toward an Economic Interpretation of
            Ceramics: Relating Vessel Size and Shape to
            Use. In *Decoding Prehistoric Ceramics,* edited
            by Ben A. Nelson, pp. 254–309. Center for
            Archaeological Investigations and Southern
            Illinois University Press, Carbondale.
Snyder, David M.
1989   Towards Chronometric Models for Palauan
            Prehistory: Ceramic Attributes. Ph.D. dis-
            sertation, Southern Illinois University,
            Carbondale. University Microfilms, Ann
            Arbor, Michigan.
Srejović, Dragoslav
1972   *Europe's First Monumental Sculpture: New
            Discoveries at Lepenski Vir.* Stein and Day,
            New York.
Stahl, Ann B.
1989   Plant-Food Processing: Implications for
            Dietary Quality. In *Foraging and Farming:
            The Evolution of Plant Exploitation,* edited by

D. R. Harris and G. C. Hillman, pp. 171–94.
            Unwin Hyman, London.
Steponaitis, Vincas P.
1983   *Ceramics, Chronology, and Community Patterns:
            An Archaeological Study at Moundville.* Aca-
            demic Press, New York.
Sterud, Eugene
1978   Prehistoric Populations of the Dinaric Alps:
            An Investigation of Interregional Interaction.
            In *Beyond Subsistence and Dating,* edited by
            C. L. Redman, pp. 381–408. Academic Press,
            New York.
Stuiver, M., and P. J. Reimer
1986   A Computer Program for Radiocarbon Age
            Calibration. *Radiocarbon* 28:1022–30.
Tasić, Nikola, and Emilija Tomić
1969   *Crnolačka Bara: Naselje Starčevačke i Vinčanske
            kulture.* Dissertationes 8. Narodni Muzej,
            Kruševac i Arheološko Društvo Jugoslavije,
            Beograd.
Todorović, J., D. Simoska, and B. Kitanoski
1977   The Settlement of Pešterica and the Problem
            of the Early Neolithic in Pelagonia. *Archae-
            ologia Iugoslavica* 18:1–8.
Touloukian, Y. S., R. W. Powell, C. Y. Ho, and
P. G. Klemeus
1970   Thermal Conductivity: Nonmetallic Solids.
            In *Thermophysical Properties of Matter 2.*
            IFI/Plenum, New York.
Touloukian, Y. S., R. W. Powell, C. Y. Ho, and
M. C. Nicolaou
1973   Thermal Diffusivity. In *Thermophysical
            Properties of Matter 10.* IFI/Plenum, New
            York.
Tringham, Ruth
1971   *Hunters, Fishers and Farmers of Eastern Europe,
            6000–3000 B.C.* Hutchinson, London.
Tringham, Ruth, and Dušan Krstić (eds.)
1990   *Selevac: A Neolithic Village in Yugoslavia.*
            UCLA Institute of Archaeology, Monumenta
            Archaeologica 15, Los Angeles.
Whittle, Alasdair
1985   *Neolithic Europe: A Survey.* Cambridge
            University Press, Cambridge.

7

Putting the Pot before the Horse

Earliest Ceramics and the Neolithic Transition in the Western Mediterranean

Explanations of the development of new subsistence economies in the past are usually based on the assumption that the principal factors driving the adoption of new economies were directly related to subsistence. These same explanations delegate a passive or reactive role to the social transformations and technological innovations that frequently accompany economic transitions. The purpose of this chapter is to question that basic premise and to propose that the manifestation of new technologies through social strategies could have been the principal mechanism for the appearance of a novel subsistence base. The early Neolithic in the western Mediterranean provides a test case for this experiment because both agriculture and novel artifact technologies, particularly pottery, appear concurrently.

Although polished axes are technically the "new stones" of the Neolithic, pottery is accepted as the *fossile directeur* of this period in Europe owing to its permanence, abundance, and variability. The names of the earliest European Neolithic "cultures" defined by Childe and other early workers are those of pottery types such as Banderkeramik, Cardial, Starčevo, and Rubanée. These ceramic types are traditionally associated with the appearance of agricultural societies and have provided a useful spatiotemporal framework for organizing culture histories. The attendant research has produced one of the most complete material bases for mid-Holocene prehistory in the world.

The interpretation of this base, however, has been more problematical. In the western Mediterranean, as in other areas of Europe, studies of ceramics in particular have focused traditionally on style, which was closely associated with "archaeological cultures" (Bailloud and Mieg de Boofzheim 1955). Little account was taken of the production and distribution of pottery, thereby preventing any consideration of how these contextual variables affected assemblages. Recent studies of Neolithic pottery production and distribution (Arnal 1989; Barnett 1989; Howard 1981) have provided a new context for the interpretation of prehistoric pottery in Europe. This new perspective has great value for viewing pottery as an item operating in an economic and social environment rather than as a cultural identifier. Many implications of this perceptual shift have yet to be realized. Because early pottery is associated with the appearance of agriculture in the western Mediterranean, its reevaluation can provide insight into the Neolithic transition.

WILLIAM K. BARNETT

Agricultural Expansion through Diffusion

The spread of agriculture has traditionally been explained through diffusionist models. These models depend on ecological or demographic stress mechanisms (Cohen 1977; Rindos 1984) and migration processes (Ammerman and Cavalli-Sforza 1984; Renfrew 1987) to explain the spread of agriculture in Europe. Whereas radiocarbon recalibration (Renfrew 1973) produced concrete evidence that all innovation did not arrive from the east, the basic trajectory of dates for the spread of agriculture from east to west has remained unchanged. Dates for the earliest pottery generally support this trend (Ammerman and Cavalli-Sforza 1984). Domesticated animals were also transported from the east. Geddes (1985) has firmly attributed Mediterranean sheep/goats to Asiatic stock. Diffusionist models, however, do not provide the only solution to the puzzle of agricultural origins. A critique of their assumptions provides an avenue for the development of an alternative perspective that focuses on adoption.

Diffusionist models for the spread of agriculture across Europe are characterized by three debatable assumptions: (1) that environmental or demographic stress was necessary to drive the spread of agriculture, (2) that preagricultural societies were generally egalitarian, neither wanting surplus nor having any hierarchical social structure for the manifestation of status or material wealth, and (3) that sedentary, production-oriented economies did not exist outside of agricultural subsistence bases (see also Arnold 1993). These assumptions cannot be supported, and therefore the models based on them must be questioned.

Diffusionist models developed to explain the invention of agriculture in the Near East have been applied to the expansion of agriculture across Europe, even though domestication processes may be little related to the subsequent expansion of agriculture westward. Demographic stress is therefore presented as a causal mechanism for the spread as well as for the invention of agriculture by citing external forces (Arnold 1993: 80). Wright (1993) currently defends the use of environmental determinism as a viable tool to understand domestication in the Near East. He underlines the difficulties in evaluating this model, however, by warning that "coincidence in time by itself is not a proof of cause and effect" (Wright 1993:468). It is possible to question the environmental drive behind the spread of agricultural because of the lack of causal links between environment and agricultural spread and because of the lack of evidence for significant environmental fluctuations (Reille and Lowe 1993).

Population imbalances also do not necessarily lead to invention or adoption. Novel technologies may not be adopted or invented during periods of stress. Population decline or starvation might happen, particularly during times of imbalance between population and resources. Alternatively, experimentation and adoption of novel technologies can occur where there is surplus and without demographic pressure, particularly when technologies can be introduced in nondependent roles as prestige items. Zvelebil (1986a) has proposed such a mechanism in his substitution model for the adoption of agriculture in western Europe.

The notion of egalitarianism in preagricultural Europe has been based largely on studies of modern foraging groups in ecologically peripheral zones (Lee and DeVore 1968) and has been perpetuated through maximized efficiency studies of Mesolithic populations (e.g., Jochim 1976). Preagricultural egalitarianism is explicit in migrationist models that view such populations as resource poor and thus overwhelmed by agriculturalists through either replacement or absorption. Egalitarianism is implicit in models of social storage (O'Shea 1981) that attribute resource storage to predicted scarcity. Recent evaluations of modern foraging groups indicate that many are far from unaffected by colonialism (Wilmsen 1989) and therefore may not be useful for modeling European Mesolithic societies. Even among such groups, social benefits may compete with subsistence in foraging strategies (Hawkes 1993), supporting the notion that foragers need not be egalitarian. Jeanne Arnold's (1993) recent discussion of complex hunter-gatherers makes a strong case for hierarchies in forager societies.

The perceptual dichotomy of mobile foragers versus sedentary agriculturalists has led to stress-based models of demic (Ammerman and Cavalli-Sforza 1984; Cohen 1977) or environmental (Wright 1993) determinism. In these models, seasonally mobile Mesolithic populations are overwhelmed by rapidly growing and expanding sedentary agricultural populations. Agriculture is not necessary for sedentism (Brown 1985; Henry 1985). In cases where Mesolithic populations can be shown to have been sedentary and to have exhibited complex foraging strategies, they likely inhabited the lowland zones required for agriculture and coastal areas with rich resource bases. Complex foragers might have been able to resist "Neolithic" subsistence strategies because early agriculture did not provide particular advantages over foraging. Alternatively, Mesolithic societies could have adopted domesticates and pottery as part of their existing hierarchical interaction strategies.

Agricultural Expansion through Adoption

To reject each principal assumption of the diffusion models requires me to propose alternative hypotheses for the agricultural transition in the western Mediterranean that focus on the activities of indigenous preagricultural populations. First, these Mesolithic populations in Europe did not adopt agricultural and other technologies as a result of stress but through attempts to integrate innovations into ritual or social activities. Such societies may already have had mechanisms for storing surpluses. Second, preagricultural societies were not strictly egalitarian and so practiced prestige or ritual activities in pursuance of social strategies. Agricultural products could have been introduced initially as prestige items (Hayden 1990) that later were slowly integrated into the subsistence repertoire (Zvelebil 1986a). Third, the transition to agriculture may have resulted not so much in a qualitative shift to sedentary agriculture as in the incorporation of new technologies into an extant economy.

Adoptionist models typically posit accumulation of prestige goods instead of stress as a causal mechanism and depend on the existence of sedentary, or at least territorial, hierarchical societies. Research focusing on the ecology and economy of Mesolithic societies, beginning with Higgs and Jarman (1969), provided models of indigenous affluence for Holocene foragers. Recently, models of complex hunter-gatherers describe foraging groups playing more active roles in the agricultural transition (Arnold 1993; Shnirelman 1992; Zvelebil 1986b). Both "adaptationist" (O'Shea 1981) and "political" (Hayden 1990; chapter 20) perspectives (see Arnold 1993:80) model preagricultural foraging societies as engaging in social and/or ritual activities to promote personal prestige or support hierarchies.

Both perspectives describe the indigenous adoption of agriculture as taking place through social factors (Bender 1978, 1985), storage of surplus (O'Shea 1981), or exchange (Lewthwaite 1986). Hodder (1990) has proposed a structuralist dialectic of *domus* (the domestic) versus *agrios* (the wild) to explain a suite of ritual, social, and economic activities that led to domestication in Europe. It is easy to envision sociopolitical

activities that could have acted as mechanisms for the adoption of novel items in resource-rich areas such as Europe. Resource-rich areas, particularly coastal zones, could have supported high population densities and social hierarchies during the Mesolithic. These adoptionist models have been actualized either as local scenarios such as frontier interaction (Dennell 1985; Moore 1985) or social territoriality (Barnett 1990a) or as broader descriptions of prestige exchange networks (Barnett 1989; Lewthwaite 1986).

The use of a "preagricultural" perspective provides a basis for proposing adoption as a mechanism for the spread of agriculture. It further allows the development of a "political" (Arnold 1993:80) accumulation model for the adoption of domesticates and Neolithic material technologies (see also Hoopes, chapter 15). Such a model proposes that sedentary, hierarchical Mesolithic societies participated in social or religious interaction that resulted in the accumulation and distribution of surplus. These societies would have enforced social identity, developed alliances, and used symbol-bearing items to assert power or define inclusion and exclusion (Aldenderfer 1993; Wiessner 1984). The suite of Neolithic traits that appears across the western Mediterranean may have been adopted through these interaction processes. The patterns of its adoption would then reflect the existence of interaction patterns along social territories.

The four criteria of accumulation models are resource abundance, social complexity, broad intergroup interaction, and a continuity of population from Mesolithic to Neolithic. These criteria overlap those of Price and Brown (1985:8) for complex hunter-gatherers: societal circumscription, resource abundance, and high population. Accumulation depends, therefore, on preagricultural hierarchies with accumulation ideologies (Testart 1982). The identification of hierarchies archaeologically would depend on the study of "craft specialization, mortuary data pertaining to status differentiation, distribution of valuables, and long-distance exchange" (Arnold 1993:82). Resource abundance can be shown through examination of Mesolithic settlements in resource-rich zones. These settlements may demonstrate year-round habitation and the residents' ability to have resource surpluses. Intergroup interaction can be examined through settlement and exchange pattern studies. Continuity of population must be demonstrated through analysis of human physical remains.

An adaptationist model (O'Shea 1981) proposes

that external forces required indigenous populations to acquire novel technologies. Nonsubsistence resource acquisition by preagricultural groups was principally accomplished from within an extended catchment, possibly related to seasonal movements. In this perspective, egalitarian groups adopted new technologies for utilitarian, principally subsistence-based needs. Symbol-bearing objects could have played a role in the adoption of these new technologies. Adaptation, however, requires neither sedentism nor social hierarchies.

The data required to evaluate adoption models are generated by studying settlement patterns, artifact production, decoration, and distribution, and the biology of populations during the Mesolithic to Neolithic transition. In general, the data sets necessary to evaluate the Mesolithic side of the transition are limited. Settlements are mostly inland cave settlements with few coastal or mortuary sites (the Muge middens in Portugal are the notable exception). Many areas that were coastal during the agricultural transition are now inundated, as evidenced by the early Neolithic site of Leucate-Corrège (Guilaine et al. 1984). Traditionally, studies of Mesolithic artifacts have been limited to typological analyses of flaked lithics.

Early pottery, because of its decorative variability and rapid distribution during the early Neolithic of the western Mediterranean, has great potential for evaluating the Mesolithic-Neolithic transition. Difficulties arise, however, because it is impossible to assume that the analysis of early Neolithic ceramics necessarily provides information about interaction among indigenous populations. Assuming the contrary—that patterns of early Neolithic ceramic production and distribution were not influenced by indigenous populations—is equally dangerous. Independent lines of evidence, discussed later, can help us evaluate the diffusion/ adoption question. Regardless of this question of identity, pottery is complex and information rich. The analysis of its decorative, technological, and spatial aspects can contribute greatly to our understanding of the processes of the Mesolithic-Neolithic transition.

An accumulation model proposes that the adoption of pottery occurred through the exchange of goods that also included ground stone and agricultural products. The prime mover in this case would have been accumulation for social, political, or economic reasons. Testart (1982) has suggested that an "accumulation ideology" explains the storage of surplus. Such accumulation could have driven logistic settlement and increased focus on storage, which would have led to investment and delayed return (Zvelebil 1986b) and

could easily have integrated a new container technology. Exchange across group boundaries could have been used to enhance personal prestige, cement intergroup alliances (Hayden 1990), or make investments that could be called upon in times of need (O'Shea 1981). In addition, pottery as a novel item could have had independent value as a prestige item.

In traditional diffusionist models, ceramics are produced and primarily used in an economic framework of migrating agriculturalists, although there may be some exchange with neighboring foragers. The advantages of ceramics in a food-producing economy (Arnold 1985) notwithstanding, the adoption of pottery is not dependent on agriculture. There are abundant examples of pottery in foraging contexts (Aikens, chapter 2; Gebauer, chapter 9; Price 1991; Sampson 1988). Food production has also appeared without pottery in the Near East (Moore, chapter 4) and in the New World (Hoopes 1994). Pottery is a material class independent of agriculture with advantages for food preparation, storage, and consumption (Arnold 1985) that would have been valuable for farmers and foragers alike.

In any of these adoption scenarios, decorated pots could have played important roles as transport containers and tokens to identify the giver. Pottery as an innovation in the context of an accumulation model is of value as a new technology for storage, food processing, and serving in social settings (Brown 1989), and also as a transport container or item of prestige. Its capacity to be highly decorated permits it to carry symbols of identity or power that would have been important in intra- and intergroup identification (Wiessner 1984) or in the ritual institutionalization of hierarchies (Aldenderfer 1993). It is necessary to consider other roles pottery might have played in the agricultural transition, including that of the agent of a prime mover —in this case, accumulation.

An accumulation model can be evaluated for the appearance of agriculture and for the adoption of pottery in the western Mediterranean. Such a model proposes that early pottery, as well as many other novel items such as domesticated animals and plants and polished stone tools, was adopted through exchange as part of an accumulation strategy, be it through competition for prestige (Hayden 1990) or guided by a domestication metaphor (Hodder 1990). Accordingly, one would expect to see sedentary Mesolithic populations, at least in high-yield coastal areas. These groups would have displayed internal hierarchies and stable territories. Symbol-bearing items would have been exchanged across boundaries and may have been accompanied by the exchange of other goods. Early highly decorated vessels would have moved great distances either as specialized prestige goods or through more local interaction among adjacent groups. Prestige items may have been of relatively uniform style and technology, but local exchanges would have reflected local group social diversity.

The Early Neolithic in the Western Mediterranean

Although there has been some controversy about early dates for Neolithic pottery (Zilhão 1993), current estimates place its first appearance in the western Mediterranean around 6800 b.p. from Liguria to Catalonia (Evin 1987; Zilhão 1993; Zvelebil 1986a). The spread of domesticates and pottery was very rapid and reached coastal Portugal by 6200 b.p., much faster than can be accounted for by Ammerman and Cavalli-Sforza's (1984) demic diffusion model (Zilhão 1993). The appearance of Neolithic items can be said to be spotty at best, occurring in most cases in apparent continuity with Mesolithic settlement patterns, economies, and lithic styles. There is no transition to a dependence on food production during the early Neolithic for up to 1,000 years (Dennell 1992; Zvelebil 1986a). Domesticated animals were transported from the east. Geddes (1985) has firmly attributed Mediterranean sheep/goats to Asiatic stock. There also was movement of other items such as obsidian (Tykot 1992) and ground stone objects (Ricq-de Bouard and Fedele 1993) across wide areas during the early Neolithic.

The initial pottery horizon shows two different distribution patterns. There are certain distinct decorative types, such as the *vrai Cardial*, or *Impressa*, wares that span wide areas. These can be also be easily identified by their technology of production and decoration (Barnett 1989). Guilaine (1976:37–38) has defined two principle zones based on these types: a central zone covering Italy to the Ligurian coast and a western zone beginning in Provence and extending to Atlantic Portugal. Whereas these types are mostly a coastal Mediterranean phenomenon, rare finds of Cardial pottery have been made in Aquitaine (Roussot-Larroque 1987) and in the central Alps (Gallay et al. 1987), indicating extensive inland access.

Within these zones, Guilaine (1976:21–22) has further identified 14 more restricted pottery "groups" that are related to the use of certain decorative tech-

niques or patterns. Many of these types are later than the "Cardial Horizon" and may indicate more local adoption of ceramic technology. All these ceramics are highly decorated and in some cases have been intentionally drilled, indicating social or ritualistic roles inconsistent with container function. Analysis of the production and distribution of early Neolithic pottery in Languedoc (Barnett 1989) has shown that the larger zones relate to long-distance movement of distinct types and the smaller groups relate to local use or smaller-scale patterns of movement—within a particular valley, for example (Barnett 1990b).

Migration versus Adoption in the Western Mediterranean

As I mentioned earlier, information on settlement patterns, interaction through artifact production and distribution, and human biology is crucial in determining the nature of the transition to agriculture in the western Mediterranean. Such information is also necessary for evaluating models of adoption via accumulation that propose the existence of preagricultural hierarchical societies and the movement of goods among relatively stable populations across the Mesolithic—Neolithic transition. The data that could enable us to explore these aspects are, as yet, incomplete. The current status of the question hinges on the comparison of adoption and migration models. In this comparison, the examination of early Neolithic pottery plays an important role.

The current case for the introduction of agriculture in the western Mediterranean has most recently been stated by Zilhão (1993). The scenario is one of an "enclave settlement" pattern by small, seafaring Neolithic groups who established far-flung agricultural enclaves and brought new technologies such as pottery. This model is similar to a pioneer colonization model (Zvelebil 1986a:11). The modus operandi of "enclave settlement" is demic diffusion caused by population or ecological stress. Such spread would have been more rapid than classic demic diffusion and is consistent with the coastal focus of some early pottery. The occurrence of pottery at inland sites would have resulted from local exchange with foragers. A pattern of upland-lowland ceramic exchange is consistent with this model (Fig. 7.1).

An accumulation model proposes a different cause for the adoption of domesticates through exchange mechanisms: the desire to accumulate surplus. It has

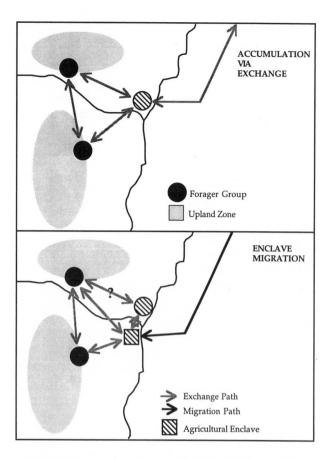

ACCUMULATION
VIA
EXCHANGE

● Forager Group
▨ Upland Zone

ENCLAVE
MIGRATION

→ Exchange Path
⇒ Migration Path
▨ Agricultural Enclave

Fig. 7.1. Diagram of migration and exchange patterns posited for an accumulation model (top) and an enclave migration model (bottom).

become clear that early agriculture had no economic advantage over complex foraging (Zvelebil 1986a). There must, therefore, have been some other motivation, such as competition or investment, for the adoption of agricultural innovations via accumulation. Adoption via accumulation would result in different patterns of ceramic exchange, particularly in regard to exchange of materials along the coast or between valleys (Fig. 7.1). There is no evidence for an abrupt economic shift to agriculture, even at submerged coastal sites such as Leucate-Corrège (Guilaine et al. 1984). The transition was instead more gradual and has been modeled by Zvelebil (1986a) as a lengthy substitution process more consistent with local adoption of pottery and domesticates through exchange.

Zilhão (1993), through close analysis of the stratigraphy of many early Neolithic sites, rejects earlier claims of the piecemeal adoption of pottery, sheep/goats, and cereals (Barnett 1989; Geddes 1985) and argues for the appearance of a Neolithic "package" of domesticates and pottery. The fact that Neolithic ra-

diocarbon dates generally have a first standard deviation of around 200 years precludes the identification of contemporaneous arrival. Even if rough contemporaneity could be shown, the adoption of exchange goods does not preclude the arrival of a suite of goods at approximately the same time. What appears to be a package, therefore, could just as easily have been somewhat staggered—we simply cannot distinguish the two.

Zilhão's (1993) critique of adoption schemes argues that a sudden appearance of the complete "Neolithic package" is more appropriately interpreted as evidence of colonization because there is no good evidence for an extant exchange system in the preceding Mesolithic phases, which would have been necessary for the adoption of these items by foragers. He notes that domesticates such as pigs are also difficult to incorporate into a foraging economy (Rowley-Conwy 1986). In addition, Zilhão (1993) notes that exchange of domesticated animals would have been more difficult than their transport with moving agriculturalists.

A case can be made for adoption through accumulation despite these criticisms. It is true that there is little evidence for Mesolithic trade—but then again, there is little material culture appropriate for such studies, and this question has yet to adequately studied. There is direct evidence for Mesolithic exchange elsewhere (Price 1991) and indirect evidence for boat travel to Melos in the Aegean during the Mesolithic (Jacobsen 1976), which would have facilitated coastal exchange. I would also argue that the rapidity with which novel material traveled across the western Mediterranean supports the hypothesis that innovations such as pottery, ground stone, and agricultural materials entered an extant network. The exchange of domestic sheep could not have been more difficult than their introduction through colonization. Both engender the same techniques of transport. The fact that swine are incompatible with a foraging economy (Zilhão 1993) is a nonissue because there is no evidence that domestic pigs were present during the early Neolithic (Helmer 1987).

It is currently difficult to interpret settlement patterns, owing to the paucity of coastal data. That most early Neolithic sites are caves is due in part to a traditional research bias. In addition, the Holocene sea-level rise inundated many of the coastal areas of the western Mediterranean during the early Holocene. The early Neolithic site of Leucate Corrège in Languedoc, for example, lies between 5 and 6 meters below current sea level (Guilaine et al. 1984). It represents a substantial, year-round, maritime-based settlement with one of the largest and most decoratively diverse, albeit fragmentary, ceramic assemblages in the western Mediterranean. Mesolithic coastal sites in this area would likely have been even further submerged.

The middens in Portugal are perhaps the only large late Mesolithic coastal sites in the western Mediterranean. They demonstrate an important coastal focus of the Atlantic Mesolithic. Zilhão (1993), in his assessment of Mesolithic and Neolithic settlement, concludes that the apparent discontinuity between Mesolithic and Neolithic settlement and lithic types in Portugal is due to the arrival of agricultural enclaves. Pottery recovered from the middens of the estuarine Sado Valley (Arnaud 1987) may, however, indicate adoption by local groups. The examination of the single Cardial vessel from one of these inland sites, Gruta do Caldeirão, indicates a remote, possibly coastal source for this vessel (Barnett 1992). Subsequent research, it is hoped, will shed light on the question of Neolithic lowland settlement in this region. It does appear, however, that late Mesolithic economies were robust and not likely to adopt new technologies as adaptations to external stresses.

Evidence of pottery movement (Barnett 1990a) provides a valuable measure of interaction. These patterns of movement are consistent with a model of accumulative exchange. There is evidence for the small-scale transport, in coastal areas and across adjacent upland zones, of impressed pottery. These exchange patterns are inconsistent with exclusive coastal-inland movement that would have resulted from mobility patterns or agriculturalist-forager exchange. These wares are highly decorated, and in the case of Cardial pottery, particular decorations and technology are consistent with its use as symbols. Long-distance movement of the classic Cardial types may have been the result of prestige trade, although this trade may have occurred through down-the-line exchange (Renfrew 1977) or other localized mechanisms. These data provide evidence that the earliest pottery was transported and that the patterns of this movement are more consistent with adoption via exchange than with migration and subsequent localized production. This long-distance exchange and the high decoration and particular technology of these wares appear contradictory to notions of their use as vessels for social storage or other adaptationist models of adoption.

Only human biology data can potentially enable us to discriminate indigenous from migrating populations. A biocultural study of the health status of Mesolithic and Neolithic populations (Meiklejohn and Zvelebil 1991) has shown no clear change in levels of stress related to the appearance of agriculture but is equivocal in identifying population migration (João Zilhão, personal communication). Previous attempts to demonstrate morphological disjunction between Neolithic and Mesolithic populations (Vencl 1986) have been similarly unsuccessful (Meiklejohn and Zvelebil 1991:135; Sokal et al. 1990). It is possible that only DNA information can ultimately provide an independent test of the migration/adoption question.

Conclusions

New perspectives on preagricultural foragers have come out of recent research on many fronts. Recent models of hierarchical foraging societies (Aldenderfer 1993; Arnold 1993) permit proposals of social or ritual behavior that could have driven the adoption of new technologies and subsistence bases through accumulation. It is possible to "put the pot before the horse" in an explanatory fashion and consider the role pottery exchange might have played in accumulation strategies that led to the transition to agriculture in the western Mediterranean. Evaluation of data on settlement, interaction through ceramic production and distribution, and human biology is consistent with a model of adoption through accumulation. These data also support notions that pottery exchange played an important role in the Neolithic transition. It is clear, however, that "Neolithization" was accomplished by interrelated social and economic processes involving both population and artifact movement. The migration-versus-adoption dichotomy has been a useful tool for fleshing out and evaluating an accumulation model for the western Mediterranean. Discussions of process and cultural dynamics should lead subsequent dialogue on this important transition.

References Cited

Aldenderfer, M.
  1993   Ritual, Hierarchy, and Change in Foraging Societies. *Journal of Anthropological Archaeology* 12:1–40.
Ammerman, A. J., and L. L. Cavalli-Sforza
  1984   *The Neolithic Transition and the Genetics of Populations in Europe.* Princeton University Press, Princeton.

Arnal, G.

1989   *Céramique et céramologie du néolithique de la France Méditerranéenne,* Mémoire no. 5, Centre de Recherche Archéologique du Haut-Languedoc, Lodéve (Hérault), France.

Arnaud, J.

1987   Os concheiros mesoliticos dos Vales do Tejo e Sado: Semelhanças e diferenças. *Arqueologia* 15:53–64.

Arnold, D.

1985   *Ceramic Theory and Cultural Process.* Cambridge University Press, Cambridge.

Arnold, J. E.

1993   Labor and the Rise of Complex Hunter-Gatherers. *Journal of Anthropological Archaeology* 12:75–119.

Bailloud, G., and P. Mieg de Boofzheim

1955   *Les civilisations néolithiques de la France dans leur contexte Européen.* Picard, Paris.

Barnett, W. K.

1989   The Production and Distribution of Early Neolithic Pottery in the Aude Valley, France. Ph.D. dissertation, Boston University. University Microfilms International, Ann Arbor, Michigan.

1990a   Production and Distribution of Early Pottery in the West Mediterranean. In *The Changing Roles of Ceramics in Society: 26,000 B.P. to the Present,* edited by D. W. Kingery, pp. 137–57. Ceramics and Civilization, vol. 5, American Ceramic Society, Westerville, Ohio.

1990b   Small-Scale Transport of Early Neolithic Pottery in the West Mediterranean. *Antiquity* 64:859–65.

1992   The Physical Analyses of Early Neolithic Impressed Pottery from Gruta do Caldeirão. In *Gruta do Caldeirão: O neolítico antigo,* edited by J. Zilhão, pp. 297–312. Trabalhos de Arqueologia 6, Instituto Português do Património Arquitectónico e Arqueológico, Lisbon.

Bender, B.

1978   Gatherer-Hunter to Farmer: A Social Perspective. *World Archaeology* 10(2):203–22.

1985   Prehistoric Developments in the American Midcontinent and in Brittany, Northwest France. In *Prehistoric Hunter-Gatherers: The Emergence of Cultural Complexity,* edited by T. D. Price and J. A. Brown, pp. 21–57. Academic Press, Orlando, Florida.

Brown, J. A.

1985   Long-Term Trends to Sedentism and the Emergence of Complexity in the American Midwest. In *Prehistoric Hunter-Gatherers: The Emergence of Cultural Complexity,* edited by T. D. Price and J. A. Brown, pp. 201–31. Academic Press, Orlando, Florida.

1989   The Beginnings of Pottery as an Economic Process. In *What's New? A Closer Look at the Process of Innovation,* edited by S. van der Leeuw and R. Torrence, pp. 203–24. Unwin Hyman, London.

Cohen, M. N.

1977   *The Food Crisis in Prehistory.* Yale University Press, New Haven.

Dennell, R.

1985   The Hunter-Gatherer/Agricultural Frontier in Prehistoric Temperate Europe. In *The Archaeology of Frontiers and Boundaries,* edited by S. Green and S. Perlman, pp. 113–39. Academic Press, New York.

1992   The Origins of Crop Agriculture in Europe. In *The Origins of Agriculture: An International Perspective,* edited by C. W. Cowan and P. J. Watson, pp. 71–100. Smithsonian Institution Press, Washington, D.C.

Evin, J.

1987   Révision de la chronologie absolue des débuts du néolithique en Provence et Languedoc. In *Premières communautés paysannes en Méditerranée occidentale,* edited by J. Guilaine et al., pp. 27–36. CNRS, Paris.

Gallay, A., R. Carazzetti, and C. Brunier

1987   Le néolithique ancien des Alpes centrales (fin Veme millénaire) et ses relations avec la Méditerranée. In *Premières communautés paysannes en Méditerranée occidentale,* edited by J. Guilaine et al., pp. 479–85. CNRS, Paris.

Geddes, D.

1985   Mesolithic Domestic Sheep in West Mediterranean Europe. *Journal of Archaeological Science* 12:25–48.

Guilaine, J.

1976   *Premiers bergers et paysans de l'occident Méditerranéen.* Mouton, Paris.

Guilaine, J., A. Freises, and R. Montjardin

1984   *Leucate-Corrège: Habitat noyé du néolithique Cardial.* Centre d'Anthropologie des Sociétés Rurales, Toulouse.

Hawkes, K.

1993   Why Hunter-Gatherers Work. *Current Anthropology* 34(4):341–61.

Hayden, B.

1990   Nimrods, Piscators, Pluckers and Planters: The Emergence of Food Production. *Journal of Anthropological Archaeology* 9:31–69.

Helmer, D.

1987   Les Suidés du Cardial: Sangliers ou cochons? In *Premières communautés paysannes en Médi-*

terranée occidentale, edited by J. Guilaine et al., pp. 215–20. CNRS, Paris.

Henry, Donald O.
1985   Preagricultural Sedentism: The Natufian Example. In *Prehistoric Hunter-Gatherers: The Emergence of Cultural Complexity,* edited by T. D. Price and J. A. Brown, pp. 365–84. Academic Press, Orlando, Florida.

Higgs, E. S., and M. R. Jarman
1969   The Origins of Agriculture: A Reconsideration. *Antiquity* 43:31–41.

Hodder, Ian
1990   *The Domestication of Europe.* Basil Blackwell, Oxford.

Hoopes, John
1994   Ford Revisited: A Critical Review of the Chronology and Relationships of the Earliest Ceramic Complexes in the New World, 6000–1500 B.C. *Journal of World Prehistory* 8(1):1–49.

Howard, Hilary
1981   In the Wake of Distribution: Towards an Integrated Approach to Ceramic Studies in Prehistoric Britain. In *Production and Distribution: A Ceramic Viewpoint,* edited by H. Howard and E. Morris, pp. 1–30. British Archaeological Reports, International Series 120, Oxford.

Jacobsen, Thomas W.
1976   17,000 Years of Greek Prehistory. *Scientific American* 234(6):76–87.

Jochim, Michael A.
1976   *Hunter-Gatherer Subsistence and Settlement: A Predictive Model.* Academic Press, New York.

Lee, Richard B., and Irven DeVore, eds.
1968   *Man the Hunter.* Aldine Publishing Co., Chicago.

Lewthwaite, J.
1986   The Transition to Food Production: A Mediterranean Perspective. In *Hunters in Transition,* edited by M. Zvelebil, pp. 53–66. Cambridge University Press, Cambridge.

Meiklejohn, C., and M. Zvelebil
1991   Health Status of European Populations at the Agricultural Transition and the Implications for the Adoption of Farming. In *Health in Past Societies: Biocultural Interpretations of Human Skeletal Remains in Archaeological Contexts,* edited by H. Bush and M. Zvelebil, pp. 129–45. British Archaeological Reports, International Series 567, Oxford.

Moore, J. A.
1985   Forager/Farmer Interactions: Information, Social Organization, and the Frontier. In *The Archaeology of Frontiers and Boundaries,* edited

by S. Green and S. Perlman, pp. 93–112. Academic Press, New York.

O'Shea, J.
1981   Coping with Scarcity: Exchange and Social Storage. In *Economic Archaeology,* edited by A. Sheridan and G. Bailey, pp. 167–83. British Archaeological Reports, International Series 96, Oxford.

Price, T. D.
1991   The Mesolithic of Northern Europe. *Annual Review of Anthropology* 20:211–33.

Price, T. D., and J. A. Brown
1985   Aspects of Hunter-Gatherer Complexity. In *Prehistoric Hunter-Gatherers: The Emergence of Cultural Complexity,* edited by T. D. Price and J. A. Brown, pp. 3–20. Academic Press, Orlando, Florida.

Reille, M., and J. J. Lowe
1993   A Re-evaluation of the Vegetation History of the Eastern Pyrenees (France) from the End of the Last Glacial to the Present. *Quaternary Science Reviews* 12:47–77.

Renfrew, Colin
1973   *Before Civilization.* Jonathan Cape, London.
1977   Alternative Models for Exchange and Spatial Distribution. In *Exchange Systems in Prehistory,* edited by T. Earle and J. Ericson, pp. 71–90. Academic Press, New York.
1987   *Archaeology and Language.* Jonathan Cape, London.

Ricq-de Bouard, M., and F. G. Fedele
1993   Neolithic Rock Resources aross the Western Alps: Circulation Data and Models. *Geoarchaeology* 8(1):1–22.

Rindos, David
1984   *The Origins of Agriculture: An Evolutionary Perspective.* Academic Press, New York.

Roussot-Larroque, Julia
1987   Les deux visages du néolithique ancien d'Aquitaine. In *Premières communautés paysannes en Méditerranée occidentale,* edited by J. Guilaine et al., pp. 681–92. CNRS, Paris.

Rowley-Conwy, Peter
1986   Between Cave Painters and Crop Planters: Aspects of the Temperate European Mesolithic. In *Hunters in Transition,* edited by M. Zvelebil, pp. 17–32. Cambridge University Press, Cambridge.

Sampson, C. Garth
1988   *Stylistic Boundaries among Mobile Hunter-Foragers.* Smithsonian Institution Press, Washington, D.C.

Shnirelman, Victor
1992   Crises and Economic Dynamics in Traditional

Societies. *Journal of Anthropological Archaeology* 11:25–46.

Sokal, R., et al.

1990   Genetics and Language in European Populations. *American Naturalist* 135(2):157–75.

Testart, Alain

1982   The Significance of Food Storage among Hunter-Gatherers: Residence Patterns, Population Densities and Social Inequalities. *Current Anthropology* 23:523–37.

Tykot, R.

1992   Regional Interaction in the Prehistoric Central Mediterranean: Chronological Variation as Evidenced by Obsidian Exchange. Paper presented at the 57th annual meeting of the Society for American Archaeology, Pittsburgh, Pennsylvania.

Vencl, S.

1986   The Role of Hunting-Gathering Populations in the Transition to Farming: A Central European Perspective. In *Hunters in Transition*, edited by M. Zvelebil, pp. 43–52. Cambridge University Press, Cambridge.

Wiessner, Polly

1984   Reconsidering the Behavioral Basis for Style:

A Case Study among the Kalahari San. *Journal of Anthropological Archaeology* 3:190–234.

Wilmsen, Edwin N.

1989   *Land Filled with Flies : A Political Economy of the Kalahari*. University of Chicago Press, Chicago.

Wright, H. E., Jr.

1993   Environmental Determinism in Near Eastern Prehistory. *Current Anthropology* 34(4):458–69.

Zilhão, João

1993   The Spread of Agro-Pastoral Economies across Mediterranean Europe: A View from the Far West. *Journal of Mediterranean Archaeology* 6(1):5–63.

Zvelebil, Marek

1986a   Mesolithic Prelude and Neolithic Revolution. In *Hunters in Transition*, edited by M. Zvelebil, pp. 5–15. Cambridge University Press, Cambridge.

1986b   Mesolithic Societies and the Transition to Farming: Problems of Time, Scale and Organization. In *Hunters in Transition*, edited by M. Zvelebil, pp. 167–88. Cambridge University Press, Cambridge.

8

The Linear Pottery Culture of Central Europe

Conservative Colonists?

PETER BOGUCKI

The Linear Pottery culture was the first farming culture of central Europe, identified in the 1870s by the German art historian-turned-archaeologist Friedrich Klopfleisch on the basis of the pottery's distinctive curvilinear incised decoration. Over the past century, the Linear Pottery culture has been referred to by a variety of different names. V. Gordon Childe called it "Danubian I" in his sequence of prehistoric European cultures, although this terminology has fallen from use. There are also a variety of national names across Europe, including Linearbandkeramik in Germany and Austria, Céramique Rubanée in France, and Ceramika Wstęgowa in Poland. Dates for the Linear Pottery culture fall between 6400 and 6000 b.p. (unrecalibrated), which are calibrated to between 5400 and 4900 B.C. in calendar years.

The spread of the Linear Pottery culture across central Europe represents one of the few colonizations that can be documented in the archaeological record, for reasons that are elaborated later. The weight of evidence indicates that the Linear Pottery culture was a case neither of in situ innovation of pottery nor of its adoption by previously aceramic peoples. Instead, the Linear Pottery culture constitutes a widespread dispersal of pottery-using peoples across an area where no ceramics had been found previously. Only in the western part of the Linear Pottery realm, in the case of the anomalous Limburg and La Hoguette wares (Lüning, Kloos, and Albert 1989), can one possibly speak of indigenous pottery traditions at this date, but even then only in direct association with the Linear Pottery culture.

There is a recent trend toward emphasizing regional and temporal diversity within the Linear Pottery culture in an effort to understand it better (e.g., Bogucki 1988; Modderman 1988). In many contexts, such an approach makes sense and does not contradict the position taken in this chapter. On the other hand, there are also situations in which the high degree of conformity within the Linear Pottery culture to a specific model of how its material world should look and the persistence of this model over time have significance. Coudart (1991), for instance, has pointed out this conformity to cultural norms and used it to support a model of egalitarian social structure. The title of Modderman's 1988 article—"The Linear Pottery Culture: Diversity in Uniformity"—indeed sums up the contrasting themes in the study of this culture.

The goal of this chapter is to explore some issues related to the agricultural colonization of central Europe, particularly some thoughts that arise from looking at the Linear Pottery ceramics in conjunction with other aspects of this culture. Linear Pottery ceramics, house forms, and settlement patterns are remarkably similar from one end of central Europe to the other, especially during the early phases of this culture. Although the Linear Pottery culture dispersed rapidly (in archaeological time), its degree of uniformity cannot be completely explained by the quickness of its spread. Instead, the full explanation must be sought in social relations and in societal approaches to innovation.

The Agricultural Colonization of Europe

Linear Pottery sites occur across central Europe from Slovakia and the western Ukraine to eastern France and Belgium (Bogucki and Grygiel 1993; Fig. 8.1). They are found primarily along the rivers and brooks of the rolling uplands of central Europe in basins filled with loess soil, which is very fertile but also somewhat dry except in stream valleys. Linear Pottery sites typ-

ically occur in small clusters separated from nearby concentrations by some distance. In the loess belt, these sites typically occur in the landscape zone where the floodplain meets the adjoining watershed. Farther north, off the loess, Linear Pottery sites also occur on the glacial soils of the North European Plain in the lower Vistula and Oder drainages.

Beginning on the Hungarian Plain and spreading through Slovakia, the Czech lands, Austria, Germany, and Poland into the Low Countries and eastern France, the expansion of the Linear Pottery culture is one of the most remarkable phenomena in prehistoric Europe, taking place over only a few centuries between approximately 5400 and 4900 B.C. The argument for the Linear Pottery dispersal as a colonization rather than an in situ development is based on several observations. First, as mentioned already, Linear Pottery material culture is extraordinarily uniform over wide areas, particularly in the earliest phases. Second, there is no known preexisting tradition of pottery manufacture in central Europe. Third, Linear Pottery flint technology

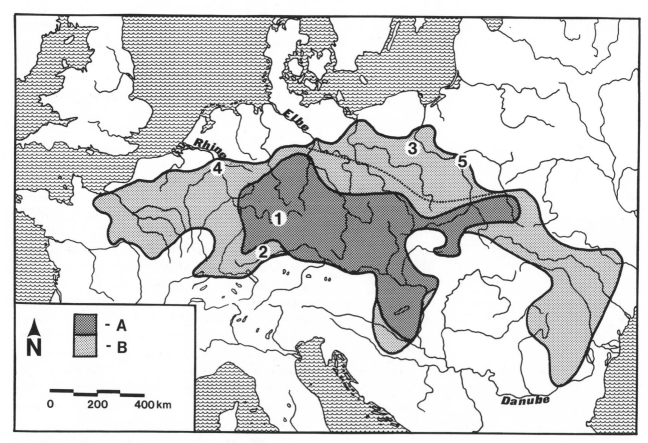

Fig. 8.1. Map of central Europe showing the distribution of Linear Pottery ceramics and key sites mentioned in chapter 8 (base map after Lüning, Kloos, and Albert 1989). Key: *A*, initial extent of Linear Pottery colonization; *B*, subsequent expansion of Linear Pottery settlement; 1, Schwanfeld; 2, Ulm-Eggingen; 3, Radziejów; 4, Sittard and Geleen; 5, Śniadków Górny.

is quite different from that of tool types used by local foraging populations. Fourth, the cereals (wheat and barley) and some of the livestock (sheep and goats) used by the Linear Pottery communities have no native counterparts in central Europe. Finally, Linear Pottery houses are completely unlike any structures found in central Europe before 5400 B.C.

The initial episode of Linear Pottery colonization in central Europe was first outlined by Quitta in 1960. The ceramics of the oldest phase, with simple incised decorations on relatively thick ware, occur primarily in Moravia, Bohemia, and Bavaria; the northern and western fringes of their distribution lie in Lower Saxony and Franconia (Fig. 8.1a). Whittle (1990) recently examined the dating of the oldest Linear Pottery. Conventional radiocarbon dates on charcoal samples had indicated an early date of 6400 b.p. or earlier. Recent accelerator dating of cereal and bone samples, however, shows a more varied picture, with some dates falling around 6300–6100 b.p. Much work remains to be done in the dating of Linear Pottery materials, especially using accelerator dating of samples that are clearly associated with specific pottery types. Whittle suggests, however, that the earliest dispersal of Linear Pottery, frequently characterized as rapid, may have been more gradual than hitherto believed or that ware considered to be the oldest Linear Pottery might have persisted for some time after its initial appearance.

The initial phase of Linear Pottery colonization in central Europe was followed by expansion into adjacent loess areas, including southern Poland and the Rhineland (Fig. 8.1b). The pottery of this phase, which has curvilinear incised decoration on thinner ware than that of the oldest phase, goes under a variety of names, including Ačkovy in Bohemia, Zofipole in southern Poland, and Flomborn in Germany. It has been found throughout the distribution zone of the oldest materials as well as beyond this area into the lower Rhine and Maas valleys of Germany and the Netherlands, along the upper courses of the Vistula and Oder in southern Poland (Kulczycka-Leciejewiczowa 1988), and recently in the western part of Ukraine (Piasets'kiy and Okhrimenko 1990).

The next Linear Pottery phase saw the development of two broad regional provinces. In the east—in Czechoslovakia, eastern Germany, and Poland—the simple curvilinear lines of the Ačkovy/Zofipole/Flomborn pottery were replaced by more complex curvilinear decoration relieved by oval impressions along the lines and at nodes where they cross. This is the so-called "music-note" (*Notenkopf*) style of Linear Pottery, the "classic" manifestation of the culture in its eastern province. During this phase, Linear Pottery sites appeared along the lower Vistula and Oder rivers in Poland and eastern Germany. In western Germany and the Low Countries, this phase of Linear Pottery saw the development of similar complex patterns of incised decoration, but without the music-note motif.

The end of Linear Pottery was marked by a further regionalization of the pottery decoration, even though the east-west dichotomy continued, and by a gradual transition to later cultures. The regional styles of Linear Pottery were distributed over fairly wide areas, and there was continued expansion of the culture into Belgium and the Paris Basin. Late Linear Pottery decoration became increasingly "baroque." In the east, the music-note ware, with its curvilinear motifs, developed into the "Želiezovce style" in Moravia and southern Poland, in which angular incised lines are intersected by large, lozenge-shaped indentations. In Silesia and Bohemia, ladder and herringbone motifs are known as the "Šarka style," which is also characterized by the in-filling of the incisions with white pigment.

Throughout this area, the use of smaller stab-and-drag ornamentation also appeared, in many cases executed with a toothed spatula to form multiple parallel rows of impressions bounded by solid incised lines. This practice is seen even more frequently toward the western part of the Linear Pottery range, and it is the dominant form of late Linear Pottery decoration in the Rhineland. The parallel incised lines bounding the small punctates gradually disappeared, resulting in the linear patterns of punctates and stab-and-drag ornament characteristic of the Rubanée Récent of the Paris Basin, the "Omalian" of Belgium, the Grossgartach group in the Rhineland, and the Hinkelstein group on the upper Rhine—all variations on the same general theme (Meier-Arendt 1972). Recently, the use of white pigment has also been documented from western Linear Pottery sites of this phase, particularly to fill in and highlight the bands of comb impressions (Modderman 1988).

Throughout the Linear Pottery culture, there is also a coarse ware that lacks the incised decoration and thin walls but instead is characterized by bands of fingernail impressions on relatively thick walls. The coarse ware is similar across central Europe. Unlike the fine ware, which was rarely tempered, the coarse ware frequently contains inclusions of sand grains.

Thin-section analyses of Linear Pottery decorated and coarse pottery indicates that it was made from local clays (Bakels 1978; Cowie 1983; Modderman 1988), probably from the loess soil found in the immediate environs of the settlements. Thus it is clear that the broad regional similarities cannot be explained by decorated ceramics' having served as trade wares (although interregional exchange did take place in various flint types, obsidian, and *Spondylus* shell artifacts).

Uniformity of Material Culture

The foregoing review indicates two salient aspects of the development of the Linear Pottery culture across central Europe. First, there are several "stadia" in the dispersal of Linear Pottery ceramics, corresponding first to the distribution of the oldest ware, then to the limit of the Ačkovy/Zofipole/Flomborn ware, and then eventually to the distribution of the music-note and more complex decoration of the middle phase. Second, within these three stadial episodes, there is considerable interregional homogeneity in Linear Pottery ceramic decoration. Only in the middle phase does some regional differentiation appear, which is amplified in the final Linear Pottery phases, in which there are a variety of regional groups. Nonetheless, the regional provinces of Linear Pottery are still very large, especially when compared with the local styles that predominate in later European prehistory.

Over this period, changes in pottery decoration are predominantly accretional: a basic repertoire of incised lines and punctates is organized in progressively more complex forms. The incised lines continue as wavy bands around the vessel, and with the exception of the use of denticulated instruments to make impressions and the highlighting of the bands with white pigment, no new elements such as stamping or cord impressions are introduced. Surface treatment and firing techniques also appear to have remained constant. In short, across the Linear Pottery realm there was a basic and simple vocabulary of ceramic decoration for which the possibilities of combination became progressively richer but which did not change in its basic components for several centuries.

Most Linear Pottery decorated vessels, from Slovakia to eastern France, take the form of a 3/4-spherical bowl (*Kümpf* in German). The largest are 60–70 centimeters in diameter, but most are considerably smaller —between 20 and 40 centimeters across (Fig. 8.2). Although those of the oldest phase are flat-bottomed and some in the latest phase have rims that flare upward to form a neck, the forms of these bowls are very consistent through the early phases of the Linear Pottery culture. Among the remaining vessel forms are shallow dishes and flasklike vessels, although in much lower frequencies.

Although minor variations are often emphasized to refine typological schemes, the very small basic number of Linear Pottery vessel forms, particularly in the

Fig. 8.2. Linear Pottery fine-ware vessels. Key: *a*, Sittard, the Netherlands (after Modderman 1958/59); *b*, Śniadków Górny, Poland (after Grygiel 1978); *c*, Ulm-Eggingen, Germany (after Kind 1989).

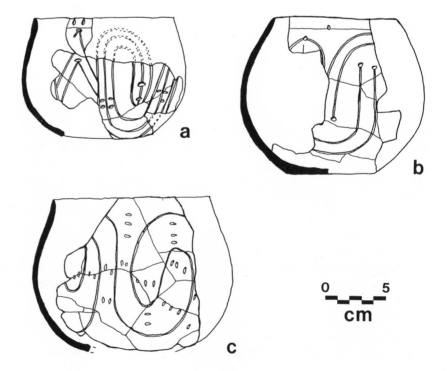

earlier phases, is in striking contrast to the virtual explosion in vessel shapes and forms that occurs later in the Neolithic and continues through later European prehistory. Moreover, the fact that so many of the vessels are *Kümpfe* suggests that this form was particularly suited to a wide range of uses, from storage and transport to food preparation and even cooking.

This uniformity extends to other aspects of Linear Pottery material culture, particularly architecture. Perhaps the most distinctive characteristic of the Linear Pottery culture was its large longhouses, up to 45 meters in length: the largest buildings in the world at this time. They were multipurpose structures, providing shelter for humans and livestock as well as storage and working space. Linear Pottery longhouses were built from massive timber posts that usually occur in five rows, two forming the exterior walls and three providing the interior support for the roof. They have rectangular plans, between 7 and 45 meters long and 5–7 meters wide. In the exterior walls, the spaces between the posts were filled with wooden wattle (woven twigs and branches) and plastered with mud taken from elongated pits dug along the walls.

The oldest Linear Pottery longhouses, known from sites such as Schwanfeld (Lüning and Stehli 1989), have somewhat complicated side extensions and a porchlike feature, but already they have the familiar elongated ground plan. By the Ačkovy/Flomborn/Zofipole phase the houses have their standard five rows of posts. Modderman (1988) has noted the tripartite division of the longhouses into three distinct modules (Fig. 8.3) that presumably had a functional

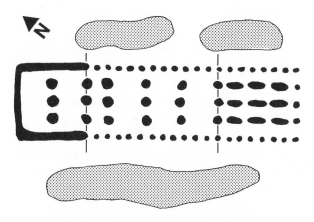

Fig. 8.3. Generalized ground plan of a Linear Pottery longhouse, showing tripartite modular design and elongated pits alongside. Orientations may vary across Europe, ranging from roughly N-S in eastern Europe to W-E in France, with NW-SE being typical of Germany and the Netherlands (after Kind 1989).

significance; some smaller houses containing only one or two of the modules are also found. Despite some regional variation in construction details (for instance, the enigmatic **Y** post pattern in early longhouses in the western Linear Pottery range), the dimensions and general organization of the longhouses is remarkably similar throughout central Europe (Fig. 8.4).

Adaptive Conservatism?

The pattern of broad regional uniformity extends beyond the material culture to the Linear Pottery subsistence and settlement system. The Linear Pottery sub-

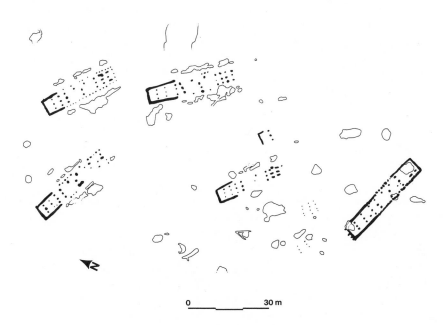

Fig. 8.4. Plan of the Linear Pottery settlement at Geleen showing uniform ground plans of longhouses and their three modules. Note the **Y** post pattern in the central module, typical of earlier Linear Pottery houses in the Rhineland and the Netherlands (after Modderman 1985).

0 _____ 30 m

sistence economy was based on crop agriculture and animal husbandry. Emmer and einkorn wheat, peas, lentils, and linseed were grown throughout the Linear Pottery area, whereas barley has an unusual limited distribution on the eastern, northern, and western periphery. Several sites in the western part of the Linear Pottery culture distribution have yielded traces of poppyseed, which has a Mediterranean origin. Although animal bones are usually poorly preserved in the loess soil, those of cattle make up the largest portion of the available Linear Pottery samples, usually over 70 percent. It is likely that cattle were used for dairy products in addition to meat. Sheep and goat are also present in smaller quantities, while pig bones are relatively rare. Bones of wild animals occur sporadically, but not in quantities that indicate that hunting made a significant contribution to the diet.

For many years, it had been thought that the Linear Pottery farmers practiced a form of slash-and-burn agriculture that quickly exhausted soil fertility and necessitated constant relocation of settlements. Since about 1970, this idea has been largely abandoned in favor of the notion of long-term occupation of settlements and cultivation of small fields located in the fertile zone where the floodplain meets the watershed. Carbonized seeds of shade-loving plants suggest that fields were surrounded by trees. Grain was harvested by cutting off the ears with a flint sickle.

Gregg (1989) studied almost 400 samples of carbonized seeds from Ulm-Eggingen in Baden-Württemburg. Based on consistent weed spectra that occur throughout the Linear Pottery occupation, she suggests that planting practices appear to have changed little over time, which in turn may reflect a lack of flexibility and ability to adjust to changing climatic conditions. In her view, the inhabitants of Ulm-Eggingen followed a conservative planting strategy, continuing "to plant their crops in the same manner, on the same types of fields from the earliest occupation phases to the latest" (Gregg 1989:390).

It seems improbable that the early Neolithic agricultural system was one of integrated yet flexible "mixed farming," which developed later in European prehistory. It is more likely that it was one of loosely connected components, with caution and redundancy as hedges against crop failure rather than integration and experimentation. Although these farmers were clearly able and successful, their agricultural system does not seem to have had the characteristics of the mixed farming systems that characterized later prehistoric and early historical periods in Europe.

Linear Pottery settlements consistently occur in particular landscape zones in central Europe, especially in the loess belt. In general, these are the lower slopes along the valleys of the brooks and streams that form the tributaries of the rivers of central Europe. Not settling on the floodplains themselves, the Linear Pottery colonists selected adjacent areas at the bases of the slopes that culminated in the watershed separating one stream from the next such drainage. On the North European Plain, Linear Pottery sites are also found in relatively low-lying locations. For instance, at Radziejów in Poland, Linear Pottery sites are clustered at the base of a long moraine next to some damp meadows. Elsewhere in northern Poland they are found consistently at the tips of small peninsulas in basins left by the retreating glaciers.

Such habitats are what ecologists would call "energy subsidized" (Odum 1983). They can consistently produce high yields without the shifting of fields or settlement locations. In large measure, the selection of such habitats by Linear Pottery colonists was good agronomy. Yet it also reflects a tendency to avoid the unpredictable and risky and to stick with the tried and true. Even on the North European Plain there was a tendency to keep to habitats that were relatively similar to those found on the loess. Predictability and consistency over time were apparently valued over high-risk/high-gain situations.

When it came to new soil types, the Linear Pottery culture followed a similarly cautious pattern. On the North European Plain, the favored soils along the lower Oder and Vistula approximated to some degree the loess found to the south, whereas settlement on other lowland soils that could also be easily cultivated was avoided. In the Paris Basin, late Linear Pottery settlement occurs on Pleistocene flood loam, a soil that also approximated the loess to a large degree (Ilett 1983).

Conservative Colonists

The chronology, material culture, and distribution of the Linear Pottery communities in central Europe create an image of a frontier of Neolithic colonization of the optimal riverine habitats (e.g., Dennell 1985). The notion of this frontier, with sedentary Neolithic communities on one side and mobile Mesolithic bands on the other, has affected our perception of the nature of agrarian communities across this area.

Much thinking in the social sciences about frontier

social processes has been influenced by the "frontier thesis" advanced by Frederick Jackson Turner (1893) concerning the American frontier. Turner saw the frontier social milieu as a catalyst for change and innovation that stamped the American national character with its practicality, individualism, and propensity for rapid social change, yet with an inherently egalitarian ethic. Although Turner was writing specifically about the American frontier of the nineteenth century, his model is often applied to other historical frontier situations to suggest that frontiers are areas where new social forms can develop unfettered by the conventions and customs of the core area.

The achievement of the Linear Pottery colonists of central Europe in their introduction of a successful economy based on food production across a vast area in a short period makes Turner's model of the frontier as a milieu for adventure, risk, and innovation very attractive. Yet if the Linear Pottery farmers were so prone to taking risks and innovating, one would expect a variety of local adaptations to appear almost immediately, leading to great variation in material culture almost from the start. Clearly longhouses and *Kümpfe* are not the only possible functional forms that such artifacts can take in the central European milieu, as later cultural variation so plainly demonstrates. Instead, Linear Pottery communities from Ukraine to France adhered to a very limited repertoire of conventions in virtually all material expressions of their culture.

In his study of African frontier societies, Kopytoff found that the conservative aspects of frontier social dynamics can also be extremely significant, and he points out that few frontierspeople possess "the yearning to construct a designed and utterly new social order." Instead, "frontiersmen bring with them preexisting conceptions of social order," and the impulse that brings them to the frontier is "culturally . . . a conservative one—to secure a way of life that is culturally legitimate and desirable but that is, for some reason, unattainable at home" (Kopytoff 1987:33). In his view, "the frontier process becomes one of cultural self-reproduction on a regional scale." At the same time, the African frontier dweller is a social entrepreneur in that to achieve this replicated social order he must take an expansive view of what constitutes kinsmen and adherents.

In his analysis of African frontiers, Kopytoff deals with societies that are organized at a somewhat greater level of complexity than the Linear Pottery culture, yet nonetheless his model may find an additional expression in the Neolithic frontier of central Europe. Instead of being an environment in which a variety of new social arrangements sprang up, the Neolithic frontier zone actually saw the replication of very similar domestic units making very similar artifacts and, by inference, having very similar patterns of social interaction. In other words, the Neolithic frontier of central Europe can be argued not to have been the scene of tremendous innovation in either material culture or social relationships.

Conclusion

The Linear Pottery colonization of central Europe meant the bringing of Near Eastern cultigens and domestic livestock to latitudes and habitats in which they had not previously been cultivated. This is indeed a stunning achievement, the importance of which cannot be diminished. Yet alongside the boldness of carving out new settlements in the forested tracts of central Europe and forever changing human society in this region, there is a clear caution visible both in functionality of architecture and pottery forms and in expression as seen in pottery decoration.

Is this a contradiction? The position taken here is that it is not. The Linear Pottery colonization was not achieved through constant local innovation but rather through a tried-and-true strategy that permitted an agricultural settlement to be established quickly and function through several generations. The houses, with their modular form and standard plans, were known quantities. Shifts in orientation and minor changes in construction details could take care of variation in local conditions. The agricultural system had enough built-in redundancy to mitigate most short-term fluctuations in yield. Variations that could not be dealt with in this way were probably mitigated socially (Bogucki 1988).

The other aspect of this highly successful adaptive system was the uniform collective identity, as expressed in the ceramic decoration, at least during the earlier phases. Although Linear Pottery settlement clusters have been characterized as "islands in the forest" (Lüning and Stehli 1989), they were certainly not insular in their social outlook. The inhabitants of these settlements did not draw symbolic boundaries through their pottery decoration until relatively late in this culture, and even then in rather open and loose ways. What factors account for this? One, almost certainly, was that these clusters needed to be exogamous, for within them everybody was probably closely related to everyone else. The constant infusion of mates from other valleys (where a similar process would be going on) would have had a certain "leveling" effect on material culture that would have produced the minor variations without any radical differences that we observe in the archaeological record.

Another reason is that a Linear Pottery community could not afford to erect rigid social boundaries around itself. Although the agricultural system was sufficiently productive to offset most calamities, there were undoubtedly times when shortfalls exceeded the ability of the local community to cope and forced it to seek external help. The Linear Pottery frontier dwellers needed to take a broad view of potential kinfolk, and explicit efforts to differentiate themselves from their neighbors could have eventually backfired when a harvest was poor.

Thus, the uniformity observed in Linear Pottery ceramics and houses, as well as that which has been argued for the subsistence and settlement system of this culture, can be seen as an important reason for the success of the initial agricultural colonization of Europe. It enabled Linear Pottery communities to go about the task of restructuring patches of the European landscape in an efficient and direct manner. Although it may appear "conservative," such a uniform technology and identity supported the radical and rapid change in subsistence and land use that laid the foundation for the development of later European prehistoric society.

References Cited

Bakels, C. C.
1978   *Four Linearbandkeramik Settlements and Their Environment: A Palaeoecological Study of Sittard, Stein, Elsloo, and Hienheim.* Analecta Praehistorica Leidensia 11. Institute of Prehistory, Leiden.
Bogucki, Peter
1988   *Forest Farmers and Stockherders: Early Agriculture and Its Consequences in North-Central Europe.* Cambridge University Press, Cambridge.
Bogucki, Peter, and Ryszard Grygiel
1993   The First Farmers of Central Europe: A Survey Article. *Journal of Field Archaeology* 20:399–426.
Coudart, Anick
1991   Social Structure and Relationships in Prehistoric Small-Scale Sedentary Societies:

The Bandkeramik Groups in Neolithic Europe. In *Between Bands and States,* edited by S. A. Gregg, pp. 395–420. Center for Archaeological Investigations, Southern Illinois University, Carbondale.
Cowie, Robert
1983   The Production and Distribution of Linear Pottery Culture Ceramics and Other Neolithic Pottery from Eastern Europe. Master's thesis, University of Sheffield.
Dennell, Robin
1985   The Hunter-Gatherer / Agricultural Frontier in Prehistoric Europe. In *The Archaeology of Frontiers and Boundaries,* edited by S. W. Green and S. M. Perlman, pp. 113–39. Academic Press, Orlando, Florida.
Gregg, Susan
1989   Palaeo-ethnobotany of the Bandkeramik phases. In *Ulm-Eggingen. Die Ausgrabungen 1982 bis 1985 in der bandkeramischen Siedlung und der mittelalterlichen Wüstung,* edited by C-J. Kind, pp. 367–99. Konrad Theiss, Stuttgart.
Grygiel, Ryszard
1978   Z problematyki oddziaływań zakarpackich we wczesnym neolicie Polski. *Acta Archaeologica Carpathica* 18:75–100.
Ilett, Mike
1983   The Early Neolithic of North-Eastern France. In *Ancient France, 6000–2000 B.C.,* edited by C. Scarre, pp. 6–33. Edinburgh University Press, Edinburgh.
Kind, Claus-Joachim, ed.
1989   *Ulm-Eggingen. Die Ausgrabungen 1982 bis 1985 in der bandkeramischen Siedlung und der mittelalterlichen Wüstung.* Konrad Theiss, Stuttgart.
Kopytoff, Igor
1987   The Internal African Frontier: The Making of African Political Culture. In *The African Frontier: The Reproduction of Traditional African Societies,* edited by Igor Kopytoff, pp. 3–84. Indiana University Press, Bloomington.
Kulczycka-Leciejewiczowa, Anna
1988   Erste Gemeinschaften der Linienbandkeramikkultur auf polnischen Boden. *Zeitschrift für Archäologie* 23:137–82.
Lüning, Jens, Ulrich Kloos, and Siegfried Albert
1989   Westliche Nachbarn der bandkeramischen Kultur: La Hoguette und Limburg. *Germania* 67:355–420.
Lüning, Jens, and Petar Stehli
1989   Die Bandkeramik in Mitteleuropa: Von der Natur- zur Kulturlandschaft. *Spektrum der Wissenschaft,* April 1989:78–88.

Meier-Arendt, Walter

1972   Zur Frage der Jüngerlinienbandkeramischen Gruppenbildung: Omalien, "Plaidter," "Kölner," "Wetterauer," und "Wormser" Typ; Hinkelstein. In *Die Anfänge des Neolithikums vom Orient bis Nordeuropa,* vol. 5a, edited by H. Schwabedissen, pp. 85–152. Böhlau Verlag, Köln.

Modderman, P. J. R.

1958/59   Die bandkeramische Siedlung von Sittard. *Palaeohistoria* 6/7:33–120.

1985   Die Bandkeramik im Graetheidegebiet. *Bericht der Römisch-Germanischen Kommission* 66:25–121.

1988   The Linear Pottery Culture: Diversity in Uniformity. *Berichten van de Rijksdienst voor het Oudheidkundig Bodemonderzoek* 38:63–139.

Odum, Eugene P.

1983   *Basic Ecology.* Saunders College Publishing, Philadelphia.

Piasets'kiy, V. K., and G. V. Okhrimenko

1990   Doslidzhennia pam'iatok kul'tury liniino-strichkovoi keramiky na Volyni. *Arkheologiia* (Kiev) 1990(4):69–82.

Quitta, Hans

1960   Zur Frage der ältesten Bandkeramik in Mitteleuropa. *Prähistorische Zeitschrift* 38:1–38, 153–89.

Turner, Frederick Jackson

1893   The Significance of the Frontier in American History. *Annual Report of the American Historical Association* 1893:190–227.

Whittle, Alasdair

1990   Radiocarbon Dating of the Linear Pottery Culture: The Contribution of Cereal and Bone Samples. *Antiquity* 64:297–302.

9

Pottery Production and the Introduction of Agriculture in Southern Scandinavia

ANNE BIRGITTE GEBAUER

Pottery production was introduced to the north European hunters, fishers, and foragers by the Linear Band Ceramic (or Linear Pottery culture) farmers. The initial adoption of ceramic production by these Mesolithic societies appears to have been purely utilitarian. As domesticates were introduced and the economy became more dependent on food production, pottery gained increasing importance for ritual purposes. With the development of a fully agrarian economy, however, the ritual significance of impressive ceramic containers declined or was replaced that of by flint and ground stone axes. This chapter focuses on two parallel developments: the introduction of pottery production and the adoption of agriculture in southern Scandinavia. The final frontier for the adoption of food production, southern Scandinavia offers a long span of time and a wealth of data for the study of the changing role of pottery in society (Price and Gebauer 1992).

In northern Europe a predominantly Mesolithic lifestyle prevailed for several centuries in areas beyond the Linear Band Ceramic (LBK) habitation (Bogucki, chapter 8; Whittle 1985:76). These Mesolithic communities included the Rhine-Meuse-Schelde group in Belgium, Swifterbant and Hazendonk in the Rhine-Meuse delta in the Netherlands, the Dümmersee group in northwest Germany, and Ellerbek/Ertebølle in the western Baltic area (Fig. 9.1). In the Rhine-Meuse delta, farming practices and pottery production were adopted simultaneously and fairly early, before 6000 B.P. (Keeley 1992:91). A ceramic Mesolithic phase with pointed-bottom vessels and Rössen influences is found in northern Germany as early as 4200–3700 b.c. (Schirnig 1979). In southern Scandinavia, pointed-bottom Ertebølle vessels and lamps appear between 3700 and 3100 b.c. (4600–3900 B.C. recalibrated; S. H. Andersen 1975:56).

The adoption of agriculture on the North European Plain appears to have been preceded by a period in which cereals were imported from farming communities rather than being locally produced. The first evidence of local farming appears everywhere in a context in which people are still heavily dependent on foraging. Hunting, fishing, and fowling remained important parts of the subsistence base; the domestic component of the economy probably served as a supplement rather than providing the main food supply (Bogucki 1988:161; Louwe Kooijmans 1987). Only after several centuries did the actual transition to a fully agrarian economy take place. The timing of these stages toward a Neolithic economy was delayed by 300 to 500 years to the north in Scandinavia.

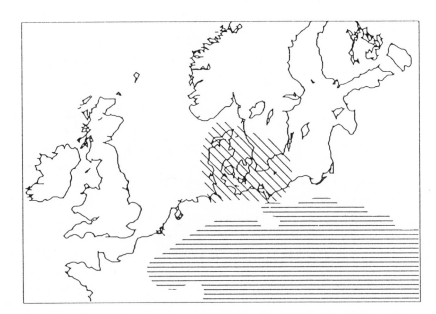

Fig. 9.1. Distribution of the Mesolithic Ertebølle groups (diagonal hatching) and the Linear Band Ceramic groups (horizontal hatching) (after Price and Gebauer 1992:Fig. 1).

The existence of food production in late Ellerbek/Ertebølle contexts from 3700 to 3100 b.c. is debated. Evidence such as carbonized grains, imprints on pottery, and traces of possible cereal pollen suggest that cereals were imported and utilized, if not locally produced (Bogucki 1988:152; Kampffmeyer 1983:129; Kolstrup 1987; Schütrumpf 1972). Remains of domestic animals have been found at a few late Ertebølle/Ellerbek sites, but their stratigraphical context has been questioned (Meurers-Balke 1983; Schwabedissen 1979, 1981).

A selective exchange of goods and information took place between the Linear Band Ceramic communities and the foraging communities on the North European Plain. Certain exotic items such as *Schuhleistkeilen* (shoe-last adzes), **T**-shaped antler axes, and bone combs were imported or copied by the foragers, along with the technology of pottery production and farming (Fischer 1982; Jennbert 1984:145). Actual import of Rössen pots from sites 80–100 kilometers away demonstrates how know-how and stylistic trends in farming communities to the south were spread to foragers on the North European Plain (Bogucki 1988:154; Fansa and Kampffmeyer 1985:109). Extensive exchange of information among the foraging communities appears to have played a critical role in the spread of pottery technology as well. A similar kind of thick-walled pottery with a pointed bottom was produced over most of the North European Plain and has also been found at Roucadour in central France and in southwestern France (Roever 1979:25; Schwabedissen 1966: 457). Interestingly, the Belgian Rhine-Meuse-Schelde group appears to have adopted both ceramics and animal husbandry from the Swifterbant group to the north rather than from the neighboring LBK (Linear Band Ceramic) communities only 40 kilometers away (Keeley 1992:90).

The **S**-profiled, pointed-bottom vessels were succeeded by Funnel Beaker pottery (Fig. 9.2). Similarities in the manufacture of Ertebølle and Funnel Beaker pottery suggest that the two groups of pottery represent different developmental stages within the same tradition of pottery production. In northern Germany and Schleswig-Holstein, a blend of pottery traditions led to the development of Dümmer pottery during the period 3700–3200 b.c. Dümmer pottery was influenced by stroke-ornamented pottery and Rössen, Bischheim, Baalberg, and Michelsberg features. This pottery appears at the Boberg sites, Rosenhof, and Siggeneben-Süd (Madsen and Petersen 1984:103; P. Nielsen 1985:117; Schindler 1962; Schirnig 1979; Schwabedissen 1979, 1981).

The early Funnel Beaker pottery found in western Scandinavia, the Volling style, was influenced by the Rössen-inspired Dümmer pottery in northwest Germany. The early Funnel Beaker pottery found in eastern Scandinavia, the Oxie style, appears to be more closely related to Baalberg, Jordanow, and early Funnel Beaker groups south of the Baltic such as Sarnowo and Pikutkowo (Lichardus 1976:53; Madsen and Petersen 1984:105; P. Nielsen 1985:117). The development of Funnel Beaker pottery on the North European Plain and in Schleswig-Holstein preceded the Scandinavian development by at least a couple of hundred

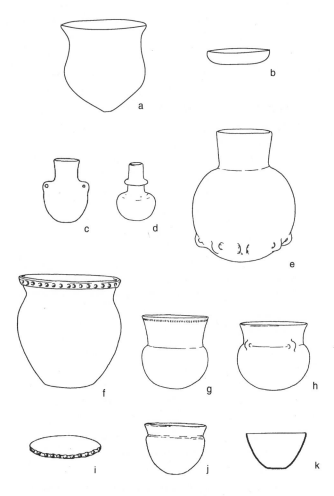

Fig. 9.2. Ertebølle (*a, b*) and early Funnel Beaker (*c–k*) vessel types. Key: *a*, pointed-bottom, **S**-shaped vessel; *b*, blubber lamp; *c*, lugged flask; *d*, collared flask; *e*, lugged jar; *f*, large funnel beaker; *g*, small funnel beaker; *h*, lugged beaker; *i*, clay disc; *j*, funnel-necked bowl; *k*, simple bowl. Clay spoons are not shown.

dling technique and the smoothing method of joining the clay coils produced pottery that was better joined together and less fragile. A smoothing finish of the surface may also have reduced porosity (Rice 1987:232).

These changes in pottery production probably required a little more work per vessel, in addition to that required for decoration (E. Nielsen 1987:114). Ertebølle and Funnel Beaker pots appear to have been fired under identical conditions in bonfires at 500–700 degrees Celsius (Hulthen 1984:202; E. Nielsen 1987:114). Both groups of pottery were most likely produced at the household level (Rice 1987:184). A few kilnlike structures found at causewayed enclosures suggest that specialized production using more controlled firings was employed to meet demands for large quantities of pottery for certain ritual purposes later in the Funnel Beaker period (N. Andersen 1977; Davidsen 1978:139, 156, figs. 22–23; Larsson 1982; Madsen and Fidel 1987). Despite arguments for the existence of specialists in other fields in Funnel Beaker society (Ebbesen 1975:272), the majority of the pottery was most likely the result of nonspecialist or semispecialist household production (Bakker and Luijten 1990:184). Evidence for local, rather than centralized, production is found in the few examples of pots' being traded (Bakker and Luijten 1990:184; Ebbesen 1975: 271; Ebbesen and Petersen 1974:103), in local idiosyncrasies in the shaping of pots, and in long-term, local stylistic traditions (Ebbesen 1978:77; Gebauer 1980:92, 1988:117). Female potters were most likely responsible for ceramic production, as is suggested by the slender finger imprints commonly found in Funnel Beaker pottery (Bakker and Luijten 1990:184; Ebbesen and Petersen 1974:104; Davidsen 1978:101). The concept of female potters is widely supported in the ethnographic literature (Balfet 1984:173; deBoer 1984; deBoer and Lathrap 1979; Krause 1984:650).

Converging trends are found in the Ertebølle pottery toward production of more Funnel Beaker–like pottery in terms of vessel wall thickness and construction method (S. H. Andersen 1975:56, 1991:30; Jennbert 1984:47; E. Nielsen 1987:114). The similarities between the two groups of pottery indicate that they represent a continuous tradition of pottery production. The decoration usually allows a distinction to be made between Ertebølle and Funnel Beaker pottery, but some of the rim designs show common features such as rows of stabs or nail and finger impressions (Jennbert 1984:55, P. Nielsen 1987:112). Beaded rims with finger and nail imprints, typical of the early Funnel Beaker Oxie group, have been found on a few Er-

years (Madsen and Petersen 1984:103). The dichotomy between east and west Scandinavia is most likely a continuation of the regional variation found during the Ertebølle period (P. Petersen 1984).

Manufacture of Ertebølle and Funnel Beaker Pottery

The introduction of Funnel Beaker pottery implied a technological improvement in pottery production. The denser and finer-grained temper in the Funnel Beaker pottery was probably related to an improvement of vessels' mechanical performance in terms of withstanding thermal shock during firing as well as cooking (Braun 1983:108; E. Nielsen 1987:109; Steponaitis 1984:113). The more pervasive use of the pad-

tebølle pots (S. H. Andersen 1975:59; P. Nielsen 1987:112; Skaarup 1983:141).

The Ertebølle and Funnel Beaker traditions of pottery production are no doubt related, and the two groups of pottery can be seen as different developmental stages within the same tradition of pottery production. Similar continuity is found in the blade technology for production of unpolished flint tools, especially within the Oxie group in eastern Scandinavia (P. Nielsen 1985:113). The implication of this continuity is that most likely the Ertebølle hunters, fishers, and gatherers were also the people responsible for the introduction of Funnel Beaker culture and food production into southern Scandinavia. Early pottery production in southern Scandinavia must be seen in the context of both the late Mesolithic Ertebølle period and the early Neolithic Funnel Beaker period.

Functional Analysis of Ertebølle Pottery

Ertebølle pottery includes two types of pots: pointed-bottom, S-shaped pots and low oval dishes usually interpreted as lamps (Mathiassen 1935; E. Nielsen 1987:115). Experiments using copies of the Ertebølle lamps as blubber lamps have produced identical charred incrustations, supporting the conventional interpretation (van Diest 1981). Only a few lamps, if any, are found in each assemblage (S. H. Andersen 1975:61; Jennbert 1984:52). Lamps disappear at the end of the Ertebølle period, and their function is not duplicated by any of the Funnel Beaker pots (E. Nielsen 1987:115).

The pointed-bottom Ertebølle vessels are found in three size classes: (1) small cups, 8–10 centimeters high and 5–6 centimeters in rim diameter; (2) medium-size vessels, 20–30 centimeters high and 10–15 centimeters in rim diameter; and (3) large vessels, 40–50 centimeters high and 15–20 centimeters in rim diameter.

The three size classes are found in the same frequencies throughout the late Ertebølle period, 3700–3100 b.c. (S. H. Andersen 1975:58). Unfortunately, no studies have been made of the possible functional differences between the size classes, perhaps owing to the high degree of fragmentation of Ertebølle pots in general.

Cooking appears to have been the primary function of Ertebølle pots, although a function as storage containers can not be excluded. At excavated settlements, potsherds are found everywhere in the cultural layers and particularly in the waste layers, but field observa-

tions on the functions of the pots are seldom possible. In the kitchen midden at Ertebølle, several large fragments of pots were found at some, but not all, of the fireplaces. In the kitchen midden at Flynderhage, five pointed bottoms from Ertebølle pots were found standing in situ in ash layers, suggesting that the pots were positioned in a layer of embers and used for cooking (Andersen and Malmros 1985:81).

A similar function is suggested by a study of Ertebølle pots at the site of Tybrind on Funen showing that food crusts were predominantly found inside the pots, especially in the bottom part. Location of the crusts likely reflects exposure to strong heat from below. Food crusts also occurred on the outside of the rim and neck section of the pots, probably remnants of food that boiled over. A build-up of the crusts was reduced by wiping the interiors of the pots; usually the crust is less than 0.1 centimeter thick (Andersen and Malmros 1985:85).

Experiments have shown that Ertebølle pots could be used for boiling foods so long as the vessel wall was saturated with starch and fat. Heating of the pots could be done externally by placing the pot in embers or internally by adding heated stones. Either way, it was important to avoid rapid temperature changes because the Ertebølle ware is fragile and sensitive to thermal shock (Andersen and Malmros 1985:81ff.).

Food crusts are commonly found on Ertebølle pots from both inland and coastal sites (Andersen and Malmros 1985:85). Several analyses—macroscopic, stable carbon isotope, and chemical—have been made of the food crusts to discover what was cooked in the Ertebølle pots. Macroscopic analysis of very solid crust formations found at Tybrind revealed fish bones and scales, mostly of cod. Traces of grass leaves suggest that either the fish were wrapped up to prevent their charring in the boiling process or else the grass leaves were added as a vegetable. Stable carbon isotope analysis of the same crusts indicates that the food cooked in these vessels was predominantly of terrestrial origin. This is surprising, considering the fish remains in the pots as well as the stable carbon isotope analysis of human bone from Ertebølle people, which shows heavy reliance on a marine diet (Tauber 1983).

Analyses of protein and amino acids in Ertebølle food crusts likewise indicate that the food cooked in the Ertebølle pots had a high vegetable content, whereas the protein content was low and cholesterol absent (Arrhenius 1984:179). Arrhenius suggested that the pots contained a nourishing porridge composed of a flour of hazelnuts and seeds along with egg whites and possibly fermented blood. The absence of the amino acid alanine indicates that cereals and milk were not used in either Ertebølle or Funnel Beaker pots from the Tybrind site, unlike what is found in later samples from the middle Neolithic Funnel Beaker period (2600–2200 b.c.) and afterward (Arrhenius 1984:179ff.).

Ertebølle cooking appears to have been based mainly on boiling or steaming of the food. Other kinds of food preparation such as drying, smoking, pickling, and fermenting may well have preceded the introduction of pottery but cannot be demonstrated in the archaeological record (Andersen and Malmros 1985: 92). Very few bones show exposure to open fire (Andersen and Malmros 1985:92). Food might have been fried over embers or heated stones, but the most common procedure was probably boiling. This could have been done by adding heated stones to containers made of stone or wood or by wrapping the food in leaves and boiling it in pits surrounded by heated stones. The introduction of pottery offered a less energy- and work-consuming way of cooking. Most importantly, the boiling process made it possible to extract the nutrition from plant foods such as roots, seeds, fruits, and greens in a more efficient manner, while preserving the juices in the meal (Andersen and Malmros 1985:92).

The Ertebølle period is named after a large kitchen midden, one of the earliest prehistoric middens to be investigated (Andersen and Johansen 1987). It is important to remember, however, that kitchen middens represent only one among several types of coastal sites within this time period. Around the Baltic Sea, no middens are found at all, owing to the brackish water. Ertebølle pottery is found at inland sites as well as coastal sites with or without middens. Pottery production is not linked in any particular way to shellfish collecting or processing of oysters.

The first pottery in southern Scandinavia was adopted for purely practical purposes such as cooking and storage; in Hayden's terms (chapter 20), it is a derivative practical pottery technology. The use of ceramic vessels increased the efficiency of food preparation in terms of work and energy consumption. Cooking in pots improved the nutritional output of meals and provided increased access to various foods. Ceramic containers became part of the technological advances that enabled complex hunters, fishers, and gatherers to exploit a wider range of resources, including species invulnerable to overexploitation such as fish and plant foods (Hayden 1992:12). No containers have been found in Mesolithic contexts in Scandinavia prior to the introduction of pottery, even at sites with superior preservation (Larsson 1990:293). The adoption of ceramics apparently was a radical change and an improvement in late Mesolithic food technology. Pottery production was introduced to Scandinavia through exchange relations between Ertebølle foragers and farming communities in continental Europe. Like the much earlier adoption of ceramics among foraging communities in the Mediterranean, this introduction reflects the importance of exchange of surplus goods for the spread of pottery production as well as agriculture (see Barnett, chapter 7).

Functions of Funnel Beaker Pottery

The introduction of Funnel Beaker pottery around 3100 b.c. (3900 B.C. recalibrated carbon dates) increased the number of pot shapes because of the employment of pottery in a wider range of domestic functions as well as for ritual purposes. The early Neolithic Funnel Beaker inventory includes nine types of pots, as opposed to only two pot shapes found in the Ertebølle period (Table 9.1). Funnel Beaker vessels can be divided into bowls, beakers/jars, and flasks according to the accessibility of the contents as defined by the relationship between height and diameter of the orifice (Braun 1983:115; Ebbesen and Mahler 1980:33; E. Nielsen 1987:115; Rice 1987:207ff.). A number of miscellaneous types of pots form a fourth group.

Beakers and jars are semiopen vessels with rim diameters equal to or smaller than their height but greater than half their height. Beakers are by far the most common category among Funnel Beaker pottery, constituting 75 percent of the pottery at one of the earliest Neolithic sites, Mosegård (Madsen and Petersen 1984:84). During the middle and late Funnel Beaker period, various double conical, barrel-shaped, and bucket-shaped vessels are included in the group of semiopen vessels in addition to the beakers. The growth of this vessel category may reflect an increased importance of storage. The beaker/jar group continues to be very common throughout the Funnel Beaker period. Beakers can be divided into three size classes similar to those of the pointed-bottom Ertebølle vessels (E. Nielsen 1987:115ff.): (1) small beakers with a rim diameter of less than 11 centimeters and a volume of up to 3/4 liter; (2) medium-size vessels with a rim diameter between 11 centimeters and 27 centimeters, holding between 3/4 liter and 10 liters; and (3) large vessels with a rim diameter larger than 27 centimeters and a volume of 10–32 liters.

Table 9.1. Functional Vessel Types of Early Scandinavian Pottery of the Ertebølle and Funnel Beaker Periods (4600–2800 B.C.)

Calib. 14C Dates	Conv. 14C Dates	Time Period	% Pots Decorated	No. Flask Shapes	No. Beaker/Jar Shapes	No. Bowl Shapes	Miscellaneous Vessels
4600	3700	Late Ertebølle	1.5		1		Blubber lamps
3900	3100	Early Funnel Beaker	30.0	3	2	2	Baking discs, clay spoons
3300	2600	Middle Funnel Beaker	30.0 84% of ritual pottery		7	11	Baking discs, pedestaled bowls, clay ladles, drums, suspension vessels, clay lids
—	2400	Late Funnel Beaker	8% rim decoration 90% finger imprints		6	6	Baking discs, suspension vessels, clay lids
2800	2200	Battle Axe Period					

The primary functions of the medium-size and large vessels of the beaker group appear to have been storage and cooking. The small funnel beakers probably served as drinking cups (Table 9.2). Their size corresponds to that of an individual serving, and their frequency of decoration suggests a serving rather than a cooking function. Medium and large vessels showed traces of food crusts and heat exposure much more frequently than did small beakers (79 percent and 88 percent, respectively, versus 31 percent of the small beakers). No difference was found between the use wear on funnel beakers and that on lugged beakers (E. Nielsen 1987:119). Food crusts appeared primarily on the inside of the upper part of the funnel beakers and lugged beakers, whereas the crusts on Ertebølle pots were found in the lower part of the pot. This difference

Table 9.2. Domestic and Ritual Functions of Early Scandinavian Pottery during the Ertebølle and Funnel Beaker Periods (4600–2800 B.C.)

Calib. 14C Dates	Conv. 14C Dates	Time Period	Domestic Functions	Elite/Funeral	Other Ritual Contexts
4600	3700	Late Ertebølle	Light cooking, storage	None	None
3900	3100	Early Funnel Beaker	Food preparation, cooking, storage, baking, drinking cups, liquid preparation and storage	Serving and drinking of liquids (flasks and cups)	Votive food deposits (cooking pots)
3300	2600	Middle Funnel Beaker	Food preparation, cooking, storage, drinking cups, baking	Food presentation and serving (pedestaled bowls, clay ladles, and open bowls), Nonelite funeral pots	Causewayed camps (food presentation and serving in open bowls)
—	2400	Late Funnel Beaker	Food preparation, cooking, storage, drinking cups, baking	Oculi bowls (skull copies?), suspension vessels, miniature domestic pots with special bottom shape and special decoration	None
2800	2200	Battle Axe Period			

may be related to the way in which pots were placed in the fire, but differences in the contents of the pots may also have played a role.

The contents of Funnel Beaker pots are largely unknown. A pig bone found in a large funnel beaker suggests that a soup or stew of pork had been cooked in the pot (Becker 1947:find no. 9; E. Nielsen 1987:118). Arrhenius's analysis of the Löddesborg pottery suggests that the same predominantly vegetable porridge was cooked in both Funnel Beaker and Ertebølle pots (Arrhenius 1984:179).

The Funnel Beaker pots with medium-size orifices —the beaker group—are the functional equivalent of the pointed-bottom Ertebølle pots. Cooking was the primary function of medium and large vessels during both time periods (E. Nielsen 1987:119). The small beakers served as drinking cups during the Funnel Beaker period, but it is not clear whether the same functional distinction exists between the small Ertebølle cups and the larger Ertebølle vessels.

A functional distinction between the three sizes of funnel beakers is supported by their distribution in domestic and ritual contexts. Medium and large vessels are dominant at the settlements (Madsen and Petersen 1984:93, fig. 22). Medium-size funnel beakers and lugged beakers, most of which had been used for cooking, dominate in ritual deposits in bogs between 3100 and 2500 b.c. (Becker 1947; E. Nielsen 1983, 1987). The deposits in bogs vary from sacrifices of individual pots, presumably with food, to evidence of large communal feastings including sacrifices of cattle and sometimes humans. Small drinking cups and flasks are the only vessels used for burial purposes during the early Neolithic (3100–2600 b.c.). Small beakers also prevail in later pottery deposits at megalithic tombs; medium-size beakers are absent, but a few large beakers, probably storage vessels, have been found (Ebbesen 1978:77; Gebauer 1980).

Bowls—the second Funnel Beaker pottery group— are defined as open vessels giving easy access to the contents because rim diameter is greater than height. During the period 3100–2600 b.c., bowls were rare, and their crude appearance suggests a function in food preparation rather than in serving; only two different shapes occur. During the middle Funnel Beaker period (2600–2400 b.c.), a wide variety of highly decorated bowls were used, especially for ceremonial purposes in relation to funerals and causewayed camps. The use of bowls for funeral purposes declined during the late Funnel Beaker period (2400–2200 b.c.).

Flasks are vessels with restricted orifices and a rim diameter equal to or smaller than half their height. This group is present only during the period from 3100 to 2600 b.c. The flask group, including lugged jars and collared and lugged flasks, was probably used for the preparation, storage, and transportation of liquids. The smaller types—the collared and lugged flasks—are often nicely decorated and may have been used in the serving of liquids.

Collared and lugged flasks occur from time to time at settlements but are especially important as funeral pottery, together with small beakers. Occasionally lugged jars were used for funeral purposes as well (S. H. Andersen 1991:49ff.). The three types of flasks and the small beakers are closely associated with elite burials in earthen long barrows and dolmens. The elite drinking ritual began a little later in eastern Denmark (2800–2630 b.c.) in relation to the construction of thousands of dolmens. The earliest Funnel Beaker burials in eastern Denmark resemble late Ertebølle burials in the absence of mounds and the composition of grave goods (E. Petersen 1974).

The group of miscellaneous types of pottery includes clay discs, clay spoons and ladles, lids, pedestaled bowls, and drums. The clay discs and spoons were used in food preparation, whereas pedestaled bowls and clay laddles served as elite funeral pottery in relation to megalithic tombs during the middle Funnel Beaker period (2600–2400 b.c.).

An extended debate has concerned the function of clay discs as plates for baking, lids for pots, plates for eating, turntables for pottery production, or stands for pots (Davidsen 1974:36). The relative small size of the discs and the perforations and decorations found on some of them suggest that a function as stands for other pots, as turntables, or as eating plates is unlikely. The unimodal distribution of the diameters of the discs, usually within the range of 11–24 centimeters, compared with the much more varied orifice sizes of TRB pottery likewise indicate that only a few of the discs could have served as lids (Davidsen 1974:37, Kjærum 1955:24). Most likely the clay discs were heated in a fire and used for baking bread. The perforations would help in pulling the warm discs out of the fire with a stick, and discs could be stacked and stored with a stick through the holes. The interpretation of discs as baking plates is further supported by their reddish color and, in several cases, by evidence of exposure to fire. The absence of a dark core indicates that the discs were fired more thoroughly than other TRB pottery, and a few finds of disc fragments have been made in fireplaces (Davidsen 1974:38).

Clay discs usually form 10–30 percent of the settlement pottery at residential sites, but it is not clear whether this number changes through time as would be expected with the increased importance of agriculture (Davidsen 1974:10). The baking function is supported by the almost total absence of clay discs at hunting stations (Skaarup 1973:134). Clay discs are also absent in ritual deposits in bogs and lakes (Davidsen 1974:10).

Clay spoons with a shape like that of modern spoons have been found at only a few sites in Scandinavia (P. Nielsen 1985:fig.7). Wooden spoons found in bogs, however, suggest that spoons may have been more widespread than it appears from the archaeological record (Troels-Smith 1960:134). The wooden spoons were found in or associated with funnel beakers, or wooden vessels (P. Nielsen 1987:118). The appearance of clay and wooden spoons suggests increased importance of the preparation and serving of food.

The Role of Pottery in Relation to the Introduction of Agriculture

The change from Ertebølle to Funnel Beaker pottery was a technological improvement increasing the performance of cooking vessels and the general resistance of vessels to mechanical stress from handling and moving. Increased ceramic production and improved technology reflect the importance of preparing, cooking, and storing food, as well as the extended use of pottery beyond the domestic sphere that is so characteristic of the Funnel Beaker period. The different functions of Funnel Beaker pottery through time are related to the transformation from a hunting, fishing, and gathering society to an agricultural society.

During the earliest Funnel Beaker period (3100–2800 b.c.), the dietary importance of domestic food sources, cereals in particular, is questionable. Evidence ranging from pollen diagrams to the absence of plowing and the very limited occurrence of harvest implements suggests a limited role for cereal growing during this time period (S. T. Andersen 1991:62; Iversen 1941; Jensen 1989; Thrane 1982, 1991:118). A mixed economy of both wild and domesticated resources persisted for several centuries after the first appearance of domesticates (Table 9.3). The local significance of wild versus domestic resources, and of stock rearing versus cereal growing, varies considerably (Madsen 1990, 1991). A definite intensification of agricultural production began around 2800 b.c. Ma-

jor forest clearings show up in the pollen diagrams, and plow marks appear under the mounds (S. T. Andersen 1991; Iversen 1941; Thrane 1982, 1991:118). However, regular sickles with heavy gloss from intensive harvesting do not appear until about 2500 b.c., or 600 years after the first appearance of domesticates. An increased number of grinding stones through time would be another indication of the importance of cereal growing, but this pattern is unknown. Cereals appear to be of little importance in the daily diet until late in the Funnel Beaker period.

The association between pots, foods, and special status is obvious at the very beginning of the Funnel Beaker period from the use of cooking pots, presumably containing food, as sacrifices in wet areas and from the use of liquid containers as elite items and funeral pottery. The new significance of food and pots was most likely related to the introduction of domesticates. As suggested by Hayden (1992:12; chapter 20), food production was likely adopted in the context of competitive feasting where labor-intensive domesticated foods were used as delicacies. The domesticated foods would demonstrate the leader's success and power to control the labor of other people. Evidence mentioned earlier, such as pollen diagrams and lack of harvest implements, suggests that cereals were not part of the staple diet for several centuries after domesticates were first introduced. But does the ceramic evidence suggest that domesticated foods initially served as delicacies rather than as staples?

New products made from cereals include flat bread baked on clay discs. Unfortunately, it is unclear whether or not the number of discs found at settlements increases through time, as would be expected with a growing dependence on cereal cultivation. However, clay discs do not appear in ceremonial contexts at funerals and ritual gatherings before about 2600 b.c., which perhaps is an indication of increased importance of bread baking at the same time the major agricultural expansion takes place.

The elite drinking ritual reflected in flasks and beakers very likely reflects the use of cereals, barley in particular, for beer production (Braidwood et al. 1953; Katz and Maytag 1991). Arguments for the importance of beer in the adoption of agriculture have been opposed by some scholars: "Did these Neolithic farmers forego the extraordinary food values of the cereals in favor of alcohol, for which they had no physiological need? Are we to believe that the foundations of Western Civilization were laid by an ill-fed people living in a perpetual state of partial intoxication?" (Mangelsdorf

Table 9.3. Economic and Cultural Changes during the Late Ertebølle and Funnel Beaker Periods in Scandinavia (4600–2800 B.C.)

Calib. ^{14}C Dates	Conv. ^{14}C Dates	Time Period	Economic and Cultural Characteristics
4600	3700	Late Ertebølle	Sedentary hunters, fishers, gatherers Coastal focus, broad-spectrum economy Cemeteries Long-distance trade, including Band Ceramic items
3900	3100	Early Funnel Beaker	First domesticates, thin-walled pottery Polished flint axes, battle axes, mace heads Copper imports Smaller, shorter-lived settlements Mix of wild and domestic resources More inland focus Elite burials in earthen long barrows and dolmens Votive food deposits and feasting at bogs Hoards and long-distance trade
3300	2600	Middle Funnel Beaker	Substantial forest clearance Agricultural expansion Larger settlements, territorial fixation Elite burials in megalithic graves Regional centers at causewayed enclosures Hoards and long-distance trade Expanded ceramic production
—	2400	Late Funnel Beaker	Fully agricultural economy Larger settlements, permanent fields and pastures Reuse of megalithic tombs Reduced ceramic production
2800	2200	Battle Axe Period	

1953:519). The Scandinavian people do not appear to have been ill-fed, and probably they were not perpetually intoxicated. It does seem likely, however, that the attraction of beer production was a means by which the elite encouraged the adoption of agriculture and the production of surpluses for ritual and political purposes. Bread and beer may very well have served as "party" foods, in accordance with the competitive feasting model, while staples came from wild resources and animal husbandry.

Interestingly, the association between flasks, beer, and elite status appears only at the beginning of the Neolithic in western Denmark. Flasks were used for funeral purposes at earthen long barrows in western Denmark during the period from 3100 to 2800 b.c. (Kristensen 1991:72). In eastern Denmark, the main evidence of ideological change at the time of the transi-tion to agriculture is deposits of cooking pots and food in wet areas. These differences might suggest that a more competitive, aggrandizing system was at work in western Denmark while a more gradual process, with emphasis on communal rituals, took place toward the east. The eastern distribution of a few examples of cereals in Ertebølle context is perhaps another reflection of a more gradual transition to the Neolithic in this region.

The Landnamm phase (Iversen 1941:1), from 2800 to 2500 b.c., appears to have been a period not only of agricultural intensification but also of territorial claims and competition for status and power. Settlements become more permanent, with substantial cultural layers. At the same time, enormous efforts were invested in monumental structures for the purposes of regional gatherings and the death cult. The largest of the bog sacrifices appear to have taken place during this period, but the function of these ceremonies seems to have been replaced by that of the causewayed camps. A pattern of local territories can be detected from the distribution of megalithic tombs, bog sites, and causewayed camps; this territorial fixation extended throughout the remainder of the TRB period (N. Andersen 1981, Madsen 1982:203; Skaarup 1985:359). The presence of a social elite is clear from the burial monuments, but a social hierarchy is not obvious. Among the few primary burials preserved, both genders and all age groups are represented without any clear status differentiation indicated by the grave goods.

During this period of agricultural intensification and social instability, an immense surplus production was invested in rituals as a way of managing society. At a local level, surplus was invested in monumental burials and funeral rites, and at a regional level, in periodical constructions of causewayed camps. Rituals were apparently related to competition for territories, control over resources, and social status among lineages and perhaps individuals. Besides the monumental constructions, a key element in the rituals was vast consumption of food and pottery in continuation of the early Funnel Beaker tradition, but at a much larger scale.

Production of pottery for ritual purposes was radically increased in terms of sheer numbers, variation of pot shapes, and degree of decoration. Ritual pottery included primarily open-type vessels such as bowls and carinated vessels suited for the presentation and serving of food. Unlike before, cooking pots were excluded from rituals. Pottery in the form of pedestaled bowls and clay spoons served as elite items restricted to people entitled to a megalithic burial. The decoration of these pots appears to reflect the local tradition of the lineage responsible for erecting a particular tomb or group of tombs (Gebauer 1988:116; Hårdh 1986:82).

Pottery styles were used in communicating social affiliation both at a local lineage level and at a regional level. Only broad regional style variation existed during the early Funnel Beaker period; during the Landnamm phase, regional style zones contracted and variation appeared at the local level, probably as an expression of the competitive environment.

The enormous consumption of pottery at megalithic funerals and at causewayed camps suggests that the importance of pottery was related both to its role as container of food and to its role as expression of social wealth. The use of large numbers (84 percent) of highly decorated pots at various ceremonies in itself reflects

a considerable expenditure of labor (Ebbesen 1975: 127). Ritual pottery was specially produced for the feasting ceremonies at the causewayed camps using more sophisticated methods of firing than those normally found at settlements. The deliberate smashing of pottery both at megalithic tombs and at causewayed camps reflects destruction of social wealth and supports the inference that high status pertained to the organizing person or lineage (N. Andersen 1977, 1988; Ebbesen 1975, 1978, 1979; Gebauer 1979, 1980, 1988; Hårdh 1986, 1990; Kjærum 1967, 1970; Larsson 1982; Madsen 1988; Strömberg 1971).

Around the time cereal cultivation appears to become more substantial (ca. 2400 b.c.), the surplus invested in rituals starts to drop. Monument construction is reduced and gradually stops. Production of pottery for ritual purposes declines in quantity, quality, and degree of variation and decoration. In the western areas, storage vessels in part replace ritual pottery (Gebauer 1979:143); in the east, oculi bowls and suspension vessels may have served as ceremonial objects rather than as food containers in the funeral rites.

During the late Funnel Beaker period (2400–2200 b.c.), village agglomerations grew bigger. No clear status differentiation is present, but apparently a more stable social system evolved, rendering overt power displays superfluous. Rituals were greatly reduced; only funeral ceremonies and a few deposits in wet areas took place. A much reduced production of funeral pottery continued. In the west, a diminished version of settlement pottery appears to have been used as food containers at burials. In some areas, different kinds of axes replaced pottery for funeral purposes. In the east, funeral pottery has more the appearance of ceremonial objects. The link between food production and the ritual function of pottery had almost disappeared.

Pottery production was initially adopted for practical purposes during the Mesolithic in southern Scandinavia. The use of ceramic containers for cooking and storage represented a technological improvement in terms of food processing, and it increased the accessibility of a wider range of resources. The basic production of pottery remained linked to the processing, cooking, storing, and serving of food. Pottery gained increasing importance as ritual objects, however, during the initial phase of adoption of domesticates and later during the actual agricultural expansion. The role of pottery as food container provided an inextricable linkage between pots and food. Pottery became associated with wealth in terms of abundance of food, control over resources, and the power of certain people to accumulate a substantial production surplus. The amount and the quality of pottery used in ritual contexts served as an expression of social wealth and political power in Funnel Beaker society, until agriculture had become the established way of living.

The relationship between elaborate pottery production and a period of agricultural expansion is not unique to the Funnel Beaker period. A similar high-quality pottery production is found during the Linear Band Ceramic period. Within Scandinavia, the next period of major agricultural expansion during the pre-Roman and Roman Iron Age is once again a period of vast expansion in types of pots, increased proportion of decorated pottery, and better quality of pottery. During periods of agricultural expansion, the capacity for food production and accumulations of surplus became a measure of social status. Display and consumption of food and pottery were vehicles in the competition for status in society.

References Cited

Andersen, N. H.
1977   Sarup. Keramikgruber fra to bebyggelsesfaser. *Kuml* 1976:11–46.
1981   Befæstede neolitiske anlæg og deres baggrund. *Kuml* 1980:63–103.
1988   The Neolithic Causewayed Enclosures at Sarup, on Southwest Funen, Denmark. In *Enclosures and Defenses in the Neolithic of Western Europe,* edited by C. Burgess, P. Topping, C. Morrant, and M. Maddison, pp. 337–63. British Archaeological Reports, International Series 403, Oxford.

Andersen, S. H.
1975   Ringkloster, en jysk indlandsboplads med Ertebøllekultur. *Kuml* 11–108.
1991   Norsminde: A "Køkkenmødding" with Late Mesolithic and Early Neolithic Occupation. *Journal of Danish Archaeology* 8:13–40.

Andersen, S. H., and E. Johansen
1987   Ertebølle Revisited. *Journal of Danish Archaeology* 5:31–61.

Andersen, S. H., and C. Malmros
1985   Madskorper på Ertebøllekar fra Tybrind Vig. *Aarbøger for Nordisk Oldkyndighed og Historie* 1984:78–95.

Andersen, S. T.
1991   Pollen Spectra from Two Early Neolithic Lugged Jars in the Long Barrow at Bjørns-holm, Denmark. *Journal of Danish Archaeology* 9:59–63.

Arrhenius, B.
1984   Analysrapport Gällande Organiskt Material på Keramikskärvor funna i Löddesborg, Löddeköpinge Sn, Skåne. In *Den Produktiva Gåvan. Tradition och innovation i Sydskandinavian för omkring 5300 år sedan,* edited by K. Jennbert, pp. 174–81. Acta Archaeologica Lundensia Series in 4. No. 16.

Bakker, J. A., and H. Luijten
1990   "Service Sets" and Other "Similarity Groups" in Western TRB Pottery. In *La Bretagne et l'Europe prehistorique. Memoire en hommage a Pierre Rebaud Giot.* Revue Archéologie Ouest, Supplément no. 2:173–87.

Balfet, H.
1984   Methods of Formation and the Shape of Pottery. In *The Many Dimensions of Pottery: Ceramics in Archaeology and Anthropology,* edited by S. E. van der Leeuw and A. C. Pritchard, pp. 171–98. University of Amsterdam, Amsterdam.

Becker, C. J.
1947   Mosefundne Lerkar fra Yngre Stenalder. Studier over Tragtbægerkulturen i Danmark. *Aarbøger for Nordisk Oldkyndighed og Historie* 1947:5–318.

Bogucki, P. I.
1988   *Forest Farmers and Stockherders: Early Agriculture and Its Consequences in North Central Europe.* New Studies in Archaeology. Cambridge University Press, Cambridge.

Braidwood, R. J., et al.
1953   Symposium: Did Man Once Live by Beer Alone? *American Anthropologist* 55:515–26.

Braun, D. P.
1983   Pots as Tools. In *Archaeological Hammers and Theories,* edited by J. A. Moore and A. S. Keene, pp. 108–34. Academic Press, Orlando, Florida.

Davidsen, K.
1974   Neolitiske Lerskiver belyst af danske fund. *Aarbøger for Nordisk Oldkyndighed og Historie, 1973,* pp. 5–72.
1978   *The Final TRB Culture in Denmark: A Settlement Study.* Arkæologiske Studier vol. 5. Akademisk Forlag, Copenhagen.

deBoer, W. R.
1984   The Last Pottery Show: System and Sense in Ceramic Studies. In *The Many Dimensions of Pottery: Ceramics in Archaeology and Anthropology,* edited by S. E. van der Leeuw and A. C. Pritchard, pp. 527–68. University of Amsterdam, Amsterdam.

deBoer, W. R., and D. W. Lathrap
1979   The Making and Breaking of Shipibo-Conibo
        Ceramics. In *Ethnoarchaeology: Implications of
        Ethnography for Archaeology,* edited by C.
        Kramer, pp. 102–38. Columbia University
        Press, New York.

Ebbesen, K.
1975   *Die jüngere Trichterbecherkultur auf den dänis-
        chen Inseln.* Arkæologiske Studier vol. 2.
        Akademisk Forlag, Copenhagen.
1978   *Tragtbægerkultur i Nordjylland.* Nordiske
        Fortidsminder 5, Copenhagen.
1979   *Stordyssen i Vedsted. Studier over Tragtbæger-
        kulturen i Sønderjylland.* Arkæologiske Studier
        vol. 6. Akademisk Forlag, Copenhagen.

Ebbesen, K., and D. Mahler
1980   Virum. Et tidligneolitisk bopladsfund. *Aar-
        bøger for Nordisk Oldkyndighed og Historie, 1979,*
        pp. 11–61.

Ebbesen, K., and E. B. Petersen
1974   Fuglebæksbanken. En jættestue på Stevns.
        Aarbøger for Nordisk Oldkyndighed og Historie
        1974:73–106.

Fansa, M., and U. Kampffmeyer
1985   Vom Jäger und Sammler zum Ackerbauern.
        In *Ausgrabungen in Niedersachen, Arkäologische
        Denkmalpflege 1979–1984,* edited by K.
        Wilhelmi, pp. 108–11. Konrad Theiss,
        Stutgart.

Fischer, A.
1982   Trade in Danubian Shaft-Hole Axes and the
        Introduction of Neolithic Economy in Den-
        mark. *Journal of Danish Archaeology* 1:7–12.

Gebauer, A. B.
1979   Mellemneolitisk Tragtbægerkultur i Syd-
        vestjylland. En analyse af keramikken.
        Kuml 1978:117–57.
1980   En analyse af en neolitisk kultur eller
        kulturperiode på grundlag af et udvalgt
        materiale indenfor et nærmere defineret
        område. Ph.D. thesis, Århus University.
1988   Stylistic variation in the pottery of the Funnel
        Beaker Culture. In *Multivariate Archaeology:
        Numerical Approaches in Scandinavian Ar-
        chaeology,* edited by T. Madsen, pp. 91–117.
        Jutland Archaeological Society Publications,
        Århus.

Hayden, B.
1992   Contrasting Expectations in Theories of Do-
        mestication. In *Transitions to Agriculture in
        Prehistory.* edited by A. B. Gebauer and T. D.
        Price, pp. 11–19. Prehistory Press, Madison,
        Wisconsin.

Hulthen, B.
1984   Teknologisk Undersökning av Keramiska
        Artefakter från Löddesborg, Löddeköpinge

Sn, Skåne. In *Den Produktiva Gåvan. Tradition
och innovation i Sydskandinavian för omkring
5300 år sedan.* edited by K. Jennbert, pp. 201–
206. Acta Lundensia Series in 4. No. 16.

Hårdh, B.
1986   *Ceramic Decoration and Social Organization:
        Regional Variation Seen in Material from South-
        Swedish Passage-Graves.* Scripta Minora.
        Studier utgivna av Kungl. Humanistiska
        Vetenskabssamfundet i Lund 1985–86:1–95.
1990   *Patterns of Deposition and Settlement: Studies on
        the Megalithic Tombs of West Scania.* Scripta
        Minora. Studier utgivna av Kungl. Human-
        istiska Vetenskabssamfundet i Lund 1988–
        89:2–107.

Iversen, J.
1941   Landnam i Danmarks stenalder. En pol-
        lenanalytisk undersøgelse over det første
        landbrugs indvirkning paa vegetation-
        sudviklingen. *Danmarks Geologiske
        Undersøgelser,* series II, no. 66, pp. 1–68.
        Copenhagen.

Jennbert, K., ed.
1984   *Den Produktiva Gåvan. Tradition och innovation i
        Sydskandinavian för omkring 5300 år sedan.* Acta
        Lundensia Series in 4. No. 16.

Jensen, H. J. J.
1989   Plant Harvesting and Processing with Flint
        Implements in the Danish Stone Age: A View
        from the Microscope. *Acta Archaeologica*
        59:131–42.

Kampffmeyer, U.
1983   Die neolitische Siedlungsplatz Hüde I a
        Dümmer. In *Frühe Bauernkulturen in Nie-
        dersachen,* edited by G. Wegner, pp. 119–34.
        Staatliches Museum für Naturkunde und
        Vorgeschichte, Oldenburg.

Katz, S. H., and F. Maytag
1991   Brewing an Ancient Beer. *Archaeology,* July,
        pp. 24–33.

Keeley, L. H.
1992   The Introduction of Agriculture to the West-
        ern North European Plain. In *Transitions to
        Agriculture in Prehistory.* edited by A. B.
        Gebauer and T. D. Price, pp. 81–95.
        Prehistory Press, Madison, Wisconsin.

Kjærum, P.
1955   Tempelhus fra Stenalderen. *Kuml* 1955:7–35.
1967   The Chronology of the Passage Graves in
        Jutland. *Palaeohistoria* 12.
1970   Jættestuen Jordhøj. *Kuml* 1969:9–66.

Kolstrup, E.
1987   Tidligt landbrug. *Skalk* 5:9–12.

Krause, R. A.
1984   Modelling the Making of Pots: An Ethno-
        archaeological Approach. In *The Many*

Dimensions of Pottery: Ceramics in Archaeology and Anthropology, edited by S. E. van der Leeuw and A. C. Pritchard, pp. 615–98. University of Amsterdam, Amsterdam.

Kristensen, I. K.
1991   Storgård IV: An Early Neolithic Long Barrow near Fjelsø, North Jutland. *Journal of Danish Archaeology* 8:72–88.

Larsson, L.
1982   A Causewayed Enclosure and a Site with Valby Pottery at Stävie, Western Scania. *Meddelanden från Lunds Universitets Historiska Museum* 1981–82. New series vol. 4, pp. 65–107.
1990   The Mesolithic of Southern Scandinavia. *Journal of World Prehistory* 4(3):257–309.

Lichardus, J.
1976   *Rössen-Gatersleben-Baalberg.* Saarbrücker Beitrage zur Altumskunde. Rudolf Habelt Verlag GMBH, Bonn.

Louwe Kooijmans, L. P.
1987   Neolithic Settlement and Subsistence in the Wetlands of the Rhine/Meuse Delta. In *European Wetlands in Prehistory,* edited by J. Coles and A. Lawson, pp. 227–51. Oxford University Press, Oxford.

Madsen, B., and R. Fidel
1987   Store Brokhøj, en foreløbig meddelelse om en ny anlægsform fra yngre stenalder. In *Arkæologiske Fund. Kulturhistorisk Museum, Randers. Virksomhed og resultater,* edited by B. Madsen and A. Berg, pp. 53–61. Kulturhistorisk Museum, Randers, Denmark.

Madsen, T.
1982   Settlement Systems of Early Agricultural Societies in East Jutland: A Regional Study of Change. *Journal of Anthropological Archaeology* 1:197–236.
1988   Causewayed Enclosures in South Scandinavia. In *Enclosures and Defenses in the Neolithic of Western Europe,* edited by C. Burgess, P. Topping, C. Morrant, and M. Maddison, pp. 301–36. British Archaeological Reports, International Series 403, Oxford.
1990   Changing Patterns of Land Use in the TRB Culture of South Scandinavia. In *Die Trichterbecherkultur. Neue Forschungen und Hypothesen. Material des Internationalen Symposiums Dymaczewo* (September 20–24, 1988, vol. 1), edited by D. Jankowska, pp. 27–41. Poznan, Poland.
1991   The Social Structure of Early Neolithic Society in South Scandinavia. In *Die Kupferzeit als historische Epoche; Symposium Saarbrücken und Otzenhausen* (November 6–13, 1988), edited by J. Lichardus, pp. 489–96.

Saarbrücker Beiträge zur Altertumskunde 55. Bonn.

Madsen, T., and J. E. Petersen
1984   Tidligneolitiske anlæg ved Mosegården. Regionale og kronologiske forskelle i tidligneolitikum. *Kuml* 1982–83:61–120.

Mangelsdorf, P. C.
1953   Comment in Symposium: Did Man Once Live by Beer Alone? by R. J. Braidwood et al. *American Anthropologist* 55:519–24.

Mathiassen, T.
1935   Blubber Lamps in the Ertebølle Culture? *Acta Archaeologica* 6:139–52.

Meurers-Balke, J.
1983   Siggeneben-Süd. Ein Fundplatz der frühen Trichterbecherkultur an der holsteinischen Ostseeküste. *Offa-Bücher* 50. Neumünster.

Nielsen, E. K.
1983   Tidligneolitiske Keramikfund. Ph.D. thesis, Copenhagen University.
1987   Ertebølle and Funnel Beaker Pots as Tools: On Traces of Production Techniques and Use. *Acta Archaeologica* 57:107–20.

Nielsen, P. O.
1985   De første bønder. Nye fund fra den tidligste Tragtbægerkultur ved Sigersted. *Aarbøger for Nordisk Oldkyndighed og Historie* 1984:96–126.
1987   The Beginning of the Neolithic: Assimilation or Complex Change? *Journal of Danish Prehistory* 5:240–43.

Petersen, E. B.
1974   Gravene ved Dragsholm. Fra jægere til bønder for 6000 år siden. *Nationalmuseets Arbejdsmark* 1974:112–20.

Petersen, P. V.
1984   Chronological and Regional Variation in the Late Mesolithic of Eastern Denmark. *Journal of Danish Archaeology* 3:7–18.

Price, T. D., and A. B. Gebauer
1992   The Final Frontier: First Farmers in Northern Europe. In *Transitions to Agriculture in Prehistory.* edited by A. B. Gebauer and T. D. Price, pp. 97–116. Prehistory Press, Madison, Wisconsin.

Rice, P.
1987   *Pottery Analysis: A Sourcebook.* University of Chicago Press, Chicago.

Roever, J. P. de
1979   The Pottery from Swifterbant: Dutch Ertebølle? *Helinium* 19:13–36.

Schindler, R.
1962   Rössener Elemente im Boberg Neolitikum. *Germania* 40:341–44. Mainz.

Schirnig, H.
1979   Die Siedlung Hüde I am Dümmer. In

Grosssteingräber in Niedersachen, edited
by H. Schirnig, pp. 239–41.

Schütrumpf, R.

1972   Stratigrahie und pollenanalytische Ergebnisse
der Ausgrabung des Ellerbek-zeitlische
Wohnplatzes Rosenhof (Ostholstein).
Arkäologisches Korrespondenzblatt 2:9–16.

Schwabedissen, H.

1966   Ein horizontierter "Breitkeil" aus Satrup und
die mannigfachen Kulturverbindungen des
beginnenden Neolitikums im Norden und
Nordwesten. *Palaeohistoria* 12:409–68.

1979   Der Begin des Neolithikums in nord-
westlichen Deutschland. In *Grosssteingräber in Niedersachen,* edited by H.
Schirnig, pp. 203–22.

1981   Ertebölle/Ellerbek: Mesolithikum oder
Neolithikum? *Veröff. Potsdam* 14/15. Potsdam.

Skaarup, J.

1973   *Hesselø-Sølager. Jagdstationen der süd-
skandinavischen Trichterbecherkultur.*
Aakæologiske Studier vol. 1. Akademisk
Forlag, Copenhagen.

1983   Submarine Stenalderbopladser i Det Sydfyn-
ske øhav. *Antikvariske Studier* 6:137–61.

1985   *Yngre Stenalder på øerne syd for Fyn.*
Meddelelser fra Langelands Museum,
Rudkøbing, Denmark.

Steponaitis, V. P.

1984   Technological Studies of Prehistoric Pottery
from Alabama: Physical Properties and Vessel
Function. In *The Many Dimensions of Pottery:
Ceramics in Archaeology and Anthropology,*
edited by S. E. van der Leeuw and A. C.
Pritchard, pp. 79–122. University of
Amsterdam, Amsterdam.

Strömberg, M.

1971   *Die Megalithgräber von Hagestad.* Acta
Archaeologica Lundensia 8. Lund.

Tauber, H.

1983 ^{14}C Dating of Human Beings in Relation to
Dietary Habits. *PACT* 8:365–75.

Thrane, H.

1982   Dyrkningsspor fra yngre stenalder i Danmark.
Skrifter fra Historisk Institut, Odense Universitet
30:20–28.

1991   Danish Plough-Marks from the Neolithic and
Bronze Age. *Journal of Danish Archaeology*
9:111–25.

Troels-Smith, J.

1960   En Elmetræs-Bue fra Aamosen og andre
Træsager fra Tidlig-Neolitisk Tid. *Aarbøger for
Nordisk Oldkyndighed og Historie* 1959:91–145.

van Diest, H.

1981   Zur Frage der "Lampen" nach den
Ausgrabungsfunden von Rosenhof
(OstHolstein). *Archäologisches Kor-
respondenzblatt* 11:301–14. Mainz.

Whittle, A.

1985   *Neolithic Europe: A Survey.* Cambridge
University Press, Cambridge.

The New World

10

Early Pottery in the Amazon

Twenty Years of Scholarly Obscurity

A. C. ROOSEVELT

Influential scholars have posited that Amazonia was occupied mainly by dispersed, small-scale societies in ancient times because of the resource poverty of the tropical rain forest habitat. Environmental factors are said to have precluded permanent settlement, population growth, and cultural complexity. Important cultural innovations such as pottery, agriculture, and complex social organization were hypothesized to have spread to the lowlands from centers of civilization in the Andes and Mesoamerica and then deteriorated in the tropical environment (Jennings 1964; Meggers 1954, 1971, 1985; Steward 1946–50). The archaeological evidence from Amazonia, however, reveals a long, complex prehistoric occupation that does not fit this picture of human cultural development in the Americas. One finding is that the age of pottery began in Amazonia about 7,500 years ago, more than 1,500 years earlier than elsewhere in the hemisphere.

Although commonly stereotyped as a resource-poor habitat with ancient, leached soils (Goodland and Irwin 1975), Amazonia possesses sizable areas of high-nutrient recent alluvial soils as well as *terra firme* soils formed on limestone or volcanic rocks (Franzinelli and Latrubesse 1993), which would not have presented severe limitations to human occupation.[1] Researchers of the period 1830–1945 uncovered evidence for diverse preceramic and ceramic-stage occupations, including rock art, numerous large, deeply stratified middens, extensive monumental earthworks, elaborate, diverse artifacts, well-preserved ancient plant and animal remains, and human skeletons (Derby 1879; Ferreira Penna 1876; Hartt 1871, 1885; Nimuendaju 1949; Roosevelt 1991). Of particular interest at the time were the large Amazonian pottery shell mounds, which were assessed as early Holocene fishing camps on the basis of geological, biological, and cultural evidence.

This early research was later dismissed as prescientific by pioneering professional archaeologists Betty Meggers and Clifford Evans of the Smithsonian Institution. In their mid-century writings they outlined a culture history in which people from the Andes brought pottery and complex culture into the Amazon in late prehistoric times (Evans and Meggers 1960; Meggers and Evans 1957). Their view of Amazonia, developed before radiocarbon dating had been applied in the Amazon, was later critiqued by Donald Lathrap and his students on environmental and archaeological grounds (Brochado and Lathrap 1982; Lathrap 1970), but it has prevailed until recently, owing to a lack of public dissemination of chronological evidence for early pottery in Amazonian sites. Since the early 1970s, sites in eastern Amazonia have consistently produced numerous radiocarbon dates for pottery that are as old as or older than those from other parts of the Americas.

Early Pottery in Ecuador and Colombia

By the 1960s, the emerging radiocarbon dates from South America had made it apparent that several shell-midden sites along coasts and estuaries of the tropical lowlands of Ecuador and Colombia in northwestern South America had pottery starting in the early fourth millennium b.p., making it the earliest pottery in the Americas at the time. The majority of sherds of these early pottery styles were sand tempered, but a small proportion of the Colombian undecorated pottery was fiber tempered. Although secondary sources on the Colombian estuarine pottery commonly refer to the early pottery as fiber tempered, most of the sherds are sand tempered, and all the decorated sherds are sand tempered, according to the site reports (Reichel-Dolmatoff 1965, 1985). By the 1970s, the dates for the early Colombian and Ecuadorian pottery had been generally accepted by archaeologists as valid, despite the facts that there were only a few dates, many of the dates were on shell, which can give unreliable dates, and none of the pottery itself had been directly dated.

Meggers and Evans, who had excavated early Ecuadorian pottery, hypothesized that knowledge of the craft had been brought to South America by ship-wrecked fishermen from Japan (Meggers, Evans, and Estrada 1965), which then as now had the earliest pottery in the world, between 12,000 and 10,000 years old (Aikens, chapter 2). (There is a possibility that earlier Japanese pottery, between 14,000 and 12,000 years old, was incorrectly dated through laboratory error; Pamela Vandiver, personal communication, 1993.) Their opponent Donald Lathrap, in contrast, argued that pottery had been brought in during the late Pleistocene, around 13,000 years ago, by root-cultivating migrants from Africa (Lathrap 1977).

Early Pottery in Eastern South America

For the most part left out of these discussions of early pottery were the many pottery shell mounds of eastern South America. Nineteenth- and early twentieth-century scholars had excavated several of the large pottery-age shell middens in the Brazilian Amazon and British Guiana and had hypothesized that the mounds were very ancient, possibly predating later agricultural

peoples (Ferreira Penna 1876; Hartt 1885; Verrill 1918). In the 1950s Meggers and Evans themselves excavated at shell middens in British Guiana but concluded that they must be campsites of late prehistoric hunter-gatherers living side by side with more advanced pottery-using peoples (Evans and Meggers 1960). They did not test this theory with radiocarbon dating, however, stating that the mounds lacked materials suitable for dating, although the mounds contained the same materials that have been dated at other sites, namely, charcoal, shell, bone, and pottery.

In the 1970s and early 1980s, seven pottery shell mounds in eastern South America produced 31 radiocarbon dates between about 4,000 and 6,000 years ago for the Mina culture in Brazil and the Alaka culture in Guyana (Simoes 1981; Williams 1981; and documents in the Smithsonian Archives).[2] This date series (Table 10.1), run by the Smithsonian Radiocarbon Laboratory, now defunct, is still the longest series available for South America; remarkably, it overlaps with the dates for the Ecuadorian and Colombian early pottery and extends back 500 to 1,000 years earlier.

Having the earliest known American pottery in tropical lowlands at the eastern edge of South America fit neither the Japanese fishermen theory nor the Andean invasion theory but was consonant with independent invention or Lathrap's African origins hypothesis. The fact that dates on shell can be too early because of the incorporation by the shellfish of early carbon from limestone did not explain the early Amazonian dates, because the dates were run on numerous charcoal samples as well as on shell samples. The possibility that later pottery had become mixed with preceramic shells or charcoal was not viable either, because the shell temper actually in the sherds also gave early dates. The radiocarbon dates were consistent, regardless of the material dated.

MINA CULTURE, BRAZIL

The first culture to be dated, the Mina pottery shell mound phase, is found on the south shore of the mouth of the Amazon in an estuarine zone called the Salgado. The culture gets its name from the use of the shell mounds as mines for lime since the European conquest.

Brazilian archaeologists associated with Meggers and Evans excavated the mounds in the 1960s and found pottery associated with shell, fish bone, charcoal, and human bones in the strata of the shell mounds. The secondary literature usually incorrectly refers to this early pottery from eastern Brazil as exclusively

Table 10.1. Early Pottery-Age Radiocarbon Dates from Shell Mounds at the Mouth of the Amazon, Eastern Para, Brazil, and Coastal Guyana

Lab No.	Date	Material	Excavation Depth	Uncalibrated Date b.p.	Date b.c.

Sites of the Mina Phase, Para, Brazil

PONTA DAS PEDRAS

Lab No.	Date	Material	Excavation Depth	Uncalibrated Date b.p.	Date b.c.
SI1030	1972	Charcoal	40–60	4500 ± 90	2550
SI1031	1972	Charcoal	60–80	4090 ± 95	2140
GX2474	—	Charcoal	80–100	3490 ± 195	1540

PORTA DA MINA

Lab No.	Date	Material	Excavation Depth	Uncalibrated Date b.p.	Date b.c.
GX2472	—	Charcoal	120–140	5115 ± 195	3165
SI1035	1972	Charcoal	60–80	4610 ± 55	2660
SI1036	1972	Charcoal	180–200	5070 ± 95	3120
SI1037	1972	Charcoal	220–240	4750 ± 65	2800
SI1038	—	Charcoal	280–300	5045 ± 95	3095
SI2543	1975	Shells	cut 2, 60–80	4740 ± 80	2790
SI2544	1975	Shell temper	cut 2, 60–80	4380 ± 80	2430
SI2545	1976	Shells	180–200	4695 ± 80	2745
SI2546	1975	Shell temper	cut 2, 180–200	5050 ± 85	3100

SAMBAQUI DE URUA

Lab No.	Date	Material	Excavation Depth	Uncalibrated Date b.p.	Date b.c.
SI1034	1972	Charcoal	200–220	5570 ± 125	3620

Sites of the Alaka Phase, Guyana

BARAMBINA MOUND

Lab No.	Date	Material	Excavation Depth	Uncalibrated Date b.p.	Date b.c.
SI4332	1980	Charcoal	Cut C-6 c. 35	4115 ± 50	2165
SI4333	1980	Charcoal	Cut C-11 c. 65	5965 ± 50	4015
SI5741	1982	Peat	Cut 1 #64 40–60	5065 ± 70	3115
SI5742	1982	Peat	Cut 1 #65 65–80	4525 ± 75	2575
SI5743	—	Peat	Cut 1 #66 100–120	5460 ± 65	3510

MABARUMA/SEBA CREEK SITE

Lab No.	Date	Material	Excavation Depth	Uncalibrated Date b.p.	Date b.c.
SI5448	1982	Peat	Cut 2, Level A 83–100	4325 ± 50	2375
SI5449	1982	Peat	Cut 2 Level B 70–82	3945 ± 50	1995
SI5451	1982	Peat	Cut 2 Level X 100–120	5455 ± 55	3505

HOSOSORO CREEK SITE

Lab No.	Date	Material	Excavation Depth	Uncalibrated Date b.p.	Date b.c.
SI6635	1984	Peat	Cut 3 #67 c. 60	3185 ± 65	1235
SI6637A	1984	Peat	Cut 3 #69 c. 90	3690 ± 90	1740

(continued)

Table 10.1. (*Continued*)

Lab No.	Date	Material	Excavation Depth	Uncalibrated Date b.p.	Date b.c.
SI6637B	1984	Shells	Cut 3 #69 c. 90	3350 ± 50	1400
SI6638A	1984	Peat	Cut 2 #70 c. 110	3975 ± 45	2025
SI6638B	1984	Shells	Cut 2 #70 c. 110	3115 ± 65	1165
SI6639C	1984	Peat, shells	Cut 2 #71 c. 120	3390 ± 55	1440
SI6639B	1984	Peat	Cut 2 #71 c. 120	3385 ± 60	1435
SI6639A	1984	Shells	Cut 2 #71 c. 120	3385 ± 85	1435
KAKAKABURI					
SI7019	1986	Charcoal	Cut 75 c. 90	4890 ± 75	2940
SI7020	1986	Charcoal	Cut 76 c. 100	4215 ± 70	2265

Note: Previously unpublished dates are shown in boldface. All the dated samples in this list were recorded as having been excavated from soil layers with pottery sherds or from peat layers that the excavator associated with the early pottery-bearing layers. The sources of the published dates are Simoes (1981) and Williams (1981). The original lab records for the unpublished dates in the list can be found in the Radiocarbon Laboratory data forms and excavation records in the Smithsonian Anthropology Archives, No. 87-035, Box 7-8, 9-10, Record Unit 387.

shell tempered, but sand-tempered pottery is also present in all levels and all sites (Simoes 1981). The shell mound pottery is described as plain, with simple bowl shapes.

Thirteen radiocarbon dates were run on charcoal or shells associated with pottery sherds and on shell temper in pottery sherds from three Mina sites: Ponta das Pedras, Porto da Mina, and Sambagui de Urua. That all the dated samples were from pottery-bearing layers of the sites is made clear in the Smithsonian sample submission forms filled out by Clifford Evans in May 1970 and on January 26, 1972, which state "assoc. with sherds, shell, and animal bones." Evans also wrote in each of the 1970 submission forms that "this and several other shell middens from north coast near mouth of Amazon dug by Simoes are very important to date the ceramic bearing shell middens of north and see if each midden was occupied at about the same time or if they moved from midden to midden and the population was never large." In the 1972 forms he wrote that it was "important to date these shell middens on North Coast of Brazil just south of mouth of Amazon for they have pottery in them and appear to be recent in occupation compared to all the shell middens of the south coast of Brazil."

To the archaeologists' and laboratory scientists' great surprise, the 13 dates on charcoal, shell, and pottery temper ran from 5,570 to 3,490 years ago, with the earliest dates coming from the lower levels, some

200–300 cm deep in the mounds (Table 10.1). (No mound was dug to sterile, according to the publications and Smithsonian records.) After the first few dates had been run, Evans wrote a memo on February 17, 1975, to Robert Stuckenrath requesting that more samples be run to check the early dates: "The pottery is important because it could be some of the oldest on the continent. We still can't understand the early dates but soon might be forced to accept them. For all practical reasons the pottery fits the early horizon material we had of Alaka Phase for British Guiana (for which we had no datable material)." The subsequent dates confirmed the first set and extended back even earlier.

The completed 13-date sequence of Brazilian dates constituted a longer and more precise series than the Colombian and Ecuadorian chronologies because numerous samples of charcoal and temper from pottery as well as shells were run, and all the sixth-millennium dates were on charcoal or on the temper in pottery. Little charcoal and no pottery had been dated from sites in Colombia at this point (Reichel-Dolmatoff 1985), and the earliest dates were on shell, the less reliable material. In fact, at this time the Colombian series had only five dates, compared to the Amazonian thirteen.

Further, the Smithsonian Radiocarbon Laboratory had carried out experiments to evaluate the possibility of old-carbon contamination of the charcoal dates by dating trees growing on the ancient shell mounds to see if they gave too-early radiocarbon dates. The dates of the trees came out modern, and Stuckenrath, the laboratory scientist, concluded that there was no evidence for an old-carbon problem with the dates. He wrote to Evans on August 29, 1973: "Hard water effect is obviously not the answer to problems posed by samples SI-1030 through SI-1038."

Nevertheless, only seven of the thirteen dates were published in Brazil in an article by the excavator, Mario Simoes (1981). No mention was made in print about the old-carbon experiment, and six of the dates that had been run by then, including the earliest and stratigraphically one of the deepest dates, SI 1034, a charcoal date of 5570 b.p., were withheld from publication. (When I asked Betty Meggers about the additional dates for Mina pottery, she stated that Simoes had published all the dates in the 1981 article [personal communication, 1990]. I wrote to Robert Stuckenrath in 1989 and 1990 to verify that the unpublished dates for the Mina and Alaka cultures had not subsequently been published, but received no answer.) The earliest date, which was 500 years earlier than any Colombian date and more than 1,000 years earlier than Ecuadorian dates at the time, made the Mina pottery the earliest pottery in the Americas. Without mentioning the date and its implications or the other dates that were left out, Simoes argued that pottery had been introduced to Brazil by migrants from Colombia and Ecuador, using virtually the same wording that Meggers and Evans (1978) used to refer to the pottery in a survey article three years earlier. Only by leaving out the Brazilian dates that were earlier than the Ecuadorian ones could this argument be justified. Nowhere in the publicly accessible correspondence at the Smithsonian Institution or the Museu Goeldi in Belem, Brazil, does either Simoes or Meggers and Evans refer to the rejection of any of these dates or any reason to reject them. These potentially revolutionary dates were consigned to obscurity without explanation.

Then as now, Brazil had the earliest and most thoroughly dated pottery in the Americas, but even those few archaeologists who have read the Brazilian article do not realize how many dates there are for the Mina culture or that the earliest date for the Brazilian pottery was earlier than those for pottery in the northwestern South American cultures. In addition, because the article is in Portuguese, which most archaeologists do not read, archaeologists were not aware of the details about the early pottery culture, relying on secondary sources instead. Many who had not read literature on the lowlands had not even heard that there was an early pottery culture in Brazil. Therefore, the implications of the Brazilian culture for the theories about the geography of cultural development in South America have not been disseminated or discussed.

In the meantine, Jose Brochado, a Brazilian scholar who earlier had worked with the Smithsonian team and later went to study with Lathrap, found at the Museu Goeldi and then circulated a mimeographed date list from the Smithsonian that included some of the unpublished dates from the Mina culture, particularly the earliest date. When Brochado gave me a copy of Smithsonian date list, I contacted the Smithsonian Archives, which are open to the public, and the staff showed me the original records from the Radiocarbon Laboratory and Anthropology Department and copied them for me with permission to publish, which I do here (Table 10.1). The previously unpublished dates are shown in boldface.

ALAKA CULTURE, GUYANA

The Mina early pottery culture was not the only one radiocarbon dated at the time. As I mentioned earlier, Meggers and Evans had excavated Alaka-phase pottery shell mounds along the coasts of then British Guiana, but they had interpreted them as the camps of recent foragers living side by side with more sophisticated people around 1,000 years ago (Evans and Meggers 1960). They did not have radiocarbon dates run from the materials they excavated, because, according to them, they found no suitable material for dating.

The early shell mounds in Guyana had produced sand-tempered plain pottery and shell-tempered plain pottery with simple shapes (Evans and Meggers 1960; Osgood 1946; Verrill 1918). As in the case of the Mina pottery, the secondary literature describes this pottery as exclusively shell tempered, but the majority of it at the majority of sites is sand tempered, with the shell-tempered pottery seriated as more recent, according to Evans and Meggers (1960). To quote:

The predominant pottery type of the middens clearly associated with the typical Alaka Phase stone artifacts is a mica and sand-tempered plain ware (Sand Creek Plain). At [two] sites . . . shell-tempered sherds (Wanaina Plain) occur; pottery with this temper was not found in any other site in the whole of British Guiana. Since Sand Creek Plain [the sand-tempered ware] is found at the largest number of sites . . . it might be considered the most characteristic pottery type of the Alaka Phase. . . . [Wanaina Plain, the shell-tempered ware, is] the most abundant pottery at the end of the Alaka Phase. (Evans and Meggers 1960:53–57)

Considering these clear statements in their site report that the sand-tempered pottery is the earliest and most characteristic of the Alaka phase, it is difficult to explain why Meggers and Evans describe the Alaka phase pottery as exclusively shell tempered in their secondary articles, leaving out any mention of the earlier and more abundant sand-tempered pottery (Meggers and Evans 1978:551–55, 1983:297). The secondary literature takes its lead from Meggers and Evans's general articles, not the site report, so the nature of the pottery's temper is misrepresented in that literature.

The Alaka pottery phase was not dated radiometrically until 1980, when the Smithsonian Institution ran dates on charcoal from Barambina, a pottery shell mound excavated by A. H. Verrill of the Museum of the American Indian at the turn of the century and later by Charles Osgood of Yale, and then reexcavated in 1980 by Denis Williams, an associate of Meggers and Evans's at the Georgetown Museum (Williams 1981). These first dates, 5965 and 4115 b.p. (Table 10.1), overlapped substantially with the Mina dates but extended back about 400 years earlier.

According to Williams's article and the Smithsonian sample submission forms, the dated materials came from layers and features that contained the plain sherds of sand-tempered Alaka pottery. However, in Evans's covering memo to the submission records and in Williams's article, these dates are attributed to a preceramic culture, an attribution that contradicts the records. To quote the summary submission form: "Associated cultural materials: Food debris of bone and shell, stone implements, few plain potsherds. Importance of dating this sample: Establish temporal relationship of this early shell midden complex with some plain pottery in Northern South America and its relationship specifically with the Mina Phase of Mouth of the Amazon." Considering that pottery was found with the dated samples and throughout the mound, and considering that the justification for dating the samples was to date the pottery, the dates are clearly empirically associated with the early pottery culture and not with a preceramic culture, which has not been documented at the site. (Both Verrill and Williams found pottery in all levels. Osgood [1946] reported that the mound was preceramic, but he did not use screens when excavating.) Nevertheless, those few archaeologists who have read Williams's article, which was published in Guyana, do not realize that these early dates have a solid stratigraphic association with the pottery.

During the two years after the publication of the first Barambina dates, 16 other samples from this site and three other Guyanese pottery shell mounds produced more early radiocarbon dates, falling in the sixth to fourth millennia before the present (Table 10.1). None of these additional dates, however, has apparently been published, according to Meggers (personal communication, 1990), and so the scholarly community has remained unaware of them in the decade since they were run.

At the time the Guyanese dates were run, just before the Smithsonian Radiocarbon Laboratory closed, eastern South America had earlier dates and more early dates on more kinds of material from more sites than did northwestern South America. Yet most of the modern excavations in the Amazonian sites were made in the upper levels of the pottery shell mounds, and no mounds had yet been sampled for dating in the lowest levels, so the dates run so far could not have been the earliest dates for the shell mound cultures.

SIGNIFICANCE OF THE MINA AND ALAKA PHASES

The archaeological evidence from the Mina and Alaka phases indicated that the coasts and estuaries of eastern South America in the vicinity of the mouth of the Amazon had early pottery-age fishing cultures just as northwestern South America did.

As I have mentioned, many archaeologists are not aware of the characteristics of the Mina and Alaka phases or of their radiocarbon dates. This seems partly due to language barriers and the fact that local literature is not usually read by people working in other areas, but part of the problem has been that the nature of the complexes was not presented clearly and accurately in the writings of those familiar with the sites, collections, and dates. For example, most of the early dates were not published, especially those that were earlier than Colombian and Ecuadorian dates, and early assemblages that contained pottery were nonetheless presented as preceramic, although preceramic cultures have not yet been scientifically documented at these sites. Additionally, although both sand-tempered pottery and shell-tempered pottery are characteristic of both cultures, in the secondary sources Meggers and Evans represented the pottery of both cultures as shell tempered, omitting reference to the sand-tempered wares even though they had written in their site report that those tempered with sand were the most common and earliest wares in the Alaka seriation.

The omissions confused comparisons among early pottery styles and obscured the fact that the Amazonian pottery sites were more abundant and earlier than the northwestern South American early pottery sites. Most archaeologists consult only the secondary literature from Amazonia and thus would not realize what information from the dating program and site reports had been left out. The information that was unpublished, of course, has only become available to the public since the closing of the Smithsonian Radiocarbon Laboratory and the archiving of its records. Because its existence was not mentioned by those involved in the research, and because Jose Brochado's discovery that the majority of the Smithsonian dates from the Amazon had not been published was mentioned only in his unpublished M.A. thesis (Brochado 1980) and an unpublished article (Brochado and Lathrap 1982), most people have not realized that there was missing chronological information accessible in the Smithsonian Archives.

That archaeologists were unaware of the Amazonian evidence for early pottery is very important because it has conditioned reaction to the recent discovery of sites with early sand-tempered pottery in the Santarem region in the lower Amazon. Because archaeologists are not aware of the dates of the Mina and Alaka pottery cultures or of the character of the pottery and its distribution in the stratigraphy, the Santarem finds seem unique and discordant.

Early Pottery in the Lower Amazon, Brazil

In addition to the Amazonian estuarine shell middens, shell middens with pottery had also been excavated by nineteenth-century scholars from the shores of rivers in the interior of Amazonia. Recently, our excavations to the basal stratigraphy of two such sites along the main channel of the Amazon in the vicinity of Santarem, in Para, Brazil, have produced dates that overlap with the earliest Mina and Alaka dates and extend from 1,000 to 1,500 years earlier. Thus, although Colombian sites have by now produced dates on pottery and on charcoal extending back to the early sixth millennium (Oyuela-Caycedo, chapter 11), as had Mina and Alaka sites earlier, the Amazonian sequence has in the meantime moved even earlier, continuing the tradition of eastern South America's having the earliest dates for pottery in the Americas.

TAPERINHA

The riverine shell middens in the lower Amazon were not investigated stratigraphically or dated until our

team worked at Taperinha mound in the vicinity of Santarem in 1987. Subsequently, we discovered a shell midden in the middle levels of a deeply stratified archaeological deposit in Caverna da Pedra Pintada, a cave at Monte Alegre, also near Santarem. We excavated in the cave in 1991 and 1992, and in 1993 we returned to excavate at Taperinha again. In both sites, our excavations were carried to the base of the cultural deposits, unlike the situtation at the Mina and Alaka sites.

Taperinha is a mound originally of about 6 hectares, 6.5 meters deep, on terra firme rain forest land overlooking early Holocene relict river terraces and the current floodplain, about 30 miles downstream from Santarem (Fig. 10.1). In 1870–71, the geologist C. F. Hartt, a student of Louis Agassiz, excavated there and concluded that the site was an early village of pottery-using foragers (Hartt 1885). I learned of the site from a book by an amateur archaeologist, Helen Constance Palmatary (1960). With the information in the book, I located Hartt's collections at Harvard and Cornell, and in 1982, with the permission of the Peabody Museum, commissioned a conventional radiocarbon date on shell from his excavations of the pottery mound. The date of 5705 b.p. (Table 10.2) supported Hartt's interpretations but was not conclusive because stratigraphic context for the sample was lacking, and freshwater shellfish may incorporate earlier carbon in their shells and thus may give erroneously early dates.

To verify the chronology and cultural contexts of the pottery, I went with Brazilian colleagues to the site in 1987 and 1993 as part of the Lower Amazon Project of research on lowland developmental sequences (Roosevelt 1989). The team mapped the mound with electronic distance-measuring (EDM) instruments, carried out geophysical survey using radar, electromagnetic conductivity, magnetometer, self-potential, resistivity, and seismic reflection, and placed ten auger holes and four stratigraphic excavations: Excavation 1 at its base, Excavation 2 on top, and Excavation 3 in between. Excavation 4 was placed outside of the mound 20 meters to the southeast. Reduced in areal extent since 1871 by lime mining, Taperinha lies on top of an ancient beach and under later prehistoric black soil refuse and recent sandy colluvium eroded from the high plateau some 50 meters above the site.

The 1987 excavations exposed 48 prehistoric strata of shells, charcoal, faunal bone, rocks, pottery fragments, rare human bones, and little soil (Fig. 10.2). The bulk of the mound is Archaic-age shell midden, with only 20–50 cm of late prehistoric black soil mid-

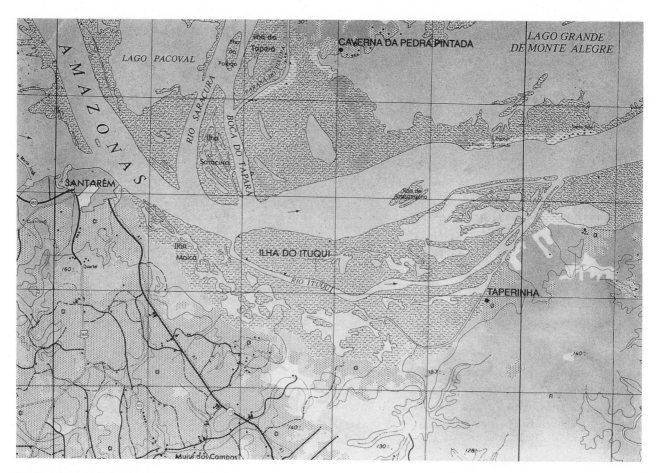

Fig. 10.1. Map of the Santarem region.

den above it. The 1993 excavations and auger holes revealed that the Taperinha phase occupation was also present in the sandy apron that sloped from the mound up to the cliffs behind the mound. There, a sand layer approximately 50 centimeters thick containing mussel shells, fish bone, turtle shells, charcoal, and pottery was reached about 1 meter below surface, under Formative and late prehistoric black soil deposits. A human skeleton was recovered from the juncture between the Archaic and Formative deposits in the apron. No preceramic deposit has yet been found below the pottery Archaic cultural layers at the site, although testing by augers was carried to a depth of more than 4 meters below the base of the deposits.

M. Imazio, S. Maranca, C. Lopes Machado, M. Eck, F. Noelli, and I, along with others, excavated the archaeological strata in natural levels by hand, leaving objects in place to be mapped and photographed before removal. The soil was sieved with one-quarter-inch to one-thirty-second-inch graduated screens. One or two 8-liter samples of soil from each layer or feature were, in addition, water floated. All material from the screens and filters was retained.

To determine the age when the mound was first occupied, radiometric dates on 12 samples from shell, charcoal, and pottery from habitation features in Excavation 1 at the base of the mound were run at Oxford University (Table 10.2; Roosevelt et al. 1991). (Samples from the middle and upper part of the mound were not run because the loose shell layers there are subject to slumping and intrusion by iguanas and armadillos, which inhabit the mound. Therefore the Taperinha dates from our project relate to the beginning of the phase only.) Accelerator mass spectrometry (AMS) radiocarbon dating was performed at Oxford by Rupert Housley on 11 samples: 4 charcoal pieces, 5 shells, and samples of the charcoal and humic and fulvic acids from the base of a broken pottery vessel. All specimens but the pottery were excavated without handling and were cleaned by abrasion and alternating washes of acids and bases to remove any depositional contaminants (Roosevelt et al. 1991). The pottery was processed to obtain two fractions: humic acids and elemental carbon. Thermoluminescence (TL) dating was performed by Deborah Stoneham of Oxford on another piece of the same pottery vessel that was dated by

Table 10.2. Early Pottery-Age Radiometric Dates from Taperinha and Caverna da Pedra Pintada

Lab No.	Material	Catalog No.	Date b.p.	δ13C ‰

TAPERINHA

Conventional radiocarbon date from Hartt Collection

GX-12844	Calcined shell	72-23-30	5705 ± 50	

Radiocarbon accelerator dates

EXCAVATION 1

Level 8B (Stratum 8)

OxA-1540	Calcined shell	6035-1	6300 ± 90	−15

Level 10 (Stratum 9A base)

OxA-1541	Charcoal	6038-1	6860 ± 100	
OxA-1542	Shell	6038-1	7010 ± 90	−15

Level 10 Feature 2 (Stratum 9B top)

OxA-1760	Charcoal	6040-14	6880 ± 80	
OxA-1543	Charcoal	6040-6	6930 ± 80	
OxA-1544	Charcoal	6040-17	6980 ± 80	
OxA-1545	Shell	6040-21	7000 ± 80	−15

Level 12 base (Stratum 10A)

OxA-2431	Carbon in sherd	6043-1	6590 ± 100	−28
OxA-2432	Org. acids in sherd	6043-1	6640 ± 80	−28

Level 13 top (Stratum 11A)

OxA-1546	Shell	6043-15	7090 ± 80	−15
OxA-1547	Shell	6049-1	7080 ± 80	−15

Thermoluminescence date from Excavation 1 (30)

Level 12

Ox581a36	Sherd from vessel 6043-1	6043-2	7110 ± 1422	

CAVERNA DA PEDRA PINTADA

Conventional Radiocarbon Date

Excavation 6, Level 6C

GX-17415	Shell	8334-13	7580 ± 215	−11

(continued)

Table 10.2. (*Continued*)

Lab No.	Material	Catalog No.	Date b.p.	δ13C ‰
Radiocarbon Accelerator Dates				
Excavation 10, Level 2C				
OxA-4321	Shell	9258	7120 ± 80	−10.9
Excavation 2 Level 6D				
GX-17401-AMS	Shell	8221	6943 ± 60	−10.8
Excavation 3 Level 4C				
OxA-4320	Shell temper	8243	6785 ± 70	−12.1
Excavation 2 Level 6D				
GX-1742A-AMS	Turtle shell	8221	6625 ± 60	−11.8
Thermoluminescence Date				
Excavation 10, Level 2C				
Ox-287a1	Sherd	9258-10	4710 ± 375	

AMS. The TL age is quoted with a ±20 percent error range because of uncertainties due to incomplete environmental data, uncertainties about the degree of lifetime saturation of the sherd and surrounding soil, and the fact that the TL date is derived from a single sherd.

The dating program produced a series of quite consistent dates. The 2-sigma ranges of the 11 AMS radiocarbon dates are 7080 to 6300 b.p., a span of almost 1,000 years in the early part of the culture. The conventional radiocarbon date on Hartt's shells, 5705 b.p., extends the span of the culture upward several hundred years to overlap with the Mina and Alaka sequences. The AMS dates on associated charcoal and shell are within 150 years of each other, and the carbon and acids from pottery differed by only 400 years from the nearest charcoal and shell dates. The mean thermoluminescence date of 7110 ± 1422 on pottery fell within the range of the radiocarbon dates, when calibrated.

These results are conclusive evidence for the age of the early pottery-age culture because the different materials and methods are not considered subject to the same sources of error. The statistically identical dates on associated shell and charcoal indicate a lack of contamination of those materials, although the possibility cannot be eliminated that the pottery could have been contaminated slightly with modern carbon from handling during excavation or with mobile humic acids from groundwater. The fact that the pottery itself gave radiocarbon and TL dates within the same range as the charcoal and shell and that no preceramic deposit has ever been documented at the site makes it highly unlikely that we have here a situation of preceramic biological materials mixed with ceramic-age cultural materials.

The fragile, red-brown to brown fragments of pottery bowls that occurred throughout the shell midden were tempered with sand, unlike the site's later prehistoric pottery, which has organic tempers of shell, sponge spicules, or *caraipe*. The 1993 excavations revealed that the archaic pottery gets darker and browner in color with time, an observation based on the distribution of sherds in superimposed strata. Some of the clay in the pottery had weathered to the point of losing its rigidity in water, a common occurrence with pottery many thousands of years old (Pamela Vandiver, personal communication, 1992). Rims were tapered or rounded, and most vessel walls ranged between about 0.5 and 1.5 centimeters. Vessel shapes were limited to hemispherical or inturned-rim bowls (often called

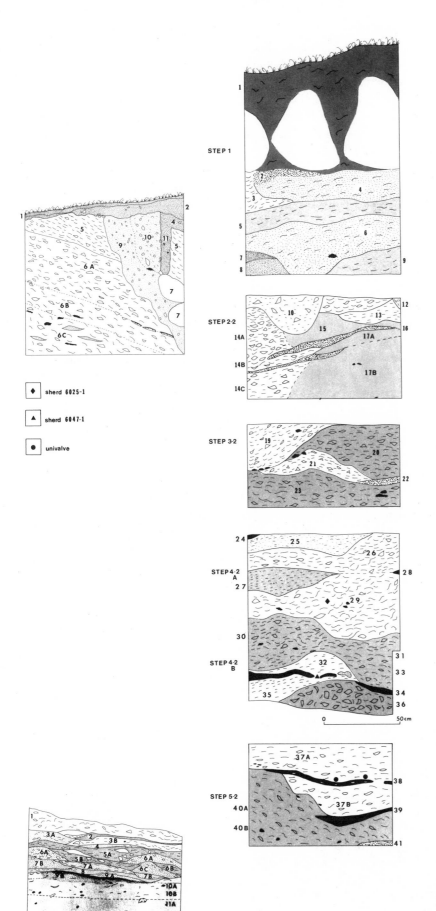

STEP 1

STEP 2-2

STEP 3-2

STEP 4-2 A

STEP 4-2 B

STEP 5-2

◆ sherd 6025-1

▲ sherd 6047-1

● univalve

Fig. 10.2. Stratigraphy of Taperinha shell mound. Top left, south cross-section, Excavation 2. Right, east cross-section, Excavation 3. Bottom left, south cross-section, Excavation 1. Sherds are shown as rectangles or triangles, shells are ovals or arcs, roots are circles or cylinders, charcoal is black, dark soil is shaded or closely stippled, and sand and rock are sparsely stippled.

Early Pottery in the Amazon 125

tecomates in American archaeology) with rounded, thickened bases. Measurable sizes varied from about 15 centimeters to 30 centimeters diameter at the rim. A number of sherds held soot on their surfaces, and some 3 percent of the 383 sherds have complex incised rim decoration (Fig. 10.3). Geometric incision on bowl rims and shoulders is the most common type of decoration throughout the Amazonian prehistoric sequence, but the Taperinha motifs are not particularly like those in any other known styles except for those of Pedra Pintada pottery, also from the Santarem area.

The function of the pottery bowls cannot be proven at this point, but presumably seafood soup or stew could have been made in them (as has been suggested by Thomas Killian for Mexican tecomates, personal communication, 1992), or they could have been used for storage or display, since a few are decorated. (The radiocarbon laboratory removed and discarded unidentified lipids from the pottery before it was dated. In the future it may be possible to save and study the DNA of such oil to determine its source. Both palm oil and turtle oil are valued fat sources in Amazonia today.) Griddles, which occur in Formative and later prehistoric cultures at the sites, do not occur in the Archaic deposits. The stratigraphic context of the pottery does not give much help in determining its function, because the pottery is found in all contexts: dispersed in garbage, scattered on living surfaces, lying in hearths. That vessels are small compared to later prehistoric vessels could be because people ate in small family groups, or because potters' command of technology did not allow for making larger vessels, or because of some other reason. In Amazonia, women are usually the potters, which may also have been the case at Taperinha.

Lithics in the shell mound were limited to hammerstones, a very few flakes, and unshaped sandstone grinding stones and hearth stones of iron-rich rock.

A bone awl, mollusc- and turtle-shell scrapers, and a shaped plug of aquatic mammal bone were also recovered. Later cultures in the area made a wide range of ground stone "axes," commonly associated with land clearing for horticulture, but none has been found in the Archaic deposits.

The faunal remains represent an economy of intensive foraging on small, abundant riverine species. Pearly freshwater mussels (identified by Richard Johnson through comparison of the archaeological shells with samples of living shellfish from the region and original type collections at the Museum of Comparative Zoology, Harvard University) predominate, with turtles and fish, mostly catfish and characins, also common. The shellfish may have furnished an abundant, year-round source of calories before cultivated plants were developed for that purpose. Interestingly, shellfish are rare in the midden during the Formative and later periods. Plant organic matter and plant remains other than charcoal are rare in the shell mound, although abundant in later prehistoric deposits at this site and in earlier deposits at Pedra Pintada. Settlement appears to have been relatively permanent, in view of the large size of the midden and the use of pottery, which is usually rare among nomads without draft animals or automobiles (Rafferty 1985). Whether the site was occupied part of the year or most of the year is difficult to say at present, but in the future study of seasonal shell rings and fish otoliths may furnish information about the seasons of occupation.

CAVERNA DA PEDRA PINTADA, MONTE ALEGRE, BRAZIL

In subsequent field seasons of the project, the team excavated a prehistoric cultural deposit in a cave in the vicinity of Monte Alegre town, opposite Taperinha on the north bank of the Amazon. The cave is one of sev-

Fig. 10.3. Incised sand-tempered pottery sherds from Taperinha shell mound.

eral hundred in the region's Serra do Erere and Serra de Paituna, low sandstone mountains between about 50 and 200 meters in elevation, overlooking extensive early Holocene and current floodplains. Vegetation in the area ranges from evergreen rain forest and seasonally dry forest to savanna and swamp. Nineteenth-century scholars had explored the caves and rock outcrops and published descriptions and drawings (Hartt 1871; Wallace 1889). In recent decades, speleologists and anthropologists have surveyed the caves and the paintings, but until our project no instrument mapping or excavations had been carried out.

After surveying with an EDM device and satellite locator and augering 10 caves in the mountains, the project staff chose for excavation a deposit about 2 meters thick with prehistoric strata in Caverna da Pedra Pintada, a painted cave in the Serra de Paituna. The deposit contained strata with material spanning the Paleoindian to late prehistoric periods, about 11,200 b.p. to A.D. 1450. Some 50–60 centimeters down in the deposit there was a thin deposit of dark gray, pottery-Archaic midden rich in freshwater pearly mussels, snails, fish bone, and turtle shell. Below this deposit was a sterile sand layer and below that a black soil Paleoindian preceramic deposit. Above and extending down into the Archaic layer was a Formative deposit with several burials, and above that a late prehistoric black soil deposit with a structure of wooden posts extending into the underlying deposits to the sterile layer over the Paleoindian deposit. The layers and features of different periods were excavated separately from one another and objects were individually recorded in place and removed without handling, for the most part, as they also were at Taperinha.

Combined in the Archaic deposit were thick sherds of red-brown, gray-brown, or brown pottery spanning the entire pottery Archaic. Most pottery was tempered with sand, but a few sherds were tempered with shell. The component is dated by five radiocarbon dates and one TL date. Three conventional radiocarbon dates were run by Geochron Labs and two accelerator dates were run by Oxford University. Geochron dated a *Paxyodon ponderosus* bivalve shell, an unidentified shell, and a turtle shell. The three dates are 7580, 6943, and 6625 b.p., respectively (Table 10.2). Oxford ran two AMS dates on mussel shells and on a shell-tempered, gray-brown, Middle Archaic sherd, to test the association of the conventional dates with pottery, as at Taperinha. The Oxford dates overlapped with the Geochron dates. They were 6785 b.p. for the shell temper in the pottery and 7120 b.p. for the shells. A TL date on a Late Archaic, brown, sand-tempered sherd from the deposit run at Oxford is 4710 b.p.

The sand-tempered Archaic pottery from Caverna da Pedra Pintada is similar to Taperinha pottery in its simple hemispherical or tecomate shapes and incised and punctate decoration, but the decoration is broader and deeper, apparently made with a larger, rounder-tipped incising tool, and rare rims bear an exterior thickening and a red horizontal band (Fig. 10.4). Some of the sand-tempered sherds bear soot on their surfaces, so a culinary function can be hypothesized. So

Fig. 10.4. Incised and (in one case) red-painted sand-tempered pottery sherds from Caverna da Pedra Pintada.

far we have found no shell-tempered sherds with decoration. Shell tempering has been found to improve the thermal properties of pottery, so perhaps the shell-tempered pottery had a cooking function too. As at Taperinha, all the early pottery at Pedra Pintada exists in pieces, due, as Pamela Vandiver has suggested, to the deterioration of the fired clay with weathering and the practice of making up pots out of clay patches rather than from clay rings.

Like the people of the early pottery culture at Taperinha, the Paituna-phase Early pottery people at Caverna da Pedra Pintada specialized in aquatic foraging. The predominent shellfish are freshwater pearly mussels of the same species as those at Taperinha. Turtle bone and fish bone are also present, but no terrestrial animal bone has yet been identified in the Archaic midden, although such bone is abundant in later prehistoric layers. In addition, as at Taperinha, carbonized plant remains other than charcoal are comparatively rare in the Archaic midden at Pedra Pintada, although very abundant in both earlier and later layers at the site. Thus, even though the cave lies a 30- to 60-minute walk or more from the floodplain lakes and river, aquatic faunal resources were so important in the diet that people hauled them to the cave and processed and ate them there. By the Formative period in the cave, dated between about 3600 and 3200 b.p., people no longer relied heavily on shellfish, perhaps because they had replaced them as a calorie source with cultivated crops such as manioc, as suggested by the Formative griddles, or maize, dried cobs of which are found in late prehistoric levels.

Conclusions

Although some have portrayed the eighth-millennium b.p. pottery from the Amazon as a unique find that contrasts with other evidence from Amazonia,[3] in fact the pottery complexes from Taperinha and Pedra Pintada are clearly part of a wider geographical phenomenon of early Holocene pottery-age cultures in the eastern part of greater Amazonia. The later dates in the early pottery sequences from Taperinha and Pedra Pintada overlap neatly with the earlier dates in the early pottery sequences from Alaka and Mina sites. The more recent dates also overlap with the earliest pottery dates from northern Colombia, and the extent of overlap would be expected to increase when more sites there are fully excavated to sterile.

When comparing the Amazonian early pottery with that from other parts of South America, it is appropriate to compare the quality and specificity of the evidence from the different regions. Rather than being a controversial, questionable, new item on the archaeological scene, Amazonian early pottery is the most securely dated early pottery in the New World. A review of the literature, site reports, and radiocarbon records shows that this observation is nothing new for Amazonia; for more than 25 years, eastern South America has been producing most of the sites and dates for early pottery and the earliest and most precise dates for pottery in the Americas.

With Taperinha and Pedra Pintada, Amazonia has even more dates than the other South American regions, and these dates are on a wider range of material. It is important to reiterate that of all early pottery in South America, only the Amazonian pottery has had its age confirmed by thermoluminescence and by radiocarbon dates directly on the pottery. None of the sixth-millennium b.p. pottery from northern South America has been dated directly (although later, Formative-age pottery there has been dated directly with radiocarbon methods [Oyuela-Caycedo, chapter 11]). To my knowledge, only in Amazonia have trees growing on the shell middens been dated to assess the old-carbon effect. Because the TL dates have come out in the same range as the radiocarbon dates and the pottery dates were the same as those on charcoal and shell, and because the modern trees came out modern despite growing on mounds of ancient shells, this region is the only one in which the possibility of an old-carbon effect has effectively been eliminated. If there is an old-carbon effect to contend with in South American early pottery studies, it remains a problem for northwestern South America, not for Amazonia.

Future research on early pottery in South America needs to deal with the incomplete stratigraphic sequences by excavating to sterile at more sites and to solve the lack of complete and secure chronometric sequences by dating a wider range of materials with more precise and focused programs of radiometric dating. The work at Taperinha and Pedra Pintada provides an example of how to clarify archaeological sequences by combining archival research, collection research, stratigraphic excavation, object conservation, the dating of multiple materials, and the use of different dating methods on the same objects.

Because at this point the Taperinha and Paituna date sequences begin between 1,000 and 1,500 years earlier than those of northern South American pottery and 3,500 years earlier than the date sequences of central

Andean and Mesoamerican pottery, it would not be reasonable to maintain that the Amazonian pottery tradition was derived by diffusion or migration from these other areas, although the reverse is possible, as is independent origins. This does not mean, however, that Amazonia was the hearth of pottery in the New World. The distinctive differences in pottery from region to region suggest that there must have been several hearths. In any case, to acquire stylistic and technological evidence for migration and diffusion will require that archaeologists in all the relevant regions excavate to the bottom of their sites to identify the styles of the truly initial periods of pottery making. Because many regions have not been investigated for early pottery, it is likely that more early phases will be discovered in the future.

Although similar in shape and temper to some other early South American pottery, Taperinha and Paituna pottery differs in some ways. The presence of incised decoration in the complexes contrasts with the plainness of the published pottery from the Mina and Alaka cultures. The early pottery from Colombia and Ecuador, however, has abundant decoration, and perhaps decoration will turn up when more Mina and Alaka sites are excavated. Possibly, also, decorated pottery was "seriated" out of these complexes as intrusive, owing to assumptions that the earliest pottery ought to be plain. Because people would presumably have decorated preexisting vessel types, such as gourds, there is no reason why early pottery would necessarily be undecorated.

What relationships the people of the Amazonian early pottery cultures might have had with their Paleoindian predecessors is not clear, because remains of the Paleoindians themselves have only just been discovered in the lower levels of Pedra Pintada cave. The thick sterile soil layers and great temporal and cultural gulf between the two cultures suggest that they may not be related, but the gulf may be an artifact of negative evidence. In the lower Amazon floodplain, there are no known cultures that date between the end of the Paleoindian period at 9,800 years ago and the first pottery shell mound people at 7,500, probably because—due to the eustatic water level rises of the intervening time period—the shores of the early Holocene river are not where the shores are today and we have not found the sites yet. Another possibility is that Amazonians began making pottery as soon as water levels rose after the end of the Pleistocene, when fish and shellfish habitats expanded greatly as the waters spread widely over the land and sediment filled the late Pleistocene canyons of

the Amazon. In any case, Lathrap's idea that pottery-using horticultural peoples from Africa came into the Amazon at 13,000 years ago does not fit the fact that there is absolutely no pottery in the 11,200- to 9,800-year-old Paleoindian site.

As to the general significance of Amazonian early pottery culture for human cultural adaptation and evolution, it seems clear that aquatic resources were key resources in the transition to the pottery age by making more permanent settlement possible and by encouraging the invention of containers for cooking fish and shellfish. In the Old World, the earliest pottery-age societies also exploited abundant aquatic species, and such resources may have underwritten the later development of horticulture (Aikens and Higuchi 1982). Thus, the archaeological record falsifies the environmental and technoeconomic determinism that decreed that tropical forest ecology would prevent the intensive agriculture that could support the sedentism that would allow the use of pottery. The Amazon is a series of huge rivers, as well as trackless forests, and the economic base for the development of pottery in the lower Amazon happened to be foraging on riverine resources. In the future, we may also discover early village sites and pottery in some of the upland forests as well, for recent geological and soil studies show that the rich soils in some areas with volcanic and limestone bedrock support dense concentrations of fruit trees and their predators (Franzinelli and Latrubesse 1993).

The first steps toward horticulture may well have taken place during the later part of the long pottery shell mound occupation in Amazonia. There is, however, so far no evidence for plant cultivation in the Amazonian Archaic sites, which instead look more like the sites of specialized river foragers.[4] Anyone wishing to interpret these cultures as evidence of early horticulture must do so with the understanding that there is no evidence to support that view. In the Santarem region, horticulture is not attested to even indirectly until griddles appear in the Formative period, between about 4,000 and 2,000 years ago. Corn cultivation in the area is not attested to until the late prehistoric period, with corncobs appearing at Caverna da Pedra Pintada in layers of the late prehistoric period, about A.D. 1000–1450. To assess the degree of sedentism and plant use at Taperinha and Pedra Pintada, studies of the sequence of botanical remains, pollen cores, and human bone morphology and chemistry are being pursued.

The prehistory of Santarem—Monte Alegre sheds

light on human cultural adaptation to a tropical environment over the millennia, revealing that riverine resources supported the earliest pottery-age cultures yet known in the western hemisphere, as well as diverse other indigenous cultures. It does not support the idea that the tropical environment was necessarily a barrier to population growth and settlement or that lowland cultures were necessarily derived from other areas.

These findings illustrate how difficult it is to correctly predict culture history with inadequate chronological and geographical information. The archaeological record frequently turns out to be different from what the grand theories predict. We need the grand theories—they are our way of thinking about the causes of things—but their routine inaccuracy and ultimate obsolescence warns us to be careful to let the archaeological record inform us even when it does not fit our theories. Rather than ignoring or obscuring the data that do not fit, we must design our research with test implications that give the theories a chance to be wrong. We can, in this way, be prepared to learn from the archaeological record.

Notes

1. The absolute size of such areas is very substantial, even though they make up a small percentage of Amazonia. For example, the entire Ecuadorian Amazon terra firme has volcanic soils, and the total area of Pleistocene and Holocene alluvium and lime-based soils in the Bolivian, Peruvian, and Brazilian Amazon and Guianas coasts (Franzinelli and Latrubesse 1993:123–26) covers an area much larger than the area of the central Andean highlands and desert coast or of the central Mexican highlands.

2. The laboratory documents and correspondence of the Smithsonian Radiocarbon Laboratory are stored in the Anthropology section of the Smithsonian Archives and are available to the public through the Freedom of Information Act. The documents that I refer to and quote in this article are classified as No. 87-035, Box 7-8, 9-10, Record Unit 387. Thanks to Susan Glen and William Cox for showing me the records and copying them. Permission to publish items from the archives has been given courtesy of the Smithsonian Institution. Facsimiles of documents will be published in a report on unpublished Smithsonian radiocarbon dates in the *Journal of Field Archaeology*.

3. Meggers, quoted in the *Washington Post* and other newspapers that carry the WP wire service, claims that the eighth-millennium Amazonian pottery is an inexplicable, unique, and impossible find. "One does not overturn large bodies of evidence that point in one direction with a single finding that points the other way, she said. . . . If [Roosevelt] has pottery at 7,000 or 8,000 years, why do we find no sign of pottery anywhere else in the Amazon until just 3,000 years ago?" (*Washington Post,* December 16, 1991, A3). The 4,000-year gap that Meggers claims exists between Santarem-area early pottery and other early pottery in Amazonia exists only if Taperinha and Pedra Pintada dates are quoted as B.P. (calibrated) and the dates from other areas are quoted as b.c. (uncalibrated), which would not be a scientifically acceptable procedure, to say the least, because it creates the impression of a gap where none exists. Thus, it is not a situation of deciding between a long and short chronology for the lower Amazon. There are no published or unpublished dates for a short chronology there, only for a long one.

4. Although some authors have stated that my colleagues and I think that the early shell midden pottery cultures are evidence for the beginning of horticulture in the eighth millennium b.p. (e.g., Moran 1993:3), this is clearly not the case (Roosevelt et al. 1991).

References Cited

Aikins, C. N., and T. Higuchi
    1982   *The Prehistory of Japan*. Academic Press, New York.

Brochado, J.
    1980   The Social Ecology of the Marajoara Culture. Unpublished M.A. thesis, Department of Anthropology, University of Illinois, Urbana.

Brochado, J., and D. Lathrap
    1982   Amazonia. Unpublished article.

Derby, O.
    1879   The Artificial Mounds of Marajo. *American Naturalist* 13:224–29.

Evans, C., and B. J. Meggers
    1960   *Archeological Investigations in British Guiana*. Bureau of American Ethnology Bulletin 177.

Ferreira Penna, D. S.
    1876   Breve noticia sobre os sambaquis do Para. *Archivos do Museu Nacional* 1:85–99. Rio de Janeiro.

Franzinelli, E., and E. Latrubesse
    1993   Resumos e contribuicoes cientificas. Abstract of papers presented at the International Symposium on the Quaternary of Amazonia. Manaus: Universidade do Amazonas and Instituto Nacional de Pesquisas da Amazonia.

Goodland, R. J. A., and H. S. Irwin
    1975   *Amazon Jungle: Green Hell to Red Desert?* Elsevier, Amsterdam.

Hartt, C. F.
    1871   Brazilian Rock Inscriptions. *American Naturalist* 5(3):139–47.

1885   Contribuicoes para a ethnologia do valle do Amazonas. *Archivos do Museu Nacional* 6:1–174. Rio de Janeiro.

Jennings, J. E., ed.
1964   *Prehistoric Man in the New World.* University of Chicago Press, Chicago.

Lathrap, D.
1970   *The Upper Amazon.* Praeger, New York.
1977   Our Father the Cayman, Our Mother the Gourd: Spinden Revisited, or a Unitary Model for the Emergence of Agriculture in the New World. In *Origins of Agriculture,* edited by C. Reed, pp. 713–51. Mouton, The Hague.

Meggers, B. J.
1954   Environmental Limitation on the Development of Culture. *American Anthropologist* 56:801–24.
1971   *Amazonia: Man and Nature in Counterfeit Paradise.* Aldine, Chicago.
1985   Aboriginal Adaptation to Amazonia. In *Key Environments: Amazonia,* edited by G. Prance and T. Lovejoy, pp. 307–27. Pergamon, Oxford.

Meggers, B. J., and C. Evans
1957   *Archaeological Investigations at the Mouth of the Amazon.* Bureau of American Ethnology Bulletin 167. Smithsonian Institution, Washington, D.C.
1978   Lowland South America and the Antilles. In *Ancient Native Americans,* edited by J. D. Jennings, pp. 543–91. W. H. Freeman, San Francisco.
1983   Lowland South America and the Antilles. In *Ancient South Americans,* edited by J. D. Jennings, pp. 286–335. W. H. Freeman, San Francisco.

Meggers, B. J., C. Evans, and E. Estrada
1965   *Early Formative Period of Coastal Ecuador.* Smithsonian Contributions to Anthropology 1. Washington, D.C.

Moran, E.
1993   *Through Amazonian Eyes: The Human Ecology of Amazonian Populations.* University of Iowa Press, Iowa City.

Nimuendaju, C.
1949   *Os Tapajo.* Boletim do Museu Paraense Emilio Goeldi, no. 10. Belem, Brazil.

Osgood, C.
1946   *British Guiana Archaeology to 1945.* Yale University Publications in Anthropology 36. New Haven, Connecticut.

Palmatary, H. C.
1960   *The Archaeology of the Lower Tapajaos Valley, Brazil.* Transactions of the American Philosophical Society 50. Philadelphia, Pennsylvania.

Rafferty, J. E.
1985   The Archaeological Record on Sedentariness: Recognition, Development, Implications. In *Advances in Archaeological Method and Theory,* edited by M. B. Schiffer, pp. 113–56. Academic Press, Orlando, Florida.

Reichel-Dolmatoff, G.
1965   *Excavaciones arqueológicas en Puerto Hormiga, Departamento de Bolívar.* Antropológica 2. Universidad de los Andes, Bogotá.
1985   *Monsú: Un sitio arqueológico.* Biblioteca Banco Popular, Bogotá.

Roosevelt, A. C.
1989   Interdisciplinary Archaeological Research at Santarem on the Lower Amazon, Brazil. Preliminary report and proposal to the National Endowment for the Humanities.
1991   *Moundbuilders of the Amazon: Geophysical Archaeology on Marajo Island.* Academic Press, San Diego.

Roosevelt, A. C., R. A. Housley, M. Imazio da Silveira, S. Maranca, and R. Johnson
1991   Eighth Millennium Pottery from a Prehistoric Shell Midden in the Brazilian Amazon. *Science* 254:1621–1624.

Simoes, M.
1981   *Coletores-pescadores ceramistas do litoral do Salgado, (Para).* Boletim do Museu Paraense Emilio Goeldi 78.

Steward, J. H., ed.
1946–50 *Handbook of South American Indians.* Bureau of American Ethnology, Bulletin 143.

Verrill, A. H.
1918   Prehistoric Mounds and Relics of the Northwest District of British Guiana. *Timehri* 5:11–17.

Wallace, A. R.
1889   *A Narrative of Travels on the Amazon and Rio Negro.* Ward, Lock and Co., London.

Williams, D.
1981   Excavation of the Barambina Shell Mound Northwest District: An Interim Report. *Archaeology and Anthropology* 4:13–38.

11

Rocks versus Clay

The Evolution of Pottery Technology in the Case of San Jacinto 1, Colombia

AUGUSTO OYUELA-CAYCEDO

What is the role of pottery production as a technology in the process of human cultural evolution? What is the effect of pottery as a selected strategy for food processing or as a form of intensification? These are the kinds of questions we should start to pursue from the perspective of cultural evolution. Studies of early pottery should be focused more on pottery's relationship to mobility and subsistence technology.

The invention or innovation of pottery has been argued to be an indicator of sedentism. It is necessary to reevaluate this relationship and not continue to take it for granted (Reid 1989:172). Part of the assumption that pottery indicates some sort of sedentism is related to two factors: a reliance on ethnographic data to infer past conditions (Arnold 1985), and archaeologists' lack of interest in demonstrating the context of pottery in relation to other aspects of the archaeological assemblage that could confirm or negate a relationship between pottery and sedentism. Part of the problem with the cross-cultural ethnographic perspective is that a strong ethnographic correlation between sedentism and pottery exists (Arnold 1985:109). The correlation is valid for the world today but is not applicable to the time when pottery was initially invented or adopted. In the end, the testing of any proposition has to come from the archaeological record if we want to generalize about the past.

The relationship of pottery to subsistence technology also has to be evaluated. Pottery may or may not be selected as a strategy for food processing and for intensification independent of resource change (see Stahl 1989). We have to ask what changed with the introduction or innovation of pottery. Did pottery have a significant impact on life-style, as is always described in the "before-and-after" scenario of pottery? Human populations knew how to cook without pots for thousands of years, but for some reason cooking with pots is generally considered a "revolution" in the same sense in which the term was once applied to the origins of agriculture. Is the model for a "pottery revolution" logical when viewed from the theories of technological invention, innovation, or adoption? The answer seems to be no. In general, such changes are gradual and can take generations or even centuries (Brown 1989:220). Another old assumption about the relationship between pots and subsistence is that pottery was invented primarily for cooking daily meals. Is this true? It is necessary to demonstrate this relationship.

One of the most appealing models for the origin of pottery is the econometric model of supply and demand developed by James Brown (1989). To test his model, Brown proposes five expectations: (1) there is an experimental period of pottery production that can be demonstrated over a span of centuries, (2) expedient technology should be present in the early phases of pottery production, (3) evidence of a decline in frequency of other technologies should be observed when pottery becomes popular, (4) the performance context in which early pottery is found will be different from place to place even within the same culture, and (5) meeting the demand for containers through other mediums should undermine pottery production in its early stages.

Brown's (1989) proposal follows the tradition of explaining cultural change as a transition between distinct stages. This stage model, however, is of little value for understanding variability in time and space (for a more in-depth discussion of the difference between a stage perspective and a processual perspective, see Drennan 1991:127–28). Brown's experimental period remains an undefined concept, especially when pottery could have been invented in such a short period of time that its development would not even be perceived in the archaeological record. The production of terracottas uses a simple technology that requires a relatively low firing temperature and does not demand the training and technical skills that porcelains demand. Furthermore, it is a technique that can be invented and perfected to a satisfying degree by a single individual. We should not expect to find in the archaeological record any evidence of "experimentation." The problem of technology is not the invention itself; it is how a new product is accepted and how the experience of its production is transmitted and improved upon through time.

In relation to Brown's second point—that expedient technology should appear in the early phases of pottery production—a look at the data available for Colombia (Correal Urrego 1986; Hurt 1977; Wolford 1994) shows that expedient technology (*tecnología* Abrience and Tequendamience) is present throughout the whole sequence from 10,000 b.c. to the European conquest. Brown's (1989:218–19) methodological approach to the cost-effectiveness of ceramics versus other containers such as baskets is very attractive and is partially considered in the model proposed in this paper.

An Alternative Model

In this chapter, a model of the origin of pottery production is presented from the perspective of cultural evolu-

tion. The objective is to understand the variability of pottery origins following principles of the evolution of culture as a process of change in which material culture has adaptive value (Bonner 1980; Cashdan 1990, 1992; Dawkins 1976:203–15; Rambo 1991). The present proposal is built partially upon the works of James A. Brown (1986, 1989), Kenneth C. Reid (1984:92–94, 1989), and Margaret C. Nelson (1991).

The origin of pottery among hunter-gatherers is seen as an adaptive strategy brought about by changing external conditions. The most active of these external changes is in the productivity of environmental resources, which is affected by such things as climatic change toward a more arid environment or prolonged dry seasons and concomitant changes such as a shift from homogeneous distribution of resources to patchiness of resources. In other words, changes toward less predictable seasonality of resources would have important consequences for hunter-gatherer adaptations. In order to cope with these changing conditions, a population has several alternatives: (1) move to a more predictable environment not occupied by another group, (2) increase the size of its territory with residential mobility, or (3) be more territorial by controlling different patchy resources through their constant monitoring. Such territoriality would favor a more logistic strategy of mobility. It is expected that this last alternative will be the preferred one, considering that these kinds of environmental changes are gradual and populations can map the distribution of resources as well as practice a spatial-temporal territoriality over the resources.

During these environmental changes, a strategy of reduced mobility would occur, leading to social or economic intensification. Pottery production can become useful, but is not necessary, in such a context. Social and economic intensifications are strategies selected to average out resources in space and time by reducing the risk of unpredictability (Cashdan 1992). Intensification of social activities could involve, for instance, an expansion of social or kin networks through activities such as feasting and raiding parties. Pottery can play a significant role as a symbolic item in food serving or food preparation (e.g., fermentation vessels) during feasting activities. As groups come together, an increase in site size is expected, as is a broader distribution of pottery styles over larger areas, even if group mobility is reduced and more territorial behavior in resource exploitation is observed.

In the case of a trajectory favoring the intensification of economic activities, a shift in focus either to one or a few abundant food resources or just to a new form of processing that enhances the nutritional quality of previously exploited resources would occur. Examples of this sort of enhancement are fermentation and detoxification. This intensification could be expressed in activities related to the processing of such food resources (Stahl 1989). Pottery would be specifically involved in the activities of processing.

Intensification in either of these forms or as a combined strategy of social and economic intensification is seen as a risk management response (see Cashdan 1990; Wills 1992) whereby such activities lend an adaptive advantage to the individual(s) participating in them under the given circumstances. In this context, pottery is just a tool that is invented or adopted to cope with resource scarcity through social or economic means of intensification.

The following are what we should expect in the context of early adoption or initial production of pottery: (1) Pottery is culturally selected for when internal social or economic conditions of the household favor the production of pottery as a response to changing conditions from a predictable to an unpredictable environment. These changing conditions require an intensification of social interactions, such as feasting, and/or of economic forms of food processing/cooking technologies. In both cases pottery will be selected for favorably. (2) The initial use of pottery involves a specialized function that is expected to vary from group to group. In some groups, pottery may have been used to extract oil from nuts; in other groups, it may have had a totally different function such as that of receptacles for the serving of feasts. The specific use is not as important as the fact of the specialized function itself. (3) Although pottery is selected by a group to assist in the process of social or economic intensification, this does not mean that it is competing against or is used instead of other kinds of technologies. It is added to the cultural assemblage because it is used for intensification and is a new form not previously exploited. A later broadening of the uses of pottery could be the result of further internal changes that favored pottery over other technologies of cooking, storing, or other activities. This last point is contrary to the expectations given by Brown (1989), in which competition between pottery and other container technologies or forms of cooking is considered to be the starting point for the development of pottery.

If these expectations hold, we would see certain patterns in the archaeological record. First, to test for internal social or economic conditions, it is necessary to establish which of the two is the selective force that favors pottery production. This can be done by determining whether pottery is found initially in an economic or in a social context of food processing. Economic contexts can be defined by archaeological evidence of cooking activities. Social contexts can be defined by evidence of activity areas that suggest feasting, by elaborate decorative styles, offerings, and associated botanical remains or chemical residues of alcoholic and/or hallucinogenic substances, or by evidence of pottery uses beyond those of normal subsistence activities.

Second, as a result of its specialized function, the earliest pottery is expected to have a reduced diversity of forms. And third, when pottery is initially adopted or invented, its presence or visibility in activity areas should be limited as a consequence of the restricted role it played as a new strategy for intensification. Through time, its presence will increase until the point comes when pottery can compete against other technologies that were at one time favorably selected for. At this point pottery will have a more dispersed pattern, occurring in multiple activity areas.

In this chapter, the first part of this model is addressed by utilizing one of the most overlooked types of evidence of cooking technologies: fire-cracked rocks. Fire-cracked rocks are among the most highly represented archaeological materials; they are used for roasting, stone boiling, and even steaming in earth ovens (Binford et al. 1970; Frison 1983; House and Smith 1975; Latas 1992; Lovick 1983; Wedel 1986). Fire-cracked rocks also have the advantage of being preserved in a variety of depositional environments. By comparing the contexts of fire-cracked rocks and pottery at the site of San Jacinto 1, I hope to present a convincing argument that considers early pottery as part of the process of cultural evolution.

The Case of San Jacinto 1

In order to understand the significance of excavation data from San Jacinto 1, it is necessary first to place it in a general regional context. The preceramic period of this region is not known, the only evidence being surface collections of artifacts representing an expedient lithic technology (Correal Urrego 1986; Reichel-Dolmatoff 1985). Our knowledge of the region is limited to sites with evidence of early pottery. The distribution of pottery in northern Colombia is restricted to the lowlands of the Magdalena River basin, especially along the Dique channel branch and the low mountains of the Serranía de San Jacinto (Figs. 11.1 and 11.2). In this region, the sites of Barlovento (Reichel-Dolmatoff and Dussan 1955), Canapote (Bischof 1966), San Marcos (Plazas and Falchetti 1986), Guajaro (An-

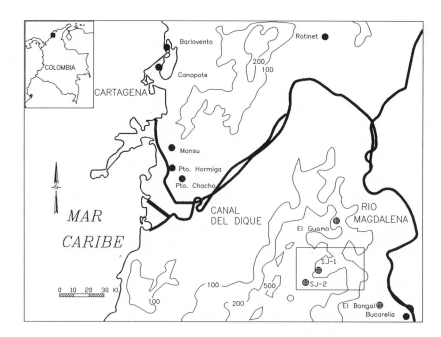

Fig. 11.1. General location of San Jacinto 1 in the lower Magdalena River drainage.

gulo Valdes 1988), Monsú (Reichel-Dolmatoff 1985, 1986), Puerto Hormiga (Reichel-Dolmatoff 1965a, 1965b), Puerto Chacho (Legros 1990; Rodríguez 1988), and San Jacinto 1 and 2 indicate that pottery was being made as early as 5940 ± 60 b.p. (all absolute dates are in uncalibrated radiocarbon years; see Table 11.1 and Fig. 11.3).

Preliminary results of the research at San Jacinto 1 and 2 indicate a sequence characterized first by an early development of pottery that was tempered with organic fiber. Later, in a gradual process, pottery utilizing sand temper was incorporated into the assemblage at sites such as Puerto Chacho, San Jacinto 2, and Puerto Hormiga. Eventually, fiber-tempered assem-

Fig. 11.2. Location of San Jacinto 1 and the town of San Jacinto.

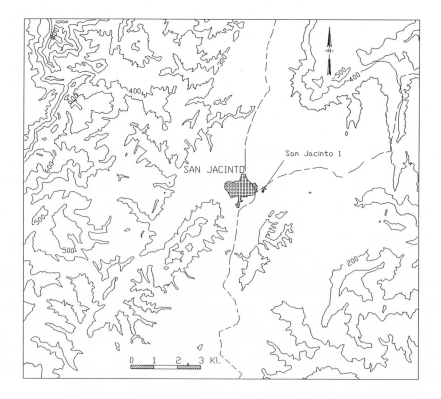

Table 11.1. Early Ceramic-Stage Radiocarbon Dates from Northern Colombia

Site	Radiocarbon Laboratory Number	Material	Radiocarbon Years b.p. (Uncalibrated)
San Jacinto 1	PITT-0155	Charcoal	5940 ± 60
	PITT-0154	Charcoal	5665 ± 75
	BETA-20352	Charcoal	5700 ± 430
Puerto Chacho	BETA-26200	Charcoal	5220 ± 90
Puerto Hormiga	SI-153	Shell	5040 ± 70
	SI-152	Shell	4970 ± 70
	I-445	Shell	4875 ± 170
	SI-151	Charcoal	4820 ± 100
	I-1123	Charcoal	4502 ± 250
San Jacinto 2	PITT-0362	Temper	4565 ± 80
	PITT-0361	Temper	3505 ± 85
San Marcos	BETA-16125	Charcoal	3650 ± 60
Monsú	UCLA-2149c	Shell	5300 ± 80
	UCLA-2149a	Shell	5000 ± 80
	UCLA-2149b	Shell	4200 ± 80
	UCLA-2565g	?	4270 ± 80
	UCLA-2568a	?	4175 ± 70
	UCLA-2568f	Bone	4170 ± 300
	TK-625a	Shell	3240 ± 60
	TK-625b	Shell	3230 ± 90
Guajaro			
Corte 7	BETA-13347	Charcoal?	4190 ± 120
Corte 6	SI-13347	Charcoal?	3800 ± 110
Canapote	Y-1317	Charcoal	3890 ± 100
	Y-1760	Charcoal	3730 ± 120
Barlovento	Y-1318	Charcoal	3510 ± 100
	W-739	Shell	3470 ± 120
	W-743	Shell	3140 ± 120
	W-741	Shell	2980 ± 120

Sources: Angulo 1988; Bischof 1966; Legros 1990; Oyuela-Caycedo 1987; Plazas and Falchetti 1986; Reichel-Dolmatoff 1965a, 1985, 1986; Reichel-Dolmatoff and Dussan 1955.

blages were completely replaced by more heat-resistant and thermally conductive pottery with temper of sand, grog, and shell (see Raymond et al. 1994; Wagner et al. 1994; Wippern 1988). This new technology replaced the older tradition around 4600 b.p., leading to the development of ceramic sequences represented by such sites as Monsú, Guajaro, Canapote, and Barlovento.

The people of this early pottery stage were exploiting diverse microenvironments that favored different kinds of adaptations, from fishing and gathering in estuaries to food gathering inland in grasslands and transitional forests (Oyuela-Caycedo 1987, 1990; Oyuela-Caycedo and Rodríguez 1990; Raymond et al. 1994; Reichel-Dolmatoff 1965a, 1985, 1986). San Ja-

cinto 1 is located in an alluvial depositional environment —in contrast to the estuarine environmental setting— close to a dynamic meandering stream system in the Serranía de San Jacinto (the northern foothills of the Cordillera Occidental of the Andes) at about 210 meters above sea level, on a small plain surrounded by low rolling hills. A bimodal seasonality of dry and wet periods, the latter characterized by precipitation and humidity, is the climatic norm; flooding episodes and vegetational changes are seasonal. The major types of sediments that contributed to the deep stratigraphy of the site are clays and silts and lower percentages of sands. The major lithic resources available to the early populations were sedimentary rocks. The site appears

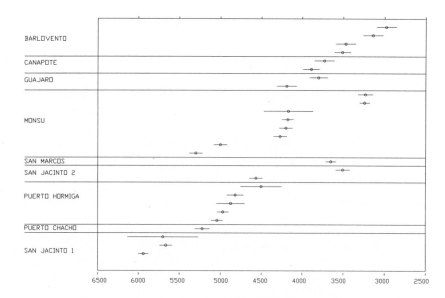

BARLOVENTO
CANAPOTE
GUAJARO
MONSU
SAN MARCOS
SAN JACINTO 2
PUERTO HORMIGA
PUERTO CHACHO
SAN JACINTO 1

6500   6000   5500   5000   4500   4000   3500   3000   2500

Fig. 11.3. Radiocarbon dates (uncalibrated) from the Early Formative sites.

to have been located at different times in its depositional history in a stream forest gallery, close to a savanna woodland, and in an open savanna.

The site was formed by long-term, seasonal human occupation and reoccupation of a point bar until the dynamic of the stream changed direction. Site activities produced a complex horizontal and vertical stratigraphy and microstratigraphy representing seven living floors of variable thickness and an abundance of features resulting from the seasonal occupation of the site. The living floors are dark bands of ash and charcoal mixed with fire-cracked rocks, stone tools, faunal remains, pottery sherds, and other remains left by the human residents of the site. Each successive cultural stratum is separated from the next by a band of lighter colored, culturally sterile sediment deposited during flooding episodes.

In 1991 and 1992 a large excavation (75 square meters) was conducted at the site (Fig. 11.4). The total area of the site at the largest expanse of its occupation (stratum 9) was close to 380 square meters. At its largest size, the site was occupied by what was probably an

Fig. 11.4. General view of the excavation of San Jacinto 1.

extended family of 10 to 25 individuals. Analysis of the material evidence indicates provisional constructions such as windbreaks or temporary structures at the site.

The initial picture that emerges of early pottery-stage lifeways is that of a population of collectors with a logistic mobility strategy that led to the reoccupation over numerous years of a favored point bar located on a permanent stream. The San Jacinto economy appears to have revolved around collecting and processing seeds of wild grasses and rhizomes by means of a ground stone technology. The diet may have been supplemented by hunting both large (deer and tapir) and small animals that were procured and processed with a diverse assemblage of unifacially flaked stone tools or with an expedient technology.

Because of the seasonality and redundancy of the occupation, it is possible to reconstruct activity areas only for stratum 9, when the nature of occupation changed from short, repetitive visits during the dry season to a more prolonged and stable occupation (for an analysis of soil formation and stratigraphy, see Oyuela-Caycedo 1993; on the nature and evidence of seasonality and redundancy of occupation, see Oyuela-Caycedo n.d.). In other words, the change was from use of the site as a special purpose camp visited frequently during the dry season to use of the site as a more permanent base camp during the last occupation of the place. Stratum 9 clearly is the most recent in formation and corresponds to the last occupation of the site by the people who manufactured fiber-tempered pottery. The thickness of this layer varies between 6 and 16 centimeters. The stratum is found at a depth of 3.0 to 3.75 meters below the present-day floodplain. It is characterized by a clay texture and a color that varies between dark brown (10YR3/3) and yellowish brown (10YR5/4), and it has a high content of phosphorus (460 ppm).

The data used for the present research consisted of weight of pottery recovered in each square meter excavated. For comparative spatial distributions, comparable data were used for fire-cracked rocks. Some exploratory analysis was also conducted to define the best approach for recognizing patterns. The technique used

for the spatial variation analysis follows that described by Charles Spencer and Kent V. Flannery (1986). For the computer graphics, however, other programs were utilized (Golden Graphics and Autocad). For determining a correlation value between the two spatial distributions, the standard Pearson's correlation was used (see Whallon 1986).

A comparison of the two sets of basic statistics for pottery and fire-cracked rocks indicates that they are not evenly dispersed over the site (Table 11.2). A multimodal distribution across the excavated area occurs in a pattern that seems far from random. Some squares have lower amounts of pottery or fire-cracked rocks or none at all, whereas others have large quantities. Pottery seems to have a more clearly defined pattern of concentration or clustering than do fire-cracked rocks.

THE POTTERY

San Jacinto 1 pottery is characterized by the use of unidentified plant fibers as temper and by being fired in reduced conditions (possibly in earth ovens). Fiber-tempered pottery seems to have been manufactured mainly by direct shaping and produced by the household for the household (Raymond et al. 1994). Ceramic forms include bowls with incurving rims, jars with spouts, and neckless globular jars with deeply incised and excised handles or luglike handles with excised and modeled zoomorphic motifs (Fig. 11.5). The San Jacinto 1 pottery is characterized by its great diversity in decorative motifs. It might represent an early stage of this technological invention when experimentation with designs appears to be the rule. Each motif is unique, unlike the case in later periods such as at Puerto Hormiga and Monsú, where decoration became repetitive and standardized.

From stratum 9 were recovered almost 9 kilograms of pottery. Together the fragments were found to form a clear pattern of distribution in 53.3 percent of the 75 square meters excavated. Only 42 fragments of pottery rims were recovered associated with this stratum, or 5.9 percent of total pottery weight (Table 11.3). The pottery analysis suggests that in the 75 square meters

Table 11.2. Basic Statistics of Pottery and Fire-Cracked Rocks by Weight, San Jacinto 1

	No. of Squares	Min. Weight (g)/Square	Max. Weight (g)/Square	Mean Weight (g)/Square	Standard Deviation	Coefficient of Variation	Variance/ Mean Ratio
Pottery	75	0	980	119.827	194.961	1.627	317.20
Rocks	75	0	9385	2327.173	1733.544	0.745	16.33

Fig. 11.5. Pottery from San Jacinto 1.

only a few vessels were present, possibly fewer than 10 concentrated in 9 peak areas (Fig. 11.6). The discrete pattern of pottery distribution, which forms clear clusters, does not indicate a direct relationship with site features or with the distribution of the fire-cracked rocks.

The low frequency of pottery also was observable

Table 11.3. Pottery from Stratum 9, San Jacinto 1

Pottery Fragments	Weight (g)	Percentage
Plain sherds	8205	91.2
Rims	468	5.2
Decorated walls	15	0.2
Decorated rims	60	0.7
Decorated lugs	239	2.7
Total	8987	100.0

during the excavation of the lower strata. This pattern contrasts radically with that observed at sites such as Monsú and Puerto Hormiga, where pottery is highly visible.

THE FIRE-CRACKED ROCKS

Fire-cracked rocks are the most abundant archaeological material recovered at San Jacinto 1 in terms of number and weight, a pattern common in base camps of collectors (Binford et al. 1970; Latas 1992). A total of 174.5 kilograms (3,511 pieces) of fire-cracked rocks were recovered in stratum 9 (Table 11.4). The mean weight of the rocks is 49.7 grams.

Fire-cracked rocks were found in three contexts: (1) dispersed over the stratum randomly (distributions below 1,000 grams per square meter seem to behave in this manner; only two square meters had no fire-cracked rocks); (2) forming clusters in piles, occasionally up to 9 kilograms of rocks in a pile; these were classified initially as features (most of the peaks observed contain more than 2,000 grams of fire-cracked rocks per square meter); and (3) in the interiors of fire pits or earth ovens (in stratum 9, only four fire pits were identified; such features were mainly associated with strata 10, 12, 14, and 16).

All the fire-cracked rocks were classified according to rock type and composition. Sedimentary rocks account for 89.91 percent of the fire-cracked rocks; the rest (10.02 percent) are composed of volcanic igneous rocks (Table 11.4).

A Pearson's correlation between pottery and fire-cracked rocks in all the excavated units is extremely low (0.083), which suggests that fire-cracked rocks are not related to pottery in the context of cooking activities (see Fig. 11.6). The distribution of fire-cracked rocks indicates a relation with cooking practices such as stone boiling, which may employ other kinds of perishable containers for which we have no direct evidence, such as bottle gourds (*Lagenaria* sp.), "totumos" (*Crescentia cujete*), leather bags, and baskets. Finally, it is clear that the main association of fire-cracked rocks is with cooking activities linked to the features— earth ovens or cooking pits—that were the chief means of cooking food at San Jacinto 1.

Conclusion

The results of this analysis suggest that there is no relationship between pottery and cooking activities as represented by fire-cracked rocks and features at San Ja-

A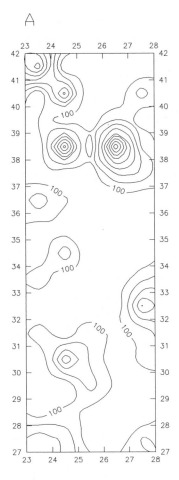

B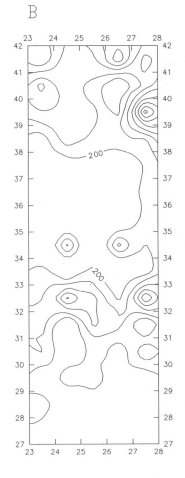

Fig. 11.6. Distributions of pottery (A) and fire-cracked rocks (B) in stratum 9. Pottery concentrations are shown in 100-gram levels, and fire-cracked rocks in 200-gram levels.

cinto 1. This interpretation favors the argument that pottery at this site had a function other than that of cooking.[1] For the moment, we have been able to achieve only partial evidence for the predictions of the model by demonstrating the restricted spatial distribution of pottery as well as its lack of relationship with fire-cracked rocks. Pottery seems not to compete at this

point in its developmental process against fire-cracked rocks. The two do not appear to be directly associated with the same activities, as the Pearson's correlation indicates and as the graphics of spatial distribution illustrate. Only with further research will it be possible to demonstrate that competition is a secondary effect occurring later in pottery's process of incorporation.

There is tentative evidence from this analysis for the third part of the model outlined above. The distribution of pottery is limited to 53.3 percent of the excavated squares. Fire-cracked rocks, on the other hand, occur in all but two squares (97.3 percent). Brown (1986:605) notes for Early Woodland archaeology a similar phenomenon: pottery's low site-wide density and its concentration in highly localized areas. The results here suggest a restricted initial role for pottery in its process of incorporation by the inhabitants of San Jacinto 1, as also seems to be the case for the Early Woodland period of North America.

Likewise, the difference between the quantity of pottery and that of fire-cracked rocks is substantial and points to a secondary and limited role for initial pot-

Table 11.4. Total Weight and Number of Fire-Cracked Rocks in Stratum 9, San Jacinto 1

Type of Rock	Number	Weight (g)
Sedimentary		
Fine-grained sandstone	1427	56078
Limestone	823	36699
Crystal limestone	573	23966
Travertine	336	25735
Igneous		
Rhyolite	78	6008
Granite	6	840
Basalt andesite	268	25212
Total	3511	174538

tery as compared to fire-cracked rocks. A later reversal in the visibility of pottery versus fire-cracked rocks at sites such as Monsú and Puerto Hormiga occurred as pottery was more fully incorporated into the inhabitants' activities and as it competed with and took over roles previously filled by other items of material culture such as fire-cracked rocks.

This work is only a first step toward understanding pottery origins as a process for which it is important to address the archaeological context. The data available from San Jacinto 1 will permit us to continue checking the expectations with more hard evidence, but only with further stratigraphic excavation of more recent sites will it be possible to follow the trajectory of the problem addressed here.

Acknowledgments

This chapter and its analysis have been made possible thanks to the hard fieldwork of students Jaime Castro, Angelica Suaza, Janneth Panche, Felipe Rueda, and Esperanza Duarte and the numerous members of the Organización Campesina Cataluña and the Urbanización la Campesina, who participated in the excavation of San Jacinto 1. The fieldwork was conducted in collaboration with Renée M. Bonzani, who, along with J. Scott Raymond, also helped edit the text. I benefited from the teaching and experience of my advisor, Dick Drennan, to whom I owe much. The research was conducted with a Dissertation Improvement Grant from the National Science Foundation, a travel grant from a Tinker Fellowship awarded by the Latin American Center of the University of Pittsburgh, and the Heinz Fellowship for dissertation writing. A Fulbright-Hays Grant for Dissertation Research was also given to Renée M. Bonzani to help partially finance living expenses during the excavation. A postdoctoral fellowship at the University of Calgary permitted me to complete this chapter.

Note

1. Other kinds of analyses are currently in progress. One of these is the organic residue analysis of the pottery, which is being conducted with the collaboration of the Department of Biochemistry of the University of Liverpool and Dr. Richard Evershed (Evershed et al. 1992). Preliminary results have not been successful in detecting organic residues (Evershed, personal communication, 1994). We also are pursuing the definition of the use of pottery as well as of

the universe of vessel forms and the spatial distribution of these forms at the site. This will allow us to pinpoint in a more exact manner the use that pottery had and will add more evidence for the general aspects of the model. For the moment the evidence seems to indicate that pottery may be more related to social aspects of intensification than to economic factors such as cooking activities.

References Cited

Angulo Valdes, Carlos
1988   *Guajaro en la arqueología del norte de Colombia.* Banco de la República, Bogotá.

Arnold, Dean E.
1985   *Ceramic Theory and Cultural Process.* Cambridge University Press, Cambridge.

Binford, Lewis R., Sally R. Binford, Robert Whallon, and Margaret Ann Hardin
1970   *Archaeology at Hatchery West.* Memoirs of the Society for American Archaeology, no. 24. *American Antiquity* 35(4).

Bischof, Henning
1966   Canapote: An Early Ceramic Site in Northern Colombia, Preliminary Report. *Actas y Memorias del XXXVI Congreso Internacional de Americanistas* 1:483–91.

Bonner, John T.
1980   *The Evolution of Culture in Animals.* Princeton University Press, Princeton, New Jersey.

Brown, James A.
1986   Early Ceramics and Culture: A Review of Interpretations. In *Early Woodland Archaeology,* edited by K. B. Farnsworth and T. E. Emerson, pp. 598–608. Center for American Archeology Press, Kampsville, Illinois.
1989   The Beginnings of Pottery as an Economic Process. In *What's New? A Closer Look at the Process of Innovation,* edited by S. E. van der Leeuw and R. Torrence, pp. 203–24. Unwin Hyman, London.

Cashdan, Elizabeth
1992   Spatial Organization and Habitat Use. In *Evolutionary Ecology and Human Behavior,* edited by E. A. Smith and B. Winterhalder, pp. 237–66. Aldine de Gruyter, New York.

Cashdan, Elizabeth, ed.
1990   *Risk and Uncertainty in Tribal and Peasant Economies.* Westview Press, Boulder, Colorado.

Correal Urrego, G.
1986   Apuntes sobre el medio ambiente pleistocenico y el hombre prehistórico en Colombia. In *New Evidence for the Peopling of the Americas,* edited by A. L. Bryan, pp. 115–31. Center for

the Study of Early Man, University of Maine, Orono.

Dawkins, Richard
1976   *The Selfish Gene.* Oxford University Press, Oxford.

Drennan, Robert D.
1991   Cultural Evolution, Human Ecology, and Empirical Research. In *Profiles in Cultural Evolution,* edited by T. Rambo and K. Gillogly, pp. 113–35. Anthropological Papers 85, Museum of Anthropology, University of Michigan, Ann Arbor.

Evershed, R. P., C. Heron, S. Charters, and L. J. Goad
1992   The Survival of Food Residues: New Methods of Analysis, Interpretation and Application. *Proceedings of the British Academy* 77:187–208.

Frison, George C.
1983   Stone Circles, Stone-Filled Fire Pits, Grinding Stones, and High Plains Archaeology. *Plains Anthropologist* 28(102):81–91.

House, John H., and James W. Smith
1975   Experiments in Replication of Fire-Cracked Rock. In *The Cache River Archaeological Project,* edited by M. B. Schiffer and J. H. House, pp. 75–80. Arkansas Archaeological Survey Research Series, no.8.

Hurt, Wesley R.
1977   The Edge-Trimmed Tool Tradition of Northwest South America. In *For the Director: Research Essays in Honor of James B. Griffin,* edited by C. E. Cleland, pp. 268–94. Anthropological Papers 61, Museum of Anthropology, University of Michigan, Ann Arbor.

Latas, Timothy W.
1992   An Analysis of Fire-Cracked Rocks: A Sedimentological Approach. In *Deciphering a Shell Midden,* edited by J. K. Stein, pp. 211–37. Academic Press, New York.

Legros, Thierry
1990   Les premieres ceramiques Americaines. *Les Dossiers d'Archeologie* 145:60–63.

Lovick, Steven K.
1983   Fire-Cracked Rocks as Tools: Wear-Pattern Analysis. *Plains Anthropologist* 28(99):41–52.

Nelson, Margaret C.
1991   The Study of Technological Organization. In *Archaeological Method and Theory, vol. 3,* edited by M. B. Schiffer, pp. 57–100. University of Arizona Press, Tucson.

Oyuela-Caycedo, Augusto
1987   Dos sitios arqueológicos con degrasante de fibra vegetal en la serranía de San Jacinto (Departamento de Bolívar). *Boletín de Arqueología* 2(1):5–26.

1990   New Evidence of Early Ceramics in the New World. Paper presented at the 55th annual meeting of the Society for American Archaeology, Las Vegas, Nevada.

1993   Sedentism, Food Production, and Pottery Origins in the Tropics: The Case of San Jacinto 1, Colombia. Ph.D. dissertation, Faculty of Arts and Science, University of Pittsburgh, Pittsburgh, Pennsylvania.

n.d.   Seasonality in the Tropical Lowlands of Northwest South America: The Case of San Jacinto 1, Colombia. In *Identifying Seasonality and Sedentism in Archaeological Sites,* edited by O. Bar-Yosef and T. R. Rocek. In preparation.

Oyuela-Caycedo, A., and C. Rodríguez
1990   Shell Midden Formation: The Case of Northwestern South America. Paper presented at the sixth international conference of the International Council for Archaeozoology, Washington, D.C.

Plazas, C., and A. Falchetti
1986   Cerámica arcaica en la sabana de San Marcos. *Boletín de Arqueología* 2:16–23.

Rambo, Terry A.
1991   The Study of Cultural Evolution. In *Profiles in Cultural Evolution,* edited by T. Rambo and K. Gillogly, pp. 23–109. Anthropological Papers 85, Museum of Anthropology, University of Michigan, Ann Arbor.

Raymond, J. Scott, Augusto Oyuela-Caycedo, and Patrick Carmichael
1994   Una comparación de las tecnologías de la cerámica temprana de Ecuador y Colombia. In *Tecnología y organización de la producción cerámica prehispánica en los Andes,* edited by I. Shimada, pp. 33–52. Fondo Editorial, Pontificia Universidad Católica del Perú, Lima.

Reichel-Dolmatoff, Gerardo
1965a   *Excavaciones arqueológicas en Puerto Hormiga (Departamento de Bolívar).* Universidad de los Andes, Bogotá.

1965b   *Colombia.* Frederick A. Praeger Publishers, New York.

1985   *Monsú.* Banco Popular, Bogotá.

1986   *Arqueología de Colombia: Un texto introductorio.* Fundación Segunda Expedición Botanica, Bogotá.

Reichel-Dolmatoff, G., and Alicia Dussan
1955   Excavaciones arqueológicas en los conchales de la costa de Barlovento. *Revista Colombiana de Antropología* 4:247–72.

Reid, Kenneth C.
1984   *Nebo Hill and Late Archaic Prehistory on the Southern Prairie Peninsula.* University of

Kansas Publications in Anthropology no. 15, Lawrence, Kansas.

1989   A Material Science Perspective on Hunter-Gatherer Pottery. In *Pottery Technology: Ideas and Approaches,* edited by G. Bronitsky, pp. 167–80. Westview Press, Boulder, Colorado.

Rodríguez, Camilo
1988   Las tradiciones alfareras tempranas en las llanuras del Caribe Colombiano. *Boletín de Arqueología* 3(2):26–40.

Spencer, Charles, and Kent V. Flannery
1986   Spatial Variation of Debris at Guilá Naquitz: A Descriptive Approach. In *Guilá Naquitz: Archaic Foraging and Early Agriculture in Oaxaca, Mexico,* edited by K. V. Flannery, pp. 331–67. Academic Press, Orlando, Florida.

Stahl, Ann B.
1989   Plant-Food Processing: Implications for Dietary Quality. In *Foraging and Farming: The Evolution of Plant Exploitation,* edited by D. R. Harris and G. C. Hillman, pp. 171–94. Unwin Hyman, London.

Wagner, U., R. Gebhard, E. Murad, J. Riederer, I. Shimada, C. Ulbert, F. E. Wagner, and A. M. Wipperns
1994   Condiciones de cocción y características de composición de la cerámica formativa: Perspectiva arqueométrica. In *Tecnología y organización de la producción cerámica prehispánica en los Andes,* edited by I. Shimada, pp. 121–56. Fondo Editorial de la Pontificia Universidad Católica del Perú, Lima.

Wedel, Dale L.
1986   Some Thoughts on the Potential of Fire-Cracked Rock Studies in Archaeology. *The Wyoming Archaeologist* 29(3–4):159–64.

Whallon, Robert
1986   A Spatial Analysis of Four Occupation Floors at Guilá Naquitz. In *Guilá Naquitz: Archaic Foraging and Early Agriculture in Oaxaca, Mexico,* edited by K. V. Flannery, pp. 369–84. Academic Press, Orlando, Florida.

Wills, W. H.
1992   Plant Cultivation and the Evolution of Risk-Prone Economies in the Prehistoric American Southwest. In *Transitions to Agriculture in Prehistory,* edited by A. B. Gebauer and T. D. Price, pp. 153–76. Prehistory Press, Madison, Wisconsin.

Wippern, Ana M.
1988   Evidencia estratigráfica en el desarrollo de la cerámica temprana de la costa Caribe de Colombia. Paper presented at the 46th International Congress of the Americanists, Amsterdam.

Wolford, Jack A.
1994   Some Problems of Theory and Method in Lithic Studies: Ecuador, Colombia, and Venezuela. In *History of Latin American Archaeology,* edited by A. Oyuela-Caycedo, pp. 155–72. Avebury, Great Britain.

12

Sites with Early Ceramics in the Caribbean Littoral of Colombia

A Discussion of Periodization and Typologies

CAMILO RODRÍGUEZ

TRANSLATED BY RENÉE M. BONZANI

This chapter presents basic data for the three sites with the earliest ceramics of the Caribbean littoral of Colombia—Puerto Chacho, Puerto Hormiga, and Monsú—with the aim of contributing to the discussion of the antiquity, periodization, and cultural affinities of each site. When one takes into account the facts that the excavations were not extensive and the published data are limited and contradictory, it becomes evident that the established typologies are based on decorations that do not serve as either cultural or chronological markers and, moreover, are unrepresentative of the materials recovered. Two or more types can be encountered in sherds from the same vessel. Decorations and motifs are similar across several millennia. These problems of typology and chronology are evident in studies of the most common receptacles, such as the vessels known as *tecomates* that can be considered a great "superfamily" for this epoch (Bray 1984).

Vessel temper appears to be an indicator of cultural dynamics in inland Colombia during this early period, as Reichel-Dolmatoff proposed in 1965. Not surprisingly, later publications by Reichel-Dolmatoff—the investigator who has worked most on this theme in the region—reconsidered temper and proposed other criteria for classifying early ceramics. Investigations on the Caribbean coast of Colombia have confirmed the great antiquity (around 6000 b.p.) of the ceramic tradition that utilized vegetable fiber as a temper (Oyuela-Caycedo 1987, 1990) and have also permitted a reinterpretation of lifeways and settlement patterns (Oyuela-Caycedo and Rodríguez 1990; Rodríguez 1988).

In somewhat younger sites, dating to around 5000–4500 b.p., the tradition of vegetable fiber temper gradually begins to coexist with that of mineral temper, as is the case at Puerto Hormiga (Reichel-Dolmatoff 1961, 1965), Puerto Chacho (Legros et al. 1988), and San Jacinto 2 (Oyuela-Caycedo 1990). The general tendency is for the use of mineral and shell temper to increase while the tradition of vegetable fiber temper disappears in sites dated up to about 4,000 years b.p., such as Canapote (Bischof 1966), Rotinet (Angulo Valdes 1986a, 1986b, 1988), and Barlovento (Reichel-Dolmatoff 1955, 1965). Vessels in the *tecomate* tradition and vessels with *budare*-like (flat griddle) profiles are divided between both temper traditions (Bray 1984). Likewise, they are similar in fundamentals such as decoration and decorative motifs.

In sites with shell middens (Puerto Chacho and Puerto Hormiga) and in sites with mounds (Monsú) located close to the estuaries and brackish lagoons (those with a mix of fresh and salt water), fish were the principal protein base in the diets of seasonal groups. The collection of mollusks and bivalves was a regular activity, although the overall quantity of protein obtained was low. The collection of seeds and the hunting of small game were secondary activities. There is insufficient paleobotanical evidence to infer agriculture, and the indirect evidence that argues for it (see Reichel-Dolmatoff 1985) is not convincing.

Comparison of Puerto Chacho with the other sites, especially Puerto Hormiga, confirms the interpretation of a pattern of settlements of groups of seasonal fishers and collectors who, over a considerable span of time, frequented the terraces of one of the estuaries of the Madgalena River. Other shell middens have been found near Puerto Chacho that have similar characteristics and physiographic positions. They also have ceramics with vegetable fiber temper and logically are considered contemporaneous. The ^{14}C dates obtained for these seasonal encampments generally coincide with the end of one of the "humid continental periods" and with a high sea level, 4 to 5 meters above that of today (Oyuela-Caycedo and Rodríguez 1990).

Puerto Chacho

Puerto Chacho, characterized by a large shell midden, is located on the right margin of the Canal del Dique close to the natural mouth of the ancient arm of the Magdalena River (Fig. 12.1). The river used to have its mouth in the Caribbean Sea south of the bay of Barbacoas, but it was displaced southward by tectonic uplift and sedimentation.

Physiographically, the site is located on a natural levee of an alluvial terrace that runs for approximately 13.5 kilometers in a straight line along the actual coast. During its formation it probably experienced several episodes of overflow from the river, especially during the rainy months of the Andean zone and the humid continental periods. The site's location on the highest part of the terrace, however, prevented its flooding. The site has a form that looks like a sideways letter S with an east-west orientation; at its largest point it is approximately 84 meters long, and its width varies between 14 and 29 meters.

Observations from more than 70 test pits that delimited the area of the site also permitted definition of the variations in height of the shell accumulations and guided the layout of the excavations. The shell accumulations, in both their vertical and their horizontal

dimensions, are neither homogeneous nor continuous over the entire site. Localized sectors exist, however, that present regularities in composition, consistency, and thickness of the layers of shells in the soil matrix (texture and color).

The alternation of similar layers of shells permits the inference that site formation was the result of many events of reoccupation. It is possible that its accumulations were initially in the form of unmixed, sequential deposits but that later reoccupations resulted in a mixing of strata. One can infer that the layers of shells were exposed for many years, even centuries, which must have made the formation of soils particularly difficult, and that soils indeed formed only after a number of millennia. For these reasons, the interpretation of the chronology of the shell midden and the "stratigraphic" localization are problematical.

The most abundant shells at Puerto Chacho are from the mollusk *Polymerada carolianiana,* present throughout the entire sequence; in fact, some layers are made up almost entirely of these mollusks (Gonzales 1990). Oysters (*Crassotrea rhizophorae* and *Ostrea plumosa*) were encountered in considerable proportions, as was the snail *Melongena melongena.* Other mollusks found in smaller quantities are the bivalve *Anomala cardiod* and the gastropod *Strombus gigas.* Small coastal snails, insignificant for dietary purposes but good indicators of areas exposed to the marine tidal surge or of the contact between fresh and salt water, were also recorded. The proportions of the mollusks, oysters, and snails, together with the soil matrix, were the principal criteria used to define the "stratigraphic" layers of the shell midden (Legros 1989).

A trench was excavated perpendicular to the midden's major axis in the middle part of the shell midden, running through one of the widest (18 m) and deepest (85 to 100 cm) sectors of the site. In quadrant J, corresponding to the flat and high part, four principal layers were defined, some with subdivisions (Legros 1989). A sample of vegetable carbon that permitted the dating of the middle part of the occupation of the east sector of the shell midden to 5220 ± 90 b.p. (Beta-26200) was obtained from layer 2B (Rodríguez 1988).

Ceramics were classified into three groups based on temper: fragments with vegetable fiber, fragments with mineral temper, and fragments that show a mix of fiber and mineral temper (*mixto*). Considering the way in which the shell midden was formed, it is unreasonable to analyze the cultural contents of the units of excavation separately, or by layers of shell or levels, to arrive at chronological interpretations about the shell

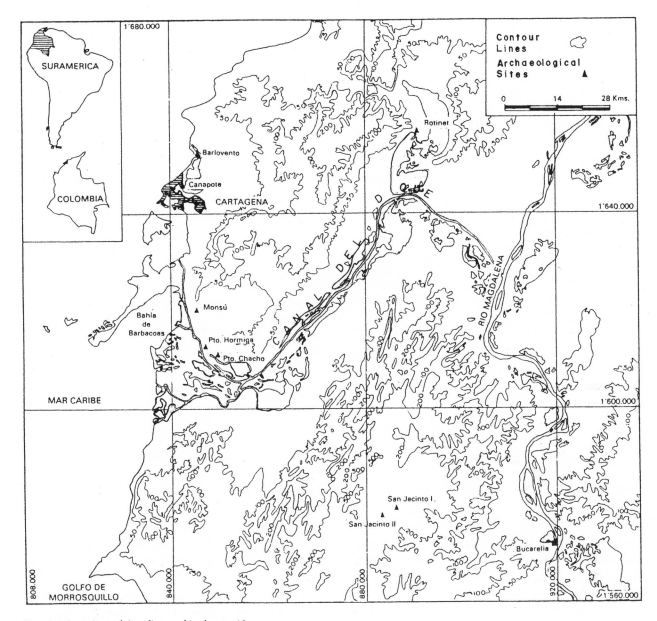

Fig. 12.1. Locations of sites discussed in chapter 12.

accumulations. For example, in probe I, excavated by arbitrary levels, cultural remains were encountered down to 120 centimeters. The recovered ceramic fragments number 334. In the higher levels of probe I, pottery fragments with mineral temper predominate, whereas the lower levels have a majority of fragments with vegetable fiber temper. However, when the proportion of each one of the three groups of ceramics is observed by level, the mixed fiber-and-mineral type predominates. For example, 30.5 percent of the total fragments were recovered from the level extending from 40 to 65 centimeters below ground surface, distributed as follows: 19.43 percent mixed temper, 8.07

percent fiber temper, and 2.99 percent mineral temper (Fig. 12.2). If the pottery from all levels of probe I is analyzed together, the percentages are as follows (Fig. 12.3): 53.29 percent mixed temper, 30.53 percent fiber temper, and 16.16 percent mineral temper (Rodríguez et al. 1988).

A total of 475 sherds was obtained from quadrant J of the trench, located 14 meters from probe I (Legros 1989). Here the layers of shell, their consistency, and the color of the matrices were considered as the guide to group or separate the remains. Stratum 2B yielded 60.63 percent of the total number of sherds—the major ceramic concentration in the quadrant—distrib-

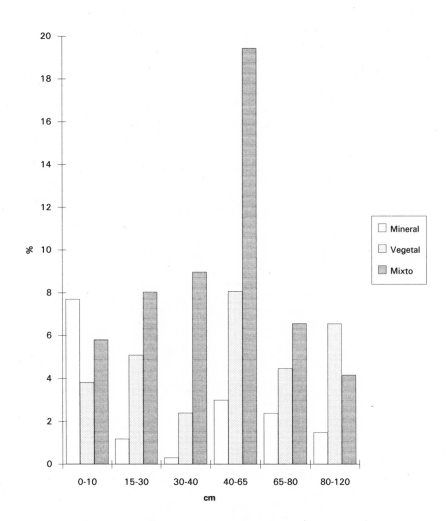

Fig. 12.2. Percentages of temper types in pottery at each level of the excavation of probe 1, Puerto Chacho.

uted as follows (Fig. 12.4): 21.68 percent mineral temper, 20.63 percent fiber temper, and 18.3 percent mixed temper. If the total potsherds in quadrant J are considered, one observes the following (Fig. 12.5): 35.36 percent mineral temper, 31.92 percent fiber temper, and 32.84 percent mixed temper (Fernández 1989).

As can be seen, the two quadrants differ from one another in their percentages of the established ceramic groups. This has been interpreted as a result of the formation process of the shell midden. There is only one characteristic shared by both quadrants: the presence of a level (40–65 cm) or stratum (2B) that has the majority of the fragments and that in general terms is encountered at the same depth.

This finding obligates us to consider the total sample, combining the data from the two quadrants in all levels, for a total of 809 fragments, which have been identified as follows: 41.28 percent mixed temper, 31.27 percent fiber temper, and 27.44 percent mineral temper (Fig. 12.6). The most common decorations are wide, deep lineal impressions (Fig. 12.7, items 6 and 9) combined with impressions, excisions, incisions, finger impressions, the application of biomorphic adornments on vessel rims, and infilling of decorations with red pigment. The wide variety of motifs that are created using each one of these types of decoration is a distinctive feature of the early ceramics of this zone. Generally, the vessels have decoration near the rim, some extending to the middle part of the body or from the maximum diameter to the mouth. Among the most frequent motifs are zoned lineal impressions with terminal points (Fig. 12.7, items 4, 5, and 7), circular excised depressions (Fig. 12.7, items 1–3), dentate-stamped impressions, and incised bands forming rectangles filled with incised dots (Fig. 12.7, item 8) or impressed points (Fig. 12.7, item 10). Vessel forms are simple with wide mouths. Semiglobular bowls with slightly inverted walls, well-defined rims, and round or thin lips are especially characteristic. These containers

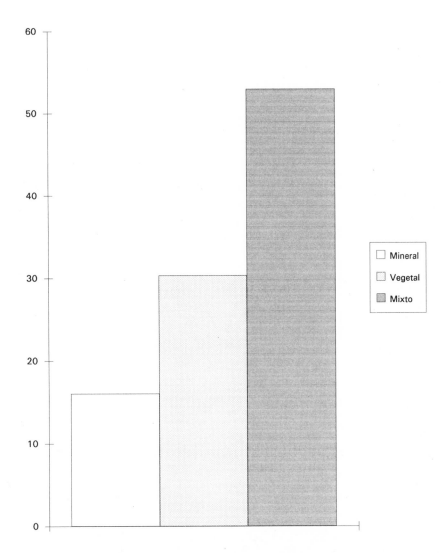

Fig. 12.3. Percentages of temper types in all pottery from probe 1, Puerto Chacho.

fall within the tradition of tecomate-type vessels (Reichel-Dolmatoff 1985).

Faunal remains, especially of marine and freshwater fish that frequent or are adapted to the brackish waters of the estuaries, were found together with ceramics and lithic artifacts in the middle strata of the shell midden. The following genera have been identified from quadrant J and stratum 2B: *Centropomus* (robalos [bass]), which is the most abundant, and *Euguerres* (*mojarras*). These two marine fishes make up more than 50 percent of the complete sample. *Trachycorystes* (*barbudos*) and *Hoplias* (*moncholos*) are also present; these are generally found in freshwater, although they do inhabit transitional waters. Other genera and species of fish identified but not present in large quantities in the total sample are *Chrymys scripta* (*icotea*), *Trichechus manatus* (*manatí*), *Procyon* sp. (*mapache* [racoon]), and *Iguana iguana* (Cooke 1990; Legros 1989).

Puerto Hormiga

This site is located on the same alluvial terrace as Puerto Chacho, 2.5 kilometers away, in an area of the natural canal formed by the overflowing of the river; the actual marine coastline is approximately 11 kilometers distant (Rodríguez et al. 1988). Reichel-Dolmatoff has given the following description of the site:

The total diameter, measured from north to south, is 77 meters; from east to west, 85 meters, that is to say, the shell mound is somewhat oval. . . . In the northeast sector it reaches its maximum width of 25 meters. It decreases then to the west and the southeast to 20 meters. The elevation over the adjacent terrain is rarely more than 1.20 meters and only in the northern middle section reaches 1.26 meters. . . . To the west there is a depression in the circle that decreases in elevation to 80 centimeters for a distance of 26 meters. It was not made by an artificial excavation as it appears that the depression is simply the result of a lesser ac-

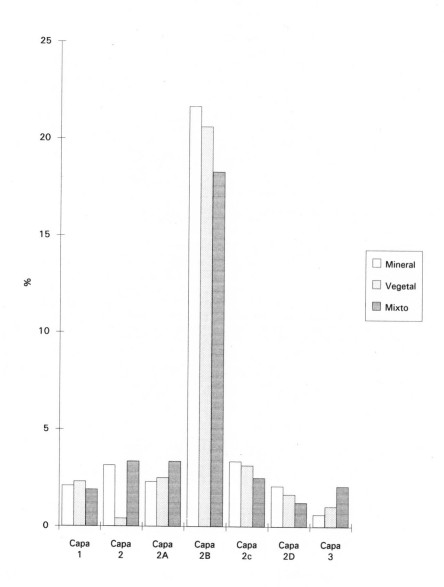

Fig. 12.4. Percentages of temper types in pottery from each shell layer of the excavation in quadrant J, Puerto Chacho.

cumulation of shell. The center of the shell mound is a circular flat area of 39 to 40 meters in diameter. (Reichel-Dolmatoff 1965:8)

Reichel-Dolmatoff interprets the shell midden by referring to the shell layers as having been formed in a manner similar to that of horizontal soil formations:

The basic structure of the shell mound consists in the superposition of four layers of shells mixed with earth, each one characterized by differences in color and consistency. Looking in more detail, one naturally observes some local variations to the stratification such as lenses of calcified shell, layers of shell dyed by red or yellow clay, floors of crushed shell, etc., but, however, in every location of the shell mound one invariably observes the same fundamental sequence of the four basic strata. (Reichel-Dolmatoff 1965:11)

The five dates published for Puerto Hormiga range from 5040 ± 70 b.p. to 4502 ± 250 b.p. (Reichel-Dolmatoff 1965:53) and present a consistent chronology. The excavated ceramics contain temper of vegetable fiber in 70 percent of the total sample; the remaining 30 percent has mineral temper. Each one of these two groups was subdivided into two types (Reichel-Dolmatoff 1965:19).

Although the exact data have not been published, the fauna recorded at Puerto Hormiga has characteristics generally similar to those of the Puerto Chacho fauna. Fishing supplied the major volume of protein; plaques of turtle shell (two species) are mentioned, and the collection of mollusks and bivalves was also considerable. As at Puerto Chacho, hunting of medium to small mammals and the collection of seeds was also secondary (Reichel-Dolmatoff 1965:42). In general, the fauna are typical of estuaries and brackish lagoons in which mangroves grow.

Monsú

The artificial mound of Monsú, approximately 100 meters in diameter (Reichel-Dolmatoff 1985:18), is located on a marine terrace approximately 3 kilometers in a straight line from the coast and 8 kilometers from Puerto Hormiga. The base of the mound is composed of impermeable silts (vertisols) without variation in texture over the entire terrace. In winter, all of the flat zone is flooded because of the poor drainage caused by these silts; this flooding required people to choose the highest points for their settlement locations. The vertisols have the property of contracting during the summer, causing surface cracks. During the winter, they expand because of water saturation. This phenome-

non of expansion and contraction can result in stratigraphic inversion, which is mentioned here as one of the possible natural causes of the alteration in this site's stratigraphy (Rodríguez et al. 1988). The discontinuity in the stratigraphy, which in some cases is abrupt (Reichel-Dolmatoff 1985:Figs. 10–17), makes plausible the supposition that the mound was not the result of a gradual accumulation of garbage but that at some points during its formation it was affected by human redeposition of earth that raised or lowered the occupied surface (Rodríguez et al. 1988).

Intrusive burials also contributed to stratigraphic alteration. In quadrant A, Reichel-Dolmatoff recorded a tomb dated to 2800 b.p.—after the abandonment of the mound—that penetrated from the surface to unit 17. Of the nine published dates from the site, seven were collected in this quadrant. Of these, Reichel-Dolmatoff accepts only four as valid.

The physiographic conditions of the marine terrace

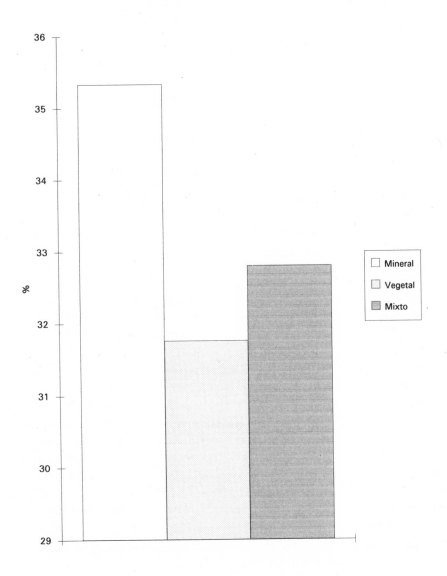

Fig. 12.5. Percentages of temper types in all pottery from quadrant J, Puerto Chacho.

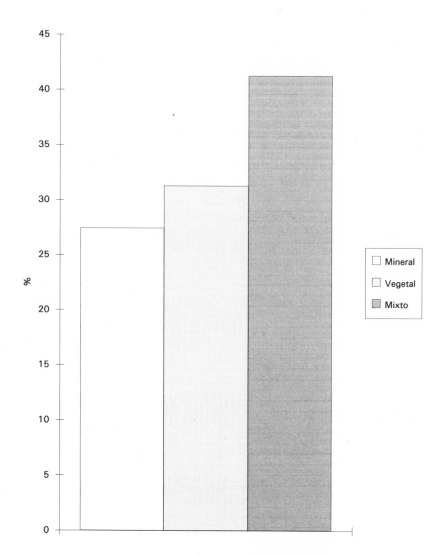

Fig. 12.6. Percentages of temper types in all pottery from probe 1 and quadrant J combined, Puerto Chacho.

where the site is located were different around 5000 b.p. from those of today. Reichel-Dolmatoff mentions a dry period, or hypsithermal, for this epoch. According to the palynological data for the Turbana and Monsú periods, it is probable that the area was covered in forest (Reichel-Dolmatoff 1985:46, 171). Between 5000 and 4000 b.p. in this zone of the Caribbean coast, a gradual drying period occurred, with a 4- to 5-meter drop in sea level until it reached practically its current level (G. Vernette, personal communication, 1988; Buriel and Vernette 1981). It is probable that the coast was closer to the site and the terrace was periodically flooded and covered with forests, eventually mangrove ones (Oyuela-Caycedo and Rodríguez 1990).

The dates accepted by Reichel-Dolmatoff run from 5275 ± 80 b.p. to 3320 ± 60 b.p. and help associate the ceramics with the early tradition. The ceramics show typological continuity with the pottery of Puerto Chacho and Puerto Hormiga. However, they differ in

that they are almost exclusively sand tempered, with the exception of a type of shell temper that appears during the final period (Barlovento) of the early tradition at this site. Ceramic fragments with vegetable temper were not recorded (Reichel-Dolmatoff 1985).

The ceramic material was classified into 40 types. Thirty-one of these types are based on variation in decoration and motifs, even though decorated material constitutes only 5.49 percent of the total. The decoration consists primarily of incisions with some variation (grooved, striated, and widened). There is only one example of modeled decoration. The motifs are all geometric and quite varied. Reichel-Dolmatoff associates specific types with periods of time. Related types that appear together in specific contexts are given the denomination *complejo cerámico*. These last were usually situated between living floors (Reichel-Dolmatoff 1985:51–52).

Reichel-Dolmatoff defined five living floors to which

he assigned chronological periods. The deepest is Turbana. It is followed by the Monsú period, radiocarbon dated to 5275 ± 80 b.p. This is followed in turn by an abandonment of the site, registered throughout the mound, for a period of 1,100 years. Reichel-Dolmatoff notes that this abandonment is simultaneous with the occupation of Puerto Hormiga. The third period, called Pangola, is dated to 4200 b.p. It is followed by the Macaví period, which does not have ¹⁴C dates; however, Reichel-Dolmatoff correlates the ceramic types of this period with those from the site of Canapote (Bischof 1966), which is dated to 3890 ± 100 b.p. The last occupation floor with early ceramics is assigned to the Barlovento period, which has dates of around 3200 b.p. (Reichel-Dolmatoff 1985).

In terms of fauna, Reichel-Dolmatoff mentions the recovery of a total of 1,700 bones of animals belonging to the following species: deer (*Odocoileus virginianus*), wild pig, *guatinaja* (*Cuniculus paca*), anteater, *manatí* (*Trichechus manatus*), bird (without specification), turtles (various species), caiman (various species), fish (without specification), and crab—all species that correspond to the present day neotropical fauna. In addition, 799 fragments of mollusks were recovered, nearly all of *Ampullarius*, an edible snail of estuaries and slow-moving waters, and of *Strombus gigas*, whose habitat is deep waters (Reichel-Dolmatoff 1985:169–70).

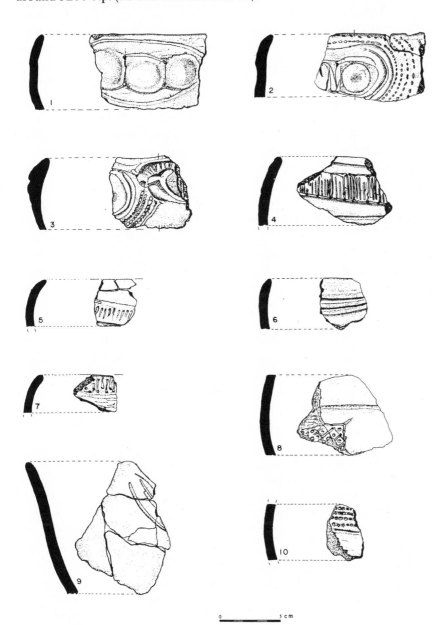

Fig. 12.7. Decoration of some ceramic fragments from Puerto Chacho.

Discussion

The ceramic materials from Puerto Chacho and Puerto Hormiga are identical; only in their classification are different aspects emphasized. The temper I have called "mixed" for the material from Puerto Chacho is also present at Puerto Hormiga but is included in the group with fiber temper there. The pottery sample from Puerto Chacho at the Instituto Colombiano de Antropología in Bogotá is identical to fragments collected by the author at Puerto Hormiga, proving the presence of mixed temper there. If, for Puerto Chacho, the percentage of pottery sherds with mixed temper is summed with that for sherds with fiber temper, the result would be 72.55 percent, similar to the percentage of sherds with fiber temper found at Puerto Hormiga. The percentages of sherds with mineral temper for both sites are similar. In addition, the types of decoration and decorative motifs are identical, as are vessel forms. Similarities among the ceramics from both sites are evident in both the kinds and percentages of tempering materials.

Reichel-Dolmatoff considered the combined ceramics of Puerto Hormiga to be clearly different from those of Monsú, although they have technical and stylistic similarities. The tecomate vessel form predominates at both Monsú and Puerto Hormiga, as do modeled adornments and incised decorative motifs (Reichel-Dolmatoff 1985:177).

Reichel-Dolmatoff's interpretations of the results of the excavations at Monsú, like his acceptance of some dates and discarding of others, are questionable in light of the stratigraphic problems mentioned earlier and noted by Reichel-Dolmatoff himself. For these reasons, the relative position of the stratum with the date of 5270 b.p., which by superposition dates one of the oldest occupations of the site of Monsú, is in question.

The established ceramic types in many cases are not well defined and tend to overlap one another. One example of this is that a single decorative motif—parallel incisions terminating in circular stamps—is distributed among various types, including Turbana Incised Punctate (Reichel-Dolmatoff 1985:Fig. 18:14), Macaví Incised Stamped (1985:Fig. 32:15 and Fig. 33:1, 8), Macaví Habana Incised (1985:Fig. 40:8), Macaví Incised Punctate (1985:Fig. 41:3 and Fig. 42:5), and Barlovento Incised Parallel (1985:Fig. 51:13). The illustrations show fragments classified under one type that are sometimes identical to fragments of other types, as occurs with the rim sherd classified as Monsú Incised Linear in Reichel-Dolmatoff's Fig. 23:3 and

as Pangola Incised Linear in his Fig. 28:9 (Reichel-Dolmatoff 1985). This is but one of many such examples.

The most controversial aspect of this typology is the equation of ceramic types with chronological periods. Types defined for the Monsú period are actually associated with all of the established periods, as occurs with fragments of Monsú Incised Linear (Reichel-Dolmatoff 1985:124). Also, one must note that the dated units of the excavation corresponding to a given period contain types that appear to be similar to those of other periods. One example of this is the presence of sherds classified as pertaining to the Turbana, Pangola, Macaví, and Barlovento periods in unit 13—the unit from which the sample used to date the Monsú period was obtained (Reichel-Dolmatoff 1985:124, 208, 210).

The last occupation of the mound of Monsú was designated the Barlovento period. It was differentiated from early occupations by the presence of artifacts of shell and abundant remains of mollusks and bones of fish, remains not encountered for the oldest periods of occupation (Reichel-Dolmatoff 1985:155). The date of the Barlovento period at Monsú falls around 3200 b.p. and coincides with a rise in sea level, after which sea level again falls (Buriel and Vernette 1981). Again, it is clear that there is an association between the humid continental periods that resulted in high sea levels and the activities of fishing and mollusk collecting in the estuaries and brackish lagoons covered by mangrove forests (Oyuela-Caycedo and Rodríguez 1990).

In the chronological periodizations proposed by Reichel-Dolmatoff (1985) and Bischof (1972), there is no convincing explanation for the absence of ceramics with fiber temper at the sites of Monsú, Canapote, and Barlovento. Before the publication of his work at Monsú, however, Reichel-Dolmatoff considered the ceramics of Puerto Hormiga as representative of the initial phase of ceramic production, noting their technical characteristics, including vegetable temper and decoration, and also their antiquity.

In his Monsú site report, Reichel-Dolmatoff (1985) attributes this absence of fiber-tempered pottery to the early dates for the Monsú period and the site's subsequent abandonment. During this abandonment, Puerto Hormiga emerged (as did, presumably, Puerto Chacho). The new occupants of the mound at Monsú during the later Pangola period did not use ceramics with vegetable fiber temper, although the most recent date for this period (4200 b.p.) is similar to that for the final occupation of Puerto Hormiga (4500 b.p.). According to Reichel-Dolmatoff, pottery of the Pangola period is related to the ceramics of the preceding Turbana and Monsú periods. Fiber-tempered pottery is also absent at Monsú during the subsequent Macaví and Barlovento periods. Reichel-Dolmatoff's explanation is that the ceramics of Puerto Hormiga, typified by vegetable fiber temper, existed only during the millennium of the abandonment corresponding to the Monsú and Pangola periods and did not have ancestors or successors. Bischof's opinion is that the ceramics of Puerto Hormiga and Puerto Chacho are later than the period proposed by Reichel-Dolmatoff and are a manifestation of local pottery production (Bischof, personal communication, 1987).

Investigations in the Serranía de San Jacinto (Oyuela-Caycedo 1987, 1990) permit the refutation of some of Reichel-Dolmatoff's and Bischof's interpretations about the origins and the antiquity of the fiber-tempered ceramic tradition. The oldest dates for the site of San Jacinto 1 are around 6000 b.p., and the latest is 5665 b.p. Vegetable fiber temper is present in 100 percent of the total ceramic sample. The decoration is incised, excised, and modeled and is similar to that of Puerto Hormiga (Reichel-Dolmatoff 1965) and Puerto Chacho (Rodríguez et al. 1988). As with the ceramics of Monsú, changes in the decorations occur (Oyuela-Caycedo 1987, 1990; Raymond et al. 1994).

For San Jacinto 2, the dates fall between 4565 and 3505 b.p. (Oyuela-Caycedo 1990); 69 percent of the ceramic sample has vegetable fiber temper, and 31 percent has sand temper. In later analyses the "mixed" temper was detected (Oyuela-Caycedo 1990). The decoration is also incised-excised (Oyuela-Caycedo 1987). The temper proportions are similar to those at the sites of Puerto Hormiga and Puerto Chacho, although there is a closer similarity in decoration with material from the site of Bucarelia (Oyuela-Caycedo 1990; Raymond et al. 1994).

The continuity of the fiber temper tradition in the periods that postdate the shell mounds of Puerto Hormiga and Puerto Chacho, when fiber-tempered ceramics coexist with mineral-tempered ceramics, has been commented on for these two sites and that of San Jacinto 2 and is also attested to at the site of El Pozón (Plazas and Falchetti 1986). El Pozón is a settlement near the Mompos Depression, far from the littoral, dated at 3600 ± 60 b.p. This date is associated with a small sample of ceramics with fiber and mineral temper, incised decoration, and modeled applications, similar to the ceramics of Puerto Hormiga.

I would like to suggest that most of the remains of the settlement at Monsú postdate the published dates for Puerto Chacho and Puerto Hormiga and that the ceramics from Monsú have a closer cultural affinity with ceramics from the settlements of Canapote, dated at 3890 ± 100 b.p., Rotinet (4190 ± 120 b.p.), and Barlovento (3470 ± 120 b.p.). The decorations of vessels with mineral and shell temper from these sites are identical to those from Monsú, and these settlements are also characterized by the absence of ceramics with vegetable fiber temper.

Acknowledgments

The investigations of the Proyecto Llanuras del Caribe (1987) and the excavations of the shell mound of Puerto Chacho (1988) were realized thanks to an agreement between the Instituto Colombiano de Antropología and the Instituto Francés de Estudios Andinos (IFEA). The investigations are in process under the direction of Thierry Legros (IFEA). Thanks to Pedro Botero (CIAF-Bogotá) for his comments on the stratigraphy and physiography of the zone and to Georges Vernette (CIOH-Cartagena) for his thoughts on changes in sea level on the Caribbean coast. Both investigators amicably visited us during the excavations. A special thanks to Richard Cooke (STRI-Panamá) for his collaboration in the identification of faunal remains. Luis Martínez Silva (INDERENA-Cartagena) identified the mollusks. Margarita Reyes drew the ceramic fragments. An earlier version of this chapter was presented as a paper at the 55th annual meeting of the Society for American Archaeology in Las Vegas, Nevada, in 1990. Colleagues Sonia Archila, Inés Cavelier, and Luisa Fernanda Herrera reviewed the present text and made important suggestions.

References Cited

Angulo Valdes, Carlos
  1986a   Arqueología de la ciénaga del Guájaro. *Boletín de Arqueología* 1(1):11–26. Fundación de Arqueológicas Nacionales, Banco de la República, Bogotá.
  1986b   Guájaro en la arqueología del norte de Colombia. *Boletín de Arqueología* 1(3):49–53. Fundación de Investigaciones Arqueológicas Nacionales, Banco de la República, Bogotá.
  1988   Modos de vida en la prehistoria de la llanura atlántico de Colombia. In *Prehistoria Sudamericana: Nuevas perspectivas,* edited by Betty J.

Meggers. Taraxacum, Washington, D.C. Printed in Santiago, Chile.

Bischof, Henning

1966   Canapote, an Early Ceramic Site in Northern Colombia (Preliminary Report). 36th International Congress of Americanists, Seville, Spain. *Actas y Memorias* 1:483–91.

1972   The Origins of Pottery in South America: Recent Radiocarbon Dates from Southwest Ecuador. 40th International Congress of Americanists, Seville, Spain. *Actas y Memorias* 1:484–91.

Bray, Warwick

1984   Across the Darien Gap: A Colombian View of Isthmian Archaeology. In *The Archaeology of Lower Central America,* edited by F. W. Lange and D. Z. Stone. University of New Mexico Press, Albuquerque.

Buriel, T. and G. Vernette.

1981   Evidencias de cambios del nivel del mar en el Cuaternario de la región de Cartagena, Bolívar. *Revista CIAF* 6(13):77–92. Bogotá.

Cooke, Richard

1990   Apuntes preliminares sobre los restos de fauna de Puerto Chacho Reporte. Unpublished manuscript on file at the Smithsonian Tropical Research Institute, Panamá.

Fernández, Eduardo

1989   Los desgrasantes del Formativo temprano en la costa Caribe Colombiana: Análisis petrográfico de la cerámica de Puerto Chacho. Field Work. Unpublished manuscript on file in the Department of Anthropology, Universidad de los Andes, Bogotá.

Gonzales, Laura

1990   Peces y pesca en el conchero de Puerto Chacho: Un estudio arqueológico. Unpublished manuscript.

Legros, Thierry

1989   Consideraciones sobre Puerto Chacho, un conchero de las Llanuras del Caribe Colombiano. In *Memorias del Simposio de Arqueología y Antropología Física, V Congreso Nacional de Antropología, Villa de Leyva,* pp. 67–76. ICFES, Bogotá.

Legros, T., C. Rodriguez, and C. Pauly

1988   Puerto Chacho, la ceramique a desgraissant de fibres vegetales et le formatif anciente du nord de la Colombie. Paper presented at the 45th International Congress of Americanists, Amsterdam.

Oyuela-Caycedo, Augusto

1987   Dos sitios arqueológicos con desgrasante de fibra vegetal en la Serranía de San Jacinto (Dpto. de Bolívar). *Boletín de Arqueología* 2(1):5–26. Fundación de Investigaciones Arqueológicas Nacionales, Banco de la República, Bogotá.

1990   New Evidence of Early Ceramics in the New World. Paper presented at the 55th annual meeting of the Society for American Archaeology, Las Vegas, Nevada.

Oyuela-Caycedo, A., and C. Rodríguez

1990   Shell Midden Formation: The Case of Northwestern South America. Paper presented at the sixth international conference of the International Council for Archaeozoology, Washington, D.C.

Plazas, C., and A. Falchetti

1986   Cerámica arcaica en la sabana de San Marcos. *Boletín de Arqueología* 2:16–23. Fundación de Investigaciones Arqueológicas Nacionales, Bogotá.

Raymond, Scott, Augusto Oyuela-Caycedo, and Patrick Carmichael

1994   Una comparación de las tecnologías de la cerámica temprana de Ecuador y Colombia. In *Tecnología y organización de la producción cerámica prehispánica en los Andes,* edited by I. Shimada, pp. 33–52. Fondo Editorial, Pontificia Universidad Católica del Perú.

Reichel-Dolmatoff, Gerardo

1955   Excavaciones en los conchales de la costa de Barlovento. *Revista Colombiana de Antropología* 4:249–72. Bogotá.

1961   Puerto Hormiga: Un complejo prehistórico marginal de Colombia (nota preliminar). *Revista Colombiana de Antropología* 10:349–54. Bogotá.

1965   *Excavaciones arqueológicas en Puerto Hormiga, Departamento de Bolívar.* Serie Antropológica no. 2. Ediciones Universidad de los Andes, Bogotá.

1985   *Monsú.* Banco Popular, Bogotá.

Rodríguez, Camilo

1988   Las tradiciones alfareras tempranas en las llanuras del Caribe Colombiano (Departamento de Bolívar y Atlántico): Periodización y comparación cerámica. *Boletín de Arqueología* 3(2):26–40. Fundación de Investigaciones Arqueológicas Nacionales, Bogotá.

Rodríguez, Camilo, Thierry Legros, and C. Pauly

1988   El Formativo de la costa Caribe Colombiana: Informe científico de 1987. Informe al Instituto Colombiano de Antropología, Bogotá.

13

The Many Contexts of Early Valdivia Ceramics

JONATHAN E. DAMP AND
L. PATRICIA VARGAS S.

Gordon Willey, on the fiftieth anniversary of the Society for American Archaeology, remarked that "the more we know about the sheer lines of culture historical structure, the better position we will be in to examine culture process" (Willey 1985:353). Willey placed only secondary importance on the integration of pottery into the sociocultural matrix. In his following brief discussion of ceramic origins in the Precolumbian New World, he directed our attention to the Valdivia ceramics of coastal Ecuador.

We have known since the work of Estrada, Meggers, and Evans (Estrada 1956; Meggers, Evans, and Estrada 1965) that Valdivia ceramics figure among the earliest ceramic assemblages in the Americas. Unfortunately, this precociousness always led discussion toward matters concerned with chronological detail, to the exclusion of concern with the "sociocultural matrix." Now that Roosevelt et al. (1991; Roosevelt, chapter 10) have emancipated Valdivia ceramics from the dubious distinction of being the earliest ceramics in the New World, we can turn our undivided attention to the many contexts of the earliest Valdivia ceramics. We hope this emancipation will also free us from what one of us called the greatest bugaboo to an understanding of Valdivia life systems—the bickering about chronology (Damp 1988:25).

We premise our discussion on an acceptance that the sociocultural matrix is important. Chronological and stratigraphic exactness may be the hallmark of good archaeology, but it lacks meaning without a consideration of the importance of socioeconomic phenomena in the lives of those we now study. We will plead for an understanding of different contexts to account for the beginnings of ceramics in the northern Andean region of coastal Ecuador between 4000 and 3000 b.c. (uncorrected and uncalibrated radiocarbon years). Some of the many details include (1) the spatial context, (2) stratigraphy and chronology, (3) site formation processes, (4) the domestic and economic context, (5) contexts of the landscape, and (6) the pre-Valdivia context.

The question of Valdivia ceramic origins once grabbed headlines. In the words of the original investigators: "Some 5000 years ago, the coasts of Japan and western America were occupied by small groups of people who subsisted by fishing and shellfish gathering, supplemented by hunting of terrestrial mammals. In addition to gathering plants, they may have taken initial steps toward cultivation" (Meggers, Evans, and Estrada 1965:167). The three then proposed that some of these Japanese Neolithic fisherfolk of the Jomon culture were lost at sea and subsequently made their way to the coast of Ecuador. In Ecuador, the Jomon fisherfolk introduced the art of pottery manufacture to the local inhabitants.

Spatial Context

Early Valdivia ceramics (Valdivia I and II, 3300 to 2300 b.c.) of coastal Ecuador have been recovered from several sites (Fig. 13.1). Some of these sites were subject to controlled excavations and others are known through the disturbed surface remains of looters. The Valdivia type site lies in the vicinity of the Santa Elena Peninsula. Most of the sites in this discussion also belong to this area. This coastal strip is one of the best studied regions of Pacific South America, and we will largely restrict our analysis to it while also making note of the presently known areal extent of Early Valdivia ceramics.

The Santa Elena Peninsula of Guayas Province of southwest coastal Ecuador juts out into the sea. Traditionally, the greater peninsula area is considered to be bounded by the Chanduy Valley on the southeast and the Valdivia Valley on the north. The Colonche Hills form a backbone to southwest coastal Ecuador and

constitute the eastern boundary of the Santa Elena Peninsula.

On the peninsula, Early Valdivia ceramics are known from several sites. Confirmed reports attribute these ceramics to the sites of Centinela and Real Alto (Lathrap, Marcos, and Zeidler 1977) in the Chanduy Valley, Punta Concepción (Hill 1972–74; Stothert 1976) near the tip of the peninsula proper, San Pablo (Zevallos and Holm 1960), La Lora, Palmar (Meggers, Evans, and Estrada 1965), and Clementina in the Colonche River drainage, and Valdivia (Meggers, Evans, and Estrada 1965) and Loma Alta (Norton 1971, 1972, 1977) in the Valdivia Valley. Spatially, there appears to be a twinning of settlement along the littoral zone, with one site located inland and an associated site established on the coast. We argue that this represents a bimodal economy for the Early Valdivia occupation of southwestern Ecuador.

Other Early Valdivia occupations are known from, for example, the Encanto site on the island of Puná in the Gulf of Guayaquil (Porras 1973), the coastal strip and interior hills north of the Valdivia Valley (Viteri Gamboa 1980), and the heavily forested hill region of southern Manabí province (Damp 1984a). In addition, a radiocarbon date of 2575 ± 75 b.c. is associated with an early occupation in the Guayas basin that

Fig. 13.1. The southwest coastal region of Ecuador, showing the major rivers of the Guayas basin, the island of Puná, the Colonche Hills, and archaeological sites on the edge of the Santa Elena Peninsula.

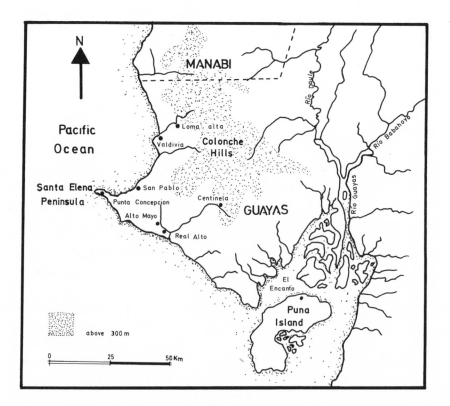

may or may not be related to Valdivia (Raymond, Marcos, and Lathrap 1980).

Stratigraphy and Chronology

The first dates on Valdivia ceramics came from the type site, G-31, investigated by Estrada (1956) and later by Meggers, Evans, and Estrada (1965). The Valdivia type site lies near the mouth of the Valdivia Valley. After their excavations at the site, Meggers, Evans, and Estrada produced a typological seriation of the ceramics from G-31. They divided the sequence into Valdivia A, B, C, and D. One date of 3200 ± 150 b.c. (M-1320; for consistency, none of the dates in this review is calibrated, corrected, or adjusted for ^{13}C content) became well known for marking the beginning of Valdivia and thus the beginning of the alleged period of contact between two sides of the Pacific.

Several authors pointed out that the M-1320 date is clearly out of sequence with other dates obtained from the same stratigraphic context. Bischof (1973:269) stated: "The critics have rejected this special result because it is out of line with the 19 remaining dates represented in the original publication, both stratigraphically and in absolute age." Bischof suggested a different interpretation because of continued excavations at the type site done by Viteri Gamboa, the original supervisor in charge of excavations (Bischof and Viteri Gamboa 1972). He suggested that the charcoal sample M-1320 "could be re-deposited from early or pre-Valdivia contexts" (Bischof 1973:271).

Bischof and Viteri Gamboa (1972) attempted to show through Viteri's continued work at the site that underlying the earliest Valdivia (A) occupation, as revealed in the definitive excavation sequence at cut J at the type site, were two previously undescribed and unrecognized preceramic or aceramic occupations. In the lower levels of Viteri's cut were a few distinctive sherds of a non-Valdivia nature. These were named San Pedro in deference to a neighboring village. The result of Bischof and Viteri's investigation was a clearer stratigraphic profile and three radiocarbon dates on the "aceramic" level (see Hill 1972–74:plates II and III): 2545 ± 100 b.c., 2560 ± 95 b.c., and 2585 ± 55 b.c. (Bischof 1973:272). Bischof felt that this layer was deposited near the end of the preceramic, "possibly correlating with the (pre-Valdivia) Vegas Phase" (Bischof 1973:272). The Valdivia sherds in this sequence were located well above the dated deposits, and the San Pedro sherds in between. It seems reasonable to assign

a date of approximately 2400 b.c. to the San Pedro sherds identified by Bischof and Viteri.

An earlier Valdivia was first recognized by Lanning. He regarded the ceramics from Punta Concepción as distinctive from the sherds reported by Meggers, Evans, and Estrada for the Valdivia type site (Hill 1972–74:2). The site of Punta Concepción, near the tip of the Santa Elena Peninsula, was occupied only during Valdivia I (Lanning 1967:16). The site lies on the seacoast near the modern village of Santa Rosa and consists of eroded mounds that produced Valdivia I sherds. Hill (1972–74:2) used the Punta Concepción assemblage, excavated by Stothert (1976), to define what she considered a pre-Valdivia A presence.

Based on these excavations and data from other sites in the peninsula region, Hill provided a new seriation that broke Meggers, Evans, and Estrada's A, B, C, and D phases down into eight phases, Valdivia I–VIII. Valdivia I, as depicted by Hill, is not represented in the Meggers, Evans, and Estrada volume (1965). The first Valdivia ceramics in their report fall into the Valdivia II category.

The date for the occupation at the site of Punta Concepción may be off by some 500 years. A date of 2510 ± 90 b.c. was seen by Hill (1972–74:8) as most clearly associated with Valdivia I at Punta Concepción. Norton (1977:6), who at the same time carried out work at the related site of Loma Alta, felt that because of mixing in the deposits at the site, this date was too recent.

The sites of Loma Alta and Punta Concepción were at least partly contemporaneous. The ceramics excavated by Stothert and described by Hill from Punta Concepción are identical to the earliest ceramics represented in the deposits from Loma Alta excavated and reported on by Norton (1971, 1972, 1977), Damp (1984b), Raymond (1987), and Stahl (1984). A good number of radiocarbon dates place the period of Valdivia I ceramics between 3300 and 2700 b.c. The preponderance of the data attests to placing all of Valdivia I within that period. Consequently, the Punta Concepción date appears somewhat anomalous.

The Encanto site on Puná Island in the Gulf of Guayaquil is another site germane to this discussion. Most of the occupation at the site would fall into Hill's Valdivia II–VIII phases. Underlying the strata that contained these occupations, however, is a preceramic layer dated at 2455 ± 90 b.c. (SI-1311; Porras 1973:134; see also Spath 1980). A confused stratigraphic picture obscures the relationship of the preceramic and the upper ceramic levels. Also scattered throughout the profile were seven sherds that resemble Bischof and

Viteri Gamboa's (1972) San Pedro sherds (Porras 1973:159). The San Pedro sherds from El Encanto probably were originally deposited in the upper levels of the preceramic debris—above the portion dated at 2455 b.c. and just below the earliest Valdivia (II) levels.

The temporal relationship of the later preceramic, termed Vegas by Lanning (1967:9; see also Stothert 1983), to San Pedro and to the Early Valdivia occupation remains inexact. Chronological context is best examined through results obtained at the site of Real Alto (Lathrap, Marcos, and Zeidler 1977; Damp 1979). Supporting evidence is available from an analysis of the ceramics from related sites.

Site Formation Processes

Excavations at the Valdivia I–VIII site of Real Alto (Fig. 13.2) began in 1974 and have continued in recent years. The first season of excavation at the site, under the direction of Lathrap, produced evidence for ceremonial life, early village structure, economic orientation, and early ceramics. It is appropriate to cite in full the initial assessment of the first occupation at Real Alto. Lathrap, Marcos, and Zeidler (1977:7) concluded that the site was first occupied by

a small, mobile group of people who practiced a fishing-gathering economy. Their remains, the earliest remains encountered at the site, indicate a culture unrelated to Valdivia. The early inhabitants were probably an itinerant group who spent the whole year along the shore. The shallow midden they left behind consists almost entirely of shell of clam-like mollusks from the mangrove swamp in the Chanduy estuary. They built flimsy houses with frames of small, flexible poles. . . . Significantly, a small amount of pottery is associated with this early period. The few fragments recovered are of a thin, hard sandy ware, lacking any kind of incised decoration. The vessel shapes and the mode of manufacture are completely outside the range of the later, more developed Valdivia ceramic tradition.

In consideration of the subsequent work at Real Alto and related sites, we argue that much of the foregoing scenario is no longer tenable.

Excavations at Real Alto in the 1970s and 1980s yielded a set of data pertaining to the Early Valdivia occupation of the Ecuadorian coast. Most of the investigation of Valdivia I and II centered on the northern portion of the site in or near what was dubbed trench C by Lathrap and Marcos. This trench cut across the site in order to give a transect of an approximately 1-meter-deep cultural deposit that contained evidence of the first occupation, later Early and Middle Valdivia ceramics, and a following Machalilla occupation.

Fig. 13.2. Excavations at Real Alto. The photograph shows the Valdivia I structure 2-77, trench C, during excavations in 1977. Wooden sticks mark the locations of post holes.

One of us (Damp) participated in the first session of fieldwork at Real Alto, returned with Zeidler to look at regional settlement patterns in 1976 and then renewed excavations at trench C in 1977. We were both able to amplify this information during the 1980s.

Crucial to an understanding of the first occupation of the site is a series of dates acquired during excavations in 1975 and 1977 from trench C (Damp 1979: 24). These dates are presented in Table 13.1. The ISGS dates (Illinois State Geological Survey) all came from contexts excavated in 1975. The GX dates (Geochron) were obtained during the 1977 excavations. The two series of dates were acquired for slightly different reasons. The 1975 series resulted from exploratory trenching of the northern part of the site to get a clear picture of the cultural sequence. The earliest date could be interpreted as relating to the non- or pre-Valdivia occupation of the site. Such was the scenario outlined by Lathrap, Marcos, and Zeidler.

The 1977 excavations, however, sought to determine the site formation processes involved in the earliest occupation of the site. At the onset of these excavations, it was believed that a pre-Valdivia occupation did exist. It was ultimately shown, however, that the "shallow midden" of mollusk shells and postholes, about 10 centimeters thick between 90 and 100 centimeters below surface (b.s.), was in fact a Valdivia I occupation. What appeared to be almost a pure shellfish, preceramic or aceramic deposit was no more than the result of refuse disposal patterns of food remains around the periphery of the Valdivia I households (Damp 1979, 1984b).

Besides the evidence for activity areas and zonation within the settlement, the 1977 excavations yielded a full repertoire of Valdivia I and II ceramics (Fig. 13.3; Damp 1982), macrobotanical remains in the form of *Canavalia plagiosperma* beans (Damp, Pearsall, and Kaplan 1981), and floor plans for the Valdivia I household (Damp 1984b).

The small amounts of pottery "outside" of the more developed Valdivia ceramics mentioned by Lathrap, Marcos, and Zeidler were mainly undecorated sherds that were probably intrusive from the overlying Machalilla occupation (1500–1000 b.c.). There was a temptation to compare these sherds to Bischof and Viteri's San Pedro sherds. Their similarity, however, could not be demonstrated. Nevertheless, the 1977 excavations did isolate five San Pedro sherds (Fig. 13.4) that could essentially have come from the same vessels illustrated by Bischof and Viteri Gamboa (1972).

The stratigraphic and chronological provenience of the San Pedro sherds found at Real Alto in 1977 provides a clear interpretation of the place of this style in Ecuadorian prehistory. The five sherds were recovered from four different 2 × 3 meter excavation units. In each case they were restricted to between 40–50 centimeters and 50–60 centimeters b.s. None were found elsewhere, above or below, during the 1977 excavations. At 40 centimeters b.s. a Valdivia II living floor (structure 1-77) was exposed. The San Pedro sherds were below this floor and well above a Valdivia I house structure (structure 2-77) uncovered at 90–100 centimeters b.s. (Damp 1984b). The Valdivia I house was dated to between approximately 3000 and 3500 b.c. The Valdivia II sequence spans a period between 2700 and 2300 b.c.

The San Pedro sherds at Real Alto were recovered within a Valdivia II context but below a single house

Table 13.1. Radiocarbon Dates from Trench C, Real Alto

Phase	Date b.c.	Lab No.	Depth (cm b.s.)	Material
Valdivia II?	2190 ± 190	ISGS-467	70–80	Wood charcoal
Valdivia II	2440 ± 75	ISGS-466	70–80	Wood charcoal
Valdivia II	2545 ± 160	GX-5266	70–80	Wood charcoal
Valdivia I	2810 ± 120	ISGS-468	80–90	Wood charcoal
?	4245 ± 215	GX-5269	80–90	Wood charcoal
Valdivia I	2950 ± 170	GX-5268	90–98	Wood charcoal
Valdivia I	3545 ± 200	GX-5267	95–102	Wood charcoal
?	3670 ± 250	ISGS-448	90–100	Wood charcoal

floor that probably dates to the end of the Valdivia II phase. The chronological and stratigraphic evidence at Real Alto indicates a placement for San Pedro pottery between 2500 and 2300 b.c. This is consistent with the dates at the Valdivia type site where Bischof and Viteri first found San Pedro sherds. The dates for the strata that are below and above San Pedro are 2545 ± 100 b.c. (Hv-4840) and 2310 ± 100 b.c. (Hv-4838), respectively (Hill 1972–74:plate III). Therefore, the San Pedro sherds were deposited at both sites around 2400 b.c., when they were also probably discarded at El Encanto.

Apart from figuring out the stratigraphic and chronological position of Early Valdivia and San Pedro pottery, investigations at Real Alto attempted to plot the village layout during Valdivia I and II. A similar goal guided research at the related site of Loma Alta. The results of this research are outlined in Damp (1984b). The Early Valdivia village was, apparently, laid out in the shape of a **U**. At both Real Alto and Loma Alta, the opening to the **U** was to the south. As population grew within the village, the size of the **U** expanded from about 145 × 90 meters in Valdivia I to about 175 × 115 meters by the end of Valdivia II. The **U**-shaped village consisted of a periphery of domestic structures and refuse that surrounded a clean central portion of the site. In Valdivia II times the entrance to the **U** was built up with ceremonial offerings or caches at Loma Alta; at Real Alto this build-up became a ceremonial mound (Marcos 1978).

This village pattern can also be observed in the surficial distribution of ceramics and other artifacts at related Valdivia sites in the peninsula area. These include San Pablo, Clementina, La Lora, and Punta Concepción, for example. At the Valdivia type site, that sort of information was not gathered during excavation and the site has subsequently been pillaged by pot hunters (Bruhns and Hammond 1983; Damp 1984c). The part of the type site excavated by Meggers, Evans, and Estrada lies on the northwest edge. This location is also where Bischof and Viteri located the San Pedro sherds.

When Bischof (1979) returned to the site to locate Valdivia I sherds, he did so in a pot hole (*becken*) that lies in the north central portion of the site. The position of this pot hole is similar to that of the area at Real Alto that also revealed Valdivia I remains. If we superimpose a 150 × 100 meter **U**-shaped pattern over a map of the type site, it shows an area that might have contained Early Valdivia households around a clean center where testing showed no evidence of Early Valdivia refuse. The original cuts made by Meggers, Evans,

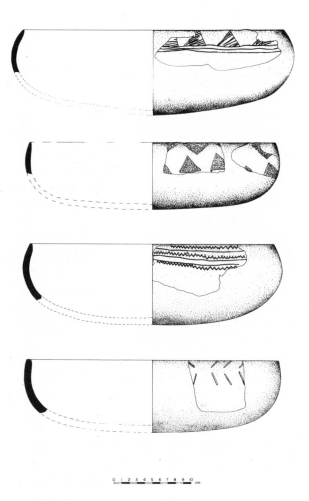

Fig. 13.3. Valdivia I ceramics from the 1977 excavations of trench C, Real Alto.

Estrada, Viteri, and Bischof lie downslope toward the seashore on the edge of the Valdivia occupation. Considering their location, these deposits were probably secondary.

The slanting stratigraphy noted in Bischof's profile (Hill 1972–74:plate II) attests to the redeposition interpretation. In addition, the sole occurrence of Valdivia I pottery in this profile is noted in an intrusive channel to the side of the San Pedro sherds. This suggests that deposition followed the San Pedro manifestation and probably resulted from later erosion of earlier deposits originally located higher up on the slope.

Domestic and Economic Context

The results of intensive study at Real Alto, in particular, and Loma Alta provide a picture of domestic life in the Early Valdivia village. The early habitations were

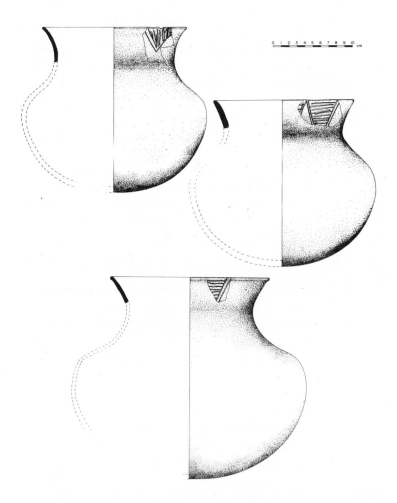

0 1 2 3 4 5 6 7 8 9 10 cm

Fig. 13.3. (continued)

elliptical pole and thatch constructions that measured less than 5 × 4 meters in size. The center of these habitations was relatively void of artifacts and is interpreted as a sleeping area. Around the house structures were scattered refuse and artifacts for craft production (lithic tools, stone spindle whorls, etc.), food preparation (pottery), and ceremony (stone and ceramic figurines). Activities, apart from sleeping, were conducted near the house. The conspicuous shell remains at Real Alto, for example, are the refuse of meals consumed by the occupants and discarded around the house. Sherds and botanical remains are also evident in the deposits.

Apart from the controversy surrounding the origins of Valdivia ceramics, the second most controversial topic is the economic orientation of the Valdivia people. We will not attempt a comprehensive overview of this important subject but will try to shed some light on the empirical evidence for Valdivia agricultural pursuits.

Meggers, Evans, and Estrada (1965) believed that Valdivia was essentially a fishing economy in which gathering and hunting also played a role. They also felt

that some inroads were being made toward agriculture. Zevallos (1966–71), because of evidence obtained at San Pablo, argued for the economic importance of corn in the Valdivia diet. Lathrap (Lathrap, Collier, and Chandra 1975; Zevallos et al. 1977), jumped on this bandwagon and championed the role of corn in the Early Formative of Ecuador. Pearsall (1978, 1979), studying opal phytoliths, concluded that corn had played a role in the Valdivia diet, along with manioc, *achira*, and other crops.

Macrobotanical evidence for agriculture in Valdivia times came in the form of *Canavalia plagiosperma* beans from Real Alto (Damp, Pearsall, and Kaplan 1981). The excavations at Loma Alta that revealed evidence of Early Valdivia houses and settlement also provided additional macrobotanical evidence. Pearsall identified one specimen from a hearth next to structure 4, a house (Damp 1984b:Fig. 5), as the fruit *cherimoya* (*Annona cherimolia*) (Pearsall 1986:151).

Hundreds of macrobotanical specimens were retrieved from our investigation of Early Valdivia deposits at Real Alto in the 1980s. These remains, iden-

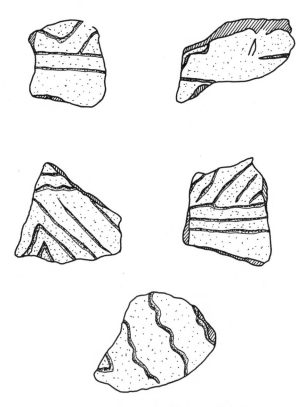

Fig. 13.4. San Pedro sherds recovered from a Valdivia II context in trench C, Real Alto.

tified by Pearsall, include *Canavalia* beans, cotton (*Gossypium barbadense;* Damp and Pearsall 1994), fruits, nuts, and a possible manioc seed. The absence of corn remains is problematical at this time. We interpret the lack of corn as reflecting a non—corn-based economy for the coastal sites, an economy more in line with the diet reflected in the inventory at the northern Peruvian site of Huaca Prieta (Bird 1948). More investigation of these possibilities is necessary before a definitive statement can be made.

One possibility is that the inland sites such as Loma Alta in the Valdivia Valley and Centinela in the Chanduy Valley had a greater emphasis on corn cultivation and the coastal sites were more specialized in fishing. This would fit the pattern of site distribution during Valdivia I times and would suggest the existence of a bimodal (farming/fishing) economic system during the Early Formative of coastal Ecuador.

On the Beach: Landscape Contexts

In the late 1980s we began to look at the possibility that coastal uplift might have affected the landscape during the Valdivia occupation of the Santa Elena Pen-insula (Damp et al. 1990). A consideration of aerial photographs, sedimentary units, and settlement distribution led us to the conclusion that the site of Real Alto, now over 2 kilometers from the coast and about 25 meters above sea level, was on the shoreline during its Early Valdivia occupation.

We were able to locate coastal sediments with associated Valdivia sherds some 2 kilometers inland. Also located were relict mangrove swamp beds and sediments with marine shell in positions that suggested an ancient shoreline adjacent to the Real Alto site. Far from being an inland, agricultural village, as posited by Lathrap, Marcos, and Zeidler (1977), Real Alto was, apparently, a seashore settlement at which the inhabitants collected shellfish, fished the shoreline, did some hunting of deer (Byrd 1976), and grew some crops such as cotton and beans.

The possibility of a shoreline settlement does not preclude the growing of corn during the Early Valdivia occupation but it makes it less feasible because the area surrounding Real Alto is composed of subsurface beds of sand. The river valley, mentioned by Lathrap, Marcos, and Zeidler, may have been an equally poor locale for corn cultivation if it was covered by a mangrove swamp. None of this, however, rules out the possibility of corn agriculture in the more inland regions of the Santa Elena Peninsula near the Colonche Hills and in the interior reaches of southern Manabí, where the densest concentration of Valdivia sites has been shown to occur (Damp 1984a).

The possibility of a restructuring of the shoreline also has implications for the archaeological record at the Valdivia type site. Because the terrain near Real Alto is relatively flat, consisting of a coastal plain, an episode of coastal uplift would have produced a broad expanse of land between an old and a new shoreline. At Valdivia, however, the terrain is more hilly. As a consequence, a former seashore settlement might not now be removed so far from the coast. In addition, the rates of coastal uplift noted for Real Alto in the Chanduy Valley are not necessarily the same as those that might have occurred elsewhere on the coast. Geological processes may easily have had different local responses.

It is interesting, however, to note that Bischof's discussion of the stratigraphy for the cut in which the San Pedro sherds were found shows that the sedimentary unit containing San Pedro lay upon a level with holes, cracks, charcoal, mussels, and fishbone but no sherds. Bischof suggested that this level had the characteristics of a mangrove swamp (Bischof 1979:351). This possible mangrove swamp level now lies some 20 meters above sea level. In a recently published study of the archaeology of the Valdivia Valley, Raymond (1987) suggested that there is no evidence for environmental change in the valley since the Valdivia occupation. Raymond does not explain what evidence he has for that statement, nor does he discuss the evidence just mentioned of a mangrove swamp left abandoned.

Evidence for relict mangrove swamps associated with Valdivia sites is also described in connection with Norton's work at the site of Salango farther north on the coast (Norton, Lunnis, and Nailing 1983). On the island of La Plata, a later Valdivia site (Damp and Norton 1987) was found on what a geologist has identified as an uplifted terrace about 25 meters above sea level (Wilkinson 1987).

All the sites in which San Pedro sherds were found (El Encanto, Real Alto, and Valdivia) were situated on the shoreline during occupation. The sherds occur in limited quantities and can be dated to around 2400 b.c., during the Valdivia II phase. We believe that the context for these sherds implies trade involving seagoing crafts that landed on the beaches at El Encanto, Real Alto, and Valdivia.

The Pre-Valdivia Context

The pre-Valdivia occupation of coastal Ecuador is imperfectly known. Lanning (1967) first defined the preceramic Vegas phase, and Stothert (1974, 1976, 1983, 1985, 1988) has contributed most of our knowledge concerning that occupation. Vegas begins in the post-Pleistocene and continues up to about 1,150 years before Valdivia. Then follows a gap in the sequence. Various authors have tried to fill this hiatus with such manifestations as Achallan (Stothert 1976) and San Pedro (Bischof and Viteri Gamboa 1972). Stothert (1985) has cogently pointed out the problems with many preceramic sequences on the peninsula, and none of the previous attempts to fill the gap has proven successful.

As an outgrowth of our study of Early Valdivia and our later investigation of landscape changes, we were drawn to consider the effects of geomorphological change on site visibility and the question of the Vegas-Valdivia gap. We surmised that if tectonic uplift was ongoing throughout the Holocene period, then pre-Valdivia shorelines were a possibility in more inland regions. We were drawn to a landform with a beachlike profile some 4.6 kilometers north of the present shore. On the surface of this site, which we called Altomayo,

lay a scatter of Valdivia phase VIII ceramics (1650–1500 b.c.). The site has been traversed by a cart track or goat trail in recent years. In the eroded portions of this trail we identified lithic debris seemingly not associated with the Valdivia occupation.

Excavation at Altomayo was carried out in 1987 as part of a field school for the Escuela Superior Politécnica del Litoral, Guayaquil, under the leadership of the senior author. The site of Altomayo (OGSECh-056B) is located 1.1 kilometers west of the Río Verde, 300 meters east of the Río Real and 4.6 kilometers north of the present shore at La Tintina point. Archaeological deposits are distributed over an area 100 × 100 meters on a small rise between 35 and 40 meters above sea level.

From 62 to 74 centimeters b.s., well below the Valdivia VIII occupation, the remains of a house were identified. This house is defined on the basis of post holes surrounded by shellfish remains. Although slightly smaller than the nearby Valdivia I houses at Real Alto, the Altomayo house is nearly identical to the Valdivia I structures.

Artifacts recovered from the Altomayo house include more than 1,000 lithic artifacts similar to both the Vegas and Valdivia lithics. The shell refuse zone also contained bone remains and macrobotanical specimens. Most significant for this review is the presence of ceramic artifacts and a small stone figurine. The ceramic artifacts are not from pots but, we feel, represent an experimental stage in ceramic production. Three figurine objects were recovered. Two of the objects are eccentric—roughly triangular—in shape and made of a soft whitish stone. The other figurine is a small (2.2 × 0.6 × .02 cm), flat stone slab with scratches, produced during its making, evident on one surface and containing traces of red pigment. This stone figure is an exact, but smaller, version of the Valdivia I plain stone figurines that sometimes have engraved faces and body parts.

No ceramic pots or sherds were found in the lower occupational refuse at Altomayo. However, several burnt clay and worked clay pieces were recovered. Several pieces of burnt clay with stick or twig impressions show that the early Altomayo house was covered in clay to make a wattle-and-daub structure. Other pieces of burnt clay include one with the impression of a single finger, another that is a strip apparently rolled between someone's hands, and a third that is a small ball of fired clay with obvious finger impressions.

No radiocarbon date is currently available for Altomayo. Because of the artifacts just mentioned that are prototypes of the Valdivia I artifacts, the stratigraphic position of the buried structure below a Valdivia VIII occupation, and the possible restructuring of the shoreline, we feel that the early occupation at Altomayo represents a pre-Valdivia and early ceramic phase on the Ecuadorian coast. Accordingly, a new phase was created to designate a period transitional from Vegas to Valdivia. This phase, Chuculunduy, dates from approximately 4650 to 3500 b.c.

Clearly, there are many problems associated with the cultural remains at Altomayo. A radiocarbon date for the occupation would go far to clear up aspects of chronology. We hope to resolve this issue soon. Another problem is the question of landscape change associated with coastal uplift. A comprehensive program of study is needed to understand how uplift might have influenced and might still influence the lives of the inhabitants of coastal Ecuador.

A third problem is the nature of the Chuculunduy occupation of the Ecuadorian coast. An investigation of this problem should prove most rewarding in terms of understanding the in situ origins of ceramics in the New World.

Conclusions

Rather than believing that culture history contributes to the sociocultural matrix, we believe an approach that evaluates the many contexts of Early Valdivia pottery will show how the environment, the economy, and the social sphere contribute to a better understanding of culture history. A simple evaluation of the stratigraphic profile from one site can be misleading. It is imperative to look at the site formation process involved in each site. We have tried to show that knowledge of the arrangement of domestic refuse and households within a village is necessary if one is to fully assess any stratigraphic profile. In addition, we have tried to look at larger processes of geological importance that may have restructured the landscape.

We have not exhausted the possibilities of context. For example, we have not discussed the designs on Early Valdivia ceramics. Elsewhere (Damp 1982), it was argued that certain design motifs on Valdivia I and II bowls represent felines and snakes. These were considered metaphors for the Early Valdivia community. We have centered our discussion on the factors that may have accounted for the physical presence of Valdivia I sherds in the archaeological record.

In making this assessment, we have come to believe that the origins of Valdivia lie not in some far-off place such as across the Pacific (Meggers, Evans, and Estrada 1965) or across the Andes in the Amazon (Lathrap 1970), but on the coast of Ecuador.

Lévi-Strauss (1974:110) once pointed out the modern-day economic motives behind colonialism and "the pursuit of archaeological research intended to stress certain analogies between pre-Columbian remains and those of the Japanese neolithic period." More recently, Marcos (1986) has instilled a growing nationalism into the study of Valdivia. He sees the beginning of the Ecuadorian nation-state as coinciding with the florescence of Real Alto, what he calls the most important Neolithic site on the continent of South America. He also ties these developments into an area, the coastal region, that he lists as the agroindustrial center of Ecuador. With all due respect to any particular individual, these attempts seem to have economic motives. It is ludicrous to assume that Real Alto is the most important early agricultural site in South America. We have tried to show that it was only part of a process. In addition, we have questioned the role of agriculture at the site of Real Alto.

When we attempt to construct culture history from any one context (e.g., time-space systematics, economic motivation), we are telling our own history and denying history to others. We believe the history of ceramic invention in Ecuador is intimately tied to the local development of culture in that area. This development has deep roots going back to the end of the Pleistocene.

Unfortunately, archaeological interpretation often crystallizes time by looking at only one moment or one event in the past. In the case of the origins of Valdivia ceramics, we have denied history to the indigenous people responsible for the invention of that way of life. As Trigger (1986:198) pointed out, "the cultural-historical approach to American archaeology, with its emphasis first on chronology and later on culture context," has made archaeologists unwilling to concede that native groups were able to innovate on their own.

The origins of Valdivia ceramics are one of the classic cases of culture history in the annals of method and theory in American archaeology. All accounts have attempted to trace the ceramic origins to migration or diffusion. We believe that our approach is radical in that it advances an indigenous cause for cultural development.

We hope that our efforts at sites such as Altomayo will prompt investigators to look not just for the origins of Valdivia ceramics but for the socioeconomic processes that accounted for transitions in the archaeological record. Then, we will be on our way toward a history of culture and not just another culture history.

References Cited

Bird, J. B.
1948   Preceramic Cultures in Chicama and Viru. In *A Reappraisal of Peruvian Archaeology*, edited by W. C. Bennet, pp. 21–28. Memoirs of the Society for American Archaeology 14.

Bischof, H.
1973   The Origins of Pottery in South America: Recent Radiocarbon Dates from Southwest Ecuador. *Atti del XL Congreso Internazionale degli Americanista* 1:269–81. Rome-Geneva.
1979   San Pedro und Valdivia: Fruhe Keramikkomplexe an der Küste Südwest-Ekuadors. In *Beiträge Zur Allgemeinen und Vergleichenden Archäologie* 1:335–89. Deutshes Archäologisches Institut, Sondedruck.

Bischof, H., and J. Viteri Gamboa
1972   Pre-Valdivia Occupations on the Southwest Coast of Ecuador. *American Antiquity* 38:548–51.

Bruhns, K., and N. Hammond
1983   A Visit to Valdivia. *Journal of Field Archaeology* 10:485–87.

Byrd, K.
1976   Changing Animal Utilization Patterns and Their Implications: Southwest Ecuador (6500 B.C.–A.D. 1400). Ph.D. dissertation, Department of Anthropology, University of Florida, Gainesville.

Damp, J.
1979   Better Homes and Gardens: The Life and Death of the Early Valdivia Community. Ph.D. dissertation, Department of Archaeology, University of Calgary.
1982   Ceramic Art and Symbolism in the Early Valdivia Community (Ecuador). *Journal of Latin American Lore* 8(2):155–78.
1984a   Environmental Variability, Agriculture and Settlement Processes of Coastal Ecuador (3300–1500 B.C.). *Current Anthropology* 25(1):106–11.
1984b   Architecture of the Early Valdivia Village. *American Antiquity* 49:573–85.
1984c   Salvaging Sites and Specimens: To Fake or Not to Fake. *Journal of Field Archaeology* 11(4):427–28.
1988   *La primera ocupación Valdivia de Real Alto: Patrones económicos, arquitectónicos e ideológicos.* Corporación Editora Nacional, Quito, Ecuador.

Damp, J., D. Jackson, P. Vargas, and P. Zambrano
1990   On the Waterfront: Quaternary Environments and the Formative Occupation of Southwestern Ecuador. *Geoarchaeology* 5(2):171–85.

Damp, J., and P. Norton
1987   Pretexto, contexto y falacias en la Isla de la Plata. *Miscelánea Antropológica Ecuatoriana* 7:109–22.

Damp, J., and D. Pearsall
1994   Early Cotton from Coastal Ecuador. *Economic Botany* 48(2):163–65.

Damp, J., D. Pearsall, and L. Kaplan
1981   Beans for Valdivia. *Science* 212:811–12.

Estrada, E.
1956   *Valdivia: Un sitio arqueológico formativo en la costa de la Provincia del Guayas, Ecuador.* Museo Víctor Emilio Estrada, Guayaquil.

Hill, B.
1972–74   A New Chronology of the Valdivia Ceramic Complex from the Coast Zone of Guayas Province, Ecuador. *Ñawpa Pacha* 10–12:1–39.

Lanning, E.
1967   Archaeological Investigations on the Santa Elena Peninsula, Ecuador. Report to the National Science Foundation on research carried out under grant GS-402, 1964–65.

Lathrap, D., D. Collier, and H. Chandra
1975   *Ancient Ecuador: Culture, Clay, and Creativity, 3000–300 B.C.* Field Museum of Natural History, Chicago.

Lathrap, D., J. Marcos, and J. Zeidler
1977   Real Alto: An Ancient Ceremonial Center. *Archaeology* 30:2–13.

Lévi-Strauss, C.
1974   *Tristes Tropiques.* Atheneum, New York.

Marcos, J.
1978   The Ceremonial Precinct at Real Alto: Organization of Time and Space in Valdivia Society. Ph.D. dissertation, Department of Anthropology, University of Illinois, Urbana.

Marcos, J., ed.
1986   *Arqueología de la costa ecuatoriana: Nuevos enfoques.* Corporación Editora Nacional, Quito, Ecuador.

Meggers, B., C. Evans, and E. Estrada
1965   *The Early Formative Period of Coastal Ecuador.* Smithsonian Contributions to Anthropology 1, Washington, D.C.

Norton, P.
1971   A Preliminary Report on Loma Alta and the Implications of Inland Valdivia A. Paper presented at the Primer Simposio de Correlaciones Antropológicos Andino-Mesoamericano, Salinas, Ecuador.
1972   Early Valdivia Middens at Loma Alta, Ecuador. Paper presented at the 37th annual

meeting of the Society for American
Archaeology, Bal Harbor, Florida.

1977   The Loma Alta Connection. Paper presented
at the 42d annual meeting of the Society for
American Archaeology, New Orleans,
Louisiana.

Norton, P., R. Lunnis, and N. Nailing

1983   Excavaciones en Salango, Provincia de
Manabí, Ecuador. *Miscelánea Antropológica Ecuatoriana* 3:9–72. Guayaquil.

Pearsall, D.

1978   Phytolith Analysis of Archeological Soils:
Evidence for Maize Cultivation in Formative Ecuador. *Science* 199:177–78.

1979   The Application of Ethnobotanical Tech-
niques to the Problem of Subsistence in the
Ecuadorian Formative. Ph.D. dissertation,
Department of Anthropology, University of
Illinois, Urbana.

1986   An Overview of Formative Period Subsistence
in Ecuador: Paleoethnobotanical Data and
Perspectives. In *Diet and Subsistence: Current
Archaeological Perspectives,* edited by B. V.
Kennedy and G. M. LeMoine, pp. 149–58.
Proceedings of the 19th annual Chacmool
Conference, University of Calgary.

Porras G., P.

1973   *El Encanto–La Puná: Un sitio insular de la fase
Valdivia asociado a un conchero anular.* Ediciones
Huancavilca, Quito.

Raymond, J. S.

1987   Patrones de subsistencia durante el Formativo
temprano en el valle de Valdivia, Ecuador.
Miscelánea Antropológica Ecuatoriana 7:101–108.
Guayaquil.

Raymond, J. S., J. Marcos, and D. Lathrap

1980   Evidence of Early Formative Settlement in the
Guayas Basin, Ecuador. *Current Anthropology*
21:700–701.

Roosevelt, A., R. Housley, M. Imazio da Silveira, S. Maranca, and R. Johnson

1991   Eighth Millennium Pottery from a Prehistoric
Shell Midden in the Brazilian Amazon. *Science*
254:1621–1624.

Spath, C.

1980   The El Encanto Focus: A Post-Pleistocene
Maritime Adaptation to Expanding Littoral
Resources. Ph.D. dissertation, Department of
Anthropology, University of Illinois, Urbana.

Stahl, P.

1984   Tropical Forest Cosmology: The Cultural
Context of the Early Valdivia Occupation at
Loma Alta. Ph.D. dissertation, University of
Illinois. University Microfilms, Ann Arbor,
Michigan.

Stothert, K.

1974   The Lithic Technology of the Santa Elena
Peninsula, Ecuador: A Method for the
Analysis of Technologically Simple Stone
Work. Ph.D. dissertation, Yale University,
New Haven. University Microfilms, Ann
Arbor, Michigan.

1976   The Early Prehistory of the Santa Elena
Peninsula, Ecuador: Continuities between
Preceramic and Ceramic Cultures. *Actas del
XLI Congreso Internacional de Americanistas*
2:88–98. Mexico City.

1983   Review of the Early Preceramic Complexes of
the Santa Elena Peninsula, Ecuador. *American
Antiquity* 48:122–27.

1985   The Preceramic Las Vegas Culture of Coastal
Ecuador. *American Antiquity* 50:613–37.

1988   La prehistoria temprana de la península de
Santa Elena, Ecuador: Cultura Las Vegas.
Miscelánea Antropológica Ecuatoriana, Serie
Monográfica 10, Guayaquil.

Trigger, B.

1986   Prehistoric Archaeology and American Society. In *American Archaeology Past and Future,* edited by D. Meltzer, D. Fowler, and J.
Sabloff, pp. 187–215. Smithsonian Institution
Press, Washington, D.C.

Viteri Gamboa, J.

1980   *Valdivia tierra adentro.* Publicación del Museo
de la Escuela Superior Politécnica del Litoral,
Guayaquil, Ecuador.

Wilkinson, A.

1987   Descripción de la Isla de la Plata. *Miscelánea
Antropológica Ecuatoriana* 7:123–28. Guayaquil.

Willey, G.

1985   Some Continuing Problems in New World
Culture History. *American Antiquity* 50:351–
63.

Zeidler, J.

1984   Social Space in Valdivia Society: Community
Patterning and Domestic Structure at Real
Alto, 3000–2000 B.C. Ph.D. dissertation,
Department of Anthropology, University
of Illinois, Urbana.

Zevallos, C.

1966–71 *La agricultura en el Formativo temprano del
Ecuador (cultura Valdivia).* Casa de la Cultura Ecuatoriana, Guayaquil, Ecuador.

Zevallos, C., W. Galinat, D. Lathrap, E. Leng, J. Marcos,
and K. Klumpp

1977   The San Pablo Corn Kernel and Its Friends.
Science 196:385–89.

Zevallos, C., and O. Holm

1960   *Excavaciones arqueológicas en San Pablo: Informe
preliminar.* Guayaquil, Ecuador.

14

Monagrillo, Panama's First Pottery

Summary of Research, with New Interpretations

RICHARD COOKE

In the first half of this chapter, I discuss the history of research into Panama's oldest known pottery, the Monagrillo Ceramic Complex, and its manufacturers. I then present my own interpretation of chronology, subsistence, and cultural geography. I collate data published in the 1950s with some results of research conducted between 1973 and 1985. The latter have been reported unevenly. Much information is available only in unpublished manuscripts and theses or in local Spanish-language journals. Some analyses (e.g., dietary bone) have not been completed. I hope that readers will soon be able to check my points of view against more detailed reports.

Research History

Willey and McGimsey (1954) based their descriptions of the Monagrillo Ceramic Complex on more than 22,000 sherds collected at four sites adjacent to Parita Bay, a mangrove-fringed embayment on the central Pacific coast of Panama: Monagrillo (He-5), Zapotal (He-15), He-12, and He-18 (Fig. 14.1).[1] This "dense, sand- and grit-tempered" ware bore slight resemblance to other prehistoric ceramics in Panama (except the partly coeval or descendant Sarigua Complex) and was simpler than any Peruvian, Middle American, or lower Central American styles known at that time. Stratigraphic, technological, and stylistic indications of considerable antiquity were confirmed directly by a charcoal date of 2140 ± 70 b.c. (Deevey et al. 1959) (2880 [2610] 2460 B.C.) and indirectly by data from Cerro Mangote, a neighboring Late Preceramic site, where grinding tools remarkably similar to those found at the Monagrillo type site (He-5) were dated to 4960 ± 110 b.c. (5930 [5660–5640] 5450 B.C.) (McGimsey 1956, 1957).[2]

Deducing from stratigraphy and aerial photographs that the coastal geomorphology of Parita Bay had changed since Monagrillo times, Willey and McGimsey related site formation processes and subsistence economy to hypothetical topographical features on a "receding" coastline. Believing that they were describing a "shellfish-gathering culture," they attributed the densest occupation at He-5 to the intensive collection of *Tivela* clams and *Natica* snails, surmising that these would have been most abundant when a shallow coastal lagoon existed nearby. They were aware, nonetheless, that screening only one test pit's sediments led to a gross underestimation of the importance of fishing. They were ambiguous about agricul-

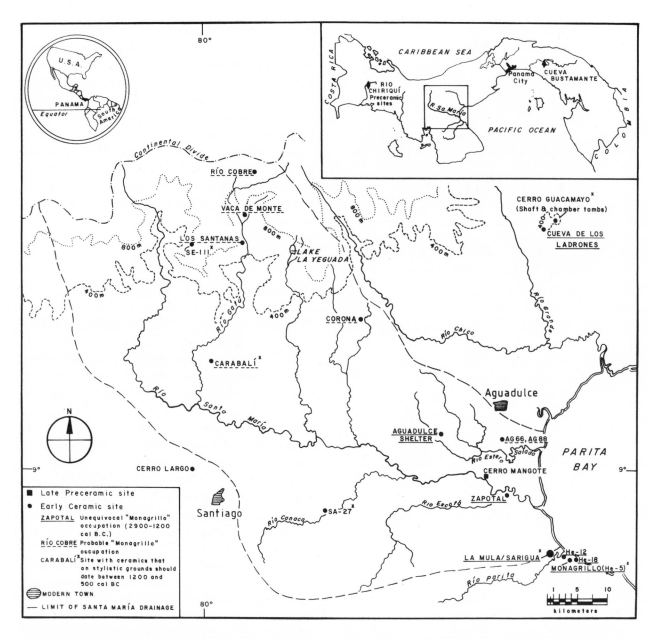

Fig. 14.1. The Santa María and neighboring drainages of central Pacific Panama, showing the locations of archaeological sites mentioned in chapter 14. Drawing by Richard Cooke.

ture: they pointed out that the "crude," "primitive," and "unspecialized" grinding stones had elsewhere been associated with a nonagricultural or marginal agricultural status, but they were reluctant to reject a priori the use of maize. The small hand-collected sample of mammal bones (n = ca. 250) alluded to the hunting of deer (*Odocoileus virginianus*) and peccaries (*Tayassu tajaçu*) in littoral and gallery woodlands and to the occasional use of stranded marine mammal carcasses.

Willey and McGimsey distinguished between "living" and "dumping" areas at He-5 and identified "clay briquettes showing pole or reed impressions." But they were unable to assign hearths or floors to the Monagrillo occupation. They offered no substantive data to back up their timid suggestion of seasonal occupation by "people who had homes in the interior." The absence of chronologically secure human remains suggested "burial at places remote from the site or cremation and dispersal of ashes."

FIRST INLAND OCCURRENCES OF THE
MONAGRILLO CERAMIC COMPLEX

Encouraged by his discovery of Preceramic sites in forested foothills drained by the Chiriquí River (650–900 m elevation; Fig. 14.1), where the subsistence economy would have received no, or minimal, input from coastal habitats (Piperno 1988:135–38; Ranere 1980a, 1980b), Ranere searched for early sites inland from Parita Bay. In 1973, he tested a midden under a huge boulder atop a rocky outcrop 18 kilometers from the present-day coast (the Aguadulce Shelter, henceforth Aguadulce). He found pottery and grinding stones similar to those reported from He-5 and isolated potteryless deposits in a compressed (0.4–0.9 m) stratigraphy. Stone tool and debitage densities far exceeded those of the strandline sites with Monagrillo ceramics. Hence, Ranere proposed that Aguadulce was not a specialized (coastal) activity center but a habitation site used by hunting-fishing-gathering peoples and, in the ceramic levels, farmers (Ranere and McCarty 1973). He excavated two more test pits in 1975 (Ranere and Hansell 1978).

In 1974, Bird and Cooke (1978) discovered Monagrillo pottery stratified over Preceramic deposits at the Cueva de los Ladrones (henceforth Ladrones, 300 m elevation), on the south slope of a prominent hill (Cerro Guacamayo) 25 kilometers inland from Parita Bay. Their interpretation of the site's economy is contradictory. On the one hand, they used the term "hunting and gathering station," inferring from the dry season barrenness of adjacent hill slopes and the absence of edge-ground cobbles (Ranere 1980b:Fig. 8/10; Willey and McGimsey 1954:Figs. 15, 49) that the environs were inappropriate for "intensive" or "extensive" agriculture. On the other hand, they speculated that small quartz and agate tools were manioc grater inserts and that small stone slabs were bases for grinding maize.

Ranere and Hansell (1978) were less ambiguous. They rejected the use of maize during the Preceramic and Monagrillo periods. They inferred from the abundance of carbonized fragments that palm nuts were a primary food source at Aguadulce and from grinding stone distributions and Ranere's (1975) replication experiments that root crops were cultivated in central Panama by the "end of the third millennium b.c."

RETESTING THE MONAGRILLO TYPE SITE

In 1975, Ranere and Linares excavated two pits (4 m² and 1.5 m²) at He-5 (Hansell 1979:Fig. 3). They added ten ^{14}C dates and confirmed Willey and McGimsey's interpretation of the site's history, proposing that the first occupation was established around 3000 B.C. on a sandbar subject to wave action. From this moment until about 1950 B.C., intermittent occupation occurred while He-5 was still directly affected by tidal events.[3] As the Parita River delta prograded, a shallow lagoon formed around the site. Occupation became more permanent. By about 1500 B.C., the expansion of a barren high- and supratidal surface (*alvina* in local parlance) diminished the site's attractiveness.[4] Sporadic occupants after this (identified by Willey and McGimsey [1954] as "Alvina" and "El Tigre" peoples) added some subsurface features.

"Literally thousands of sardine-sized vertebrae . . . and hundreds upon hundreds of crab claws" recovered with fine screens suggested that He-5's economy was "unquestionably oriented towards aquatic resources for the procurement of animal protein," in contrast to that of Ladrones, which was "understandably dependent on terrestrial sources for animal protein" (Ranere and Hansell 1978).

Hansell (1979) analyzed shell extracted from a 0.3-m² column in the south wall of Ranere's block 2. She confirmed Willey and McGimsey's major inference—the alternate abundance of clams (*Tivela*) and oysters (*Ostrea*)—and related the latter's decline to a shift from brackish water to saline lagoonal conditions after 1950 B.C. (SI-2840). She proposed, however, that clams may not have been collected inside the lagoon but on a sandy beach exposed to wave action, perhaps on the seaward side of a bar, citing in support ecological data on *Tivela byronensis* and the coabundance of two other sand beach bivalves, *Donax* and *Mactra*. The low representation of salt-marsh species (e.g., *Anadara tuberculosa*) suggested that mangroves and mud flats were not favored collection habitats or were not present nearby. Although acetate peels taken from *Tivela byronensis* clams alluded to dry season occupation, Hansell wisely refrained from exaggerating the precision of this inference because life history data on this species were deficient.

Dere (1981) collected surface sediment samples and took four cores on a 1,600-meter northeast-trending topographic profile through He-5, perpendicular to Parita Bay. Core MG-1, immediately to the north of the cultural deposits, indicated that a supratidal environment was rapidly transgressed by rising sea level about 3750 B.C. At 1045 B.C. (TEM-149) the environment changed to that of a mangrove-covered mid-tidal zone, which gradually filled in. A bare alvina surface had formed by the end of the first millennium B.C.[5]

RADIOMETRIC DATING OF THE MONAGRILLO CERAMIC COMPLEX

The five dates associated with Monagrillo sherds at Ladrones (Eldredge 1979) have a 2-sigma range of 3830–2010 B.C. At Aguadulce, only three of the ten ^{14}C dates occurred in the same levels as pottery (Monagrillo, cf. Sarigua, and later categories). Their 2-sigma range is 1480–500 B.C.

Ranere rejected two He-5 dates—4530 (4340) 4050 B.C. (TEM-109) and 4450 (4240) 3980 B.C. (SI-2841)—because soil textural analysis and the water-worn condition of potsherds indicated mixing of cultural and beach-deposited materials (Cooke 1984: 273; Hansell 1979:96, 117–18; Hansell and Adams 1980). (They were also out of sequence with a date run on water-deposited shells stratified well below them [TEM-208]). Block 1 dates are very inconsistent. Block 2 dates are in predictable stratigraphic sequence above the natural beach deposits. This suggests that the densest occupation (above 0.9 m below surface and equivalent to Willey and McGimsey's stratum 8) took place between 1950 B.C. (SI-2840) and 1510 B.C. (SI-2843) (Ranere and Hansell 1978).

The new chronology induced Cooke (1984:277–78) to propose that 3000 b.c. (ca. 3800 B.C.) was a good "round figure date" for the inception of the Monagrillo Ceramic Complex. Correctly cautious about He-5's basal stratigraphy and dating discrepancies at Ladrones, Ranere (in Cooke 1984:273) counterproposed that it postdated 2500 b.c. (ca. 3000 B.C.).

PHYTOLITH AND POLLEN ANALYSIS

Piperno's analysis of phytoliths in archaeological soils and lake sediments engendered a reevaluation of Monagrillo subsistence by (1) associating pottery at Aguadulce (dated there to 2000–1000 b.c.) with maize and horticulture (Piperno 1979, 1988:171–74),[6] (2) suggesting that this cultigen appeared at Ladrones and, less convincingly, Los Santanas (SE-189) during the Late Preceramic (5000 b.c.),[7] and (3) proposing that maize was accepted by a society that had begun to cultivate some indigenous crops (e.g., arrowroot) by

about 6600 B.C. (Piperno 1985:Tables 3–4, 1988: 171–73; Piperno and Clary 1984; Piperno et al. 1985).[8]

These claims for early archaeological maize were substantiated at Lake La Yeguada, located at 650 meters elevation in the same drainage as Aguadulce and 40 kilometers west of Ladrones, where maize phytoliths first occurred at about 4000 b.p. (ca. 2500 B.C.) and maize pollen at about 3600 b.p. (ca. 1975 B.C.) (Piperno 1991:Table V).[9]

Reviews of Monagrillo subsistence written in the 1980s and 1990s (e.g., Cooke 1984:281–83; Cooke and Ranere 1992b:269–74) have underlined the compatibility of these phytolith and pollen distributions with a pre–6000 B.C. movement of maize down the Central American land bridge into Colombia and Ecuador (Pearsall 1992; Piperno 1991; Pearsall and Piperno 1990). Since then, Piperno (1989a, 1991; Piperno et al. 1991, 1992) has consistently argued that (1) human disturbance of central Panamanian Pacific slope forests goes back to the Pleistocene/Holocene transition, (2) pre-maize domestication of indigenous crops was causally linked to the anthropogenically induced proliferation of successional plant taxa, and (3) this region was inhabited during Late Preceramic and Monagrillo times by small groups of hamlet-dwelling shifting cultivators.

Puzzled by the absence of polished stone celts in Monagrillo deposits, Ranere (1992:30) speculated that fire alone may have been sufficient to clear the land in the foothills of central Panama.[10]

THE SANTA MARÍA PROJECT

Between 1981 and 1985, the Santa María Project conducted surveys and test excavations in the eponymous drainage (Cooke and Ranere 1984, 1992a, 1992b). Only one site along 84 linear kilometers of 0.5-kilometer-wide, randomly located transects contained Monagrillo sherds: Los Santanas (SE-189), a rockshelter at 800 meters elevation, 70 kilometers from Parita Bay. At six other sites located during off-transect ("purposive") surveys, a few ostensibly Monagrillo sherds were found in small test pits: four rockshelters—Carabalí (SF-9), Corona (CL-2), Río Cobre (SE-201), and Vaca de Monte (CL-6)—and two shellmounds, AG-66 and AG-88. At La Mula–Sarigua (PR-14), an extensive open site near the Parita Bay coast, Hansell (1988, vol. 2, Fig. 37a–g) recorded a surface scatter of Monagrillo sherds, including seven rims.

Santa María Project archaeologists opened a small

(1 × 2 m) cut at Zapotal (He-15), where Willey and McGimsey (1954:91–100) excavated six 3-m pits in 1952. They found only Monagrillo pottery in three clearly differentiated natural strata and obtained a ^{14}C date for the lowest one: 1630 (1410) 1190 B.C. (Beta-9574). Fine-screened sediments contained large amounts of shell and animal bone. Their site map suggested that Zapotal's refuse covered more than 3 hectares. In 1987, Giausserand, a Yale graduate student, initiated *décapage* excavations at Zapotal. She found one Monagrillo period structure, apparently the edge of an oval dwelling with a central hearth, stratified over a shell date of 1660 (1430) 1220 B.C. (Beta-20850). Alongside it lay a possible cache of edge-ground cobbles. She recovered about 1,200 Monagrillo sherds and at least one crude ceramic figurine.[11]

Although the 1981–85 surveys suggested that Monagrillo-period populations were active over the entire Santa María drainage—from the Parita Bay shoreline to Río Cobre (SE-201) in humid premontane forest (more than 4,000 mm rainfall, 1,100 m elevation)—sherds that Cooke originally identified as Monagrillo were very sparse at all the tested sites: at none of the inland localities did they approach the densities observed at Aguadulce and Ladrones.

Cooke and Ranere (1992b:270) suggested that two interrelated features lessened the objectivity of opinions concerning population distribution and settlement patterns: (1) the friability of Monagrillo sherds, which disappeared at open sites with shallow or surface deposits, and (2) identical core reduction techniques (and hence flake morphology) during Late Preceramic and Monagrillo times. These features complicated the chronological differentiation of sherdless deposits dated between 5000 b.c. and 1000 b.c. They summarized the situation in the following manner (1992b:273–74):

not enough information is available for the Monagrillo period to enable us to distinguish objectively between aggregation-dispersion patterns typical of family-based small-scale societies and an evolutionary trend towards the formation of local groups with a specialized agrosystem and a structured order of economic integration. . . . Nevertheless, site hierarchies and occupation specialization are more apparent than in the Late Preceramic. This intimates that some segments of the regional population were becoming larger, less self-sufficient, and more sedentary, perhaps because scheduling, procurement, and manufacturing activities were responding to increasing demands on the land, diminishing possibilities for emigration, and a growing dependence on cultivated plants.

Central Panama, circa 3800–500 B.C.: A Brief Reassessment

MONAGRILLO AND SARIGUA AS CLASSIFICATORY CATEGORIES

Willey and McGimsey (1954:58, 95, 128) considered the distinctive features of their Monagrillo Phase to be (1) the ceramic types included in their Monagrillo Ceramic Complex,[12] (2) pebble chopping and grinding tools, and (3) stone bowls with incised decoration similar to that present on the pottery. "Associated traits," which were not "of sufficient distinctiveness to serve as hallmarks of the Monagrillo Phase," comprised multifaceted grinding stones, stone pestles, spherical pebble hammers, metates, and chipped stone scrapers.

They listed characteristic features of the Monagrillo Ceramic Complex as (1) temper of fine sand and angular and rounded quartz particles, (2) variable fire-clouded, dirty-buff surfaces, (3) average thickness 9 millimeters, (4) average hardness (Moh) 4.5 to 5.0, (5) notable predominance of plain or undecorated surfaces, (6) moderately good firing but poor oxidation or reduction control, (7) no handles, added bases, spouts, or other appendages, (8) very few shapes (ollas, bowls, and plates without necks, collars, flared rims, or composite silhouettes), and (9) very rare decoration limited to (a) red pigment applied and fired to exterior or interior surfaces and (b) incised lines and punctations with curvilinear designs imprinted in exterior surfaces prior to firing (Willey and McGimsey 1954:58).

This description applies well to the samples assigned by Cooke in the 1970s to the Monagrillo Ceramic Complex from Ladrones (n = 3,470) and Aguadulce (n = 497).[13] Vessel shapes, rim forms, and lip treatments are very similar at these sites, He-5, and Zapotal (Fig. 14.2). The Ladrones sample differs from that of He-5 principally with regard to surface color (much more variable at He-5) and surface hardness (Ladrones sherds are generally much more friable). The latter feature is related to preservation environment: the few Monagrillo sherds from dry floor deposits have surfaces as hard as those of He-5. The Aguadulce sample includes a larger number of sherds with a homogeneous paste tempered with fine quartz sand than Ladrones and He-5. Monagrillo Red sherds are also more abundant there (n = 23 [4.6 percent]).

On the other hand, plastic decoration at the two rockshelters is very different from the modes recorded at He-5. The 17 Ladrones sherds that present incised, scratched, punctated, appliqué, and fabric(?)-impressed

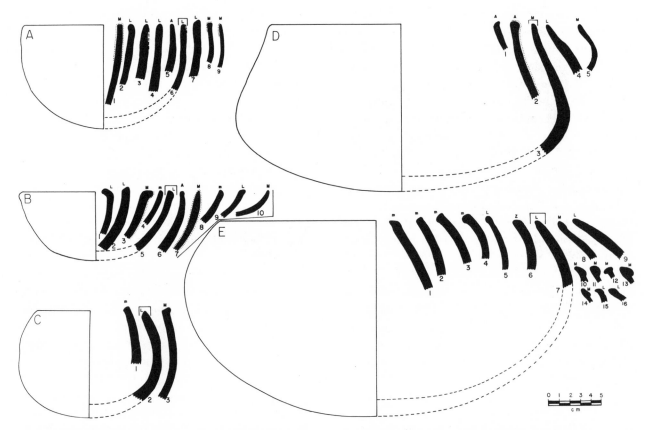

Fig. 14.2. Hypothetical vessel shapes and associated rim form variability in the Monagrillo Ceramic Complex, Monagrillo Plain and Monagrillo Red types, based on materials from excavations at Monagrillo (He-5) (M = Willey and McGimsey's sample, 1948–52; m = Ranere's sample, 1975), La Cueva de los Ladrones (L), the Aguadulce Shelter (A), and Zapotal (Z, Giausserand's 1987 excavations). The dotted line around rim profiles signifies the extent of red paint. Drawing by Lindsay Wall and Richard Cooke.

markings (Fig. 14.3) were restricted to the top third of the ceramic levels (Bird and Cooke 1978:Fig. 7). No curvilinear motifs are complete enough to be assigned to Willey and McGimsey's Monagrillo Incised type (although the sherds illustrated in Fig. 14.3, *l–n*, could be fragments). Some motifs, however, were recorded formerly in the Sarigua Complex, which Willey and McGimsey (1954:126) thought was "either contemporary with some portion of the Monagrillo Phase or else immediately postdated it." Paste and surface characteristics of these cf. Sarigua sherds are so similar to those of the rest of the Ladrones sample that Bird and Cooke would surely have classified undecorated or rimless sherds of decorated vessels as Monagrillo.[14]

At Aguadulce, one sherd is clearly Monagrillo Incised (Fig. 14.4, *g*). The five other plastically decorated sherds, however, bear motifs that were absent at He-5 (Fig. 14.4, *b–f*).

At He-5, Monagrillo Incised represented less than 0.5 percent of the Monagrillo sample. Willey and McGimsey (1954:65) considered it to be "of later in-

ception than 'Monagrillo Plain' or 'Monagrillo Red.'" Since the cf. Sarigua sherds at Ladrones occurred in the uppermost ceramic levels, it is possible that Monagrillo Incised and Sarigua coevally represent the tail end of the Monagrillo Ceramic Complex, when new kinds of decoration and new shapes were being added to a tradition that continued to use the same clays, tempers, and firing techniques. Supportive of contemporaneity is an incurved bowl rim sherd with a unique modeled and incised decoration (Fig. 14.4, *a*), which was associated at Zapotal with a date of 1630 (1410) 1200 B.C. (Beta-9574) and with typical Monagrillo rims.

An alternate (and, in my opinion, more likely) hypothesis is that the cf. Sarigua materials at Ladrones and Aguadulce postdate Monagrillo Incised. Supporting evidence is stylistic and stratigraphic. A few decorated sherds from the rockshelters are from small collared vessels with subglobular or cylindrical bodies (Fig. 14.3, *a, b, ?c, d;* Fig. 14.4, *e*). These forms are absent in the lower ceramic levels of Ladrones and Aguadulce and in the entire He-5 Monagrillo sample. They occur, however, at (1) the Sarigua type site (He-16), a shallow, one-component coastal deposit (Willey and McGimsey 1954:105–10),[15] (2) Carabalí, where cf. Sarigua sherds are stratified just above a date of 1520 (1120) 780 B.C. (Valerio 1987), and (3) SA-27, where surface-collected materials represent a short-term, single-component occupation. At SE-111, Cooke and Ranere collected sherds from small jars with collars but no incised decorations, above a date of 1300 (1000) 810 B.C. (Beta-19,497).

Small collared vessels with globular and subglobular bodies and a variety of incised and impressed decorations—unlike those of Monagrillo Incised—have been recorded in undated hilltop shaft-chamber tombs excavated by amateurs and looters: (1) Cerro Largo near Santiago (Biese 1967), (2) Cerro Guacamayo, on the flat peak of the hill of the same name, 3 kilometers east of Ladrones (Harte 1966), and (3) El Limón, 15 kilometers northeast of Cerro Guacamayo (Fig. 14.3, insert A; Stirling and Stirling 1964:Fig. 17).

Another characteristic shape found in the Cerro Guacamayo and El Limón tombs is a thin, tall chalice with a flat base, everted collar, and exterior incised and appliqué decoration (Harte 1966; Stirling and Stirling 1964:Plate 27). Fig. 14.3, *p*, from Ladrones, is a sherd from the raised, beveled "waist" of such a chalice. Fig. 14.3, *q–r*, from Ladrones, and Fig. 14.4, *c*, from Aguadulce, are probably sherds from the cylindrical part beneath the waist (see Fig. 14.3, insert B). This distribution implies that the flat-bottomed chalices called "Guacamayo" in Panamanian literature are co-eval with the cf. Sarigua materials described here and belong to an imperfectly defined "post-Monagrillo" (1200–800 B.C.) development. I expatiate on this possibility later.

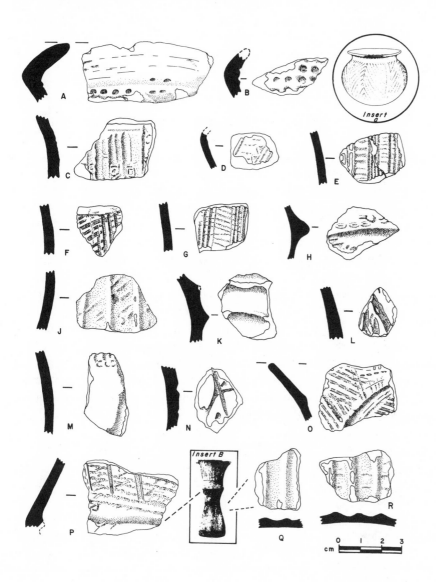

Fig. 14.3. Plastically decorated sherds from the Cueva de los Ladrones (1974 excavations). Some motifs recall the Sarigua Complex of Willey and Mc-Gimsey (1954). Sherds *a, b, d* and perhaps *c* are from collared vessels, as in insert A; *p–r* are from cylindrical vessels, as in insert B. Sherds *a* and *b* have punctate decoration; *c* and *k* are ridged; *j, q,* and *r* are fluted; *d, e, f, g,* and *p* are impressed, apparently with some kind of fabric; *o* is impressed and ridged; *n* is incised. Sherds *h, l, m:* decorative medium unclear. Drawing by Lindsay Wall and Richard Cooke.

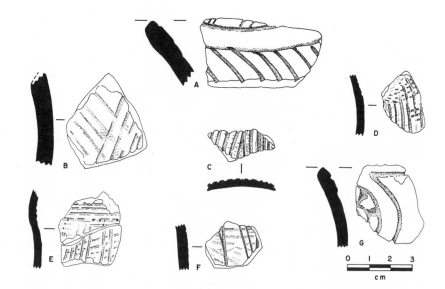

Fig. 14.4. Plastically decorated sherds from Zapotal (*a*, 1987 excavations) and the Aguadulce Shelter (*b–g*). Sherd *g* is Monagrillo Incised; *a–f* recall the Sarigua Complex of Willey and McGimsey; *c, f,* and *g* have incised decoration; *a* is incised above and below an appliqué ridge; *b, d,* and *e* are impressed, apparently with some kind of fabric. Drawing by Lindsay Wall.

MONAGRILLO AS A TEMPORAL CONCEPT[16]

Ladrones presents the earliest dates for Monagrillo pottery: 3830 (3620) 3350 B.C. (TEM-119) and 3510 (3310–3125) 2910 B.C. (TEM-124). Both samples were found in the same feature—a basin-shaped pile of wood charcoal, dietary refuse, and stones located just outside the drip line of the shelter (Cooke 1984:Fig. 10.1), which may have been a "fire pit" or oven.

A later group of dates (TEM-120, 121, 122) was recovered from beneath the diagnostic peak in abundance of Monagrillo sherds in the talus profiles (15 to 50 cm below surface [Cooke 1984:277]). This suggests that the major Monagrillo occupation at Ladrones postdates 2670–2010 B.C. Hence, although 621 Monagrillo sherds were extracted from this basin feature, it could conceivably be a trash pit into which materials of different ages (including Late Preceramic "sweepings") were dumped when the shelter floor was swept clean.

Only three of the ten Aguadulce ^{14}C samples were collected in the same levels as pottery: 1270 B.C. (TEM-126), 790 B.C. (TEM-107), and 770 B.C. (TEM-125). In block 3, where cultural deposits were 40 centimeters deep, dates are stratigraphically quite consistent, if one eliminates the clearly anomalous TEM-110. In each level, the majority of sherds are Monagrillo, but a few are not. This is probably why their 2-sigma range (1480–500 B.C.) is later than those recorded at Ladrones and He-5. Perhaps the occupants of this small shelter did not take pottery there during the second millennium B.C. even though it was in use regionally.

I agree with Ranere that the two fourth-millennium B.C. dates at Monagrillo (He-5) (TEM-109, SI-2841) seem disproportionately early: the dated charcoal may represent sporadic Preceramic use of the basal beach deposits.[17] Dates SI-2842 (2970 B.C.) and SI-2844 (2660 B.C.) should be ignored because they are clearly incompatible with stratigraphy. Hence, two major periods of Monagrillo activities can be identified: an earlier, intermittent one during the third millennium B.C. and a more regular or more permanent one from about 2000 to 1500 B.C. Willey and McGimsey's and Ranere's interpretations of He-5's site topographic history coincide broadly: the two types of occupation are surely related to coastal progradation and concomitant resource availability and/or abundance. Dere's prediction that abandonment of the locale is connected to the formation of a mangrove swamp around the site at approximately 1050 B.C. is compatible with the very scant representation of cf. Sarigua sherds at He-5.

Two-sigma ranges for five dates at Zapotal span 2470–1190 B.C. Interpretation of the site's history awaits Giausserand's analyses. The sandy basal strata suggest that it was near a beach when first occupied. Since I have not handled the 1948–52 sherd sample, I cannot comment on possible temporal differences between Willey and McGimsey's Monagrillo Plain and Zapotal Plain.

With regard to the small inland rockshelters, I retract my earlier identification of "early" sherds as *unequivocally* Monagrillo (Cooke and Ranere 1992b: 270). Some may well be, but the few rims are not diagnostic and could be coeval with the cf. Sarigua decorated sherds described earlier. Whichever its real temporal position, this material is scarce. It appears, then, that rockshelters more than 25 kilometers from Parita Bay either were not used much between 3800 and 500 B.C. or pottery was taken to them only occasionally.

In the light of the foregoing data, what is the best term for the time period during which the Monagrillo pottery sensu Willey and McGimsey was manufactured? Conscious of the confusion that has occurred in Panama because of the adoption of the same names for pottery categories, phases, and "cultures," Cooke and Ranere (1992b) suggested "Early Ceramic A" for the period during which central Panama pottery lacked black paint and appendage modes. Their terminology has since been modified by Isaza (1993). She suggested that the Monagrillo ceramics, as originally defined by Willey and McGimsey, be assigned to the Early Ceramic A (3000–1100 b.c.). She transferred the La Mula Group (Cooke 1992b:Figs. 8, 9) to the "Middle Ceramic B" period (500–100 b.c.), adducing that its apogee coincided with important technological and social developments: (1) the use of three painted colors on carefully fired collared vessels with fine pastes, (2) the specialization of agriculture upon maize, (3) greater standardization of stone tools, and (4) regional population nucleation.

Between these two clearly defined ceramic complexes she identified two provisional groupings: (1) the cf. Sarigua and Guacamayo materials referred to previously, which she assigned to the Early Ceramic B (1100–900 b.c.), and (2) fragments of 11 vessels found in feature 242S417E at La Mula–Sarigua, for which she chose the term "Middle Ceramic A" in recognition of the fact that this feature includes the earliest ^{14}C-dated painted designs in red and black on a pale slip (Cooke and Ranere 1992b:Fig. 9m; Hansell 1988, vol. 2, Fig. 41d). A dendrocalibrated version of Isaza's (1993) model is shown in Table 14.1.

SUBSISTENCE

Plant Use

Maize pollen and phytolith distributions at Ladrones and Aguadulce and in Lake La Yeguada sediments suggest that Early Ceramic A peoples, like their Late Preceramic predecessors, grew a small-eared maize in small garden plots as part of a rotating (slash-and-burn) cultivation system (Piperno et al. 1985, 1991). They also cultivated arrowroot, although Piperno (1989b, 1991) suggests that it was already in decline by this time. Mora (personal communication, 1994) identified the following phytoliths in a carbon residue encrusted on the surface of a Monagrillo sherd from Ladrones: wild grasses, sedges, Compositaceae, Chrysobalanaceae (a tropical tree family), palms (sperical forms like those of *Scheelea* and *Elaeis*), and cucurbits. These may or may not be food remains.

Table 14.1. Suggested Chronology (Dendrocalibrated) for Isaza's Ceramic Classification Scheme

Period	Pottery Complex	2-Sigma Range
Early Ceramic A	Monagrillo	3800/2900–1200 B.C.*
Early Ceramic B	In need of revision Collared round-bodied and flat-bottomed cylindrical vessels Plastic decorative motifs mostly linear and paneled	1200–800? B.C.
Middle Ceramic A	cf. Feature 242S417E at La Mula–Sarigua	780–380 B.C.
Middle Ceramic B	La Mula	180 B.C.–230 A.D.†

*I suggest two alternative dates for the inception of the Monagrillo Ceramic Complex in deference to the possibility that the feature from which TEM-119 and TEM-124 were recovered at Ladrones may contain chronologically mixed materials (i.e., charcoal and shell older than the pottery). The younger alternate date, 2900 B.C., is the outer 2-sigma figure for Y-585, which I accept as the most reliable date for the intermittent basal occupation at He-5. The latest reliable date for the Monagrillo Ceramic Complex sensu Willey and McGimsey is Beta-9574 from Zapotal.

†La Mula Group pottery is dominant in features at La Mula–Sarigua and Sitio Sierra in which the following dates were recovered: Beta-12728, Beta-12729, Beta-12931, I-9702, 97603, 9704.

No carbonized remains of maize have yet been identified in Early Ceramic deposits from central Panama. A charcoal sample (541 fragments) taken over one-sixteenth-inch mesh at Aguadulce is dominated by the American oil palm (*Elaeis oleifera*) and the wine palm (*Acrocomia mexicana*), which were primary food sources (Table 14.2).[18] The former produces large bunches of an orange-colored, hard, oily nut that is pounded before boiling. Especially abundant in seasonal swamps and along streams, it produces most fruit at the beginning of the dry season (December–February). The nuts of *A. mexicana*, abundant today in seasonally dry pastures to about 800 meters elevation, are rich in fats and protein. The fermented sap is a useful source of sugars (Lentz 1990).

No information is yet available on plant foods at Monagrillo (He-5); no pollen or phytoliths were recovered there, and the sorted charcoal is all wood. At Ladrones, Myint-Hpu reports *nance* (a tree fruit, *Byrsonima crassifolia*).

The foregoing data invite speculation about the possible uses of the characteristic edge-ground cobbles and their bases that accompany Monagrillo and cf. Sarigua pottery. Palm nut preparation? Doubtfully, in my opinion, unless the nuts were steadied in a perishable base rather than a "nutting stone," a tool type that is absent. Extraction of fibers? Possibly, but there are no confirmatory data. Ranere (1972, 1975, 1980b; Ranere and Hansell 1978) has argued that they were used for pounding root crops. The tuberous organs of many wild and some domesticated tuberous taxa must be heated or traumatized in order to release harmful toxins (e.g., Hawkes 1989) and reduce fibers inimical to nutrient absorption (e.g., Stahl 1989). So far as I

know, no arrowroot cultivars have toxic roots. However, because bruising is a precondition of starch grain release, Precolumbian peoples probably prepared arrowroot with stone tools.

Edge-ground cobbles have a remarkably wide distribution in Panama and Colombia, from sea level to more than 3,000 meters, on the coast, in forested interiors, and in *páramos* (Cooke 1993). Hence it is doubtful that they were used for processing only one plant species. McGimsey (1956) and Willey and McGimsey (1954) thought they may have been used for grinding seeds. In view of the dietary importance of wild grass seeds at Peruvian Middle Preceramic sites such as Paloma and Chilca (4500–2500 B.C.; Weir et al. 1988) and the apparently early movement of a small-grained (cultivated) maize through Central America, their hypothesis is not unreasonable. Specialists should search for identifiable phytoliths encrusted in cobble grinding surfaces. In central Panama, edge-ground cobbles first occur at Carabalí in the Early Preceramic (Ranere and Cooke 1993; Valerio 1987). By the end of the first millennium B.C. they had dropped out everywhere, being replaced by well-manufactured metates and cylindrical manos. Hence, the disappearance of edge-ground cobbles could conceivably be related not to a root crop–seed crop hiatus but to the replacement of primitive small-kerneled varieties with larger-kerneled "flour" maizes.

In disagreement with the "seed hypothesis," however, is the absence of edge-ground cobbles at Ladrones —the site whose microbotanical data most firmly suggest the use of maize! Some abraded pebbles and small grinding stone bases, however, were found in the Early Ceramic levels (Bird and Cooke 1978).

Table 14.2. Carbonized Plant Remains from Early Ceramic Levels at Aguadulce Shelter

Taxon	Plant Part	Fragments	Weight (g)
Cochlospermaceae: *Cochlospermum vitifolium*	Whole seed	1	0.2
Cucurbitaceae: *Momordica charantia*	Seed coat	1	0.5
Leguminoseae	Seed	2	0.1
Hymenea courbaril	Exocarp	4	0.1
Palmae: *Acrocomia mexicana*	Endocarp	63	0.9
Bactris mayor	Endocarp	11	0.2
Elaeis oleifera	Endocarp	456	8.4
Scheelea zonensis	Endocarp	3	0.4

Hunting and Fishing

Lists of exploited terrestrial taxa at Ladrones, Aguadulce, Zapotal (1984 excavations), and Monagrillo have been reported (Cooke and Ranere 1989:Fig. 26.5, 1992c:Table 2). The white-tailed deer dominates the mammalian samples (whose MNI totals are low), except at Ladrones, where the collared peccary (*Tayassu tajaçu*) is almost as abundant.[19] These data suggest that people stayed around long enough at all the sites to organize hunting parties. At Monagrillo (He-5), some marine turtles and iguanids were taken. Aguadulce's fauna is more diverse and contains more small animals, such as mud turtles (*Kinosternon*). This is compatible with the site's occasional use by small gathering and foraging groups or as a temporary shelter while people planted or tended crops.[20]

Fish remains were found at Aguadulce and Ladrones, as well as at Parita Bay littoral sites. Aguadulce's fisherfolk divided their time between freshwater and estuaries. The Ladrones sample includes primary freshwater taxa—catfish (*Rhinoloricaria* [Loricariidae]), *Rhamdia* [Pimelodidae]), a small characid (*Curimata*), and a gymnotine eel (*Sternopygus*)—and a few estuarine taxa of marine origin (e.g., thread-herring [*Opisthonema*] and croakers [*Ophioscion*]), which were probably brought in dried and salted from the Parita Bay coast. Fifteen marine shellfish species were identified in the basinlike feature discussed earlier. In spite of the site's minimum distance of 18 kilometers from the sea (due to marine transgression), the consumption of (presumably fresh) mollusks suggests that Ladrones was "home enough" either to attract kinsmen on social trips or to send people on a long walk in search of something different to eat.

Data on fishing at Monagrillo and Zapotal promise to add information relevant to the reconstruction of contiguous exploited habitats at different stages in these sites' histories. One He-5 sample of roughly 8,500 bones (MNI = 525), taken over one-eighth-inch mesh and associated with date SI-2838, 1880 [1678] 1511 B.C., points to the capture of inshore species, all of which have been recorded in catches in intertidal fish traps in Parita and Panama bays (Cooke and Tapia n.d.). Rank-order abundance is (1) thread-herring (*Opisthonema* cf. *libertate*, Clupeidae, 31 percent MNI), (2) Pacific lookdown (*Selene peruviana*, Carangidae, 17 percent), (3) Pacific bumper (*Chlorosocombrus orqueta*, Carangidae, 7 percent), (4) yellow bobo (*Polydactylus opercularis*, Polynemidae, 4 percent), and (5) a marine catfish (*Cathorops* species A,

Ariidae) and a longfin herring (*Ilisha furthii*, Pristigasteridae, less than 4 percent). These distributions, in addition to the lower dominance of marine catfish than at other Parita Bay sites, imply that Monagrillo's fisherfolk operated mainly in shallow but not too turbid water, at least partly over sandy substrates.[21]

Neither boats nor gill nets would have been necessary (despite Cooke 1992). The minimal representation of eleotrid gobies suggests that alvinas and mangrove channels were not exploited. The low frequency of the catfish *Arius seemanni* suggests that the Parita River did not enter the sea where the fish were being caught. The most logical conclusion is that barrier tidal traps were placed at the seaward outlet of the shallow embayment that is visible in aerial photographs just to the east of the site of Monagrillo (Willey and McGimsey 1954:Fig. 36). Most of the fish are small (less than 200 g). No bones were burnt or charred. It is likely that a major activity at Monagrillo during its peak occupation was the salting, sun drying, and transport inland of small estuarine fish.[22]

Conclusion

The Monagrillo Ceramic Complex, described 40 years ago at a few sites located on a former Holocene strandline, is almost certainly the earliest pottery in central Panama and, perhaps, in lower Central America. It is probably of local origin, made somewhat extemporaneously with whichever clay was available near each site. The fact that it is much more abundant within 25 kilometers of the present-day coast than farther inland could be interpreted as suggesting that most people lived near Parita Bay. Zapotal may have been a coastal "village," albeit occupied seasonally. Lake sediment and Santa María Project archaeological survey data, however, do not support such a dichotomy in regional population distribution. Perhaps the activities for which small collarless bowls and plates were used were more important near coastal habitats than away from them.[23]

If it was as long-lived as the existing ^{14}C chronology suggests (2-sigma range 3800–1200 B.C., intercept range 3620 B.C. [TEM-119]–1410 B.C. [Beta-9574]), the Monagrillo Ceramic Complex was technologically and conceptually very conservative. It is clear, however, that small test pits and slit trenches excavated in shell mounds and rockshelters with differential preservation and steep taluses are not appropriate for tight chronological control. The oldest part of the sequence is still confusing. Hence, I offer an alternative maximum 2-sigma time span of 2900–1200 B.C.

Exactly when Monagrillo pottery sensu Willey and McGimsey acquired the composite shapes and heterogeneous plastic decorative motifs to which archaeologists have inconsistently assigned the names Sarigua and Guacamayo is still unclear. Current data suggest that this was an endogenous process. I have suggested that it is likely to have occurred between 1200 and 800 B.C. However, it is wise not to discard the possibility that collared and cylindrical vessels found in hilltop grave sites in Coclé and Veraguas provinces represent a funerary ware that was partially coeval with "classic" Monagrillo sherds found in refuse dumps at sites located within 25 kilometers of Parita Bay. If these grave sites prove to date from the period 2900–1200 B.C., they would lend support to the hypothesis that the Monagrillo (Early Ceramic A) people of central Panama were slash-and-burn horticulturalists who lived for most of the year at some distance from the coast, to which they moved and congregated seasonally to harvest and preserve marine and estuarine foods. This situation was tentatively proposed by Willey and McGimsey.

Specialists have argued that the Late Preceramic and Early Ceramic in central Panama were periods of considerable cultural stability: stone tool technology seems to be as "conservative" as the pottery. The fact that more differences are noticeable in inferred subsistence economies and stone tool assemblages among sites, rather than through time, suggests that future fieldwork should concentrate on (1) opening out rockshelters and doing a better job of identifying time-specific occupations and activities, and (2) locating single-component open sites that would clarify important uncertainties, such as the morphology of dwellings, the seasonality of habitat exploitation, the relationship of stone tools to specific plant resources, and diachronic typological changes within the Monagrillo Ceramic Complex and its imperfectly understood sequel.

Notes

1. Willey and McGimsey's nomenclature. The *He-* prefix signifies Herrera province.

2. Dendrocalibrations were generously provided by M. Tamers (Beta Analytic). Data set references are M. Stuiver and T. F. Brazunias, 1993, *Radiocarbon* 35:137–89; M. Stuiver and G. W. Pearson, 1993, *Radiocarbon* 35:1–23; G. W. Pearson and M. Stuiver, 1993, *Radiocarbon* 35:25–33. Bidecadal weighted averages are from E. Bard, M. Arnold, R. G. Fairbanks, and B. Hamelin, 1993, *Radiocarbon* 35:191–99; T. W. Linick, A. Long, P. E. Damon, and C. W. Ferguson, 1986, *Radiocarbon* 28:93–104; G. W. Pearson, B. Becker, and F. Qua, 1993, *Radiocarbon* 35:93–104. A δ13C value of 0.0‰ was assumed for uncorrected shell samples, which resulted in 410 years being added to the uncorrected dates. ΔR = 5 ± 50 was assumed for the reservoir effect. Where single dates are quoted, the figure given is the intercept date. In the text, dates are rounded to the nearest ten years.

3. Willey and McGimsey (1954:53) state that their strata 2–6 are "primarily the result of natural agencies with human deposition playing a minor role in their formation."

4. Alvinas are characteristic landforms of the Parita Bay littoral. After heavy or prolonged rains or during the highest spring tides, they are covered with a thin sheet of water. During the dry season, their barren, alga-covered surface desiccates. The strong northerly winds whip up saline sediments and deposit them inland.

5. Although the major marine transgression had ended by approximately 5000 b.c., Dere's sequence perhaps identified a brief reversal event at approximately 3000 b.c. (Clary et al. 1984).

6. Piperno (1983:253–54) assessed four characteristics of cross-shaped phytoliths: (1) size (cf. Pearsall 1978, 1979), (2) three-dimensional structures, (3) dumbbell to cross-shaped phytolith ratios, and (4) the percentage of cross-shaped phytoliths of all sizes in the deposits.

7. The date 5000 b.c. was based on estimations for the beginning of the Late Preceramic of central Panama (Cooke 1984:Table 10.1; Cooke and Ranere 1984:Fig. 2) and on the basal position of the earliest 14C date at Ladrones, 4910 b.c. (5940 [5690] 5530 B.C.) (Cooke 1984:277).

8. Marantaceae phytoliths, attributed by Piperno (1989b) to domesticated arrowroot (*Maranta arundinacea*), occur in deposits dated to 7960 (7540) 7260 B.C. (Beta-5101) at the Cueva de los Vampiros (Cooke and Ranere 1984). At Aguadulce, they are abundant in the potteryless levels but drop out in ceramic strata.

9. Identification of maize phytoliths was based on the size (13 microns) of the Variant 1 cross-shapes.

10. Two polished ax flakes were recovered at Ladrones by Bird and Cooke (1978) in sherdless layers. Their occurrence near pit wall junctions, however, casts doubt on their stratigraphic validity. Hence, this association should be rejected until confirmed by subsequent excavations.

11. Giausserand did not return to finish the excavations. I have not been able to evaluate her pottery sample because it is still in her possession in France.

12. Monagrillo Plain, Plain Variant, Thin Yellow, Incised, and Red; Zapotal Plain.

13. Ladrones pastes are friable, sand- and grit-tempered

(with crushed rock additions on thicker vessels). Fewer than 2 percent of the sherds are homogenously oxidized (usually thinner ones with a yellow-brown wall, Munsell 10YR 4/6, 5/6, cf. Willey and McGimsey's "Thin Yellow"). More than 90 percent of surfaces have fire clouds. Soot-free surfaces are dark brown (10YR 4/2, 3/4, 3/2) or strong brown (7.5YR 4/6). Surfaces are roughly smoothed but not polished. Wall thicknesses range from 4 to 9 millimeters (average: 7 ± 1.3 mm). A few sherds (probably thickened bases) are up to 14 millimeters thick. Rims are generally uneven and often have an interior or exterior fold. Three short collars were the only appendages recorded in the Precolumbian samples (cf. Sarigua). So many rim sherds are eroded or very small that the precise proportionality of shapes cannot be calculated. However, they can be rank ordered: (1) wide-mouthed (15–30 cm) subglobular bowls with slightly incurved walls, (2) vessels with more restricted mouths (6–15 cm) and more incurved walls (i.e., tecomates), (3) bowls with straight or slightly outcurved walls and widish mouths, and (4) plates (see Fig. 14.2). Fifty-eight Ladrones sherds (1.7 percent) have red paint (cf. Monagrillo Red [Willey and McGimsey:Fig. 12e–j]): their designs are restricted to circumferential bands of color below the exterior and/or interior rim.

14. At Ladrones and all other central Panama rockshelters, sherds of handmade historic pottery occurred in the upper layers and on the surface. They were also common at He-5, where they were assigned to the El Tigre complex (Willey and McGimsey 1954). Rims, decorated sherds, and well-preserved bodies are usually distinguishable from those of the Monagrillo complex. Eroded fragments, however, can easily be confused; hence, body sherd counts in deposits where Monagrillo and El Tigre materials occur together are suspect. Cooke and Fonseca discovered a fire pit exposed on the surface at He-5 in 1991. It contained exclusively El Tigre pottery and very large amounts of wood charcoal. A date of A.D. 1654 (1683–1954) 1955 confirms a modern chronological placement.

15. Sarigua (He-16) was apparently located within the limits of the 200-hectare, multicomponent La Mula–Sarigua (PR-14) site, where the distribution of surface materials and features suggests constant (if not continuous) occupation from Monagrillo times (1.3 ha) to the beginning of the Christian era (more than 50 ha; La Mula Complex) (Hansell 1988).

16. It will be clear from the preceding section that there are serious obstacles to calculating the age and longevity of the Monagrillo Ceramic Complex: (1) The only site where décapage techniques have been employed is Zapotal (by Giausserand in 1987, material unpublished). At some sites (He-5, Ladrones), long trenches were employed; at others, small test pits. This hampers the identification of natural strata and the sequential removal of disturbances and features. Under these conditions, it is very difficult to be certain of the contemporaneity of artifacts and datable

materials. (2) Rockshelter deposits are proportionally much deeper down humid taluses than on dry floors. At Ladrones, for example, maximum depths inside and outside the drip line are 0.5 meter and 1.50 meters respectively (Cooke 1984:Fig. 10.2). Consequently, dry cultural deposits, where preservation of sherds and organic materials is best, tend to comprise materials belonging to different time periods. This is particularly true of the top 0.25 meter or so, where the transition from Monagrillo sensu stricto into later "complexes" is recorded. (3) More ^{14}C dates have been calculated with shells than with charcoal. All are shallow-water marine taxa. Carbon 14 specialists are still uncomfortable about the correlation between marine shell and terrestrial (wood) carbon dates. Some would recommend not using marine calibrations for shells from shallow estuaries near river mouths. I have followed Tamers's advice herein, using the marine dendrocalibration for all "marine" shells (irrespective of their tolerances of freshwater influences), a ΔR value of 5 ± 50, and an estimated δ^{13}C value of 0.0 ‰ (somewhat more positive than the -5.4 to -1.3 values determined empirically for Late Preceramic and Early and Middle Ceramic shell samples from the region). In some cases, shell and charcoal dates calibrated independently are compatible with stratigraphy and stylistic appreciations of cultural evolution; in others, they are not.

17. In October 1993, I found an approximately 100-m^2 lithic scatter a few hundred meters south of He-5, which appears to be Preceramic in age.

18. These remains come from block 3, 10–25 centimeters below surface, and block 5, 5–35 centimeters below surface. C. Earle Smith identified them with a binocular microscope in 1985, but without referring to a comparative collection. They were reanalyzed by A. Blanco in 1987 and by K. Myiint-Hpu in 1992–93. They are associated with mostly Monagrillo and a few cf. Sarigua sherds.

19. MNI indicates minimum numbers of individuals. The quite large sample of terrestrial fauna from Giausserand's 1987 dig at Zapotal has not been analyzed.

20. Small shelters such as Aguadulce and Ladrones may well have served as dwellings or storehouses within larger communities. This has not been demonstrated by survey. However, Los Santanas (SE-189), where Piperno has reported early maize, is close to quite large, probably Late Preceramic "sites," which may well have belonged to a single community with dispersed dwellings.

21. This reconstruction is in accordance with the shellfish data for the later, denser period of occupation. *Tivela byronensis* is a filter feeder with a very long syphon that reflects a burrowing existence in high-energy sandy substrates. It is unlikely to have occurred in a shallow lagoon.

22. None of the top-ranked fish appears to show any categorical seasonal preference for the Parita Bay estuarine littoral. It is possible, however, that prolongation of actualistic studies of artisanal fishing in Parita Bay will re-

veal patterns of inshore abundance that will be relevant to the problem of seasonal human occupancy. If Monagrillo (He-5) were used for salting and drying fish, the sunny and windy months (December–April) would have been the most favorable.

23. Some pottery technologically quite similar to Monagrillo but possessing short "Sarigualike" collars has been reported outside the Santa María basin and littoral adjacent to Parita Bay—for example, at the Cueva Bustamante site in the Bayano Valley (Cooke 1984; and see Fig. 14.1). However, this material has not been dated.

References Cited

Biese, L.
1967   Cerro Largo: An Atypical Gravesite in Central Panama. *Ethnos* 1967:26–34.

Bird, J. B., and R. G. Cooke
1978   La Cueva de los Ladrones: Datos preliminares sobre la ocupación Formativa. *Actas del V Symposium Nacional de Antropología, Arqueología y Etnohistoria de Panamá*, pp. 283–304. Instituto Nacional de Cultura, Panama.

Clary, J., P. Hansell, A. Ranere, and T. Buggey
1984   The Holocene Geology of the Western Parita Bay Coastline of Central Panama. In *Recent Developments in Isthmian Archaeology*, edited by F. W. Lange, pp. 55–83. British Archaeological Reports, International Series 212, Oxford.

Cooke, R. G.
1984   Archaeological Research in Central and Eastern Panama: A Review of Some Problems. In *The Archaeology of Lower Central America*, edited by F. W. Lange and D. Z. Stone, pp. 263–302. University of New Mexico Press, Albuquerque.

1992   Prehistoric Nearshore and Littoral Fishing in the Eastern Tropical Pacific: An Ichthyological Evaluation. *World Archaeology* 6:1–49.

1993   Etapas tempranas de la producción de alimentos en la baja Centroamérica y partes de Colombia ("Región Histórica Chibcha-Chocó"). *Revista de Arqueología Americana* 6:35–70.

Cooke, R. G., and A. J. Ranere
1984   The "Proyecto Santa María": A Multidisciplinary Analysis of Prehistoric Adaptations to a Tropical Watershed in Panama. In *Recent Developments in Isthmian Archaeology*, edited by F. W. Lange, pp. 3–30. British Archaeological Reports, International Series 212, Oxford.

1989   Hunting in Prehistoric Panama: A Diachronic Perspective. In *The Walking Larder: Patterns of Domestication, Pastoralism and Predation*, edited by J. Clutton-Brock, pp. 295–315. Unwin Hyman, London.

1992a   Prehistoric Human Adaptations to the Seasonally Dry Forests of Panama. *World Archaeology* 24:114–33.

1992b   The Origin of Wealth and Hierarchy in the Central Region of Panama (12,000–2,000 B.P.), with Observations on Its Relevance to the History and Phylogeny of Chibchan-Speaking Polities in Panama and Elsewhere. In *Wealth and Hierarchy in the Intermediate Area*, edited by F. W. Lange, pp. 243–316. Dumbarton Oaks, Washington, D.C.

1992c   Human Influences on the Zoogeography of Panama: An Update Based on Archaeological and Ethnohistorical Evidence. In *Biogeography of Mesoamerica*, edited by S. P. Darwin and A. L. Welden, pp. 21–58. Proceedings of a Symposium (Mérida, Yucatán, México, October 26–30, 1984). Special Publication of the Mesoamerican Ecology Institute, Tulane University, New Orleans.

Cooke, R. G., and G. Tapia
n.d.   Stationary Intertidal Fish Traps in Estuarine Inlets on the Pacific Coast of Panama: Descriptions, Evaluations of Early Dry Season Catches and Relevance to the Interpretation of Dietary Archaeofaunas. *Offa*. In press.

Deevey, E. S., L. J. Gralenski, and V. Hoffren
1959   Yale Natural Radio-Carbon Measurements, IV. *American Journal of Science, Radio-Carbon Supplement* 1:142–72.

Dere, C.
1981   The Geological and Paleographic Setting of an Archeological Site on the Southwestern Coast of Parita Bay, Panama. M.A. thesis, Department of Geography, Temple University.

Eldredge, K.
1979   Temple University Radiocarbon Dates 1. *Radiocarbon* 21:472–76.

Hansell, P.
1979   Shell Analysis: A Case Study from Panama. M.A. thesis, Department of Anthropology, Temple University, Philadelphia.

1988   The Rise and Fall of an Early Formative Community: La Mula-Sarigua, Central Pacific Panama. Ph.D. dissertation (2 vols.), Temple University, Philadelphia.

Hansell, P., and J. K. Adams
1980   The Application of Textural Analysis to the Interpretation of Cultural Deposits. Paper presented at the 45th annual meeting of the

Society for American Archaeology, Philadelphia.

Harte, N.
1966   El Sitio Guacamayo. *Boletín del Museo Chiricano* 3:3–7.

Hawkes, J. G.
1989   The Domestication of Roots and Tubers in the American Tropics. In *Foraging and Farming: The Evolution of Plant Exploitation,* edited by D. R. Harris and G. C. Hillman, pp. 481–503. Unwin Hyman, London.

Isaza, I.
1993   Desarrollo estilístico de la cerámica pintada del Panamá central con énfasis en el período 500 a.c.–500 d.c. Graduation thesis, Universidad Autonómica de Guadalajara, México.

Lentz, D. L.
1990   *Acrocomia mexicana:* Palm of the Ancient Mesoamericans. *Journal of Ethnobiology* 10:183–94.

McGimsey, C. R., III
1956   Cerro Mangote: A Preceramic Site in Panama. *American Antiquity* 22:151–61.
1957   Further Data and a Date from Cerro Mangote, Panama. *American Antiquity* 23:434–35.

Pearsall, D. M.
1978   Phytolith Analysis of Archaeologial Soils: Evidence for Maize Cultivation in Formative Ecuador. *Science* 199:177–78.
1979   The Application of Ethnobotanical Techniques to the Problem of Subsistence in the Ecuadorian Formative. Ph.D. dissertation, Department of Anthropology, University of Illinois, Urbana.
1992   The Origins of Plant Cultivation in South America. In *The Origins of Agriculture: An International Perspective,* edited by C. W. Cowan and P. J. Watson, pp.173–205. Smithsonian Institution Press, Washington, D.C.

Pearsall, D. M., and D. R. Piperno
1990   Antiquity of Maize Cultivation in Ecuador: Summary and Reevaluation of the Evidence. *American Antiquity* 55:324–37.

Piperno, D. R.
1979   Phytolith Analysis of Archaeological Soils from Central Panama. M.A. thesis, Department of Anthropology, Temple University, Philadelphia.
1983   The Application of Phytolith Analysis to the Reconstruction of Plant Subsistence and Environments in Prehistoric Panama. Ph.D. thesis, Department of Anthropology, Temple University, Philadelphia.
1985   Phytolith Taphonomy and Distributions in Archeological Sediments from Panama. *Journal of Archaeological Science* 12:247–67.
1988   *Phytolith Analysis: An Archaeological and Geological Perspective.* Academic Press, San Diego.
1989a   Non-affluent Foragers: Resource Avaliability, Seasonal Shortages and the Emergence of Agriculture in Panamanian Tropical Forests. In *Foraging and Farming: the Evolution of Plant Domestication,* edited by D. R. Harris and G. C. Hillman, pp. 538–54. Unwin Hyman, London.
1989b   The Occurrence of Phytoliths in the Reproductive Structures of Selected Tropical Angiosperms and Their Significance in Tropical Paleoecology, Paleoethnobotany and Systematics. *Review of Paleobotany and Palynology* 61:141–73.
1991   The Status of Phytolith Analysis in the American Tropics. *Journal of World Prehistory* 5:155–91.

Piperno, D. R., M. B. Bush, and P. Colinvaux
1991   Paleoecological Perspectives on Human Adaptation in Panama, II: The Holocene. *Geoarchaeology* 6:227–50.
1992   Patterns of Articulation of Culture and the Plant World in Prehistoric Panama: 11,500 B.P.–3000 B.P. In *Archaeology and Environment in Latin America,* edited O. R. Ortiz-Troncoso and T. van der Hammen, pp. 109–27. Instituut voor Pre- en Protohistorische Archeologie Albert Egges van Giffen, Universiteit van Amsterdam, Amsterdam.

Piperno, D. R., and K. H. Clary
1984   Early Plant Use and Cultivation in the Santa María Basin, Panama: Data from Phytoliths and Pollen. In *Recent Developments in Isthmian Archaeology,* edited by F. W. Lange, pp. 85–121. British Archaeological Reports, International Series 212, Oxford.

Piperno, D. R., K. H. Clary, R. G. Cooke, A. J. Ranere, and D. Weiland
1985   Preceramic Maize in Central Panama. *American Anthropologist* 87:871–78.

Ranere, A. J.
1972   Early Human Adaptations to New World Tropical Forests: The View from Panama. Ph.D. dissertation, Department of Anthropology, University of California at Davis.
1975   Toolmaking and Tool Use among the Preceramic Peoples of Panama. In *Lithic Technology,* edited by E. S. Swanson, pp. 173–210. Mouton, The Hague.
1980a   Preceramic Shelters in the Talamancan Range. In *Adaptive Radiations in Prehistoric Panama,*

edited by O. F. Linares and A. J. Ranere, pp. 16–43. Peabody Museum Monographs 5. Harvard University, Cambridge, Massachusetts.

1980b   Stone Tools from the Río Chiriquí Shelters. In *Adaptive Radiations in Prehistoric Panama,* edited by O. F. Linares and A. J. Ranere, pp. 316–53. Peabody Museum Monographs 5. Harvard University, Cambridge, Massachusetts.

1992   Implements of Change in the Holocene Environments of Panama. In *Archaeology and Environment in Latin America,* edited O. R. Ortiz-Troncoso and T. van der Hammen, pp. 45–57. Instituut voor Pre- en Proto-historische Archeologie Albert Egges van Giffen, Universiteit van Amsterdam, Amsterdam.

Ranere, A. J., and R. G. Cooke

1993   Evidencia de ocupación humana en Panamá a postrimerías del Pleistoceno y a comienzos del Holoceno. In press.

Ranere, A. J., and P. Hansell

1978   Early Subsistence Patterns along the Pacific Coast of Central Panama. In *Prehistoric Coastal Adaptations,* edited by B. L. Stark and B. Voorhies, pp. 31–48. Academic Press, New York.

Ranere, A. J., and R. L. McCarty

1976   Informe preliminar sobre la excavación de un sitio precerámico en Coclé, Panamá. *Actas del IV Simposium Nacional de Antropología, Ar-queología y Etnohistoria de Panamá, octubre, 1973,* pp. 483–93. Universidad de Panamá e Instituto Nacional de Cultura.

Stahl, A. B.

1989   Plant-Food Processing: Implications for Dietary Quality. In *Foraging and Farming: the Emergence of Plant Exploitation,* edited by D. R. Harris and G. C. Hillman, pp. 171–98. Unwin Hyman, London.

Stirling, M. W., and M. Stirling

1964   *El Limón, an Early Tomb Site in Coclé Province, Panamá.* Smithsonian Institution, Bureau of American Ethnology, Bulletin 191, Anthropological Paper 71, Washington, D.C.

Valerio, W.

1987   Análisis funcional y estratigráfico de Sf-9 (Carabalí), un abrigo rocoso en la región central de Panamá. Undergraduate thesis, University of Costa Rica.

Weir, G., R. Benfer, and J. Jones

1988   Preceramic to Early Formative Subsistence on the Central Coast. In *Economic Prehistory of the Central Andes,* edited by E. S. Wing and J. C. Wheeler, pp. 55–94. British Archaeological Reports, International Series 427, Oxford.

Willey, G. R., and C. R. McGimsey III

1954   *The Monagrillo Culture of Panama.* Papers of the Peabody Museum of Archaeology and Ethnology 49(2). Harvard University Press, Cambridge, Massachusetts.

15

Interaction in Hunting and Gathering Societies as a Context for the Emergence of Pottery in the Central American Isthmus

JOHN W. HOOPES

The origin and development of pottery in Central America remains a complex issue. New data from South America suggest that pottery was being made by nonhorticultural, semisedentary populations in the Amazon basin as early as 7000 b.p. (Roosevelt, chapter 10) and in northern Colombia around 6000 b.p. (Oyuela-Caycedo, chapter 11). Ceramics were also being manufactured in Ecuador shortly after 6000 b.p. (Damp and Vargas, chapter 13). To the north, the earliest Mesoamerican pottery appears in the context of sedentary populations practicing maize horticulture around 3500 b.p. (Clark and Gosser, chapter 17). Although the Central American isthmus is a geographical bridge between the continents, and dates for its earliest pottery complexes are intermediate between those for South America and Mesoamerica, straightforward diffusionary models fail to account for variability in technology and style. This chapter explores the possibility that ceramic technology appeared as a result of independent invention (or perhaps "dependent invention" as discussed by Clark and Gosser, chapter 17) within the region, emphasizing factors besides basic subsistence considerations.

Current models for the appearance of pottery production in the Central American isthmus can be grouped into ectothonous and autochthonous types. The former link ceramic production to the migration or diffusion of incipient horticulturalists from the north or south (Ford 1969; Lathrap 1977; Linares 1980; Snarskis 1978, 1984) and emphasize similarities among Central American complexes and those of Mesoamerica and South America. Ceramics, which improved the food value of maize, manioc, beans, and other cultigens, are assumed to have arrived together with these species. The emergence of ceramic production was an adjunct to demographic expansion as farming populations to the north and south increased at the expense of indigenous hunters and gatherers.

There is an unmistakable trend in the dates of the appearance of the earliest ceramics from south to north; however, it is difficult (if not impossible) to derive the earliest Panamanian complexes from northern Colombia or the earliest Costa Rican ceramics from Panama. Although ceramic technology may have a South American origin, independent invention is just as plausible as diffusion (Hoopes 1994a). Diffusionary models provide few insights into the distribution of ceramic forms or styles. They are also relatively sterile with regard to questions about why ceramics were used at all.

An alternative, autochthonous model for the emergence of ceramic production in Central America removes pottery from an implicit context within the expansion of horticultural societies and the diffusion of horticultural traditions. Instead, it sees ceramic production as an adjunct to two important processes: (1) the intensive utilization of seasonally abundant wild resources, and (2) symbiotic relationships between sedentary and mobile populations. Specific patterns of social interaction, facilitated by the use of pottery, helped improve strategies for the broad-based utilization of tropical forest resources. The uses of native tree crops made possible by ceramic containers, for example, may have helped to predispose incipient sedentarists to the adoption of exogenous seed crops such as maize.

Geographical Contexts for the Emergence of Ceramics

The earliest pottery in Central America appears in a variety of contexts and regions over a period of about two thousand years beginning around 4500 b.p. The most important of these regions (in order of temporal priority) are (1) central Panama, especially Parita Bay and the Río Santa María drainage, (2) northern Costa Rica, including parts of Greater Nicoya and the San Carlos region, (3) the central highlands of Costa Rica, and (4) the Pacific watershed of southern Costa Rica (Fig. 15.1).

CENTRAL PANAMA

In central Panama, Monagrillo pottery has been found in deposits stratified over Late Preceramic ones at five rockshelters (Cooke, chapter 14; Cooke and Ranere 1992:270). It has been associated with 18 radiocarbon dates from Cueva de los Ladrones, Monagrillo, and Zapotal, ranging from 4800 ± 100 b.p. (TEM-119, Cueva de los Ladrones) to 3180 ± 80 b.p. (Beta-9574, Zapotal). Sherds have been reported from coastal sites with shell middens and from inland sites like Carabalí and Río Cobre, the latter located at over 1,000 meters

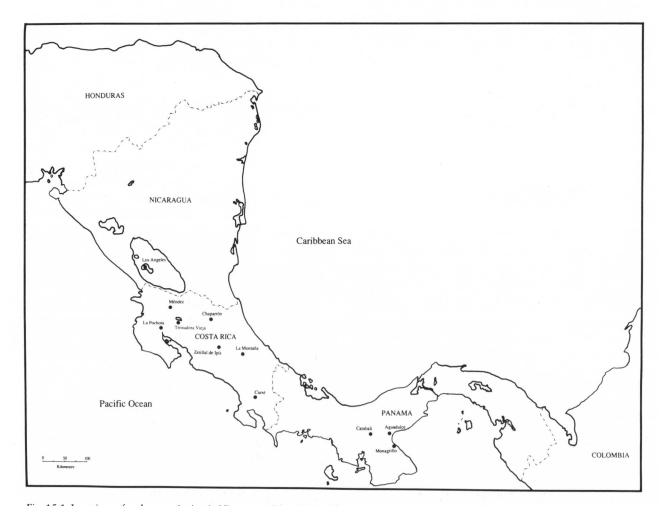

Fig. 15.1. Locations of early ceramic sites in Nicaragua, Costa Rica, and Panama.

in montane rain forest with annual precipitation in excess of 4,000 millimeters. Cooke and Ranere (1992: 270) find Monagrillo pottery sufficiently different from early South American complexes to be considered "completely endogenous." The pottery is extremely simple and unrefined. Its manufacture was probably informal. The principal forms are large, deep bowls with simple, unthickened rims (Cooke and Ranere 1992: Fig. 7). Necks or collars are absent, as are specialized supports or bases. Decoration, restricted to red painted rims and incised motifs, is absent from the earliest examples and rare in later assemblages.

NORTHERN COSTA RICA AND SOUTHWESTERN NICARAGUA

The earliest ceramic complexes from northern Costa Rica are all closely related. They differ, however, from Monagrillo and from early complexes to the north, such as the Barra ceramics of coastal Chiapas, Mexico (Clark and Gosser, chapter 17) and Bostan of coastal El Salvador (Arroyo, chapter 16). Their distribution extends from the Tempisque Valley in Guanacaste province across the volcanic cordillera into the broad San Carlos Plains. They appear in a wide variety of ecological zones, ranging from swamp margins at inland lakes to riverine habitats and islands in Lake Nicaragua.[1] Radiocarbon dates and volcanic tephra strata suggest that Tronadora ceramics from sites on Lake Arenal date as early as 3700 b.p. (Hoopes 1987, 1994b; Sheets et al. 1991).

The discovery near the Tronadora type site of a fluted projectile point manufactured from locally available chalcedony indicates that the Arenal region was first occupied in Paleoindian times (Sheets et al. 1991). Both radiocarbon dates and lithic assemblages document the presence of preceramic Archaic populations. A series of radiocarbon dates in association with aceramic deposits with chipped stone debitage situated below strata containing early ceramics suggests that Tronadora Vieja represents the reoccupation of an earlier, open-air Late Preceramic site by a ceramic-producing Early Formative population (Hoopes 1994b). Although ground stone tools dominated Tronadora lithic assemblages and chipped stone tools were rare, chalcedony biface thinning flakes—more typically associated with Preceramic industries—were found together with early pottery at Tronadora Vieja. These suggest continuity across the Preceramic/Ceramic boundary. The association of pottery with simple structures and with both macro- and microbotanical remains of maize, as well as with fragments of manos

and metates, indicates that Tronadora pottery was manufactured by sedentary or semisedentary horticulturalists. At La Pochota, in lowland Guanacaste, a ceramic complex similar to Tronadora has been found in association with a large, rectangular stone mound identified as a habitational platform (Odio 1992:3).

Apart from Tronadora, none of the other northern complexes has been dated directly.[2] Early pottery from the Tronadora, Chaparrón, Dinarte, and Naranjo complexes is known exclusively from fragmentary remains, and only one partial vessel has been reported (Fig. 15.2; Hoopes 1987:Fig. 6.4). Principal vessel types include massive, incurving-rim bowls with heavily bolstered rims; wide bowls with comma-shaped rims; and squat, necked jars. Tall, flat-based cylinders decorated with wide incisions and fine, shell-edge stamping stand out as special-purpose vessels for the serving of beverages. Handles and supports are absent, as are figurines and other clay objects. Decoration is represented by the sophisticated application of thick red slips and paints in combination with a wide variety of plastic techniques that include punctation, shell stamping, reed stamping, wide incision, modeling, scraping, and gouging (Hoopes 1987, 1994b).

Fig. 15.2. Tall, cylindrical serving vessels from Early Formative complexes at Tronadora Vieja and Zetillal de Ipís.

Central Highlands of Costa Rica

The central highlands region provided the first dated early pottery complex in Costa Rica (Snarskis 1978, 1984). La Montaña pottery, identified at the type site near Turrialba, has been associated with five ^{14}C dates. The earliest is 3465 ± 160 b.p. (UCLA-2113A). Three others overlap from 800 to 400 B.C. at the 2-sigma range, and the fifth dates to the third century B.C. Although the earliest date was initially rejected, similarities between La Montaña and Tronadora ceramics suggest that it may, in fact, be valid. Barba ceramics, closely related to La Montaña, are found in small quantities at sites such as nearby Guayabo de Turrialba, and similar pottery has been reported from Guacimo, Tatisco, Pavas, and Barrial de Heredia (Snarskis 1984:206). Like Tronadora, La Montaña pottery is found in a region that supported hunting and gathering populations from Paleoindian times. The type site is not far from a Paleoindian chert quarry and large Paleoindian and Early Archaic sites near Turrialba (Snarskis 1979). It is situated on a terrace of one of the largest rivers in Costa Rica, in an area characterized by fertile soils derived from volcanic tephra.

Early ceramics from the central highlands of Costa Rica share several modes with northern complexes. The most common vessels are large-capacity, incurving-rim bowls with bolstered rims. Flat-based, cylindrical vessels similar to those from the Arenal region are also known, including one almost complete example from the site of Zetillal de Ipís (Fig. 15.2; Snarskis 1978:Fig. 25a). The ceramics differ, however, from those of the Tronadora and Chaparrón complexes in important respects. Painting and slipping are virtually absent, and vessel forms include *budares*—ceramic griddles that may have been used to toast cakes of bitter manioc.

Southern Costa Rica

The earliest pottery in southern Costa Rica is known as Curré, from sites in the Térraba–Coto Brús valley (Corrales 1985, 1989). Although it is not directly dated, its stratigraphic position and stylistic traits suggest that it appeared around 3500 b.p. Emphasis on plastic decoration, with punctation and shell stamping predominant, indicates relationships between Curré and complexes to the north. Curré's closest analogies, however, are with Sarigua pottery of central Panama. The predominant vessel forms are short-necked jars with outcurving rims. Slipping and painting are ab-

sent. Present, however, are flat-based cylindrical vessels decorated with shell stamping of the type found at Tronadora Vieja and Zetillal de Ipís. These distinctive forms are unknown outside of Costa Rica. Although it is the southernmost of the Costa Rican complexes, there are few similarities between Curré and Monagrillo pottery. The former is dominated by necked jars, whereas these are absent in the latter.

Corrales (1985, 1989) has suggested that Curré populations cultivated bitter manioc, a suggestion based on the presence of lithic artifacts interpreted as manioc grater chips. Although Corrales noted that budare fragments were absent, they have since been identified in type collections of Curré pottery. There is little information available on Curré settlement patterns, but the type site is situated in the fertile Río Térraba floodplain. The continuity of occupation at this site is noteworthy. Curré deposits are overlain by those of the subsequent Aguas Buenas complex, and the site is today the location of an indigenous settlement. Preceramic sites have not yet been reported for the Térraba–Coto Brús region.

Preceramic Contexts for the Emergence of Ceramics

One of the most significant problems with the evaluation of cultural contexts for the emergence of pottery in southern Central America is the dearth of information on Preceramic societies. The most data are available for Archaic period populations in western and central Panama. In western Panama, mobile populations occupied wet tropical forests from at least 7000 b.p. The earliest period, Boquete, is characterized by small bands of hunters and gatherers. During the Talamanca phase, ground stone tools suggest the beginnings of forest clearing. In central Panama, estuarine resources were adequate for the support of semipermanent occupations, as indicated by sites such as Cerro Mangote (McGimsey 1956).

In central Panama, lithic, macrobotanical, and microbotanical data indicate that root crops, palms, and other tree crops were important components of the diet as early as the ninth millennium b.p. (Cooke and Ranere 1992:260). At Carabalí Shelter (Valerio Lobo 1985), where the earliest occupations date to about 8000 b.p., carbonized seeds included palm fruits, Sapotaceae (*Sideroxylon* or *Bumelia*), and *nance* (*Byrsonima crassifolia*) (Cooke and Ranere 1992:261; Smith 1988:166). In western Panama, the earliest macrobotanical remains are fragments of palm fruits (*Scheelia* sp. and *Acrocomia* sp.), nance seeds, and *algarrobo* (*Hymenaea courbaril*) (Smith 1980, 1988) dating to about 6600 b.p. At Aguadulce Shelter, deposits dating to about 5600 b.p. contained many palm fragments, including *pejibaye* (*Bactris gasipaes*) (Smith 1988:166).

The great variety and range of palms in Central America were undoubtedly assisted by human activity. After 8600 b.p. there is a rapid increase in charred grass and in the abundance of palm phytoliths—a pattern suggestive of intentional burning (Cooke and Ranere 1992:257; Piperno et al. 1990). The use of fire to encourage the spread of useful palm species probably increased with their utilization. Creation of a suitable environment and the protection and use of palms represent the first step toward horticulture in Central America.

Cooke and Ranere (1992:261) suggest that Carabalí and similar sites be termed "incipient agrilocalities," where "human populations collected certain plant species intensively and initiated the coevolutionary processes that subsequently led to horticulture." Citing the number of palm and tuberous genera that are probably indigenous to Panama, they remark that it is likely that "indigenous agroecologies that used such genera predate horticultural systems dominated by exogenous cultigens on the Central American land bridge" (Cooke and Ranere 1992:261).

The relationship between ceramics and maize remains problematical. The earliest radiocarbon date for Monagrillo ceramics is 4800 ± 100 b.p. (TEM-119) from Cueva de los Ladrones, and maize phytoliths dating between 4850 and 4750 b.p. and maize pollen from between 4750 and 3320 b.p. (Cooke and Ranere 1992:273) at Lake Gatun suggest that the cultigen was contemporaneous with early pottery. By 4000 b.p., there is evidence for the alteration of forest growth by slash-and-burn strategies that may have included maize cultivation, but there is not enough information to enable us to recognize the formation of specialized horticulture during Monagrillo times. Ceramic use is not accompanied by significant shifts in the kinds of resources that were being used at existing Preceramic sites. In central Panama, household artifacts remain simple (Cooke and Ranere 1992:271), and there are few changes in either chipped or ground stone tools between Late Preceramic and early Monagrillo assemblages. On the other hand, there is evidence for settlement change. Coastal sites increase in size and number during the Monagrillo phase, and

there is evidence for simple wattle-and-daub structures (Cooke and Ranere 1992:273).

Monagrillo pottery has not yet been found in direct association with maize. Cooke and Ranere suggest, however, that evidence for increased site specialization during the period of early ceramic production "intimates that some segments of the regional population were becoming larger, less self-sufficient, and more sedentary, perhaps because scheduling, procurement, and manufacturing activities were responding to increasing demands on the land, diminishing opportunities for emigration" (Cooke and Ranere 1992:274).

The Late Preceramic cultural landscape was far from uniform. Monagrillo-style pottery has not been found in either western Panama or southern Costa Rica. Given divergent adaptations in western and central Panama by the Late Preceramic, it can be argued that

equally strong intuitive cases can be made for (a) a relic (i.e., indigenous) foraging population that survived in humid montane forests above 800 m (too wet for primitive races of maize), while "intrusive" maize farmers occupied the drier foothills, or (b) the economic/ecological fissioning of a homogeneous endogenous population, which led to a symbiotic relationship between a humid forest foraging lifestyle and a more "agrilocal" or horticultural variant in the seasonally dry forests of the Pacific mid-elevation slopes. (Cooke and Ranere 1992:264)

The dynamic between mobile and sedentary populations in the Central American isthmus may also have played an important role in the emergence of ceramic production. Maize, however, may not have been the foremost cultigen in the emergence of early sedentism. It was probably preceded by the utilization of seasonally available tree-crop products, particularly nutrient- and oil-rich palm fruits.

Tree Crops

One of the principal questions about the Archaic period has been the nature of the prehorticultural subsistence base. Tropical forests are difficult habitats for human foragers. In a study of two areas of tropical forest in Costa Rica and Panama, Piperno (1989) noted that (1) wild plant sources with high caloric content, such as starches, are rare, (2) useful plants are widely dispersed, (3) many species produce small fruits, (4) palms and tuberous plants are rare in climax forests, (5) many taxa show unpredictable variability in productivity, and (6) a high proportion of wild plants are toxic. In a "pure" foraging economy (with minimal human intervention and simple technology), there would be significant advantage to small, highly dispersed populations.

Smith (1988:170) suggested that "the cultivation of annual crops, maize, and beans was superimposed on an old dietary pattern which relied heavily on palms and broad leafed fruit trees." Among the tree crops subject to intense, periodic exploitation in Central America during the Late Preceramic were palm fruits from pejibaye, *coyol* (*Acrocomia vinifera*), American oil palm (*Elaeis oleifera*), *corozo* (*Orbignya* spp.), and *palma real* (*Scheelia rostrata*). Deciduous trees such as nance, *guayabo* (*Psidium guajava*), *jocote* (*Spondias* sp.), papaya (*Carica papaya*), *cherimoya* (*Annona cherimola*), *guanabana* (*Annona muricata*), and members of the Sapotaceae such as mamey and *chico sapote* are also likely to have been important food sources.

Palms, in particular, were sources of valuable products with both nutritional and social utility. Among these were palm starch (sago) and palm oil, which could provide otherwise scarce carbohydrates and fats. The preparation and serving of beverages such as palm wine, *chicha* beer (which could be made from a wide variety of palm and other fruits as well as pumpkins, manioc, and maize), and cacao probably played key roles in the development of early Central American social systems. Because their production and consumption were dramatically improved with the use of pottery, the development of these products and the development of ceramic systems are likely to have gone hand in hand.

The domestication of palms is still poorly understood. Valuable species such as pejibaye—documented to have hundreds of varieties—are unknown in the wild. Its wild relatives are native to the Amazon, and it is believed to have originated in the eastern foothills of the Andes (Prance 1984:91), but it is still not known whether its introduction to Central America was natural or cultural. Palm utilization, however, may provide a key to understanding the development of pottery in southern Central America.

Gourds were undoubtedly the original containers for preparing, serving, and storing fermented beverages. The most important species in Central America would have been the bottle gourd (*Lagenaria siceraria*) and the tree gourd, or *jícaro* (*Crescentia alata*). Pottery, however, was important because it enhanced the *scale* of food preparation. Large-capacity pottery vessels improved a group's ability to control and plan the avail-

ability of fermented products. Through their conversion into beverages, surplus fruits would not go to waste. Palm fruit crops would have provided abundant, seasonal resources to mobile foragers. When fruits were available, there was no significant risk of their overexploitation by small populations. Individual pejibaye trees can produce annually for up to 50 years, and the species is easily propagated. (Spanish records report the existence of plantations numbering trees in the tens of thousands near Sixaola, on the Atlantic coast [Lothrop 1944].) Gathering of pejibaye is not especially labor intensive because all it involves is scaling the spiny tree and cutting loose a bunch of fruit. The fruit, however, must be boiled and peeled before it is consumed. As Chagnon notes (1968:30), "it takes a lot of work to get filled up on palm fruits."

Ceramic vessels would have vastly improved people's ability to exploit abundant tree-crop resources during the period of their maximum availability. Improvements in boiling, brewing, pickling, and storing would have had significant impact on the qualitative and quantitative effects of tree crops on human subsistence.

PALM STARCH

In eastern Malaysia, sago is a staple of the Penan, living foragers who occupy a tropical forest ecosystem that remains mostly undisturbed by previous clearance (Brosius 1991). Sago is also utilized by lowland South American groups (Heinen and Ruddle 1974) and was probably an important staple in tropical Central America. Sago exploitation can provide a stable subsistence base. The Western Penan, for example, are unusual among documented foragers in that they are characterized by (1) bands of 60–200 individuals, (2) long-term occupations of settlements, often for more than a year, (3) long-term stability of band composition, and (4) "what appears to be a nascent form of aristocratic leadership" (Brosius 1991:136). Sago use made it possible for foragers to inhabit tropical rain forests. In doing so, it "influenced the distribution of important faunal resources, placed people within and near faunally rich environmental zones, and balanced conventional patterns of labor input between the sexes in ways that agriculture did not" (Dwyer and Minnegal 1991:209).

PALM OIL PRODUCTION

The extraction of oils from meats and nuts by indirect cooking has been suggested as one of the uses for early pottery in the southeastern United States (Sassaman, chapter 18). Oils and fats are highly valued among foraging societies, especially where animal resources tend to be lean and highly dispersed. Tropical palms are well known as a source of high-quality oils, and there are a large number of species available for oil production. In South America, *babassu* palms (*Orbignya* spp.), whose kernels contain up to 70 percent oil, have been the subject of both traditional indigenous and large-scale commercial production (Balée 1989; Hecht and Anderson 1988). The most important species for Precolumbian Central American populations was probably the American oil palm. Although palm oil production is possible without pottery, the availability of large-capacity containers would have been a significant contribution to an increase in the scale of production. Palm oil extraction is typically done by mashing fruits and slowly boiling the pulp, then scooping out the oil as it rises to the surface. Pots would have been more durable than gourds in the extraction of palm oil through indirect stone boiling. Direct cooking would have resulted in even more dramatic increases in oil production.

SWEET AND FERMENTED BEVERAGES

The principle of fermentation was undoubtedly known to all tropical hunting and gathering groups. Many indigenous Central American fruits, among them pineapples and papayas, ferment naturally soon after maximum ripeness. Natural fermentation would have been evident among tree crops, when bunches of *Scheelia* and *Acrocomia* palm fruits—with a higher sugar content than pejibaye—begin to ferment on the tree. Integration of ritual alcohol intoxication into community gatherings may have first occurred when indigenous hunter-gatherers consumed fermented fruits toward the end of a season of abundance. Fruits of pejibaye, coyol, and other palms have been used to make a fermented chicha beer by several Central American societies (Johnson 1963; Kirchhoff 1963).

The production of palm wine from sweet sap was undoubtedly discovered during forest clearing, when sap collected and fermented in damaged trunks of fallen palms. The sweet sap of *Bactris* and *Acrocomia* can be collected and fermented as palm wine (*coquelo*). Palm wine, however, is traditionally collected and fermented in the trunk of a fallen tree (Balick 1990). Vessels are required only for serving and short-term storage of wine, but they would have been more important for pickling. Coyol wine must be consumed

shortly after fermentation; it turns to vinegar after a few days. Today it is used for making *salsa* with pickled peppers and onions (Balick 1990:90). There is no doubt that pottery permitted a dramatic improvement in early Central American cuisines, and the availability of drink and tasty foods in quantity would have provided a significant incentive for social gatherings.

Competitive Feasting as a Model

Prehorticultural exploitation of Central American tree crops for starch, oil, and beverages, when considered in the context of a cultural landscape marked by societies with variable degrees of sedentism, suggests an alternative to diffusionary models for the emergence of pottery on the Central American isthmus. A modification of the competitive feasting model suggested by Hayden (1990) for the emergence of agriculture can explain an autochthonous genesis of ceramic production, motivated and encouraged by both nutritional and social factors. Whether ceramic technology was invented in a variety of locations or had a single source of origin, early ceramics were undoubtedly first produced in the midst of mobile hunting and gathering societies. Pottery vessels are likely to have enhanced communication and interchange between ceramic producers and nonproducers and were important not only for their specific contributions to the preparation and storage of specific subsistence products but also for their contribution to the diversification of subsistence strategies for *both* mobile and sedentary populations through cooperative interchanges.

There are significant similarities between the processes leading to the adoption of horticulture in Hayden's model and those that would have encouraged the adoption of ceramic technology. As a general principle, Hayden suggests that subsistence innovations related to competitive feasting are most likely to have occurred in rich environments with abundant resources, where the accumulation of resources by individuals would not have threatened the population's survival. This principle would have been especially applicable to strategies focusing on r-selected resources (fish, shellfish, certain fruits, and seeds) rather than on K-selected species (deer, birds). Early pottery also improved people's ability to exploit seasonally abundant r-selected species. Hayden predicts that food production will first appear in areas where obligatory sharing was not essential for survival and where ownership of produced food was "no longer anathema" (Hayden

1991:12). This shift would have occurred where resources were abundant, reliable, and invulnerable to overexploitation. Once undertaken, competitive practices are not detrimental to the resource base. A primary goal of competitive feasting was control over labor. Foods and beverages prepared in quantity are still widely used in Central and South American social contexts as payment for group labor.

Pottery offers significant advantages in the processing of *r*-selected species such as fruits and seeds. It plays a specific role in the preparation of crops like beans and maize, which are easily stored when dry but require softening (and cooking, in the case of beans) to become palatable. It enhances opportunities for food preservation and storage through fermentation and pickling. It also made it possible to extend the "shelf life" of fish and game through the preparation of soups and stews—an important addition to techniques of drying and smoking. Perhaps most important from a social point of view, ceramics greatly facilitated the preparation of large quantities of food and beverages. The largest ceramic vessels from the earliest ceramic complexes in Colombia and Costa Rica have a capacity greater than that of the available gourds. Although chicha is often prepared in wooden troughs, a practice still common in parts of Central America (Johnson 1963:249), it is usually stored in pottery (Kirchhoff 1963:221). One of the most important contributions of storage jars is that they can facilitate transportation and serving to large groups of people.

Hayden (1990:12) predicts that the first domesticated foods should be items suitable for feasting rather than staples, and that they could be expected to occupy a very minor position for a relatively long time in the overall subsistence emphasis within a community. These same factors would have encouraged the emergence of ceramic technology. In the context of an abundant resource, ceramics enhance the functions of storage and serving. As with horticulture in Hayden's model, pottery is more likely to have appeared in the context of abundant than scarce resources. Its production requires a significant investment of energy in the acquisition and preparation of raw materials, vessel manufacture, gathering of fuel and firing, and use and transport of the vessels themselves. Ceramic technology shows a high degree of correlation with sedentism because of manufacture and transport costs (Arnold 1985). A population under dietary stress is not likely to invest in technology that will restrict mobility and require increased investment of energy in nonsubsistence activities. Ceramic manufacture may have been regarded by many mobile, preceramic populations as falling into the same category as early domestication: more trouble than it was worth. It was easier—and probably necessary—to move and find other resources than to stay in one place and make pottery.

Competitive feasting, according to Hayden, encourages cultivation because of the positive feedback received by the organizer(s) sponsoring the feasting activity. Special crops are cultivated because of their specific contributions to feasting. The value of ceramics for feasting-related activities emphasized (1) preparation of large quantities of special foodstuffs, (2) accumulation and storage of these items for high-volume, short-duration consumption, (3) efficient serving of participants, and (4) the vessels' role in impressing participants with the wealth and generosity of the feast's sponsor(s). The quality of "impressiveness" would have been particularly important for the emergence of ceramic styles. It reinforced the identity of the ceramics' producers and either their difference from or their similarity with competitive groups. Persons emulating or imitating the "aggrandizer/accumulators" would copy ceramic styles. Where innovation was valued, stylistic distinction would have served to emphasize differences.

Although Hayden's model concentrates on the effect of competitive feasting on cultivation and domestication, status competition would have affected technology even in the absence of domesticates. The ability to prepare, store, and serve desired comestibles in sufficient quantities for large-scale, integrative consumption does not require domesticated products. Periodic feasting is not an essential subsistence activity. When the technology for taking advantage of natural abundance is improved, however, it can make a significant contribution to the integration of groups and to increasing the efficiency of wild resource use.

THE CASE OF SOCONUSCO

Clark and Blake (1994) suggest that the adoption of Barra ceramics in coastal Chiapas, Mexico, represents an example of the emergence of pottery in the context of early domestication. Early Barra vessels imitate gourds, with an emphasis on vessels used for serving liquids. Their form and decoration suggest ritual significance and prestige value. Clark and Blake suggest that maize was introduced to coastal Soconusco prior to the adoption of ceramics, for the purpose of making chicha. It was a special cultigen grown for its use in competitive feasting activities. Pottery vessels communicated status through competitive use and display, and their production was enhanced and encouraged by these activities.

In this model, maize is an initial component of competitive feasting activities, with ceramics appearing as a technical and stylistic adjunct. Chicha, however, can be made from foods other than maize—including nondomesticated products. As I noted earlier, palms, present in undisturbed tropical forests (and even more abundant in areas that have been cleared) would have been available to prehorticultural populations. Maize —or any specific cultigen—may well have been *secondary* to ceramic technology in the promotion of rituals of social integration. Changes in food preparation made possible by ceramic vessels facilitated the incorporation of beverages and foodstuffs into social gatherings. The enhanced social interaction made possible by new products (and increased quantities of familiar ones) encouraged intergroup exchange of commodities and information. At a more intensive level, feasting promoted gatherings for the periodic concentration of human labor for projects beyond the capacity of small or dispersed populations. Although beverages like maize chicha and cacao eventually achieved primary importance, they probably appeared in the context of existing, prehorticultural repertoires of similar beverages. The earliest foods and beverages prepared in pottery and served at social gatherings were probably not cultivated products. Maize and cacao, when they entered the subsistence system as prestige products, were elaborated in the context of an already existing tradition of brewing and consuming beverages during ritual exchanges of resources and labor intensification.

Interactions between Sedentary and Mobile Societies

The dynamic of interaction between food producers and foragers was undoubtedly an important one in the emergence of early horticulture. It was probably preceded by interactions between contemporaneous early ceramic and preceramic (or, more accurately, aceramic) societies.

In describing foragers of the Malaysian rain forest, Endicott and Bellwood (1991:181) remark: "If we may venture one modest generalization: an apparent result of the paucity of resources in the tropical forest is that the peoples living off them are opportunistic rather than conservative in outlook. They are ever eager to experiment, to try new ways to improve their

lives. And one of the opportunities they are quick to take up is the opportunity to trade for horticultural produce."

The existence of populations producing reliable sources of carbohydrates would have supported the existence of interdependent, semisedentary or nomadic populations who were better able to take advantage of wild game and seasonally available fruits in areas away from sedentary settlements. Exchange between these groups would have permitted a broader exploitation of the entire tropical ecosystem. It would also have counteracted the effects that sedentary populations can have on the availability of game.

The dynamic of interchange between sedentary and mobile populations would have been seasonal, emphasizing the variability of resources available to each group. Ceramics were the technological contribution of sedentary groups, assisting with storage and preparations for gatherings and other integrating activities. Sedentary groups provided the place and the facilities for periodic sedentary-mobile exchange. They also provided the opportunity and context for joint feasting. The advantages conferred by ceramics in preparation and storage increase with quantities of available foodstuffs. Storage is most important when more food is available than can be consumed when fresh, and when there is an incentive to preserve this food for later consumption.

There has been a great deal of commentary on the ability of tropical forests to support "pure" hunters and gatherers (Bailey et al. 1989; Bailey and Headland 1991; Headland 1987). Bailey et al. assert that there is little documentary evidence for societies that rely exclusively on tropical rain forest resources for their survival. They conclude that these ecosystems could not have supported populations of "pure" hunter-gatherers and remark that in almost all known cases such groups have found it advantageous, if not essential, to establish reciprocal relationships with horticultural societies for the purposes of resource exchange. The principal reason for this is a dearth of fats, carbohydrates, and other nutrients in a diet based on tropical forest foraging.

Tropical ecosystems are the most speciose in the world, with large numbers of plants that produce edible seeds and fruits. These plants, however, are most abundant in clearings, along waterways, and at forest margins. In climax forests, most resources are concentrated in the inaccessible canopy. A number of researchers have pointed to deficiencies in protein, fats, and carbohydrates in tropical rainforests. But whereas extensive Amazonian tropical forests may have been problematical in terms of nutrients, rain forest landscapes in small countries such as Costa Rica and Panama are far from uniform. Periodic volcanic activity created large areas of early succession species. Climax forests on steeply dissected terrain are riddled with openings created by tree falls that are colonized by forest margin species. Furthermore, the geographical extent of any landform is highly restricted. A foot traverse from the Caribbean to the Pacific can be accomplished in a matter of days. As Cooke and Ranere (1992:269) remark: "Living on a narrow isthmus means that one is never very far from the sea and that one can easily go and live on the beach for a while if it is worth the effort." Mobile populations were unlikely to have experienced significant dietary stress. With adequate extractive technologies, rivers, estuaries, and swamps would have provided an abundance of protein from fish or birds. The variety of the Preceramic diet is demonstrated clearly in faunal assemblages from sites such as Cerro Mangote (Cooke and Ranere 1989, 1992; McGimsey 1956), which included estuarine mollusks, marine catfish, deer, raccoons, iguanas, and small reptiles.

In central Panama, Late Preceramic populations appear to have been composed of both mobile hunter-gatherers and "agrilocal" incipient horticulturalists (Cooke and Ranere 1992). Around 4000 B.C., a change in stone tools signals the beginning of forest clearing, possibly associated with incipient root-crop horticulture. The advantages of root-crop cultivation to mobile hunting and gathering societies were great. Manioc (*Manihot esculenta*), tiquisque (*Xanthosoma* sp.), arrowroot (*Maranta* sp.), and other root crops did not require the degree of sedentism necessary for maize cultivation, principally because of the self-storing qualities of root crops and their resistance to animal predation. Their cultivation could therefore be undertaken by mobile populations seeking to increase sources of carbohydrates while utilizing abundant but widely dispersed tropical forest resources. In combination with more seasonally available tree crops such as the American oil palm or the pejibaye, tubers would have provided important sources of necessary carbohydrates.

Exogenous seed crops, on the other hand, were more demanding. Races of maize that had been developed in dry highland environments were unsuitable for wet tropical forests without selection and modification. The first populations to cultivate maize in Central America accepted a high degree of risk, which

needed to be offset in some fashion. One way this could have been accomplished was through reciprocal relationships between sedentary and mobile segments of the population. Considering that prime hunting season would have coincided with the harvest, such relationships would have benefited from the contributions of both sedentary and mobile strategies.

An important motivation for feasting on the part of early sedentary or semisedentary societies would have been a desire to reinforce reciprocal relationships that developed between segments of the population corresponding to incipient horticulturalists and tropical forest foragers. Resources that could be extracted in sufficient quantities allowed some populations to remain in a given location for all or most of an annual period. The local surplus implied by this pattern would also have attracted the attention of mobile groups reliant upon more dispersed resources.

Early horticulture limited hunting by horticulturalists when crop harvesting and optimal hunting occurred in the same season. On the other hand, forest clearing and "garden hunting" (Linares 1976) would have improved the availability of some species. Mobile populations, always opportunistic, probably encroached upon the territory of sedentary or semisedentary populations when "disturbance" resources, whose availability was enhanced by human activities, were available. Simultaneous use of complimentary resources created a situation in which reciprocal relationships between sedentary horticulturalists and mobile hunter-gatherers would have been advantageous. Feasting is one mechanism that could have promoted exchanges, encouraged pooled labor, and established reciprocal relationships based on the exchange of resources and marriage partners.

The earliest Central American pottery probably appeared in the context of dynamic social relationships between sedentary and mobile populations. An important aspect of this dynamic was the maintenance of ongoing relationships between groups with distinct subsistence strategies. Subsistence strategies of early ceramic producers should be considered within a broad network of social interactions characterized by ongoing, periodic interaction between sedentary and mobile societies. Whether or not sedentarism preceded horticulture, sedentary societies would have been able to concentrate resources in ways unavailable to mobile groups while the latter retained flexible subsistence strategies that brought them into regular contact with a broader subsistence base than that available to sedentarists.

Social gatherings made possible by the preparation and serving of special foods and beverages provided a focal point for interaction between populations with differing subsistence bases. This interaction became especially important as knowledge of species and the technology for the extraction of fats and carbohydrates improved. The availability of surpluses and the need for additional labor may have motivated sedentary groups to use their improved technology for preparing and serving large quantities of foods and beverages in order to reciprocate the contributions of mobile groups within their social network. Regular gatherings, facilitated by ceramic vessels, would have reinforced a continuing dynamic of interaction. Although the contributions of hunters and gatherers declined with the expansion of swidden horticulture and the pressure of sedentary populations on finite hunting resources, competition for the attention of different groups and the diversification of the social landscape became driving forces behind the emergence of regional diversification in artifact styles and subsistence strategies.

There is a great deal of empirical support for the presumption of continued interaction between sedentary, horticultural populations and mobile hunter-gatherers (Bailey et al. 1989; Headland and Reid 1989). Efficient preparation of tree and root crops by sedentary populations enhanced their ability to attract and negotiate with mobile populations for resources prone to local overexploitation by sedentary groups. Sedentarists' ability to prepare and serve surplus carbohydrates, fats, and oils would have attracted the interest of tropical forest hunters, particularly when these resources were scarce in the wild. In situations where the hunter-gatherers were able to obtain a surplus of animal protein, an advantageous reciprocity would result. This type of resource exchange provided positive feedback for an increase in horticultural production as well as the spread of ceramic technology. It would also have motivated hunters and fishers to utilize ceramics to prepare and transport protein resources for exchange. Marine products at the inland sites of Aguadulce Shelter and Cueva de los Ladrones (Cooke and Ranere 1992:268) suggest that utilization of both inland and coastal resources was common.

A Hypothetical Scenario for the Emergence of Pottery

As populations increased, habitats with higher densities of palms and other fruiting trees—the result of gardens and orchards tended by mobile incipient horticulturalists to increase sources of carbohydrates and fats—would have become the objects of competition from different human groups. Establishment of semipermanent communities near these plantings helped protect them from encroachment. Although a portion of the society remained mobile to take advantage of dispersed resources, periodically the group assembled to consume root and tree-crop products. There may also have been a sense of "ownership" of a particular landscape and its associated resources, a pattern suggested by intensive use of quarries as early as the Paleoindian period (Cooke and Ranere 1992:263; Snarskis 1979). Cooke and Ranere (1992:262) suggest that "archaeologists should look for the beginnings of 'provincial stability or instability' in the Intermediate Area long before the introduction of ceramics and the development of sedentary (Formative) villages."

Palm resources and other tree crops tend to be highly seasonal but abundant when available. Toward the end of the rainy season, trees like pejibaye produce enormous clusters of nutritious fruit. In South America, palm species like *Mauritia flexuosa* provide starch (sago) in seasonal cycles (Heinen and Ruddle 1974). Ceramics represented a vast improvement in a group's ability to prepare, consume, and store palm products such as fruits, oils, and starches. Pottery vessels made it possible to process large quantities of fruit without a high loss percentage. Not only would they have allowed for fruits to be cooked quickly and efficiently, but they also increased the percentage of the tree crop harvest that could be processed during a season. As I noted earlier, pottery vessels also facilitated the production of food products such as oils and alcoholic beverages that were valuable to intergroup social exchange.

To return to Hayden's model of competitive feasting, the intensive utilization of tree crops permitted by ceramic vessels was an effective strategy for taking advantage of the seasonal abundance of an *r*-selected resource that was not prone to overexploitation. This assessment also applies to shellfish and other seasonal *r*-selected resources. Ceramics broadened the subsistence base by enhancing social interaction through the introduction of desirable foods and beverages produced and distributed in quantity.

The use of vessels for feasting on wild or semicultivated products would have preadapted communities to the introduction of other status foods and beverages. In historic times, the favored beverages of indigenous Central Americans have been maize chicha and chocolate. In southern Central America, both are based on exogenous crops that would have been more labor intensive than palm fruits. It is these crops, together with other specialty foods (meats from the hunt? deepsea fish?), that would have formed the basis for competitive feasting—accompanied by the elaboration of the vessels for preparing and serving feasted foods. Maize and cacao, as special feasting foods, should appear in the context of existing sedentary populations. This corresponds to Cooke and Ranere's (1992:266) interpretation of "the adoption of exogenous plants . . . as the internal adaptive response of segments of a forest-oriented population, which having developed a simple 'agrilocal' ecology based on native palms and tubers prior to 7000 B.P. was predisposed to accept new plant domesticates." The timing of their adoption, however, may have been quite variable. With regard to maize, this model suggests that in agrilocalities favorable for the production of tubers and palm fruits, initial preference for maize would focus on varieties appropriate for brewing.

Conclusion

Past models for the appearance of ceramic traditions in southern Central America have emphasized the role of the isthmus as a land bridge between Mesoamerica and northern South America. As a result, there has been a tendency to interpret prehistoric culture change in the region as a result of the diffusion of innovations from external hearths of cultural development. Current evidence makes it difficult to attribute the earliest pottery complexes to diffusion or migration from culture areas to the north or south. Ceramic production may have arisen locally as a strategy for intensive utilization of tree and root crops in the context of tropical forest hunter-gatherer/horticulturalist interaction. Social factors, in particular periodic feasts that united mobile and sedentary segments of the population, are suggested to have been as important as nutritional advantages in the emergence of ceramic production.

The emergence of pottery in southern Central America parallels, if not accompanies, the adoption of horticulture. Ceramics increased the variety and quantity of foodstuffs available for social interactions. Early ceramic-using societies not only modified the way they used existing resources but also invented new products and increased the scale of their consumption. In some societies, ceramics offered versatility to individual self-aggrandizers (Blake et al. 1992; Clark and Blake 1991) who sought to obtain the benefits of concentrated la-

bor or trade items. They provided an advantage in situations of competitive feasting, where large quantities of food were accumulated, prepared, and served. In other situations, noncompetitive feasting improved by ceramics helped to sustain stable relationships between different segments of the population.

One implication of this model is that ceramic production will first appear in the context of seasonal, rather than year-round, occupations. Another is that early ceramic-producing sites will represent only part of the regional settlement pattern. There may be some overlap of preceramic/early ceramic traditions at sites where regular interchange between mobile and sedentary populations occurred. In southern Central America, the earliest ceramics should precede intensive maize cultivation. Early ceramic sites are also most likely to appear in locations characterized by centuries (and perhaps millennia) of anthropogenically altered habitats with an enhanced abundance of economically useful indigenous tree and root crops rather than abundant hunting or fishing resources.

Notes

1. Recently discovered ceramics from sites east of the lake in Chontales, Nicaragua, may also be related (Espinoza and Rigat 1994).

2. One exception is a date for the Naranjo phase of 3500 ± 60 b.p. (UCLA-2167A), but its association with ceramics is not clear.

References Cited

Arnold, D. E.
    1985   *Ceramic Theory and Culture Process.* Cambridge University Press, New York.
Bailey, R. C., G. Head, M. Jenike, B. Owen, R. Rechtman, and E. Zechenter
    1989   Hunting and Gathering in Tropical Rain Forest: Is It Possible? *American Anthropologist* 91:59–82.
Bailey, R. C., and T. N. Headland
    1991   The Tropical Rain Forest: Is It a Productive Environment for Human Foragers? *Human Ecology* 19(2):261–85.
Balée, W.
    1989   The Culture of Amazonian Forests. In *Resource Management in Amazonia: Indigenous and Folk Strategies,* edited by D. A. Posey and W. Balée, pp. 1–21. *Advances in Economic Botany* 7.

Balick, M. J.

1990   Production of Coyol Wine from *Acrocomia mexicana* (Arecaceae) in Honduras. *Economic Botany* 44(1):84–93.

Blake, M., B. Chisolm, J. Clark, and K. Mudar

1992   Non-agrarian Staples and Agricultural Supplements: Early Formative Subsistence in the Soconusco Region, Mexico. In *Transitions to Agriculture in Prehistory,* edited by A. B. Gebauer and T. D. Price, pp. 131–51. Prehistory Press, Madison, Wisconsin.

Brosius, J. P.

1991   Foraging in Tropical Rain Forests: The Case of the Penan of Sarawak, East Malaysia (Borneo). *Human Ecology* 19(2):123–50.

Chagnon, N.

1968   *Yanomamo: The Fierce People.* Holt, Reinhart, and Winston, New York.

Clark, J. E., and M. Blake

1994   The Power of Prestige: Competitive Generosity and the Emergence of Rank Societies in Lowland Mesoamerica. In *Factional Competition and Political Development in the New World,* edited by E. Brumfiel and J. W. Fox, pp. 17–30. Cambridge University Press, Cambridge.

Cooke, R., and A. J. Ranere

1989   Hunting in Prehistoric Panama: A Diachronic Perspective. In *The Walking Larder: Patterns of Domestication, Pastoralism and Predation,* edited by J. Clutton-Brock, pp. 295–315. Unwin Hyman, London.

1992   The Origin of Wealth and Hierarchy in the Central Region of Panama (12,000–2,000 B.P.), with Observations on Its Relevance to the History and Phylogeny of Chibchan-Speaking Polities in Panama and Elsewhere. In *Wealth and Hierarchy in the Intermediate Area: A Symposium at Dumbarton Oaks, 10th and 11th October 1987,* edited by F. W. Lange, pp. 43–84. Dumbarton Oaks, Washington, D.C.

Corrales U., F.

1985   Prosepección y excavaciones estratigráficas en el sitio Curré (P-62-Ce), Valle Diquís, Costa Rica. *Vínculos* 11:1–16.

1989   La ocupación agricola temprana del sitio arqueológico Curré, Valle del Diquís. Tesis de Licenciatura, Escuela de Antropología y Sociología, Facultad de Ciencias Sociales, Universidad de Costa Rica.

Dwyer, P. D., and M. Minnegal

1991   Hunting in a Lowland, Tropical Rain Forest: Towards a Model of Non-agricultural Subsistence. *Human Ecology* 19(2):187–212.

Endicott, K., and P. Bellwood

1991   The Possibility of Independent Foraging in the Rain Forest of Peninsula Malaysia. *Human Ecology* 19(2):151–85.

Espinoza P., E., and D. Rigat

1994   Gran Nicoya y la región de Chontales, Nicaragua. *Vínculos* 18–19 (1992–93):139–56.

Ford, J.

1969   *A Comparison of Formative Cultures in the Americas: Diffusion or the Psychic Unity of Man?* Smithsonian Contributions to Anthropology, vol. 11. Smithsonian Institution, Washington, D.C.

Hayden, B.

1990   Nimrods, Piscators, Pluckers, and Planters: The Emergence of Food Production. *Journal of Anthropological Archaeology* 9:31–69.

1991   Models of Domestication. In *Transitions to Agriculture in Prehistory,* edited by A. B. Gebauer and T. D. Price, pp. 11–19. Prehistory Press, Madison, Wisconson.

Headland, T. N.

1987   The Wild Yam Question: How Well Could Independent Hunter-Gatherers Live in a Tropical Rainforest Ecosystem? *Human Ecology* 15:465–93.

Headland, T. N, and L. A. Reid

1989   Hunter-Gatherers and Their Neighbors from Prehistory to the Present. *Current Anthropology* 30(1):43–66.

Hecht, S. B., and A. B. Anderson

1988   The Subsidy from Nature: Shifting Cultivation, Successional Palm Forests, and Rural Development. *Human Organization* 47(1):25–35.

Heinen, H. Dieter, and K. Ruddle

1974   Ecology, Ritual, and Economic Organization in the Distribution of Palm Starch among the Warao of the Orinoco Delta. *Journal of Anthropological Research* 30:116–38.

Hoopes, J. W.

1987   Early Ceramics and the Origins of Village Life in Lower Central America. Ph.D. dissertation, Harvard University, Cambridge, Massachusetts. University Microfilms, Ann Arbor, Michigan.

1994a   Ford Revisited: A Critical Review of the Chronology and Relationships of the Earliest Ceramic Complexes in the New World, 6000–1500 B.C. *Journal of World Prehistory* 8(1):1–49.

1994b   The Tronadora Complex: Early Formative Ceramics in Northwestern Costa Rica. *Latin American Antiquity* 5(1):3–30.

Johnson, F.

1963   The Caribbean Lowland Tribes: The

Talamanca Division. In *Handbook of South American Indians, vol. 4: The Circum-Caribbean Tribes,* edited by J. H. Steward, pp. 231–52. Cooper Square Publishers, New York.

Kirchhoff, P.
1963   The Carribbean Lowland Tribes: The Mosquito, Sumo, Paya, and Jicaque. In *Handbook of South American Indians, vol. 4: The Circum-Caribbean Tribes,* edited by J. H. Steward, pp. 219–29. Cooper Square Publishers, New York.

Lathrap, D. W.
1977   Our Father the Cayman, Our Mother the Gourd: Spinden Revisited or a Unitary Model for the Emergence of Agriculture in the New World. In *Origins of Agriculture,* edited by C. A. Reed, pp. 713–52. Mouton, The Hague.

Linares, O.
1976   Garden Hunting in the American Tropics. *Human Ecology* 4:331–49.
1980   Conclusions. In *Adaptive Radiations in Prehistoric Panama,* edited by O. Linares and A. Ranere, pp. 233–49. Peabody Museum Monographs no. 5, Harvard University, Cambridge, Massachusetts.

Lothrop, S. K.
1944   The Sigua: Southernmost Aztec Outpost. *Proceedings: Eighth American Scientific Congress* (Lima), pp. 104–16.

McGimsey, C. R., III
1956   Cerro Mangote: A Preceramic Site in Panama. *American Antiquity* 23(4):301–13.

Odio O., E.
1992   La Pochota: Un complejo cerámico temprano en las tierras bajas del Guanacaste, Costa Rica. *Vínculos* 17(1991):1–16.

Piperno, D.
1989   Non-affluent Foragers: Resource Availability, Seasonal Shortages and the Emergence of Agriculture in Panamanian Tropical Forests. In *Foraging and Farming: The Evolution of Plant Domestication,* edited by D. R. Harris and G. Hillman, pp. 538–54. Allen and Unwin, London.

Piperno, D. R., M. B. Bush, and P. A. Colinvaux
1990   Paleoenvironments and Human Settlement in Late-Glacial Panama. *Quaternary Research* 33:108–16.

Prance, G. T.
1984   The Pejibaye, *Guilielma gasipaes* (HBK) Bailey, and the Papaya, *Carica papaya* L. In *Precolumbian Plant Migration,* edited by D. Z. Stone, pp. 85–104. Papers of the Peabody Museum of Archaeology and Ethnography, vol. 76, Cambridge, Massachusetts.

Sheets, P. D., J. Hoopes, W. Melson, B. McKee, T. Sever, M. Mueller, M. Chenault, and J. Bradley
1991   Prehistory and Volcanism in the Arenal Area, Costa Rica. *Journal of Field Archaeology* 18:445–65.

Smith, C. E.
1980   Plant Remains from the Chiriquí Sites and Ancient Vegetational Patterns. In *Adaptive Radiations in Prehistoric Panama,* edited by O. F. Linares and A. J. Ranere, pp. 151–74. Peabody Museum Monographs no. 5, Harvard University, Cambridge, Massachusetts.
1988   The Recovery of Plant Remains from Intermediate Area Sites. In *Diet and Subsistence: Current Archaeological Perspectives,* edited by B. V. Kennedy and G. M. LeMoine, pp. 165–71. University of Calgary Press, Calgary.

Snarskis, M. J.
1978   The Archaeology of the Central Atlantic Watershed of Costa Rica. Ph.D. dissertation, Columbia University. University Microfilms, Ann Arbor, Michigan.
1979   Turrialba: A Paleo-Indian Quarry and Workshop Site in Eastern Costa Rica. *American Antiquity* 44:125–38.
1984   Central America: The Lower Caribbean. In *The Archaeology of Lower Central America,* edited by F. W. Lange and D. Z. Stone, pp. 195–232. University of New Mexico Press, Albuquerque.

Valerio Lobo, W.
1985   Investigaciones preliminares en dos abrigos rocosos en la región central de Panamá. *Vínculos* 11(1–2):17–29.

16

Early Ceramics from El Salvador

The El Carmen Site

BARBARA ARROYO

The Early Formative period of southern Pacific Meso-america has attracted the attention of many scholars in recent years. An understanding of this time period is critical to any theory of cultural evolution in Meso-america. A series of significant changes took place at this time: the settling of permanent villages, the initial adoption of agriculture, the use of pottery, and incipient social developments. The distribution of Early Formative sites with similar cultural traits extends from the coast of Veracruz and continues along the Isthmus of Tehuantepec and the Pacific coast of southern Meso-america. These traits include similar pottery (hemispherical bowls, or *tecomates,* with a red band around the rim), obsidian technology, and preferential settlement location near estuaries and mangroves.

Research on the Early Formative in southern Meso-america began with Coe's work at La Victoria, Guatemala (Coe 1961). Several other early sites have been investigated (Coe and Flannery 1967; Lowe 1975; Shook and Hatch 1979; Ceja Tenorio 1985; Clark et. al. 1987, 1990; Demarest et. al. 1988; Love 1989; Pye 1990, 1992; Arroyo 1991, 1992). Most of our knowledge of the Early Formative, however, has been limited to areas in Chiapas and the western Pacific coast of Guatemala. Although it was thought that there was a more extensive contemporaneous settlement system along the coast farther south, a lack of research precluded its study. Discovery of the site of El Carmen in El Salvador (Amaroli 1986) has brought new information on the distribution of Early Formative settlements along the Pacific coast of southern Mesoamerica.

Amaroli (1986) noted that El Carmen pottery had characteristics similar to those of ceramics of the Ocós phase from sites in Mexico and Guatemala. In 1988, a Vanderbilt University project directed by Demarest (Arroyo et. al. 1989) carried out excavations at the site in conjunction with a survey of the area. The main objectives of the project were to learn about the site's chronology, its relationship with sites to the west, and the subsistence and social organization of its ancient inhabitants.

Previous Early Formative Research in El Salvador

Several projects trying to explain the cultural evolution of complex society in Prehispanic El Salvador have focused on large sites with public architecture and sculpture (Longyear 1944; Haberland 1960; Andrews 1976; Sharer 1978; Demarest 1986). Other projects

have been oriented toward rescue because of the flooding of extensive areas caused by the building of dams
and ditches (Black 1983; Sheets 1983; Fowler and Earnest 1984). These studies have been useful in providing
a more complete view of the prehistory of some regions, but they have tended to be narrow in focus.

One of the few research projects focusing on early
settlements was at the shell midden of Playa el
Huizcoyol (Perla 1968). This site is located 100 meters
from the beach between the Chichihua and Las Cañas
rivers in terrain on the Hacienda Miralvalle in the department of Sonsonate. Excavations at the site were
carried out by Perla (1968), who describes the site as
having several mounds, three of them of significant size
and height. According to Sharer (1978), the material at
the site seems to date to the Early Formative. His interpretation is based on other Early Formative findings,
including four sherds with Ocós phase characteristics
in a deposit at the Laguna Cuzcachapa (Sharer 1978).
These sherds were similar to some of the pottery found
at El Carmen.

Other early findings have been reported in the eastern region of El Salvador. Footprints were found at the
site of La Rama, southeast of Usulután, for which
Haberland (1960:26) suggested a dating of 1500 b.c.
Some sites, such as Atiquizaya in Ahuachapán and At-
alaya and Barra Ciega in Sonsonate, have been alleged
to have a Middle Formative occupation. These sites
have traits similar to those of the Providencia phase in
Kaminaljuyú and the Conchas phase on the Pacific
coast (Casasola 1975). Other early references are limited to two Middle Formative sites. One is reported by
Black (1983) for the Zapotitán Valley, and the other by
Fowler and Earnest (1985) at El Perical. Another Middle Formative site was reported by Amaroli (1986) and
later excavated by Demarest and his colleagues. During the Late Formative the presence of sites is larger,
suggesting demographic growth and social change.

The scarce evidence for Early Formative sites in El
Salvador does not mean they do not exist. The lack of
research focusing on this period, in addition to the vulcanism (Sheets 1983) that has affected El Salvador, has
impaired the finding of early sites, which may have
been buried under thick, heavy layers of volcanic ash.

The Site of El Carmen

El Carmen is located on the western Pacific coast of El
Salvador in the department of Ahuachapán, 3 kilometers from the Pacific Ocean (Fig. 16.1). The mountain

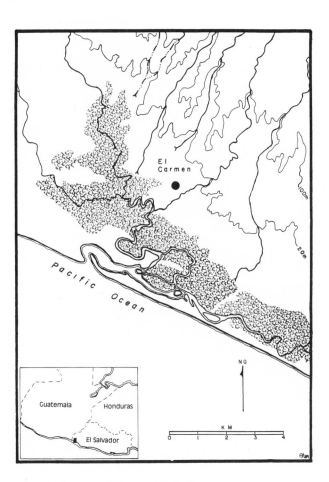

Fig. 16.1. Location of the site of El Carmen.

range begins approximately 800 meters north of the
site, and the mangroves are 200 meters to the south.
This zone represents the eastern limit of the greater
coastal plain that extends from Oaxaca to El Salvador,
crossing the coasts of Chiapas and Guatemala. In contrast with the size of the coastal plain and piedmont in
Guatemala and Chiapas, the area of the coastal formation in western El Salvador is compressed: the coastal
plain is only 4 kilometers wide in this part of the
country.

El Carmen consists of a single mound measuring 60
by 50 meters and standing 3 meters high. The site lies
in El Zapote estuary, one of the most important estuary and mangrove systems of the region.

El Carmen Excavations

Excavations were carried out during the summer of
1988, and the materials were analyzed between 1988
and 1989. The excavations covered a total area of 32
square meters. In this large sample, the earliest evi-

dence of human activity is three ovens excavated into sterile soil at the base of the mound. The association of the ovens with the deeper levels, their location at the base and center of the mound, and the way they were excavated into sterile soil suggest an earlier occupation than the subsequent ones. According to the physical appearance of the ovens, they were subject to high temperatures and in constant use. Some thick fragments of Trujillo coarse pottery were found associated with them, suggesting a special function of the site at the time of its first human occupation.

The excavations of the upper levels exposed a series of compact clay floors separated by fill of sandy clay. Definition and exposure of the floors were easy because of their hardness. Some human footprints were identified in one of the floors. The compact clay floors suggest a permanent and constant occupation of El Carmen.

Seven stages of construction have been identified at the site. Some are associated with storage pits (Fig. 16.2), 14 of which were found. They were cylindrical in shape and varied in depth to a maximum of 80 centimeters. Their diameters measured between 80 and 100 centimeters. Some of the storage pits had a sherd layer at the base. The contents of the pits at the time of excavation consisted of fill material with burnt clay chunks and carbonized seed remains.

Several midden deposits were found south of the mound. These deposits were sometimes associated with floors. The remains associated with these deposits and with the storage pits suggest a mixed subsistence pattern involving both marine and agricultural products.

Four radiocarbon dates show that the site of El Carmen was contemporaneous with Locona-Ocós sites from Chiapas and Guatemala. The ceramic style also helps to confirm this dating. The oldest date, Beta 29795, 3430 ± 90 b.p., was obtained from one of the storage pits associated with a floor located 2 meters deep. Two other dates (Beta 29797, 3220 ± 90, and Beta 29794, 3130 ± 90 b.p.) were associated with later superimposed floors. (All these dates are uncalibrated, uncorrected).

A number of features suggest seasonal use of the Carmen mound during its first occupation. These features include low variation in ceramic forms (only bowls occur in the deeper levels), ceramics without decoration, and the lack of domestic features such as floors, ground stone, or obsidian. The discrete deposits of sand, carbon, and ash and the makeup of the hearths indicate that they were used more than once. This occupation probably depended on the seasonal availability and exploitation of certain resources and may reflect the mobile nature of the society of that time.

The second occupation of the mound covers a larger area. The superimposed clay floors show a number of reconstructions and extensions, which suggest a more permanent occupation at the site or an expansion related to population growth and an increased need for more activity areas. Another possibility is that El Carmen became a specialized site. Considering how close the highlands are to the coastal plain in El Salvador, the site was perfectly located to process estuarine resources such as shellfish, fish, and mollusks that were later transported inland.

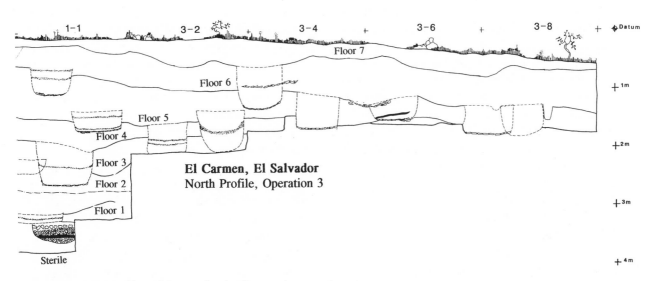

Fig. 16.2. Excavation profile at El Carmen showing floors and storage pits.

El Carmen Ceramics

The ceramic sequence from El Carmen is the result of analysis of sherds recovered from stratigraphic contexts. El Carmen is the only known site with an occupation at the beginning of the Early Formative in El Salvador. The only relevant comparative material is from sites in Guatemala and Chiapas, Mexico.

The ceramic classification follows the general basic concepts of the type-variety system as it was defined by Smith, Willey, and Gifford (1960), Smith and Gifford (1965:502), and Sabloff and Smith (1969). The ceramic classifications of Quelepa (Andrews 1976) and Cihuatán (Fowler 1981) were also useful.

The group definition follows Sabloff and Smith's (1969:279) definition of a group: "a collection of types closely related showing a consistency in the variation of form and color." According to them, the ceramic group belongs within a single ware in which other members share paste composition and surface finish.

El Carmen ceramics shared traits with the Locona and Ocós phases as defined by Coe (1961) and Clark (Clark et. al. 1987). A modal analysis was carried out in order to determine whether the principal characteristics reflected chronological differences. Once this analysis was done, comparative analysis was used to establish distribution patterns for the early pottery.

Six ceramic groups have been noted for El Carmen. The following descriptions include paste, surface treatment, decoration, and vessel forms.

METALÍO GROUP

Metalío Type
Paste: Texture varies from medium to fine, regular hardness, although very porous in some examples. Sand was used as temper in 64 percent of the total sample, and ferruginous particles were used as temper in 25 percent. Pumice was also used for temper. Paste color varies from orange brown 2.5YR 5/5/6 to orange gray 2.5YR N3/0.

Surface treatment: Surfaces are burnished without slip. The exterior rim generally presents a band of specular red paint.

Color: Surface color ranges from buff 10YR 7/3 to orange 2.5YR 5/8 and black 2.5YR 2.5/0. The red band varies from red 10R 3/3 to 7.5YR 6/4.

Forms: Hemispherical bowls, or tecomates, with thin walls (Fig. 16.3, *a*), and tear-shaped tecomates (Fig. 16.3, *b*). Reconstructed diameters of the vessels range from 11 to 21 centimeters, and sherd thicknesses from 0.6 to 1.2 centimeters.

Decoration: Surface decoration consisted of a red band around the rim. Several body sherds were found showing parallel burnished and crisscrossed lines as decorative patterns (Fig. 16.3, *c*). Other decorated body sherds had rocker stamping and textile impressions. These were not common, but their physical characteristics related them to this type.

Metalío White Type
Paste: Same as that of the Metalío type.

Surface: The surface of this type has a white wash or slip and is burnished. A red band around the rim on top of the white wash or slip was noted. Sometimes this band is replaced by a red line on the lip.

Color: White 10YR 8/1 to 10YR 8/3. The red band varies between 10R 3/6/6 and 7.5YR 6/4/4.

Forms: Tecomates and tear-shaped tecomates. Sometimes the lip is rounded, although there are several examples of pointed and square lips. Diameters vary between 11 and 19 centimeters, and sherd thickness varies from 0.6 to 1.2 centimeters.

Decoration: A band of red paint around the rim or a red paint line over the lip.

Metalío Grooved Type
Paste: Same as the previous two types.

Surface: White wash or white slip, burnished.

Color: A band of red paint around the rim over buff, orange, or white.

Forms: Tecomates and tear-shaped tecomates. Diameters and thicknesses of the sherds are the same as those of the preceding types.

Decoration: A band of red paint around the rim with one or more grooves in the same position delimits the rest of the body of the vessel (Fig. 16.3, *d*). There are a few examples of red-slipped surfaces with one groove around the rim (Fig. 16.3, *e*). Some body sherds had burnished parallel or crisscrossed lines (Fig. 16.3, *f*).

Metalío Incised Type
Except for being incised rather than grooved, this type has the same characteristics as Metalío Grooved, but in addition to the red band around the rim, this type has two incised lines around it (Fig. 16.3, *g*). The paste, forms, and surface treatment are the same as those of Metalío Grooved. This type is not as common as the previously described types.

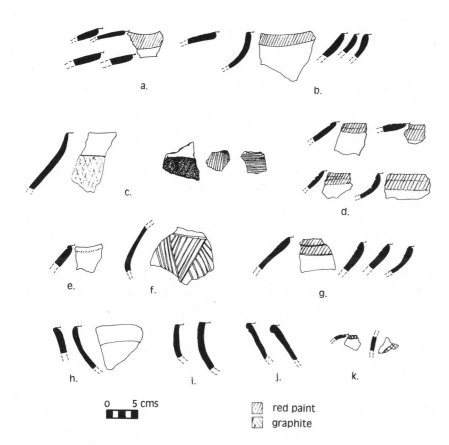

Fig. 16.3. Pottery from El Carmen. Key: *a–c*, Metalío type; *d–f*, Metalío Grooved; *g*, Metalío Incised; *h*, Ahuachapío Slipped; *i–j*, Trujillo Coarse; *k*, Izcanal Graphite.

0   5 cms

▨ red paint
◨ graphite

AHUACHAPÍO GROUP

Ahuachapío Slipped Type

Paste: Paste texture varies from medium to fine grained, regular hardness. Temper consists of coarse sand and ferruginous particles. Paste color ranges from orange brown 2.5YR 5/5/6 to orange gray 2.5YR N3/0.

Surface: The interior surface is slipped and burnished, whereas the exterior is only coarsely smoothed.

Color: The surface color is red 7.5R 3/4. The exterior presents the same color as the paste.

Forms: Open, thick-walled bowls, which are not a common form (Fig. 16.3, *h*). The diameter varies from 21 to 23 centimeters.

Decoration: No decoration was present.

Ahuachapío White Type

Paste: Same as that described for Ahuachapío Slipped.

Surface: The interior surface has a white slip or wash and a band of red paint around the rim. The interior is burnished, the exterior coarsely smoothed.

Color: White 10YR 8/1 and 10YR 8/2.

Forms: Open bowls. Diameter around 15 centimeters.

TRUJILLO GROUP

Trujillo Coarse Type

Paste: The paste texture is medium to fine, with fine sand as temper. Paste color is orange 7.5YR 6/8 and 7.5YR 5/8.

Surface: The exterior surface is coarsely smoothed. No slip or wash.

Color: Same as the paste.

Forms: Bowls with thick walls, and globular bowls with rims slightly curved toward the inside (Fig. 16.3, *i*). The lip is rounded, although sometimes there is a groove in the center (Fig. 16.3, *j*). Diameters vary from 12 to 14 centimeters and rim sherds are 1 centimeter thick. Several body sherds 1.6 centimeters thick were recovered, but their associated vessel shapes could not be determined.

Decoration: None.

KUNIMENA GROUP

Kunimena Slipped Type

Paste: The paste of this type is very fine and hard. The temper consists of small particles of ferruginous inclusions and pumice. The color is orange 7.5 YR 6/8. It is important to note the absence of sand as temper, in contrast with previous groups.

Surface: Orange slip or wash, burnished. Sometimes there is no slip or wash and the surface is only burnished because of the quality of the paste.

Color: Orange 7.5 YR 6/8.

Form: Bowls with thin walls and flat bases, and hemispherical bowls with concave bases. The lip on the flat-based bowls is generally rounded, whereas on the hemispherical bowls it is grooved. The flat-based bowls measure 21 centimeters in diameter, and the hemispherical bowls, 15 centimeters. Sherds are approximately 0.8 centimeters thick.

Decoration: Some have an incised line around the exterior rim.

IZCANAL GROUP

Izcanal Grooved Type

Paste: Paste texture varies from fine to medium. Temper consists of fine-grained sand with some ferruginous inclusions. Paste color is orange brown 2.5 YR 5/5/6.

Surface: The surface is burnished, with deep, thick grooves that form geometric line patterns that crisscross.

Color: Dark orange 2.5 YR 4/6, buff 10 YR 7/3, or white 10 YR 8/1.

Forms: No rims were found, but the body sherds suggest that they were parts of tecomates. The tecomates appear to have been globular, although the shapes of the bases cannot be determined. Sherds measured 0.8 centimeters thick.

Decoration: Grooved line patterns.

Izcanal Graphite Type

Paste: Same as Izcanal Grooved.

Surface: Somewhat eroded, but it seems to have been burnished on the exterior. There is a graphite band 2.5 Y 4/0 around the rim over red slip.

Color: Graphite on red.

Forms: Miniature tecomates with a rounded lip and a deep groove around the exterior rim (Fig. 16.3, *k*). The walls are very thin (0.5 cm), and diameter is 5 centimeters. This type was not common.

Decoration: Grooves around the rim and graphite lines on red slip.

AMATILLO GROUP

Amatillo Polished Type

Paste: Medium texture, with coarse-grained sand as temper. Sometimes there are ferruginous inclusions.

Surface: Well-polished micaceous slip.

Color: Black 7.5 R 2.5/0.

Forms: Globular tecomates and tear-shaped tecomates with thin walls. Lips are rounded and bases are possibly concave. Diameters vary between 12 and 15 centimeters.

Decoration: Some tecomates have one groove around the exterior rim. The decoration on the body consists of burnished lines on top of the slip or a burnished surface. It is the same pattern as that of the Metalío and Metalío Burnished types. There are some examples of globular tecomates with a red band around the exterior rim.

The Bostan Phase and Discussion

The regional and singular characteristics of El Carmen pottery required the definition of a new ceramic phase, named Bostan. The phase was dated by four radiocarbon dates and placed between 1450 and 1200 b.c., before the Tok phase (Fig. 16.4) originally defined by Sharer (1978). It is interesting to note that even though no superimposed Bostan-Tok deposits were found, this sequence is similar to that from western sites in Guatemala. The Tok ceramics are stylistically similar to the Cuadros phase ceramics, which in Chiapas and Guatemala are found after the Ocós phase and are later in date than El Carmen ceramics.

Prior to the discovery of and excavations at El Carmen, the earliest ceramic phase for El Salvador was the Tok phase (Sharer 1978). This phase was defined from pottery at the sites of El Trapiche and Laguna Cuzcachapa in Chalchuapa. It is characterized by the presence of plain tecomates with interior rim thickening, red-rimmed tecomates, flaring-wall flat-bottomed bowls, modeling on jar shoulders, fluting, and other traits. Other vessel characteristics appear more restricted and demonstrate the close relationship between the Pacific coast and the Gulf Coast (flat-bottomed bowls with flaring walls and exterior-thickened rims, groove-incising and the double and triple line break motif, exterior brushing, interior finger punching, differential smudging, red-on-cream slipping, etc.) (Sharer 1978:124). These ceramic materials indicate

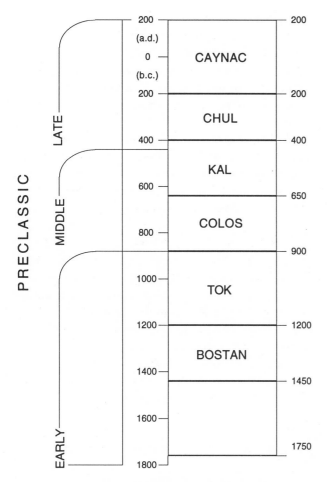

Fig. 16.4. Chronological chart showing the placement of the Bostan phase in relationship to the Chalchuapa ceramic phases.

close affinities with the ceramic tradition (Cuadros complex) of the Pacific coast of Guatemala and Chiapas (Sharer 1974:169), which dates to the later part of the Early Preclassic period.

Sharer suggested that the "earliest settlers were a part of an expanding lowland maize-cultivating cultural tradition" (Sharer 1974:169). He referred to Lowe's idea (Green and Lowe 1967:53–79) that the early maize farmers may have migrated slowly from Chiapas toward El Salvador along the natural corridor of the Pacific coastal plain. According to this theory, the migration of people from the west to the southeast occurred toward the end of the Early Formative. The archaeological evidence from El Carmen, however, suggests that if a migration did take place, it happened earlier.

The migration hypothesis is supported by cultural traits shared between the regions to the west (Chiapas and the western Guatemala Pacific coast) and El Car-

men. In contrast to Sharer's hypothesis of an expanding maize-cultivating tradition, however, El Carmen evidence suggests that agriculture was a later development. The first migration may have been part of an early expansion along the coast of temporary settlements oriented toward productive estuarine microenvironments by mobile hunter-gatherer-fishers. The shell middens in Tlacuachero, Chiapas (Voorhies 1976), and El Huiscoyol in El Salvador (Perla 1968) may represent examples of such groups. Each estuarine microenvironment on the coast can be very productive if it is managed and exploited carefully. It is possible that the ancient preceramic inhabitants living along the Pacific coast of southeastern Mesoamerica understood that the environment could be exhausted if it was not exploited properly. They may have been constantly moving to find new productive estuarine areas.

The first occupation at El Carmen is associated with ovens dug into sterile soil. The people who dug them may have been using the site as a seasonal station while they exploited a local estuarine resource. They may also have been the first people to settle permanently at El Carmen, although the artifacts associated with the ovens suggest a seasonal occupation. The people who settled there later may have learned how to manage the coastal environment and take advantage of the productive location. The coastal plain at El Carmen measures around 4 kilometers, so access to resources farther inland from the coast must have been fairly easy, making the location a favorable one. The strategic position may have promoted contact with inland groups or other coastal settlements.

Maize agriculture may have diffused to the coast through such contact. Although farming was probably not the main subsistence strategy, it was practiced to a some small degree. Early deposits found in the deeper storage pits at El Carmen contained fragments of corncobs. The existence of maize at an early date has also been documented by Blake et. al. (1992) and Coe and Flannery (1967) on the western coast of Mesoamerica. Recent evidence from the Tecojate region in central Pacific Guatemala (Arroyo 1991, 1992) also corroborates the use of maize at an early date. There, pottery with corncob impressions is associated with a radiocarbon date of 1500 b.c.

The pottery at El Carmen shows a very particular pattern in comparison with ceramic material from Chiapas and western Guatemala. The presence of white washes and slips is limited to El Carmen. White slips appear later, in the Middle Formative, in Guatemala and Chiapas. The tear-shaped tecomate form is also highly characteristic of El Carmen, whereas in other areas it seems to be limited to the earlier part of the Locona phase (John E. Clark, personal communication, 1989). The absence of the large feet on tecomates that are representative of the material in Chiapas and Guatemala is another unique feature of El Carmen ceramics. It is possible that the absence of these tripod supports in El Carmen can be explained by the use of rocks to hold the vessels over fire. Large numbers of fire-cracked rocks were recovered from the excavations.

Although basic traits are shared by the ceramics from throughout Early Formative Pacific southeastern Mesoamerica, each area presents its own regional variants. These variants were based not only on style or aesthetics but also on the organization of these early societies. Although some of these societies (such as the examples from the Chiapas coast presented by Clark and Gosser, chapter 17) attained a high degree of social complexity at an early date, other regional cultures had different developments that shaped them distinctively. In contrast with the pottery of Chiapas, El Carmen ceramics had a predominantly utilitarian function. Although there is evidence of both a cooking and a serving ware, the latter is not elaborate and cannot be considered a prestige item.

The first mobile groups of coastal El Salvador may have had alliance systems through which information was exchanged with other groups to the west and east. We know of the existence of similar alliance systems among contemporary and archaeologically known hunter-gatherers (Lourandos 1983; Walters 1992). The mobile groups in El Salvador may not have used ceramics at first; more than likely, they used gourds as containers. Lowe (1971) and Clark and Blake (1990) have proposed that the first pottery found in Chiapas may replicate natural gourds.

The later pottery with unique local characteristics but similar styles from areas to the west suggests that the network of information that existed while groups were mobile continued after they became sedentary. It may be that the ancient inhabitants of El Carmén knew about pottery through the exchange of information and adopted it by incorporating local traits (such as the lack of tripod supports because of the abundance of rocks). Until earlier deposits are found, however, only speculations can be made about the origins of Salvadoran ceramics.

Differences in available resources and in the degree of contact between regions may have contributed to the widespread sharing of stylistic traits. As Demarest (1989) has proposed for the later Olmec horizon, it is possible that a series of networks of interaction existed during the Early Formative. This multidirectional interaction resulted in the sharing of traits that varied in local interpretation and representation. This does not adequately account for the origins of pottery in the area, however. Until we find the antecedents of the Bostan phase, we can only infer that its origins lay somewhere to the west or east of El Carmen.

In summary, the Bostan phase pottery represents the earliest appearance of ceramics in El Salvador. It depicts the initial ceramic industry of that region. The potters were not full-time agriculturalists but had a subsistence system dependent on estuarine resources. The general characteristics of El Carmen pottery share stylistic traits with ceramics from other, contemporaneous sites across Mesoamerica during the Early Formative. The Bostan pottery, however, has important dissimilarities suggesting regional variation in both the styles and functions of ceramic vessels. Only future research will help us understand the origins of the Bostan ceramics.

References Cited

Amaroli, P. E.
1986   Registro de sitios del departamento de Ahuachapán. Manuscrito en el Museo David J. Guzman, San Salvador, El Salvador.

Andrews, E. W., V
1976   *The Archaeology of Quelepa*. Middle American Research Institute, Publication 42. Tulane University, New Orleans, Louisiana.

Arroyo, B.
1991   Informe preliminar del proyecto Tecojate, temporada 1991. Submitted to the Instituto de Antropología e Historia, Guatemala.
1992   Informe preliminar del proyecto Tecojate, temporada 1992. Submitted to the Instituto de Antropología e Historia, Guatemala.

Arroyo, B., A. A. Demarest, and P. E. Amaroli
1989   The El Carmen Site, El Salvador: New Information on the Early Preclassic of Southeastern Mesoamerica. Paper presented at the 54th annual meeting of the Society for American Archaeology, Atlanta, Georgia.

Black, K.
1983   The Zapotitán Valley Archaeological Survey. In *Archaeology and Volcanism in Central America: The Zapotitán Valley of El Salvador,* edited by

P. D. Sheets, pp. 62–97. University of Texas Press, Austin.

Blake, M., J. E. Clark, B. Chisholm, and K. Mudar
1992   Non-agricultural Staples and Agricultural Supplements: Early Formative Subsistence in the Soconusco Region, Mexico. In *Transitions to Agriculture,* edited by A. B. Gebauer and T. D. Price, pp. 133–52. Prehistory Press, Madison, Wisconsin.

Casasola, L.
1975   Panorama general de la arqueología de El Salvador. *America Indígena* 25:4–14.

Ceja Tenorio, J. F.
1985   *Paso de la Amada: An Early Preclassic Site in the Soconusco, Chiapas.* Papers of the New World Archaeological Foundation, no. 49. Provo, Utah.

Clark, J. E., and M. Blake
1990   The Development of Early Formative Ceramics in the Soconusco, Chiapas, Mexico. Paper presented at the 55th annual meeting of the Society for American Archaeology, Las Vegas, Nevada.

Clark, J. E., M. Blake, B. Arroyo, M. Pye, R. Lesure, V. Feddema, and M. Ryan
1990   Proyecto Investigaciones del Formativo Temprano en el Litoral Chiapaneco. Final report submitted to the Instituto de Antropología e Historia de México. New World Archaeological Foundation, San Cristóbal de las Casas, Chiapas, Mexico.

Clark, J. E., M. Blake, P. Guzzy, M. Cuevas, and T. Salcedo
1987   Final Report on the Early Preclassic Pacific Coastal Project. Submitted to the Instituto de Antropología e Historia de México. New World Archaeological Foundation, San Cristóbal de las Casas, Chiapas, Mexico.

Coe, M. D.
1961   *La Victoria: An Early Site on the Pacific Coast of Guatemala.* Peabody Museum, Harvard University, Archaeological and Ethnological Papers 53. Cambridge, Massachussetts.

Coe, M. D., and K. V. Flannery
1967   Early Cultures and Human Ecology in South Coastal Guatemala. *Smithsonian Contributions to Anthropology* no. 3. Smithsonian Institution, Washington, D.C.

Demarest, A. A.
1986   *The Archaeology of Santa Leticia and the Rise of Maya Civilization.* Middle American Research Institute, Publication no. 52. Tulane University, New Orleans, Louisiana.
1989   The Olmec and the Rise of Civilization in Eastern Mesoamerica. In *Regional Perspectives on the Olmec,* edited by R. J. Sharer and D. C. Grove, pp. 303–44. Cambridge University Press, Cambridge.

Demarest, A. A., M. E. Pye, J. Myers, and R. Méndez
1988   Informe preliminar de las excavaciones de 1987–1988 Proyecto Arqueológico El Mesak. Submitted to the Instituto de Antropología e Historia, Guatemala.

Fowler, W. R.
1981   The Pipil-Nicarao of Central America. Ph.D. dissertation, Calgary University, Calgary.

Fowler, W. R., and H. Earnest
1985   Settlement Patterns and Prehistory in the Paraíso Basin of El Salvador. *Journal of Field Archaeology* 12:19–32.

Green, D. F., and G. W. Lowe
1967   *Altamira and Padre Piedra: Early Preclassic Sites in Chiapas, Mexico.* Papers of the New World Archaeological Foundation, no. 38, Provo, Utah.

Haberland, W.
1960   Ceramic Sequences in Salvador. *American Antiquity* 26(1):21–29.

Longyear, J. M.
1944   *Archaeological Investigations in El Salvador.* Memoirs of the Peabody Museum of Archaeology and Ethnology. Harvard University, Cambridge.

Lourandos, H.
1983   Intensification: A Late Pleistocene-Holocene Archaeological Sequence from Southwestern Victoria. *Archaeology in Oceania* 18:81–94.

Love, M. W.
1989   Early Settlements and Chronology of the Río Naranjo, Guatemala. Ph.D. dissertation, University of California, Berkeley.

Lowe, G. W.
1971   The Civilizational Consequences of Varying Degrees of Agricultural and Ceramic Dependency within the Basic Ecosystems of Mesoamerica. In *Observations on the Emergence of Civilization in Mesoamerica,* edited by J. A. Graham, pp. 212–48. Contributions of the University of California Archaeological Research Facility 11.
1975   *The Early Preclassic Barra Phase of Altamira, Chiapas: A Review with New Data.* Papers of the New World Archaeological Foundation, no. 38. Provo, Utah.

Perla, C.
1968   Informe preliminar de la excavación de un montículo de concheros en la zona del Río Huizcoyol, Sonsonate. Manuscript.

Pye, M. E.
1992   Informe final del proyecto Río Jesús. Sub-
        mitted to the Instituto de Antropología e
        Historia, Guatemala.
Pye, M. E. (ed.)
1990   Informe preliminar de los resultados del
        análisis de laboratorio del proyecto El Mesak.
        Submitted to the Instituto de Antropología e
        Historia, Guatemala.
Sabloff, J. A., and R. E. Smith
1969   The Importance of Both Analytic and Tax-
        onomic Classification in the Type-Variety
        System. *American Antiquity* 34:278–85.
Sharer, R. J.
1974   The Prehistory of the Southeastern Maya
        Periphery. *Current Anthropology* 15(2):165–87.
Sharer, R. J. (ed.)
1978   *The Prehistory of Chalchuapa, El Salvador, vol.
        3, Pottery and Conclusions*. University of Penn-
        sylvania Press, Philadelphia.
Sheets, P. D.
1983   *Archaeology and Vulcanism in Central America:
        The Zapotitán Valley of El Salvador*. University
        of Texas Press, Austin.

Shook, E. M., and M. P. Hatch
1979   The Early Preclassic Sequence in the Ocós-
        Salinas La Blanca Area, South Coast of
        Guatemala. *Contributions of the University of
        California Archaeological Research Facility*
        41:143–75.
Smith, R. E., and J. C. Gifford
1965   Pottery of the Maya Lowlands. In *Handbook
        of Middle American Indians,* vol. 2, edited by
        R. Wauchope and G. Willey, pp. 498–534.
        University of Texas Press, Austin.
Smith R. E., G. R. Willey, and J. C. Gifford
1960   The Type-Variety Concept as a Basis for the
        Analysis of Maya Pottery. *American Antiquity*
        25:330–40.
Voorhies, B.
1976   *The Chantuto People: An Archaic Period Society
        of the Chiapas Littoral, Mexico*. Papers of the
        New World Archaeological Foundation, no.
        41. Provo, Utah.
Walters, I.
1992   Farmers and Their Fires, Fishers and Their
        Fish: Production and Productivity in Pre-
        European Southeastern Queensland. *Dia-
        lectical Anthropology* 17:167–82.

17

Reinventing Mesoamerica's First Pottery

JOHN E. CLARK AND DENNIS GOSSER

The widely held belief that Mesoamerica's first pottery originated in the central highlands of Mexico about 2300 b.c. springs from an uncritical acceptance of a few uncorroborated radiocarbon dates run in the 1960s. When these anomalous dates are removed from serious consideration, the picture that emerges of the oldest pottery in Mesoamerica is much more complicated than previously thought. At least three pottery complexes are known to have been present in Mexico by 1600 b.c., and possibly earlier, none of which can convincingly be related to local antecedents or to each other. Published data are currently available for two of these: the Purron pottery of the central highlands of Mexico and the Barra pottery from the coastal region of Chiapas, Mexico, known as the Soconusco. The striking differences between the plain Purron pottery of the highlands and the decorated Barra pottery of the coastal lowlands have given rise to two competing explanations concerning the origins of ceramic technology in Mesoamerica. These explanations represent, respectively, the notion of independent invention of the ceramic arts and the notion of direct borrowing. As we will discuss, neither explanation adequately accounts for the distribution of early pottery in Mesoamerica or in adjoining regions.

The best evidence for diffusion of ceramic technology is the overall distribution of the earliest pottery in North, South, and Central America, shown in Fig. 17.1 and Table 17.1. The earliest pottery is found in northern South America, and the earliest recorded pottery becomes increasingly younger as one moves northward from this region toward Mexico. The other expectation of diffusion is not met, however, because each adjacent early ceramic assemblage is stylistically different from its closest neighboring complex. The chronological progression of ceramic technology shown in Fig. 17.1, coupled with the stylistic disparity of neighboring assemblages, suggests that the standard, dichotomous possibilities of diffusion and independent invention of the ceramic arts should be reconsidered, because neither explains the extant data.

The reliable evidence for early pottery in Mesoamerica, we think, suggests a third process that involved what David Kelley (personal communication to Clark, 1992) calls "dependent invention." This variant of stimulus diffusion involves the acceptance of ideas and technical knowledge by a borrowing group and the technology's rapid application and modification in ways foreign to its use by the donor group. In archaeological time, the rapid transformation of technology is essentially instantaneous, thus making its

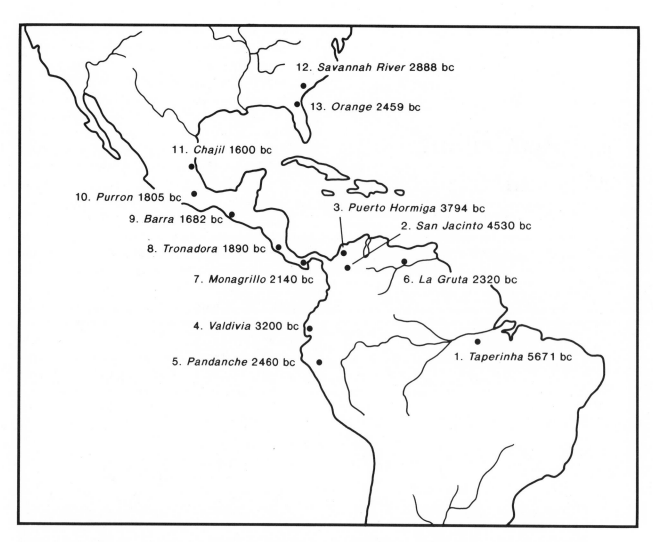

Fig. 17.1. Earliest documented occurrence of pottery in various regions of North, South, and Central America, showing the probable northward progression of ceramic technology from northern South America to Mesoamerica. The movement of ceramic technology from the southeastern United States is unknown. Site numbers and intercept mean dates b.c. correspond to those in Table 17.1.

specific source difficult to trace. Our ambiguous title refers to this process of dependent invention or rapid "reinvention" as well as to the current need to reconsider the "Tehuacan myth" of independent ceramic origins in the highlands of Mexico. In the following discussion we briefly consider the question of early ceramic dates and then pursue the implications of our analysis of the various early Mesoamerican ceramic complexes. We focus principally on the origins of Barra pottery from the Pacific coast of Chiapas and argue that the reinvention of ceramic technology must be seen in its social and political context.

A Reconsideration of Early Ceramic Dates

When one considers critically the absolute dates available for the earliest pottery in Mesoamerica, the number of primary contenders can be reduced to three. Contrary to popular misconception, the early "Pox" pottery from Puerto Marquez, Guerrero, can be dismissed or subsumed under the better-known Early Ajalpan pottery from Tehuacan Valley and the Tierras Largas pottery from the Valley of Oaxaca. Pottery from all three assemblages is technically, stylistically, and formally similar (Brush 1965; Coe 1964; Flannery and Marcus 1994:59; MacNeish et al. 1970; Marcus 1983).

Pocked pottery from layer 33 of Brush's single test pit at Puerto Marquez was dated to 2440 ± 140 b.c. An aceramic date of 2940 ± 130 b.c. was obtained from layer 38 (Brush 1965:149), thus suggesting stratigraphic consistency for the date of the earliest ceramics in level 33. However, a third date from layer 35, left out of the *Science* article but mentioned in the thesis, dates the late preceramic horizon to 2250 ±

135 b.c. (cited in Johnson and MacNeish 1972: Table 9; MacNeish et al. 1970:22; Voorhies 1976:6). The inconsistency of these two dates from upper levels, the arbitrary selection of the early date over the later date, and the fact that the single date for the pocked pottery came from the lowermost ceramic level and from shell (i.e., material in probable contact with the underlying aceramic levels) all suggest that we should not accept the early date for "Pox" pottery at face value. There is no reason to assign a date earlier than 2000 b.c. for this pottery (the lower one-sigma range for the date from level 35), and it would be considerably later if an Archaic shell from a previous occupation was dated. Marcus (personal communication, 1994) suggests a date of 1300 b.c. for the Puerto Marquez pottery based upon its similarities to Tierras Largas pottery.

The Purron phase dates from 2300 to 1500 b.c. and is the phase that witnessed the origins of pottery (MacNeish et al. 1970:21). Uncritical reading of the Tehuacan data has fostered the widespread and unwarranted view that Purron pottery dates to 2300 b.c. (see Hoopes 1992 for an excellent comparative summary). The Purron phase is the most poorly dated phase of the Tehuacan sequence, and determination of its beginning and ending dates involved considerable conjecture, including, among other things, the proposed date for the "Pox" pottery (Johnson and MacNeish 1972:24–25; MacNeish et al. 1970:22). Only 127 sherds were found in the two components (K and K_1) from Purron Cave that provided the basis for defining this ceramic complex. Two radiocarbon dates from component K provided a mean date of 1925 ± 131 b.c. for 67 sherds, and four pooled radiocarbon dates for the overlying component K_1 provided a mean date of 1531 ± 91 b.c. for another 60 sherds (MacNeish et al. 1970:21). This suggests an uncalibrated range for Purron pottery of 1900 to 1400 b.c. (see Flannery 1983:28; Marcus 1983:42).

The recent identification at San José Mogote, Hacienda Blanca, and Tierras Largas, Oaxaca, of Espiri-

Table 17.1. Radiocarbon Dates for Early Ceramic Assemblages in North, South, and Central America

No.	Region/*Phase*	No. Dates Averaged*	Oldest Date (Years b.p.)	Average Years b.p.	Calibrated Age B.C.†	Intercept Mean B.C.	References
1	Brazil/*Taperinha*	6	6980 ± 80	6826 ± 35	5693–5626	5671	Roosevelt et al. 1991
2	Colombia/*San Jacincto*	1	5700 ± 430	5700 ± 430	5055–4043	4530	Oyuela 1987
3	Colombia/*Puerto Hormiga*	6	5300 ± 80	5025 ± 38	3931–3775	3794	Reichel-Dolmatoff 1985
4	Ecuador/*Valdivia*	28	5275 ± 175	4516 ± 22	3335–3104	3200	Damp 1984
5	Peru/*Pandanche*	2	4018 ± 80	3955 ± 77	2563–2335	2460	Kaulicke 1981; Hoopes 1987
6	Venezuela/*La Gruta*	4	4090 ± 106	3864 ± 45	2452–2206	2320	Rouse and Allaire 1978
7	Panama/*Monagrillo*	14	4800 ± 100	3750 ± 24	2191–2050	2140	Cooke 1984
8	Costa Rica/*Tronadora*	4	3730 ± 100	3560 ± 52	1946–1779	1890	Hoopes 1987
9	Mexico/*Barra*	9	3570 ± 110	3398 ± 36	1738–1637	1682	Blake et al. n.d.
10	Mexico/*Purron*	4	3725 ± 180	3483 ± 90	1900–1680	1805	Johnson and MacNeish 1972
11	Mexico/*Chajil*	NA	NA	NA	c.1600–1400	1600?	Castañeda Z. 1992
12	Southeast U.S./*Savannah River*	9	4465 ± 95	4272 ± 37	2911–2880	2888	Sassaman 1993
13	Southeast U.S./*Orange*	3	4210 ± 60	3937 ± 35	2466–2364	2459	Russo 1992

Note: Numbers in first column refer to Fig. 17.1.

*Represents number of dates associated with earliest ceramic phase.

†Calibrated using Calib program version 3.0 using bicadal dataset at one-sigma confidence interval (Stuiver and Pearson 1993).

dión pottery (Marcus 1983; Ramírez 1993), a local variant of Purron Plain, corroborates the early date for Purron pottery. Although no dates are available for the 262 sherds identified at San José Mogote with this Oaxaca assemblage, Espiridión sherds are antecedent to Tierras Largas ceramics that are securely dated to 1400 to 1150 b.c. (Drennan 1983:364; Flannery et al. 1981; Flannery and Marcus 1994; Ramírez U. 1993). This suggests an ending date for the Espiridión and Purron pottery of 1400 b.c., a conclusion that fits well with the dates from component K_1 of Purron Cave. The beginning date for the Purron ceramic complex is placed at 1900 b.c., but considering the small size of the extant collections and the one-sigma ranges of the available dates, an upper limit of 1650 b.c. (the rounded average of all six dates) seems more reasonable. As Lowe (1971:219) argued: "It would seem much more to the point to emphasize that these Purron vessel forms are the same as those of the Early Ajalpan phase which *follows*. If we move these few pieces of pottery toward the late end of this tremendously long phase (they can hardly span all 800 years of it!), then there seems little need to project any meaningful gap between them and the beginnings of the Early Ajalpan subphase."

Until more data are forthcoming, we will consider the Purron and Espiridión pottery as variants of the same early complex of simple highland pottery that dates from 1650 to 1400 b.c. The technological and stylistic continuity of these early assemblages with those that follow in each region (Early Ajalpan and Tierras Largas) supports this view of highland ceramics (see Flannery and Marcus 1994). All this is to suggest that these early highland ceramics are not as ancient as commonly thought.

One implication of the revision proposed here is that highland Purron and Espiridión pottery was contemporaneous with the sophisticated Barra pottery of the Pacific coast of Chiapas, Mexico (see Ceja 1985; Lowe 1975). Considering our research focus, this implication can easily be interpreted as self-serving revisionism, but we think any dispassionate view of the extant data would arrive at a similar conclusion. Purron ceramics may be slightly earlier than Barra ceramics, but not significantly so, and both complexes were clearly contemporaneous for several centuries. Our recent work on the Chiapas coast has resulted in a revision of the Early Formative phase sequences there. Based upon 11 uncalibrated radiocarbon dates, we now place the Barra phase at 1550 to 1400 b.c. (overall mean date of 1448 ± 36 b.c.). It is important to note that 20 radiocarbon dates for the following Locona phase (1400 to 1250 b.c.) leave little room to negotiate the terminal date of the Barra phase, although the beginning date is an open question. Given the dating of Late Archaic deposits, a beginning date before 1800 b.c. for the Barra phase is highly unlikely (see Blake et al. n.d. for a summary of the chronology).

The third candidate for early pottery comes from northern Veracruz. Few data are yet available for the Chajil complex and phase (Castañeda Z. 1992), but the initial radiocarbon dates for the following phase suggest contemporaneity of the Chajil complex with the Purron and Barra complexes; stylistically, however, the thin, carefully painted Chajil pottery (predominantly deep bowls and necked jars) is unlike anything else in Mesoamerica (Castañeda Z. 1992; cf. Ekholm 1944; MacNeish 1954, 1958; Merino and García Cook 1987).

In summary, at least three early pottery sequences have been documented for Mesoamerica. The highland Purron-Espiridión complex and the lowland Chajil complex appear to have been coeval with the lowland Barra complex. It appears unlikely that any of the three complexes derived from or was significantly related to the other two. We suggest that all three pottery complexes result from different lines of "dependent invention." The patent differences among these early ceramic complexes may derive from (1) differences in the reasons for the initial adoption of pottery vessels in each region, (2) different perishable container prototypes, and perhaps (3) significant differences in the social and political settings. In the following discussion we explore these possibilities by focusing on the Barra complex from the Soconusco.

The Barra Complex

Analysis of Barra pottery recovered in our recent excavations in the Mazatán region of coastal Chiapas, Mexico, generally confirms Lowe's (1975) and Ceja's (1985) earlier evaluations of this early ceramic complex. Other than a small proportion of relatively coarse, buff vessels (these are extremely elaborate but are slipped only on the red rim-band and sometimes on a basal band), all Barra vessels are finely slipped and highly burnished. Besides the small grooved red vessels described by Lowe (1967, 1975), we found tall orange fluted vessels, a variety of bichrome neckless jars, or *tecomates*, and numerous burnished brown bowls (Fig. 17.2). Bichrome vessels include red-on-buff, red-

Fig. 17.2. Reconstruction drawing of the Barra ceramic assemblage from the Mazatán region of southeastern Mexico.

10 cms

on-white, black-on-orange, black-on-red, and black-on-white. Black paint is confined to thin line designs and appears somewhat fugitive; other colors and hues are from highly burnished slips. We have also recovered numerous trichrome sherds (black, red, and white or buff; black, red, and orange), but these easily erode into bichromes because of the poor preservation of the fugitive black. Brown, red, orange, and white monochromes predominate, with gray and black monochromes being rare. Bichrome and trichrome decorations comprise less than 10 percent of the Barra assemblage. Small tecomates and simple, flat-bottomed, incurved bowls are the most common vessel forms. Open shallow bowls, dishes, and plates are not known for the Barra complex.

Cross-cutting all of these vessel forms are a variety of surface decorations. Deep, multiple, parallel-line incising, fluting, grooving, gadrooning, lobing, squashlike segmentation, zoned cross-hatching, and zoned punctation in a variety of geometric designs occur. Indeed, an unmodified surface on a Barra sherd is unusual. Stick-punctate, zoned designs are present, but rocker stamping is absent. All the Barra vessels were thinwalled, with coarse sand temper, and were fired at high temperatures. Fire clouding is infrequent.

The Origins of Pottery in the Soconusco

Both Coe (1960) and Lowe (1975) favored a southern origin for the spread of ceramic technology into the Soconusco. Many of the shared decorative modes that Coe (1960) documented between Ocós pottery from coastal Guatemala and Chorrera pottery from Ecuador are striking and could indicate a significant relationship. But Coe's hypothesis is adversely affected by

the discovery of the earlier and more sophisticated Barra pottery in the Soconusco. In his study of the first sample of Barra sherds, Lowe (1967) noted some modal similarities between Barra pottery and pottery from Ecuador, Colombia, and Central America and argued for some kind of long-range diffusion or contact. But these similarities are much less convincing than those described by Coe for Ocós and Chorrera pottery. In comparing early ceramics from Costa Rica and the Intermediate Area, Mesoamerica, and South America, Hoopes (1987:3) notes that "even the most general patterns [of tecomates] display at best distinct stylistic 'spheres' rather than a modal 'fall-off' from a center of precocious development."

Lowe (1971:217, 221) has suggested four possibilities for the spread of ceramic technology to Mesoamerica. Ceramics could have been (1) introduced by immigrant people, (2) traded in as objects, (3) made locally by itinerant craftspersons, or (4) a result of diffusion of ideas about how to make and use pottery vessels. Lowe compared the Soconusco case with the Mexican highland case and suggested that the differences in the earliest assemblages may be due to different local traditions of perishable containers, different subsistence systems, and different needs for ceramic vessels. In both cases, technology could have been spread by a variety of means, with the spread of ideas being the most important.

The idea of ceramic technology diffusing to Mesoamerica from Central or South America has met mixed reviews among Americanists and continues to be a topic of some debate (see Marcus 1983). Many would see this pottery tradition as evolving indigenously, in either the highlands or the lowlands. Unfortunately, debate about ceramic origins has shifted attention from what may be equally important issues concerned with social process and technological change and innovation. If pottery was brought in from elsewhere, why was it brought in and how?

In considering these questions, Lowe linked the "origins" question to larger issues of adaptation and social context. When the spread of ceramic technology is viewed as an *option* rather than as something that just happened, it seems clear that the adoption of this new technology was probably linked to the use and function of the ceramic vessels in question. If true, this link could explain the differences noted within Mesoamerica in the occurrence of the first ceramics in the highlands and lowlands and the character of each ceramic assemblage.

With the recent recovery of larger and more varied collections of Barra pottery in the Soconusco, and with the realignment of ceramic types and complexes, it is clear that some of Lowe's and Coe's arguments should be revised. The striking similarities between some Ocós and some Chorrera pottery (in both form and decoration) are now problematical. The shared modes (such as striped iridescent painting on bowl interiors, fingernail gouging of vessel exteriors, and rocker stamping) are characteristic of Locona pottery and are slightly earlier (1400 to 1250 b.c.) than previously thought; recent research in Ecuador has shown that the Chorrera complex is younger than once thought (Burger 1992; Lippi 1983). The contemporaneity of the Barra and Machalilla complexes also appears to be in doubt. Barra is older and Machalilla is younger than once thought. The widening chronological gap makes it unlikely that there was a significant relationship between the two, and in any case, Barra ceramics now appear to be older than their supposed predecessors to the south.

Explanations of early Soconusco ceramics have been polarized between the possibility of local development and that of site unit intrusion. In fact, neither model adequately explains the data in hand. Independent development within the Soconusco has been dismissed for lack of credible local antecedents. On the other hand, possibilities of a site unit intrusion, trade of finished vessels, or stimulus diffusion of the ceramic arts seem minor given the limited similarities between Barra pottery and contemporaneous pottery to the south or north.

The Functions of Ceramic Vessels as a Clue to Origin

The fact that Barra ceramics do not appear to be obviously derived from earlier ceramics to the south or to result from local, in situ development suggests that we may be making inappropriate assumptions about the processes of invention, innovation, and reinvention of ceramic technology. If we place these processes in their likely sociopolitical context, we may be able to arrive at a more plausible model that can account for more of the data. In addressing the question of the spread of ceramic technology we assume that potential donors and borrowers each exercised a choice in the matter. Groups adopting this technology had the option of accepting it or rejecting it, or of selecting parts of the total package.

Lowe (1971:213) speculated that people "made pottery only when it was economically or socially essential to their survival in increasingly competitive situations." This is to acknowledge that sufficient incentive was required on the part of the borrowing group. Lowe found incentive in the guise of population pressure. In his view, the spread of ceramic technology occurred only when ecological circumstances forced growing populations to accept it because of their increasing need to harvest and process more resources, such as corn and beans, more efficiently (see Brown 1989 for a critique of such adaptationist arguments). We think it equally plausible that the spread of ceramic technology was due to perceived opportunities for personal benefit and was not just a welcome escape valve from reproductive mismanagement.

The logical implication of Lowe's argument is that pots were adopted as tools for processing food; pottery vessels allowed more efficient use of caloric resources. Thus, pottery technology should have been adopted at about the same time as, or slightly after, the first use of the foods in question or the first evidence for changes in the processing techniques for traditional foods. On the other hand, the hypothesis that ceramics were adopted for personal political advantage has no necessary a priori implications for the timing, content, or context of adoption. Clark and Blake (1994) argue that the first pottery vessels in the Soconusco were used in competitive displays of ritual drinking among aggrandizers rather than as food-processing implements. We can evaluate the relative merits of these two hypotheses by considering the functions of the earliest vessels.

Clues to vessel function are evident in use-wear and breakage patterns, residues, and vessel form. In his initial study of Ocós pottery, Coe (1961:115) was unable to find clear evidence that vessels had been used for cooking. Analysis of tecomates from following phases, however, suggested that such vessels may have been used to steam food. The neckless jar form would be ideal for this function. Coe and Flannery (1967:81) noted that the bases of some vessels were charred inside and outside, indicating that some boiling was done with very little water, probably indicating the vessels' use to steam food. Considering the formal similarities between Ocós tecomates and later tecomates, Coe and Flannery (1967:81) conjectured that earlier tecomates may have been used in the manner documented for the later vessels.

Lowe did not discuss the uses of Barra vessels but did allude to their possible use to store water or cook. With his focus on manioc as a possible staple for the early coastal groups of the Soconusco, he was interested in the absence of ceramic griddles, the one ceramic form that would have supported his argument. Following Coe (1961), Lowe suggested that manioc, if available, may have been eaten as dough balls or tamales. This possibility now seems unlikely because the basal fragments of Barra vessels we have recovered lack traces of thermal alteration from having been used in a fire.

The overall impression of Barra pottery is that of fancy vessels with a limited range of forms. Treatment of vessel exteriors is exhaustive and labor intensive, with no true plain ware being present. The range of vessel forms appears quite limited; the Barra complex lacks plates, dishes, shallow open bowls, or vessels that could be construed as utilitarian. All the vessels shown in Fig. 17.2 are tecomates or deep, round-sided bowls with restricted openings. They are clearly patterned after the gourd form, as noted by Lowe (1971). Storage and serving of liquids appear, on formal grounds, to be their most appropriate usages.

Other clues to vessel functions are changes in assemblage composition through time. The Barra assemblage appears formally more restricted than the following Locona assemblage. The Locona complex includes a wide variety of forms and treatments not present previously (see Clark and Blake 1994:Fig. 2.6). Tecomates and deep bowls continued to be important, but one sees for the first time vessels that approach "utilitarian" forms. The most obvious change from the Barra phase was the addition of plates, dishes, and wide, open bowls. The differences between these two assemblages are strong evidence that the restricted inventory of Barra vessels represents a similarly restricted set of uses and functions. It is worth mentioning here that the restricted Barra inventory is not a result of sampling problems favoring special contexts but considers all Barra deposits recovered from a range of contexts.

The quantity of fire-cracked rock in Barra and Locona deposits suggests that Late Archaic period cooking techniques (roasting in pits?) continued into the Early Formative. It is highly significant that the frequency of fire-cracked rocks declined steadily throughout the Early Formative as the relative proportion of utilitarian tecomates increased, as shown in Fig. 17.3. These data suggest an inverse relationship between the different food preparation techniques and, thus, a probable replacement process of one by the other. This possibility is corroborated by a similar increase in formal grinding implements through time (Clark 1994). More importantly, these data suggest that the introduction of ceramic vessels during the Barra phase did not immediately affect the previous food-preparation techniques carried over from the Late Archaic period and that the transition to Early Formative food preparation techniques (boiling in pots) occurred over a period of several centuries. In short, modification of pottery technology to utilitarian ends appears to have occurred gradually, and well after the adoption of fancy pottery for other purposes.

Our expectation for Lowe's hypothesis is basically a utilitarian view of pots as tools to process food, probably by boiling; this expectation is not supported by the nature of the Barra vessels or use-wear traces, as Lowe himself has shown. As is apparent in Fig. 17.2, Barra vessels are functionally limited and stylistically appear not to have been appropriate for general food preparation. Lowe's expectations are better met by the early highland pottery, as we will discuss later.

As a basis for an alternative hypothesis, we point to the following: (1) The limited form inventory suggests that Barra ceramic vessels were used in a restricted (or

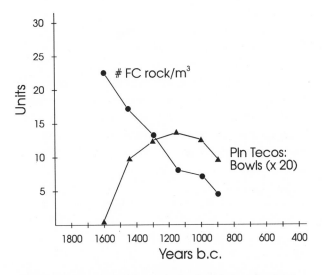

Fig. 17.3. Comparison of fire-cracked rock with the ratio of plain tecomates to bowls from the Mazatán region of coastal Chiapas, Mexico.

specialized) way. (2) The vessel forms are functionally best suited for uses involving liquids with restricted access and minimum transport. (3) The technical quality and stylistic elaboration of these vessels further suggest an important and highly visible function within the society. (4) The labor and skill investment points to a function of these early vessels as "primitive valuables" or luxury goods. All of the foregoing lead to the strong inference that ceramic technology was not adopted in the Soconusco for pedestrian reasons of food preparation. The limited data for changes in cooking techniques in subsequent phases bolster this inference. Clark and Blake (1994) have suggested that these first ceramic vessels were special containers used to serve especially important liquids on special occasions, such as ritual drinking. In particular, they argue for chocolate, *atole* (a drink of ground corn and chocolate), or corn beer. There is no direct evidence to support these speculations at present, but we plan to evaluate the idea through residue analysis of some of the pottery.

Old Wine in New Bottles: A Model for Barra Ceramic Vessels

Two related questions about early pottery in lowland Mesoamerica not previously addressed are (1) what impact did the adoption of ceramic technology have on the borrowing society? and (2) how was it able to have such impact? For Lowe (and implied in Coe and Flannery's work), the significance was increased adaptive fitness; but this appears to be a clear case of the theoretical perspective overpowering the data. Our objection to this utilitarian explanation is brought out well in Lowe's own puzzlement: "One can well ask what these lagoon fishermen, peneplain farmers, and piedmont pioneers were doing with such excellent pottery" (Lowe 1971:223). Lowe leaves this question unanswered. We think they were "showing off" in contests for prestige.

Our explanation of early pottery has been informed by a model of social action and agency described elsewhere (Clark and Blake 1994). We assume that knowledge of ceramic arts was brought into the Soconusco region by local individuals and groups for their own purposes, which may have had little to do with how the donors of this technology were using it. We further conjecture that adoption of pottery involved a process of replacement of perishable containers with nonperishable containers. Since the range of containers and container functions need not have been the same

between donors and borrowers, it would be naive to maintain that ceramic vessels in the two societies had to have been used in the same ways. All this is prelude to the suggestion that ceramic technology, vessel styles, and decorative modes need not have spread as a coherent package; they could have been adopted singly or in various combinations. Considering each of these features as potentially separate provides a basis for understanding Barra pottery.

We need to consider probable historical antecedents to the adoption of ceramics. Archaeological data for the Soconusco indicate that groups of hunter-fisher-gatherers had inhabited this coastal zone for at least 2,000 years prior to the first known use of ceramics (Clark 1994; Voorhies 1976). Undoubtedly, these Archaic foragers and collectors knew how to get along in this tropical and subtropical coastal environment. Minimally, this adaptation would have included a viable container technology and food preparation techniques. The spread of ceramic technology to the Soconusco, therefore, should probably be viewed as a process of replacement of some types of perishable containers with ceramic vessels. Attributes of the first ceramic vessels suggest they served a specialized function.

Lowe (1971) demonstrated that Barra vessels mimic gourd forms. All the surface modifications noted for Barra pots (painting, slipping, fine burnishing, incising, and carving) are techniques still used today to decorate gourds—simple techniques with great antiquity (see Lathrap 1977). We suppose that many of the decorative techniques employed to embellish Barra vessels were already known and being used to decorate gourds before they were applied to the new medium of fired clay.

If ceramic technology was brought in fully developed, how do we explain the differences in pottery styles between the borrower and donor areas? These differences may be explicable by technological transfer within the social milieu of competitive displays among aggrandizers. If perishable gourd vessels were already functioning in a competitive sphere of public/ritual display, the containers most likely imitated by ceramic forms would already have been stylistically elaborate and socially bounded. That is, vessel style would have been socially meaningful and semantically complex within special social contexts. Reproducing these vessels in a new and more expensive medium (fired clay) would have enhanced their value but not tampered with meaningful social conventions (see Clark and Blake 1994 for discussion). Such an adaptation of imported ceramic technology to local conventions would be a clear case of dependent invention.

The idea of technological transfer in a milieu of competing aggrandizers can account for those aspects of early Mesoamerican ceramic technology that investigators have found most puzzling. It would explain (1) the timing of the adoption, (2) the possible replacement of gourd containers, (3) vessels as gourd skeuomorphs, (4) vessel decorative modes, (5) general workmanship, (6) the specialized function of these first vessels, and (7) the subsequent development of ceramics during following phases as pottery became more utilitarian.

The data on hand suggest that Barra ceramic vessels served a special function and were not for cooking. (Indeed, the first pottery vessels in the Soconusco may have functioned as luxury goods.) If Barra vessels were homologues of Late Archaic gourd drinking vessels, this would imply the presence of decorated perishable containers in pre-Barra times. It would follow that the principal value of the first pots probably lay in the novelty of the new clay medium. Only after the Barra phase, when knowledge of the ceramic arts became more pervasive, were ceramics adapted to more utilitarian functions.

A Note on Early Highland Pottery

Comparison of the highland Purron-Espiridión ceramic complex to the early Barra pottery highlights the remarkable differences between them. Lowe's utilitarian expectations for the adoption of ceramic technology appear better met in the plain highland pottery. As is evident in Table 17.2, the two early ceramic complexes show a complementary organization in both time and space. At first, the differences are striking, but subsequent development in each complex tended toward unity. We see a greater range of vessel forms in each ceramic complex through time. The plain pottery of the highlands became more decorated (and in ways that directly paralleled coeval developments in coastal ceramics), and the early coastal ceramics started to include more plain pots. It is as if each early assemblage was incomplete and a full assemblage was created from their union.

We think it likely that these notable differences between highland and lowland pottery are clear evidence that the earliest ceramics in each region were used in different ways and adopted for different reasons. We attribute the elaboration of Barra pottery to the context of an evolving rank society and intense competition among aggrandizers for renown (see Clark and Blake 1994). Such behavior would probably have been inappropriate among the small groups occupying the highland valleys at this time. Indeed, one could argue that the highland peoples deliberately avoided producing decorated and marked pottery to maintain their egalitarianism. We do not think the absence of decoration (of any kind) on the earliest highland pottery can be attributed to lack of technical knowledge because the pottery is extremely thin and technologically complex. Social and political factors involved in the "reinvention" process were probably more important. (All of this presumes that additional samples of highland pottery and associated artifacts will demonstrate that the technology was brought in from the outside rather than discovered and developed locally.)

Concluding Remarks

Questions of the origins of Mesoamerican ceramic technology will not be resolved until more extensive, well-dated samples are available from numerous regions. We have attempted to show here that the acceptable data currently available suggest a complex process for the spread of ceramic technology to Mesoamerica and within Mesoamerica. We discussed briefly two different models for the adoption of ceramic technology in Mesoamerica, one proposed for the highland pottery and another for the lowland complexes. These data are sufficient to demonstrate a wide diversity in the forms and decorations of the earliest ceramic vessels and the contemporaneity of the different complexes. All this suggests that a model of stimulus diffusion is needed to account for the coeval development of stylistically distinct ceramic assemblages. We think a model of "dependent invention" or rapid "reinvention" best accounts for the timing and content of, and the formal and stylistic diversity among, the earliest ceramic assemblages. It is important to realize that such a process would have been in effect for many centuries as additional regions within Mesoamerica adopted the technology. In some cases we can demonstrate a borrowing *en toto* from region to region in Mesoamerica; in other cases, the source of the technology is not presently apparent (e.g., Swasey) and may never be determined because the technology was so quickly converted to local stylistic norms.

This model for the development of ceramic technology raises the question of phytomorphism and skeuo-

Table 17.2. Comparison of Early Highland and Lowland Ceramic Complexes in Mesoamerica

Attribute	Purron	Espiridión	Barra
No. sites	1 (Purron Cave, components K, K₁)	3 (San José Mogote, Hacienda Blanca, Tierras Largas)	38 (6 excavated)
No. ^{14}C dates	6	0	11*
Probable years b.c.	1650–1400	1500–1400 (?)	1550–1400
Probable max. years b.c.	1900–1400	1600–1400 (?)	1800–1400
No. sherds	127	>262	>2,500
Manufacture technique	?	Poss. press molded and clay rings	Clay rings
Firing	Poor	Irregular	Excellent, oxidized, hard-fired ware
Paste color	Light	Light	Light
Temper	Coarse-grained	Coarse	Sand
Sherd thickness	3–15 mm	3–15 mm Espiridión Thin, 2–2.5 mm	8–15 mm
Predominant forms	Tecomates, jars, bowls	Bowls, jars	Flat-bottomed tecomates, deep bowls, composite tecomates
Copied natural forms	Bottle and vine gourds	Bottle gourds	Vine and tree gourds, squash, pumpkins
Paints	None	None	Fugitive black
Slips	None	None	Orange, white, red, brown, red-rim modeled vessels, bichromes, trichromes
Plastic decoration	None	None	Multiple, deep-growing; fluting, gadrooning, lobing, squashlike segmentation, zoned cross-hatching, zoned punctation, geometric designs
Surface treatment	Coarse or smoothed	Coarse or burnished	Modeled or highly burnished
Major changes in the following phase	Early Ajalpan: red slip, red-rim vessels, deep outsloping flat-bottomed bowls	Tierras Largas: red slip, red-rim vessels, red-on-buff designs (chevrons and parallel bands), flat-bottomed outleaned-wall bowls, zoned dentate rocker stamping	Locona: plain red-rim tecomates, vessel feet, flat-bottomed plates, dishes and shallow bowls, pink and red striped designs (chevrons and parallel bands), specular red vessels predominate, zoned shell-edge and shell-back rocker stamping, negative-resist designs, censers, effigy pots
Trade wares in the following phase	Possible Barra sherds	Possible Locona and Ocós sherds	None
Probable sociopolitical context	Egalitarian	Egalitarian	Transegalitarian
References	MacNeish et al. 1970	Flannery and Marcus 1994; Flannery et al. 1981; Marcus 1983, 1990; Ramírez 1993	Ceja 1985; Clark 1991; Clark and Blake 1994; Lowe 1975

*Includes nine recent dates (Table 17.1) as well as two dates reported by Ceja (1985:34).

morphism noted by all investigators for the earliest Mesoamerican pottery (see Lowe 1971; Marcus 1983). We think the forms of the earliest vessels are more indicative of a replacement process in each region than of a process of development of ceramic technology. The earliest ceramic vessels copied the forms of some of the perishable vessels already in use among those who adopted and modified the new technology. This copying may not always have been the case, but it should be considered a possibility. The notion of dependent invention suggests that the technical knowledge of a craft and specific applications of it in donor and borrowing regions should be considered as potentially separate or separable. This separability creates problems archaeologically because the connection between donors and borrowers cannot always be traced, and some technologies appear to come from nowhere and to be unrelated to surrounding developments. This certainly appears to be true of the Barra ceramic assemblage.

Our primary thesis here is that ceramic technology was adopted by various groups in Mesoamerica at different times and for different reasons. Some of these reasons can be reconstructed by examining each assemblage. Each case should be seen in its wider sociopolitical context and on its own merits. In modern society we have become so accustomed to seeing technological development from a utilitarian and evolutionary point of view that we often lose sight of other functions of technology and objects. In the case of pottery, the literature shows a general expectation that the earliest pottery vessels were most esteemed as tools associated with boiling technology. The Barra case demonstrates that pottery vessels were also esteemed as special goods, perhaps as a form of primitive valuables. We suspect that many other cases of adoption of ceramic technology around the world can be shown to conform to this pattern.

Acknowledgments

We would like to thank Joyce Marcus, Michael Blake, Elizabeth M. Brumfiel, Kenneth E. Sassaman, and John W. Hoopes for their comments on a previous draft of this chapter.

References Cited

Blake, Michael, John E. Clark, Barbara Voorhies, George Michaels, Michael W. Love, Arthur A. Demarest, Mary E. Pye, and Barbara Arroyo
n.d.   The Archaic and Early Formative Chronology for the Soconusco Region of Mexico and Guatemala. *Ancient Mesoamerica.* In press.

Brown, James A.
1989   The Beginnings of Pottery as an Economic Process. In *What's New: A Closer Look at the Process of Innovation,* edited by S. E. van der Leeuw and R. Torrence, pp. 203–24. Unwin Hyman, London.

Brush, Charles E.
1965   Pox Pottery: Earliest Identified Mexican Ceramic. *Science* 149:194–95.

Burger, Richard L.
1992   *Chavin and the Origins of Andean Civilization.* Thames and Hudson, London.

Castañeda Z., Laura Adriana
1992   Altamirano: Un sitio del Formativo al noreste de Mexico. B.S. thesis, Escuela Nacional de Antropología e Historia, Mexico City.

Ceja, Jorge Fausto
1985   *Paso de la Amada: An Early Preclassic Site in the Soconusco, Chiapas, Mexico.* Papers of the New World Archaeological Foundation, no. 49. Provo, Utah.

Clark, John E.
1991   The Beginnings of Mesoamerica: Apologia for the Soconusco Early Formative. In *The Formation of Complex Society in Southeastern Mesoamerica,* edited by W. R. Fowler, Jr., pp. 13–26. CRC Press, Boca Raton, Florida.
1994   The Development of Early Formative Rank Societies in the Soconusco, Chiapas, Mexico. Ph.D. dissertation, University of Michigan, Ann Arbor.

Clark, John E., and Michael Blake
1994   The Power of Prestige: Competitive Generosity and the Emergence of Rank Societies in Lowland Mesoamerica. In *Factional Competition and Political Development in the New World,* edited by E. M. Brumfiel and J. W. Fox, pp. 17–30. Cambridge University Press, Cambridge.

Coe, Michael D.
1960   Archaeological Linkages with North and South America at La Victoria, Guatemala. *American Anthropologist* 62:363–93.
1961   *La Victoria: An Early Site on the Pacific Coast of Guatemala.* Papers of the Peabody Museum of Archaeology and Ethnology, no. 53. Harvard University, Cambridge, Massachusetts.

1964   Review of *Second Annual Report of the Tehuacán Archaeological-Botanical Project,* by R. S. MacNeish. *American Antiquity* 29:525.

Coe, Michael D., and Kent V. Flannery

1967   *Early Cultures and Human Ecology in South Coastal Guatemala.* Smithsonian Institution Press, Washington, D.C.

Cooke, Richard

1984   Archaeological Research in Central and Eastern Panama: A Review of Some Problems. In *The Archaeology of Lower Central America,* edited by F. W. Lange and D. Z. Stone, pp. 263–302. University of New Mexico Press, Albuquerque.

Damp, Jonathan

1984   Architecture of the Early Valdivia Village. *American Antiquity* 49(3):573–85.

Drennan, Robert D.

1983   Appendix: Radiocarbon Dates for the Oaxaca Region. In *The Cloud People: Divergent Evolution of the Zapotec and Mixtec Civilizations,* edited by K. V. Flannery and J. Marcus, pp. 363–70. Academic Press, New York.

Ekholm, Gordon F.

1944   Excavations at Tampico and Pánuco in the Huasteca, Mexico. *Anthropological Papers of the National Museum of Natural History,* vol. 38, part 5. American Museum of Natural History, New York.

Flannery, Kent V.

1983   Tentative Chronological Phases for the Oaxaca Preceramic. In *The Cloud People: Divergent Evolution of the Zapotec and Mixtec Civilizations,* edited by K. V. Flannery and J. Marcus, pp.26–29. Academic Press, New York.

Flannery, Kent V., and Joyce Marcus

1994   *Early Formative Pottery of the Valley of Oaxaca, Mexico.* Memoirs of the Museum of Anthropology, University of Michigan, no. 27. (Prehistory and Human Ecology of the Valley of Oaxaca, vol. 10.) Ann Arbor.

Flannery, Kent V., Joyce Marcus, and Stephen A. Kowalewski

1981   The Preceramic and Formative of the Valley of Oaxaca. In *Handbook of Middle American Indians: Supplement 1,* edited by J. A. Sabloff, pp. 48–93. University of Texas Press, Austin.

Hoopes, John W.

1987   Early Ceramics and the Origins of Village Life in Lower Central America. Ph.D. dissertation, Harvard University. University Microfilms International, Ann Arbor, Michigan.

1992   Early Formative Cultures in the Intermediate Area: A Background to the Emergence of Social Complexity. In *Wealth and Hierarchy in the Intermediate Area,* edited by F. W. Lange, pp. 43–83. Dumbarton Oaks, Washington, D.C.

Johnson, Frederick, and Richard S. MacNeish

1972   Chronometric Dating. In *The Prehistory of the Tehuacan Valley, vol. 4: Chronology and Irrigation,* edited by F. Johnson, pp. 3–55. University of Texas Press, Austin.

Kaulicke, Peter

1981   Keramik der fruhen Initialperiode aus Pandanche, Dpto. Cajamarca, Peru. *Beitrage zur Allegemeinen und Vergleichenden Archaologie* 3:363–89.

Lathrap, Donald W.

1977   Our Father the Cayman, Our Mother the Gourd: Spinden Revisited, or a Unitary Model for the Emergence of Agriculture in the New World. In *Origins of Agriculture,* edited by C. A. Reed, pp. 713–51. Mouton, The Hague.

Lippi, Ronald D.

1983   La Ponga and the Machalilla Phase of Coastal Ecuador. Ph.D. dissertation, Department of Anthropology University of Wisconsin, Madison. University Microfilms, Ann Arbor, Michigan.

Lowe, Gareth W.

1967   Discussion. In *Altamira and Padre Piedra, Early Preclassic Sites in Chiapas, Mexico,* by D. F. Green and G. W. Lowe, pp. 53–79. Papers of the New World Archaeological Foundation, no. 20. Provo, Utah.

1971   The Civilizational Consequences of Varying Degrees of Agricultural and Ceramic Dependency within the Basic Ecosystems of Mesoamerica. *Contributions of the University of California Archaeological Research Facility* 11:212–48.

1975   *The Early Preclassic Barra Phase of Altamira, Chiapas: A Review with New Data.* Papers of the New World Archaeological Foundation, no. 38. Provo, Utah.

MacNeish, Richard S.

1954   An Early Archaeological Site near Panuco, Veracruz. *Transactions of the American Philosophical Society,* vol. 44, part 5. Philadelphia.

1958   Preliminary Archaeological Investigations in the Sierra de Tamaulipas, Mexico. *Transactions of the American Philosophical Society,* vol. 48, part 6. Philadelphia.

MacNeish, Richard S., Frederick A. Peterson, and Kent V. Flannery

1970   *The Prehistory of the Tehuacan Valley, vol. 3: Ceramics.* University of Texas Press, Austin.

Marcus, Joyce

1983   The Espiridión Complex and the Origins of
        the Oaxacan Formative. In *The Cloud People:
        Divergent Evolution of the Zapotec and Mixtec
        Civilizations,* edited by K. V. Flannery and J.
        Marcus, pp. 42–43. Academic Press, New
        York.

1990   Oaxaca's First Ceramics. Paper presented at
        the 55th annual meeting of the Society of
        American Archaeology, Las Vegas, Nevada.

Merino C., B. Leonor, and Angel García Cook

1987   Proyecto Arqueológico Huaxteca. *Arqueología*
        1:31–72.

Oyuela-Caycedo, Augusto

1987   Dos sitios arqueológicos con desgrasante de
        fibra vegetal en la serranía de San Jacinto (De-
        partamento de Bolívar). *Boletín de Arqueología*
        2(1):5–26. Fundación de Investigaciones
        Arqueológicas Nacionales, Bogotá.

Ramírez U., Susana

1993   Hacienda Blanca: Una aldea a través del
        tiempo, en el valle de Etla, Oaxaca. B.S.
        thesis, Escuela de Antropología, Universi-
        dad Autónoma de Guadalajara, Jalisco.

Reichel-Dolmatoff, Gerardo

1985   *Monsú: Un sitio arqueológico.* Fondo de Pro-
        moción de la Cultura del Banco Popular,
        Bogotá, Colombia.

Roosevelt, A. C., R. A. Housley, M. Imazio da Silveira, S.
Maranca, and R. Johnson

1991   Eighth Millennium Pottery from a Prehistoric
        Shell Midden in the Brazilian Amazon. *Science*
        254:1621–1624.

Rouse, Irving, and Louis Allaire

1978   Caribbean. In *Chronologies in New World Ar-
        chaeology,* edited by R. E. Taylor and C. W.
        Meighan, pp. 431–81. Academic Press, New
        York.

Russo, Michael

1992   Chronologies and Cultures of the St Marys
        Region of Northeast Florida and Southeast
        Georgia. *The Florida Anthropologist* 45:107–26.

Sassaman, Kenneth E.

1993   *Early Pottery in the Southeast: Tradition and
        Innovation in Cooking Technology.* Univer-
        sity of Alabama Press, Tuscaloosa.

Stuiver, Minze, and G. W. Pearson

1993   High Precision Calibration of the Radiocarbon
        Time Scale, A.D. 1950–500 B.C. and 2500–
        6000 B.C. *Radiocarbon* 35(1):839–62.

Voorhies, Barbara

1976   *The Chantuto People: An Archaic Period Society
        of the Chiapas Littoral, Mexico.* Papers of the
        New World Archaeological Foundation, no.
        41. Provo, Utah.

18

The Social Contradictions of Traditional and Innovative Cooking Technologies in the Prehistoric American Southeast

KENNETH E. SASSAMAN

Pottery in the American Southeast, as in so many other regions across the globe, was first made and used by small-scale, mobile, hunter-gatherer populations, not by sedentary agriculturalists. Although this observation is nothing new to the contributors to this volume and other specialists, the tendency to link technological innovations such as pottery with pivotal events in human history permeates much of the logic and reasoning of modern archaeology. For instance, to reconcile the knowledge that mobile hunter-gatherers made and used pottery with the conceptual baggage we inherited from V. Gordon Childe, the Neolithic has been expanded to include certain preagricultural populations, and hunter-gatherer pottery has been downgraded to the status of subceramic or "gadget" (Reid 1989; Schiffer and Skibo 1987). Aside from the fact that this reveals the weakness of typologies in accommodating variation, the problem boils down to a conflation between modes of subsistence and forms of societal organization. Put another way, we still have a hard time disentangling technology from subsistence economy and from society, and many of us still expect certain traits to evolve in a unified, structural way (for a historical sketch of this problem in hunter-gatherer studies, see Bender and Morris 1988).

The emergence of pottery in the American Southeast was anything but structural and unified. In the Savannah River valley, for example, pottery was added to an existing hunter-gatherer economy with little perceptible change in subsistence organization. What is more, pottery was used in limited and varied contexts, taking several centuries to be adopted across the valley and many more before it was incorporated into the inventories of panregional populations (Sassaman 1993a). Innovations to improve the thermal efficiency of early pottery were equally slow in being accepted. As is true in other places worldwide, the first ceramic vessels were used at sites where shellfish middens accumulated, but there is no apparent functional link between pottery and shellfish, and many more examples of early shellfishing in the Southeast did not involve the use of pottery (Klippel and Morey 1986; Milanich and Fairbanks 1980).

As the variegated temporal and geographical patterns of early pottery in the Southeast gain greater archaeological resolution, explanations for them remain vague. On the one hand, the onset of shellfishing and pottery production is viewed as a symptom of broader economic changes stemming from decreased settlement mobility (e.g., Goodyear 1988). Under the general rubric of "economic intensification," the use of pottery is construed as a solution to needs for increased efficiency in processing food. It follows that other tasks, perhaps new ones, required more time and energy than ever before. Unfortunately, such demands are not readily apparent. Indeed, without specifying mechanisms for "internal" economic change, and lacking a clear "external" impetus for the development of pottery, there exists no cause for technological change.

On the other hand, the question of what was being done with the gains in time and energy pottery afforded may be understood in the broader context of hunter-gatherer social life. If we allow that social strategies are the first-order response to economic stress among hunter-gatherers (Ellen 1988; Wiessner 1982), then changes in technology must be precipitated by social process. In this sense, "economic intensification" is preceded by "social intensification" that adds demands on the time and energy budgets of production, and technological change may ensue (Bender 1978, 1985; Lourandos 1988). Conversely, the processes that ensure successful social responses to subsistence stress can inhibit technological change, even though they create increased demands on personal labor. Under both sets of circumstances contradictions arise: an effective social solution to stress may stimulate technological change that undermines the effectiveness of the social solution, and technological change may be thwarted even when social solutions to stress encourage more efficient use of time and energy.

To situate technology within hunter-gatherer society and to examine the contradictions involved, it is useful to integrate explanatory models that have heretofore been considered incompatible. The alternative perspectives I have briefly introduced provide different readings of the archaeological record on early pottery, but importantly, they expose the contradictions that are inherent in the hunter-gatherer social contexts in which early pottery emerged. In combining the two, I hope to avoid overgeneralization about technological change and instead look at the specific regional and historical circumstances involved.

The Savannah River valley lends itself as an especially good case study. Not only is it among the earliest settings for pottery in North America, but its patchwork of alternative cooking technologies also provides ample opportunity to examine differences in the economic and social contexts of pottery innovation. Technofunctional, chronological, and distributional data on cooking alternatives in the area are more than adequate for these purposes. Finally, the lessons learned from this case study can be used to develop some pre-liminary hypotheses about the spread of pottery across the greater Southeast.

Traditional and Innovative Cooking Technology in the Savannah River Valley

The earliest ceramic vessels in the Savannah River valley, a fiber-tempered ware referred to as Stallings, appeared at about 4500 b.p. in the context of small, freshwater shellfish middens (Fig. 18.1). The ware has long been considered the earliest pottery known for the southeastern United States (Sassaman 1993a; Stoltman 1972, 1974), but recent research in the St. Johns basin of Florida has shown that fiber-tempered pottery of the Orange tradition may date as early as Stallings (Russo et al. 1992). Debate over the inception of these traditions occupied the attention of archaeologists throughout the 1960s and 1970s. James Ford (1966, 1969) championed a South American origin for the wares, but others argued for indigenous development (Peterson 1971, 1980; Stoltman 1972, 1974). The issue of ultimate origins for fiber-tempered pottery is beyond the scope of this chapter, but suffice it to say that Ford's argument should not be dismissed on theoretical grounds alone, and until a concerted effort is made to locate earlier sites along the Atlantic Coast, the samples at hand should not be considered adequate. If evidence exists for the use of pottery before 4500 b.p., it will likely be found in buried estuarine or offshore locations of the south Atlantic coast (Brooks et al. 1990; Ste.Claire 1990).

The earliest pottery vessels in the Savannah River valley are from interior coastal plain sites where small shellfish middens accumulated from the short-term and probably repeated occupations of small, mobile hunter-gatherer bands. Most of the earliest vessels are shallow basins with semi-flat bases, almost always plain and often outfitted with thickened or flanged lips that lend some morphological variation to an otherwise simple design (Fig. 18.2). Another variety includes round-bottomed, hemispherical bowls with straight to slightly incurvate wall profiles. The bowl form makes up a minor component of the earliest assemblages but gains increased popularity over the fourth millennium. When and where the bowls appear is a significant piece of the puzzle in understanding early pottery in the Savannah River valley. Similarly, the distribution and evolution of the basin form, which in the fifth millennium was widespread but later became more restricted in use, provides important infor-

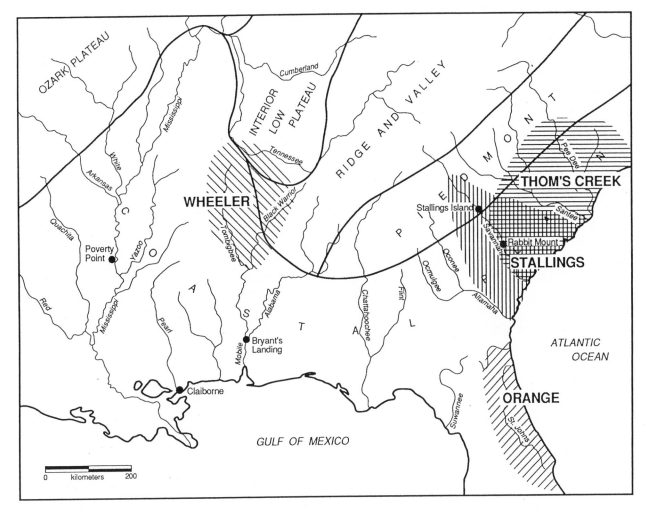

Fig. 18.1. Locations of major fiber-tempered pottery traditions in the American Southeast, circa 4500–3000 b.p.

mation about cultural resistance to certain cooking innovations. An understanding of both of these patterns revolves around interpretations of pot function.

Until recently, little information was available on the functions of fiber-tempered pottery in the Savannah River valley. Researchers had implicitly assumed that pots were used for cooking, but virtually no one speculated about what foods were prepared with pots or how (see Anderson and Joseph 1988:201 and Goodyear 1988 for exceptions). In 1990, I set out to examine functional variation in fiber-tempered pottery with a sample of sherds representing over 1,200 vessels from 29 sites in the region (Sassaman 1993a). My review of the literature on vessel form and function was hindered by that literature's bias toward the pottery of sedentary agricultural societies.

One notable exception was the work of Kenneth Reid (1989), who, from his discovery of fiber-tempered pottery in Missouri (Reid 1984), began to investigate

the uses and design of hunter-gatherer pottery from the ethnographic literature. His work was bringing to light the relevance of indirect moist cooking, a common North American cooking technique (Driver and Massey 1957:229), to pottery design. Simultaneously, James Skibo and Michael Schiffer began a series of studies, some in collaboration with Reid and some with David Hally, to examine the mechanical performance of experimental and archaeological fiber-tempered pottery (Schiffer and Skibo 1987; Skibo et al. 1988, 1989). Combining these results with related information on the mechanical performance of cooking pots (Braun 1983; Bronitsky and Hamer 1886; Hally 1986; Linton 1944; Rice 1987:207–42; Rye 1981), I developed a list of performance criteria to apply to the analysis of my archaeological sample (Table 18.1). I also examined use-alteration of the sherds, particularly the incidence of soot deposits (Hally 1983; Skibo 1992), as an independent line of functional data.

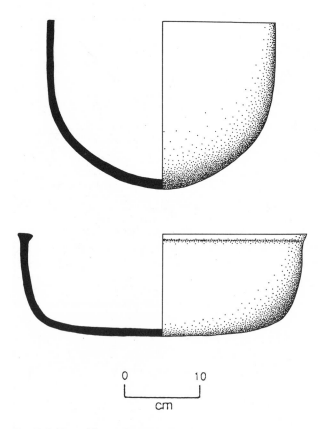

Fig. 18.2. Typical forms of Stallings fiber-tempered vessels from the Savannah River valley (*top,* hemispherical bowl; *bottom,* flat-bottomed basin).

These vessels have properties that enabled effective use of an indirect-heat cooking technique: the form and temper lend insulating properties to the vessel, the flat bottom is ideal for radiating internal heat, and the wide orifice provides for the manipulation of vessel contents, especially cooking stones. Conversely, the basins lack the design specifications for effective direct-heat cooking: they are relatively poor thermal conductors and have limited resistance to thermal shock.

Compared to basins, bowl designs in the Savannah River valley meet many of the mechanical performance criteria for direct-heat cooking. Thinner, more uniform vessel walls, smoother, more rounded body curvature, and a lower orifice-to-volume ratio than that of basins are all features conducive to direct-heat moist cooking. Observations on the use-alteration of basin and bowl forms support the functional inferences. Only 12 of the 133 basins (9 percent) with noneroded external surfaces show definite or probable traces of soot, whereas 98 out of 447 noneroded bowls (22 percent) exhibit traces of soot.[1] I concluded from these analyses that bowls were indeed made and used for direct-heat moist cooking, and that basins were ceramic containers for indirect-heat moist cooking, serving essentially as above-ground, portable "pits."

Having derived general functional interpretations from the forms of early vessels, what remains to be established are the technological precedents for these vessels. This is of obvious importance if we are to evaluate the relative efficiency of pottery among several alternatives (e.g., Brown 1989; van der Leeuw 1984:59). It follows as well that more specific information on

The results of this analysis are critical to understanding the emergence and spread of pottery in the Southeast. The results show that the flat-bottomed basins that are so prevalent in early assemblages were designed for indirect moist cooking or "stone boiling."

Table 18.1. Mechanical Performance Attributes of Direct- and Indirect-Heat Cooking Vessels

Attribute	Direct Heat	Indirect Heat
Heating effectiveness	Thin vessel walls (conduct) Sand temper Round bottom	Thick vessel walls (insulate) Fiber temper Flat bottom
Vessel content heat loss	Reduce permeability Constricted orifice Low orifice : volume ratio	Reduce permeability Thick vessel walls (insulate)
Thermal shock resistance	Temper Smooth wall curvature Uniform wall thickness	Temper
Manipulation and removal of vessel contents		High orifice : volume ratio

the resources processed with pottery and its alternatives is required to interpret the particular choices made among them.

INDIRECT-HEAT MOIST COOKING

Archaeological evidence for food preparation by Late Archaic populations of the Savannah River valley is very limited. The usual array of edible plant and animal species exploited by eastern woodland Indians has been documented in subsistence studies for sites in the region (e.g., Dye 1976; Freer 1992; Gardner 1986; Moore 1985; Stoltman 1974; Trinkley 1976, 1980, 1986; Weinand 1992). In addition, species of saltwater and freshwater shellfish constitute conspicuous remains at scores of coastal and riverine sites (Claassen 1986). When these data are combined with ethnohistorical and ethnographic materials on North American Indians, three resources emerge as likely candidates for indirect-heat moist cooking: nut oils, meat and bone grease, and gastropods.

Nut Oils

Nut oils were a major subsistence item for historic era Indians of the eastern woodlands (Swanton 1946: 364–67). Judging from the occurrence of nutshell fragments in archaeological contexts from 9000 b.p. onward, nut oils were important to prehistoric groups as well (Cowan 1985:218). In the Southeast, hickory nuts were rendered for oil, as were walnuts, acorns, and other species. Whereas the nutmeats of most of these varieties can be consumed in various ways, hickory nuts have a thick shell and an internal structure that make them especially difficult to eat. Southeastern Indians crushed hickory nuts, shell and all, into a meal that was then submerged in water to extract oils. Hudson (1976:301) reports that about a gallon of oil could be extracted from 100 pounds of hickory nuts. In historic times the oil was used as a condiment to flavor breads, stews, and cereals. Prehistorically, the resource may have provided an important storable product for overwintering (Ozker 1982).

All of the accounts of hickory nut processing involve ceramic vessels, but the accounts are split between processes involving boiling water (Asche 1682 cited in Waddell 1980:40; Bartram 1940 cited in Swanton 1946:366) and those involving only cold water (Adair 1930:439). Acorn processing to remove tanins usually involved only cold water, but at least two accounts describe prolonged boiling of, apparently, the sweet variety (Swanton 1946:273, 366). Detailed accounts of acorn processing among California Indians (e.g., Ebeling 1986; Gayton 1948:178–79; Kroeber 1925; O'Neale 1932:48) show that cold water leaching was accomplished in sand basins or baskets, and that an indirect-heat cooking technique using baskets was sufficient to prepare acorn mush, the local staple.

Archaic period sites in the Savannah River valley often yield charred hickory nutshell fragments when flotation or fine water-screening is used to process archaeological deposits. Walnuts and acorns make up smaller fractions of nut remains, but this possibly reflects a preservation bias for the thicker-shelled hickories. Although quantitative data are not available, there appears to have been a greater reliance on hickory nuts at sites in the piedmont province than in the coastal plain and on the coast. The northward expansion of southern pine communities at about 8000 b.p. in the Atlantic Coastal Plain (Delcourt and Delcourt 1987) likely weakened the competitive edge of hickory and other mast-bearing species in the province, making them a less reliable, or at least less abundant, food resource.

Bone Grease

Grease rendered from animal fat and bone was a critical resource for hunter-gatherer populations exposed to cold winters (Speth and Spielman 1983:19). Most notable, perhaps, was the use of bone grease for pemmican and other storable products among Plains Indians. The process began by smashing bones into small pieces with a mortar. Stones were heated to a high temperature and then transferred to a hide- or clay-lined pit containing water and the bone fragments. The grease was then skimmed from the surface and stored in skins or gourds.

Accounts of indirect-heat moist cooking among Northwestern Indians include some examples of stone cooking with clay pots. In Reid's (1989) discussion of these examples, he notes that the oft-used term "boiling" is a misnomer for the moist-cooking technique of rendering grease from bones or animal fat. At boiling temperatures, protein coagulates, causing the product to toughen and shrink. Moreover, the rolling surface of boiling water is not conducive to skimming off grease. In contrast, simmering temperatures (85–88°C) are ideal for reducing connective tissue or collagen to a gel, and the product is readily collected from the water's surface. This distinction is anything but trivial when we contemplate the origins of ceramics, because it shows that certain types of moist cooking do not implicate the performance requirements necessary for sustained boiling, namely, good thermal conductivity.

The importance of fat or grease rendering to Southeastern Indians is unknown. During the early historic era, bear fat was rendered for an oil that was rubbed into hair and on skin for cosmetic and religious purposes (Adair 1930:4, 64, 115; Hudson 1976:300–301). This was accomplished in ceramic vessels placed directly over heat. Other, prehistoric examples of bone grease rendering can be inferred cautiously from archaeological evidence. At Late Archaic shell midden sites along the south Atlantic Coastal Plain, deer bone is often highly fragmented, suggesting to Waring (1968: 156, 191) that fat was extracted by boiling (*sic*) (see also Goodyear 1988; Trinkley 1980:245). Similar evidence is not found at sites in the piedmont province. Again, the diminished capacity for mast-bearing resources in the coastal plain may serve to explain the divergent subsistence practices.

Small Gastropods

Both freshwater (pond snail) and saltwater (periwinkle) species of gastropods are common to shell middens in the Savannah River valley region. The meat of small snails is difficult to separate from the shell, even after cooking, and because shells in middens are usually whole, the technique used to cook them did not damage the shell. It thus seems reasonable to conclude that snails were cooked in a liquid-filled container to make a broth (Goodyear 1988). The time and temperatures it took to render snails into broth are unknown.

Also unknown is the importance of snails to the Late Archaic diet. Although small gastropod shells are not uncommon in middens of the Savannah River valley region, their proportions pale in comparison to those of the middens of northeast Florida and central Tennessee (Klippel and Morey 1986; Milanich and Fairbanks 1980). Freshwater gastropods in these areas pre-date the local inception of pottery technology, thus testifying to the existence of effective preceramic moist-cooking technology. Combined with the knowledge that species of bivalves were cooked without pottery, this testimony lessens the likelihood that pottery was adopted because of some specific functional demand for shellfish processing (cf. Goodyear 1988).

Discussion

Each of the resources just discussed was processed with an indirect-heat moist cooking technique long before pottery and the innovation of direct-heat moist cooking emerged. The relative importance of these re-

sources to the Late Archaic diet is hard to discern. The data suggest that nut oil and bone grease may have been important seasonal resources that were processed in bulk, perhaps involving considerable time investment. Moreover, the relatively limited capacity for mast resources and deer in the coastal plain may have put a premium on processes that saved time and energy. Because preceramic technologies were seemingly effective in meeting these needs before pottery emerged, changes in technology imply that the demands on time and energy exceeded the production capacities of traditional technology.

PRECERAMIC TECHNOLOGIES FOR INDIRECT-HEAT MOIST COOKING

Indirect-heat moist cooking worldwide involves the use of a solid medium to transfer heat and containers to hold liquid (Driver and Massey 1957:229–31). In the Savannah River valley, fragments of locally available rock are common to assemblages dating as early as the early Holocene, and this class of artifact (fire-cracked rock) is especially abundant in Late Archaic assemblages (Tippitt and Marquardt 1984; White 1982). The technique of stone cooking has been documented in many ethnographic settings, but the relative efficiency of this technique has never been measured. It is obvious, however, that a major problem with stone cooking is fragmentation. Most rock types have poor thermal shock resistance and thus break easily when subjected to rapid changes in temperature, as happens in stone cooking. In an experiment using whole quartz cobbles from a geological source in the upper coastal plain of the Savannah River valley, nearly every cobble fractured after five successive episodes of heating and rapid cooling (Sassaman 1993b; Fig. 18.3). Besides revealing how resource consumptive stone cooking can be, the experiment corroborates what physical anthropologists have noted for years—that preceramic cooking techniques introduced a lot of grit to the hunter-gatherer diet and caused accelerated tooth attrition.

The limitations of a stone cooking technology were apparently the impetus behind an important innovation that appeared in the middle Savannah River valley at about 5000 b.p. Soapstone outcrops in the lower piedmont of the valley began to be exploited for the manufacture of perforated cooking slabs (Fig. 18.4). With its high level of thermal shock resistance and exceptional heat retention qualities, soapstone was a natural solution to the age-old problem of stone—and tooth—attrition. Slabs were ground from naturally

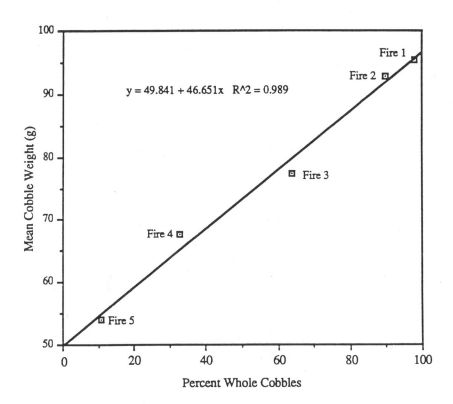

$$y = 49.841 + 46.651x \quad R^2 = 0.989$$

Fig. 18.3. Bivariate plot of the percentage of whole cobbles and mean cobble weight from five successive episodes of heating and rapid cooling using quartz cobbles from a geological source in the Aiken Plateau of the upper coastal plain of the Savannah River valley (after Sassaman 1993b).

occurring nodules to a uniform thickness and then perforated off-center with a cane or stone drill. Described as "netsinkers" for years (Claflin 1931), the Savannah River valley examples are similar to the soapstone cooking stones made and used by late prehistoric and historic California Indians for moist cooking, as well as for baking. From California accounts we know that the hole was used to transfer the slab from fire to container using a stick or antler tine (Hudson and Blackburn 1983).

It is noteworthy that the perforated slab was not widely used in the Southeast, being restricted largely to the middle Savannah River valley and adjacent, smaller valleys. But as the slabs were made and used over the fifth millennium in the area, soapstone was used to manufacture vessels in other parts of the Southeast. Soapstone vessels were not made and used in the Savannah River valley until after 3500 b.p., at least 1,000 years after pottery was available locally.

That soapstone slabs represented an improvement over other types of boiling stones is unequivocal, but the major shortcoming of soapstone is its limited geological distribution. Sites located near soapstone quarries in the Savannah River valley contain abundant remains of soapstone slabs, and, predictably, the amount of soapstone diminishes with distance from source

5 cm

Fig. 18.4. Examples of perforated soapstone cooking stones from the Savannah River valley.

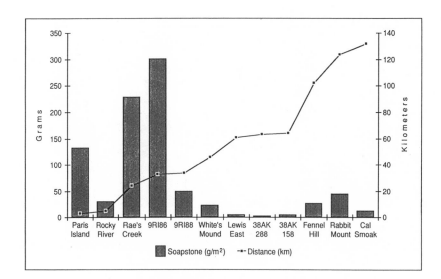

Fig. 18.5. Volume of soapstone per unit excavation (g/m²) at sites along the Savannah River, plotted against distance from soapstone source.

(Fig. 18.5). Away from sources, soapstone conservation was practiced. Measured by the incidence of repair and reperforation, the level of soapstone conservation is directly attributable to distant from source (Fig. 18.6). This conservation, of course, lends a bias to the archaeological record of soapstone similar to that seen in the use and maintenance of chipped stone raw materials. Thus, when the minimum number of individual slabs at sites is calculated from a sample of sites along the Savannah River (Fig. 18.7), it can be seen that the actual use of soapstone slabs is not as limited as the record seems. This indicates that efforts to bring soapstone into the soapstoneless coastal plain were significant.

CERAMIC VESSELS AND INNOVATIONS FOR DIRECT-HEAT MOIST COOKING

It is in contexts where soapstone was used in the coastal plain, far from sources of raw material, that we find evidence for the earliest pottery in the Savannah River valley. As the functional data described earlier show, the earliest vessels were used as containers for stone cooking, no doubt with soapstone, and they therefore represent a variation on the traditional indirect-heat moist cooking theme.

Shortly after the time these early sites were occupied, coastal populations began to develop innovations in pottery technology to improve its use directly

Fig. 18.6. Mean number of perforations per slab at sites along the Savannah River, plotted against distance from soapstone source.

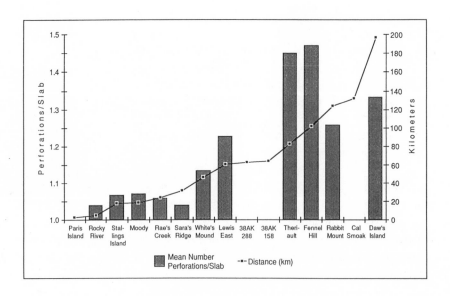

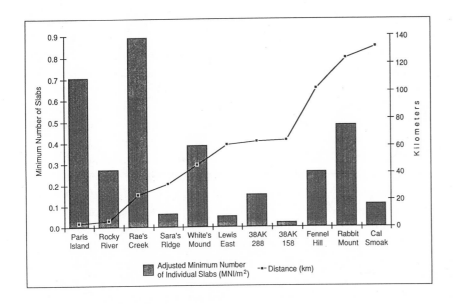

Fig. 18.7. Minimum number of slabs per unit excavation at sites along the Savannah River, plotted against distance from soapstone source.

over fire. The innovations included increased vessel height, thinner walls, rounded bottoms, more uniform thickness, and increased sand in temper. Use-alteration data confirm the increased emphasis on direct-heat cooking: of the 269 coastal vessels with noneroded surfaces I analyzed, 105 (39 percent) showed definite or probable traces of soot. Very little soapstone was used at sites during this time (ca. post-4000 b.p.), and there was virtually no local stone for indirect-heat cooking. Clay substitutes for stone, so-called baked-clay objects, were once thought to have functioned in moist cooking, but because they lack temper, they lack thermal shock resistance and would thus be ill suited to a cooking technique involving rapid changes in temperature. Instead, baked-clay objects were probably used for slow roasting in pits (DePratter 1979:19).

DISCUSSION

The evolution of moist cooking technology in the Savannah River valley appears to have followed a logical trajectory when the inputs and outputs of alternatives are evaluated against a constant demand for increased efficiency. The relative values of the alternatives are modeled in Fig. 18.8. Typical stone cooking media such as quartz entailed few procurement costs and no manufacturing costs but were expensive to use because of their limited use-life. The technique also entailed the costs of making and using containers, principally clay- or hide-lined pits, and baskets. The use of soapstone introduced new procurement costs to indirect-heat cooking, but these were offset by the protracted use-life of this material. Also, the costs of cycling stones from

heat source to container were alleviated somewhat by the superior heat retention properties of soapstone. Compared to soapstone, pottery involved few procurement costs (suitable clay was widely available), although manufacturing costs were undoubtedly higher. The technique of direct-heat cooking with pottery eliminated all of the use-costs involved in stone cooking, and I presume that vessels enjoyed a longer use-life than their nonceramic counterparts.

Problems with the foregoing comparisons are twofold. First, there is no inherent reason for suggesting

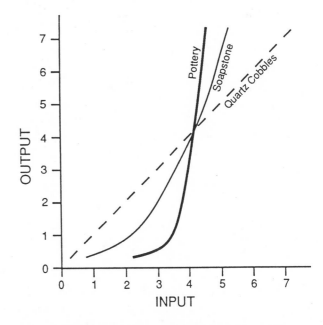

Fig. 18.8. Model of the relative inputs and outputs of alternative moist cooking technologies in the Savannah River valley.

that occupants of the Savannah River valley experienced continuous demand for increased cooking efficiency. It seems apparent, instead, that the observed changes from indirect-heat cooking to the use of pottery have been read as manifestations of broader economic trends for increased efficiency (e.g., Caldwell 1958; Goodyear 1988). This is not to say that demands for increased efficiency were not realized, only that the sources of the demands are not specified.

Second, the unit of analysis implicit to the input-output comparison is the individual or individual production unit (e.g., household), so it does not take into account factors important to social relations among individuals. This is especially significant for soapstone because it was traded from piedmont source areas to the coastal plain and thus had some role in replicating relations of exchange that minimized the costs of procurement.

Both of these analytical shortcomings can be addressed in a consideration of the roles of alternative technologies in social reproduction. My use of the term *social reproduction* here refers to the social actions individuals take to reproduce conditions necessary for production (Hindess and Hirst 1975). Such actions include reciprocal exchange, alliance building, defense, boundary maintenance, marriage, and anything else that involves obligations, benevolent or otherwise, among individuals that affect decisions about the allocation of personal time and energy. I maintain that demands stemming from social reproduction, even efforts to assert egalitarian relations (Trigger 1990; Woodburn 1980, 1982), often lead to technological change (Bender 1978, 1985), and conversely, that change may be resisted even when the benefits of new technology, measured in simple microeconomic terms, represent a substantial improvement over traditional technology. Moreover, because social reproduction is manipulated through exchanges or alliances that affect individual decisions about the allocation of labor and time, technological changes are, at best, only indirectly related to particular subsistence or environmental conditions (Bender 1978).

Alternative Cooking Technology and Social Reproduction

Traditional indirect-heat stone cooking involved few obligations among individuals. Access to raw materials for cooking stones was likely direct for all individuals, and the construction and maintenance of nonceramic

containers posed few opportunities for differentiation or specialization. I hasten to note, however, that the use of an indirect-heat cooking technology for the bulk processing of nut oil may have entailed a technical division of labor to accommodate what surely were costly investments in collecting, grinding, and rendering nuts. Unfortunately, there are currently no means to explore this proposition empirically.

The inception of soapstone use at about 5000 b.p. presented a potentially different set of social relations. Other sources of cooking stones were used in the area for well over four millennia. The superiority of soapstone over the alternatives is unequivocal, but the costs of procurement were high except for users close to outcrops. The volume of use near source areas was considerable, but as I demonstrated earlier, soapstone was also used in significant quantities at sites more than 150 kilometers from outcrops. At these distances, the benefits of using soapstone probably did not outweigh the costs of procurement. Instead, the benefits of soapstone resided not in the material itself but in the social obligations it represented. In the first few centuries of the Late Archaic period, many different sources of soapstone were introduced into the Atlantic Coastal Plain, reflecting, perhaps, the existence of a wide, decentralized network of trading partners. Accordingly, I suggest that soapstone was simply one among many media of exchange that symbolized relations of reciprocity within the local population.

But to attract and keep trading partners, coastal plain inhabitants had to engage in nonsubsistence production that increased demands on personal time and energy. It is at this level that incentives for the adoption of ceramic vessel technology were likely realized. It is significant, however, that for at least two centuries, vessel use among recipients of soapstone in the coastal plain was limited to indirect-heat cooking. What is more, the simple innovation of an indirect-heat ceramic basin was not adopted by piedmont groups who produced soapstone for exchange. I read this pattern as a network of interdependence and mutual obligation wherein the loss of individual gains to be experienced by using more efficient vessel technology was offset by social benefits. In this sense, social reproduction took precedence over individual production.

This scenario becomes all the more interesting when we consider that innovations for direct-heat cooking were eventually adopted across the area, but pots were not routinely used over fire by interior inhabitants. For the period after which these innovations appeared (i.e., after 4000 b.p.) only 13 of 236 vessels (6 percent) with noneroded surfaces from interior sites have traces of soot, compared to 105 of 269 vessels (39 percent) from coastal sites (Sassaman 1993a:162–63). Like those from the coast, vessels from large interior sites such as Stallings Island (Claflin 1931) embody all the design properties of direct-heat cooking vessels, yet they continued to be used as containers for stone cooking. Was the innovation of direct-heat cooking with pottery a threat to the perpetuation of social obligations predicated on soapstone exchange?

Examples of social constraints on technological choice are legion in ethnographic and ethnohistoric literature. Individuals in all Yanomamö villages know how to make pottery, and suitable clays are ubiquitous, but pottery manufacture is restricted to certain villages that export it to nonproducing villages through reciprocal exchange alliances (Chagnon 1977:100–101). In this case, the desire to maintain exchange alliances outweighs any desire for economic autonomy. Similarly, the Chumash Indians of California are said to have resisted the imposition of ceramic vessel technology by neighboring groups in the interest of perpetuating the exchange networks of their traditional basket and soapstone cooking technology (Hudson and Blackburn 1983:207–209).

That the introduction of new technology can undermine traditional social relations is well documented in anthropological literature. Snowmobile use among Eskimos (Hall 1978) and the introduction of steel axes in Australia (Sharp 1952) are two famous examples. In an archaeological case, Bronze Age Europe experienced significant social and economic transformation with the spread of iron metallurgy in the seventh century b.c. Wealth in Bronze Age society was dependent on one's access to copper and tin. Because these resources were highly localized, individuals with direct access gained power and wealth through control of their distribution. Being more widely available, iron ore was obtainable by practically everyone, so positions of privilege were undermined as individuals abandoned bronze technology for iron (Sander van der Leeuw, personal communication, 1987). Similarly, the introduction of the bow and arrow and ceramic vessel innovations in the Late Woodland period of eastern North America may have weakened the prestige structure of exchange networks by diminishing the need for economic cooperation among households (Blitz 1988; Muller 1986:148).

Each of these cases illustrates the importance of certain individuals or groups in influencing the pathways and rates of innovation diffusion. I suggest that this sort of importance was likewise a critical element in the emergence of pottery in the Savannah River valley. Individuals with direct access to soapstone had the potential to manipulate alliances and hence control labor. A variety of strategies may have been used to meet social demands on labor (e.g., communal fishing, storage), some of which placed constraints on groups' ability to fission (e.g., Filios 1990; Root 1983), and these strategies probably contributed to the need for more efficient technology. Yet because the medium of traditional cooking technology (soapstone) was fundamental to social transactions, individuals were reluctant to adopt an innovation that would render traditional technology obsolete. Obviously, other media of exchange were important to social transactions in the Late Archaic, so why would a single material have so much influence on the technological decisions of individuals? The answer, I believe, lies in the power of certain individuals to manipulate soapstone exchange in ways that produced benefits, real or perceived, to those in less privileged positions of access. Such power was probably legitimated in the contexts of public ceremony and ritual.

Settlement patterns after about 4000 b.p. in the middle Savannah River valley included relatively large-scale aggregations at sites such as Stallings Island (Claflin 1931) and Lake Spring (Miller 1949). These occupations provided opportunities for public ritual, including mortuary rites, marriages, and rites of passage. Although hard evidence for such ritual eludes us, the immense accumulation of food refuse, including much shellfish, is suggestive, if not convincing, evidence for public feasting. Pottery presumably played an important role in feasting, as did soapstone cooking slabs, which have been found at Stallings Island by the thousands.

These sites have also yielded many sherds of an unusual vessel form that is not found elsewhere in appreciable numbers. The carinated bowl, reminiscent of Mississippian-period *casuela* bowls (Hally 1986), was evidently a serving vessel. A variety of sizes have been observed, but many bowls are large (orifice diameter greater than 40 cm), and all are highly decorated with incising and punctation. Both attributes point to a public context for their use (Hally 1986; Wobst 1977). Interestingly, of the few vessels from Savannah River valley sites that show traces of soot, many are carinated bowls. This suggests that the local acceptance of a direct-heat technique (presumably to *re*heat food) took place in the context of public feasting, a finding similar to that of Clark and Blake's (1993) for the emergence of pottery in coastal Chiapas. But despite this innovative use, I point out again that the vast majority of vessels were used in traditional ways. Thus, while the public context of feasting served to reaffirm social obligations and legitimate positions of prestige, any social demands individuals experienced in the allocation of labor were not mitigated by technological change.

The social contradictions of these conditions appear to have been played out in at least two ways. First, settlement in the middle Savannah River valley involved fall dispersal at sites along tributaries (Sassaman et al. 1990). Camps were small in size and widely distributed across the upland zone. Although dispersed groups were probably autonomous, it was hardly a time of social isolation. Dispersed well into the uplands, individuals had direct access to neighbors from adjacent river valleys. Through visiting and exchange, alternative alliances may have formed. Importantly, there appear to have been no social or political constraints to building alliances, or at least none that could be enforced in the decentralized, private contexts of upland settlement. The innovations of pottery and direct-heat cooking may have served these alliance-building efforts well, especially considering that nut oil processing for overwintering provided opportunities for channeling production into alliance formations. Some empirical support for this model has been amassed (Sassaman 1993a), but there is much to be done to test specific propositions stemming from the model. The important point is that pottery innovations in the Savannah River valley probably moved more quickly and unfettered in the peripheral areas of territory occupied by the river-based population. This has implications for the regional spread of pottery that I will later return to briefly.

A second way in which social contradictions were played out is in the stylistic expression of potters. Stallings fiber-tempered pottery is highly diverse in its surface treatments, which include plain, random punctated, linear punctation, "drag and jab" punctated, incised, and simple stamped (Fig. 18.9). Among the 459 punctated vessels I examined recently (Sassaman 1993a), 18 different punctation styluses were used, and variations in the placement, orientation, and execution of the punctations ensured that no two vessels were alike.

How does all this individualistic expression represent the resolution of social contradiction? A recent article by Polly Wiessner (1989) provides one possible

Fig. 18.9. Sample of design variation of Stallings fiber-tempered pottery from sites in the Savannah River valley.

answer. Wiessner examines the role of style in the social identification of individuals. Drawing on the psychological theory of social identification via comparison, she suggests that efforts to project individuality are important in contexts of social conformity, and while this is abundantly evident in complex societies, such "motivation may be linked to the evolution of reciprocity in that those who can present positive images to others will be more likely to be successful in relationships of delayed reciprocity that are critical for economic security" (Wiessner 1989:57). Thus, the expression of individual style on fiber-tempered pottery from sites such as Stallings Island may signify the efforts of individuals to manipulate alliances outside of soapstone exchange.

This scenario begs the issue of gender relations, for if we assume that women in Late Archaic society made and decorated pottery, then the expression of individualism may represent a sort of alternative discourse in public contexts. Elsewhere I addressed the issue of gender relations as it pertains to shellfishing, the emergence of pottery, and changing political roles of women (Sassaman 1992), but I have not yet examined style from a gender perspective. This indeed seems a promising avenue for future investigations.

Expanding the Scale of Analysis

The centripetal forces that caused people to aggregate at riverine sites in the middle Savannah River valley dissolved around 3500 b.p. The outcome was a complete reorganization of the social landscape, with groups occupying upland sites more frequently and for longer periods of time. Alternative, dispersed networks of social alliance, as I alluded to earlier, took the place of the centralized networks and served to catalyze the spread of innovations associated with direct-heat moist cooking. As traditional alliances dissolved and new ones emerged, stylistic variation in pottery appears to have burgeoned,[2] suggesting that options for individual enterprise in concert with dissolution of the traditional social order encouraged individuals (women) to find new solutions to demands on their labor. I suspect that adopting new technology and building new alliances went hand in hand. I should add that elaborate decoration on fiber-tempered pottery disappears after about 3400 b.p., reflecting perhaps a period of stability in the changing social order, or, more simply, that pottery was no longer an important medium of individual expression.

This time period also marked the beginnings of pottery use in other parts of the greater Southeast. Fiber-tempered pottery of the Wheeler series and related wares appears in limited areas of the Midsouth and Gulf Coast as early as 3600 b.p. (New World Research 1988:10–13; Stowe 1991), gaining increasing use over the ensuing centuries, particularly in the middle Tennessee and Tombigbee river valleys of Alabama, until supplanted by sand-tempered wares around 2500 b.p. (Jenkins and Krause 1986:43). Jenkins and colleagues proposed years ago that the westward spread of pottery was facilitated by the Poverty Point trade network (Webb 1982), particularly the commerce in soapstone vessels that involved the westward exportation of raw material from sources in the Alabama-Georgia piedmont (Jenkins 1982; Jenkins et al. 1986; Walthall and Jenkins 1976). The model implies that individuals in

the Poverty Point exchange network were key agents in innovation diffusion, and the development of such a trading network was a precondition for the westward spread of pottery.

As an alternative to the Jenkins model, I suggest that Poverty Point soapstone exchange inhibited technological change much in the same manner that soapstone exchange inhibited change in the Savannah River valley (Sassaman 1993a:222–28). This argument is supported by the fact that pottery was not widely used across the greater Southeast until 2500 b.p., after the social formations that supported the Poverty Point exchange network dissolved. Processes of dissolution similar to those I described for the Savannah River valley may be implicated here, and I suggest that the processes are indeed regional in scale. This implies a certain amount of interconnectedness among the constituent societies of the greater Southeast that affected both the regional distribution of labor (e.g., Kowalewski 1995) and the decisions individuals made concerning the allocation of personal labor. But in continued efforts to understand these processes, we should avoid generalizations about the particular forms and directions of technological change in particular settings. Indeed, historical and cultural contexts will be of the utmost importance in explaining the change, or lack of change, in a given area. Alternating scales of analysis from local to regional, from individual to society, and from synchronic to diachronic is an effective approach to unraveling these processes (e.g., Marquardt 1985, 1992).

Conclusion

An economic model of technological change that focuses on the inputs and outputs of energy or other currency is an effective tool for understanding technological choice from the perspective of isolated production units. It is not as effective, however, in illuminating the relative costs and benefits of perpetuating the social relations that are a precondition for production. If we are willing to argue that hunter-gatherer societies are composed of relatively autonomous production units of equal abilities and with egalitarian relations among them, then we are left with no basis for internally generated change and are forced to put external inputs like climatic change at the forefront of explanation. Current thinking among hunter-gatherer specialists, however, renders this line of reasoning untenable (e.g., chapters in Ingold et al. 1988a, 1988b; Leacock and Lee 1982; Schire 1984). A model of social reproduction brings to the fore the fundamental social basis of hunter-gatherer production (reciprocity) while also emphasizing the potential for inequality to effect change. My analysis of the pottery in the Savannah River valley suggests that technology capable of improving the productivity of individual labor was subordinated by options that served to perpetuate social obligations among individuals. It also shows that obligations were not symmetrical because of the manipulation of a localized medium of exchange. Manipulation extended to the perpetuation of traditional technology and became manifested, for some, as a contradiction between tradition and innovation.

It is important to note that my argument about the relevance of social factors in technological change does not deny the relevance of technofunctional or energetic data in explaining choices among alternatives. Rather, the juxtaposition of what makes sense economically and what is socially acceptable exposes the contradictions that effect change. No social theory would have helped to document the technofunctional variation of fiber-tempered pottery seen in the Southeast. Similarly, no theory ignoring the social contexts of technology could explain the technofunctional patterns so documented.

Acknowledgments

I thank Bill Barnett and John Hoopes for inviting me to contribute to their symposium on early pottery at the 1993 SAA meetings in St. Louis, and to this volume. My thanks also to John Clark and Augusto Oyuela-Caycedo for comments on an earlier draft of this chapter. Support for this research was provided by the United States Department of Energy–Savannah River under contract number DE-FC09-88SR15199. Figures 18.5–18.7 are reproduced from Sassaman (1993a) by permission of the University of Alabama Press.

Notes

1. The association yields a chi-square value of 11.101 with 1 degree of freedom at < .01 level of significance.

2. A thorough comparison of stylistic change is the subject of another paper altogether, but suffice it to say that upland assemblages such as the one from Tinker Creek (38AK224) (Sassaman et al. 1990) reflect as much, if not more, stylistic diversity than Stallings Island assemblages, despite their relatively small size.

References Cited

Adair, James
1930   *Adair's History of the American Indians* (originally published 1775), edited by Samuel Cole Williams. Promontory Press, New York.

Anderson, David G., and J. W. Joseph
1988   *Prehistory and History along the Upper Savannah River: Technical Synthesis of Cultural Resource Investigations, Richard B. Russell Multiple Resource Area.* Russell Papers, Atlanta Interagency Archaeological Services Division, National Park Service.

Bender, Barbara
1978   Gatherer-Hunter to Farmer: A Social Perspective. *World Archaeology* 10:204–23.
1985   Emergent Tribal Formations in the American Midcontinent. *American Antiquity* 50:52–62.

Bender, Barbara, and Brian Morris
1988   Twenty Years of History, Evolution and Social Change in Gatherer-Hunter Studies. In *Hunters and Gatherers 1: History, Evolution and Social Change,* edited by T. Ingold, D. Riches, and J. Woodburn, pp. 4–14. Berg, Oxford.

Blitz, John H.
1988   Adoption of the Bow in Prehistoric North America. *North American Archaeologist* 9:123–45.

Braun, David P.
1983   Pots as Tools. In *Archaeological Hammers and Theories,* edited by J. A. Moore and A. S. Keene, pp. 107–34. Academic Press, New York.

Bronitsky, G., and R. Hamer
1986   Experiments in Ceramic Technology: The Effects of Various Tempering Materials on Impact and Thermal Shock Resistance. *American Antiquity* 51:89–101.

Brooks, Mark J., Donald J. Colquhoun, and Kenneth E. Sassaman
1990   Buried Sites in South Carolina's Estuaries: Possibilities and Implications. *COSCAPA Newsletter* 11(1):5.

Brown, James A.
1989   The Beginnings of Pottery as an Economic Process. In *What's New? A Closer Look at the Process of Innovation,* edited by S. E. van der

Leeuw and R. Torrence, pp. 203–24. Unwin
Hyman, London.

Caldwell, Joseph R.
1958   *Trend and Tradition in the Prehistory of the
        Eastern United States.* American Anthro-
        pological Association Memoir 88.
        Washington, D.C.

Chagnon, Napoleon
1977   *Yanomamö: The Fierce People.* 2d ed. Holt,
        Reinhart and Winston, New York.

Claassen, Cheryl
1986   Shellfishing Seasons in the Prehistoric South-
        eastern United States. *American Antiquity*
        51:21–37.

Claflin, William H., Jr.
1931   *The Stalling's Island Mound, Columbia County,
        Georgia.* Peabody Museum of American Ar-
        chaeology and Ethnology Papers 14(1).

Clark, John E., and Michael Blake
1993   The Power of Prestige: Competitive
        Generosity and the Emergence of Rank
        Societies in Lowland Mesoamerica. In
        *Factional Competition and Political Development
        in the New World,* edited by E. M. Brumfiel
        and J. W. Fox, pp. 17–30. Cambridge
        University Press, Cambridge.

Cowan, C. Wesley
1985   Understanding the Evolution of Plant
        Husbandry in Eastern North America:
        Lessons from Botany, Ethnography and
        Archaeology. In *Prehistoric Food Production in
        North America,* edited by R. I. Ford, pp. 205–
        43. Anthropological Papers 75, Museum of
        Anthropology, University of Michigan, Ann
        Arbor.

Delcourt, Paul A., and Hazel R. Delcourt
1987   *Long-Term Forest Dynamics of the Temperate
        Zone.* Springer-Verlag, New York.

DePratter, Chester B.
1979   Shellmound Archaic on the Georgia Coast.
        South Carolina Antiquities 11(2):1–69.

Driver, Harold E., and William C. Massey
1957   *Comparative Studies of North American Indians.*
        Transactions of the American Philosophical
        Society 47(2). Philadelphia.

Dye, David H.
1976   The Bilbo Site Revisited: Archaeological
        Investigations from Chatham County,
        Georgia. M.A. thesis, Department of
        Geography and Anthropology, Louisiana
        State University, Baton Rouge.

Ebeling, Walter
1986   *Handbook of Indian Foods and Fibers in Arid
        America.* University of California Press,
        Berkeley.

Ellen, Roy
1988   Foraging, Starch Extraction and the Sedentary
        Lifestyle in the Lower Rainforest of Central
        Seram. In *Hunters and Gatherers 1: History,
        Evolution and Social Change,* edited by T.
        Ingold, D. Riches, and J. Woodburn,
        pp. 117–34. Berg, Oxford.

Filios, Elena L.
1990   Thresholds to Group Fissioning among
        Hunters and Gatherers: An Archaeological
        Perspective. Ph.D. dissertation, Department
        of Anthropology, University of Massachu-
        setts, Amherst.

Ford, James A.
1966   Early Formative Cultures in Georgia and
        Florida. *American Antiquity* 31:781–99.
1969   *A Comparison of Formative Cultures in the
        Americas.* Smithsonian Contributions to
        Anthropology 11. Washington, D.C.

Freer, Jennifer A.
1992   Late Archaic Subsistence Economy at Midden
        Point, Georgia. Paper presented at the 49th
        annual meeting of the Southeastern Ar-
        chaeological Conference, Little Rock,
        Arkansas.

Gardner, Paul S.
1986   Carbonized Plant Remains from Paris Island
        South (9EB21), Sara's Ridge (38AN29), and
        Simpson's Field (38AN8). In *Prehistory in the
        Richard B. Russell Reservoir: The Archaic and
        Woodland Periods of the Upper Savannah River,*
        edited by W. D. Wood, pp. 387–92. Russell
        Papers, Atlanta Interagency Archaeological
        Services Division, National Park Service.

Gayton, A. H.
1948   Yokuts and Western Mono Ethnography,
        II: Northern Foothill Yokuts and Mono
        Ethnography. *University of California
        Anthropological Records* 10:143–301.

Goodyear, Albert C.
1988   On the Study of Technological Change.
        Current Anthropology 29:320–23.

Hall, Edwin S., Jr.
1978   Technological Change in Northern Alaska.
        In *Archaeological Essays in Honor of Irving B.
        Rouse,* edited by R. C. Dunnell and E. S.
        Hall, Jr., pp. 209–29. Mouton, The Hague.

Hally, David J.
1983   Use Alterations of Pottery Vessel Surfaces:
        An Important Source of Evidence for the
        Identification of Vessel Function. *North
        American Archaeologist* 4:3–26.
1986   The Identification of Vessel Function: A Case
        Study from Northwest Georgia. *American
        Antiquity* 51:267–95.

Hindess, B., and P. Hirst
1975   *Precapitalist Modes of Production.* Routledge and Kegan Paul, London.

Hudson, Charles M.
1976   *The Southeastern Indians.* University of Tennessee Press, Knoxville.

Hudson, Travis, and Thomas C. Blackburn
1983   *The Material Culture of the Chumash Interaction Sphere, vol. II: Food Preparation and Shelter.* Ballenna Press, Menlo Park, California.

Ingold, Tim, David Riches, and James Woodburn (eds.)
1988a   *Hunters and Gatherers 1: History, Evolution and Social Change.* Berg, Oxford.
1988b   *Hunters and Gatherers 2: Property, Power and Ideology.* Berg, Oxford.

Jenkins, Ned J.
1982   Archaeology of the Gainesville Lake Area: Synthesis. In *Archaeological Investigations in the Gainesville Lake Area of the Tennessee-Tombigbee Waterway,* vol. 5. Report of Investigations 23, Office of Archaeological Research, University of Alabama, Tuscaloosa.

Jenkins, Ned J., David H. Dye, and John A. Walthall
1986   Early Ceramic Development in the Gulf Coastal Plain. In *Early Woodland Archaeology,* edited by K. B. Farnsworth and T. E. Emerson, pp. 546–63. Kampsville Seminars in Archaeology, no. 2. Center for American Archaeology Press, Kampsville, Illinois.

Jenkins, Ned J., and Richard A. Krause
1986   *The Tombigbee Watershed in Southeastern Prehistory.* University of Alabama Press, Tuscaloosa.

Klippel, Walter, and Darcy Morey
1986   Contextual and Nutritional Analysis of Freshwater Gastropods from Middle Archaic Deposits at the Hays Site, Middle Tennessee. *American Antiquity* 51:799–813.

Kowalewski, Stephen A.
1995   Large-Scale Ecology in Aboriginal Eastern North America. In *Native American Interaction: Multiscalar Analyses and Interpretations in the Eastern Woodlands,* edited by M. S. Nassaney and K. E. Sassaman. University of Tennessee Press, Knoxville. In press.

Kroeber, A. L.
1925   *Handbook of the Indians of California.* Bureau of American Ethnology Bulletin 78. Smithsonian Institution, Washington, D.C.

Leacock, Eleanor B., and Richard B. Lee (eds.)
1982   *Politics and History in Band Societies.* Cambridge University Press, Cambridge.

Linton, Ralph
1944   North American Cooking Pots. *American Antiquity* 9:369–80.

Lourandos, Harry
1988   Palaeopolitics: Resource Intensification in Aboriginal Australia and Papua New Guinea. In *Hunters and Gatherers 1: History, Evolution and Social Change,* edited by T. Ingold, D. Riches, and J. Woodburn, pp. 148–60. Berg, Oxford.

Marquardt, William H.
1985   Complexity and Scale in the Study of Fisher-Gatherer-Hunters: An Example from the Eastern United States. In *Prehistoric Hunter-Gatherers: The Emergence of Cultural Complexity,* edited by T. D. Price and J. A. Brown, pp. 59–98. Academic Press, Orlando, Florida.
1992   Dialectical Archaeology. In *Archaeological Method and Theory,* vol. 4, edited by M. B. Schiffer, pp. 101–40. University of Arizona Press, Tucson.

Milanich, Jerald T., and Charles H. Fairbanks
1980   *Florida Archaeology.* Academic Press, New York.

Miller, Carl F.
1949   The Lake Spring Site, Columbia County, Georgia. *American Antiquity* 15:254–58.

Moore, Josselyn F.
1985   Archaeobotanical Analyses at Five Sites in the Richard B. Russell Reservoir, Georgia and South Carolina. In *Prehistoric Human Ecology along the Upper Savannah River: Excavations at the Rucker's Bottom, Abbeville and Bullard Site Groups,* assembled by D. G. Anderson and J. Schuldenrein, pp. 673–94. Russell Papers, Atlanta Interagency Archaeological Services Division, National Park Service.

Muller, Jon
1986   *Archaeology of the Lower Ohio Valley.* Academic Press, Orlando, Florida.

New World Research
1988   *Cultural Resource Testing on the Mobile Bay Pipeline Project, Choctaw, Washington, and Mobile Counties, Alabama.* New World Research, Inc., Report of Investigations 167. Ft. Walton Beach, Florida.

O'Neale, Lila M.
1932   Yurok-Karok Basket Weavers. *University of California Publications in American Archaeology and Ethnology* 32:1–184.

Ozker, Doreen
1982   *An Early Woodland Community at the Schultz Site 20SA2 in the Saginaw Valley and the Nature of the Early Woodland Adaptation in the Great Lakes Region.* Anthropological Papers 70, Museum of Anthropology, University of Michigan, Ann Arbor.

Peterson, Drexel
1971   Time and Settlement in the Archaeology
        of Groton Plantation. Ph.D. dissertation,
        Department of Anthropology, Harvard
        University.
1980   The Introduction, Use and Technology of
        Fiber-Tempered Pottery in the Southeastern
        United States. In *Early Native Americans,*
        edited by D. L. Browman, pp. 363–72.
        Mouton, The Hague.

Reid, Kenneth C.
1984   Fire and Ice: New Evidence for the Pro-
        duction and Preservation of Late Archaic
        Fiber-Tempered Pottery in the Middle-
        Latitude Lowlands. *American Antiquity*
        49:55–76.
1989   A Materials Science Perspective on Hunter-
        Gatherer Pottery. In *Pottery Technology: Ideas•
        and Approaches,* edited by G. Bronitsky,
        pp. 167–80. Westview Press, Boulder,
        Colorado.

Rice, Prudence M.
1987   *Pottery Analysis: A Sourcebook.* University of
        Chicago Press, Chicago.

Root, Dolores
1983   Information Exchange and the Spatial Con-
        figurations of Egalitarian Societies. In
        Archaeological Hammers and Theories, edited
        by J. A. Moore and A. S. Keene, pp. 193–219.
        Academic Press, New York.

Russo, Michael, Barbara A. Purdy, Lee A. Newsome, and
Ray M. McGee
1992   A Reinterpretation of Late Archaic Adap-
        tations in Central-East Florida: Groves'
        Orange Midden (8-Vo-2601). *Southeastern
        Archaeology* 11:95–108.

Rye, O. S.
1981   *Pottery Technology.* Taraxacum Manuals in
        Archaeology 4. Taraxacum, Washington,
        D.C.

Sassaman, Kenneth E.
1992   Gender and Technology at the Archaic-
        Woodland "Transition." In *Exploring Gender
        through Archaeology: Selected Papers from the
        1991 Boone Conference,* edited by C. Claassen,
        pp. 71–79. Prehistory Press, Madison,
        Wisconsin.
1993a   *Early Pottery in the Southeast: Tradition and
        Innovation in Cooking Technology.* University
        of Alabama Press, Tuscaloosa.
1993b   *Early Woodland Settlement in the Aiken Plateau:
        Archaeological Investigations at 38AK157,
        Savannah River Site, Aiken County, South
        Carolina.* Savannah River Archaeological
        Research Papers 3, South Carolina Institute

of Archaeology and Anthropology, Univer-
        sity of South Carolina, Columbia.

Sassaman, Kenneth E., Mark J. Brooks, Glen T. Hanson,
and David G. Anderson
1990   *Native American Prehistory of the Middle
        Savannah River Valley: A Synthesis of Ar-
        chaeological Investigations on the Savannah
        River Site, Aiken and Barnwell Counties, South
        Carolina.* Savannah River Archaeological Re-
        search Papers 1, South Carolina Institute of
        Archaeology and Anthropology, University
        of South Carolina, Columbia.

Schiffer, Michael B., and James M. Skibo
1987   Theory and Experiment in the Study of
        Technological Change. *Current Anthropol-
        ogy* 28:595–622.

Schrire, Carmel (ed.)
1984   *Past and Present in Hunter-Gatherer Studies.*
        Academic Press, Orlando, Florida.

Sharp, Lauriston
1952   Steel Axes for Stone Age Australians. In
        *Human Problems in Technological Change: A
        Casebook,* edited by E. H. Spicer, pp. 69–90.
        Sage, New York.

Skibo, James M.
1992   *Pottery Function: A Use-Alteration Perspective.*
        Plenum Press, New York.

Skibo, James M., David J. Hally, and Michael B. Schiffer
1988   *The Manufacture and Use of Fiber-Tempered
        Pottery from the Southeastern United States.* Paper
        presented at the 53d annual meeting of the
        Society for American Archaeology, New
        Orleans, Louisiana.

Skibo, James M., Michael B. Schiffer, and
Kenneth C. Reid
1989   Organic-Tempered Pottery: An Experimental
        Study. *American Antiquity* 54:122–46.

Speth, John D., and Katherine A. Spielmann
1983   Energy Source, Protein Metabolism, and
        Hunter-Gatherer Subsistence Strategies.
        Journal of Anthropological Archaeology
        2:1–31.

Ste.Claire, Dana
1990   The Archaic in East Florida: Archaeological
        Evidence for Early Coastal Adaptations. *The
        Florida Anthropologist* 43:189–97.

Stoltman, James B.
1972   The Late Archaic in the Savannah River
        Region. In *Fiber-Tempered Pottery in
        Southeastern United States and Northern
        Colombia: Its Origins, Context and Significance,*
        edited by R. P. Bullen and J. B. Stoltman,
        pp. 37–62. Florida Anthropological Society
        Publications, no. 6. *The Florida Anthropologist*
        25(2), part 2.

1974   *Groton Plantation: An Archaeological Study of a
         South Carolina Locality.* Monographs of the
         Peabody Museum 1, Harvard University,
         Cambridge.

Stowe, Noel R.
1991   The Gulf Formational Stage on the North
         Central Gulf Coast. Paper presented at the
         12th annual meeting of the Mid-South Ar-
         chaeological Conference, Mississippi State,
         Mississippi.

Swanton, John R.
1946   *The Indians of the Southeastern United States.*
         Bureau of American Ethnology Bulletin 137.
         Smithsonian Institution, Washington, D.C.

Tippitt, V. Ann, and William H. Marquardt
1984   *Archaeological Investigations at Gregg Shoals, A
         Deeply Stratified Site on the Savannah River.*
         Russell Papers, Atlanta Interagency Ar-
         chaeological Services Division, National
         Park Service.

Trigger, Bruce G.
1990   Maintaining Economic Equality in
         Opposition to Complexity: An Iroquoian
         Case Study. In *The Evolution of Political
         Systems: Sociopolitics in Small-Scale Sedentary
         Societies,* edited by Steadman Upham,
         pp. 119–45. Cambridge University Press,
         Cambridge.

Trinkley, Michael B.
1976   Paleoethnobotanical Remains from Archaic-
         Woodland Transitional Shell Middens along
         the South Carolina Coast. *Southeastern
         Archaeological Conference Bulletin* 19:64–67.
1980   Investigation of the Woodland Period along
         the South Carolina Coast. Ph.D. dissertation,
         Department of Anthropology, University of
         North Carolina, Chapel Hill.

Trinkley, Michael B. (ed.)
1986   *Indian and Freedman Occupation at the Fish Haul
         Site (38BU805), Beaufort County, South Caro-
         lina.* Chicora Foundation Research Series 7.
         Columbia, South Carolina.

van der Leeuw, Sander
1984   Pottery Manufacture: Some Complications for
         the Study of Trade. In *Pots and Potters: Current
         Approaches in Ceramic Archaeology,* edited by P.
         M. Rice, pp. 55–70. Monograph 24, Institute
         of Archaeology, University of California, Los
         Angeles.

Waddell, Gene
1980   *Indians of the South Carolina Lowcountry 1562–
         1751.* Southern Program Studies, University
         of South Carolina, Columbia.

Walthall, John A., and Ned J. Jenkins
1976   The Gulf Formative Stage in Southeastern
         Prehistory. *Bulletin of the Southeastern Ar-
         chaeological Conference* 19:43–49.

Waring, Antonio J., Jr.
1968   The Bilbo Site, Chatham County, Georgia
         (originally published 1940). In *The Waring
         Papers: The Collected Works of Antonio J.
         Waring, Jr.,* edited by S. Williams, pp. 152–97.
         Papers of the Peabody Museum of Ar-
         chaeology and Ethnology, vol. 58. Harvard
         University, Cambridge, Massachusetts.

Webb, Clarence H.
1982   *The Poverty Point Culture.* 2d ed. *Geoscience and
         Man* 17. School of Geoscience, Louisiana State
         University, Baton Rouge.

Weinand, Daniel
1992   Vertebrate Remains from the Late Archaic
         Stallings Island Site: Economic Interpretation
         through Zooarchaeological Techniques. Paper
         presented at the 49th annual meeting of the
         Southeastern Archaeological Conference,
         Little Rock, Arkansas.

White, John W.
1982   An Integration of Late Archaic Settlement
         Patterns for the South Carolina Piedmont.
         M.A. Thesis, Department of Anthropology,
         University of Arkansas, Fayetteville.

Wiessner, Polly
1982   Risk, Reciprocity and Social Influences on
         !Kung San Economics. In *Politics and History in
         Band Societies,* edited by E. B. Leacock and R.
         B. Lee, pp. 61–84. Cambridge University
         Press, Cambridge.
1989   Style and Changing Relations between the
         Individual and Society. In *The Meaning of
         Things: Material Culture and Symbolic Ex-
         pression,* edited by I. Hodder, pp. 56–63.
         Unwin-Hyman, London.

Wobst, H. Martin
1977   Stylistic Behavior and Information Exchange.
         In *Papers for the Director: Research Essays in
         Honor of James B. Griffin,* edited by C. E.
         Cleland, pp. 317–42. Anthropological Papers
         61, Museum of Anthropology, University of
         Michigan, Ann Arbor.

Woodburn, James
1980   Hunters and Gatherers Today and
         Reconstruction of the Past. In *Soviet and
         Western Anthropology,* edited by E. Gellner,
         pp. 95–117. Duckworth, London.
1982   Egalitarian Societies. *Man* 17:431–51.

19

Economic Intensification and the Origins of Ceramic Containers in the American Southwest

PATRICIA L. CROWN
AND W. H. WILLS

The greater American Southwest is famous for its wealth of archaeological resources, but only since about 1980 has the chronology of initial ceramic production become well established. Similarly, research during the 1980s and 1990s has dramatically revised the timing of incipient agriculture and the beginnings of sedentary lifeways, making it possible to compare these economic developments with the emergence of ceramic container technology. Consequently, we can now describe the origins of Southwestern ceramic containers with sufficient detail that we can suggest at least the outlines of an explanatory model.

In this chapter we suggest that pottery containers were produced in conjunction with increasing sedentism, reduced territories, and a greater dependence on cultigens. The burdens of pottery production and its associated food processing techniques outweighed the advantages until increased sedentism and increased dependence on cultigens necessitated watertight, pest-resistant containers for storage and thermal shock resistant vessels for direct-fire cooking. The changes in processing and storage technology associated with ceramic containers increased the effective yield and nutritional value of crops. Pottery production altered the labor contribution of women, and scheduling conflicts between pottery production and subsistence pursuits may have delayed the adoption of ceramic containers.

The Earliest Southwestern Ceramic Containers

The American Southwest is an immense region exceeding 400,000 square miles that includes greater biological habitat diversity than any other portion of North America, ranging from extremely hot deserts in the southern Basin and Range province to cold alpine zones in the southern Rocky Mountains. Although generally characterized by aridity, many parts of the region, especially highland areas above 2,000 meters, receive enough precipitation to support dense evergreen forests. Several major river systems, including the Colorado, Gila, and Rio Grande, originate in the montane regions of the northern Southwest but course through lowland deserts. Prehistorically, these river systems represented a predictable and steady source of water for areas of extremely low precipitation. In general, temperature and aridity vary inversely, with areas of high temperatures characterized by low precipitation. Because elevations in the Southwest tend to increase from the low deserts in the south to the higher northern elevations in the Colorado Plateau and adjacent mountainous areas, modern growing season length is generally greatest in the south, while precipitation is higher in the north. Archaeologists divide the entire region after the introduction of ceramic containers into three major culture areas, largely on the basis of architecture, burial practices, and ceramic technology and decorative style: the Hohokam of southern Arizona, the Mogollon in mountainous highlands to the north and east, and the Anasazi of the Colorado Plateau and southern Rocky Mountain areas (Fig. 19.1).

The earliest ceramics consist of figurines from the Milagro site, a Late Archaic pithouse settlement in southeastern Arizona dating to approximately 800 B.C. (Huckell 1990:238–40). Ceramic containers also appeared first in the deserts of southern Arizona, but not until about A.D. 1, during the Red Mountain phase of the Hohokam cultural sequence (Doyel 1991:236). The oldest ceramic vessels in the cooler, northern portions of the Southwest postdate those in the Hohokam region. Ceramic containers in the Anasazi culture area appear between A.D. 200 and 300, and those from the

Mogollon culture area are currently associated with dates ranging from A.D. 200 to 400 (Blinman and Wilson 1993:72; Burton 1991; Eddy 1966:384; Haury and Sayles 1947; LeBlanc 1982; Varien 1990:88–91; Wilson and Blinman 1991). All of the earliest Southwestern ceramics were brown wares with sand inclusions (Wilson and Blinman 1991). In all areas, pottery is recovered in low frequencies until two to three centuries after its initial appearance.

Interestingly, the inception of ceramic container technology was unrelated to the beginning of agriculture. Plant cultivation was clearly important during the Late Archaic period, between 1500 and 1000 B.C., when maize and squash were introduced from Mesoamerica. Moreover, some indigenous plant cultivation (particularly chenopodium and amaranth) probably preceded the acquisition of maize and squash, although this has not yet been confirmed (see Toll and Cully 1983; Winter and Hogan 1986). In contrast, the oldest ceramic containers date a thousand years or more after the adoption of maize and squash, so the use of ceramic containers in the Southwest did not originate with the beginnings of plant cultivation.

Fig. 19.1. Major cultural divisions in the greater American Southwest.

Nevertheless, ceramic containers were first made by populations experiencing distinct shifts toward greater reliance on food production. The evidence for this conclusion consists in part of larger and more residentially stable settlements characterized by substantial pithouse architecture, numerous and large storage pits, dense midden deposits, burials, and chronometric indications of extended site use. Because extended settlement occupation required greater productivity from smaller catchment areas, cultigens are assumed to have comprised a larger portion of the diet than they did during the Archaic, an assumption supported by pollen and macrobotanical data, the presence of larger and more numerous storage facilities, and the development of specialized milling tools (trough metates and two-hand rectangular manos).[1]

The earliest evidence for qualitative changes in residential stability occurred during the Late Archaic in the broad river valleys of southeastern Arizona, where researchers have documented numerous large pithouse sites dating to about 800 B.C. (Eddy 1958; Huckell 1988, 1990; Roth 1989). Late Archaic peoples could harvest the rich plant foods of the southern Arizona desert over longer portions of each yearly seasonal cycle than in other portions of the Southwest, owing to lengthy growing seasons, and apparently the addition of maize promoted a fairly rapid adoption of at least seasonally sedentary strategies (Fish, Fish, and Madsen 1990; Huckell 1990). Manufacture of ceramic containers during the Red Mountain phase in southern Arizona thus followed several centuries of locally intensive residential systems in which maize cultivation and storage played a major role. Doyel (1991: 242) suggests, however, that the Red Mountain phase may have been characterized by more intensive farming techniques, with permanent villages located along major drainages.

A different picture of the temporal relationships among ceramic containers, agriculture, and sedentism emerged in other portions of the Southwest. In the cool temperate Colorado Plateau and adjoining montane areas, the oldest dates for maize, squash, and beans pre-date the oldest dates for cultigens in the deserts of southern Arizona, yet evidence for residential stability comparable to that found by 800 B.C. in Arizona does not appear in the northern Southwest until 200 B.C., and not widely until after A.D. 200.[2] As in the desert regions, however, the development of ceramic containers coincided with a trend toward greater emphasis on local economies and possibly territoriality. In these cool temperate environments, the shorter growing sea-

sons and greater availability of mobile large game created conditions in which plant cultivation may not initially have had the economic importance it had in warmer regions (Wills 1992).

In this respect it is probably significant that in addition to evidence for intensive site occupation, storage, and specialization in milling stones, many early ceramic-period sites in the northern Southwest produced *maíz de ocho*, an 8-row variety of corn that apparently evolved during the early ceramic period, by A.D. 200–400 (Ford 1981; Galinat 1988; Minnis 1985). Maíz de ocho is an early-flowering variety with large, soft kernels that provided increased productivity per plant and greater ease in milling over earlier maize types. Maíz de ocho is adapted for short growing seasons, and its intentional selection by humans undoubtedly was important in enabling local populations to establish extended occupations in upland regions. In sum, temporal and distributional patterns for early Southwestern ceramic containers clearly indicate that their initial manufacture was closely tied to greater residential stability based on plant cultivation, rather than to food production per se.

Researchers have offered a variety of explanations for the origins of pottery production in the Southwest. Many argued for indigenous development from basketry, with initial mud-coating of basket interiors followed by fiber-tempered vessels made without basket molds and finally by the firing of clay vessels (Amsden 1949; Cushing 1886:485; Holmes 1886; Morris 1927:159). This developmental model incorporates the assumption that "pottery arose to meet certain unfulfilled needs because of its functional superiority" (Brown 1989:210), but it does not identify the social or economic context in which such superiority became advantageous.

In contrast, other researchers contended that pottery technology was introduced from Mesoamerica (Haury 1976, 1983:164; Huckell 1984; LeBlanc 1982:43; Schroeder 1965). LeBlanc (1982; cf. Schroeder 1965) presents a particularly detailed argument that pottery was part of a trait complex that appeared in the Southwest about A.D. 200–300 and included large, deep pithouses; storage pits/annexes; trough metates and two-handed manos; ground stone axes; and possibly new cultigens and the bow and arrow. New dates for the Hohokam and Anasazi areas require that LeBlanc's time of introduction be revised, particularly given the evidence for ceramic figurines at 800 B.C. Moreover, the traits described by LeBlanc can all be interpreted as the culmination or reorganization of technological features present in the Late Archaic, and therefore the Mesoamerican origin of this "complex" is uncertain. Whether ceramic technology as evidenced by the figurines ultimately derived from Mesoamerica remains to be addressed, but for our purposes here it suffices to indicate that the production of ceramic containers utilized a technology extant in the Southwest by 800 B.C. (Huckell 1990). Recent researchers have focused less on the ultimate origins of ceramics in the Southwest and more on establishing when they first appeared or how they were utilized (Blinman and Wilson 1993; Mills 1992; Wilson et al. 1993).

Current evidence thus indicates that knowledge of techniques for the manufacture of ceramic objects was present long before those techniques were used to make containers, and that the manufacture of ceramic containers followed the first use of cultigens by centuries. This situation is not unique. Although ceramics and agriculture are correlated (Driver and Massey 1957:231), careful dating reveals that ceramics precede agriculture in some societies and postdate agriculture in others (Arnold 1985; Birket-Smith 1965; Brown 1989:211; several chapters in this volume). Furthermore, ceramic technology was used to manufacture figurines centuries or even millennia before it was used for containers in many portions of the world (Klima 1953; Mellaart 1975).

The primary question for the American Southwest remains why increasing sedentism in the context of economic intensification made ceramic containers useful. In proposing an answer to this question, we turn to the recent economic model for pottery origins suggested by James Brown (1989). In the remainder of this chapter we assess the power of Brown's model for explaining the origins of Southwestern ceramic container technology.

James Brown's Model for the Origins of Pottery

In basic outline, Brown (1989) argues that ceramic containers are manufactured when the need for watertight containers exceeds the existing, or rapidly manufactured, supply. Such a situation may arise either when existing vessels are used up at a faster rate or when new tasks are added to the existing repertoire of activities requiring containers. For the former situation, he specifically cites increases in stone boiling, parching, or other methods of food processing involv-

ing fire as wearing containers out more rapidly. For the latter situation, he notes the new processing requirements of foods such as small-sized seeds and nuts (long-term boiling, in particular). He argues that sedentism would heighten the suitability of pottery production as a response to the increased demand:

Cooperating with this potential on demand are many constraints that constrict the capacity of supply to respond. Chief among these is the impact on tethered households in sedentary and partly sedentary settlement systems. This condition fosters the adoption of pottery due to the cheapness of this craft as an alternative to increased production of containers from other raw materials when labour can be readily deployed to satisfy some of the unsatisfied demand. (Brown 1989:222)

The economy of scale makes pottery a particularly desirable product under these conditions. The manufacture of ten ceramic vessels in a single potting episode takes considerably less than ten times as long as the manufacture of ten vessels in ten potting episodes. In contrast, the manufacture of ten baskets or ten bags requires equivalent amounts of time whether they are manufactured in a single episode or over the course of months (Brown 1989:218–19).

Following Arnold (1985), Brown (1989:215) also argues that pottery has time-budget advantages for partly or fully sedentary groups because their settlements "usually have women who are occupied in a pattern of activities around the base settlement. These are tasks around which craft production of many types easily fits the odd bits of time left over. Consequently, under these settlement practices, labour has negligible costs" (1989:216).

In considering the applicability of the Brown model to the Southwestern cases, we turn first to the supply-and-demand portion of his argument, and following that, we evaluate the argument that the production of ceramic containers had negligible costs in early Southwestern villages. If the supply-and-demand portion of the Brown model is correct, we expect (1) pottery containers to replace containers that are more labor intensive to produce, and (2) a rise in demand for containers just prior to their initial manufacture, because of either a faster rate of use (lower use-life) for existing vessels or new tasks for container assemblages.

In terms of the supply side of the equation, early Southwestern pottery containers were used for cooking, as drinking and serving vessels, for storing water, food, and seed crops, and for carrying water for pot irrigation. Baskets, bags, gourds, and pits served these purposes prior to the adoption of ceramic vessel technology. Manufacture of bags and most types of baskets was particularly labor intensive, but all four container types probably had longer use-lives than the average pottery vessel.[3] Bags, baskets, and pits, however, lack the "economy of scale" advantages of pottery manufacture. The manufacture of ceramics in the Southwest would thus provide a means of producing many containers in a relatively cost-effective manner. For instance, although it may be argued that digging a pit for storing food is less labor intensive than making a ceramic vessel, pits probably cost more to construct than is commonly assumed.[4]

To examine the issue of container demand, we must explore the specific uses of containers and how these might have changed with greater residential stability. First, the partly sedentary populations who occupied Southwestern sites at the time pottery production began were apparently more dependent on cultivated plant foods than were Late Archaic populations, an inference based on pollen and macrobotanical records. Foraging remained a major source of food throughout the Southwest, and perhaps the primary source in many local areas, but domesticated plants increased in dietary significance everywhere during the early ceramic period (Minnis 1989). The combination of increasing residential stability and increasing dependence on cultigens required larger and more permanent storage facilities. In the Anasazi area, the period just preceding the appearance of pottery is called "Basketmaker II," a name that recognizes an increase in the amount and complexity of basketry as one of the main defining characteristics (Amsden 1949). In both the Anasazi and Mogollon areas, the earliest ceramic-period settlements show a dramatic increase in the number and size of storage pits over preceding Late Archaic sites (LeBlanc 1982; Morris and Burgh 1954; Smiley 1985). Many of these "storage" pits may have been containers for containers—that is, a variety of objects and material cached or kept in a single, large facility.

Pottery had several advantages over other containers. First, the watertight nature of pottery presented a distinct improvement over pits and baskets for food storage because reduced moisture lessened the possibility of seeds germinating during storage. The large number of seed jars dating to this early time period indicates that ceramic vessels were important containers for storage of seed crops from harvest to planting. Second, with longer site occupation, pests became an increasing problem, and pottery is not permeable, perishable, or penetrable in the way that baskets or pits might be. The soft maíz de ocho variety of corn that appeared at this time was more susceptible to insect damage than the earlier flint and pop kernel types (Lisa Huckell, personal communication, 1993), perhaps necessitating more pest-resistant containers. Third, using leather bags, woven bags, or tightly woven baskets for long-term storage removed containers that took many hours to construct from use for other tasks.

In addition, pottery had advantages over pits in being portable for groups who still moved on a semi-annual basis, and in being multifunctional. People could use individual vessels to segregate a variety of items within the same storage pit, making access more efficient and reducing the possibility of losing the entire contents of a pit to contamination. Furthermore, the contents of pottery were hidden from view, masking the success of a particular harvest from the prying eyes of non–family members. Finally, people often buried pots beneath the floors of dwellings, banking stored foods for future use while protecting them from human and nonhuman intruders. Pottery was thus a superior container for storing the larger harvests associated with this time period.

Prior to the advent of pottery, Southwestern cooks could stone-boil plant food in baskets, parch it in trays, or roast or steam it in pits. Changing residential patterns did not necessarily require a change in these food processing techniques, but pottery was a superior product for cooking the corn and beans that formed the major portion of the cultivated crops at this time. Pottery permitted direct application of fire to a container holding water and food, increasing the range of food preparation techniques (Arnold 1985:136). The earliest ceramic vessels found in Southwestern sites have thin walls, rounded bases, simple profiles, and sand temper (Burton 1991:50–52; Haury and Sayles 1947:326–29). These properties promote heat effectiveness and thermal conduction and are most appropriate for vessels used over a fire; in contrast, vessels used for stone boiling generally have thick walls and flat bases to improve heat insulation (Hally 1986; Sassaman 1993:141). Where researchers report use alteration of early Southwestern vessels, many of the vessels have exterior sooting on the base, indicating use over a fire (Burton 1991:50–52).

The advantage of direct heating as a cooking technique would be to increase the nutritional yield of foods such as corn. Food processing aids both in detoxifying foods and in altering the accessibility of nutrients. Soaking and long-term boiling served to remove fiber and concentrate the carbohydrate fraction, including starch, of corn, slowing the movement of the food through the digestive tract and thus promoting greater absorption of nutrients (Stahl 1989:177; grinding had a similar effect, making food more digestible and speeding its absorption [Stahl 1989:174]). Moist heat produced a more readily digested product than dry heat (Stahl 1989:181), and prolonged boiling sterilized food as well (Arnold 1985:135). Long-term boiling also permitted rendering of fat from animal bones.[5] Pottery would also have provided a container for fermentation of grains or legumes (Arnold 1985: 136), which also improved their digestibility through the increase in soluble sugars, and which inhibited spoilage (Stahl 1989:179–80). Following Stahl (1989:185), we maintain that use of pottery in food processing was a means of intensifying food production by increasing the nutritional yield of a given crop.

In terms of demand then, increased storage needs and more intensive food processing accelerated the use of existing containers. Cultivated plants could be processed with the technology available prior to pottery, but greater dependence on cultigens required more frequent use of existing containers, leading to rapid wear and destruction. Most importantly, the use of pottery for long-term boiling of cultigens and meat or bones over a fire and possibly for fermentation of cultigens enhanced the nutritional yields from these sources of food.[6] Pottery thus served the functions of existing containers and was used for new tasks. Increased residential stability and increased dependence on cultigens necessitated a larger number of containers, and pottery may well have been produced to fill the demand.

There is a social dimension to container manufacture that we must consider in evaluating Brown's largely economic model. In a recent critique of the Brown model, Sassaman (1993; chapter 18) argues that social constraints may retard innovation in container technology. In the Southwestern case, the highly elaborate basketry manufactured during the preceramic period had an important role in marking social status and defining social relationships (Hays-Gilpin 1993). The social consequences of basketry may have impeded the adoption of pottery as an innovation in material culture, although ceramic containers never superseded all of the functions of baskets, and basket manufacture continued into the historic period.

The Division of Labor and the Origins of Pottery Production

The economic and social contexts within which early Southwestern ceramics appeared seem to support James Brown's hypothesis that supply and demand associated with sedentism were important factors in the inception of the craft. We disagree, however, with the second part of his model that assumes the costs of this new technology were negligible. As we noted earlier, Brown (1989:216) argues that in partly or fully sedentary villages, women are occupied in tasks at home and that pottery production "easily fits the odd bits of time left over" between these tasks. This labor, he states, has "negligible costs" (1989:216) and "can be readily deployed" (1989:222). In order to evaluate these statements for the Southwestern situation, it is necessary to take a closer look at the division of labor in societies that practice a mixed horticultural and foraging economy and produce pottery.

We justify this use of cross-cultural comparison because, as we discussed earlier, ethnobotanical, palynological, and faunal data demonstrate that prehistoric Southwestern populations had a mixed foraging-horticultural economy at the time they began producing pottery. Farming during this time period involved nonintensive hoe agriculture, although most Southwestern populations adopted more intensive farming practices later. The first evidence for settlements consisting of multiple households also occurs during this time, in the form of large pithouses with interior storage facilities and specialized maize grinding tools and grinding areas within houses (Kohler 1993; Plog 1990; Wills 1992; Wilshusen and Blinman 1992). It is therefore reasonable to assume that ethnographic records of household economic organization in societies with a mixed horticultural and foraging economy and multiple household settlements can provide insight into the conditions underlying the decision to make ceramic containers in the prehistoric Southwest.

Cross-cultural studies indicate that women perform the majority of wild plant gathering in mixed economies (Murdock and Provost 1973) and that agriculturalists utilize a greater variety of wild plants than do strictly foraging groups (Johns 1990:245). They also spend several hours per day in activities associated with horticulture, particularly in societies that lacked the plow (Boserup 1970:35; Murdock and Provost 1973:212, 215). Although men often clear the land and prepare the soil for gardens, women generally do the actual planting and typically undertake the day-today tasks of crop tending more than men in horticultural societies. Harvesting is also more often a female task (or a task undertaken by both sexes) than an exclusively male task (Murdock and Provost 1973). Ember (1983:Table 1) provides figures on women's contributions to food production, with an average of 4.68 hours spent each day by women in simple agricultural societies. Estimates of women's contributions to the diet in horticultural societies range from 70 to 90 percent of the total calories (Hewlett 1991:26).[7] Greater dependence on cultigens might thus entail an initial investment in time by men in clearing and preparing the land, but women were likely responsible for the daily farming burden (Martin and Voorhies 1975). Activities such as hunting, warfare, and trade may have limited men's contribution to horticulture (Ember 1983:297).

In addition to their contribution to food production, women in most societies perform virtually all tasks associated with food processing, with the exception of butchering and fire starting. Such activities include preservation of meat and fish, fuel and water gathering, preparation of drinks, preparation of vegetal foods, and cooking (Kurz 1987; Murdock and Provost 1973). Women also generally launder, spin, manufacture clothing, weave, make mats, make baskets, and carry burdens; they often prepare skins and manufacture leather products as well (Murdock and Provost 1973). Women are also the primary care-givers for children, although older children, women other than the mother, and the elderly may help with this task (Brown 1970:1075; Ember 1983:296; Hewlett 1991). In groups in which ceramics are manufactured for household consumption, women perform the majority of activities involved in the production of pottery (Arnold 1985:102; Murdock and Provost 1973:209; White, Burton, and Brudner 1977).[8]

Production of pottery required not only collection and forming of materials for the pottery itself, but also collection of firewood and water and manufacture of tools for forming, finishing, and firing the vessels. If pottery production was associated with new cooking technology, the labor requirements of this new technology must be accounted for as well. Processing of cultigens, particularly cereals, necessitated collection of firewood and water in quantities much greater than those for most wild plant foods, and processing of dried cultigens necessitated more time and effort than did preparation of fresh cultigens (Ember 1983:291). Stone boiling of cultigens required more labor but less time than direct boiling (Driver and Massey 1957:

231). It has been argued that a cook could engage in other activities while food cooked in a pot over a fire (Arnold 1985:128), but the cook was nevertheless tied to the immediate vicinity of the hearth.

In any event, increased dependence on cultigens meant increased processing and cooking time. Historically, for example, the Zunis cooked hominy from dried corn kernels by removing the corn from the husk, placing it in cold water with ash, and boiling and stirring it for three hours. They then carried the cooked corn to the river and washed it. Milling the corn prior to cooking reduced the boiling time but necessitated hours of grinding (Ember 1983:290). Historic accounts report that the Hopis ground corn for three hours daily (Dorsey 1899:741). Once Southwestern groups became partly sedentary and began storing crops dry (rather than, for instance, roasting and eating green corn), the processing requirements of those dried crops added a heavy burden to women's daily tasks. Schiffer's (1975:Table 9) behavioral chain analysis of maize preparation among the Hopis in A.D. 1900 reveals that women assumed fourteen tasks from harvesting to serving, with seven of those tasks performed several mornings a week and four tasks performed twice daily.

Considering the heavy labor contribution of women to household production in mixed foraging-horticultural economies, it is difficult to argue that pottery production "easily" fit "the odd bits of time left over" or that the costs of adding this activity and the food processing tasks associated with it would be negligible. Indeed, Claassen (1991:286) notes that by arguing that horticulture and pottery production were simply added to foraging women's existing workload, "we have written into prehistory a time management crisis for women."

Such a crisis would be particularly acute in environmental zones where climatic factors were such that the portion of the year when pottery production was feasible conflicted with farming activities (Arnold 1985: 100). Although rainfall did not present a significant problem for pottery production in the Southwest, cold, harsh winters did, particularly outside the southern Arizona desert. Pueblo potters today generally cannot fire pottery during the winter months. Although potters in some parts of the world made pottery despite severe environmental limitations (Brown 1989:204), potters in the Southwest probably manufactured pottery during the spring, summer, and fall, when cold temperatures would not threaten their success—precisely the months when they would be most involved in subsistence activities. Arnold (1985: 103) notes that such scheduling conflicts may serve to prevent the introduction of pottery production in societies in which women undertake extensive gathering activities. As we discussed earlier, women at this time in the Southwest were likely responsible for gathering as well as hoe farming. The resulting scheduling conflicts between pottery making and subsistence would not exist for the manufacture of basketry or textiles, which can be made at night or during the winter. It is perhaps not surprising, then, that Southwestern pottery was first produced in the southern Arizona desert, where milder winters presented fewer scheduling conflicts.

Given women's heavy labor contribution and scheduling problems, we must consider why women rather than men produce pottery at the household level of organization. Brown (1989:215) cites Arnold's (1985: 100–101) argument that women make pottery because it is compatible with child care responsibilities, is performed in the domestic sphere, is not dangerous, is monotonous, can be easily interrupted and resumed, can be performed in spare time within the household, and requires attention from individuals tied to the domestic sphere. In making his argument, Arnold is largely relying on the work of Judith Brown, who examined ethnographic accounts of women's subsistence activities and suggested that "women are most likely to make a substantial contribution when subsistence activities have the following characteristics: the participant is not obliged to be far from home; the tasks are relatively monotonous and do not require rapt concentration; and the work is not dangerous, can be performed in spite of interruptions, and is easily resumed once interrupted" (Brown 1970:1074).

Judith Brown's model has received some support from cross-cultural studies (Murdock and Provost 1973; White, Burton, and Brudner 1977). Several researchers, however, point to numerous alternative child care arrangements that free mothers from close supervision of children (Gero 1991:171; Hewlett 1991; Mukhopadhyay and Higgins 1988; Nerlove 1974; Peacock 1991; Wright 1991). Reviewing Arnold's work in particular, Wright (1991:n6) argues that pottery production does require concentration, that some steps in pottery production are not easily interrupted because the rhythm of the potter's work is important, that firing pottery may be dangerous, and that any restrictions imposed by child care would entail only a portion of a potter's lifetime. Even distance from the domestic sphere need not be a constraint on

potting; Castetter, Bell, and Grove (1938:48) note that Papago women may manufacture pottery away from settlements in areas where their husbands are collecting agave.

Nerlove (1974) demonstrates that where women are heavily involved with agricultural pursuits, early supplemental feeding is common, permitting lactating mothers to spend more time away from infants. Peacock (1991) found that Pygmy women performed numerous activities at a distance from the household, even when pregnant or nursing, and suggested that the energetic constraints of pregnancy and lactation were a more appropriate limiting factor to the specific activities undertaken by women than the logistic constraints of child care. Potting does not produce insurmountable logistical or energetic constraints for nursing mothers. Ethnoarchaeologists report that a lactating potter may keep her child on her back in a sling during potting and move it to the front for nursing (William A. Longacre, personal communication, 1993) or may have a mother's helper (older child or relative) watch the child and bring it when it is hungry (Melissa Hagstrum, personal communication, 1993).

There are several formulations for the relationship between women and pottery production in horticultural societies alternative to that suggested by Judith Brown. Wright (1991:201) notes that women do tend to perform activities (including pottery production) near their homes, but that this patterning is not due exclusively to child care responsibilities (see also White, Burton, and Brudner 1977). Citing the work of others, Wright suggests that ecological factors may account for this division of labor. White, Burton, and Brudner (1977) analyze the Murdock and Provost (1973) task list (discussed earlier) and argue that tasks in a single production sequence tend to be performed by the same sex, but that men are more likely to undertake tasks requiring distant travel and danger (cf. Peacock 1991), including procurement of raw materials for craft production.

In general, then, women tend to produce the tools they use in food procurement and processing, and pottery manufacture might be viewed as part of a production sequence that involves food gathering, crop tending, harvesting, water fetching, food preparation, and cooking. Yet another viewpoint suggested by Amiran (1965) is that preparation of bread or porridge and production of pottery required a similar series of motor skills, techniques, and instruments. The individual socialized to perform one activity would already have the skills and tools to undertake the other.

Conclusions

We posit that the mixed foraging and horticultural economies present in the Southwest between 300 B.C. and A.D. 300 entailed a heavy workload of gathering, hoe farming, and food preparation by women. Child care, tool manufacture, and domestic chores required complex scheduling of activities throughout the year. Adding pottery manufacture to this workload demanded the acquisition of new skills, tools, and food preparation techniques. The new methods of food processing associated with ceramics also meant additional burdens of time, in food preparation itself and perhaps in gathering water and fuel. As Brown (1989) maintains, if the superior qualities of ceramic containers were of primary importance to Archaic peoples, they had the technology to produce pottery long before they actually did. Unlike Brown, however, we do not believe that the production and use of the first pottery fit easily into the odd bits of time that prehistoric women had. Pottery production in the Southwest lagged behind incipient agriculture at least in part because ceramic manufacture created scheduling problems that added to the workload of women and conflicted with farming and gathering activities.

Why, then, was pottery manufactured at all? Probably for a number of reasons, some of which may have been interdependent or mutually reinforcing. First, pottery provided a means of altering the technology of food processing extant in the Late Archaic that enhanced the nutritional yield from a given crop. Direct-fire boiling using pottery was thus a strategy for optimizing the available harvest even when the actual hectarage under cultivation was not increased. Such processing required considerably more time, but as Stahl (1989:185) postulates, "the increased availability of nutrients in processed versions of otherwise fibrous foods offsets the costs of processing, and . . . [the] increased extraction of nutrients becomes more critical with increased specialization on these high-fibre resources." As dependence on cultigens for nutrients became greater, processing of these foodstuffs took on more importance, and we should expect to see increasing specialization in the tools designed to extract nutrients (cf. Mills 1992). For instance, the appearance of trough metates and two-hand manos during the early ceramic period permitted more effective milling of seeds into smaller particles, while pottery forms and materials may have become more efficient for boiling, parching, or baking cultigens.

We suggest, then, that as Southwestern populations became increasingly sedentary, they had three choices for increasing their effective yield from cultigens: (1) increase the hectarage, (2) intensify the cultivation of existing hectarage, or (3) alter their storage and food processing techniques. Considering the low population densities and small residential groups found during the early ceramic period, it is unlikely that adequate labor existed to expand field systems. However, evidence for genetic isolation of maize during this period suggests that intensive management of small gardens or plots indeed occurred (see Ford 1981, 1985). The third alternative would be the most easily visible in the archaeological record, through the appearance of pottery and changes in other tool forms. It is possible that all three strategies were employed at various times and places.

Second, scheduling conflicts between foraging, horticulture, and food processing became more complex problems with increasing dependence on cultigens, particularly cereals. Nerlove (1974) demonstrated that women frequently accommodate incompatible subsistence and child care activities by early introduction of weaning foods. Thus, she found a positive correlation between a high contribution by women to subsistence and early introduction of solid foods (the exceptions tended to be among strictly foraging groups). Gruels made by boiling and grinding cereal grains such as maize make suitable weaning foods.

One consequence of the early use of weaning foods, however, would be increased fertility. For the midwestern United States, Buikstra and others (1987:79) argued that the change in food preparation technology associated with the appearance of pottery forms appropriate for boiling cultigens (citing Braun 1987) facilitated early weaning and led to a decrease in birth intervals and an increase in fertility. They argued that it was not a dietary change that led to the demographic changes in the archaeological record but rather a change in food processing technology. Although we do not currently have the data to test this relationship in the American Southwest, the development of pottery and an associated shift in the processing of cultigens would have allowed the early introduction of solid foods and partial weaning. Advances in determining the age of supplementation with solid foods from skeletal material (Sillen and Smith 1984) may eventually permit us to evaluate whether such supplementation correlates with sedentism in the Southwest. Of course, as Nerlove's work suggests, this early weaning may have been necessitated by scheduling conflicts brought on by women's increasing workload.

Third, the new varieties of maize that evolved roughly contemporaneously with the appearance of pottery containers may have been processed differently from earlier varieties, encouraging the shift in cooking technology. For example, the floury maíz de ocho is well suited for ground and boiled preparations such as gruel.

Finally, cooking technology using ceramics may have resulted in greater equality between individuals in the nutritional value of foods consumed. Speth (1990) argued that meat sharing practices among foragers may be nutritionally and quantitatively inequitable, with women typically receiving less desirable portions, even when pregnant or ill. Preparation of stews utilizing ceramic containers could have improved women's access to critical nutrients by equalizing the distribution of foods within a social unit sharing meals from a single vessel and by making more fats available from the rendering of bone.

The empirical record for the origins of Southwestern pottery containers supports Brown's model that sedentism is the critical social context for pottery production. But the evidence for economic intensification during this time period suggests that women's contributions to subsistence were greater than during the preceramic period, and therefore we suspect that Brown's argument for low labor costs associated with pottery production does not accurately reflect the Southwestern situation. The functional superiority of pottery did not bring about its manufacture, but rather increasing residential stability and increasing dependence on cultigens made the increased costs of this technology and associated processing techniques acceptable to prehistoric Southwestern populations.

Acknowledgments

Patricia Crown would like to thank the participants in the spring 1993 "Archaeological Ceramics" and "Gender in Archaeology" graduate seminars at Arizona State University for their intelligent discussions of many of the issues raised in this chapter. John Hoopes, Bruce Huckell, and Lisa Huckell provided useful comments on an earlier draft.

Notes

1. The issue of why localized economic production increased at this time is an extremely complex problem, and we do not attempt to address its causality in this chapter. We note, however, that these shifts are not correlated with episodes of "environmental stress," as many Southwestern archaeologists have speculated, and are in fact more closely tied to periods of increasing or high natural resource productivity. One of us (Wills 1992) has argued that competition for high-return resource zones may have been a key factor in the decision by Late Archaic populations to invest more heavily in food production as a tactic enabling local groups to control important areas through residential permanence.

2. Pithouses pre-date the arrival of maize in most parts of the Southwest but are small, typically occur as isolates, and are not associated with subsurface storage features. Recent research in northeastern Arizona indicates that pithouses were associated with maize use by about 1000 B.C. (Gilpin 1992), but so far investigators have failed to find large, multiple pithouse sites similar to those documented by Huckell (1990) in southeastern Arizona at 800 B.C.

3. A possible exception to this statement is the manufacture of large storage baskets made by coarsely coiling bundles of grass. This manufacturing technique was used to make above-ground storage granaries in the historic Southwest. Such baskets would have been relatively cost-effective to manufacture.

4. A pit of 1.0 m³ probably took a full day to excavate, on average, using digging sticks. Storage pits were often clay lined and fire hardened, requiring plastering material and fuel in addition simply to excavation. Moreover, storage pits in many early Anasazi sites were lined with sandstone slabs that were covered with plaster. Although pits are sometimes referred to as "permanent facilities," historic Navajo storage pits were seldom used more than two years without remodeling or abandonment (Russell 1983). Consequently, storage pits as containers not only had limited functions compared to ceramic pots but may also have had relatively short use lives.

5. Binford (1978:158–59) describes stone boiling for rendering bone grease as possible but considerably more labor intensive than direct boiling. Reid (1989) suggests that simmering may be more appropriate for rendering grease from meat and bone.

6. Brown (1989:207) and Stahl (1989:183) point out that containers made of materials such as stone or basketry were used directly over a fire in some parts of the world, but there is no evidence that such containers were used for boiling food over a fire in the Southwest.

7. As agriculture intensifies, men generally contribute more hours, while women's contribution tends to remain stable (Ember 1983) or even decline (Burton and White 1984). Anthropologists posit numerous reasons for this shift, including increasing processing time for cereal crops "pulling" women out of agriculture (Martin and Voorhies 1975), increasing household size increasing the domestic workload, increasing fertility increasing childcare respon-

sibilities (Ember 1983), and increasing environmental degradation with sedentism forcing women to spend more time gathering firewood and water and decreasing their contribution to farming (Burton and White 1984). For the Southwest during the historic period, women at Zuni maintained gardens near the pueblo while men cultivated outlying fields (Parsons 1919), suggesting that men were gradually "pulled" into agriculture but that women's contribution to food production remained constant. Arnold (1985:100) argues that where scheduling conflicts between subsistence activities and pottery production exist, societies may assign these different activities to different sexes. The importance of hunting in the early ceramic period in the Southwest may well have precluded greater involvement in other activities by men.

8. Women generally prepare the materials and form and fire the vessels, whereas men may quarry clay and gather other materials for paste preparation. Wright (1991:198–99) provides a more detailed discussion of gender and the organization of tasks involved in pottery production.

References Cited

Amiran, R.
1965   The Beginnings of Pottery-Making in the Near East. In *Ceramics and Man,* edited by F. R. Matson, pp. 240–47. Aldine Publishing Company, Chicago.

Amsden, C. A.
1949   *Prehistoric Southwesterners from Basketmaker to Pueblo.* Southwest Museum, Los Angeles.

Arnold, D. E.
1985   *Ceramic Theory and Cultural Process.* Cambridge University Press, Cambridge.

Binford, L. R.
1978   *Nunamiut Ethnoarchaeology.* Academic Press, New York.

Birket-Smith, K.
1965   *The Paths of Culture.* University of Wisconsin Press, Madison.

Blinman, E., and C. D. Wilson
1993   Ceramic Perspectives on Northern Anasazi Exchange. In *The American Southwest and Mesoamerica: Systems of Prehistoric Exchange,* edited by J. E. Ericson and T. G. Baugh, pp. 65–94. Plenum Press, New York.

Boserup, Ester
1970   *Women's Role in Economic Development.* St. Martin's Press, New York.

Braun, D. P.
1987   Coevolution of Sedentism, Pottery Technology, and Horticulture in the Central Midwest, 200 B.C.–A.D. 600. In *Emergent Horticultural Economies of the Eastern Woodlands,* edited by W. F. Keegan, pp. 153–82. Center for Archaeological Investigations Occasional Paper no. 7. Southern Illinois University, Carbondale.

Brown, J. A.
1989   The Beginnings of Pottery as an Economic Process. In *What's New? A Closer Look at the Process of Innovation,* edited by S. E. van der Leeuw and R. Torrence, pp. 203–24. Unwin Hyman, London.

Brown, J. K.
1970   A Note on the Division of Labor by Sex. *American Anthropologist* 72:1072–1078.

Buikstra, J. E., J. Bullington, D. Charles, D. Cook, S. Frankenberg, L. Konigsberg, J. Lambert, and L. Xue
1987   Diet, Demography, and the Development of Horticulture. In *Emergent Horticultural Economies of the Eastern Woodlands,* edited by W. F. Keegan, pp. 67–86. Center for Archaeological Investigations Occasional Paper no. 7. Southern Illinois University, Carbondale.

Burton, J. F.
1991   *The Archeology of Sivu'ovi: The Archaic to Basketmaker Transition at Petrified Forest National Park.* Publications in Anthropology 55. Western Archeological and Conservation Center, National Park Service, Tucson.

Burton, M. L., and D. R. White
1984   Sexual Division of Labor in Agriculture. *American Anthropologist* 86:568–83.

Castetter, E. F., W. H. Bell, and A. R. Grove
1938   *Ethnobiological Studies in the American Southwest, VI: The Early Utilization and the Distribution of Agave in the American Southwest.* The University of New Mexico Bulletin, Albuquerque.

Claassen, Cheryl P.
1991   Gender, Shellfishing, and the Shell Mound Archaic. In *Engendering Archaeology,* edited by J. M. Gero and M. W. Conkey, pp. 276–300. Basil Blackwell, London.

Cushing, F. H.
1886   A Study of Pueblo Pottery as Illustrative of Zuni Culture Growth. *Fourth Annual Report of the Bureau of Ethnology,* pp. 467–521. Smithsonian Institution, Washington, D.C.

Dorsey, George A.
1899   The Hopi Indians of Arizona. *Popular Science Monthly* 55:732–50.

Doyel, D. E.
1991   Hohokam Cultural Evolution in the Phoenix Basin. In *Exploring the Hohokam,* edited by G. Gumerman, pp. 231–78. University of New Mexico Press, Albuquerque.

Driver, H. E., and W. C. Massey

1957   Comparative Studies of North American Indians. *Transactions of the American Philosophical Society* 47(2):165–456.

Eddy, F. W.

1958   A Sequence of Cultural and Alluvial Deposits in the Cienega Creek Basin, Southeastern Arizona. Master's thesis, Department of Anthropology, University of Arizona, Tucson.

1966   *Prehistory in the Navajo Reservoir District, Northwestern New Mexico.* Papers in Anthropology 15. Museum of New Mexico, Santa Fe.

Ember, C. R

1983   The Relative Decline in Women's Contribution to Agriculture with Intensification. *American Anthropologist* 85:285–304.

Fish, S. K., P. R. Fish, and J. Madsen

1990   Sedentism and Settlement Mobility in the Tucson Basin prior to A.D. 1000. In *Perspectives on Southwestern Prehistory,* edited by P. E. Minnis and C. L. Redman, pp. 76–90. Westview Press, Boulder, Colorado.

Ford, R. I.

1981   Gardening and Farming before A.D. 1000: Patterns of Prehistoric Cultivation North of Mexico. *Journal of Ethnobiology* 1:6–27.

1985   Patterns of Prehistoric Food Production in North America. In *Prehistoric Food Production in North America,* edited by R. I. Ford, pp. 341–64. Anthropology Papers no. 75. Museum of Anthropology, University of Michigan, Ann Arbor.

Galinat, W. C.

1988   The Origin of Maiz de Ocho. *American Anthropologist* 90:682–83.

Gero, J. M.

1991   Genderlithics: Women's Roles in Stone Tool Production. In *Engendering Archaeology,* edited by J. M. Gero and M. W. Conkey, pp. 163–93. Basil Blackwell, Oxford.

Gilpin, D.

1992   Salina Springs and Lukachukai: Late Archaic/Early Basketmaker Habitation Sites in the Chinle Valley, Northeastern Arizona. Paper presented at the 57th annual meeting of the Society for American Archaeology, Pittsburgh, Pennsylvania.

Hally, D. J.

1986   The Identification of Vessel Function: A Case Study from Northwest Georgia. *American Antiquity* 51:267–95.

Haury, E. W.

1976   *The Hohokam: Desert Farmers and Craftsmen.* University of Arizona Press, Tucson.

1983   Concluding Remarks. In *The Cochise Cultural Sequence in Southeastern Arizona,* by E. B. Sayles, pp. 158–66. Anthropological Papers of the University of Arizona 42. University of Arizona Press, Tucson.

Haury, E. W., and E. B. Sayles

1947   An Early Pit House Village of the Mogollon Culture, Forestdale Valley, Arizona. *University of Arizona Bulletin* vol. 18, no. 4. Social Sciences Bulletin no. 16.

Hays-Gilpin, Kelley

1993   Symbolic Archaeology, Science, and Other False Dichotomies: Learning about the Broken Flute Basketmakers. Paper presented at the New Mexico Archaeological Council meetings, Albuquerque.

Hewlett, Barry S.

1991   Demography and Childcare in Preindustrial Societies. *Journal of Anthropological Research* 47(1):1–37.

Holmes, W. H.

1886   Origin and Development of Form and Ornament in Ceramic Art. *Fourth Annual Report of the Bureau of American Ethnology,* pp. 443–65. Smithsonian Institution, Washington, D.C.

Huckell, B. B.

1984   *The Archaic Occupation of the Rosemont Area, Northern Santa Rita Mountains, Southeastern Arizona.* Arizona State Museum Archaeological Series 147. Tucson.

1988   Late Archaic Archaeology of the Tucson Basin: A Status Report. In *Recent Research on Tucson Basin Prehistory: Proceedings of the Second Tucson Basin Conference,* edited by W. H. Doelle and P. R. Fish, pp. 57–79. Anthropological Papers no. 10. Institute for American Research, Tucson.

1990   Late Preceramic Farmer-Foragers in Southeastern Arizona: A Cultural and Ecological Consideration of the Spread of Agriculture into the Arid Southwestern United States. Ph.D. dissertation, Arid Lands Resource Sciences, University of Arizona, Tucson.

Johns, T.

1990   *With Bitter Herbs They Shall Eat It: Chemical Ecology and the Origins of Human Diet and Medicine.* University of Arizona Press, Tucson.

Klima, B.

1953   Paleolithic Huts of Dolni Vestonice. *Antiquity* 27:4–14.

Kohler, T. A.

1993   News from the Northern Anasazi Southwest: Prehistory on the Edge of Chaos. *Journal of Archaeological Research* 1:267–321.

Kurz, R. B., Jr.
1987   Contributions of Women to Subsistence in Tribal Societies. *Research in Economic Anthropology* 8:31–59.

LeBlanc, S. A.
1982   Temporal Change in Mogollon Ceramics. In *Southwestern Ceramics: A Comparative Review,* edited by A. H. Schroeder, pp. 107–28. *The Arizona Archaeologist* 15. Arizona Archaeological Society, Phoenix.

Martin, M. K., and B. Voorhies
1975   *Female of the Species.* Columbia University Press, New York.

Mellaart, J.
1975   *The Neolithic of the Near East.* Thames and Hudson, London.

Mills, B. J.
1992   The Organization of Ceramic Production in Household Economies. Ms. on file, Department of Anthropology, University of Arizona, Tucson.

Minnis, P.
1985   Domesticating Plants and People in the Greater American Southwest. In *Prehistoric Food Production in North America,* edited by R. I. Ford, pp. 309–40. Anthropological Papers no. 75. Museum of Anthropology, University of Michigan, Ann Arbor.
1989   Prehistoric Diet in the Northern Southwest: Macroplant Remains from Four Corners Feces. *American Antiquity* 54:543–63.

Morris, E. H.
1927   The Beginnings of Pottery Making in the San Juan Area: Unfired Prototypes and the Wares of the Earliest Ceramic Period. *Anthropological Papers of the American Museum of Natural History,* vol. 28, part 2. New York City.

Morris, E. H., and R. F. Burgh
1954   *Basketmaker II Sites near Durango, Colorado.* Publication no. 604. Carnegie Institution of Washington, D.C.

Mukhopadhyay, C. C., and P. J. Higgins
1988   Anthropological Studies of Women's Status Revisited: 1977–1987. *Annual Review of Anthropology* 17:461–95.

Murdock, G. P., and C. Provost
1973   Factors in the Division of Labor by Sex: A Cross-Cultural Analysis. *Ethnology* 12:203–25.

Nerlove, S. B.
1974   Women's Workload and Infant Feeding Practices: A Relationship with Demographic Implications. *Ethnology* 13:207–14.

Parsons, E. C.
1919   Waiyautitsa of Zuni, New Mexico. *Scientific Monthly* 9:443–57.

Peacock, N. R.
1991   Rethinking the Sexual Division of Labor: Reproduction and Women's Work among the Efe. In *Gender at the Crossroads,* edited by M. di Leonardo, pp. 339–60. University of California Press, Berkeley.

Plog, S.
1990   Agriculture, Sedentism, and Environment in the Evolution of Political Systems. In *The Evolution of Political Systems: Sociopolitics in Small-Scale Sedentary Societies,* edited by S. Upham, pp. 177–202. Cambridge University Press, Cambridge.

Reid, K. C.
1989   A Materials Science Perspective on Hunter-Gatherer Pottery. In *Pottery Technology: Ideas and Approaches,* edited by G. Bronitsky, pp. 167–80. Westview Press, Boulder, Colorado.

Roth, B.
1989   Late Archaic Settlement and Subsistence in the Tucson Basin. Ph.D. dissertation, Department of Anthropology, University of Arizona, Tucson.

Russell, S. C.
1983   Factors Affecting Agricultural Production in a Western Navajo Community. Ph.D. dissertation, Department of Anthropology, Arizona State University, Tempe.

Sassaman, K. E.
1993   *Early Pottery in the Southeast: Tradition and Innovation in Cooking Technology.* University of Alabama Press, Tuscaloosa.

Schiffer, M. B.
1975   Behavioral Chain Analysis: Activities, Organization, and the Use of Space. In *Chapters in the Prehistory of Eastern Arizona, IV. Fieldiana: Anthropology* 65:103–19.

Schroeder, A. H.
1965   Unregulated Diffusion from Mexico into the Southwest prior to A.D. 700. *American Antiquity* 30:297–309.

Sillen, A., and P. Smith
1984   Weaning Patterns are Reflected in Strontium-Calcium Ratios of Juvenile Skeletons. *Journal of Archaeological Science* 11:237–45.

Smiley, F. E.
1985   Chronometric and Early Agricultural Adaptations in Northeastern Arizona: Approaches to the Interpretation of Radiocarbon Dates. Ph.D. dissertation, Department of Anthropology, University of Michigan, Ann Arbor.

Speth, J. D.
1990   Seasonality, Resource Stress, and Food Sharing in So-Called "Egalitarian" Foraging

Societies. *Journal of Anthropological Archaeology* 9:148–88.

Stahl, A. B.

1989   Plant-Food Processing: Implications for Dietary Quality. In *Foraging and Farming: The Evolution of Plant Exploitation,* edited by D. R. Harris and G. C. Hillman, pp. 171–94. Unwin Hyman, London.

Toll, M. S., and A. C. Cully

1983   Archaic Subsistence in the Four Corners Area: Evidence for a Hypothetical Seasonal Round. In *Economy and Interaction along the Lower Chaco River,* edited by P. Hogan and J. C. Winter, pp. 385–92. Office of Contract Archaeology, University of New Mexico, Albuquerque.

Varien, M.

1990   *Excavations at Three Prehistoric Sites along Pia Mesa Road, Zuni Indian Reservation, McKinley County, New Mexico.* Revised Zuni Archaeology Program Report no. 233. Zuni, New Mexico.

White, D. R., M. L. Burton, and L. A. Brudner

1977   Entailment Theory and Method: A Cross-Cultural Analysis of the Sexual Division of Labor. *Behavior Science Research* 12:1–24.

Wills, W. H.

1992   Plant Cultivation and the Evolution of Risk-Prone Economies in the Prehistoric American Southwest. In *Transitions to Agriculture in Prehistory,* edited by A. B. Gebauer and T. D. Price, pp. 153–76. Monographs in World Prehistory no. 4, Prehistory Press, Madison, Wisconsin.

Wilshusen, R. H., and E. Blinman

1992   Pueblo I Village Formation: A Reevaluation of Sites Recorded by Earl Morris on the Ute Mountain Ute Tribal Lands. *The Kiva* 57:251–69.

Wilson, C. D., and E. Blinman

1991   Early Anasazi Ceramics and the Basketmaker Transition. Paper presented at the Anasazi Symposium, Mesa Verde National Park, Colorado.

Wilson, C. D., E. Blinman, J. M. Skibo, and M. B. Schiffer

1993   The Designing of Southwestern Pottery: A Technological and Experimental Approach. Revised version of a paper presented at the Third Southwest Symposium, Tucson, Arizona.

Winter, J. C., and P. F. Hogan

1986   Plant Husbandry in the Great Basin and Adjacent Northern Colorado Plateau. In *Anthropology of the Desert West: Essays in Honor of Jesse D. Jennings,* pp. 117–44. University of Utah Anthropological Papers, no. 110. Salt Lake City.

Wright, Rita P.

1991   Women's Labor and Pottery Production in Prehistory. In *Engendering Archaeology,* edited by J. M. Gero and M. W. Conkey, pp. 194–223. Basil Blackwell, London.

Part
3

Theory and Critique

20

The Emergence of Prestige Technologies and Pottery

BRIAN HAYDEN

Scant theoretical attention has been paid in the past to the conditions under which prestige technologies emerge. Certainly, archaeologists have been cognizant of the obvious—that prestige technologies are used by the elites—but this does not advance our understanding of the issue very far. It does, however, relate the question to the more thorny problem of the conditions under which socioeconomic inequalities emerge. The purpose of this chapter is to advance the inquiry into the conditions under which prestige technologies develop, with specific reference to pottery.

For 99 percent of human existence, there are *no* indications of the existence of any prestige technology. Not until the Upper Paleolithic (and even then, not until the later half of this period) do clear material indicators of prestige occur in the world prehistoric record. A number of prehistorians interpret the appearance of art and prestige material items in the Upper Paleolithic as due to the arrival of a new genetic variant of human beings on the scene: *Homo sapiens sapiens,* or anatomically modern humans. In this scenario, Neandertals and other pre-modern human types were incapable of much foresight, language, art, or culture, not to mention status distinctions and the ability to craft items to communicate these distinctions symbolically (Binford 1981, 1985; Chase and Dibble 1987; Gargett 1989; Stringer and Andrews 1988; for a more complete review, see Mellars 1989).

The view that Neandertals were incapable of symbolism, language, and culture has always appeared unrealistic to me for several reasons. First, not all modern human groups produce prestige items or have economically based socioeconomic inequalities, nor was this the case prehistorically. In fact, the occurrence of prestige goods is initially restricted to only a very few, largely subarctic or temperate regions. Only after the Pleistocene do prestige technologies become relatively widespread. This distribution indicates that economics, not genetics, is the key variable in understanding the occurrence of prestige items.

The second reason I view the genetic model as unsatisfactory for explaining the emergence of prestige technologies is because at the end of the Pleistocene, prestige goods largely disappeared from most of the areas where they had developed, at least for a while. This disappearance, too, indicates that economic factors were more likely than genetics to have played critical roles in the development of prestige technologies.

The third reason I reject the genetic model is that my experience with Mousterian and other early industries indicates that pre-modern people were extremely sophisticated in terms of their lithic technology, and on this basis it is inconceivable to me that their behavior was dramatically different from our own behavior. These arguments and supporting observations have been presented in detail elsewhere (Hayden 1993a).

Before exploring alternative explanations for the development of prestige technologies, it is useful to define exactly what is meant by the term. The distinction I have made between a *practical* and a *prestige* technology (Hayden 1993b:203) is that a practical technology is based on the principle of performing tasks in the most efficient and effective fashion possible. The less time and work involved, the better. In contrast, a prestige technology is based on the principle of displaying or showing off one's wealth, power, or control over labor and resources. Therefore, as much time and labor as can be spared are used to produce prestige items. The more time and work spent in obtaining or making them, the better. Thus the thousands of shell disk beads interred with the burials at Sungir (White 1993), the elaborately carved (and delicate) antler spear throwers from the Grotte des Trois-Frères and Mas d'Azil, and the long-distance trade in dentalium shells to decorate garments in Natufian burials all constitute prestige technologies.

The argument I make to explain the emergence of prestige technologies is based on economics (in the sense of cultural materialism and cultural ecology) and relies on the critical distinction between generalized hunter-gatherers (foragers, in Binford's terms) and complex hunter-gatherers (roughly equivalent to collectors). The important differences between these two types of hunter-gatherers for the discussion of prestige technologies revolve around *economically based* competition.

Among generalized hunter-gatherers, resources are so scarce, unpredictable, and vulnerable to overexploitation that sharing of food is an absolute imperative, while private ownership and the competitive use of food resources is anathema because of the detrimental effects for other members of the community (see Hayden 1981, 1993a, 1993b). I have argued that it is only when technological advances occur in subsistence procurement and food storage, such as those that typified many Mesolithic, Epipaleolithic, and Archaic groups (but which began in the Upper Paleolithic in some areas), that the restrictions on economically based competition are removed. With these technological advances, resources become much more abundant, invulnerable to overexploitation, and perhaps more constant, thereby permitting the private owner-

ship of foods (especially stored foods), the private ownership of resource locations, increased sedentism, logistical mobility patterns, and most importantly, the emergence of economically based competition together with the resultant socioeconomic inequalities that this implies.

It is under these conditions, I have argued, that prestige technologies emerge among hunter-gatherers such as some favored Upper Paleolithic groups in Europe and many more Mesolithic, Epipaleolithic, and Archaic groups. Some of the key food resources upon which complex hunter-gatherers are based include fish, reindeer, and grass seeds, together with the intensive labor required to dry and process these foods for storage. The emergence of agriculture in most instances simply amplifies all of the above developments among complex hunter-gatherers. Indeed, a number of prehistorians have noted the fundamental similarities between complex hunter-gatherers and simple horticulturalists (e.g., Shnirelman 1992).

Once technologies evolve to the point where private ownership and economically based competition can be sustained without immediate detrimental effects, it seems that some individuals in every community will attempt to aggrandize themselves and acquire material, social, and political benefits for themselves and their families. Such aggrandizing individuals occur in all human populations and probably are part of the natural genetic variability in personality types that characterizes human populations, even if they do not constitute a very large proportion of the population. This condition may ultimately be responsible for observations like those of Sahlins (1958:1), Voytek and Tringham (1989:496), Beteille (1981), and Saitta (Saitta and Keene 1990), who view tendencies toward inequality and class process as inherent in all societies.

According to the degree of aggrandizers' success and their social and technological starting points, these individuals can be viewed as developing prestige technologies to advertise their success and thereby attract supporters. In the terms of other vocabularies, prestige items are the material manifestations of the asymmetry inherent in economically based aggrandization. Although Sassaman (1993) suggests that aggrandization does not necessarily lead to asymmetrical relationships, this seems to me to be a contradiction by definition and certainly is inconceivable where *economically* based aggrandization is involved. The range of prestige technologies is constrained only by the materials available, the ingenuity of the craftsmen, and the degree of power that aggrandizers are capable of acquiring. It is difficult to conceive of a more profound and far-reaching change in the nature of human culture than the emergence of economically based competition and prestige technologies at the end of the Pleistocene.

Prestige Technologies

I have argued elsewhere that many of the most important cultural developments of the last 30,000 years have initially been the products of prestige technologies in various forms. During the Upper Paleolithic, the heavy emphasis on finely curried skin garments (Hayden 1990) and the development of both movable and parietal art (Hayden 1993a) can be viewed as prestige undertakings. These are the distinctive hallmarks of European Upper Paleolithic culture. White (1992:560, 1993:289, 296) has similarly proposed that beads and other ornamentation evolved in the context of socioeconomic hierarchies during the Upper Paleolithic in Europe.

METALS

The earliest use of metals both in the western hemisphere and in the Old World was clearly for prestige purposes rather than practical ones. Moreover, the first appearances are not in agricultural communities but in communities of complex hunter-gatherers. In the area where I have been excavating on the Northwest Plateau of North America, copper appears first and exclusively in the form of tubular beads, ornamental disks, and ornamental sheeting at least 1,000–2,000 years ago (see Blake et al. 1993; Morrison and Myles 1992). The Old Copper culture around the Great Lakes used prestige copper items as early as 4000 B.C. (Binford 1962). In a recent analysis, Rosen (1993) points out that in the Near East, metals were introduced first and foremost as prestige display items (as is generally true of Chalcolithic cultures throughout the world), and that it was only after the use of metals had evolved to some degree as a prestige technology that people began to realize that certain metalic combinations (such as bronze) also had practical uses that made them technically superior to stone tools. The practical benefits of using metals appeared only incidentally to, and considerably after, the use of metals in the prestige sphere (see also Bradley 1984; Darvill 1987; Fallers 1973; Randsborg 1982; Shennan 1982).

The same process has continued in the development of new metal technologies: iron was used as a prestige metal long before techniques were developed to produce it economically for practical purposes. And initially, aluminum was so difficult to extract that its value surpassed that of gold, so that it was used only by the richest families for such things as Napoleon's tea set. Similarly, plastics were initially used primarily as elite jewelry.

The development of metals is an extremely instructive example for examining the development of pottery. A good case can be made that a very similar process occurred in the course of pottery development (as exemplified by many of the studies in this volume). We can then use the metals example as a template for examining the emergence of pottery—a topic to which I shall return shortly.

Metals made an ideal prestige medium for several reasons: the most common native metals (copper, silver, gold) were soft and plastic enough that they could be shaped by cold hammering into a wide variety of ornamental shapes. Moreover, their softness rendered them relatively useless for most practical purposes. The native metals were also relatively rare (much rarer than cherts, flints, chalcedonies, and quartzites), thus requiring considerable search time to procure. They were also time consuming to work and fashion into ornaments of any significant size. And finally, they were shiny and bright, thereby catching observers' attention. All these characteristics made metals extremely useful for displaying economic power.

SLAVES AND CRAFTS

In other areas of technology and economics, I believe that good arguments can be made that slavery initially appeared as an institution to display power and prestige (again, initially among complex hunter-gatherers such as those in the North American Northwest). Craft specialization similarly emerges first among complex hunter-gatherers as part of elite prerogatives (shamans, exclusive hunters, carvers) or to provide labor-intensive craft items for elites (see Clark and Parry 1990). I would suggest that nephrite or jade adzes functioned as specialist-produced items for elites, along with the first woven textiles of cotton and wool and finely woven basketry. Cauvin (1978:100) similarly argues that the first ground stone tools in the Levant were prestige items. Architectural elaborations such as the use of adobe brick construction, lime plaster, and arches can similarly be argued to have been initially introduced as more labor-intensive forms of architecture used for the display of wealth and power.

Perhaps of even greater importance for the present discussion, I have suggested that domesticated plants and animals initially developed as parts of prestige technologies used in the context of reciprocal and competitive feasts (Hayden 1990, 1992)—an argument presaged by Cauvin's discussions (1978:77ff., 116–17) of domestication as resulting from social rather than ecological pressures. There can be little doubt that special efforts were made by the organizers of these feasts to indebt or impress guests by providing unusual quantities of the most desired types of foods and drinks, especially delicacies and highly labor-intensive foods (requiring either intensive procurement or intensive preparation). Organizers clearly competed to outproduce each other in quantity and quality; this assertion is based empirically on both emic and etic observations. It is my contention that this competition is an entirely new type of motivation on the evolutionary scene and that it logically leads to the investment of additional labor in food production that characterizes many aspects of initial food production. This aspect of the argument is the easiest to establish.

It is much more problematical to satisfactorily explain precisely what motivated some people to initiate (and other people to support) these competitive and reciprocal feasts. I have made one suggestion involving the use of these feasts in the creation of debts, the mobilization of manpower and womanpower, and the acquisition of power via the manipulation of debts and gifts. In this context, prestige items are used partly in order to attract people to participate in the production and debt system (much as in contemporary industrial society), partly to advertise the success of the organizers (thereby attracting supporters or desirable allies and mates), and partly to magnify or facilitate the creation of debts based on wealth. Other scenarios, however, may be just as viable. Such issues are not critical for the present discussion.

If we accept the premise that prestige displays—especially those involving food—were an integral part of reciprocal and competitive feasts, no matter what the ultimate motivation, then there are some extremely important implications for the technologies associated with food preparation and, particularly, food serving. If the biggest, best, most valuable, tastiest, and most succulent foods that feast organizers could procure were being offered to guests as a display of the group's success and wealth, or to create a favorable impression on guests so that they would enter into alliances with

the hosts rather than with enemy groups, it seems highly unlikely that the presentation of foods meant to impress would not also be made in special, impressive containers. The use of containers meant to impress in the contexts of feasts may even be a universal cultural characteristic; it is certainly an integral part of our own culture and many others.

There are many possible food container technologies, including wood, basketry, stone, metal, shell, and ceramic. On the Northwest Coast of North America, in Melanesia, and in Polynesia, elaborately carved bowls, sometimes worth hundreds or thousands of dollars, were used to serve food at these feasts. Stone bowls and plates appear in Mesoamerica, South America, the Nile Valley, and the Near East in elite contexts. Gero (1989:104) has explicitly linked their appearance in Peru to a prestige technology, and stone bowls appear in the Near East before pottery (Schmandt-Besserat 1977). And, most importantly, highly decorated, labor-intensive bowls constitute initial ceramic developments in many centers such as the Chiapas coast (Clark and Gosser, chapter 17), Melanesia and Polynesia (Kirch 1988), the European Neolithic (Barnett 1990, chapter 7; Gebauer, chapter 9), North Africa and Greece (Close, chapter 3; Vitelli, chapter 5), the Central American isthmus and Colombia (Hoopes, chapter 15; Oyuela-Caycedo, chapter 11), and many other locations examined in the chapters of this book.

POTTERY

The exact form that prestige food containers take in each culture is probably dependent upon the materials most readily available, the climate, degrees of mobility, and the preceding traditions and values of the culture. Although we can expect a prestige food-serving technology to emerge in an almost deterministic fashion with the development of competitive feasts among complex hunter-gatherers and early horticulturalists, there is no guarantee that ceramics themselves will be included in the choice of technological media being used for prestige food containers.

In view of the lack of pottery prior to the development of complex hunter-gatherer and horticultural communities, it is tempting to view the initial development of pottery as a prestige technology in the same fashion that metals can be viewed as having initially developed as a prestige technology. Like metals, ceramics had a number of important qualities that probably made them a very useful prestige medium. At the outset, the potter's art would probably have been a difficult one to master. Clay sources had to be carefully selected for proper construction and firing properties. Tempers compatible with specific clays had to be obtained and processed, sometimes with a great deal of labor, as in the grinding up of sherds and calcite. Construction techniques themselves would have required considerable practice in order to make pottery that would be both functional and attractive. Surface finishing and decorations would have required further expertise, practice, and materials. Drying and firing would also have been extremely critical and subject to many initial failures. In order to produce the finest painted and burnished examples with the thinnest walls, a great deal more specialized expertise would have been required.

During the development phase of pottery manufacture, then, pottery may have represented a very labor-intensive endeavor with many problems and failures. It is perhaps this labor-intensive aspect, the shiny surfaces, and the sheer novelty of the forms and appearances that made pottery a favored prestige medium for food-serving vessels in many communities throughout the world. Another advantage of ceramics for prestige display is the extremely plastic nature of the medium, in contrast to the much more rigid and constrained mediums of stone and even wood or basketry. As in the case of metals, plasticity in ceramics could be used to emphasize the specialness of objects, such as in the ornate forms of Jomon ritual pottery. Finally, prestige pottery could be dramatically broken during feasts where the destruction of property occurred as a display of wealth (see Gebauer, chapter 9).

There may be other production costs and prestige advantages that have not been adequately appreciated as well, but the ones just mentioned are some of the most obvious. It is also possible that some ceramics were developed in order to permit the preparation of prestigious types of food such as those requiring long periods of boiling or brewing or straining (e.g. Myers 1989:3).

If the prestige scenario bears any relevance to the initial development of pottery in some, many, or even all geographical areas, there are a number of logical expectations that follow. The first is that pottery should initially occur in the form of food-serving vessels such as plates, bowls, and liquid containers—for example, beakers, *tecomates,* and cups. It must also be recognized, however, that some instances may occur in which pottery was initially (or coterminously) developed for the processing of prestige foods (boiling, brewing, or straining). Moreover, a rapid evolution to-

ward labor-intensive, specialized production of highly decorated forms should occur, with great emphasis on control of the medium and craft expertise. Even in instances where pottery appears to be cruder than anticipated by this model, the possibility that organic surface decorations covered over rough surfaces needs to be examined. For instance, resin coatings existed on some Jomon and Southeast Asian pottery (e.g., Aikens and Higuchi 1982:125), and exterior bark decorations have been recovered from some Neolithic Swiss vessels (Corboud and Seppey 1991).

Second, because competitive and hierarchical societies often use marriages and burials as occasions to reaffirm exchange relationships and advertise the wealth and success of the group, prestige ceramics might also be expected to feature frequently in these contexts.

Finally, the initial appearance and spread of pottery technology should occur among societies for whom feasting can be inferred to have been competitive or reciprocal for the purpose of creating allies or wealth-exchange partners, that is, among complex hunter-gatherers and most horticultural groups with incipient or developed socioeconomic inequalities. In addition to a number of other chapters in this volume that present cases consistent with this model, Gebauer (chapter 9) and Shennan (1986:135) have argued that European beakers used for drinking were essentially prestige items often used at ritual events.

The Role of Ritual

Although many archaeologists and anthropologists treat ritual and socioeconomics as distinct spheres of activity, recourse to the ethnographies of complex hunter-gatherers and horticulturalists shows repeatedly that these two domains are nearly inseparable in the context of competitive and reciprocal feasting. There are many possible reasons for this. Without going into detail, the reason I favor is that feast organizers use ritual as a pretext and a lever to gain the cooperation of large numbers of families within their own communities. Everyone in a community is generally viewed as having an obligation to keep the guardian spirits happy, or else calamity may visit the community in the form of crop failures, disease, pests, and battle defeats. Ritual can also be construed as demanding unusual and exotic items pleasing to gods and spirits—the procurement of which involves extra labor, production, and debts. Even more importantly, if leaders can convincingly portray their own ancestors as powerful supernatural allies, this would enhance or help validate existing leaders' claims to power. Such leaders try to bury their immediate ancestors in as lavish a fashion as possible and maintain periodic sacrifices or feasts to them. Finally, the organizers of competitive feasts can easily appropriate the role of ritual and dance organizers, thereby enabling them to manipulate participants even more.

From this vantage, it should not be surprising that many of the prestige items used in competitive feasts take the form of unusually elaborate ritual items: incense burners, flower holders, offering vessels, and finely made figurines. Because of their plasticity, ceramics lend themselves admirably to the expression of ritual ideologies, the portrayal of deities, and the creation of ornate ritual forms. Whether the relatively crude ceramic figurines of cultures like that of the pre-pottery Neolithic of the Levant (Cauvin 1978) should be viewed as an expression of ritual elaboration generated and supported by the organizers of competitive or reciprocal alliance feasts is a difficult question to address. Other explanations may be equally useful, but the feasting scenario needs to be kept in mind.

In terms of other possibilities, we should not forget, for example, that the earliest use of ceramics involved the simple and crude creation of clay figurines from the easily molded loess of central Europe, apparently for shamanic divinations or spell workings (Vandiver et al. 1989). Crude ceramic figurines also occur among the complex hunter-gatherers of the North American Northwest (Mack 1991; Stenger 1986) and among the Epipaleolithic complex hunter-gatherers of the Near East and Japan. Although these figurines were products of quite complex hunting and gathering cultures, other developments of ceramic technologies, such as the creation of ceramic hearth stones in Australia (Harry Allen, personal communication, 1994) and the creation of simple, flat ceramic lamps among the Inuit (McCartney and Savelle 1989:40), appear to reflect the convenient use of the ceramic medium when other, more suitable materials were scarce. These are some of the best-documented initial occurrences of ceramic innovations as part of practical technologies. When we turn to pottery, however, in contrast to the broader range of ceramics, there is a stronger argument to be made for its development as stemming predominantly from its role in prestige technologies, including the storage and preparation of prestige foods. In order to consider the problem fully from an archaeological perspective, it is necessary to take into account the dynamics of prestige technologies.

The Dynamics of Prestige Technologies

There is another important lesson to be learned from the example of metal technology. It is that in some cases where a new medium is developed in order to supply prestige items partly because of its labor-intensive nature, craft specialists may generate technological advances that render the new medium useful in the practical sphere. This may be because of improvements in the technology, such as creating more durable cutting edges through alloying, in the case of metals, or creating heat-shock–resistant ceramics, in the case of pottery. Alternatively, prestige technologies can give rise to practical technologies due to technological improvements that greatly reduce the time and effort necessary to make the products. The previously cited examples of iron, aluminum, and plastics are important instances in which technological improvements greatly reduced costs. I have similarly argued that the initial domestication of plants and animals was a prestige technological development but that once genetic manipulation and gardening techniques had advanced to the point where domesticated foods could compete in terms of returns with wild foods, then domesticates spread to a much broader range of communities as part of a practical food producing technology and could even be adopted by groups without socioeconomic hierarchies.

At the point when a more efficient, cost-effective alternative to existing technological strategies is introduced, the new technology generally spreads throughout the surrounding area, as in the case of the replacement of stone tools with bronze in most technological domains in the Levant (Rosen 1993) and perhaps the spread of cooking ceramics in many parts of the world. It is important to recognize that even where communities lack the kind of competitive feasting structures that would make the diffusion of the original prestige technologies adaptive, the diffusion of the practical, cost-effective derivatives of prestige technologies can easily occur. This condition tends to confuse situations in which we have only a few glimpses of regional and areal diachronic developments.

Thus, whereas metals may have been developed originally as prestige technologies and initially diffused to hierarchical communities as prestige items, it was their later, practical, derivative products that were most eagerly sought by communities still using stone and often lacking socioeconomic complexity, including remote tribal communities in the nineteenth and twentieth centuries. Similarly, food production may have originated in—and initially diffused to—communities with socioeconomic inequalities and competitive feasts, but once food production became cost effective compared to wild food gathering, agriculture must have spread to all environments where it provided a better return than wild foods, whether the inhabitants had complex communities or not. The same scenario may well have characterized the development of pottery. That is, even if the first pottery emerged as prestige items within broader prestige technologies, subsequent improvements in pottery technology may have created a derivative *practical* pottery technology used primarily for cooking or storage. This derivative practical pottery technology could have arrived first in peripheral areas where prestige technologies were not supported by the socioeconomic system, thus making it appear that practical pottery forms were the first to evolve in some localities.

Whether practical pottery technology or prestige pottery technology was the first to emerge in an evolutionary sense may thus not be as easy to determine as one might first expect. Either prestige pottery or practical pottery or both could have emerged independently, but it is at least worth exploring the possibility that the ultimate priority in all regions and areas lies with the development of pottery in the prestige technological realm.

Finally, it is worth pointing out that when technologies become affordable by a large number of people in communities, elites or incipient elites generally abandon the prestige forms that they initially pioneered. When this happens, elites go on to develop other prestige items and techniques that are not affordable by most people (see Bradley 1984; Cannon 1989; Fallers 1973; Randsborg 1982; Shennan 1982). If the cost of specific prestige items remains high, as in the case of gold and furs, prestige technologies and items persist for long periods, often along with practical derivatives that are more widely available, such as iron tools and leather shoes. If the cost of initial prestige items comes down dramatically over time, as in the case of aluminum and plastics, elites may completely abandon these technologies for the production of new prestige items. Alternatively, elites may find ways to embellish the value of objects through either expensive hand-crafted decoration or technical elaboration, as in the case of increasingly elaborate glassware and ceramics used even today to display prestige and impress guests. In many respects we can perceive the legacy of prestige technologies, including prestige pottery technology, in our own culture. The roots of these develop-ments go back to the end of the Pleistocene, and one of the most challenging problems in contemporary archaeology is to understand the origins of prestige technologies and the impact they have had on the rest of culture.

References Cited

Aikens, C. M., and Takayasu Higuchi
1982   *Prehistory of Japan.* Academic Press, New York.

Barnett, William
1990   Small-Scale Transport of Early Neolithic Pottery in the West Mediterranean. *Antiquity* 64:859–65.

Beteille, A.
1981   The Idea of Natural Inequality. In *Social Inequality,* edited by G. Berreman, pp. 59–80. Academic Press, New York.

Binford, Lewis
1962   Archaeology as Anthropology. *American Antiquity* 28:217–25.
1981   *Bones: Ancient Men and Modern Myths.* Academic Press, New York.
1985   Human Ancestors: Changing Views of Their Behavior. *Journal of Anthropological Archaeology* 4:292–327.

Blake, Michael, Gary Coupland, and Brian Thom
1993   Dating the Scowlitz Site. *The Midden* 25:7–8.

Bradley, Richard
1984   *The Social Foundations of Prehistoric Britain.* Longman, New York.

Cannon, Aubrey
1989   The Historical Dimension in Mortuary Expressions of Status and Sentiment. *Current Anthropology* 30:437–58.

Cauvin, Jacques
1978   *Les premiers villages de Syrie-Palestine du IXème au VIIème millénaire avant J.C.* Maison de l'Orient, Lyon.

Chase, Philip, and Harold Dibble
1987   Middle Paleolithic Symbolism: A Review of Current Evidence and Interpretations. *Journal of Anthropological Archaeology* 6:263–96.

Clark, John, and William Parry
1990   Craft Specialization and Cultural Complexity. *Research in Economic Anthropology* 12:289–346.

Corboud, Pierre, and Véronique Seppey
1991   Les stations littorales préhistoriques du Petit-Lac et la céramique Néolithique moyen de Corsier-Port GE. *Archéologie Suisse* 14:181–89.

Darvill, Timothy
1987   *Prehistoric Britain*. Batsford, London.
Fallers, Lloyd
1973   *Inequality: Social Stratification Reconsidered*. University of Chicago Press, Chicago.
Gargett, Rob
1989   The Evidence for Neandertal Burial. *Current Anthropology* 30:157–90.
Gero, Joan
1989   Assessing Social Information in Material Objects. In *Time, Energy, and Stone Tools,* edited by R. Torrence, pp. 92–105. Cambridge University Press, Cambridge.
Hayden, Brian
1981   Research and Development in the Stone Age: Technological Transitions among Hunter-Gatherers. *Current Anthropology* 22:519–48.
1990   The Right Rub: Hide Working in High Ranking Households. In *The Interpretative Possibilities of Microwear Studies,* edited by B. Graslund, pp. 89–102. Societas Archaeologica Upsaliensis, Uppsala.
1993a   The Cultural Capacities of Neandertals: A Review and Re-evaluation. *Journal of Human Evolution* 24:113–46.
1993b   *Archaeology: The Science of Once and Future Things*. W. H. Freeman, New York.
Kirch, Patrick (ed.)
1988   *Archaeology of the Lapita Cultural Complex: A Critical Review*. Research Report no. 5, Thomas Burke Memorial Washington State Museum, Seattle.
McCartney, Allen, and James Savelle
1989   A Thule Eskimo Stone Vessel Complex. *Canadian Journal of Archaeology* 13:21–49.
Mack, Joanne
1991   Ceramic Figurines of the Western Cascades of Southern Oregon and Northern California. In *The New World Figurine Project,* vol. 1, edited by Terry Stocker, pp. 99–110. Research Press, Provo, Utah.
Mellars, Paul
1989   Major Issues in the Emergence of Modern Humans. *Current Anthropology* 30:349–85.
Morrison, Sandra, and Heather Myles
1992   The Sacred Mounds of Scowlitz. *The Midden* 24(4):2–4.
Myers, Thomas
1989   The Role of Pottery in the Rise of American Civilizations: The Ceramic Revolution. In *Ceramic Ecology 1988: Current Research on Ceramic Materials,* edited by Charles Kolb, pp. 1–28. British Archaeological Reports, Oxford.

Randsborg, Klavs
1982   Rank, Rights and Resources: An Archaeological Perspective from Denmark. In *Ranking, Resource and Exchange,* edited by C. Renfrew and S. Shennan, pp. 132–40. Cambridge University Press, Cambridge.
Rosen, Stephen
1993   The Decline and Fall of Flint. Paper presented at the Conference on Theory in Lithic Analysis, University of Tulsa, Tulsa, Oklahoma.
Sahlins, Marshall
1958   *Social Stratification in Polynesia*. University of Washington Press, Seattle.
Saitta, Dean, and Arthur Keene
1990   Politics and Surplus Flow in Prehistoric Communal Societies. In *The Evolution of Political Systems: Sociopolitics in Small-Scale Sedentary Societies,* edited by Steadman Upham, pp. 203–24. Cambridge University Press, Cambridge.
Sassaman, Kenneth
1993   *Early Pottery in the Southeast: Tradition and Innovation in Cooking Technology*. University of Alabama Press, Tuscaloosa.
Schmandt-Besserat, Denise
1977   The Beginnings of the Use of Clay in Turkey. *Anatolian Studies* 27:133–50.
Shennan, Stephen
1982   Ideology, Change and the European Early Bronze Age. In *Symbolic and Structural Archaeology,* edited by I. Hodder, pp. 155–61. Cambridge University Press, Cambridge.
1986   Central Europe in the Third Millenium B.C. *Journal of Anthropological Archaeology* 5:115–46.
Shnirelman, Victor
1992   Complex Hunter-Gatherers: Exception or Common Phenomenon? *Dialectical Anthropology* 17:183–96.
Stenger, Alison
1986   *The Prehistoric Ceramics of Lake River: A Preliminary Report*. Ceramic Analysis Laboratory, Portland State University, Portland, Oregon.
Stringer, C. B., and P. Andrews
1988   Genetic and Fossil Evidence for the Origin of Modern Humans. *Science* 239:1263–1268.
Vandiver, Pamela, O. Soffer, B. Klima, and J. Svoboda
1989   The Origins of Ceramic Technology at Dolni Vestonice, Czechoslovakia. *Science* 246:1002–1008.
Voytek, Barbara, and Ruth Tringham
1989   Rethinking the Mesolithic: The Case of South-East Europe. In *The Mesolithic in Europe,*

edited by Clive Bonsall, pp. 492–99. John Donald Publishers, Edinburgh.

White, Randall

1992   Beyond Art: Toward an Understanding of the Origins of Material Representation in Europe. *Annual Review of Anthropology* 21:537–64.

1993   Technological and Social Dimensions of "Aurignacian-Age" Body Ornaments across Europe. In *Before Lascaux,* edited by H. Knecht, A. Pike-Tay, and R. White, pp. 277–99. CRC Press, Boca Raton, Florida.

21

Social Strategies and Economic Change

Pottery in Context

IAN ARMIT AND BILL FINLAYSON

Recent interpretations of the Mesolithic-Neolithic transition in Europe have tended to stress the social basis of the change (e.g., Hodder 1990; Thomas 1988) as an alternative to previous models based primarily on environmental and economic factors and those based on colonization by farming groups. It has been suggested that the Neolithic was a cultural and ideological package "composed of an integrated set of cultural media and practices which served to promote and reproduce a particular way of thinking about the world" (Thomas 1991:18). The "package" comprised such elements as pottery, formal burial monuments, sedentism, domesticated animals, and agriculture itself.

We have suggested elsewhere (Armit and Finlayson 1992) that in contrast to this view, the set of media and practices that composed the Neolithic formed an assemblage of traits, elements of which may have been adopted by Mesolithic populations in the context of their own changing cultures. Rather than displacing indigenous cultures, "material symbols associated with agriculture or derived from agricultural practice provided a new means of symbolic expression for Mesolithic groups" (Armit and Finlayson 1992:674). Empirical evidence for this view includes the adoption of pottery by the Mesolithic Ertebølle communities of southern Scandinavia, and other examples have been cited elsewhere (Armit and Finlayson 1992). Because of the diversity of European Mesolithic communities, the transition to agriculture varied markedly, not only in its rate but also in the manner of change (Armit and Finlayson 1992).

This chapter examines one element of these complex transformations: the adoption of pottery. By expanding on the mechanisms of socioeconomic change and using comparative work in modern development studies, we will attempt to set our archaeological concept of cultural change in its wider context. Within this framework we will examine the adoption and initial development of pottery in northern and western Europe, specifically in Scotland, in the context of the transition from Mesolithic to Neolithic.

Development Studies

Although environmental pressures may frequently be significant, they cannot be translated into social and economic change without appropriate social mechanisms. This is a lesson that modern studies in development have recognized. The value of agricultural "improvements" may appear clear to an aid worker, for example, but their value has to be perceived by the recipient group. Modern development agencies have realized that the value of radical new methods is seldom self-evident and that a package cannot simply be imposed, despite the presence of serious environmental pressures (Yadav 1980). Even when development is not only required urgently for survival but is also supported from outside, "massive infusions of outside money for agriculture will not result in development unless individual farmers themselves decide it will" (Miller 1990:1).

Development studies have additionally highlighted a number of social issues affecting local adoption of development programs. These include socioeconomic structures, age, sex, education, language, religion, race, social status, income, land-tenure status differences, and illiteracy (Uphoff 1978). Although some of these issues are clearly irrelevant to the transformation of prehistoric hunter-gatherers into farmers, others are likely to have affected the ways in which individuals responded to farming. Uphoff noted, for example, that people are more likely to be able to participate in the decision-making process if they are members of organizations such as co-ops, unions, and so on. The presence of such institutions affects the economic and political context of decision making. Although our understanding of the nature and scale of late Mesolithic social institutions is presently poor, there are indications of substantial regional variations (Gendel 1984; Jacobi 1978), and we can postulate that differing local institutions will have had a profound affect on local development patterns.

Hagan has argued that change is rarely deliberate: "All farmers . . . conduct their operations by some kind of plan. Perhaps the general plan is a traditional one handed down from generation to generation. . . . Operating plans and day-by-day work procedures often become habitual and the manager rarely takes time to question what he is doing, how the work is performed, and whether or not some other way would be more productive and profitable for the time and effort applied" (Hagan 1971a:10). And: "Farming is predominantly a 'way of life' . . . instead of a business. Farming and family living are closely entwined and farm business decisions often are conditioned and altered by the necessities of family life. Farmwork and some kinds of management decisions often are shared among husband, wife and other members of the family unit" (Hagan 1971b:3). In other words, economic rationality is rarely to the fore, and subsistence practices

become inextricably entwined with social practices and the wider culture of the community. We would argue that these characteristics are not unique to farming (as Hagan maintains) but apply to subsistence economies in general, including those of hunter-gatherers.

It has also been argued that change will most likely occur where it can be absorbed with the minimum of effort: "The analysis indicates that in three different farming systems . . . farmers adopt new technologies where their characteristics are compatible with needs" (Pachico 1981). Change must be *compatible* with perceived needs. Congruence with the existing social order is important, "stronger than age, education, income and the economic importance of the innovation considered" (Amerasinghe and Vithanadurage 1974: 2). Miller argues that "congruence with culture understood as the total way of life of a people is a reasonable condition for the adoption of innovations in any line, not only in agriculture" (Miller 1990:21).

It is hard to see how, in the context of Third World societies, a cultural package could be imposed. Availability of new economic practices is not sufficient cause for their adoption, even if they are potentially more efficient and productive. Even severe environmental stress may not always have been sufficient to force an abandonment of traditional practices. These observations have important implications for the way we view economic change in prehistory.

Congruence and Opposition

VARIATION IN THE EUROPEAN MESOLITHIC

Our perceptions of Mesolithic society have changed markedly in recent years. The idea of homogenous, egalitarian hunter-gatherer societies has largely given way to a greater awareness of the complexity and variation in Mesolithic subsistence economies. At least two major dietary variations have been observed, one based on a mixed diet of plant foods, meat, and fish, and one based heavily on aquatic sources (Meiklejohn and Zvelebil 1991). Given the small number, size, and limited distribution of the skeletal samples analyzed to date, this generalization must represent a highly simplified picture of the patchwork of Mesolithic adaptations across Europe. Additional variations have been suggested in terms of population density and social stratification—suggestions made on the basis of site density, semipermanent occupation, and presence of large cemeteries, especially in southern Scandinavia

(Brinch-Petersen 1973; Zvelebil and Rowley-Conwy 1986). Added to this picture is pathological evidence for increased violence and dietary stress, which might indicate conflict and instability (Meiklejohn and Zvelebil 1991). Social differentiation is suggested by the variation in grave goods and rites and the correlation of various skeletal features with patterns of grave good deposition (Meiklejohn and Zvelebil 1991).

Rowley-Conwy has suggested the use of the term "complex" hunter-gatherers to describe societies such as the Ertebølle, which have a degree of sedentism, and notes that if hunter-gatherer societies do not conform to a few of the characteristics normally associated with hunter-gatherers, then they usually fail to conform to most of the characteristics (Rowley-Conwy 1983). The use of pottery by the Ertebølle is one such indication of complexity. There is an implication that complex hunter-gatherers have a substantially different mindset from that of their traditionally nomadic relations. We would further suggest that the division of complex and traditional hunter-gatherers is somewhat artificial and based on the relative wealth of preservation in southern Scandinavia. We suggest that the range of other deviations from the hunter-gatherer norm is wide, and that all hunter-gatherer societies will tend to deviate from the theoretical egalitarian norm. It is only where the evidence is better preserved (for example, within shell midden contexts) that we recognize complex societies (Finlayson n.d.).

RESISTANCE TO CHANGE

There is clear evidence that the rapid expansion of farming associated with the Linearbandkeramik (LBK) culture stalled in northern and western Europe. For centuries after the establishment of farming groups in the inland areas, indigenous Mesolithic populations continued to thrive and develop (see Gebauer, chapter 9). Various ideas have been put forward to explain the resistance of hunter-gatherers to farming. In the context of the Ertebølle, these explanations have ranged from the economic investment of many hunter-gatherer groups in specialized economic practices (Zvelebil 1990) to the ideological opposition to agriculture proposed by Hodder (1990).

In Hodder's view, it was initially impossible for the Ertebølle to adopt farming because of its association with the alien ideology of farming groups—an ideology centered on the domestic sphere, which Hodder has characterized as the "domus." They did, however, adopt pottery (although they developed their own distinctive forms) and shaft-hole axes from farming communities. Hodder believes these were elements that could be effectively dissociated from the "domus," the central structuring concept of the neighboring farming communities, whereas other traits, such as farming and longhouse construction, could not. Pottery and axes could thus be adopted by the Ertebølle without undermining their own distinctive ideology. Hodder's model of opposition itself requires its opposite: a concept of congruence close to that discussed earlier in the context of contemporary developing societies.

One key factor in the interaction of the Ertebølle with contemporary farming communities was the adoption of pottery. Ertebølle pottery, with its distinctive forms and decoration, clearly does not represent an ideological borrowing; the material and technology were adopted, but not the form or decoration. Considering that few other Neolithic traits were adopted, it seems reasonable to suppose that Ertebølle pottery became an integral part of the Ertebølle symbolic repertoire and was not seen as an alien or exotic product.

This malleability of cultural meanings has important implications for the adoption of other conventionally Neolithic traits elsewhere in Europe. The Ertebølle were exposed to farming communities with a radically different ideology and range of economic systems. It would not be surprising if the symbolic associations of Neolithic traits with alien ideologies was strongest in the areas where radically different communities were exposed to each other. These are the areas in which we might expect to see evidence for an indivisible Neolithic package. Instead, we see in the Ertebølle, for example, the piecemeal adoption of congruent traits that rapidly acquire culturally specific symbolic associations. This sort of cultural "frontier zone" is not the context in which Neolithic traits were adopted in Britain, and certainly not in Scotland. Once such traits had been adopted and effectively divorced from any concept of a Neolithic ideology, their spread among more closely related hunter-gatherer communities may have been considerably more rapid.

Pottery

POTTERY AND SYMBOLIC ELABORATION

The case of the Ertebølle demonstrates that there is no necessary connection between pottery and agriculture. Elsewhere, aceramic Neolithic communities are well documented, for example in the early Neolithic of the

Near East, and pottery spread independently of food production in much of Africa (Close, chapter 3). Although ceramic technology may have been introduced into Europe by farming societies, its spread appears to have been at least partially independent of the spread of agriculture.

To the archaeologist interested in the analysis of material culture and exploration of its social and symbolic meanings, the emergence of pottery is of the utmost significance. In much of Europe the rich decoration and range of forms seem to offer the potential for a detailed reconstruction of past ideologies if only we could "read" the material properly—crack the symbolic code. We should not, however, let this sudden emergence of archaeological potential blind us to the existence, prior to the adoption of pottery, of equally rich and diverse cultures with their own, perishable forms of symbolic expression.

Before ceramics there are few artifactual survivals from hunter-gatherer communities that have the potential to display status differentiation. Despite this relative poverty of survival, there have been significant attempts to define social territories in the Mesolithic in Europe and Britain (Gendel 1984; Jacobi 1979:63–68); evidence for these territories is based on stylistic differences in lithic manufacture. There are other indications that status differentiation and/or ethnic identity was displayed in organic materials such as clothing (Finlayson n.d.), and there are rare examples of elaborated organic artifacts, such as the canoe paddles from Tybrind Vig (Andersen 1983).

In Scotland, most Mesolithic stone artifacts, particularly microliths, are too small to have ever been used as overt symbols, whether as armatures or as other tool elements. Although the arrangement of these artifacts as armatures and the arrow shafts and other items with which they were associated may well have been loaded with symbolic meaning, these meanings are not generally available to us from the archaeological record. Thus the one surviving, typologically diagnostic tool of the period is unlikely to have been used directly in an emblematic manner.

With the adoption of pottery, we need not be seeing the emergence of status differentiation in portable artifacts but simply the ability of evidence for status differentiation for the first time to survive in quantity in the archaeological record. Thus we should not be too surprised if, with the emergence of pottery, we appear suddenly to witness an explosion of symbolic behavior and an equally dramatic upsurge in ethnic identification and social differentiation.

POTTERY AND THE MESOLITHIC

It is hard to assess the adoption of pottery in the context of nonfarming societies in Scotland. The central problem is that the very presence of pottery has been taken as evidence of the existence of a Neolithic community. Because the Neolithic has been seen as a package, there has been little consideration of the possibility that pottery was adopted by hunter-gatherer groups. This is particularly odd since pottery is manifestly found in the upper levels of otherwise apparently clearly Mesolithic sites in Scotland, as at Ulva Cave (Bonsall, Sutherland et al. 1989) and Kinloch, Rhum (Wickham-Jones 1990). At the latter site these "Neolithic" levels, although not substantially different in character from the Mesolithic deposits, were thought to indicate a peripheral part of a Neolithic settlement whose focus (presumably a permanent, farming settlement) must lie off-site.

The use of pottery to signal the presence of "Neolithic" culture, combined with the belief that the Neolithic is an indivisible package, has served to deny the possibility of pottery use in nonfarming communities in Scotland. In fact, there is no reason to believe that pottery and agriculture were adopted at the same time, and the evidence from sites like Ulva and Kinloch clearly demonstrates the possibility of pottery use within economic systems that show no appreciable change from the Mesolithic. This use would seem to parallel that of pottery in a Mesolithic context in southern Scandinavia.

THE INITIAL ADOPTION OF POTTERY

The earliest pottery in Scotland is characterized by a wide diversity of styles, most of which have a strong regional concentration (Fig. 21.1). These styles are defined generally on the basis of a loose mix of morphological and decorative characteristics. A more consistent and objective classification is still required. Nonetheless, it is clear that compared with styles of later periods, the earliest pottery styles were highly diversified across Scotland, with styles such as Unstan Ware, Beacharra Ware, Hebridean Ware, Rothesay/Achnacree Ware, and others all representing local forms (Fig. 21.2).

The number of distinct pottery styles and their varying, though often overlapping, geographical distributions suggest that pottery at this stage tended to be related to specific groups of people associated with particular areas. As well as supporting the case for

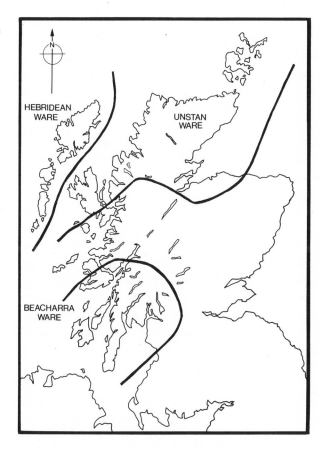

Fig. 21.1. Distribution of selected pottery styles of the earlier Neolithic in Scotland (data from Kinnes 1985).

indigenous development rather than colonization (which would surely have produced a more consistent ceramic tradition), this geographical diversity suggests that different populations across Scotland were using ceramics as a medium for the expression of group identity or ethnicity. This suggestion does not mean, however, that any simplistic equation can be made between pottery typology and ethnicity. This Scottish pattern seems to be broadly representative of the rest of Britain, where the early Neolithic is characterized by a diversity of ceramic styles. Bradley (1984:12) even notes that "the major styles of Neolithic pottery in southern England are distributed over rather the same areas as the artifacts which define several of the 'social territories' of the Late Mesolithic."

Nonceramic evidence, too, supports the case for continuity into the early Neolithic; for example, the continuing use of "Obanian" sites indicates the persistence of a specialized economic practice within a logistic economy and the continuing use of Mesolithic occupation sites (Armit and Finlayson 1992).

SUBSEQUENT DEVELOPMENT

The later Neolithic in Scotland, as in the rest of Britain, is characterized by the emergence of pottery styles that are much more widespread in distribution and more uniform in morphology and decoration. The first of these styles is Grooved Ware (Fig. 21.3), generally

Fig. 21.2. Scottish Neolithic pottery: Unstan, Hebridean, and Beacharra styles.

HEBRIDEAN WARE

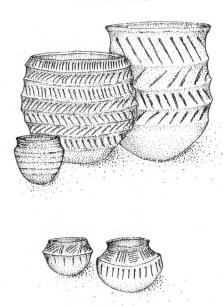

BEACHARRA WARE

UNSTAN WARE

Fig. 21.3. Scottish Neolithic pottery: Grooved Ware.

bucket-shaped, flat-based pots with incised and applied zoned decoration (Kinnes 1985:49). Grooved Ware has been described as the first "genuinely national ceramic style" (Kinnes 1985:43). Despite a number of possible substyles, the pottery is recognizably in the same tradition from Orkney to the south of England.

Grooved Ware is succeeded by a series of other "national" (and "international") styles—beakers, food vessels, and cordoned and collared urns (Bradley 1984:72)—which, although they overlap in chronological span, seem to represent successive traditions. As new styles were developed, the older styles appear to have declined in quality and symbolic force. Bradley (1984:72) has suggested that this happened through a process of "emulation" as successive styles became more widely available and lost their initial symbolic associations, necessitating the creation of novel prestige material.

POTTERY IN CONTEXT

In the terms used by Barnett in his discussion of Neolithic pottery in southern France (Barnett 1990), the earlier Neolithic in Scotland appears to have been characterized by a series of delimiting styles focused on distinct geographical regions. Pottery appears to have played a part in the material construction of the ethnicity of different communities. In the absence of detailed work on the sources and movement of various types of ceramics, the pattern of regional diversity suggests that pottery was not routinely exchanged over great distances, in contrast to the pattern in other areas, notably the west Mediterranean (Barnett 1990).

By the later Neolithic, however, a series of successive unifying styles became dominant in which ethnic distinctions between communities were no longer made explicit through the medium of ceramics. Although our analyses of ceramic variation have a long way to go, and apparent typological uniformity may mask what were originally significant variations, there is little doubt that a broad-scale transformation had occurred in the social and symbolic role of pottery from the earlier to the later Neolithic.

The processes involved in the adoption of pottery apply equally to the other conventional indicators of the Neolithic, such as monuments and domesticates. There are interesting parallels, for example, between the development of monumentality and that of pottery. Burial monuments in the early Neolithic seem to have strong local styles and have been interpreted as being associated with territoriality and resource control, the same concerns with the autonomy and identity of the local group that are manifested in the adoption and embellishment of local pottery styles. The use of totemism to identify and distinguish group affiliations has also been suggested on the basis of animal and bird deposits in Orcadian chambered tombs (Hedges 1984). Indeed, territoriality and resource control may have required greater emphasis in the earlier Neolithic, when communities were less heavily dependent on identifiable agricultural resources.

It is significant that local burial monuments disappear in the later Neolithic to be replaced by fewer, larger monuments indicative of the cooperation of larger groups marshaled by more outward-looking authorities. Grooved Ware appears in the archaeological record in association with these new monument types. At Balfarg in Fife, Grooved Ware first appears in association with the henge monument, having been absent in the previous phases of more transient activity (Barclay and Russell-White n.d.). The same pattern can be discerned at Wellbrae in Strathclyde, where early Neolithic domestic activity without apparent permanent structures is succeeded by a large enclosure complex associated with Grooved Ware (Alexander and Armit 1993). In Orkney, the emergence of Grooved Ware may also be associated with the appearance of nucleated village settlements like Skara Brae, replacing isolated farmsteads like Knap of Howar (Ritchie 1983).

The phenomenon of early, local pottery styles may reflect the relevance of ceramics to early, semimobile communities, who had a need to define their identity through their artifacts. The widespread networks of communication witnessed by the dispersal of pottery styles such as Grooved Ware imply not only the existence of larger, less mobile communities but also a substantially different symbolic role for ceramics within those societies.

With the appearance of more settled communities and more extensive authorities, the overt display of local identity, through both pottery and other aspects of material culture such as burial monuments, seems to have receded. Perhaps the establishment of more powerful hierarchies had been accompanied by the formalizing of rights to land and resources; such formal divisions of land can be seen, for example, in the upstanding Neolithic field systems of Shetland (Whittle 1986).

Conclusions

Available Neolithic traits were thus adopted when they were congruent, when their symbolic associations did not undermine those of the existing ideology, and when they had a perceived social and symbolic role within existing social strategies. Some Neolithic traits need have had no direct economic impact: funerary monuments and pottery, for example, are potential means of status differentiation, theoretically open to adoption by hunter-gatherers within a seasonally mobile economy. Artifacts may have been used, for instance, in the circulation of prestige objects or the reinforcement of different social roles within the community. The latter may have been the case with the adoption of pottery in the Ertebølle and, in another context, the former with the circulation of Western exotica in the cargo cults of Polynesia.

Other traits could in time have had profound economic effects. There is little reason to suppose that traditional economic indicators, such as sheep and crops, should be regarded any differently from exotic items of material culture: man-made agricultural developments have a social as well as an economic aspect, especially in the context where they are novel and their associated knowledge may be restricted. Thus, social strategies of hunter-gatherers can lead to lasting economic change, determining the archaeologically perceived change from Mesolithic to Neolithic.

There is great regional variation in the nature of the Mesolithic-Neolithic transition (Armit and Finlayson 1992), and it is therefore possible to envisage a number of mechanisms by which Neolithic traits might have become socially congruent. Barnett (chapter 7) has suggested that the impetus for the adoption of conven-

tionally Neolithic traits in the western Mediterranean was the desire to accumulate surplus for competitive social display and consumption. In Scotland the evidence for such practices is so far lacking; for example, pottery does not appear to have been exchanged over any great distances. The multiplicity of early styles suggests that pottery was adopted as a congruent cultural element well suited to displaying ethnicity and identity in communities where these were already significant concerns. The diversity of regional traditions in both ceramics and burial, the continuity of settlement on existing sites, and the persistence of specialized activity sites such as those manifested by the Obanian "culture" all confirm the basic continuity of population through a protracted period of social and economic transition.

In Britain, the evidence of both ceramics and monuments suggests that the principal, identifiable period of social change came at the beginning of the later Neolithic. Whereas earlier communities appear to have maintained the social and economic trajectories of their Mesolithic ancestors, the later Neolithic witnessed a dramatic transformation in social organization, ideology, and the display of power. Evidence for a major economic shift, however, is still ambiguous and variable between regions: we have not sought simply to shift the "Neolithic revolution" forward in time. Rather, we hope to have highlighted some of the social factors that conditioned the social and economic transformations undergone by societies in northern and western Europe.

Acknowledgment

The authors would like to thank Diane Nelson for her comments on a previous draft of this chapter.

References Cited

Alexander, D., and I. Armit
1993   Unstratified Stratigraphy: Methodologies for the Interpretation and Presentation of Cropmark Sites. In *Interpreting Stratigraphy*, edited by J. W. Barber, pp. 37–41. AOC Scotland Ltd., Edinburgh.
Amerasinghe, N., and N. Vithanadurage
1974   Some Socio-economic Determinants of the Adoption of Improved Management Practices in Paddy Production. *Journal of the National*

Agricultural Society of Ceylon (Sri Lanka)
11(12):1–17.

Andersen, S. H.
1983   Patterned Oar Blades from Tybrind Vig. *Kuml*
1982–83: 11–30.

Armit, I., and B. Finlayson
1992   Hunter-Gatherers Transformed: The
Transition to Agriculture in Northern and
Western Europe. *Antiquity* 66:664–76.

Barclay, G. J., and C. J. Russell-White
n.d.   Excavations in the Ceremonial Complex
at Balfarg/Balbirnie, Glenrothes, Fife.
Proceedings of the Society of Antiquaries
of Scotland 123. In press.

Barnett, W. K.
1990   Small-Scale Transport of Early Neolithic
Pottery in the West Mediterranean. *Antiquity*
64:859–65.

Bonsall, J. C., D. G. Sutherland, et al.
1989   *Ulva Cave: Excavation Report Number 3.*
Department of Archaeology, University
of Edinburgh.

Bradley, R.
1984   *The Social Foundations of British Prehistory.*
Longman, London.

Brinch-Petersen, E.
1973   A Survey of Late Palaeolithic Denmark. In
The Mesolithic in Europe, edited by Z. K.
Kozlowski, pp. 77–127. Warsaw University Press, Warsaw.

Finlayson, B.
n.d.   Complexity in the Mesolithic of the Western
Scottish Seaboard. In *Proceedings of the Man,
Sea, and the Mesolithic Conference, Horsholm,
Denmark.* In press.

Gendel, P. A.
1984   *Mesolithic Territories in Northwestern Europe.*
British Archaeological Reports, International
Series 218, Oxford.

Hagan, A. R.
1971a *Farm Planning at the Micro-Level.* EAPD Staff
Paper no. 2, HMGN, Ministry of Food and
Agriculture, Kathmandu.
1971b *Suggestions for Farm Management Research in
Nepal.* EAPD Staff Paper no. 7, HMGN,
Ministry of Food and Agriculture,
Kathmandu.

Hedges, J.
1984   *Tomb of the Eagles.* John Murray, London.

Hodder, I.
1990   *The Domestication of Europe.* Cambridge
University Press, Cambridge.

Jacobi, R.
1978   Northern England in the Eighth Millennium
B.C.: An Essay. In *The Early Postglacial

Settlement of Northern Europe,* edited by P.
Mellars, pp. 295–332. Duckworth, London.
1979   Early Flandrian Hunters in the South-West.
Proceedings of the Devon Archaeological Society
37:48–93.

Kinnes, I.
1985   Circumstance, Not Context: The Neolithic of
Scotland as Seen from the Outside. *Proceedings
of the Society of Antiquaries of Scotland* 115:
15–57.

Meiklejohn, C., and M. Zvelebil
1991   Health Status of European Populations at the
Agricultural Transition and the Implications
for the Adoption of Farming. In *Health in Past
Societies,* edited by H. Bush and M. Zvelebil,
pp. 129–45. British Archaeological Reports,
International Series 218, Oxford.

Miller, C. J.
1990   *Decision Making in Village Nepal.* Sahayogi
Press, Kathmandu.

Pachico, E. H.
1981   Small Farmer Decision Making: An Economic
Analysis of Three Farming Systems in the
Hills of Nepal. *World Agricultural Economics and
Rural Sociology Abstracts* 1981:394–95.

Ritchie, A.
1983   Excavation of a Neolithic Farmstead at Knap
of Howar, Papa Westray, Orkney. *Proceedings
of the Society of Antiquaries of Scotland* 113:40–
121.

Rowley-Conwy, P.
1983   Sedentary Hunters: The Ertebolle Example. In
Hunter-Gatherer Economy, edited by G. Bailey,
pp. 111–26. Cambridge University Press,
Cambridge.

Thomas, J.
1988   Neolithic Explanations Revisited: The
Mesolithic-Neolithic Transition in Britain
and South Scandinavia. *Proceedings of the Prehistoric Society* 54:59–66.
1991   *Re-thinking the Neolithic.* Cambridge
University Press, Cambridge.

Uphoff, N.
1978   Problems Inhibiting Achievement of Broader
People's Participation. In *People's Participation
in Rural Development in Nepal,* pp. 68–71.
Agricultural Projects Services Centre
(APROSC), Kathmandu.

Whittle, A.
1986   *Scord of Brouster: An Early Agricultural
Settlement on Shetland.* Oxford University
Committee for Archaeology Monograph 9,
Oxford.

Wickham-Jones, C.
1990   *Rhum: Mesolithic and Later Sites at Kinloch: Ex-

cavations 1984–86. Society of Antiquaries of Scotland, Monograph Series 7, Edinburgh.

Yadav, Ram P.
1980   *People's Participation: Focus on Mobilisation of the Rural Poor. Local Level Planning and Rural Development.* Concept Publishing Co., New Delhi.

Zvelebil, M.
1990   Economic Intensification and Postglacial Hunter-Gatherers in North Temperate Europe. In *The Mesolithic in Europe,* edited by J. C. Bonsall, pp. 80–88. John Donald, Edinburgh.

Zvelebil, M., and P. Rowley-Conwy
1986   Foragers and Farmers in Atlantic Europe. In *Hunters in Transition: Mesolithic Societies of Temperate Eurasia and Their Transition to Farming,* edited by M. Zvelebil, pp. 67–93. Cambridge University Press, Cambridge.

22

Why Did They Invent Pottery Anyway?

For more than a hundred years, archaeologists have been intrigued by pottery. They have discovered it, classified it, dated it, used it to infer cultural affiliations, wondered about its use, and speculated about its origin. My own ethnoarchaeological fieldwork has focused upon pottery as it is made and used by various societies in the Philippines and in China. My work and that of my students has attempted to understand the sources of variation of pottery in an effort to strengthen archaeological inference. Can such research shed light on the origins of pottery? Yes, I would argue, for a variety of reasons.

But since I know the origin of pottery making among the Kalinga people of northern Luzon, let me share that knowledge with you at this point.

How Pottery Making Came to the Kalinga
As Told by Lingayo in Dangtalan, 29 October 1975

People here in the mountains originally came from the lowlands. Ever since, they have called their god Kabunyan. During those early days Kabunyan was traveling in the mountains with his son. The first place they reached was the region of Benguet. He saw many pine trees in Benguet and even today that region has many pine trees. From Benguet, Kabunyan went to Bontoc. From there he proceeded to Sumadel. While he was in Sumadel, he planted sugar cane there. And even today, there is plenty of sugar cane that grows there.

Every night, Kabunyan worked in his sugar mill and, because of the noise, he created a disturbance in Sumadel. The people became so angry that they killed his son.

As a punishment for the people of Sumadel, he left their town, and he gave every family a large cooking pot. No matter how large or small their family, even though they filled this pot with rice, they would never feel filled up; they would always feel hungry. And that is true even today.

He put his son on his back and left Sumadel. He passed through Lubuagan and, upon reaching Lonong, he was already tired. He lay down and slept there and today one can see the spot because there is a large depression there. He stuck his spear in the ground and ever since, there has been a spring flowing from the hole.

The next morning, he went down to Dangtalan and there he looked for a container so he could cook his rice. Because he could not find a pot, he made one out of clay that he dug up right at Dangtalan. He cooked his rice and that evening he left his pot where he had cooked. So the people saw the pot made by Kabunyan and they also knew how he had made it because they had watched him. The people now knew how to make pots and that is why the women of Dangtalan are potters today.

WILLIAM A. LONGACRE

When Kabunyan left Dangtalan, he crossed the Pasil River and went up to Kuta Kupa. Because his son, whom he was carrying on his back, was covered with blood, he struck a stone and water poured out. He bathed his child. After this, he continued to climb uphill.

When he reached Galdang, he was very thirsty, so he struck a stone with his spear and, again, water flowed from that spot. Today, that spring is the source of water for the people of Galdang. After he had drunk the water, he put his son up on his back and continued his journey to Abra.

When he reached Abra, the people were very kind; they respected him, were polite, and they gave him food. He was grateful to the hospitable people of Abra, so he blessed them and gave them a bountiful life with plenty of food. He also planted bamboo for the people and even today there is plenty of bamboo in Abra.

That is the end of the story of Kabunyan, the god of the peoples here in the mountains.

Early Pottery Elsewhere

Thus, in at least one case, we know the explanation for the origin of the ceramic cooking pot. Let me now turn to the rest of the world, painting with a broad brush, drawing upon the preceding chapters and other statements about the beginnings of pottery making. I do so to explore the possible explanations for pottery and to attempt to add to an understanding of that incredible invention. I will start by reviewing what we know, or at least what we think we know.

In a recent paper, Skibo and Schiffer (1993) concluded, correctly in my opinion, that pottery was invented by women and remained a woman's technology for millennia. Others have made similar arguments (e.g., Sassaman 1992). As they point out, pottery is one of the few technologies controlled by women, and it was a revolutionary invention. It permitted the opening up of broader ranges of foodstuffs for consumption through processing by ceramic-assisted cooking. These foodstuffs included an incredible array of seeds and grains, both wild and domestic, as well as a variety of bivalves, shellfishes, and snails. It may be, too, that pottery figured in fermentation and detoxification, especially in tropical environments. The broadening of available and usable foods would surely have conferred advantage—selective advantage—on peoples using pots.

As Brown documented some time ago (1989), familiarity with clay and the firing of clay is not sufficient to explain the beginning of pottery making. Such familiarity was well developed by the late Pleistocene, at least in the Old World. The first pots, most of which are cooking vessels, begin to show up in various parts of the world at the end of the Pleistocene and into the earlier part of the Holocene period. It is clear that these earliest clay pots are associated with foraging-collecting economies and somewhat mobile lifeways. Earliest pottery does *not* appear to be associated with sedentary agricultural economies.

The chapters in this volume document the earliest known appearances of pottery and the sociopolitical and economic contexts of those occurrences. A few go further and attempt to explain the first appearance of pottery in a region or to discuss the possible social nexus of its first use. But more on that later.

The recent emphasis on materials-science appraisals of pottery in terms of performance characteristics holds great promise for shedding light on its earliest development. Several of the chapters mention performance characteristics of tempers and vessel wall thickness in discussing vessel function. Cooking over an open fire is best done with pots lacking abrupt angles, with a thermal-shock–resistant temper, and a clay combination with good thermal conductivity.

Several chapters and Brown's earlier contribution (1989) mention the cooking technique called "stone boiling," or better (following Sassaman, chapter 18), "indirect moist cooking." Sassaman's chapter is the only one that reports attempts to discern actual pot use from the study of surface alterations. He used presence of exterior sooting to conclude that a pot was used over an open fire. Lacking such sooting, indirect moist cooking was inferred. He makes a case for the rendering of oils or grease using an indirect cooking technology.

But one could also cook shellfish, a process that also opens the shell, or cook gastropods. The Kalinga seine their rice fields after each harvest and collect a small snail, a long-legged water spider, and a large black water beetle with orange flesh. All three are cooked with water in ceramic pots to form a highly popular soup. The snail's meat is easily sucked from the shell after cooking, with a distinctive sound. It has always made me nervous eating this delicacy, because the snail is the vector for schistosomiasis.

Vessel shape is also important to Sassaman's argument. He notes that vessels that lack exterior sooting tend to have flat bottoms, making them stable containers for "stone boiling" technology. In many parts of the world, flat-bottomed pots are associated with cooking on coals to produce porridgelike foods (e.g., Japan and Korea). Cooking on coals would not produce large accumulations of exterior sooting.

Experimentation is called for to assess the technology of "stone boiling" using low-fired, friable, fiber-tempered pottery. It is hard for me to imagine using stones—dropping them into the water and later recovering them—without damaging such a fragile pot.

Many of the suggestions concerning advantages of pots for food processing discuss the actual foods being cooked, fermented, detoxified, and so forth. What seems to be called for next is the application of a suite of techniques for identifying the actual uses of pottery. Sassaman makes a good start, but more sophisticated surface-alteration studies are the logical next step. We need not only to assess the distribution of external sooting but also to identifiy organic residues as an aid to inferring pottery use. Residue analysis is far more complex than we originally thought, but it holds enormous promise of strong functional inference in pottery analysis. I would think that nut oil versus animal grease extraction would be easily identified through residue analysis, for example. To strengthen this technique and others, clearly we need more experimental studies tied closely to additional ethnoarchaeological research programs.

From Kobayashi's (1994) and Skibo's (1992) work with Kalinga pottery, we know that there is a strong pattern of sooting on the inside walls of rice-cooking pots that is easily recognized. The pattern of interior soot accumulation associated with the cooking of meats and vegetables is quite different from the pattern observed in the rice pots. Thus, it is fairly easy to identify rice-cooking pots and vegetable/meat-cooking vessels by examining the interior patterns of sooting. Kobayashi is studying prehistoric Japanese pottery from the Jomon-Yayoi transition to see if rice cooking is evidenced in the cooking pots dating to that period, which saw the introduction of rice to Japan.

Beyond adding to the available foods through improvements in cooking technology, the use of pottery confers other advantages to peoples employing ceramic technology. Brown (1989) points to several in his seminal article, including the impact on time and labor through the freeing of time for doing other things while cooking.

But what about the social advantages that pottery bestows? Several of the chapters refer to the importance of feasting. Hoopes, for example, suggests the possibility that the explanation for the origin of potting might lie in the context of small group or individual feasting rather than in daily cooking functions. He sees group cohesion and projection of power through wealth display and generosity in feasting—what he and others refer to as the "aggrandizer/accumulation model." Of course, among the best ethnographic examples—Northwest Coast Indians in North America and ranked systems in Polynesia—there are no pots! How widespread feasting and social factors turn out to be across our world sample is unclear. This may be a tropical forager pattern and thus a special case.

But there is a clear association between the earliest pottery and the enlargement of the array of foods more efficiently processed. And some foods were not able to be processed readily at all, prior to the advent of cooking pots. Because food processing and potting seem to be women's technology, and because there is a link between these tasks and the increasing use of seeds requiring simmering, I wonder whether women played a primary role in the process of plant domestication. If we have Man the Hunter and Woman the Potter, Cook, and Gatherer (albeit stereotypical and inaccurate models), might women have been the driving force in seed selection for planting versus cooking, thus—gradually—contributing to the domestication process (Watson and Kennedy 1991)?

I hope these forays into understanding the beginnings of pottery making continue. I urge more and better analyses employing use-alteration, including residue studies. Let us try our best to find out just what these pots were being used for. And I hope we will continue to pursue the social context of early pottery, exploring social advantages of pottery use, aspects of gender, and social cohesion and group identification and solidarity. For the latter, one must keep in mind the lack of visibility of much measurable stylistic variation, as well as the context of pottery use and thus its audience. To be applied broadly, stylistic signals of significant social boundaries must be conspicuous and unambiguous (loud and clear). Pottery would seem to be a poor vehicle for such important information, compared with a flag, headdress, or color of dress.

References Cited

Brown, James A.
1989   The Beginnings of Pottery as an Economic Process. In *What's New? A Closer Look at the Process of Innovation,* edited by S. van der Leeuw and R. Torrence, pp. 203–24. Unwin Hyman, London.

Kobayashi, Masashi

1994   Use-Alteration Analysis of Kalinga Pottery: Interior Carbon Deposits of Cooking Pots. In *Kalinga Ethnoarchaeology: Expanding Archaeological Method and Theory,* edited by W. A. Longacre and J. M. Skibo, pp. 127–68. Smithsonian Institution Press, Washington, D.C.

Sassaman, Kenneth E.

1992   Gender and Technology at the Archaic-Woodland "Transition." In *Exploring Gender through Archaeology: Selected Papers from the 1991 Boone Conference,* edited by C. Claassen, pp. 71–79. Prehistory Press, Madison, Wisconsin.

Skibo, James M.

1992   *Pottery Function: A Use-Alteration Perspective.* Plenum Press, New York.

Skibo, James M., and Michael B. Schiffer

1993   The Clay Cooking Pot: An Exploration of Women's Technology. Paper presented at the annual meeting of the Society for American Archaeology.

Watson, Patty Jo, and M. Kennedy

1991   The Development of Horticulture in the Eastern Woodlands of North America: Women's Role. In *Engendering Archaeology: Women and Prehistory,* edited by J. Gero and M. Conkey, pp. 255–75. Basil Blackwell, Oxford.

Index

Manos. *See under* Lithics

Manufacture, pottery. *See* Production

Maranta sp. (arrowroot). *See under* Root crops

Marine resources. *See* Fish; Mammals; Molluscs; Turtles

Material culture studies, 134, 142, 246, 270, 273

Meggers, Betty, 115, 116, 130

Mesolithic, 5, 27, 30–31, 39, 80–85, 99–103, 258, 267, 268, 269, 270, 271, 273; pottery, 5, 30–31, 99, 102–103, 108, 270; social organization, 81–82, 102, 268, 270, 271; subsistence, 30–31, 80–81, 85, 99, 268

Metallurgy, 2, 48, 62, 233

Metate. *See under* Lithics

Meuse pottery. *See* Rhine-Meuse-Schelde pottery

Mexico, 5, 187, 192, 199, 202, 209, 210, 212, 215

Microliths. *See under* Lithics

Middens, shell, 13–14, 15, 82, 85, 102–103, 115–18, 120, 121, 124, 125, 128, 130, 145–50, 155, 186, 200, 205, 228, 269. *See also* Shellfishing

Migration, 80, 83, 85, 128, 166, 185, 196, 205, 267, 271

Milagro, 242

Mina culture, 116, 119, 120, 121, 128, 129

Mobility, 133, 134

Modal analysis, 202, 213

Mogollon, 242, 245

Molluscs, 30–31, 122, 126; bivalves, 127, 146, 150, 169, 171, 228, 278; gastropods, 146, 153, 169, 227, 228, 279

Monagrillo, 169, 170, 172, 173, 175, 179, 181, 182, 187, 188, 189; ^{14}C dates, 169, 172, 173, 176, 189; dates, 176, 177, 179; phase, 171, 176, 189; pottery, 169, 171–82, 186, 187, 189; sites, 169, 171, 172, 173, 176; structures, 173; subsistence, 172, 177, 178, 179, 181

Monsú, 136, 137, 139, 140, 142, 145, 151–54, 155

Moravia, 91

Morgan, L. H., 4

Mosegården, 103

Muge, 82

Mureybat, 42, 46

Nabta, 25, 27–29, 32

Nahal Oren, 42

Nance. See under Tree crops

Naranjo phase, 196

Natsushima, 13–14, 17

Neolithic, 2–5, 12, 23, 26, 28, 31–32, 39–51, 55, 62, 65, 70–71, 74, 79–85, 93–95, 99, 106–107, 157, 166, 223, 261, 262, 267, 269–72, 273; Balkan, 73; "cultural package," 84; Early, 58, 60, 66, 79, 83–84, 102–103, 105, 272; Final, 58, 62; Late, 58, 272, 273; revolution, 39, 273; Saharo-Sudanese, 26, 30

Nicaragua, 186, 187, 196

Nile Valley, 23, 25–27, 30, 32, 260

Nomads, 126

Nosa, 70

Nutrition, 3–5, 6, 58, 72, 103, 134, 178, 190, 191, 193, 196, 241, 245, 246, 249, 250

Obanian culture, 271, 273

Obre, 70

Obsidian, 44, 47, 58, 83, 92, 199, 201. *See also* Exchange; Lithics

Ocós phase, 199–204, 213–15

Oil, 31, 126, 135, 178, 189–91, 194, 195, 227, 228, 279; nut, 227, 228, 232, 234, 279; palm, 126, 190, 191; turtle, 126

Olla. *See under* Vessel form

Omalian pottery, 91

Orkney Islands, 272

Ostrich eggshell, 27, 28

Padina, 69

Paituna phase, 128

Paleoindians, 129

Palm trees. *See under* Tree crops

Panama, 169–73, 177, 178–81, 185, 186, 188, 189, 194

Pangola phase, 153, 154, 155

Paris Basin, 91, 94

Parita Bay, 169, 171–73, 177, 179, 180–82, 186

Peccary. *See* Fauna: collared peccary

Penan, 190

Performance characteristics of pottery, 3, 72, 225–27, 279; hardness, 42, 47, 60, 173, 202, 203; porosity, 71, 72–73, 101; thermal alteration, 215; thermal coefficient, 72–73; thermal conductivity and diffusivity, 72–73, 228, 279; thermal performance, 72–74, 127, 137; thermal shock resistance, 72–73, 101–102, 226, 228, 231, 241; use-alteration, 214, 215

Philippines, 273

Phytoliths. *See under* Floral remains

Phytomorphism, 217. *See also* Skeuomorphism

Pithouses, 242, 243, 246, 250

Plants. *See* Agriculture; Domestication; Horticulture; Root crops; Seed crops; Tree crops

Plaster, 45–46, 48, 51, 93

Playa el Huizcoyol, 200, 205

Pleistocene, 25, 27, 94, 116, 129, 164, 166, 278; transition to Holocene, 17–19, 172, 257, 259, 263

Poland, 89, 90–91, 94

Pollen. *See under* Floral remains

Ponta das Pedras, 118

Population: distribution, 4, 73, 81, 173, 179; growth, 19, 31, 115, 130, 201; pressure, 80, 83, 195, 214

Porosity. *See under* Performance characteristics of pottery

Porto da Mina, 118

Portugal, 82, 83, 85

Potters, 42, 46, 55–56, 58–60, 62, 73–74, 206, 234, 247; shamans as, 62; women as, 61, 101, 126, 273

Pottery: classification, 47; coarse ware, 26, 42–43, 47–48, 57, 58–60, 66–67, 71, 73, 91; color, 40, 60–61; economic aspects, 1–2, 28, 30, 74, 79, 82, 85, 135, 193, 195; manufacture, 1–3, 4, 6, 15, 26, 32, 40, 46, 48, 101; religious aspects, 1, 81, 192, 193, 214, 216, 261, 262; social aspects, 135, 142, 177, 186, 191, 192, 194–96, 214, 216, 217, 224, 232, 233, 246, 250, 271, 272, 279

Potting, 3, 39, 44, 244, 248, 279. *See also* Firing; Forming of pottery; Shape

Poverty Point, 235

Pox pottery, 210, 211

Practical technology, 258

Preagricultural, 5, 80–82, 83, 85. *See also* Archaic period

Preceramic, 4–6, 115, 116, 120, 122, 124, 127, 135, 159, 160, 161, 164, 187, 192, 193, 196, 205, 210, 228, 246, 250

Prestige and prestige technology, 3–4, 6, 15, 16, 62, 80–83, 85, 192, 193, 206, 216, 233, 234, 257, 258, 259, 260, 261–63, 272, 273

Production, 4–5, 7, 134; domestic mode of, 73; household, 6, 15, 58, 70, 101, 247; local, 26, 31–32, 56, 99–101; organization of, 60, 101; nonspecialist, 101; scheduling of, 241, 248, 249, 251

Puerto Chacho, 136, 145–50, 152, 154, 155

Puerto Hormiga, 136, 139, 140, 142, 145, 146, 149, 150–55

Puerto Marquez, 210

Punta Concepción, 158, 159, 162

Purron pottery, 209, 211, 212, 217

Quartz, 171, 173, 228, 229, 231

Radiocarbon dating. *See* Carbon 14 dating

Rain forests, tropical, 115, 121, 127, 187, 193, 194

Rarámuri, 4

Ras Shamra, 42–43

Real Alto, 158, 160–66

Red Mountain phase, 242, 243

Residential: mobility, 73, 134; stability, 73, 74, 243, 245, 246, 250. *See also* Settlement

Residues, 2, 47–48, 135, 142, 177, 214, 216, 279

Rhine-Meuse-Schelde pottery, 99, 100

Río Cobre, 172, 173, 186

Rio Grande, 241

Risk reduction, 134

Ritual, 3, 14–15, 45–46, 81–82, 85, 99, 101, 105–108, 191–93, 214, 216, 228, 233, 261, 262

Riverine resources, 30, 31, 130